EMORY UNIVERSITY STUDIES IN LAW AND RELIGION

John Witte Jr., General Editor

BOOKS IN THE SERIES

Faith and Order: The Reconciliation of Law and Religion
Harold J. Berman

Rediscovering the Natural Law in Reformed Theological Ethics
Stephen J. Grabill

The Ten Commandments in History:
Mosaic Paradigms for a Well-Ordered Society
Paul Grimley Kuntz

Theology of Law and Authority in the English Reformation
Joan Lockwood O'Donovan

Religious Liberty in Western Thought
Noel B. Reynolds and W. Cole Durham Jr.

Political Order and the Plural Structure of Society
James W. Skillen and Rockne M. McCarthy

The Idea of Natural Rights:
Studies on Natural Rights, Natural Law, and Church Law, 1150-1625
Brian Tierney

The Fabric of Hope: An Essay
Glenn Tinder

Religious Human Rights in Global Perspective: Legal Perspectives
Johan D. van der Vyver and John Witte Jr.

GOD'S JOUST, GOD'S JUSTICE

Law and Religion in the Western Tradition

John Witte Jr.

William B. Eerdmans Publishing Company
Grand Rapids, Michigan / Cambridge, U.K.

Published 2006 by
Wm. B. Eerdmans Publishing Co.
2140 Oak Industrial Drive N.E., Grand Rapids, Michigan 49505 /
P.O. Box 163, Cambridge CB3 9PU U.K.

Printed in the United States of America

11 10 09 08 07 06   7 6 5 4 3 2 1

Library of Congress Cataloging-in-Publication Data

Witte, John, 1959-
God's joust, God's justice: law and religion in the Western tradition /
John Witte Jr.
p.   cm.
Includes bibliographical references and index.
ISBN-10: 0-8028-4421-9 / ISBN-13: 978-0-8028-4421-7 (pbk.: alk. paper)
1. Religion and law. 2. Human rights — Religious aspects.
I. Title.

BL65.L33W58   2006
201'.72 — dc22

2006018222

www.eerdmans.com

To Alison,
God's Gift

Contents

Foreword

In 1998, the Lilly Endowment, Inc., in Indianapolis was kind enough to furnish me with a very generous grant to write a series of studies on the historical contributions of mainline Protestantism, particularly Reformed Calvinism, to the development of Western law. This grant provided me with something that every academic covets dearly — time. Time to visit archives and libraries, time to read and reflect, time to translate and interpret, time to plan and write. This grant has provided me with the luxury of thinking through and mapping out a series of studies on cardinal issues of law, politics, and society. I want to offer my heartfelt thanks to Craig Dykstra and his colleagues at Lilly for their generous solicitude and confidence in me, and to Don Browning of the University of Chicago, who recommended my project so enthusiastically to the Endowment.

Over the past decade, The Pew Charitable Trusts, Inc., in Philadelphia was kind enough to furnish our Center for the Study of Law and Religion at Emory University with several very generous grants to run a series of projects on religious liberty and human rights; marriage, children, and family life; and Christian Jurisprudence. In the past three years, the Alonzo McDonald Family Foundation has blessed us with two further generous grants to extend this work into new fields of scholarship on religious freedom and the rule of law. These grants provided me with a second thing that every academic covets dearly — conversation. Serious conversations have been the happy hallmarks of the dozens of faculty seminars, roundtable conferences, public forums, and major conferences that our Center has been able to convene over the past few years. It has been edifying to converse with so many distinguished colleagues and visiting scholars and to watch their ideas explode into vibrant new lectures and writings. I want to offer a special word of appreciation and admiration to the Senior Fellows in our Center who have been so vital to this conversation — particularly Frank S. Alexander, Don S. Browning, Martin E. Marty, Philip L. Reynolds, and Steven M. Tipton, who co-directed projects with me, as well as Abdullahi Ahmed An-Na'im, David R. Blumenthal, Michael J. Broyde, Paul B. Courtright, Martha Albertson Fineman, E. Brooks Holifield, Timothy P. Jackson, Luke Timothy Johnson, Mark D. Jordan, Michael Perry, and Johan D. van der Vyver, who were particularly generous in offering their sage counsel and keen insights. I want to express my heartfelt thanks to our friends at Pew, particularly Rebecca Rimel, Luis Lugo, Susan Billington Harper, Diane Winston, and Julie Sulc, and to our friends at the McDonald Family Foundation, especially Alonzo McDonald, Suzie McDonald, Peter McDonald, and Robert Pool, for the generous grants that have made these conversations possible.

These grants have allowed me to embark on two multi-volume monograph series — one series on *Law and Protestantism: The Legal Teachings of the Reformation* (Lutheran, Calvinist, Anglican, and Anabaptist), and a second series on *Sex, Marriage, and Family Life in John Calvin's Geneva.* They have also allowed me to complete several freestanding monographs and anthologies and several dozen scholarly articles and essays.

In the course of this new research and writing, I have been able to sort out more clearly my preferred methodology as a historian. I had learned from my great college mentor, the late Dr. H. Evan Runner, the importance of trying to discern the religious sources and commitments implicit or explicit in historical and modern ideas and institutions. I continue to learn from my great law school mentor and now colleague, Professor Harold J. Berman, the importance of trying to discern the shifting belief systems in the development of the Western legal tradition. Both these great scholars have confirmed the wisdom of the providential view of history I was taught on the knee of my parents and at the feet of my pastors — that history can have divine meaning and purpose, that time and tradition can be teachers for those who learn to listen. I have translated all this schoolboy instruction into a commitment to doing history with an eye to discerning the most enduring teachings of the tradition, particularly those that echo and elaborate the eternal teachings of Scripture.

I try to study history with three *r*'s in mind — retrieval of the religious sources and dimensions of law, politics, and society in the Western tradition, reconstruction of the most enduring teachings of the tradition for our day, and reengagement of a historically informed religious viewpoint

with the hard issues that now confront Church, state, and society. I also try
to bear three i's in mind. Much of my historical work is interdisciplinary in
perspective, seeking to bring the wisdom of religious traditions into greater
conversation with law, the humanities, and the social sciences. It is international in orientation, seeking to situate American debates over interdisciplinary issues within a comparative historical and emerging global conversation. And it is interreligious in inspiration, seeking to compare the legal
teachings of Catholicism, Protestantism, and Orthodoxy, and sometimes
those of Judaism and Islam as well. This volume is something of an apologia for and application of this historical methodology.

There are three things that people will die for — their faith, their freedom, and their family. This volume focuses on all three. Included herein is
a series of compact historical studies of religious liberty and human rights
in the Western tradition, of law and religion in American history, and of
marriage, children, and family life in America and beyond. A few of the
chapters are distillations of book-length studies already in print. Most of
them are sketches of ideas for monographs that I aim to pursue. Putting
these studies together into a single volume will, I hope, provide readers
with a convenient scholarly resource, a useful historical guide, and an accessible textbook for colleges and graduate schools, seminaries and law
schools.

I had the privilege of trying out a number of these chapters in the
form of public lectures and learned much from the questions and discussions that followed. Included were the Abraham Kuyper Lecture at Princeton Theological Seminary, the Gould Lecture at the University of Vermont,
the John Courtney Murray Lecture at the American Enterprise Institute,
the Reardon Lecture at Cumberland Law School, the Daniel J. Meador Lecture at the University of Virginia School of Law, the Donald Gianella Memorial Lecture at Villanova Law School, the Lane Lecture at Creighton University School of Law, the John Paul II Lecture at Catholic University of
America, the John Witherspoon Lecture in Washington, D.C., the Earl
Warren Institute Lecture at the University of California at Berkeley, the
Snuggs Lectures in Religion at the University of Tulsa, the Geneva Lectures
at the University of Iowa and Queens University, Kingston, the Bradley Lecture at Boston College, the Timbers Lecture at Dartmouth College, and the
Whiteside Lecture, Richard A. Kessler Reformation Lecture, Distinguished
Faculty Lecture, and Alonzo L. McDonald Lecture all at Emory University. I
was privileged in this same period to offer other lectures on some of the
other chapters at conferences and workshops at Arizona State University,

University of Chicago, Columbia University, the District of Columbia Court of Appeals, University of Edinburgh, Harvard University, University of Heidelberg, McGill University, the Interdisciplinary Center in Herzlyia, Israel, the Ohio State Bar Association, Princeton University, Tel Aviv University, University of Toronto, and University of Texas at Austin. I want to express my appreciation to the hosts of these lecture series and public forums, as well as to the curators of the libraries at most of these institutions who allowed me to use their collections.

I want to offer my warmest thanks to several Emory colleagues who helped me in preparing this volume — Amy Wheeler and Janice Wiggins, who worked so expertly on the manuscript; Will Haines and Kelly Parker, who provided such valuable library services; Eliza Ellison and April Bogle, who offered critical insights; Anita Mann and Melanie Still, who provided expert grant management; and Erin Englebrecht, Laurie Ann Fallon, Heather Good, David Harris, Charles Hooker, Wallace McDonald, Jimmy Rock, and Tony Winter, who provided helpful research assistance.

This volume, which dwells on God's joust and justice in history, is dedicated to my daughter, Alison, who attests to God's gifts and mercy here and now.

John Witte Jr.

Abbreviations

Adams, Works	C. F. Adams, ed., *The Works of John Adams, Second President of the United States, with a Life of the Author, Notes, and Illustrations,* 10 vols. (Boston: Little, Brown and Company, 1850-1856)
Berman, LR I	Harold J. Berman, *Law and Revolution: The Formation of the Western Legal Tradition* (Cambridge, Mass.: Harvard University Press, 1983)
Berman, LR II	Harold J. Berman, *Law and Revolution, II: The Impact of the Protestant Reformations on the Western Legal Tradition* (Cambridge, Mass.: Harvard University Press, 2003)
Bohatec, CSK	Josef Bohatec, *Calvins Lehre von Staat und Kirche mit besonderer Berücksichtigung des Organismusgedankens* (Breslau: M. and H. Marcus, 1937)
Brundage	James A. Brundage, *Law, Sex, and Christian Society in Medieval Europe* (Chicago: University of Chicago Press, 1987)
CO	*Ioannis Calvini opera quae supersunt omnia,* ed. G. Baum et al., 59 vols. (Brunswick: C. A. Schwetschke et Filium, 1863-1900) (Corpus Reformatorum Series, vols. 29-87)
Ehler and Morrall	Sidney Z. Ehler and John B. Morrall, eds., *Church and State through the Centuries: A Collection of Historic Documents with Commentaries* (Newman, Md.: Burns and Oates, 1954)
FSC	John Witte Jr., *From Sacrament to Contract: Marriage, Religion, and Law in the Western Tradition* (Louisville: Westminster John Knox, 1997)

Institutes (1536)	*Ioannis Calvini Institutio Religionis Christianae* (Basel, 1536), CO 1:1, translated as John Calvin, *Institutes of the Christian Religion,* trans. Ford Lewis Battles (Atlanta: John Knox, 1975)
Institutes (1559)	*Ioannis Calvini Institutio Religionis Christianae* (Basel, 1559), CO 2:1, translated as *Institutes of the Christian Religion,* ed. John T. McNeill, trans. Ford Lewis Battles (Philadelphia: Westminster, 1960)
LP	John Witte Jr., *Law and Protestantism: The Legal Teachings of the Lutheran Reformation* (Cambridge: Cambridge University Press, 2002)
LW	*Luther's Works,* trans. and ed. Jaroslav Pelikan and Helmut T. Lehmann (Philadelphia: Fortress, 1955-1968), 55 vols.
POR	John Witte Jr. and Michael Bourdeaux, eds., *Proselytism and Orthodoxy in Russia: The New War for Souls* (Maryknoll, N.Y.: Orbis, 1999)
RCE	John Witte Jr., *Religion and the American Constitutional Experiment,* second ed. (Boulder, Colo.: Westview, 2005)
RHR I	John Witte Jr. and Johan D. van der Vyver, eds., *Religious Human Rights in Global Perspective: Religious Perspectives* (The Hague: Martinus Nijhoff, 1996)
RHR II	Johan D. van der Vyver and John Witte Jr.. eds., *Religious Human Rights in Global Perspective: Legal Perspectives* (The Hague: Martinus Nijhoff, 1996)
RR	John Witte Jr., *The Reformation of Rights: Law, Religion, and Human Rights in Early Modern Calvinism* (Cambridge: Cambridge University Press, 2007)
SB	John Witte Jr. and Richard C. Martin, eds., *Sharing the Book: Religious Perspectives on the Rights and Wrongs of Proselytism* (Maryknoll, N.Y.: Orbis, 1999)
Stephenson and Markham	Carl Stephenson and Frederick B. Markham, *Sources of English Constitutional History,* rev. ed. (New York: Harper and Row, 1972)
WA	*D. Martin Luthers Werke: Kritische Gesamtausgabe,* repr. ed. (Weimar: H. Böhlaus Verlager, 1883-1987), 78 vols.

God's Joust, God's Justice

"History is God's theatre, . . . God's jousting place."

Martin Luther[1]

"All things are ruled and governed by the one God as He pleases, but if God's motives are hid, are they therefore unjust?"

St. Augustine[2]

In the spring of 1995, I visited the great Saxon capital of Dresden. I stood on the banks of the Elbe River at the site of the Frauenkirche — the monumental domed Church consecrated in 1734, graced by one of Johann Sebastian Bach's greatest organ concerts in 1736, and celebrated in German music, art, and literature ever since.

It was a sobering moment, for the great Church lay in ruins. A guide explained that the Church did not survive the firebombing of Dresden near the end of World War II. On February 13 and 14, 1945, 773 Allied bombers emptied their payloads on Dresden. No bombs hit the Church directly. But the fires were enough. First the art, the woodwork, the pulpit, the organ, and the altars were consumed. As the fires penetrated more deeply, scores of people hidden in the Church's catacombs were burned to death. Eventually, the intense heat of the fires weakened the Church so much that it simply collapsed under its own weight. Large chunks of the dome, charred

1. WA 15:32.
2. Augustine, *City of God*, bk. v, chap. 21.

and cracked, still lay where they had fallen some fifty years before. A large piece of the steeple still protruded from the ground at a grim angle. Only one wall of the nave still stood, its top jagged and pocked where the roof had torn away.

It was also an exhilarating moment, for stretching out from the wall of the nave in all directions were dozens of rows of scaffolds, where workers were storing the ten thousand–odd pieces of stone that had been collected from the rubble of the fallen Church. The Frauenkirche, the guide informed me, would be reconstructed, using as many of the original stones as possible. A giant blueprint assigned each of the recovered stones to its original place in the structure. New stones were being collected from the same quarry that had been mined for the original construction. A massive outpouring of charity had made this reconstruction possible.[3]

I have often given thanks for that brief moment on the banks of the Elbe River, for this small frame captured several themes that are at the center of my life — as a Christian believer and as a legal historian.

The story of the Dresden Church is a metaphor of life. Construction, destruction, and reconstruction. Work, judgment, and purgation. Birth, death, and resurrection. Creation, fall, and redemption. These are the stages of life. These are the passages of faith. The old must pass away so that the new may come forth. We must die so that we can be reborn. Our bodies must be buried so that they can be resurrected. Our works must be burned so that they can be purified. Our bonds must be broken so that we can be reconciled. This is the nature of biblical religion.[4] It gives life its power. It gives pain its purpose. It gives time its pattern.

These basic biblical themes — that time has a pattern, that history has a purpose, that life has an end of reconciliation — inform my understanding of history. The Bible teaches that time is linear, not cyclical. Biblical history moves forward from a sin-trampled garden to a golden city, from a fallen world to a perfect end-time. Our lives move, circuitously but inevitably, toward a reconciliation with God, neighbor, and self — if not in this life, then in the life to come; if not with the true God, then with a false god; if not in the company of heaven, then in the crowds of hell.

Human history cannot be fully understood without reference to this divine mystery. God is beyond time, yet has chosen to reveal a part of him-

---

3. Dieter Nadolski, *Die Frauenkirche zu Dresden* (Dresden: n.p., 1994).
4. Matthew 24–25; John 11:25-26; Romans 6:5-11; 8:18-39; 1 Corinthians 3:10-15; 1 Corinthians 15:12-57; 2 Corinthians 5:1-5, 16-19.

self within it. Through the creation and incarnation, God pours out a measure of his being and grace. Through the law and Gospel, God sets forth a measure of his word and will. Through miracles and messengers, God puts forth a measure of his power and judgment. All of history, in Martin Luther's words, is "a demonstration, recollection, and sign of divine action and judgment, how God upholds, rules, obstructs, rewards, punishes, and honors the world, especially the human world."[5] We are within time, yet we are able in part to transcend it. Through our conscience and imagination, we gradually discover something of the meaning of God's plan for each creature. Through our creativity and experimentation, we slowly uncover something of the majesty of God's plan for the creation. Through our liturgies and epiphanies, we slowly uncover something of the mystery of God's incarnation for the Church. Through our texts and traditions, we gradually accumulate something of the wisdom of God's revelation for all people.

To be sure, God's plan and our history are not identical. God's plan consists of much more than what God chooses to reveal to us or what we are able to discern of it. Much of what we see appears to be the work of a concealed God, even at times a seemingly capricious God. In Martin Luther's (1483-1546) colorful image, history is "God's mummery and mystery," "God's joust and tourney." History is "God's theatre," in which the play cannot be fully understood until it ends and until we exit.[6] To equate one act or actor, one speech or text, with the divine play itself is to cast a partial and premature judgment. To insist on one interpretation of the play before it ends is to presume the power of eternal discernment. To judge the play on the basis of a few episodes is to insult the genius of the divine playwright.

Human history, in turn, consists of much more than our conscientious struggle to follow God's word and will in our lives, to reflect God's image and immanence in our world. Much of what we see in our personal lives is the "war between our members," the struggle between the carnal and the spiritual, the sinner and the saint.[7] Much of what we see in our collective lives is the sinful and savage excesses of corrupt creatures, the diverse and perverse choices of free human agents. But there is simply too much order in our world, too much constancy in our habits, too much jus-

5. WA 50:383-84.
6. WA 15:32ff.; WA 50:383ff.
7. Romans 8:1-17; James 4:1.

tice in our norms for us to think that the course of human events is not somehow channeled by God's providential plan.

God is thus both revealed and concealed in history. "All events," as John Calvin (1509-1564) put it, "are governed by God's secret plan."[8] If God were completely revealed in history, there would be no reason for faith. History would simply be a mechanical execution of a predetermined plan. There would be no eternal mystery for which faith could yearn. But if God were completely concealed in history, there would also be no reason for faith. History would simply be a random and rudderless exercise of chaos. There would be no eternal justice in which faith could trust. "Somewhere between those two the Christian has to find his own balance between concealment and revelation."[9]

This is the balance I try to find in my work as a Christian historian. For me, history is more than a series of tricks that we play on the dead, or that the dead play on us. History is more than simply an accidental chronology of first one thing happening, and then another. For me, history is also a source of revelation, a collection of wisdom. The archive is a treasure trove. Old books are windows on truth. The challenge of the Christian historian is to search within the wisdom of the ages for some indication of the eternal wisdom of God. It is to try to seek God's revelation and judgment over time without presuming the power of divine judgment. It is to try to discern God's justice within God's joust.

The Binocular of Law and Religion

These basic convictions about history inform my work on the interaction of law and religion in Western history, and they have been informed by the same. I start with the assumption that somehow God is both hidden and revealed in human laws, and that human laws, in turn, both reflect and deflect God's teachings. I believe that the patterns of human laws over time will reflect something of the meaning of religious truth, and that the patterns of religious truth over time will, in turn, reflect something of the measure of divine laws. Law will reveal a religious dimension. Religion will reveal a legal dimension.

8. Calvin, Institutes (1559), bk. 1, chap. 16.2.

9. E. Harris Harbison, *Christianity and History: Essays* (Princeton, N.J.: Princeton University Press, 1964), p. 102.

Western history bears out these assumptions. In the Western tradition, systems of law and systems of religion have coexisted from the beginning. The contents of these legal and religious systems, of course, have differed dramatically over time and across cultures. At points, they have converged or contradicted each other. Every religious tradition in the West has known both theonomism and antinomianism — the excessive legalization and the excessive spiritualization of religion. Every legal tradition has known both theocracy and totalitarianism — the excessive sacralization and the excessive secularization of law. But the dominant reality in the West is that law and religion stand not in monistic unity, nor in dualistic antinomy, but in dialectical harmony. Each political community struggles to balance law and religion by counterpoising justice and mercy, rule and equity, discipline and love. Each religious tradition strives to come to terms with law by striking a balance between the rational and the mystical, the prophetic and the priestly, the structural and the spiritual. Each legal tradition struggles to link its formal structures and processes with the beliefs and ideals of its people.

This dialectical interaction has allowed the spheres and sciences of law and religion to combine and to cross-fertilize each other in a variety of ways.[10] Law and religion interact conceptually. They embrace overlapping concepts of sin and crime, covenant and contract, righteousness and justice. Law and religion interact formally. They both have interlocking patterns of liturgy and ritual, common habits of tradition and precedent, shared sources of authority and power. Law and religion interact methodologically. They maintain analogous hermeneutical methods of interpreting texts, casuistic and rhetorical methods of argument and instruction, systematic methods of organizing their doctrines. Law and religion relate professionally. They both have officials charged with the formulation, implementation, and demonstration of the norms and habits of their respective fields. Law and religion interact institutionally, through the multiple relations between political and ecclesiastical officials and institutions.

Law and religion thus serve, in Jaroslav Pelikan's apt phrase, as a "binocular" to view afresh many familiar ideas and institutions that have been studied principally through the "monocular of law" or the "monocular of religion" alone.[11] This binocular is available to scholars of many con-

---

10. See further the Conclusion herein.

11. The phrase is from Jaroslav Pelikan, foreword to *The Weightier Matters of the Law: Essays on Law and Religion in Tribute to Harold J. Berman,* ed. John Witte Jr. and Frank S. Alexander (Atlanta: Scholars, 1988), pp. xi-xii.

fessions and professions who work within and beyond the Western tradition. Indeed, some of the best work in law and religion of late has come from Hindu, Muslim, and Jewish scholars working on Asia, Africa, and the Middle East.[12]

I use this interdisciplinary binocular as a Christian legal historian working primarily within the Western tradition. The binocular reveals three kinds of pictures: (1) grand civilizational pictures, (2) narrower denominational pictures, and (3) discrete doctrinal pictures of law and religion in Western history. Much of this volume will be devoted to sketching the second and third types of pictures — how historical Christian denominations, particularly Protestant denominations, have influenced Western legal ideas and institutions, and how discrete legal doctrines, particularly respecting human rights and family law, have been shaped and colored by religious teachings.

In this introduction, I use the binocular of law and religion at its most panoramic setting to survey the grand civilizational pictures of law and religion in Western history. Here, I focus on the interaction between the dominant belief-systems of a civilization and the major forms and norms of its dominant legal system. What are the dominant beliefs and values, myths and metaphors that inform this legal system? What happens to the legal system when those beliefs and values change, especially abruptly through revolution, conquest, or force majeure?

My great mentor, Harold J. Berman, offers a splendid example of viewing the history of Western law and religion at this panoramic setting. There is a distinct Western legal tradition, Berman argues, a set of legal ideas and institutions that has evolved by accretion and adaptation over the centuries. The exact shape of these legal ideas and institutions at any given time is determined, in part, by the underlying belief systems of the people ruling and being ruled. Six great revolutions, however, have punctuated the gradual evolution of the Western legal tradition: the Papal Revolution of 1075, the German Lutheran Revolution of 1517, the English Puritan Revolution of 1640, and the American, French, and Russian Revolutions of 1776, 1789, and 1917. These revolutions were, in part, rebellions against a legal and political order that had become outmoded and os-

---

12. See, e.g., F. C. DeCoste and Lillian MacPherson, *Law, Religion, Theology: A Selective Annotated Bibliography* (West Cornwall, Conn.: Locust, 1997) (a 326-page list of recent work); "Reviews on New Books in Law and Religion," *Journal of Law and Religion* 16 (2001): 249-1035, and 17 (2002): 97-459.

sified, arbitrary and abusive. But, more fundamentally, these revolutions were products of radical shifts in the dominant metaphors, in the dominant belief-systems of the people — shifts from Catholicism to Protestantism to Deism to Marxist-Leninism. Each of these new belief-systems offered a new eschatology, a new apocalyptic vision of the perfect end-time, whether that be the second coming of Christ, the arrival of the heavenly city of the Enlightenment philosophers, or the withering away of the state. Each of these revolutions triggered massive changes in prevailing legal forms and norms — movements from canon law to civil law to common law; from the supremacy of the Church, to the supremacy of the state, to the supremacy of the individual and the collective. Each of these revolutions, in its radical phase, sought the death of an old legal order to bring forth a new order that would survive its understanding of the Last Judgment. Eventually, each of these revolutions settled down and introduced fundamental legal changes that were ultimately subsumed in and accommodated to the Western legal tradition. Today, this Western legal tradition has been drawn into increasing cooperation and competition with other legal traditions from around the globe, in the struggle to define a new common law and a new legal language for the world order.[13]

Berman's is but one grand civilizational picture of law and religion in the West. The German jurist Otto von Gierke (1841-1921) offered a quite different picture based on shifting images of the individual and the collective, the *Volk* and the *Volksgeist*, the citizen and the association *(Genossenschaft)*.[14] The English legal historian Sir Henry Maine (1822-1888) offered another grand civilizational picture in elaborating his thesis about the millennium-long shifts in the West from status to contract, from equity to legislation, from custom to code.[15] The Dutch jurist and philosopher Herman Dooyeweerd (1894-1977) offered still another grand picture based

---

13. See Berman, LR I and II; Harold J. Berman, *Faith and Order: The Reconciliation of Law and Religion* (Grand Rapids: Eerdmans, 1993); Howard O. Hunter, *The Integrative Jurisprudence of Harold J. Berman* (Boulder, Colo.: Westview, 1996); Symposium, "The Foundations of Law," *Emory Law Journal* 54 (2005): 1-375.

14. See esp. Otto von Gierke, *Das deutschen Genossenschaftsrecht* [1868-1913], 4 vols. (Graz: Akademische Druks- und Verlagsanstalt, 1954).

15. Henry Sumner Maine, *Ancient Law* [1861] (New Brunswick, N.J.: Transaction, 2001); Henry Sumner Maine, *Village Communities in the East and the West* [1871] (New York: Arno, 1974); Henry Sumner Maine, *Lectures on the Early History of Institutions* [1875] (Kitchener, Ontario: Batoche, 1999); Henry Sumner Maine, *Dissertations on Early Law and Custom* [1883] (Kitchener, Ontario: Batoche, 1999).

on the founding religious motifs of each legal age — contrasting what he called the motifs of Greek "form and matter," Catholic "grace and nature," Protestant "creation, fall, and redemption," and Enlightenment "nature and freedom" and the concrete manifestations of these shifting motifs in legal, political, and cultural life.[16]

The civilizational picture that I see reflects some of these master-pieces of historiography. There is, indeed, a distinctive Western legal tradi-tion — rooted in the ancient civilizations of Israel, Greece, and Rome. This Western legal tradition was nourished for nearly two millennia by Chris-tianity and for more than two centuries by the Enlightenment. The Western legal tradition has developed enduring postulates about justice and mercy, rule and equity, nature and custom, canon and commandment. It has fea-tured evolving ideas about authority and power, rights and liberties, indi-viduals and associations, public and private. It has developed distinctive methods of legislation and adjudication, of negotiation and litigation, of le-gal rhetoric and textual interpretation, of legal science and legal philoso-phy. The precise shape and balance of the Western legal tradition at any pe-riod has been determined, in part, by the Western religious tradition. And when the prevailing ideas, officials, symbols, and methods of the Western religious tradition have changed, the shape and balance of the Western le-gal tradition have changed as well.

Four major shifts in the Western religious tradition have triggered the most massive transformations of the Western legal tradition: (1) the Christian conversion of the Roman Empire in the fourth through sixth cen-turies; (2) the Papal Revolution of the late eleventh to thirteenth centuries; (3) the Protestant Reformation of the sixteenth century; and (4) the En-lightenment movements of the eighteenth and nineteenth centuries. The Western legal tradition was hardly static between these four watershed pe-riods. Regional and national movements — from the ninth-century Carolingian Renaissance to the Russian Revolution of 1917 — had ample ripple effects on the tradition. But these were the four watershed periods, the civilizational moments and movements that permanently redirected the

16. Herman Dooyeweerd, *Encyclopaedie der Rechtswisssenschaft*, 2 vols. (Amster-dam: Drukkerei D.A.V.I.D., 1946); Herman Dooyeweerd, *De wijsbegeerte der wetsidee* (Amsterdam: H. J. Paris, 1935-1936), 3 vols., translated by D. Freeman and W. Young as *A New Critique of Theoretical Thought* (Philadelphia: Presbyterian and Reformed Pub-lishing Company, 1969), 4 vols.; Herman H. Dooyeweerd, *Roots of Western Culture: Pa-gan, Secular, and Christian Options*, trans. J. Kraay, ed. M. Vander Vennen and B. Zylstra (Toronto: Wedge, 1979).

Western legal tradition. What follows in this Introduction are brief sketches of the interaction of law and religion in these four watershed eras, which later chapters will help to fill in.

Law and Religion in Ancient Rome

The first watershed period came with the Christian conversion of the Roman emperor and empire in the fourth through sixth centuries. Prior to that time, Roman law reigned supreme throughout much of the West. Roman law defined the status of persons and associations and the legal actions and procedures available to them. It proscribed delicts (torts) and crimes. It governed marriage and divorce, households and children, property and inheritance, contracts and commerce, slavery and labor. It protected the public property and welfare of the Roman state.

Roman law also established the imperial cult. Rome was to be revered as the eternal city, ordained by the gods and celebrated in its altars and basilicas. The Roman emperor was to be worshipped as a god and king in the rituals of the imperial court and in the festivals of the public square. The Roman law itself was viewed as the embodiment of an immutable divine law, appropriated and applied through the sacred legal science of imperial pontiffs and jurists.

A refined legal theory began to emerge at the dawn of the new millennium, built in part on Greek prototypes. Cicero (106-43 B.C.E.), Seneca (d. 65 C.E.), and other Roman philosophers cast in legal terms Aristotle's topical methods of reasoning, rhetoric, and interpretation as well as Aristotle and Plato's concepts of natural, distributive, and commutative justice. Gaius (d. ca. 180 C.E.), Ulpian (ca. 160-228), and other Roman jurists drew what would become classic Western distinctions among (1) civil law *(ius civile)*, the statutes and procedures of a particular community to be applied strictly or with equity; (2) common law *(ius gentium)*, the principles and customs common to several communities and often the basis for treaties; and (3) natural law *(ius naturale)*, the immutable principles of right reason, which are supreme in authority and divinity and must prevail in cases of conflict with civil or common laws.[17] The Roman jurists also began to develop a concept of subjective rights *(iura)* and freedoms *(libertates)*.[18]

---

17. See Chapter 3 herein.
18. See Chapter 1 herein.

The early Christian Church stood largely opposed to this Roman legal system, as had the Jewish communities in which the Church was born. Christians could not accept the imperial cult nor readily partake of the pagan rituals required for participation in commerce, the military, litigation, and other public forums and activities. The early Church thus organized itself into separate communities, largely withdrawn from official Roman society. Early Church constitutions, such as the *Didache* (c. 120) and *Didascalia Apostolorum* (c. 250), set forth internal rules for Church organization and offices, clerical life, ecclesiastical discipline, charity, education, family, and property relations.[19] Early Christian leaders, building on the injunctions of Christ and St. Paul, generally taught obedience to the political authorities up to the limits of Christian conscience. The clergy also urged upon their Roman rulers political and legal reforms consonant with Christian teachings. Such legal independence and legal advocacy by the Church brought forth firm imperial edicts from the mid first century onward, condemning Christians to intermittent waves of brutal persecution.[20]

The Christian conversion of Emperor Constantine (ca. 272-337) in 312 and the formal establishment by law of Trinitarian Christianity as the official religion of the Roman Empire in 380 ultimately fused these Roman and Christian laws and beliefs. The Roman Empire was now understood as the universal body of Christ on earth, embracing all persons and all things. The Roman emperor was viewed as both pope and king, who reigned supreme in spiritual and temporal matters. The Roman law was viewed as the pristine instrument of natural law and Christian morality.

This new syncretism of Roman and Christian beliefs allowed the Christian Church to imbue the Roman law with a number of its basic teachings, and to have those enforced throughout much of the empire — notably and most brutally against such heretics as Arians, Apollinarians, and Manicheans. Particularly in the great synthetic texts of Roman law, the *Codex Theodosianus* (438) and the *Corpus Iuris Civilis* (534), Christian teachings on the Trinity, the sacraments, liturgy, holy days, Sabbath Day observance, sexual ethics, charity, education, and much else were copiously defined and regulated. This firm legal establishment of Trinitarian Christianity contributed enormously both to its precocious expansion throughout the West and to its canonical preservation for later centuries.[21]

19. See Chapters 2 and 12 herein.
20. See Chapter 7 herein.
21. See Chapter 7 herein.

This new syncretism of Roman and Christian beliefs, however, also subordinated the Church to imperial rule. Christianity was now, in effect, the new imperial cult of Rome, presided over by the Roman emperor. The Christian clergy were, in effect, the new pontiffs of the Christian imperial cult, hierarchically organized and ultimately subordinate to imperial authority. The Church's property was, in effect, the new public property of the empire, subject both to its protection and to its control. Thus Roman emperors and other political rulers convoked many of the Church councils and major synods; appointed, disciplined, and removed the higher clergy; administered many of the Church's parishes, monasteries, and charities; and legally controlled the acquisition, maintenance, and disposition of Church property.

This "caesaropapist" pattern of substantive influence but procedural subordination of Church to state, and of the Christian religion to law, was largely accepted in the Orthodox Churches of the Byzantine Empire and its successor polities. Following the political theology of John Chrysostom (d. 407), Gregory of Nyssa (ca. 335-ca. 394), and others, Eastern Orthodox clerics readily merged Christian and secular law and life, leaving legal and political matters primarily to the emperor or magistrate as vicar of Christ and devoting themselves primarily to Christian liturgy and teaching.[22] This caesaropapist pattern sometimes met with more resistance in the West as strong clerics such as Ambrose of Milan (339-397), Pope Gelasius (d. 496), and Pope Gregory the Great (ca. 540-604) insisted on a sharper separation of spiritual and secular law and authority.[23] But with the rise of strong Germanic monarchs in the eighth and ninth centuries, notably the Frankish emperor Charlemagne (ca. 742-814) and the Saxon king Alfred the Great (c. 848-900), the Western Church, too, was subjected to firm political rule and control. This pattern was often exacerbated by the growing practice in the West of placing Church properties under feudal tenure and thus placing their clerical occupants under the control of local feudal lords.

Law and Religion in the Papal Revolution

The second watershed period of the Western legal tradition came with the Papal Revolution or Gregorian Reform of the late eleventh through thir-

22. See Chapter 4 herein.
23. See Chapter 7 herein.

teenth centuries. Beginning in 1075, the Catholic clergy, led by Pope Gregory VII (1015-1085), threw off their civil rulers and established the Roman Catholic Church as an autonomous legal and political corporation within Western Christendom. This event was part and product of an enormous transformation of Western society. The West was renewed through the rediscovery and study of the ancient texts of Roman law, Greek philosophy, and patristic theology. The first modern Western universities were established in Bologna, Rome, and Paris with their core faculties of theology, law, and medicine. A number of towns were transformed into city-states. Trade and commerce boomed. A new dialogue was opened with the sophisticated cultures of Judaism and Islam. Great advances were made in the natural sciences, in mechanics, in literature, and in art, music, and architecture. The revolutionary era of the twelfth and thirteenth centuries, Harold Berman tells us, was the "first modern age" of the West.[24]

In this period, the Church came to claim a vast new jurisdiction — literally the power "to speak the law" (jus dicere). The Church claimed personal jurisdiction over clerics, pilgrims, students, the poor, heretics, Jews, and Muslims. It claimed subject matter jurisdiction over doctrine and liturgy; ecclesiastical property, polity, and patronage; sex, marriage, and family life; education, charity, and inheritance; oral promises, oaths, and various contracts; and all manner of moral, ideological, and sexual crimes.[25] The Church also claimed temporal jurisdiction over subjects and persons that also fell within the concurrent jurisdiction of one or more civil authorities.

These jurisdictional claims rendered Church officials both the new legislators and new judges of the West. From the late eleventh century onward, Church authorities issued a steady stream of papal decretals and bulls, conciliar and synodical decrees and edicts, and orders by local bishops and abbots. Church courts adjudicated cases in accordance with the substantive and procedural rules of the canon law. Periodically, the pope or a strong bishop would deploy itinerant ecclesiastical judges, called inquisitores, with original jurisdiction over discrete questions that would normally lie within the competence of the Church courts. The pope also sent out his legates, who could exercise a variety of judicial and administrative powers in the name of the pope. Cases could be appealed up the hierarchy of Church courts, ultimately to the papal rota. Cases raising novel questions could be referred to distinguished canonists or law faculties

---

24. Berman, LR I.
25. See Chapters 3, 10, 13, and 14 herein.

called assessors, whose learned opinions *(consilia)* on the questions were often taken by the Church court as edifying if not binding.

Church authorities grounded their claims to make and to enforce canon law on three main arguments. First, this new jurisdiction was seen as a simple extension of the Church's traditional authority to govern the seven liturgical sacraments — baptism, confirmation, penance, Eucharist, marriage, ordination, and extreme unction. By the fifteenth century, some of the sacraments supported whole bodies of sophisticated canon law. The sacrament of marriage supported the canon law of sex, marriage, and family life.[26] The sacrament of penance supported the canon law of crimes and torts (delicts) and, indirectly, the canon law of contracts, oaths, charity, and inheritance. The sacrament of ordination became the foundation for a refined canon law of corporate rights and duties of the clergy. The sacraments of baptism and confirmation supported a new constitutional law of natural rights and duties of Christian believers.[27]

Second, the Church predicated its jurisdictional claims on Christ's famous delegation to the apostle Peter: "I will give you the keys of the kingdom of heaven, and whatever you bind on earth shall be bound in heaven, and whatever you loose on earth shall be loosed in heaven."[28] According to conventional canonical lore, Christ had conferred on St. Peter two keys — a key of knowledge to discern God's word and will, and a key of power to implement and enforce that word and will throughout the Church. St. Peter had used these keys to help define the doctrine and discipline of the apostolic Church. Through apostolic succession, the pope and his clergy had inherited these keys to define the doctrine and discipline of the contemporary Church. This inheritance, the canonists believed, conferred on the pope and his clergy a legal power, a power to make and enforce canon laws. This argument of the keys readily supported the Church's claims to subject matter jurisdiction over core spiritual matters of doctrine and liturgy — the purpose and timing of the mass, baptism, Eucharist, confession, and the like. The key of knowledge, after all, gave the pope and his clergy access to the mysteries of divine revelation, which, by use of the key of power, they communicated to all believers through the canon law. The argument of the keys, however, could be easily extended. Even the most mundane of human affairs ultimately have spiritual and moral dimensions. Resolution of a

26. See Chapters 10-14 herein.
27. See Chapters 1 and 3 herein.
28. Matthew 16:19 (RSV).

boundary-line dispute between neighbors implicates the commandment to love one's neighbor. Unaccountable failure to pay one's civil taxes or feudal dues is a breach of the spiritual duty to honor those in authority. Printing or reading a censored book is a sin. Strong clergy, therefore, readily used the argument of the keys to extend the subject matter jurisdiction of the Church to matters with more attenuated spiritual and moral dimensions, particularly in jurisdictions where they had no strong civil rivals.[29]

Third, the Church predicated its jurisdictional claims on the belief that the canon law was the true source of Christian equity. Canonists and moralists of the day referred to the canon law variously as "the mother of exceptions," "the epitome of the law of love," and "the mother of justice." As the mother of exceptions, canon law was flexible, reasonable, and fair, capable either of bending the rigor of a rule in an individual case through dispensations and injunctions, or of punctiliously insisting on the letter of an agreement through orders of specific performance or reformation of documents. As the epitome of love, canon law afforded special care for the disadvantaged — widows, orphans, the poor, the handicapped, abused wives, neglected children, maltreated servants, and the like. It provided them with standing to press claims in Church courts, competence to testify against their superiors without their permission, methods to gain succor and shelter from abuse and want, opportunities to pursue pious and protected careers in the cloister. As the mother of justice, canon law provided a method whereby the individual believer could reconcile himself or herself at once to God and to neighbor. This was a critical reason for the enormous popularity and success of the Church courts in much of medieval Christendom. Church courts treated both the legality and the morality of the conflicts before them. Their remedies enabled litigants to become "righteous" and "just," not only in their relationships with opposing parties and the rest of the community but also in their relationship to God.[30]

On the strength of these arguments, the Church developed an elaborate pan-Western system of canon law. Thousands of legal and ethical teachings drawn from the apostolic constitutions, patristic writings, and Christianized Roman law were collated and synthesized in the famous *Decretum Gratiani* (ca. 1140), the anchor text of medieval canon law. The *Decretum* was then heavily supplemented by collections of papal and conciliar legislation and juridical glosses and commentaries, which were

29. See Chapters 2, 3, and 7 herein.
30. See LP, pp. 33-42.

later integrated in the five-volume *Corpus Iuris Canonici* (1586). A vast hierarchy of Church courts and officials administered this canon law in accordance with sophisticated new rules of procedure and evidence. A network of ecclesiastical officials presided over the Church's executive and administrative functions. The medieval Church registered its citizens through baptism. It taxed them through tithes. It conscripted them through crusades. It educated them through Church schools. It nurtured them through cloisters, monasteries, chantries, foundations, and guilds. The medieval Church was, in F. W. Maitland's famous phrase, "the first true state in the West."[31] Its medieval canon law was the first international law of the West since the eclipse of the classical Roman law half a millennium before.

This complex new legal system of the Church attracted sophisticated new legal and political theories. The most original formulations came from such medieval jurists as John of Salisbury (d. 1180), Hostiensis (1200-1271), and Baldus de Ubaldis (c. 1327-1400), and such medieval theologians and moralists as Hugh of St. Victor (ca. 1096-1141), Thomas Aquinas (1225-1274), and John of Paris (ca. 1240-1306). These writers reclassified the sources and forms of law, ultimately distinguishing (1) the eternal law of the creation order; (2) the natural laws of the Bible, reason, and conscience; (3) the positive canon laws of the Church; (4) the positive civil laws of the state; (5) the common laws of all nations and peoples; and (6) the statutes and customs of local communities. They developed enduring rules for the resolution of conflicts among these types of laws, and contests of jurisdiction among their authors. They developed refined concepts of legislation, adjudication, and executive administration, and core constitutional concepts of sovereignty, election, and representation. They developed a good deal of the Western theory and law of chartered corporations, private associations, foundations, and trusts. And they developed sophisticated new theories and forms of individual and corporate rights *(iura,* the plural of *ius)* for both Christians and non-Christians alike.[32]

Law and Religion in the Protestant Reformation

The third watershed period in the Western legal tradition came with the transformation of canon law and civil law, and of Church and state, in the

31. Quoted by Berman, LR I, p. 113.
32. See Chapter 3 herein.

Protestant Reformation. The Protestant Reformation was inaugurated by Martin Luther of Wittenberg in his famous posting of the Ninety-Five Theses in 1517 and his burning of the canon law and confessional books in 1520.[33] The Reformation, however, was the culmination of more than two centuries of dissent within the Church against some of its sacramental theology, liturgical practice, canon law, and ecclesiastical administration. The Reformation ultimately erupted in various quarters of Western Europe in the early sixteenth century, settling into Lutheran, Calvinist, Anglican, and Free Church branches.

The early Protestant Reformers — Luther, Calvin, Menno Simons (1496-1561), Thomas Cranmer (1489-1556), and others — taught that salvation comes through faith in the Gospel, not by works of law. Each individual stands directly before God, seeks God's gracious forgiveness of sin, and conducts life in accordance with the Bible and Christian conscience. To the Protestant Reformers, the Catholic canon law obstructed the individual's relationship with God and obscured simple biblical norms for right living. The early Protestant Reformers further taught that the Church is at heart a community of saints, not a corporation of politics. Its cardinal signs and callings are to preach the Word, to administer the sacraments, to catechize the young, to care for the needy. To the Reformers, the Catholic clergy's legal rule in Christendom obstructed the Church's divine mission and usurped the state's role as God's vice-regent. To be sure, the Church must have internal rules of order to govern its own polity, teaching, and discipline. The Church must critique legal injustice and combat political illegitimacy. But, according to classic Protestant lore, law is primarily the province of the state, not of the Church; of the magistrate, not of the minister.[34]

These new Protestant teachings helped to transform Western law in the sixteenth and seventeenth centuries. The Protestant Reformation permanently broke the international rule of the Catholic Church and the canon law, splintering Western Christendom into competing nations and regions, each with its own often conjoined religious and political rulers. The Protestant Reformation also triggered a massive shift of power, property, and prerogative from the Church to the state. State rulers now assumed jurisdiction over numerous subjects previously governed principally by the Church and its canon law — marriage and family life, property and testamentary matters, charity and poor relief, contracts and oaths,

33. See Chapter 2 herein.
34. See Chapters 2, 3, 7, and 9 herein.

moral and ideological crimes. Particularly in Lutheran and Anglican polities, the state also came to exercise considerable control over the clergy, polity, and property of the Church, in part in self-conscious emulation of the laws and practices of Christianized Rome.

These massive shifts in legal power and property from cleric to magistrate, from Church to state, did not suddenly deprive Western law of its dependence upon religion. Catholic canon law remained an ineradicable part of the common law and civil law of the West, in Catholic and Protestant polities alike. It was readily used both by Church officials to govern their internal religious affairs and by civil authorities to govern matters of state.[35] Moreover, in the Catholic polities of France, Spain, Portugal, and Italy, and their many Latin American and African colonies, the legal and moral pronouncements of the Catholic episcopacy still often had a strong influence on the content of the state law, and Catholicism was the de facto if not de jure established and protected religion of many of these communities until modern times.

In Protestant polities of early modern Europe and their North American (and eventual Asian and African) colonies, many new Protestant theological views came to direct and dramatic legal expression. For example, Protestant theologians replaced the traditional sacramental understanding of marriage with a new idea of the marital household as a "social estate" or "covenantal association" of the earthly kingdom. On that basis, Protestant jurists developed a new state law of marriage, featuring requirements of parental consent, state registration, Church consecration, and peer presence for valid marital formation, a severely truncated law of impediments and annulment, and the introduction of absolute divorce on grounds of adultery, desertion, and other faults, with subsequent rights to remarry, at least for the innocent party.[36] Protestant theologians replaced the traditional understanding of education as a teaching office of the Church with a new understanding of the public school as a "civic seminary" for all persons to prepare for their peculiar vocations. On that basis, Protestant magistrates replaced clerics as the chief rulers of education, state law replaced Church law as the principal law of education, and the general callings of all Christians replaced the special calling of the clergy as the *raison d'être* of education.[37] Protestant theologians introduced a new theology of the "three

35. See Chapters 10, 11, and 14 herein.
36. See Chapters 10 and 11 herein.
37. LP, pp. 257-92.

uses" of the moral law set out in the Bible, particularly the Ten Commandments. On that basis, Protestant jurists developed arresting new theories of
natural law and equity; introduced sweeping changes in civil laws of social
welfare and moral discipline; and developed an integrated theory of the retributive, deterrent, and rehabilitative functions of criminal law and ecclesiastical discipline.[38]

Lutheranism

Each of the four original branches of Protestantism developed its own distinctive theories of politics and of Church-state relations. The Lutheran
Reformation territorialized the Christian faith, and gave ample new political power to the local Christian magistrate. Luther replaced medieval
teachings with a new two kingdoms theory. The "invisible" Church of the
heavenly kingdom, he argued, was a perfect community of saints, where all
stood equal in dignity before God, all enjoyed perfect Christian liberty, and
all governed their affairs in accordance with the Gospel. The "visible"
Church of this earthly kingdom, however, embraced saints and sinners
alike. Its members still stood directly before God and still enjoyed liberty of
conscience, including the liberty to leave the visible Church itself. But, unlike the invisible Church, the visible Church needed both the Gospel and
human law to govern its members' relationships with God and with fellow
believers. The clergy must administer the Gospel. The magistrate must administer the law.[39]

Luther insisted that the Church was not a political or legal authority.
The Church had no sword, no jurisdiction, no daily responsibility for the
administration of law and politics. To be sure, Church officers and theologians must be vigilant in preaching and teaching the law of God to magistrates and subjects alike, and in pronouncing prophetically against injustice and tyranny. But formal legal authority lay with the state rather than
the Church, with the magistrate rather than the cleric.

Luther and his followers regarded the local magistrate as God's vice-
regent called to elaborate natural law and to reflect divine justice in his local domain. The best source and summary of natural law was the Ten Commandments and its elaboration in the moral principles of the Bible. The

38. See Chapter 9 herein.
39. LP, pp. 89-119.

magistrate was to cast these general principles of natural law into specific precepts of human law, designed to fit local conditions. Luther and his followers also regarded the local magistrate as the "father of the community" (*Landesvater, paterpoliticus*). He was to care for his political subjects as if they were his children, and his political subjects were to "honor" him as if he were their parent. Like a loving father, the magistrate was to keep the peace and to protect his subjects in their persons, properties, and reputations. He was to deter his subjects from abusing themselves through drunkenness, sumptuousness, gambling, prostitution, and other vices. He was to nurture his subjects through the community chest, the public almshouse, the state-run hospice. He was to educate them through the public school, the public library, the public lectern. He was to see to their spiritual needs by supporting the ministry of the local Church and encouraging attendance and participation through civil laws of religious worship and tithing.[40]

These twin metaphors of the Christian magistrate — as the lofty vice-regent of God and as the loving father of the local community — described the basics of Lutheran political theory for the next three centuries. Political authority was divine in origin but earthly in operation. It expressed God's harsh judgment against sin but also his tender mercy for sinners. It communicated the law of God but also the lore of the local community. It depended upon the Church for prophetic direction but it took over from the Church all jurisdiction. Either metaphor of the Christian magistrate standing alone could be a recipe for abusive tyranny or officious paternalism. But both metaphors together provided Luther and his followers with the core ingredients of a robust Christian republicanism and budding Christian welfare state.

Accordingly, Lutheran magistrates in early modern Germany and Scandinavia replaced traditional Catholic canon laws with new Lutheran civil laws on religious doctrine and worship, Church administration and supervision, marriage and family life, education and poor relief, public morality and discipline for each local polity. Many of these local Lutheran legal reforms found constitutional protection in the principle of *cuius regio, eius religio* guaranteed in the Peace of Augsburg (1555) and again in the Peace of Westphalia (1648).[41] Under this principle, each local magistrate was authorized to establish by civil law the appropriate forms of religious doctrine, worship, liturgy, charity, and education for his polity — with reli-

40. LP, pp. 119-99.
41. In Ehler and Morrall, pp. 164-73, 189-93; see Chapters 4 and 8 herein.

gious dissenters granted the right to worship and educate their children privately in their homes or to emigrate peaceably from the polity. This new constitutional policy rendered the German region of the Holy Roman Empire, with its 350 plus polities, a veritable honeycomb of religious and political pluralism.

Anabaptism

Contrary to Lutherans, Anabaptists advocated the separation of the redeemed realm of religion and the Church from the fallen realm of politics and the state. In their definitive Schleichtheim Confession (1527), the Anabaptists called for a return to the communitarian ideals of the New Testament and the ascetic principles of the apostolic Church.[42] The Anabaptists eventually splintered into various groups of Amish, German Brethren, Hutterites, Mennonites, Swiss Brethren, and others. Some of these splinter groups were politically radical or utopian, particularly those following the tradition of Thomas Müntzer of Germany. But most Anabaptist communities by the later sixteenth century had become Christian separatists.

Anabaptist communities ascetically withdrew from civic life into small, self-sufficient, intensely democratic communities. When such communities grew too large or too divided, they deliberately colonized themselves, eventually spreading the Anabaptist communities from Russia to Ireland to the furthest frontiers of North America. These communities were governed internally by biblical principles of discipleship, simplicity, charity, and nonresistance. They set their own internal standards of worship, liturgy, diet, discipline, dress, and education. They handled their own internal affairs of property, contracts, commerce, marriage, and inheritance without appeal to state law.

The state, most Anabaptists believed, was part of the fallen world, which was to be avoided so far as possible. Though once the perfect creation of God, the world was now a sinful regime beyond the perfection of Christ and beyond the daily concern of the Christian believer. God had allowed the world to survive through his appointment of state magistrates who were empowered to use coercion and violence to maintain a modicum of order and peace. Christians should thus obey the political authorities, so far as Scripture enjoined, such as in paying their taxes or registering their

---

42. See Chapters 3, 6, and 7 herein.

properties. But Christians were to avoid active participation in and interaction with the world. Most early modern Anabaptists were pacifists, preferring derision, exile, or martyrdom to active participation in war. Most Anabaptists also refused to swear oaths, or to participate in political elections, civil litigation, or civic feasts and functions. This aversion to political and civic activities often triggered severe reprisal by Catholics and Protestants alike. Anabaptists suffered waves of bitter repression throughout the early modern era.

While unpopular in its genesis, Anabaptist theological separatism ultimately proved to be an influential source of later Western political arguments for separation of religion and politics and for protection of the civil and religious liberties of religious minorities. Equally important for later political developments was the new Anabaptist doctrine of adult baptism. This doctrine gave new emphasis to religious voluntarism as opposed to traditional theories of birthright or predestined faith. In Anabaptist theology, the adult individual was called to make a conscious and conscientious choice to accept the faith — metaphorically, to scale the wall of separation between the fallen world and the realm of religion to come within the perfection of Christ. Later Free Church followers, in both Europe and North America, converted this cardinal image into a powerful platform of liberty of conscience and free exercise of religion not only for Christians but eventually for all peaceable believers.[43]

Calvinism

The Calvinist Reformation charted a course between the Erastianism of Lutherans that subordinated the Church to the state, and the asceticism of Anabaptists that withdrew the Church from the state and society. Like Lutherans, Calvinists insisted that each local polity be an overtly Christian commonwealth that adhered to the general principles of natural law and that translated them into detailed positive laws of religious worship, Sabbath observance, public morality, marriage and family life, social welfare, public education, and more. Like Anabaptists, Calvinists insisted on the basic separation of the offices and operations of Church and state, leaving the Church to govern its own doctrine and liturgy, polity and property, without interference from the state. But, unlike both groups, Calvinists in-

---

43. See Chapters 6 and 7 herein.

sisted that both Church and state officials were to play complementary roles in the creation of the local Christian commonwealth and in the cultivation of the Christian citizen.

Building on the work of the Genevan Reformer John Calvin, Calvinists emphasized more fully than other Protestants the educational use of the natural and positive law. Lutherans stressed the civil and theological uses of the natural law — to deter sinners from their sinful excesses and to drive them to repentance. Calvinists emphasized the educational use of the natural law as well — to teach persons both the letter and the spirit of the law, both the civil morality of human duty and the spiritual morality of Christian aspiration. While Lutheran followers of Philip Melanchthon (1497-1560) had included this educational use of the natural law in their theology, Calvinists made it an integral part of their politics as well. They further insisted that not only the natural law of God but also the positive law of the state could achieve these three civil, theological, and educational uses.[44]

Calvinists also emphasized more fully than other Protestants the legal role of the Church in a Christian commonwealth. Lutherans, after the first two generations, left law largely to the Christian magistrate. Anabaptists gave the Church a strong legal role, but only for voluntary members of the ascetically withdrawn Christian community. Calvinists, by contrast, drew local Church officials directly into the enforcement of law for the entire Christian commonwealth and for all citizens, regardless of their Church affiliation. In Calvin's Geneva, this political responsibility of the Church fell largely to the consistory, an elected body of civil and religious officials, with original jurisdiction over cases of marriage and family, charity and social welfare, worship and public morality. Among most later Calvinists — French Huguenots, Dutch Pietists, Scottish Presbyterians, German Reformed, and English and American Puritans — the Genevan-style consistory was transformed into the body of pastors, elders, deacons, and teachers that governed each local Church congregation, and played a less structured political and legal role in the broader Christian commonwealth. But local clergy still had a strong role in advising magistrates on the positive law of the local community. Local Churches and their consistories also generally enjoyed autonomy in administering their own doctrine, liturgy, charity, polity, and property and in administering ecclesiastical discipline over their members.[45]

---

44. See Chapters 5 and 9 herein.
45. See Chapters 6 and 7 herein.

Anglicanism

Anglicanism struck something of a middle way among these competing Lutheran, Anabaptist, and Calvinist political models. The sixteenth-century English Reformation pressed to extreme national forms the Lutheran model of a unitary Christian commonwealth under the final authority of the Christian magistrate. Building in part on Lutheran and Roman law precedents, King Henry VIII severed all legal and political ties between the Church in England and the pope. The Supremacy Act (1534) declared the monarch to be "the only Supreme Head in Earth of the Church of England," with final spiritual and temporal authority in the Church and Commonwealth of England. Thus the English monarchs, through their Parliaments, established a uniform doctrine and liturgy and issued the *Book of Common Prayer* (1559), Thirty-Nine Articles (1576), and Authorized (King James) Version of the Bible (1611). They also assumed final legal responsibility for poor relief, education, and other activities that had previously been carried on under the Catholic Church's auspices. Communicant status in the Church of England was rendered a condition for citizenship status in the Commonwealth of England. Contraventions of royal religious policy were punishable both as heresy and as treason.[46]

The Stuart monarchs moved slowly, through hard experience, toward greater toleration of religious pluralism and greater autonomy of local Churches. From 1603 to 1640, King James I (1566-1625) and Charles I (1600-1649) persecuted Protestant nonconformists with a vengeance, driving tens of thousands of them to the Continent and often from there to North America. In 1640, those who remained led a revolution against the English Crown, and ultimately deposed and executed King Charles I. In 1649, they passed laws that declared England a free Christian commonwealth under the protectorate of Oliver Cromwell. Royal rule was reestablished in 1660, however, and repression of Protestant dissenters renewed. But when the dissenters again rose up in revolt, Parliament passed the Bill of Rights and Toleration Act of 1689 that guaranteed freedom of association, worship, self-government, and basic civil rights to all peaceable Protestant Churches. Many of the remaining legal restrictions fell into desuetude in the following decades, though Catholicism and Judaism remained formally proscribed in England until the Emancipation Acts of 1829 and 1833.[47]

46. See Chapters 7 and 8 herein.
47. See Chapters 3 and 7 herein.

Law and Religion in the Enlightenment

The fourth watershed period in the Western legal tradition came with the eighteenth- and nineteenth-century Enlightenment. The Enlightenment was no single, unified movement, but a series of diverse ideological movements in various academic disciplines and social circles of Western Europe and North America. Enlightenment philosophers, such as David Hume (1711-1776), Jean Jacques Rousseau (1712-1778), and Thomas Jefferson (1743-1826), offered a new secular theology of individualism, rationalism, and nationalism to supplement, if not supplant, traditional Christian beliefs. To Enlightenment exponents, the individual was no longer viewed primarily as a sinner seeking salvation in the life hereafter. Every individual was created equal in virtue and dignity, vested with inherent rights of life and liberty and capable of choosing his or her own means and measures of happiness. Reason was no longer the handmaiden of revelation, rational disputation no longer subordinate to homiletic declaration. The rational process, conducted privately by each person, and collectively in the open marketplace of ideas, was considered a sufficient source of private morality and public law. The nation-state was no longer identified with a national Church or a divinely blessed covenant people. The nation-state was to be glorified in its own right. Its constitutions and laws were sacred texts reflecting the morals and mores of the collective national culture. Its officials were secular priests, representing the sovereignty and will of the people.[48]

Such sentiments were revolutionary in their time and were among the driving forces of the national revolutions in America and France and a principal catalyst for the reformation of many Western legal systems. They inspired sweeping changes in late-eighteenth- and nineteenth-century law — new constitutional provisions for limited government and ample civil liberties, new injunctions to separate Church and state, new criminal procedures and methods of criminal punishment, new commercial, contractual, and other laws of the private marketplace, new laws of private property and inheritance, shifts toward a harm-based law of delicts and torts, the ultimate expulsion of slavery in America, and the gradual removal of discrimination based on race, religion, culture, and gender.[49] Many Western nations also developed elaborate new codes of public law and private

48. See Chapters 8, 10, and 16 herein.
49. See Chapters 6-9 herein.

law, transformed the curricula of their faculties of law, and radically reconfigured their legal professions.

The secular theology of the Enlightenment penetrated Western legal philosophy. Spurred on by Hugo Grotius's (1583-1645) famous hypothesis that natural law can exist even without the existence of God, jurists offered a range of secular legal philosophies — often abstracted from or added to earlier Christian and Graeco-Roman teachings. Writers from John Locke (1632-1704) to Thomas Paine (1737-1809) postulated a mythical state of nature that antedated and integrated human laws and natural rights. Nationalist myths were grafted onto this paradigm to unify and sanctify national legal traditions: Italian jurists appealed to their utopic Roman heritage; English jurists to their ancient constitution and Anglo-Saxon roots; French jurists to their Salic law; German jurists to their ancient constitutional liberties.

As these secular myths dissipated under the hot lights of early modern philosophical skepticism, a triumvirate of new legal philosophies came to prominence in the later eighteenth and nineteenth centuries. Legal positivists, such as Jeremy Bentham (1748-1832) and John Austin (1790-1859), contended that the ultimate source of law lies in the will of the legislature and its ultimate sanction in political force.[50] Natural law theorists, as diverse as Immanuel Kant (1724-1804) and John Adams (1735-1826), sought the ultimate source of law in pure reason and conscience and its ultimate sanction in moral suasion.[51] Historical jurists, such as Friedrich Karl von Savigny (1814-1875) and Otto von Gierke (1841-1921), contended that the ultimate source of law is the custom and character of the *Volk,* and that its ultimate sanction is communal condemnation. These juxtaposed positivist, naturalist, and historicist legal philosophies have persisted in legal academies to this day. They are now heavily supplemented by an array of realist, socialist, feminist, and other schools of legal thought and with a growing number of interdisciplinary approaches that study law in interaction with the methods and texts of theology, economics, science, literature, psychology, sociology, and anthropology.[52]

The secular theology of the Enlightenment also transformed and secularized modern legal institutions. The cardinal secular beliefs of the Enlightenment have come to prominent legal expression in the twentieth and

---

50. See the Conclusion herein.
51. See Chapter 8 herein.
52. See the Conclusion herein.

twenty-first century — individualism in constitutional doctrines of privacy; rationalism in the doctrines of freedom of speech, press, and assembly; nationalism in the totalitarian laws and polities of democracy, fascism, and socialism.[53] In socialist polities, ambitious interpretation of the Enlightenment doctrine of separation of Church and state led to campaigns to eradicate theistic religion altogether, a policy often manifest in the brutal martyrdom of the faithful and massive confiscations of religious property.[54] In democratic polities, ambitious interpretation of the same separation of Church and state doctrine and laicization theories have served to privatize theistic religion and to drive many religious communities from active participation in the legal and political process.[55]

Though these recent secular movements have removed most traditional forms of religious influence on Western law, contemporary Western law still retains important connections with Christian and other religious ideas and institutions. Even today, law and religion continue to cross over and cross-fertilize each other in a variety of ways.[56] Even today, the laws of the secular state retain strong religious dimensions and depend upon some of the enduring religious teachings of the West in crafting our modern understanding of law and order,[57] rights and duties,[58] crime and punishment,[59] Church and state,[60] marriage and family,[61] and more.

Outline of the Volume

The balance of this volume seeks to make this latter case. The first cluster of chapters traces the religious sources and dimensions of Western rights talk, particularly the rights protecting religious individuals and groups. Chapter 1 sets out the main stages of Western rights talk in classical Rome, the Papal Revolution, the Protestant Reformation, and the Enlightenment era. It then documents both the explosion and the attenuation of our mod-

---

53. See Chapters 1, 4, and 8 herein.
54. See Chapter 4 herein.
55. See Chapters 7 and 8 herein.
56. See the Conclusion herein.
57. See Chapters 2 and 5 herein.
58. See Chapters 1 and 8 herein.
59. See Chapter 9 herein.
60. See Chapters 6-8 herein.
61. See Chapters 10-12 and 14 herein.

ern rights talk, and calls for a firmer philosophical and theological grounding of human rights, a call which Chapters 2 to 4 aim to answer. Chapter 2 analyzes Martin Luther's distinctive theological theory of human dignity, liberty, and equality, and shows how Luther's views continue to shape Protestant instincts about human rights today. Chapter 3 offers a lengthy analysis of the complex interactions between religion and human rights today, calls for a new hermeneutic of rights talk within religious traditions, and then applies this hermeneutic to the history of rights in the Catholic, Protestant, and Orthodox traditions. Chapter 4 takes on one serious contemporary issue of religious liberty, briefed already in Chapter 3, namely, the growing clash between Russian Orthodox and Western Christian understandings of proselytism and conversion and attendant theories of Church-state relations.

The second cluster of chapters focuses more directly on American understandings of law and religion, Church and state. Chapter 5 illustrates how Calvinist Puritan theories helped to shape the theory and law of ordered liberty and orderly pluralism in seventeenth- and eighteenth-century New England, especially Massachusetts. Chapter 6 shows how the Puritan, Evangelical, Enlightenment, and Republican traditions together helped to forge America's essential rights and liberties of religion — liberty of conscience, free exercise of religion, religious pluralism and equality, separation of Church and state, and disestablishment of religion. It then explores how these principles of religious liberty informed the First Amendment religion clauses forged in 1789. Chapter 7 seeks to exorcise the many historical and political myths surrounding the separation of Church and state. It argues that separation of Church and state has a long and complex history in the Western tradition, and that it should remain a vital principle of religious liberty still today so long as its application is buffered by the other principles of religious liberty distilled in the prior chapter. Chapter 8 continues this argument by showing how America's history of religious liberty was driven by competing Protestant and Enlightenment understandings of Church and state, which are now converging in a new theory of the freedom of public religion. Chapter 9 makes a comparable case in the realm of criminal law and punishment. It documents the past and potential convergences between Protestant theologies of the civil, theological, and educational uses of the moral law and Enlightenment theories of deterrent, retributive, and rehabilitative purposes of the state's law of crime and punishment.

The final cluster of chapters trains the binocular of law and religion on issues of marriage and family life. Chapter 10 documents how much of our modern marriage and family are the products of Catholic, Protestant, and Enlightenment theology and law, and urges the reconstruction of some of the most common enduring teachings of these traditions to help with the marriage and family reforms of our day. One such enduring teaching, taken up in detail in Chapter 11, is the view that marriage is a good institution for the couple, the children, and the broader communities of which they are part. This teaching recurs repeatedly in Graeco-Roman, patristic, medieval Catholic, early modern Protestant, and modern philosophical sources, and has recently been documented in a new social science literature as well. A second such teaching, taken up in detail in Chapter 12, is that marriage is fundamentally a contract between husband and wife, but also much more than a contract. Christians share with Jews and Muslims the view that marriage is a covenant, at once private and public, contractual and spiritual, voluntary and natural, psychological and civilizational in origin, nature, and function. Not all the family teachings of the tradition have been so edifying. Chapter 13 shows some of the perils of Catholic mandatory clerical celibacy, both historically and today. Chapter 14 traces the sorry history of illegitimacy doctrine in the Western legal tradition. It argues that a fundamental misreading of the story of Ishmael and other biblical texts has led canon law, civil law, and common law alike to routinized discrimination against bastards, and urges instead better theories and law of adoption and personal responsibility. Chapter 15 takes up the more wholesome subject of the historical duties of love that parents and children owe to each other at different stages of a child's formation — a subject treated at length in the household manuals that have survived from the fourteenth to the nineteenth centuries.

The Conclusion and Afterword step back from this trio of specialized studies and make both the generic case for the study of law and religion, and the more specific case for modern Christian engagement of fundamental issues of law, politics, and society.

LAW, RELIGION, AND HUMAN RIGHTS

1

A Short History of Western Rights

Rights are so commonplace today that the term is in danger of becoming cliché. Rights talk has become a dominant mode of political, legal, and moral discourse in the modern West, and rights protections and violations have become increasingly important issues in international relations and diplomacy. Most nation-states now have detailed bills or recitations of rights in their constitutions, statutes, and cases. The United Nations and various other groups of nation-states have detailed catalogues of rights set out in treaties, declarations, conventions, and covenants. Many Christian denominations and ecumenical groups, alongside other religious groups, have their own declarations and statements on rights as well. Thousands of governmental, intergovernmental, and nongovernmental organizations are now dedicated to the defense of rights around the world, including a large number of Christian and other religious lobbying and litigation groups.

Various classes of rights are now commonly distinguished.[1] One common distinction is between public or constitutional rights (those which operate vis-à-vis the state) and private or personal rights (those which operate vis-à-vis other private parties). A second distinction is between individual rights and the rights of associations or groups (whether private groups, like businesses or Churches, or public groups, like munici-

---

1. The classic formulation remains W. N. Hohfeld, *Fundamental Legal Conceptions* (New Haven: Yale University Press, 1919). In the vast modern literature on point, see sources and discussion in Carl Wellman, *An Approach to Rights* (The Hague: Kluwer Academic, 1997); Michael J. Perry, *The Idea of Human Rights: Four Inquiries* (New York: Oxford University Press, 1998); Michael J. Perry, *Rights As Morality, Rights As Law* (Cambridge: Cambridge University Press, 2006); Joel Feinberg, *Rights, Justice, and the Bounds of Liberty* (Princeton, N.J.: Princeton University Press, 1980).

palities or political parties). A third is between human rights (those that inhere in a human qua human) and civil rights (those that inhere in citizens or civil subjects). A fourth is between natural rights (those that are based on natural law or human nature) and positive rights (those that are based in the positive law of the state). A fifth is between unalienable or nonderogable rights (those that cannot be given or taken away) and alienable or derogable rights (those that can be voluntarily given away or can be taken away under specified legal conditions). Increasingly today, distinctions are also drawn among the discrete claims of particular parties and groups, many of whom have historically not received adequate rights protection — women, children, workers, migrants, minorities, prisoners, captives, indigenous peoples, religious parties, the mentally and physically disabled, and more. And distinctions are also increasingly drawn among "first generation" civil and political rights, "second generation" social, cultural, and economic rights, and "third generation" rights to peace, environmental protection, and orderly development.

Different types of legal claims and jural relationships are inherent in these classifications of rights. Some scholars distinguish rights (something that triggers a correlative duty in others) from privileges (something that no one has a right to interfere with). Others distinguish active rights (the power or capacity to do or assert something oneself) and passive rights (the entitlement or claim to be given or allowed something by someone or something else). Others distinguish rights or privileges (claims or entitlements to something) from liberties or immunities (freedoms or protections from interference). This latter distinction is also sometimes rendered as positive liberty or freedom (the right to do something) versus negative liberty or freedom (the right to be left alone).

In all these foregoing formulations, the term "right" and its equivalents is being used in a "subjective sense." A "subjective right" is vested in a subject (whether an individual, group, or entity), and the subject usually can have that right vindicated before an appropriate authority when the right is threatened or violated. This subjective sense of right is quite different from right in an "objective sense." "Objective right" (or "rightness") means that something is the objectively right thing or action in the circumstances. Objective right obtains when something is rightly ordered, is just or proper, is considered to be right when judged against some objective or external standard. "Right" is here being used as an adjective, not as a noun: it is what is correct or proper — "due and meet," as the Victorians used to put it.

These subjective and objective senses of right can cohere, even overlap. You can say that "a victim of theft has a right to have his property restored" or that "it is right for a victim of theft to have his property restored." Knowing nothing else, these are parallel statements. But if the victim is a ruthless tycoon and the thief a starving child, the parallel is harder to draw: even though the subject (tycoon) has a right, it might not always be objectively right to respect or enforce it. Sometimes the subjective and objective senses of right are more clearly dissociated: even if it is objectively right for someone to perform an action, it does not always mean the beneficiary of that action has a subjective right to its performance. Though it might be right for you to give alms to the poor, a poor person has no right to receive alms from you. Though it might be right for a parishioner to give tithes to the Church, a Church has no right to receive tithes from that parishioner.

This basic tension between the subjective and objective senses of the English term "right" has parallels in other languages. *Recht* in German, *droit* in French, *diritto* in Italian, *ius* in Latin, all can be used in both subjective and objective senses — and sometimes in other senses as well. And, like English, each of these languages has developed its own terms for privileges, immunities, powers, capacities, freedoms, liberties, and more, which are used to sort out various types of rights.

These linguistic tensions and tangles of our rights talk today are products of a two-millennium-long evolution in the West. The intellectual history of Western rights talk is still very much a work in progress, with scholars still discovering and disputing in earnest the basic roots and routes of the development of rights concepts and structures. What follows is a brief sampling of some of the highlights of this still highly contested story.

Classical Formulations[2]

The classical Roman jurists of the first centuries C.E. used the ancient Latin term *ius* to identify right in both its objective and subjective

2. See sources and discussion in Charles A. Donahue, "Ius in the Subjective Sense in Roman Law: Reflections on Villey and Tierney," in *A Ennio Cortese,* ed. D. Maffei, 2 vols. (Rome: Il cigno Galileo Galilei, 2001), 1:506-35; Max Kaser, *Ius Gentium* (Cologne: Böhlau, 1993); Max Kaser, *Ausgewählte Schriften,* 2 vols. (Naples: Jovene, 1976-1977); Tony Honoré, *Ulpian: Pioneer of Human Rights,* second ed. (Oxford: Oxford University Press, 2002); C. Wirszubski, *Libertas As a Political Idea at Rome During the Late Republic and Early Principate* (Cambridge: Cambridge University Press, 1950).

senses.[3] The objective sense of *ius* — to be in proper order, to perform what is right and required, "to give to each his due" (*ius suum cuiuque tribuere*) — dominated the Roman law texts. But these texts also occasionally used *ius* subjectively, in the sense of a person "having a right" (*ius habere*). Many of the subjective rights recognized at Roman law involved property: the right to own or co-own property; the right to possess, lease, or use property; the right to build or prevent building on land; the right to gain access to water; the right to be free from interference or invasion of one's property; the right or capacity to alienate property; the right to bury one's dead; and more. Several texts dealt with personal rights: the rights of testators and heirs, the rights of patrons and guardians, the rights of fathers over children, masters over slaves, mothers over orphaned children and their affairs. Other texts dealt with public rights: the right of an official to punish or deal with his subjects in a certain way, the right to delegate power, the right to appoint and supervise officials. Others dealt with procedural rights in criminal and civil cases. Charles Donahue has recently identified 191 texts on subjective rights in the *Digest* alone (one of the four books of Justinian's *Corpus Iuris Civilis*) and speculates that hundreds if not thousands more such texts can be found in other books of Roman law.[4]

The classical Roman law also referred to subjective rights using the Latin term *libertas,* which roughly translates as liberty. One's *libertas* at Roman law turned in part on one's status in Roman society: men had more *libertas* than women, married women more than concubines, adults more than children, free persons more than slaves, and so on. But each person at Roman law had a basic *libertas* inherent in his or her social status. This included a basic right to be free from subjection or undue restraint from others who had no rights (*iura*) or claim (*dominium*) over them. Thus the wife had *libertas* from sexual relations with all others besides her husband. The child had *libertas* from the direction of all others save the paterfamilias or his delegates. Even the slave had *libertas* from the discipline of others besides his or her master. And those rights could be vindicated by filing actions before a judge or other licensed official, directly or through a representative.[5]

Some *libertas* interests recognized at Roman law were cast more gen-

---

3. *Ius* also meant law or legal order more generally.
4. Donahue, "Ius in the Subjective Sense in Roman Law."
5. Wirszubski, *Libertas;* Honoré, *Ulpian: Pioneer of Human Rights.*

erally, and not necessarily conditioned on the correlative rights or duties of others. A good example was the freedom of religion guaranteed to Christians and others under the Edict of Milan (313) passed by Emperor Constantine. This included "the freedom *(libertas)* to follow whatever religion each one wished"; "a public and free liberty to practice their religion or cult"; and a "free capacity" *(facultas)* to follow their own religion and worship "as befits the peacefulness of our times."[6]

Echoes of both *ius* and *libertas* recurred occasionally in later Frankish and Anglo-Saxon texts. In fact, in a few late-ninth- and tenth-century Anglo-Saxon texts these terms were variously translated as "ryhtes," "rihtes," and "rihta(e)."[7] The careful Roman law differentiation of objective and subjective senses of right, however, seems to have been lost in the last centuries of the first millennium C.E. — though a systematic study of the possible rights talk of the Germanic texts of this period is apparently still a desideratum. And what apparently is also still needed is a close study (at least in a Romance language) of the possible rights talk of Muslim and Jewish scholars in this same period. After all, both Muslim and Jewish scholars had access to the ancient Roman law texts that were lost in the West after the sixth century, and both worked out a refined theological jurisprudence in the eighth through tenth centuries C.E.[8]

Medieval Formulations

The rediscovery of the ancient texts of Roman law in the late eleventh and twelfth centuries helped to trigger a renaissance of subjective rights talk in the West. Brian Tierney has shown that, already in the twelfth century, medieval canonists differentiated all manner of rights *(iura)* and liberties *(libertates)*.[9] They grounded these rights and liberties in the law of

6. In Ehler and Morrall, pp. 4-6; Lactantius, *De Mortibus Persecutorum* [c. 315], 48.2-12, ed. and trans. J. L. Creed (Oxford: Oxford University Press, 1984), pp. 71-73.

7. O.E.D., s.v. "right"; Alfred Kiralfky, "Law and Right in English Legal History," in *La formazione storica de diritto moderno in Europa* (Florence: Leo S. Olschki, 1977), 3:1069-1086.

8. See George Makdisi, *Religion, Law, and Learning in Classical Islam* (Aldershot, Hampshire: Varorium, 1991); George Makdisi, *The Rise of Humanism in Classical Islam and the Christian West with Special Reference to Scholasticism* (Edinburgh: Edinburgh University Press, 1990).

9. See further Chapter 3 herein.

nature *(lex naturae)* or natural law *(ius naturale)* and associated them variously with a power *(facultas)* inhering in rational human nature and with the property *(dominium)* of a person or the power *(potestas)* of an office of authority *(officium)*. The early canonists repeated and glossed many of the subjective rights and liberties set out in the Roman law — especially the public rights and powers of rulers, the private rights and liberties of property, and what Gratian in circa 1140 called the "rights of liberty" *(iura libertatis)* enjoyed by persons of various stations in life and offices of authority.[10] They also began to weave these early Roman law texts into a complex latticework of what we now call rights, freedoms, powers, immunities, protections, and capacities for different groups and persons.

Most important to the medieval canonists were the rights needed to protect the "freedom of the Church" *(libertas ecclesiae)*. Freedom of the Church from civil and feudal control and corruption had been the rallying cry of Pope Gregory VII (1073-1085), which had inaugurated the Papal Revolution of 1075. In defense of this revolution, medieval canonists specified in great detail the rights of the Church to make its own laws, to maintain its own courts, to define its own doctrines and liturgies, to elect and remove its own clergy. They also stipulated the exemptions of Church property from civil taxation and takings, and the right of the clergy to control and use Church property without interference or encumbrance from secular or feudal authorities. They also guaranteed the immunity of the clergy from civil prosecution, military service, and compulsory testimony, and the rights of Church entities like parishes, monasteries, charities, and guilds to form and dissolve, to accept and reject members, and to establish order and discipline. In later twelfth- and thirteenth-century decrees, the canon law defined the rights of Church councils and synods to participate in the election and discipline of bishops, abbots, and other clergy. It defined the rights of the lower clergy vis-à-vis their superiors. It defined the rights of the laity to worship, evangelize, maintain religious symbols, participate in the sacraments, travel on religious pilgrimages, and educate their children. It defined the rights of the poor, widows, and needy to seek solace, succor, and sanctuary within the Church. It defined the rights of husbands and wives, parents and children, masters and servants within the house-

---

10. C. 16, q. 3, dictum post c. 15, quoted in Brian Tierney, *The Idea of Natural Rights: Studies on Natural Rights, Natural Law, and Church Law, 1150-1625* (Grand Rapids: Eerdmans, 1997), p. 57.

hold.[11] The canon law even defined the (truncated) rights that Jews, Muslims, and heretics had in Christian society.[12]

These medieval canon law rights were enforced by a hierarchy of Church courts and other administrative offices, each with distinctive rules of litigation, evidence, and judgment, and with ultimate appeal to Rome. These rights formulations were rendered increasingly sophisticated and systematic in the fourteenth through sixteenth centuries through the work of such scholars as William of Ockham (ca. 1285–ca. 1349), John Wycliffe (d. 1384), Conrad Summenhart (1465-1511), Richard Fitzralph (d. 1360), Jean Gerson (1363-1429), Francisco de Vitoria (ca. 1486-1546), Fernando Vázquez (b. 1512), Francisco Suárez (1548-1617), and others. Particularly the formulations of William of Ockham in the fourteenth century and the Spanish neo-scholastic jurists of the sixteenth century were of monumental importance to the evolution and expansion of Western rights talk. They provided a good deal of the intellectual arsenal for the later rights theories of Johannes Althusius (1557-1638), Hugo Grotius (1583-1645), Samuel von Pufendorf (1632-1694), and others.[13]

The medieval canon law formulations of rights and liberties had parallels in medieval common law and civil law. Particularly notable sources were the thousands of treaties, concordats, and charters that were issued from the eleventh to the sixteenth centuries by various religious and secular authorities. These were often detailed, and sometimes very flowery, statements of the rights and liberties to be enjoyed by various groups of clergy, nobles, barons, knights, municipal councils, citizens, universities, monasteries, and other corporate entities. A good example was the Magna Carta (1215), the great charter issued by the English Crown at the behest of the Church and barons of England. The Magna Carta guaranteed that "the Church of England shall be free (*libera*) and shall have all her whole rights

---

11. Charles J. Reid Jr., *Power over the Body, Equality in the Family: Rights and Domestic Relations in Medieval Canon Law* (Grand Rapids: Eerdmans, 2004).

12. See further Chapter 3 herein.

13. See sources in Chapter 3 herein, and further in A. S. Brett, *Liberty, Right, and Nature: Individual Rights in Later Scholastic Thought* (Cambridge: Cambridge University Press, 1997); R. W. Davis, ed., *The Origins of Modern Freedom in the West* (Stanford, Calif.: Stanford University Press, 1995); Richard Tuck, *Natural Rights Theories: Their Origins and Development* (Cambridge: Cambridge University Press, 1979); Michel Villey, *La formation de la pensée juridique moderne* (Paris: Montchrestien, 1968); Michel Villey, *Le droit et les droits de l'homme* (Paris: Presses universitaires de France, 1983); Michel Villey, *Leçons d'histoire de la philosophie du droit,* new ed. (Paris: Dalloz, 1977).

(*iura*) and liberties (*libertates*) inviolable" and that all "free-men" (*liberis hominibus*) were to enjoy their various "liberties" (*libertates*). These liberties included sundry rights to property, marriage, and inheritance, to freedom from undue military service, and to freedom to pay one's debts and taxes from the property of one's own choosing. The Magna Carta also set out various rights and powers of towns and of local justices and their tribunals, various rights and prerogatives of the king and of the royal courts, and various procedural rights in these courts (including the right to jury trial).[14]

These medieval charters of rights became important prototypes on which later revolutionaries would call to justify their revolt against arbitrary authorities. A good example of this was the Dutch Declaration of Independence of 1581, by which the estates of the Netherlands justified their revolt against Spanish religious and political tyranny on the strength of "the law of nature" and of the "ancient rights, privileges, and liberties" set out in their medieval charters.[15]

Protestant Formulations

The sixteenth-century Protestant Reformation grounded its revolt not on ancient charters of rights but on biblical calls for freedom. Particularly the New Testament is amply peppered with all manner of aphorisms on freedom: "For freedom, Christ has set us free." "You were called to freedom." "Where the Spirit of the Lord is, there is freedom." "You will know the truth, and the truth will make you free." "You will be free indeed." You have been given "the glorious liberty of the children of God."[16] These and other biblical passages inspired Martin Luther (1483-1546) to unleash the Reformation in Germany in 1517 in the name of freedom (*libertas, Freiheit*) — freedom of the Church from the tyranny of the pope, freedom of the laity from the hegemony of the clergy, freedom of the conscience from the strictures of canon law. "Freedom of the Christian" was the rallying cry of the early Protestant Reformation. It drove theologians and jurists, clergy

14. *The Statutes at Large of England and of Great Britain from the Magna Carta to the Union of the Kingdoms of Great Britain and Ireland,* 20 vols. (London: G. Eyre and J. Strahan, 1811), 1:1.

15. In E. H. Kossmann and A. Mellink, eds., *Texts Concerning the Revolt of the Netherlands* (London: Cambridge University Press, 1974).

16. Galatians 5:1, 13; 2 Corinthians 3:17; John 8:32, 36; Romans 8:21.

and laity, princes and peasants alike to denounce the medieval Church authorities and legal structures with unprecedented alacrity. The Church's canon law books were burned. Church courts were closed. Monastic institutions were confiscated. Endowed benefices were dissolved. Church lands were seized. Clerical privileges were stripped. Mendicant begging was banned. Mandatory celibacy was suspended. Indulgence trafficking was condemned. Annates to Rome were outlawed. Ties to the pope were severed. Each nation, each Church, and each Christian was to be free.[17]

Left in such raw and radical form, this early Protestant call for freedom was a recipe for lawlessness and license, as Luther learned the hard way during the Peasants' Revolt of 1525. Luther and other Protestants soon came to realize that structures of law and authority were essential to protecting order and peace, even as guarantees of liberties and rights were essential to preserving the message and momentum of the Reformation. The challenge for Protestants was to strike new balances between authority and liberty on the strength of cardinal biblical teachings.

One important Protestant contribution to Western rights talk, offered by Philip Melanchthon (1497-1560), John Calvin (1509-1564), and others, was to comb through the Bible in order to redefine the nature and authority of the family, the Church, and the state vis-à-vis each other and their constituents. The Reformers regarded these three institutions as fundamental orders of creation, equal before God and each other, and vested with certain natural duties and qualities that the other authorities could not trespass. To define these respective offices clearly not only served to check the natural appetite of the *paterfamilias, patertheologicus,* and *paterpoliticus* for tyranny and abuse. It also helped to clarify the liberties of those subject to their authority, and to specify the grounds on which they could protest or disobey.[18]

A second contribution was the Reformers' habit of grounding rights in the duties of the Decalogue and of other biblical texts. The First Table of the Decalogue prescribes duties of love that each person owes to God — to honor God and God's name, to observe the Sabbath day and to worship, to avoid false gods and false swearing. The Second Table prescribes duties of love that each person owes to neighbors — to honor one's parents and other authorities, not to kill, not to commit adultery, not to steal, not to bear false witness, not to covet. The Reformers cast the person's duties to-

17. See further Chapter 2 herein.
18. See further Chapters 2 and 5 herein.

ward God as a set of rights that others could not obstruct — the right to religious exercise: the right to honor God and God's name, the right to rest
and worship on one's Sabbath, the right to be free from false gods and false
oaths. They cast a person's duties towards a neighbor, in turn, as the neighbor's right to have that duty discharged. One person's duties not to kill, to
commit adultery, to steal, or to bear false witness thus gives rise to another
person's rights to life, property, fidelity, and reputation.

A third contribution was the effort of later Protestants to unpack the
political implications of the signature Reformation teaching that a person is
at once sinner and saint *(simul iustus et peccator).*[19] On the one hand, Protestants argued, every person is created in the image of God and justified by
faith in God. Every person is called to a distinct vocation, which stands equal
in dignity and sanctity to all others. Every person is a prophet, priest, and
king, and responsible to exhort, to minister, and to rule in the community.
Every person thus stands equal before God and before his or her neighbor.
Every person is vested with a natural liberty to live, to believe, to love and
serve God and neighbor. Every person is entitled to the vernacular Scripture,
to education, to work in a vocation. On the other hand, Protestants argued,
every person is sinful and prone to evil and egoism. Every person needs the
restraint of the law to deter him from evil, and to drive him to repentance. Every person needs the association of others to exhort, minister, and rule her
with law and with love. Every person, therefore, is inherently a communal
creature. Every person belongs to a family, a Church, a political community.

By the later sixteenth century, Protestant groups began to recast these
theological doctrines into democratic norms and forms designed to protect
human rights. Protestant doctrines of the person and society were cast into
democratic social forms. Since all persons stand equal before God, they
must stand equal before God's political agents in the state. Since God has
vested all persons with natural liberties of life and belief, the state must ensure them of similar civil liberties. Since God has called all persons to be
prophets, priests, and kings, the state must protect their constitutional
freedoms to speak, to preach, and to rule in the community. Since God has
created persons as social creatures, the state must promote and protect a
plurality of social institutions, particularly the Church and the family.
Protestant doctrines of sin, in turn, were cast into democratic political
forms. The political office must be protected against the sinfulness of the

19. For Luther's exposition of this doctrine, see Chapter 2 herein and LP, pp. 87-
117.

political official. Political power, like ecclesiastical power, must be distributed among self-checking executive, legislative, and judicial branches. Officials must be elected to limited terms of office. Laws must be clearly codified, and discretion closely guarded. If officials abuse their office, they must be disobeyed. If they persist in their abuse, they must be removed, even if by revolutionary force and regicide.[20]

These Protestant teachings were among the driving ideological forces behind the revolts of the French Huguenots, Dutch Pietists, and Scottish Presbyterians against their monarchical oppressors in the later sixteenth and seventeenth centuries. They were also critical weapons in the arsenal of the seventeenth-century English revolutionaries, whose efforts yielded the Petition of Right (1628) and the Bill of Rights (1689).[21] Both these documents set firm limits on royal authority and prescribed rules for royal succession and Parliamentary election in England. The Bill of Rights went further in guaranteeing English citizens various "undoubted rights and liberties" — the rights to speech, petition, and election, the right to bear arms, and various criminal procedural protections (right to jury trial, freedom from excessive bail and fines and from cruel and unusual punishment). These were important public law rights that were added to the growing body of private law rights already recognized by the common law and civil law.

Enlightenment Formulations

While medieval canonists grounded rights in natural law and ancient charters, and while Protestant Reformers grounded them in biblical texts and theological anthropology, Enlightenment writers in Europe and North America grounded rights in human nature and the social contract. Building in part on the ancient ideas of Cicero, Seneca, and other Stoics of a prepolitical state of nature, John Locke (1632-1704), Thomas Hobbes (1588-1679), Jean Jacques Rousseau (1712-1778), Thomas Jefferson (1743-1826), and others argued for a new foundation of rights and political order.[22] Every individual, they argued, was created, or was by nature, equal in

20. See elaboration of this theme in RR.

21. Stephenson and Markham, pp. 450-53, 599-604; See also the Toleration Act (1689), in Stephenson and Markham, pp. 607-8, that granted toleration to English Protestants who dissented from the Church of England.

22. These "state of nature" theories were also circulating in the early Protestant

virtue and dignity, and vested with inherent and unalienable rights of life, liberty, and property. Each person was naturally capable of choosing his or her own means and measures of happiness without necessary external reference or commandment. In their natural state, the state of nature, all persons were free to exercise their natural rights fully. But life in this state of nature was at minimum "inconvenient," as Locke put it — if not "brutish, nasty, and short," as Hobbes put it. For there was no means to balance and broker disputes between one person's rights against all others, no incentive to invest or create property or conclude contracts when one's title was not sure, no mechanism for dealing with the needs of children, the weak, the disabled, the vulnerable. As a consequence, rational persons chose to move from the state of nature to a society. They did so by entering into social contracts and ratifying constitutions to govern their newly created societies. By these instruments, persons agreed to sacrifice or limit some of their natural rights for the sake of creating a measure of social order and peace. They also agreed to delegate their natural rights to self-rule to elected officials who would represent and exercise executive, legislative, and judicial authority on their behalf. But, at the same time, these social contracts and political constitutions insisted on the protection of various "inalienable" rights that they were to enjoy, and on the specification of the conditions of "due process of law" under which "alienable" rights could be abridged or taken away. And they also insisted on individuals' right to elect and change their representatives in government, and to be tried in all cases by their peers.

Particularly the American and French constitutions reflected these new Enlightenment views. The Virginia Declaration of Rights (1776), for example, provided in Article I:

> That all men are by nature equally free and independent, and have certain inherent rights, of which, when they enter into a state of society, they cannot, by any compact, deprive or divest their posterity; namely, the enjoyment of life and liberty, with the means of acquiring and possessing property, and pursuing and obtaining happiness and safety.[23]

world. See, e.g., the views of Johannes Eisermann (1533), John Ponet (1556), Christopher Goodman (1558), and Johannes Althusius (1614), described in LP, chap. 4, and RR, chaps. 2 and 3.

23. In Francis N. Thorpe, ed., *The Federal and State Constitutions, Colonial Charters, and Other Organic Laws,* 7 vols. (Washington, D.C.: Government Printing Office, 1909), 7:3813. See further Chapter 7 herein.

The Declaration went on to specify the rights of the people to vote and to run for office, their "indubitable, unalienable, and indefeasible right to reform, alter or abolish" their government if necessary, various traditional criminal procedural protections, the right to jury trial in civil and criminal cases, freedom of press, and various freedoms of religion. But the Declaration also reflected traditional Christian sentiments in providing that "no free government, or the blessings of liberty, can be preserved to any people but by a firm adherence to justice, moderation, temperance, frugality, and virtue and by frequent recurrence to fundamental principles," and further by insisting that it was "the mutual duty of all to practice Christian forbearance, love, and charity towards each other."[24] Even stronger such traditional Christian formulations stood alongside the new Enlightenment views in the 1780 Massachusetts Constitution.[25]

The Bill of Rights of 1791, which amended the United States Constitution of 1787, was more forceful in its articulation of basic Enlightenment sentiments on rights. While the Constitution spoke generically of the "blessings of liberty" and specified a few discrete "privileges and immunities," it was left to the Bill of Rights to enumerate the rights of American citizens.[26] The Bill of Rights guaranteed the freedoms of religion, speech, assembly, and press, the right to bear arms, the freedom from forced quartering of soldiers, freedom from illegal searches and seizures, various criminal procedural protections (the right to grand jury indictment and trial by jury, the right to a fair and speedy trial, the right to face accusers and have them compelled to appear, freedom from double jeopardy, the privilege against self incrimination, freedom from excessive bail and cruel and unusual punishment), the right to jury trial in civil cases, the guarantee not to be deprived of life, liberty, or property without due process of law, and the right not to have property taken for public use without just compensation.[27] This original Bill of Rights was later augmented by several other amendments, the most important of which were the right to be free from slavery and involuntary servitude, the right to equal protection and due process of law, and the right for all adults, male and female, to vote.[28]

24. Virginia Declaration of Rights, arts. 15 and 16, in *The Federal and State Constitutions*, 7:3814.

25. See Chapters 5 and 8 herein.

26. U.S. Const., preamble, Arts. 1.9, 1.10.

27. U.S. Const. Am. 1-8.

28. U.S. Const. Am. 13-15, 19, 24, 26.

The French Declaration of the Rights of Man and Citizen (1791) enumerated various "natural, unalienable, and sacred rights," including liberty, property, security, and resistance to oppression, "the freedom to do everything which injures no one else," the right to participate in the foundation and formulation of law, a guarantee that all citizens are equal before the law and equally eligible to all dignities and to all public positions and occupations, according to their abilities. The Declaration also included basic criminal procedure protections, freedom of (religious) opinions, freedoms of speech and press, and rights to property.[29] Both the French and American constitutions and declarations were essential prototypes for a whole raft of constitutional and international documents on rights that were forged in the next two centuries.

Modern Age

While these Enlightenment foundations and formulations of rights have remained prominent among some theorists, a concept of universal rights predicated on "human dignity" has become increasingly common today. In the mid twentieth century, the world stared in horror into Hitler's death camps and Stalin's gulags, where all sense of humanity and dignity had been brutally sacrificed. In response, the world seized anew on the ancient concept of human dignity, claiming this as the "ur-principle" of a new world order.[30] The *Universal Declaration of Human Rights* of 1948 opened its preamble with what would become classic words: "recognition of the inherent dignity and of the equal and inalienable rights of all members of the human family is the foundation of freedom, justice, and peace in the world."[31]

The United Nations and several nation-states issued a number of landmark documents on human rights thereafter. Foremost among these were the two great international covenants promulgated by the United Nations in 1966. Both these covenants took as their starting point the "inherent dignity" and "the equal and inalienable rights of all members of the human

29. In Léon Duguit, *Les Constitutions et Les Principales Lois Politiques de la France Depuis 1789* (Paris: Librairie Générale de Droit et de Jurisprudence, 1952), p. 1.

30. The term "ur-principle" is from Louis Henkin et al., *Human Rights* (New York: Foundation, 1999), p. 80.

31. Reprinted in Ian Brownlie, ed., *Basic Documents on Human Rights,* third ed. (Oxford: Oxford University Press, 1992), p. 21.

family," and the belief that all such "rights derive from the inherent dignity of the human person."[32] The *International Covenant on Economic, Social, and Cultural Rights* (1966) posed as essential to human dignity the rights to self-determination, subsistence, work, welfare, security, education, and various other forms of participation in cultural life. The *International Covenant on Civil and Political Rights* (1966) set out a long catalogue of rights to life and to security of person and property, freedom from slavery and cruelty, basic civil and criminal procedural protections, rights to travel and pilgrimage, freedoms of religion, expression, and assembly, rights to marriage and family life, and freedom from discrimination on grounds of race, color, sex, language, and national origin. A number of other international and domestic instruments took particular aim at racial, religious, and gender discrimination in education, employment, social welfare programs, and other forms and forums of public life, and the protection of children, migrants, workers, and indigenous peoples.[33] Later instruments, like the 1981 *UN Declaration on the Elimination of All Forms of Intolerance and of Discrimination Based on Religion or Belief* and the 1989 *Vienna Concluding Document,* provided important foundations for the protection of religious rights for individuals and groups.[34]

Christian and other religious communities participated actively as midwives in the birth of this modern rights movement. Individual religious groups issued bold confessional statements and manifestos on human rights shortly after World War II. Several denominations and budding ecumenical bodies joined with Jewish nongovernmental organizations in the cultivation of human rights at the international level. The Free Church tradition played a critical role in the civil rights movement in America and beyond, as did the Social Gospel and Christian Democratic movements in Europe and Latin America.[35]

Various Christian groups also provided an active nursery for the cul-

---

32. See the preambles to both documents in *Basic Documents on Human Rights,* pp. 114, 125.

33. *International Convention on the Elimination of All Forms of Racial Discrimination* (1969), preface, in *Basic Documents on Human Rights,* p. 148. See comparable language in *International Convention on Suppression and Punishment of the Crime of Apartheid* (1973), in *Basic Documents on Human Rights,* p. 162, and in *Convention on the Elimination of all Forms of Discrimination against Women* (1979), in *Basic Documents on Human Rights,* p. 169.

34. See further Chapter 3 herein.

35. See RHR I and II.

tivation of new global understandings of human rights predicated on human dignity.[36] In *Dignitatis Humanae* and several other documents produced during and after the Second Vatican Council (1962-1965), the Roman Catholic Church took some of the decisive first steps, reversing earlier statements like the 1864 *Syllabus of Errors* that had stood foursquare against human rights.[37] Every person, the Church now taught, is created by God with "dignity, intelligence and free will . . . and has rights flowing directly and simultaneously from his very nature."[38] Such rights include the right to life and adequate standards of living, to moral and cultural values, to religious activities, to assembly and association, to marriage and family life, and to various social, political, and economic benefits and opportunities. The Church emphasized the religious rights of conscience, worship, assembly, and education, calling them the "first rights" of any civic order. It also stressed the need to balance individual and associational rights, particularly those involving the Church, family, and school. Governments everywhere were encouraged to create conditions conducive to the realization and protection of these inviolable rights and encouraged to root out discrimination, whether social or cultural, whether based on sex, race, color, social distinction, language, or religion.[39] Within a decade, various ecumenical groups, some Protestants, and even a few Orthodox Christian groups crafted comparable comprehensive declarations on human rights — albeit with varying emphases on the concept of human dignity.[40]

36. John Nurser, *For All Peoples and All Nations: Christian Churches and Human Rights* (Geneva: World Council of Churches Publications, 2005); Allen D. Hertzke, *Freeing God's Children: The Unlikely Alliance for Global Human Rights* (Lanham, Md.: Rowman and Littlefield, 2004); Robert Traer, *Faith in Human Rights: Support in Religious Traditions for a Global Struggle* (Washington, D.C.: Georgetown University Press, 1991). See further Chapter 3 herein.

37. See further Chapter 7 herein.

38. *Pacem in Terris* (1963), paragraph 9, in *The Documents of Vatican II*, ed. Walter M. Abbott and J. Gallagher (New York: Herder and Herder, 1966), p. 675.

39. *Pacem in Terris; Dignitatis Humanae (1965)*, in *Documents of Vatican II*, p. 675.

40. See, e.g., Allen O. Miller, ed., *A Christian Declaration on Human Rights* (Grand Rapids: Eerdmans, 1977) (a Calvinist statement, with full endorsement of the concept of human dignity); Lutheran World Federation, *Theological Perspectives on Human Rights* (Geneva: Lutheran World Federation, 1977) (a Lutheran document that largely eschews the concept of human dignity); *Human Rights and Christian Responsibility,* 3 vols. (Geneva: World Council of Churches, 1975) (ecumenical statements with only passing references to human dignity). See detailed analysis in Wolfgang Huber and Heinz Eduard Tödt, *Menschenrechte: Perspektiven einer menschlichen Welt* (Stuttgart: Kreuz

Today, the concept of human dignity has become ubiquitous to the point of cliché — a moral trump frayed by heavy use, a general principle harried by constant invocation. We now read regularly of the dignity of luxury, pleasure, and leisure; the dignity of poverty, pain, and imprisonment; the dignity of identity, belonging, and difference; the dignity of ethnic, cultural, and linguistic purity; the dignity of sex, gender, and sexual preference; the dignity of aging, dying, and death. At the same time, the corpus of human rights has become swollen to the point of eruption — with many recent rights claims no longer anchored in universal norms of human dignity or comparable ontological claims, but aired as special aspirations of an individual or a group. We now hear regularly of the right to peace, health, and beauty; the right to rest, holidays, and work-breaks; the right to work, development, and economic expansion; the right to abortion, suicide, and death.[41]

On the one hand, the current ubiquity of the principle of human dignity testifies to its universality. And the constant proliferation of human rights precepts speaks to their power to inspire new hope for many desperate persons and peoples around the world. Moreover, the increased pervasiveness of these norms is partly a function of emerging globalization. Since the first international documents on human dignity and human rights were issued in the mid twentieth century, many new voices and values have joined the global dialogue — especially those from Africa, Asia, and Latin America, and from various Buddhist, Confucian, Hindu, Islamic, and Traditional communities. It is simple ignorance to assume that the first international documents were truly universal statements on human dignity and human rights. The views of Western Christians, Jews, and Enlightenment exponents dominated them. And it is simple arrogance to assume that the 1940s through 1960s were the golden age of human dignity and human rights. Such theological and legal constructions are in need of constant reformation. The recent challenges of the South and the East to the prevailing Western paradigm of human dignity and human rights might well be salutary.

On the other hand, the very ubiquity of the principle of human dig-

---

Verlag, 1977); Wolfgang Vögele, *Menschenwürde zwischen Recht und Theologie: Begründungen von Menschenrechte in der Perspektive öffentlicher Theologie* (Gütersloh: Chr. Kaiser, 2001).

41. See, e.g., sources and discussion in Carl Wellman, *The Proliferation of Rights: Moral Progress or Empty Rhetoric?* (Boulder, Colo.: Westview, 1999); Mary Ann Glendon, *Rights Talk: The Impoverishment of Political Discourse* (New York: Free Press, 1991).

nity today threatens its claims to universality. And the very proliferation of new human rights threatens their long-term effectiveness for doing good. Human dignity needs to be assigned some limits if it is to remain a sturdy foundation for the edifice of human rights. Human rights need to be founded firmly on human dignity and other moral principles lest they devolve into a gaggle of wishes and wants. Fairness commands as broad a definition of human dignity as possible, so that no legitimate human good is excluded and no legitimate human rights claim is foreclosed. But prudence counsels a narrower definition of human dignity, so that not every good becomes part of human dignity, and not every aspiration becomes subject to human rights vindication.

The task of defining the appropriate ambit of human dignity and human rights today must be a multidisciplinary, multireligious, and multicultural exercise. Many disciplines, religions, and cultures around the globe have unique sources and resources, texts and traditions that speak to human dignity and human rights. Some endorse dignity and rights with alacrity and urge their expansion into new arenas. Others demur, and urge their reform and restriction. It is essential that each community be allowed to speak with its own unique accent, to work with its own distinct methods on human dignity and human rights — that the exercise be multi- rather than inter-disciplinary, -religious, and -cultural in character. It is also essential, however, that each of these disciplines, religions, and cultures develops a capacity for bilingualism — an ability to speak with insiders and outsiders alike about their unique understanding of the origin, nature, and purpose of human dignity and human rights.

2

Freedom of a Christian:
Human Dignity, Liberty, and Equality
in the Theology of Martin Luther

The previous chapter ended with a call for each religious community to re-trieve, reconstruct, and reengage its own distinctive theological founda-tions of human rights, and to compare these teachings with those of other faith traditions. The next three chapters take up this call. This chapter probes the distinctive teachings of human dignity, liberty, and equality of-fered by the great Protestant founder Martin Luther (1483-1546). The two chapters thereafter compare these early Protestant teachings with those of the Roman Catholic and Eastern Orthodox traditions.

In this chapter, I argue that Martin Luther developed a deep and dis-tinctive understanding of human dignity, which has had and can still have a monumental influence on our modern understanding of human equality and human rights. Luther found the essence of human dignity in the juxta-position of human depravity and human sanctity. For him, human dignity was something of a divine fulcrum that keeps our depravity and sanctity in balance. Luther found the essence of human liberty in our right and duty to serve God, neighbor, and self at once. For him, human liberty was the di-vine calling that keeps our individuality and community in balance. And Luther found the essence of human equality in the ominous assurance that we all stand equal before God, and before God's law and judgment. For him, human equality was divinely measured, not socially constructed.

This understanding of human dignity, liberty, and equality, I argue, was already adumbrated in Martin Luther's famous little tract, *Freedom of a Christian* (1520). Luther's tract was something of a Protestant *Dignitatis Humanae* in its day, an enduring theological statement on the essence of human dignity and human freedom. Several theological teachings in this little tract were filled with radical political implications. While Luther did not draw out these implications, a number of later Protestants did, eventually rendering Protestantism a formidable force for the construction of modern Western human rights theories and laws.[1] The last part of this chapter reflects on the enduring efficacy of Luther's cardinal insights for our understanding of human dignity and human rights.

Saint and Sinner, Priest and King

Martin Luther's *Freedom of a Christian* (1520) was one of the defining documents of the Protestant Reformation, and it remains one of the classic tracts of the Protestant tradition still today.[2] Written on the eve of his excommunication from the Church, this was Luther's last ecumenical gesture toward Rome before making his incendiary exit. Much of the tract was written with a quiet gentility and piety that belied the heated polemics of the day and Luther's own ample perils of body and soul. Luther dedicated the tract to Pope Leo X (1475-1521), adorning it with a robust preface addressed to the "blessed father." He vowed that he had to date "spoken only good and honorable words" concerning Leo, and offered to retract anything that might have betrayed "indiscretion and impiety." "I am the kind of person," he wrote in seeming earnest, "who would wish you all good things eternally."[3]

Luther was concerned, however, that the papal office had saddled Leo with a false sense of dignity. "You are a servant of servants" (*servus servorum*) within the Church, Luther wrote to Leo, citing the classic title of the Bishop of Rome.[4] And as a "servant of God for others, and over others, and for the sake of others," you properly enjoy a "sublime dignity" of office.[5] But the "obsequious flatterers" and "pestilential fellows" of your papal court do not regard you as a humble servant. Instead, they treat you as "a vicar of Christ," as "a demigod [who] may command and require whatever you wish." They "pretend that you are lord of the world, allow no one to be considered a Christian unless he accepts your authority, and prate

1. This later point is developed in Chapters 3, 5, and 6 herein.
2. *De Libertate Christiana* (1520), in WA 7:49-73, translated in LW 31:327-77. A shorter German edition, *Die Freiheit eines Christenmenschen,* appears in WA 7:20-38.
3. LW 31:334-36.
4. LW 31:341.
5. LW 31:341, 342. The quote is from *Luther: Lectures on Romans* [1515-1516], trans. Wilhelm Pauck (Philadelphia: Westminster, 1961), p. 8. Many of the teachings from these *Lectures* are repeated in Luther's *Freedom of a Christian.*

that you have power over heaven, hell and purgatory." Surely, you do not
believe any of this, Luther wrote to Leo, tongue near cheek. Surely, you can
see that "they err who ascribe to you alone the right of interpreting Scripture" and "who exalt you above a council and the Church universal." "Perhaps I am being presumptuous" to address you so, Luther wrote presump-
tuously at the end of his preface. But when a fellow Christian, even a pope,
is exposed to such "dangerous" teachings and trappings, God commands
that a fellow brother offer him biblical counsel, without regard for his "dignity or lack of dignity."[6]

In later pages of *Freedom of a Christian* and in several other writings in
that same crucial year of 1520, Luther took aim at other persons who were
"puffed up because of their dignity."[7] He inveighed at greatest length against
the lower clergy, who, in his view, used the "false power of fabricated sacraments" to "tyrannize the Christian conscience" and to "fleece the sheep" of
Christendom.[8] He criticized jurists for spinning the thick tangle of special
benefits, privileges, exemptions, and immunities that elevated the clergy
above the laity and inoculated them from legal accountability to local magistrates.[9] He was not much kinder to princes, nobles, and merchants — those
"harpies," as he later called them, "blinded by their arrogance," and trading
on their office, pedigree, and wealth to lord it over the languishing commoner.[10] What all these pretentious folks fail to see, Luther wrote, is that
"there is no basic difference in status . . . between laymen and priests,
princes and bishops, religious and secular."[11] Before God all are equal.

Luther's *Freedom of a Christian* thus became, in effect, his *Dignitatis
Humanae* — his bold new declaration on human nature and human freedom that described all Christians in his world regardless of their "dignity
or lack of dignity," as conventionally defined. Pope and prince, noble and
pauper, man and woman, slave and free — all persons in Christendom, Lu-

6. LW 31:341-42. See similar sentiments in Luther's *Address to the Christian Nobil-
ity of the German Nation Concerning the Reform of the Christian Estate* (1520), LW 44:123-
217, at 136.

7. Quotation is from Luther's *Lectures on Genesis 38–44* (1544), LW 7:182.

8. See esp. LW 44:126-55; Martin Luther, *The Babylonian Captivity of the Church*
(1520), LW 36:11-126; Martin Luther, *Treatise on Good Works* (1520), LW 44:21-114, at
87-94, with expansion in Martin Luther, *The Keys* (1530), LW 40:321-70. See also LW
44:129, 158; LW 36:117.

9. LW 44:157ff., 202ff.

10. LW 7:182ff.; LW 44:203ff. See also Luther's fuller statement in *Temporal Authority: To What Extent It Should be Obeyed* (1523), in LW 45:75-129.

11. LW 44:129.

ther declared, share equally in a doubly paradoxical nature. First, each person is at once a saint and a sinner, righteous and reprobate, saved and lost — *simul iustus et peccator,* in Luther's signature phrase.[12] Second, each person is at once a free lord who is subject to no one, and a dutiful servant who is subject to everyone. Only through these twin paradoxes, Luther wrote, can we "comprehend the lofty dignity of the Christian."[13]

Every Christian "has a two fold nature," Luther argued in expounding his doctrine of *simul iustus et peccator.* We are at once body and soul, flesh and spirit, sinner and saint, "outer man and inner man." These "two men in the same man contradict each other" and remain perennially at war.[14] On the one hand, as bodily creatures, we are born in sin and bound by sin. By our carnal natures, we are prone to lust and lasciviousness, evil and egoism, perversion and pathos of untold dimensions.[15] Even the best of persons, even the titans of virtue in the Bible — Abraham, David, Peter, and Paul — sin all the time.[16] In and of ourselves, we are all totally depraved and deserving of eternal death. On the other hand, as spiritual creatures, we are reborn in faith, and freed from sin. By our spiritual natures, we are prone to love and charity, goodness and sacrifice, virtue and peacefulness. Even the worst of persons, even the reprobate thief nailed on the cross next to Christ's, can be saved from sin. In spite of ourselves, we are all totally redeemed and assured of eternal life.[17]

It is through faith and hope in the Word of God, Luther argued, that a person moves from sinner to saint, from bondage to freedom. This was the essence of Luther's doctrine of justification by faith alone. No human work of any sort — even worship, contemplation, meditation, charity, and other supposed meritorious conduct — can make a person just and righteous before God, for sin holds the person fast, and perverts his or her every work. "One thing, and only one thing, is necessary for Christian life, righteousness, and freedom," Luther declared. "That one thing is the most holy Word of God, the gospel of Christ."[18] To put one's faith in this Word, to accept its gracious promise of eternal salvation, is to claim one's freedom

---

12. LW 31:344-47, 358-61. The theme recurs repeatedly in Luther's later writings. See, e.g., LW 12:328, 27:230ff., 32:173; WA 39/1:21, 492, 552.

13. LW 31:355.

14. LW 31:344.

15. LW 31:344, 358-61; see also LW 25:120-30, 204-13.

16. LW 19:47-48; LW 23:146.

17. LW 31:344-54, 368-77.

18. LW 31:345.

from sin and from its attendant threat of eternal damnation. And it is to join the communion of saints that begins imperfectly in this life and continues perfectly in the life to come.

A saint by faith remains a sinner by nature, Luther insisted, and the paradox of good and evil within the same person remains until death. But there is "a difference between sinners and sinners," Luther wrote. "There are some sinners who confess that they have sinned but do not long to be justified; instead, they give up hope and go on sinning so that when they die they despair, and while they live, they are enslaved to the world. There are other sinners who confess that they sin and have sinned, but they are sorry for this, hate themselves for it, long to be justified, and under groaning constantly pray to God for righteousness. This is the people of God," the saints who are saved, despite their sin.[19]

This brought Luther to his second, related paradox of human nature — that each Christian is at once a lord who is subject to no one, and a priest who is servant to everyone. On the one hand, Luther argued, "every Christian is by faith so exalted above all things that, by virtue of a spiritual power, he is [a] lord."[20] As a redeemed saint, as an "inner man," a Christian is utterly free in his conscience, utterly free in his innermost being. He is like the greatest king on earth, who is above and beyond the power of everyone. No earthly authority — whether pope, prince, or parent — can impose "a single syllable of the law" upon her.[21] No earthly authority can intrude upon the sanctuary of her conscience, can endanger her assurance and comfort of eternal life. This is "the splendid privilege," the "inestimable power and liberty" that every Christian enjoys.[22]

On the other hand, Luther wrote, every Christian is a priest, who freely performs good works in service of his or her neighbor and in glorification of God.[23] "Christ has made it possible for us, provided we believe in him, to be not only his brethren, co-heirs, and fellow-kings, but also his fellow-priests," Luther wrote. And thus, in imitation of Christ, we freely serve our neighbors, offering instruction, charity, prayer, admonition, and sacrifice even to the point of death.[24] We abide by the law of God so far as

---

19. *Lectures on Romans*, p. 120. See also LW 23:146; LW 12:328-30; LW 8:9-12.
20. LW 31:354.
21. LW 36:70, echoing LW 31:344-46.
22. LW 31:355-58.
23. LW 31:355-56; see also LW 36:112-16, 138-40; LW 40:21-23; LW 13:152, and esp. the long diatribe in LW 39:137-224.
24. LW 31:355; see also LW 36:241.

we are able so that others may see our good work and be similarly impelled to seek God's grace. We freely discipline and drive ourselves to do as much good as we are able, not so that we may be saved but so that others may be served. "A man does not live for himself alone," Luther wrote, "he lives only for others."[25] The precise nature of our priestly service to others depends upon our gifts and upon the vocation in which God calls us to use them.[26] But we are all to serve freely and fully as God's priests.

"Who can then comprehend the lofty dignity of the Christian?" Luther wrote. "By virtue of his royal power he rules over all things, death, life, and sin." The person is entirely free from the necessity of doing good works and fully immune from the authority of anyone. But by virtue of "his priestly glory, he is omnipotent with God because he does the things which God asks and requires."[27] He devotes himself entirely to doing good works for his neighbor, he submits himself completely to the needs of others. Not everyone who is charitable has faith. But everyone who has faith is charitable. Charity is a form of divine service, of priestly service, whereby God, neighbor, and self are served at once.

Such are the paradoxes of the Christian life in Luther's view. We are at once sinners and saints; we are at once lords and servants. We can do nothing good; we can do nothing but good. We are utterly free; we are everywhere bound.[28] The more a person thinks himself a saint, the more sinful he in fact becomes. The more a person thinks herself a sinner, the more saintly she in fact becomes. The more a person acts like a lord, the more he is called to be a servant. The more a person acts as a servant, the more in fact she has become a lord. This is the paradoxical nature of human life. And this is the essence of human dignity.

Luther intended his *Freedom of a Christian* to be a universal statement for his world of Christendom — a summary of "the whole of the Christian life in a brief form," as he put it in his preface to Leo.[29] He grounded his views in the Bible, liberally peppering his tract with all manner of biblical citations and quotations. He wove into his narrative several strong threads of argument pulled selectively from a number of Church Fathers and late

25. LW 31:364-65; see also LW 51:86-87.
26. LW 38:188; LW 28:171-72.
27. LW 31:355; see also LW 17:209ff.
28. Cf. Jean Jacques Rousseau, *The Social Contract* [1762], ed. Lester G. Crocker (New York: Simon and Schuster, 1967), bk. 1, chap. 1: "Man was born free, but everywhere he is in chains."
29. LW 31:343.

medieval Christian mystics. He published his tract both in Latin and in simple German, seeking to reach both the scholar and the commoner alike. He wrote with a pastoral directness and emotional empathy, convinced that if he could point out the Jekyll and Hyde in everyone, his readers would find both ample humility and ample comfort. So convinced was Luther of the veracity and cogency of his views that he believed even the Jews, the one perennial sojourner in his world of Christendom, would convert *en masse* to the Gospel once they heard it in this simple form.[30] Though this latter aspiration proved fanciful, Luther's views on human dignity did command an impressive readership among Christians. *Freedom of a Christian* was a best-seller in its day — going through twelve printings in its first two years, and five editions by 1524. It remained a perennial favorite of commentaries and sermons long after Luther's passing, and well beyond the world of Lutheranism.[31] It is no small commentary on the enduring ecumenical efficacy of Luther's views of human nature, dignity, and freedom that they lie at the heart of the "Joint Declaration on the Doctrine of Justification," signed by Catholic and Evangelical leaders on October 31, 1999.

The Lutheran Reformation of Law and Liberty

What all this elegant dialectic theology meant for the nature of freedom of the Christian in this world, Luther's little tract did not so clearly say. Luther did make clear that all Christians have the freedom and duty to follow the Bible conscientiously and to speak out against human ideas and institutions that conflict with the Bible. The Bible was for Luther the great equalizer of Christians — to the remarkable point of allowing Luther, a lowly Augustinian monk from an obscure German town, to address His Holiness Leo X as if he were the pope's equal.

Luther also made clear that clergy and laity are fundamentally equal in dignity and responsibility before God. The traditional assumption that the clergy were superior to the laity, and entitled to all manner of special privileges, immunities, and exemptions, was anathema to Luther. Luther's doctrine of the priesthood of all believers at once "laicized" the clergy and "clericized" the laity. He treated the traditional "clerical" office of preach-

---

30. Martin Luther, *That Jesus Christ Was Born a Jew* (1523), in LW 45:129.
31. Mark U. Edwards Jr., *Printing, Propaganda, and Martin Luther* (Berkeley: University of California Press, 1981), pp. 39, 64, 100-101.

ing and teaching as just one other godly vocation alongside many others that a conscientious Christian could properly and freely pursue. He treated all traditional "lay" offices as forms of divine calling and priestly vocation, each providing unique opportunities for service to one's peers. Preachers and teachers in the Church must carry their share of civic duties and pay their share of civil taxes just like everyone else. And they should participate in earthly activities such as marriage and family life just like everyone else.[32]

This radical new theory of the clergy and the laity, of the person and society, had dramatic implications for Church and state, for spiritual life and temporal life. Luther, together with a whole coterie of distinguished theologians, jurists, and moralists, drew out these implications as the Reformation unfolded in the first half of the sixteenth century.[33]

The Lutheran Reformation brought fundamental change to German ecclesiastical and spiritual life. It radically resystematized dogma. It truncated the sacraments. It revamped spiritual symbolism. It vernacularized the Bible and the worship service. It transformed corporate worship and congregational music. It gave new emphasis to the pulpit and the sermon. It expanded catechesis and religious instruction. It truncated clerical privileges and Church properties. It dissolved ecclesiastical foundations and endowments. It outlawed the cult of religious artifacts. It rejected the veneration of nonbiblical saints and the cult of the dead. It outlawed the payment of indulgences and mortuaries. It discouraged religious pilgrimages. It reduced the number of holy days. It lightened spiritual rules of diet and dress. It reformed and democratized ecclesiastical discipline and Church administration, and much more. All of these changes in spiritual and ecclesiastical life in Lutheran Germany were driven in no small part by Luther's cardinal call for freedom — freedom of the Christian conscience from unnecessary traditions and rules, freedom of the congregation from clerical monopoly and control, freedom of the Gospel from the intrusions of the law.

The Lutheran Reformation also brought fundamental change to German legal and political life through direct expression of Luther's new theology, especially his new views of the person and society. For example, Lutheran Reformers replaced the traditional understanding of education as a teaching office of the Church with a new understanding of the public

32. Martin Luther, *Concerning the Ministry* (1523), in LW 40:21ff.
33. This is the thesis of LP.

school as a "civic seminary" for all children, girls and boys alike, to prepare for their distinctive Christian vocations. On that basis, magistrates replaced clerics as the chief rulers of education, civil law replaced canon law as the principal law of education, and the general callings of all Christians replaced the special calling of the clergy as the principal good and goal of education. And the modern public school was born. Lutheran Reformers replaced the traditional idea of marriage as a sacrament with a new idea of the marital household as a social estate which all adults — clerical and lay alike — are free to enter. On that basis, the Reformers developed a new civil law of marriage, featuring the freedom of marital contract for all fit parties, freedom to divorce on grounds of adultery, desertion, and other serious faults, freedom to remarry after divorce or death of the other spouse. And there were many more such reforms.

Luther's *Freedom of a Christian,* however, was no manifesto of political freedom. Spiritual freedom may well coexist with political bondage, Luther insisted. The spiritual equality of persons and vocations before God does not necessarily entail a social equality with all others. Luther became doubly convinced of this discordance after witnessing the bloody Peasants' Revolt in Germany in 1525, as well as the growing numbers of radical egalitarian and antinomian experiments engineered out of his favorite theological doctrines of the priesthood of all believers and justification by faith alone. Indeed in his later life, Luther defended with increasing stridency and belligerence traditional social, economic, political, and ecclesiastical hierarchies as a necessary feature of this earthly life.

Luther came to defend this disparity between the spiritual and temporal dimensions of human freedom, dignity, and status with his doctrine of the two kingdoms. God has ordained two kingdoms or realms in which humanity is destined to live, Luther argued, the earthly or political kingdom and the heavenly or spiritual kingdom. The earthly kingdom is the realm of creation, of natural and civic life, where a person operates primarily by reason, law, and passion. The heavenly kingdom is the realm of redemption, of spiritual and eternal life, where a person operates primarily by faith, hope, and charity. These two kingdoms embrace parallel forms of righteousness and justice, truth and knowledge, but they remain separate and distinct. The earthly kingdom is distorted by sin, and governed by the law. The heavenly kingdom is renewed by grace and guided by the Gospel. A Christian is a citizen of both kingdoms at once, and invariably comes under the distinctive jurisdiction of each kingdom. As a heavenly citizen, the Christian remains free in his conscience, called to live fully by the light of the Word of God. But as an earthly citizen, the Christian is bound by law and called to obey the structures and strictures of ecclesiastical, political, and parental authority, even if they are sometimes hard and abusive.[34]

Protestant Instincts about Human Dignity, Liberty, and Equality Today

Some five centuries after its publication, Luther's *Freedom of a Christian* still gives a distinctive orientation to many contemporary Protestants' instincts about human dignity, human freedom, and human rights.

First, Luther's doctrine that a person is at once sinner and saint renders many Protestants today instinctively skeptical about too optimistic a view of human nature, and too easy a conflation of human dignity and human sanctity.[35] Such views take too little account of the radicality of human sin and the necessity of divine grace. They give too little credibility to the inherent human need for discipline and order, accountability and judgment. They give too little credence to the perennial interplay of the civil, theological, and pedagogical uses of law, to the perpetual demand to balance deterrence, retribution, and reformation in discharging authority within the Church, state, home, school, and other associations.[36] They give too little insight into the necessity for safeguarding every office of authority from abuse and misuse. A theory of human dignity that fails to take into account the juxtaposed depravity and sanctity of the human person is theologically deficient, and politically dangerous.

This cardinal insight into the twofold nature of humanity was hardly unique to Martin Luther and is readily amenable to many other formulations. Luther's formula of *simul iustus et peccator* was a crisp Christian distillation of a universal insight about human nature that can be traced to the earliest Greek and Hebrew sources of the West. The gripping epics of Homer, Hesiod, and Pindar are nothing if not chronicles of the perennial dialectic of good and evil, virtue and vice, hero and villain in the ancient Greek world. The very first chapters of the Hebrew Bible paint pictures of these same two human natures, now with Yahweh's imprint on them. The

---

34. This two kingdoms theory is more fully described in LP, pp. 87-117.

35. See esp. Timothy P. Jackson, *The Priority of Love: Christian Charity and Social Justice* (Princeton, N.J.: Princeton University Press, 2003).

36. See further Chapters 5 and 9 herein.

more familiar picture is that of Adam and Eve, who were created equally in the image of God and vested with a natural right and duty to perpetuate life, to cultivate property, to address and keep the creation.[37] The less familiar picture is that of their first child Cain, who murdered his brother Abel and was called into judgment by God and condemned for his sin. Yet "God put a mark on Cain," Genesis reads, both to protect him in his life and to show that he remained a child of God despite the enormity of his sin.[38] One message of this ancient Hebrew text is that we are not only the beloved children of Adam and Eve, who bear the image of God, with all the divine perquisites and privileges of Paradise. We are also the sinful siblings of Cain, who bear the mark of God, with its ominous assurance both that we shall be called into divine judgment for what we have done and that there is forgiveness even for the gravest of sins we have committed.

Luther believed that it is only through faith and hope in Christ that we can ultimately be assured of divine forgiveness and eternal salvation. He further believed that it is only through a life of biblical meditation, prayer, worship, charity, and sacramental living that a person can hold his or her depravity in check and aspire to greater sanctity. I believe that, too, as do many Christians today. But this is not to say that, in this life, Christians have the only insights into the twofold nature of humanity, and the only effective means of balancing the realities of human depravity and the aspirations for human sanctity. Any religious tradition that takes seriously the Jekyll and Hyde in all of us has its own understanding of ultimate reconciliation of these two natures, and its own methods of balancing them in this life. And who are we Christians to say how God will ultimately judge these?

Luther also believed that the ominous assurance of the judgment of God is ultimately a source of comfort, not of fear. The first sinners in the Bible — Adam, Eve, and Cain — were given divine due process: They were confronted with the evidence, asked to defend themselves, given a chance to repent, spared the ultimate sanction of death, and then assured of a second trial on the Day of Judgment, with appointed divine counsel — Christ himself, our self-appointed "advocate before the Father."[39] The only time

37. Genesis 1:26-30; 2:7, 15-23.
38. Genesis 4:1-16. This is but one of numerous interpretations of the story of Cain and Abel. For alternatives, see Ruth Mellinkoff, *The Mark of Cain* (Berkeley: University of California Press, 1981); Claus Westermann, *Genesis 1–11: A Commentary*, repr. ed. (Minneapolis: Augsburg, 1990).
39. 1 John 2:1.

that the God of the New Testament deliberately withheld divine due process was in the capital trial of his Son — and that was the only time it was and has been necessary. The political implications of this are very simple: If God gives due process in judging us, we should give due process in judging others. If God's tribunals feature at least basic rules of procedure, evidence, representation, and advocacy, human tribunals should feature at least the same. The demand for due process is a deep human instinct, and it has driven Protestants over the centuries, along with many others before and with them, to be strident advocates for procedural rights.

Second, Luther's doctrine of the lordship and priesthood of all believers renders many Protestants instinctively jealous about liberty and equality — but on their own quite distinct theological terms. In the modern liberal tradition, liberty and equality are generally defended on grounds of popular sovereignty and inalienable rights. The American Declaration of Independence (1776) proclaimed it a "self-evident truth" "that all men are created equal [and] . . . are endowed with certain unalienable rights." The Universal Declaration of Human Rights (1948) proclaimed "[t]hat all men are born free and equal in rights and dignity." Protestants can resonate more with the norms of liberty and equality in these documents than with the theories of popular sovereignty and inalienable rights that generally undergird them.

The heart of the Protestant theory of liberty is that we are all lords on this earth. We are utterly free in the sanctuary of our conscience, entirely unencumbered in our relationship with God. We enjoy a sovereign immunity from any human structures and strictures, even those of the Church, when they seek to impose upon this divine freedom. Such talk of "sovereign immunity" sounds something like modern liberal notions of "popular sovereignty." And such talk of "lordship" sounds something like the democratic right to "self-rule." Protestants have thus long found ready allies in liberals and others who advocate liberty of conscience and democratic freedoms on these grounds. But, when theologically pressed, many reflective Protestants will defend liberty of conscience not because of their own popular sovereignty but because of the absolute sovereignty of God, whose relationship with his children cannot be trespassed. Many Protestants will defend certain unalienable rights, like freedom of conscience, not in the interest of preserving their personal privacy, but in the interest of discharging their divine duties.

The heart of the Protestant theory of equality is that we are all priests before God. "You are a chosen race, a royal priesthood, a holy nation, God's own people."[40] Among you, "[t]here is neither Jew nor Greek, there is neither slave nor free, there is neither male nor female; for you are all one in Christ Jesus."[41] These and many other biblical passages, which Luther highlighted and glossed repeatedly, have long inspired a reflexive egalitarian impulse in Protestants. All are equal before God. All are priests who must serve their neighbors. All have vocations that count. All have gifts to be included. This common calling of all to be priests transcends differences of culture, economy, gender, and more.

Such teachings have led a few Protestant groups over the centuries to experiment with intensely communitarian states of nature where life is gracious, lovely, and long. Most Protestant groups, however, view life in such states of nature as brutish, nasty, and short, for sin invariably perverts them. Structures and strictures of law and authority are necessary and useful, most Protestants believe. But such structures need to be as open, egalitarian, and democratic as possible. Hierarchy is a danger to be indulged only so far as necessary. To be sure, Protestants over the centuries have often defied these founding ideals, and have earnestly partaken of all manner of elitism, chauvinism, racism, anti-Semitism, tyranny, patriarchy, slavery, apartheid, and more. And they have sometimes engaged in outrageous hypocrisy and casuistry to defend such shameful pathos. But an instinct for egalitarianism — for embracing all persons equally, for treating all vocations respectfully, for arranging all associations horizontally, for leveling the life of the earthly kingdom so none is obstructed in access to God — is a Lutheran gene in the theological genetic code of Protestantism.

Third, and finally, Luther's notion that a person is at once free and bound by the law has powerful implications for our modern understanding of human rights. For Luther, the Christian is free in order to follow the commandments of the faith — or, in more familiar and general modern parlance, a person has rights in order to discharge duties. Freedoms and commandments, rights and duties belong together in Luther's formulation. To speak of one without the other is ultimately destructive. Rights without duties to guide them quickly become claims of self-indulgence. Duties without rights to exercise them quickly become sources of deep guilt.

Protestants have thus long translated the moral duties set out in the Decalogue into reciprocal rights.[42] The First Table of the Decalogue pre-

---

40. 1 Peter 2:9; cf. Revelation 5:10; 20:6.
41. Galatians 3:28; cf. Colossians 3:10-11; Ephesians 2:14-15.
42. See detailed discussion in RR.

scribes duties of love that each person owes to God — to honor God and God's name, to observe the Sabbath day of rest and holy worship, to avoid false gods and false swearing. The Second Table prescribes duties of love that each person owes to neighbors — to honor one's parents and other authorities, not to kill, not to commit adultery, not to steal, not to bear false witness, not to covet. Church, state, and family alike are responsible for the communication and enforcement of these cardinal moral duties, Protestants have long argued. But it is also the responsibility of each person to ensure that he and his neighbors discharge these moral duties. This is one important impetus for Protestants to translate duties into rights. A person's duties toward God can be cast as the rights of religion: the right to honor God and God's name, the right to rest and worship on one's Sabbath, the right to be free from false gods and false oaths. Each person's duties toward a neighbor, in turn, can be cast as a neighbor's right to have that duty discharged. One person's duties not to kill, to commit adultery, to steal, or to bear false witness thus give rise to another person's rights to life, property, fidelity, and reputation. For a person to insist upon vindication of these latter rights is not necessarily to act out of self-love. It is also to act out of neighborly love. To claim one's own right is in part a charitable act to induce one's neighbor to discharge his or her divinely ordained duty.

∽ 3 ∽

A Dickensian Era of Religious Rights: Catholic, Protestant, and Orthodox Contributions

"It was the best of times, it was the worst of times, it was the age of wisdom, it was the age of foolishness, it was the epoch of belief, it was the epoch of incredulity, it was the season of Light, it was the season of Darkness, it was the spring of hope, it was the winter of despair."[1] Charles Dickens penned these famous words to describe the paradoxes of the late-eighteenth-century French Revolution fought for the sake of "the rights of man and citizen."[2] These same words aptly describe the paradoxes of the late-twentieth-century world revolution fought in the name of human rights and democratization for all.

The world has entered something of a "Dickensian era"[3] in the past two decades. We have seen the best of human rights protections inscribed on the books, but some of the worst of human rights violations inflicted on the ground. We have celebrated the creation of more than thirty new constitutional democracies since 1980, but lamented the eruption of more than thirty new civil wars. We have witnessed the wisest of democratic statecraft and the most foolish of autocratic belligerence. For every South African spring of hope, there has been a Yugoslavian winter of despair, for every Ukrainian season of light, a Sudanese season of darkness.

These Dickensian paradoxes of the modern human rights revolution

1. Charles Dickens, *A Tale of Two Cities* (Leipzig: Bernhard Tauchnitz, 1859), p. 1.

2. "Declaration des droits de l'homme et du citoyen (1789)," in *Les Constitutions et Les Principales Lois Politiques de la France Depuis 1789,* by Léon Duguit (Paris: Librairie Générale de Droit et de Jurisprudence, 1952), p. 1.

3. The phrase is from Irwin Cotler, "Jewish NGOs and Religious Human Rights: A Case Study," in *Human Rights in Judaism: Cultural, Religious, and Political Perspectives,* ed. Michael J. Broyde and John Witte Jr. (Northvale, N.J.: Jason Aronson, 1998), p. 165.

are particularly striking when viewed in their religious dimensions. On the one hand, the modern human rights revolution has helped to catalyze a great awakening of religion around the globe. In regions newly committed to democracy and human rights, ancient faiths once driven underground by autocratic oppressors have sprung forth with new vigor. In the former Soviet bloc, for example, Buddhist, Christian, Hindu, Jewish, Muslim, and other faiths have been awakened, alongside a host of exotic goddess, naturalist, and personality cults.[4] In post-colonial and post-revolutionary Africa, these same mainline religious groups have come to flourish in numerous conventional and inculturated forms, alongside a bewildering array of Traditional groups.[5] In Latin America, the human rights revolution has not only transformed long-standing Catholic and mainline Protestant communities but also triggered the explosion of numerous new Evangelical, Pentecostal, and Traditional movements.[6] Many parts of the world have seen the prodigious rise of a host of new or newly minted faiths — Adventists, Baha'is, Hare Krishnas, Jehovah's Witnesses, Mormons, Scientologists, and Unification Church members, among many others — some wielding ample material, political, and media power. Religion today has become, in Susanne Rudolph's apt phrase, the latest "transnational variable."[7]

One cause and consequence of this great awakening of religion around the globe is that the ambit of religious rights has been substantially expanded. In the past two decades, more than 150 major new statutes and constitutional provisions on religious rights have been promulgated — many replete with generous protections for liberty of conscience and freedom of religious exercise, guarantees of religious pluralism, equality, and nondiscrimination, and several other special protections and entitlements for religious individuals and religious groups.[8] These national guarantees

4. See POR.

5. Abdullahi Ahmed An-Na'im and Francis M. Deng, eds., *Human Rights in Africa: Cross-Cultural Perspectives* (Washington, D.C.: Brookings Institution, 1990); Abdullahi Ahmed An-Na'im, ed., *Proselytization and Communal Self-Determination in Africa* (Maryknoll, N.Y.: Orbis, 1999); Symposium: "The Problem of Proselytism in Southern Africa," *Emory International Law Review* 14 (2000): 491-1303.

6. Paul E. Sigmund, ed., *Religious Freedom and Evangelization in Latin America: The Challenge of Religious Pluralism* (Maryknoll, N.Y.: Orbis, 1999).

7. Susanne Hoeber Rudolph, introduction to *Transnational Religion and Fading States*, ed. Susanne Hoeber Rudolph and James Piscatori (Boulder, Colo.: Westview, 1997), p. 6.

8. Natan Lerner, *Religion, Beliefs, and International Human Rights* (Maryknoll, N.Y.: Orbis, 2000), pp. 129-47; Tad Stahnke and J. Paul Martin, eds., *Religion and Human*

have been matched with a growing body of regional and international norms, notably the 1981 *UN Declaration on the Elimination of All Forms of Intolerance and of Discrimination Based on Religion or Belief* and the long catalogue of religious-group rights set out in the 1989 *Vienna Concluding Document* and its progeny.[9]

On the other hand, this very same world human rights revolution helped to catalyze new forms of religious and ethnic conflict, oppression, and belligerence that have reached tragic proportions. In some communities, such as the former Yugoslavia, local religious and ethnic rivals, previously kept at bay by a common oppressor, converted their new liberties into licenses to renew ancient hostilities, with catastrophic results.[10] In other communities, such as Sudan and Rwanda, ethnic nationalism and religious extremism conspired to bring violent dislocation or death to hundreds of rival religious believers each year, and persecution, false imprisonment, forced starvation, and savage abuses to thousands of others.[11] In other communities, most notably in North America and Western Europe, political secularism, laicization, and nationalism have combined to threaten a sort of civil denial and death to a number of believers, particularly "sects" and "cults" of high religious temperature or of low cultural conformity. In still other communities, from Asia to the Middle East, Christians, Jews, and Muslims, when in minority contexts, have faced sharply increased restrictions, repression, and sometimes even martyrdom.[12] And, in many parts of the world today, a new barbaric fringe of Islamicist terror-

---

Rights: Basic Documents (New York: Center for the Study of Human Rights, Columbia University, 1998).

9. See Tore Lindholm, W. Cole Durham Jr., and Bahia G. Tahzib-Lie, *Facilitating Freedom of Religion or Belief: A Deskbook* (Leiden: Martinus Nijhoff, 2004); Malcolm D. Evans, *Religious Liberty and International Law in Europe* (Cambridge: Cambridge University Press, 1997); Bahia G. Tahzib, *Freedom of Religion or Belief: Ensuring Effective International Legal Protection* (The Hague: Martinus Nijhoff, 1996); RHR I and II.

10. Julie A. Mertus, *Kosovo: How Myths and Truths Started a War* (Berkeley: University of California Press, 1999); Paul Mojzes, *Yugoslavian Inferno: Ethnoreligious Warfare in the Balkans* (New York: Continuum, 1995); Michael A. Sells, *The Bridge Betrayed: Religion and Genocide in Bosnia* (Berkeley: University of California Press, 1996).

11. Francis M. Deng, *War of Visions: Conflict of Identities in the Sudan* (Washington, D.C.: Brookings Institution, 1995), pp. 9-31.

12. T. Jeremy Gunn, *Dieu en France et aux États-Unis: Quand les mythes font la loi* (Paris: Berg International, 2005); T. Jeremy Gunn, "Religious Freedom and Laïcité: A Comparison of the United States and France," *Brigham Young University Law Review* (2004): 419-506.

ists have wrapped their cunning and cruel belligerence and terrorism around a distorted and destructive theory of jihad against all manner of enemies real and imagined.

In parts of Russia, Eastern Europe, Africa, and Latin America, this human rights revolution has brought on something of a new war for souls between indigenous and foreign religious groups. This is the most recent, and the most ironic, chapter in the modern Dickensian drama. With the political transformations of these regions in the past two decades, foreign religious groups were granted rights to enter these regions for the first time in decades. Beginning in the early 1990s, they came in increasing numbers to preach their faiths, to offer their services, to convert new souls. Initially, local religious groups — Orthodox, Catholic, Protestant, Sunni, Shi'ite, and Traditional alike — welcomed these foreigners, particularly their foreign co-religionists with whom they had lost contact for many decades. Today, local religious groups have come to resent these foreign religions, particularly those from North America and Western Europe who assume a democratic human rights ethic. Local religious groups resent the participation in the marketplace of religious ideas that democracy assumes. They resent the toxic waves of materialism and individualism that democracy inflicts. They resent the massive expansion of religious pluralism that democracy encourages. They resent the extravagant forms of religious speech, press, and assembly that democracy protects.[13]

A new war for souls has thus broken out in these regions, a war to reclaim the traditional cultural and moral souls of these new societies, and a war to retain adherence and adherents to the indigenous faiths.[14] In part, this is a theological war, as rival religious communities have begun to demonize and defame each other and to gather themselves into ever more dogmatic and fundamentalist stands. The ecumenical spirit of the previous decades is giving way to sharp new forms of religious balkanization. In part, this is a legal war, as local religious groups have begun to conspire with their political leaders to adopt statutes and regulations restricting the constitutional rights of their foreign religious rivals. Beneath shiny constitutional veneers of religious freedom for all and unqualified ratification of international human rights instruments, several countries of late passed firm new anti-proselytism laws, cult registration requirements, tightened

13. Symposium: "Pluralism, Proselytism and Nationalism in Eastern Europe," *Journal of Ecumenical Studies* 36 (1999): 1-286. See further Chapter 4 herein.

14. See POR.

visa controls, and various other discriminatory restrictions on new or newly arrived religions. Indeed, many parts of the world seem to be on a new dawn of Islamic or Christian religious establishment.[15]

Such Dickensian paradoxes have exposed the limitations of a secular human rights paradigm standing alone. They also have inspired the earnest search for additional resources to deter violence, resolve disputes, cultivate peace, and ensure security through dialogue, liturgical healing, reconciliation ceremonies, truth commissions, and other means.[16] Human rights principles are as much the problem as they are the solution in a number of current religious and cultural conflicts. In the war for souls in Russia and Latin America, for example, two absolute principles of human rights have come into direct conflict: the foreign religion's free exercise right to share and expand its faith versus the indigenous religion's liberty-of-conscience right to be left alone on its own territory.[17] Or, put in Christian theological terms, it is one group's right to abide by the Great Commission ("Go ye therefore, and make disciples of all nations") versus another group's right to insist on the Golden Rule ("Do unto others as you would have done unto you").[18] Further rights talk alone cannot resolve this dispute. Likewise, some of the nations given to the most belligerent forms of religious nationalism have ratified more of the international human rights instruments than the United States has, and have crafted more elaborate bills of rights than what appears in the United States Constitution. Here, too, further rights talk alone is insufficient.

These paradoxes of the modern human rights revolution underscore an elementary, but essential, point — that human rights norms need a human rights culture to be effective. "[D]eclarations are not deeds," John Noonan reminds us. "A form of words by itself secures nothing. . . . [W]ords pregnant with meaning in one cultural context may be entirely

15. Gabriel A. Almond, R. Scott Appleby, and Emmanuel Sivian, *Strong Religion: The Rise of Fundamentalism around the World* (Chicago: University of Chicago Press, 2003). For sample new legislation reflecting this, see *Laws on Religion and the State in Post-Communist Europe*, ed. W. Cole Durham Jr. and Silvio Ferrari (Leuven: Peeters, 2004).

16. R. Scott Appleby, *The Ambivalence of the Sacred: Religion, Violence, and Reconciliation* (Lanham, Md.: Rowman and Littlefield, 2000); Wolfgang Huber and Hans-Richard Reuter, *Friedensethik* (Stuttgart: W. Kohlhammer, 1990).

17. Symposium: "Soul Wars: The Problem of Proselytism in Russia," *Emory International Law Review* 12 (1998): 1-738.

18. Matthew 28:19-20; 7:12; Mark 16:15-18; Acts 1:8. See SB.

barren in another."[19] Human rights norms have little salience in societies that lack constitutional processes that will give them meaning and measure. They have little value for parties who lack basic rights to security, succor, and sanctuary, or who are deprived of basic freedoms of speech, press, or association. They have little pertinence for victims who lack standing in courts and other basic procedural rights to pursue apt remedies. They have little cogency in communities that lack the ethos and ethic to render human rights violations a source of shame and regret, restraint and respect, confession and responsibility, reconciliation and restitution. As we have moved from the first generation of human rights declaration following World War II to the current generation of human rights implementation, this need for a human rights culture has become all the more pressing.

These paradoxes, when viewed in their religious dimensions, further suggest that religion and human rights need to be brought into a closer symbiosis.

On the one hand, human rights norms need religious narratives to ground them. There is, of course, some value in simply declaring human rights norms of "liberty, equality, and fraternity" or "life, liberty, and property" — if for no other reason than to pose an ideal against which a person or community might measure itself, to preserve a normative totem for later generations to make real. But, ultimately, these abstract human rights ideals of the good life and the good society depend on the visions and values of human communities and institutions to give them content and coherence — to provide what Jacques Maritain (1882-1973) once called "the scale of values governing [their] exercise and concrete manifestation."[20] It is here that religion must play a vital role. Religion is an ineradicable condition of human lives and human communities. Religions invariably provide many of the sources and "scales of values" by which many persons and communities govern themselves. Religions inevitably help to define the meanings and measures of shame and regret, restraint and respect, responsibility and restitution that a human rights regime presupposes. Religions must thus be seen as indispensable allies in the modern struggle for human rights. To exclude them from the struggle is impossible, indeed catastrophic. To include them, by enlisting their unique resources and protecting their unique

19. John T. Noonan Jr., "The Tensions and the Ideals," in RHR II, p. 594; see also John T. Noonan Jr., *The Lustre of Our Country: The American Experience of Religious Freedom* (Berkeley: University of California Press, 1998), pp. 265-84.

20. Jacques Maritain, introduction to *Human Rights: Comments and Interpretations*, by UNESCO (New York: Columbia University Press, 1949).

rights, is vital to enhancing the regime of human rights and to easing some of the worst paradoxes that currently exist.

Conversely, religious narratives need human rights norms both to protect them and to challenge them. There is, of course, some value in religions simply accepting the current protections of a human rights regime — the guarantees of liberty of conscience, free exercise, religious group autonomy, and the like. But passive acquiescence in a secular scheme of human rights ultimately will not prove effective. Religious communities must reclaim their own voices within the secular human rights dialogue, and reclaim the human rights voices within their own internal religious dialogues. Contrary to conventional wisdom, the theory and law of human rights are neither new nor secular in origin. Human rights are, in no small part, the modern political fruits of ancient religious beliefs and practices — ancient Jewish constructions of covenant and *mitzvot*,[21] original Qur'anic texts on peace and the common good,[22] classic Christian concepts of *ius* and *libertas*, freedom and covenant.[23]

Religious communities must be open to a new human rights hermeneutic — a fresh method of interpreting their sacred texts and traditions that will allow them to reclaim their essential roots and roles in the cultivation of human rights. Religious traditions cannot allow secular human rights norms to be imposed on them from without; they must rediscover them from within. It is only then that religious traditions can bring their full doctrinal rigor, liturgical healing, and moral suasion to bear on the problems and paradoxes of the modern human rights regime.

Both these theses — about the place of religion in human rights and about the place of human rights in religion — are highly controversial. In the next two sections, I shall try to parse these controversies and press these theses a bit more concretely. The final section will wrestle with a few of the difficult theological and legal conundrums that are raised by a closer symbiosis between religion and human rights.

---

21. David Novak, *Covenantal Rights: A Study in Jewish Political Theory* (Princeton, N.J.: Princeton University Press, 2000).

22. Abdullahi Ahmed An-Na'im, *Toward an Islamic Reformation: Civil Liberties, Human Rights, and International Law* (Syracuse, N.Y.: Syracuse University Press, 1990).

23. See Chapters 1-2, 5, and 12 herein and RR.

Religion and Human Rights

My first response to our modern Dickensian paradoxes is that religion, in all of its denominational multiplicity, must play a more active role in the modern human rights revolution. Many would consider this thesis to be fundamentally misguided. Even the great Religions of the Book do not speak unequivocally about human rights, and none has amassed an exemplary human rights record over the centuries. Their sacred texts and canons say much more about commandments and obligations than about liberties and rights. Their theologians and jurists have resisted the importation of human rights as much as they have helped in their cultivation. Their internal policies and external advocacy have helped to perpetuate bigotry, chauvinism, and violence as much as they have served to propagate equality, liberty, and fraternity. The blood of thousands is at the doors of our Churches, temples, and mosques. The bludgeons of pogroms, crusades, jihads, inquisitions, and ostracisms have been used to devastating effect within and among these faiths.

Moreover, the modern cultivation of human rights in the West began in the 1940s when both Christianity and the Enlightenment seemed incapable of delivering on their promises. In the middle of the twentieth century, there was no second coming of Christ promised by Christians, no heavenly city of reason promised by enlightened libertarians, no withering away of the state promised by enlightened socialists. Instead, there had been world war, gulags, and the Holocaust — a vile and evil fascism and irrationalism to which Christianity and the Enlightenment seemed to have no cogent response or effective deterrent.

The modern human rights movement was thus born out of desperation in the aftermath of World War II. It was an earnest attempt to find a world faith to fill a spiritual void. It was an attempt to harvest from the traditions of Christianity and the Enlightenment the rudimentary elements of a new faith and a new law that would unite a badly broken world order. The proud claims of Article I of the 1948 *Universal Declaration of Human Rights* — "That all men are born free and equal in rights and dignity [and] are endowed with reason and conscience"[24] — expounded the primitive truths of Christianity and the Enlightenment with little basis in post-War

24. United Nations, General Assembly, *Universal Declaration of Human Rights* [A/Res/217 A (III)], December 10, 1948, in *Religion and Human Rights*, ed. Stahnke and Martin, p. 57.

world reality. Freedom and equality were hard to find anywhere. Reason and conscience had just blatantly betrayed themselves in the gulags, battle-fields, and death camps.

Though desperate in origin, the human rights movement grew preco-ciously in the decades following World War II. The United Nations issued a number of landmark documents on human rights in the 1960s. Foremost among these were the two great international covenants promulgated by the United Nations in 1966 — *The International Covenant on Economic, So-cial, and Cultural Rights* and *The International Covenant on Civil and Politi-cal Rights*.[25] Other international and domestic instruments issued in the later 1960s took particular aim at racial, religious, and gender discrimina-tion in education, employment, social welfare programs, and other forms and forums of public life. Various nations pressed their own human rights movements. In America, the rights revolution yielded a powerful grassroots civil rights movement and a welter of landmark cases and statutes imple-menting the Bill of Rights and Fourteenth Amendment. In Africa and Latin America, it produced agitation, and eventually revolt, against colonial and autocratic rule. Academics throughout the world produced a prodigious new literature urging constant reform and expansion of the human rights regime. Within a generation, human rights had become the "new civic faith" of the post-war world order.

Christian and Jewish communities participated actively as midwives in the birth of this modern rights revolution, and special religious rights protections were at first actively pursued. Individual religious groups issued bold confessional statements and manifestos on human rights shortly after World War II. Several denominations and budding ecumenical bodies joined Jewish nongovernmental organizations (NGOs) in cultivating human rights at the international level.[26] The Free Church tradition played a critical role in the civil rights movement in America and beyond, as did the Social Gospel and Christian Democratic Party movements in Europe and Latin America.[27]

After expressing some initial interest, however, leaders of the rights revolution consigned religious groups and their particular religious rights

25. See Chapter 1 herein and RHR I and II.
26. Cotler, "Jewish NGOs and Religious Human Rights," pp. 177-87.
27. John Nurser, *For All Peoples and All Nations: Christian Churches and Human Rights* (Geneva: World Council of Churches Publications, 2005); Allen D. Hertzke, *Freeing God's Children: The Unlikely Alliance for Global Human Rights* (Lanham, Md.: Rowman and Littlefield, 2004); Robert Traer, *Faith in Human Rights: Support in Religious Traditions for a Global Struggle* (Washington, D.C.: Georgetown University Press, 1991).

to a low priority. Freedom of speech and press, parity of race and gender, provision of work and welfare captured most of the energy and emoluments of the rights revolution. After the 1960s, academic inquiries and activist interventions into religious rights and their abuses became increasingly intermittent and isolated, inspired as much by parochial self-interest as by universal golden rules. The rights revolution seemed to be passing religion by.

This deprecation of the special roles and rights of religions from the later 1960s onward introduced several distortions into the theory and law of human rights in vogue today.

First, without religion, many rights are cut from their roots. The right to religion, Georg Jellinek (1851-1911) once wrote, is "the mother of many other rights."[28] For the religious individual, the right to believe leads ineluctably to the rights to assemble, speak, worship, proselytize, educate, parent, travel, or to abstain from the same on the basis of one's beliefs. For the religious association, the right to exist invariably involves rights to corporate property, collective worship, organized charity, parochial education, freedom of press, and autonomy of governance. To ignore religious rights is to overlook the conceptual, if not historical, source of many other individual and associational rights.

Second, without religion, the regime of human rights becomes infinitely expandable. The classic Religions of the Book adopt and advocate human rights in order to protect religious duties. A religious individual or association has rights to exist and act not in the abstract but in order to discharge discrete religious duties.[29] Religious rights provide the best example of the organic linkage between rights and duties. Without them, rights become abstract, with no obvious limit on their exercise or their expansion.

Third, without religion, human rights become too captive to Western libertarian ideals. Many religious traditions — whether of Buddhist, Confucian, Hindu, Islamic, Orthodox, or Traditional stock — cannot conceive of, nor accept, a system of rights that excludes, deprecates, or privatizes religion. Religion is for these traditions inextricably integrated into every facet of life. Religious rights are, for them, an inherent part of rights of speech,

28. Georg Jellinek, *Die Erklärung der Menschen- und Bürgerrechte: ein Beitrag zur modernen Verfassungsgeschichte* (Leipzig: Duncker and Humblot, 1895), p. 42.

29. An-Na'im, *Toward an Islamic Reformation*, pp. 1-10; Novak, *Covenantal Rights*, pp. 3-12; World Council of Churches, *Human Rights and Christian Responsibility*, 3 vols. (Geneva: World Council of Churches, 1975); Wolfgang Huber and Heinz Eduard Tödt, *Menschenrechte: Perspektiven einer menschlichen Welt* (Stuttgart: Kreuz-Verlag, 1977).

press, assembly, and other individual rights as well as ethnic, cultural, linguistic, and similar associational rights. No system of rights that ignores or deprecates this cardinal place of religion can be respected or adopted.

Fourth, without religion, the state is given an exaggerated role to play as the guarantor of human rights. The simple state versus individual dialectic of many modern human rights theories leaves it to the state to protect and provide rights of all sorts. In reality, the state is not, and cannot be, so omnicompetent. Numerous "mediating structures" stand between the state and the individual, religious institutions prominently among them.[30] Religious institutions, among others, play a vital role in the cultivation and realization of rights. They can create the conditions (sometimes the prototypes) for the realization of first-generation civil and political rights. They can provide a critical (sometimes the principal) means to meet second-generation rights of education, health care, child care, labor organizations, employment, and artistic opportunities, among others. They can offer some of the deepest insights into norms of creation, stewardship, and servanthood that lie at the heart of third-generation rights.

The challenge of the next century will be to transform religious communities from midwives to mothers of human rights — from agents that assist in the birth of rights norms conceived elsewhere, to associations that give birth to and nurture their own unique contributions to human rights norms and practices.

The ancient teachings and practices of Judaism, Christianity, and Islam have much to commend them to the human rights regime. Each of these traditions is a religion of revelation, founded on the eternal command to love one God, oneself, and all neighbors. Each tradition recognizes a canonical text as its highest authority — the Torah, the Bible, and the Qur'an, respectively. Each tradition designates a class of officials to preserve and propagate its faith, and embraces an expanding body of authoritative interpretations and applications of its canons. Each tradition has a refined legal structure — the Halacha, the canon law, and the Shari'a — that has translated its enduring principles of faith into evolving precepts of works. Each tradition has sought to imbue its religious, ethical, and legal norms into the daily lives of individuals and communities. Each tradition has produced a number of the basic building blocks of a comprehensive theory and law of

30. James W. Skillen and Rockne M. McCarthy, eds., *Political Order and the Plural Structure of Society* (Atlanta: Scholars, 1991); Michael Walzer, *Spheres of Justice: A Defense of Pluralism and Equality* (New York: Basic, 1983).

religious rights — conscience, dignity, reason, liberty, equality, tolerance, love, openness, responsibility, justice, mercy, righteousness, accountability, covenant, and community, among other cardinal concepts. Each tradition has developed its own internal system of legal procedures and structures for the protection of rights, which historically have and still can serve as both prototypes and complements for secular legal systems. Each tradition has its own advocates and prophets, ancient and modern, who have worked to achieve a closer approximation of human rights ideals.

Human Rights and Religion

This leads to my second response to the Dickensian paradoxes of the modern human rights revolution: human rights must have a more prominent place in the theological discourse of modern religions. Many would consider this second thesis to be as misguided as the first. It is one thing for religious bodies to accept the freedom and autonomy that a human rights regime allows. This at least gives them unencumbered space to pursue their divine callings. It is quite another thing for religious bodies to import human rights within their own polities and theologies. This exposes them to all manner of unseemly challenges.

Human rights norms, religious skeptics argue, challenge the structure of religious bodies. While human rights norms teach liberty and equality, most religious bodies teach authority and hierarchy. While human rights norms encourage pluralism and diversity, many religious bodies require orthodoxy and uniformity. While human rights norms teach freedoms of speech and petition, several religions teach duties of silence and submission. To draw human rights norms into the structures of religion would seem only to embolden members to demand greater access to religious governance, greater freedom from religious discipline, greater latitude in the definition of religious doctrine and liturgy. So why import them?

Moreover, human rights norms challenge the spirit of religious bodies. Human rights norms, religious skeptics argue, are the creed of a secular faith born of Enlightenment liberalism, humanism, and rationalism. Human rights advocates regularly describe these norms as our new "civic faith," "our new world religion," "our new global moral language."[31] The

---

31. Johan D. van der Vyver, "Universality and Relativism of Human Rights: American Relativism," *Buffalo Human Rights Law Review* 4 (1998): 43-78.

influential French jurist Karel Vasak has pressed these sentiments into a full confession of the secular spirit of the modern human rights movement:

> The Universal Declaration of Human Rights [of 1948], like the French Declaration of the Rights of Man and Citizen in 1789, has had an immense impact throughout the world. It has been called a modern edition of the New Testament, and the Magna Carta of humanity, and has become a constant source of inspiration for governments, for judges, and for national and international legislators. . . . [B]y recognizing the Universal Declaration as a *living* document . . . one can proclaim one's faith in the future of mankind.[32]

In demonstration of this new faith, Vasak converted the "old trinity" of *"liberté, égalité, et fraternité"* taught by the French Revolution into a "new trinity" of "three generations of rights" for all humanity.[33] The first generation of civil and political rights elaborates the meaning of liberty. The second generation of social, cultural, and economic rights elaborates the meaning of equality. The third generation of solidarity rights to development, peace, health, the environment, and open communication elaborates the meaning of fraternity. Such language has become not only the *lingua franca* but also something of the *lingua sacra* of the modern human rights movement. In the face of such an overt confession of secular liberalism, religious skeptics conclude, a religious body would do well to resist the ideas and institutions of human rights.

Both these skeptical arguments, however, presuppose that human rights norms constitute a static belief system born of Enlightenment liberalism. But the human rights regime is not static. It is fluid, elastic, and open to challenge and change. The human rights regime is not a fundamental belief system. It is a relative system of ideas and ideals that presupposes the existence of fundamental beliefs and values that will constantly shape and reshape it. The human rights regime is not the child of Enlightenment liberalism, nor a ward under its exclusive guardianship. It is the *ius gentium* of

32. Karel Vasak, "A 30-Year Struggle," *UNESCO Courier,* November 1977, p. 29; see also Karel Vasak, foreword to *The International Dimensions of Human Rights,* ed. Karel Vasak (Westport, Conn.: Greenwood, 1982), p. xv; Karel Vasak, "Pour une troisième génération des droits de l'homme," in *Études et Essais sur le Droit International Humanitaire et sur les Principes de la Croix-Rouge en l'Honneur de Jean Pictet,* ed. Christophe Swinarski (The Hague: Martinus Nijhoff, 1984), pp. 837-45.

33. Vasak, "Pour une troisième génération," p. 837.

our times, the common law of nations, which a variety of Hebrew, Greek, Roman, Christian, and Enlightenment movements have historically nurtured in the West and which today still needs the constant nurture of multiple communities, in the West and well beyond. It is beyond doubt that many current formulations of human rights are suffused with fundamental libertarian beliefs and values, some of which run counter to the cardinal beliefs of various religious traditions. But libertarianism does not and should not have a monopoly on the nurture of human rights; indeed, a human rights regime cannot long survive under its exclusive patronage.

I use the antique term *ius gentium* advisedly — to signal the place of human rights as "middle axioms" in our moral and political discourse.[34] Historically, Western writers spoke of a hierarchy of laws — from natural law (*ius naturale*), to common law (*ius gentium*), to civil law (*ius civile*). The natural law was the set of immutable principles of reason and conscience, which are supreme in authority and divinity and must always prevail in instances of dispute. The civil law was the set of enacted laws and procedures of local political communities, reflecting their immediate policies and procedures. Between these two sets of norms was the *ius gentium*, the set of principles and customs common to several communities and often the basis for treaties and other diplomatic conventions. The contents of the *ius gentium* did gradually change over time and across cultures as new interpretations of the natural law were offered, and as new formulations of the positive law became increasingly conventional. But the *ius gentium* was a relatively consistent body of principles by which a person and a people could govern themselves.

This antique typology helps us to understand the intermediate place of human rights in our hierarchy of legal and cultural norms today. Human rights are the *ius gentium* of our time, the middle axioms of our discourse. They are derived from and dependent upon the transcendent principles that religious traditions (more than any other group) continue to cultivate. They also inform, and are informed by, shifts in the customs and conventions of sundry state law systems. These human rights norms do gradually change over time: just compare the international human rights instruments of 1948 with those of today. But human rights norms are a relatively stable

34. Abdullahi Ahmed An-Na'im, "Towards an Islamic Hermeneutics for Human Rights," in *Human Rights and Religious Values: An Uneasy Relationship?* ed. Abdullahi Ahmed An-Na'im et al. (Grand Rapids: Eerdmans, 1995), pp. 229-42; Robert P. George, "Response," in *A Preserving Grace: Protestants, Catholics, and Natural Law,* ed. Michael Cromartie (Grand Rapids: Eerdmans, 1997), pp. 157-61.

set of ideals by which a person and community might be guided and judged.

This antique typology also helps us to understand the place of human rights within religion. My argument that human rights must have a more prominent place within religions today is not an attempt to import libertarian ideals into their theologies and polities. It is not an attempt to herd Trojan horses into Churches, synagogues, mosques, and temples to assail secretly their spirit and structure. My argument is, rather, that religious bodies must again assume their traditional patronage and protection of human rights, bringing to this regime their full doctrinal vigor, liturgical healing, and moral suasion. Using our antique typology, religious bodies must again nurture and challenge the middle axioms of the *ius gentium* using the transcendent principles of the *ius naturale*. This must not be an effort to monopolize the discourse, nor to establish by positive law a particular religious construction of human rights. Such an effort must be part of a collective discourse of competing understandings of the *ius naturale* — of competing theological views of the divine and the human, of good and evil, of individuality and community — that will serve constantly to inform and reform, to develop and deepen, the human rights ideals now in place.[35]

An Emerging Human Rights Hermeneutic

A number of religious traditions of late have begun the process of reengaging the regime of human rights, of returning to their traditional roots and routes of nurturing and challenging the human rights regime. This process has been incremental, clumsy, controversial, and at times even fatal for its proponents. But the process of religious engagement of human rights is now under way in Christian, Islamic, Judaic, Buddhist, Hindu, and Traditional communities alike. Something of a new "human rights hermeneutic" is slowly beginning to emerge among modern religions.[36]

35. Wolfgang Huber, *Gerechtigkeit und Recht: Grundlinien christlicher Rechtsethik* (Gütersloh: Chr. Kaiser, 1996), pp. 252ff., 366ff., 446ff.; Jerome J. Shestack, "The Jurisprudence of Human Rights," in *Human Rights in International Law: Legal and Policy Issues,* ed. Theodor Meron (Oxford: Clarendon, 1984), p. 75; David Tracy, "Religion and Human Rights in the Public Realm," *Daedalus* 112, no. 4 (1983): 237-54.

36. See, e.g., An-Na'im, *Toward an Islamic Reformation;* Huber and Tödt, *Menschenrechte;* Novak, *Covenantal Rights;* Max L. Stackhouse, *Creeds, Society, and Human Rights* (Grand Rapids: Eerdmans, 1984); William Theodore de Bary, *Asian Values*

This is, in part, a "hermeneutic of confession." Given their checkered human rights records over the centuries, religious bodies have begun to acknowledge their departures from the cardinal teachings of peace and love that are the heart of their sacred texts and traditions. Christian Churches have taken the lead in this process — from the Second Vatican Council's confession of prior complicity in authoritarianism, to the contemporary Church's repeated confessions of prior support for apartheid, communism, racism, sexism, fascism, and anti-Semitism.[37] Other communities have also begun this process — from recent Muslim academics' condemnations of the politicization of "jihad" to the Dalai Lama's recent lamentations over the "sometimes sorry human rights record" of both his own and rival traditions.[38]

This is, in part, a "hermeneutic of suspicion," in Paul Ricoeur's famous phrase. Given the pronounced libertarian tone of many recent human rights formulations, it is imperative that we not idolize or idealize these formulations. We need not be bound by current taxonomies of "three generations of rights" rooted in liberty, equality, and fraternity. Common law formulations of "life, liberty, and property," canon law formulations of "natural, ecclesiastical, and civil rights," or Protestant formulations of "civil, theological, and pedagogical uses" of rights might well be more apt classification schemes. We need not accept the seemingly infinite expansion of human rights discourse and demands. Rights bound by moral duties, by natural capacities, or by covenantal relationships might well provide better boundaries to the legitimate expression and extension of rights. We also need not be bound only to a centralized legal methodology of articulating and enforcing rights. We might also consider a more pluralistic model of interpretation that respects "the right of the [local] community to

and Human Rights: A Confucian Communitarian Perspective (Cambridge, Mass.: Harvard University Press, 1998); William Theodore de Bary and Tu Weiming, eds., *Confucianism and Human Rights* (New York: Columbia University Press, 1998); Irene Bloom et al., eds., *Religious Diversity and Human Rights* (New York: Columbia University Press, 1996); Joanne R. Bauer and Daniel A. Bell, eds., *The East Asian Challenge for Human Rights* (Cambridge: Cambridge University Press, 1999); Arvind Sharma, *Hinduism and Human Rights: A Conceptual Approach* (New Delhi: Oxford University Press, 2004).

37. See Luke Timothy Johnson, "Religious Rights and Christian Texts," in RHR I, pp. 70-73; Charles Villa-Vicencio, *A Theology of Reconstruction: Nation-Building and Human Rights* (Cambridge: Cambridge University Press, 1992).

38. An-Na'im, *Toward an Islamic Reformation,* pp. 171-72; Farid Esack, "Muslims Engaging the Other and the Humanum," in SB, pp. 119-20; Dalai Lama, *Commencement Address of the Dalai Lama at Emory University,* May 11, 1998.

be the living frame of interpretation for [its] own religion and its normative regime."[39]

This is, in part, a "hermeneutic of history." While acknowledging the fundamental contributions of Enlightenment liberalism to the modern rights regime, we must also see the deeper genesis and genius of many modern rights norms in religious texts and traditions that antedate the Enlightenment by centuries, even by millennia. We must return to our religious sources. In part, this is a return to ancient sacred texts freed from the casuistic accretions of generations of jurists and freed from the cultural trappings of the communities in which these traditions were born. In part, this is a return to slender streams of theological jurisprudence that have not been part of the mainstream of the religious traditions, or have become diluted by too great a commingling with it. In part, this is a return to prophetic voices of dissent, long purged from traditional religious canons, but, in retrospect, prescient of some of the rights roles that the tradition might play today.

Permit me to illustrate this budding new human rights hermeneutic using my own tradition of Christianity. There are various ways to tell the Christian part of this story. One can analyze the rights contributions of seminal figures from Christ and the early Church Fathers onward. One can sift through the complex patterns of rights talk of various regional and national Christian groups. One can dig into the daily rights narratives of discrete communities of the faithful in different social and political contexts. Ultimately, these and other genres of analysis will need to be pursued and combined to come to full terms with the Christian Church's past and potential contribution to human rights, including religious rights.

To outline the main Christian story here, permit me to analyze briefly the rights contributions of the three main traditions of Christianity: Catholic, Protestant, and Orthodox. Other chapters herein elaborate the particular positions of Lutheranism, Calvinism, and Russian Orthodoxy.[40]

Human Rights and Catholicism

The Roman Catholic Church is, paradoxically, the first and the last of the three great traditions of Christianity to embrace the doctrine of human

---

39. An-Na'im, *Toward an Islamic Reformation*, p. 235.
40. See Chapters 1-2 and 4-6 herein.

rights. At the opening of the second millennium of the common era, the Catholic Church led the first great human rights movement of the West in the name of "freedom of the Church" (*libertas ecclesiae*). During the Papal Revolution of Pope Gregory VII (1015-1085) and his successors, the Catholic clergy threw off their royal and civil rulers and established the Church as an autonomous legal and political corporation within Western Christendom.[41] For the first time, the Church claimed jurisdiction over such persons as clerics, pilgrims, students, Jews, and Muslims. It also claimed jurisdiction over such subjects as doctrine and liturgy, ecclesiastical property, polity, patronage, marriage and family relations, education, charity, inheritance, oral promises, oaths, various contracts, and all manner of moral and ideological crimes.[42]

The medieval canon law was based, in part, on the concept of individual and corporate rights (*iura*).[43] The canon law defined the rights of the clergy to their liturgical offices and ecclesiastical benefices, their exemptions from civil taxes and duties, and their immunities from civil prosecution and compulsory testimony. It defined the rights of ecclesiastical organizations like parishes, monasteries, charities, and guilds to form and dissolve, to accept and reject members, to establish order and discipline, to acquire, use, and alienate property. It defined the rights of Church councils and synods to participate in the election and discipline of bishops, abbots, and other clergy. It defined the rights of the laity to worship, evangelize, maintain religious symbols, participate in the sacraments, travel on religious pilgrimages, and educate their children. It defined the

41. See further Chapter 1 herein.

42. Brian Tierney, *Origins of Papal Infallibility, 1150-1350: A Study on the Concepts of Infallibility, Sovereignty, and Tradition in the Middle Ages* (Leiden: E. J. Brill, 1972), pp. 39-45, 82-121; R. H. Helmholz, *The Spirit of Classical Canon Law* (Athens, Ga.: University of Georgia Press, 1996), pp. 1-32; Paul Wilpert, ed., *Lex et Sacramentum im Mittelalter* (Berlin: de Gruyter, 1969).

43. Brian Tierney, *Rights, Law, and Infallibility in Medieval Thought* (Aldershot, Hampshire: Varorium, 1997); Brian Tierney, *The Idea of Natural Rights: Studies on Natural Rights, Natural Law, and Church Law, 1150-1625* (Grand Rapids: Eerdmans, 1997); Brian Tierney, *Religion, Law, and the Growth of Constitutional Thought, 1150-1650* (Cambridge: Cambridge University Press, 1982); Charles J. Reid Jr., "Rights in Thirteenth Century Canon Law: An Historical Investigation" (Ph.D. dissertation, Cornell, 1994); Charles J. Reid Jr., "Thirteenth Century Canon Law and Rights: The Word *ius* and Its Range of Subjective Meanings," *Studia Canonica* 30 (1996): 295; Charles J. Reid Jr., "Roots of a Democratic Church Polity in the History of the Canon Law," *Canon Law Society of America Proceedings* 60 (1998): 150.

rights of the poor, widows, and the needy to seek solace, succor, and sanctuary within the Church. A good deal of the rich latticework of medieval canon law was cast, substantively and procedurally, in the form and language of rights.

To be sure, such rights were not unguided by duties, nor were they available to all parties. Only the Catholic faithful — and notoriously not Jews, Muslims, or heretics[44] — had full rights protection, and their rights were to be exercised with appropriate ecclesiastical and sacramental constraints. But the basic medieval rights formulations of exemptions, immunities, privileges, and benefits, and the free exercise of religious worship, travel, speech, and education, have persisted, with ever greater inclusivity, to this day. Many of the common formulations of individual and collective rights and liberties in vogue today were first forged not by John Locke (1632-1704) or James Madison (1751-1836) but by obscure canonists and theologians four centuries before them.

It was, in part, the perceived excesses of the sixteenth-century Protestant Reformation that closed the door to the Catholic Church's own secular elaboration of this refined rights regime. The Council of Trent (1545-1563) confirmed, with some modifications, the internal rights structure of the canon law. These formulations were elaborated in the vast and influential writings of Spanish and Portuguese neo-scholastics in the later sixteenth and seventeenth centuries.[45] But the Church left it largely to non-Church bodies and non-Catholic believers to draw out the secular implications of the medieval human rights tradition. The Catholic Church largely tolerated Protestant and humanist rights efforts in the later sixteenth century and beyond, which built, in part, on common biblical and canon law foundations. The Church grew increasingly intolerant, however, of the rights theories of the Enlightenment, which built on secular theories of individualism and rationalism. Enlightenment teachings on liberties, rights, and separation of Church and state conflicted directly with Catholic teachings on natural law, the common good, and subsidiarity. The Church's intolerance of such formulations gave way to outright hostility after the French Revolution, most notably in the blistering *Syllabus of Errors* of

44. Solomon Grayzel, *The Church and the Jews in the XIIIth Century* (Detroit: Wayne State University Press, 1989); W. J. Sheils, ed., *Persecution and Toleration* (Oxford: Blackwell, 1984); James Parkes, *The Jew in the Medieval Community: A Study of His Political and Economic Situation,* second ed. (New York: Hermon, 1976).

45. Tierney, *The Idea of Natural Rights;* Brian Tierney, "Historical Roots of Modern Rights: Before Locke and After," *Ave Maria Law Review* 3 (2005): 23-43.

1864.[46] Notwithstanding the provocative social and political teachings of subsequent instruments, such as *Rerum Novarum,* in 1891, and *Quadragesimo Anno,* in 1934, the Catholic Church hierarchy had little patience with the human rights reforms and democratic regimes of the later nineteenth and early twentieth centuries. It acquiesced more readily in the authoritative, if not authoritarian, regimes and policies that governed the European, Latin American, and African nations where Catholicism was strong.[47]

The Second Vatican Council (1962-1965) (Vatican II) and subsequent initiatives transformed the Catholic Church's theological attitude toward human rights and democracy. In a series of sweeping new doctrinal statements, from *Mater et Magistra* (1961) onward, the Church came to endorse many of the very same human rights and democratic principles that it had spurned a century before. First, the Church endorsed human rights and liberties — not only in the internal, canon law context, but also now in a global, secular law context. Every person, the Church taught, is created by God "with intelligence and free will" and has rights "flowing directly and simultaneously from his very nature."[48] Such rights include the right to life and adequate standards of living, to moral and cultural values, to religious activities, to assembly and association, to marriage and family life, and to various social, political, and economic benefits and opportunities. The Church emphasized the religious rights of conscience, worship, assembly, and education, calling them the "first rights" of any civic order. It also stressed the need to balance individual and associational rights, particularly those involving the Church, family, and school. Governments everywhere were encouraged to create conditions conducive to the realization and protection of these "inviolable rights" and encouraged to root out every type of discrimination, whether social or cultural, whether based on sex, race, color, social distinction, language, or religion. Second, as a corol-

---

46. In Ehler and Morrall, p. 281. See further Chapter 7 herein.

47. David Hollenbach, *Claims in Conflict: Retrieving and Renewing the Catholic Human Rights Tradition* (New York: Paulist, 1979), p. 42; John Courtney Murray, *The Problem of Religious Freedom* (Westminster, Md.: Newman, 1965), pp. 3-6; Mary Elsbernd, "Papal Statements on Rights: A Historical Contextual Study of Encyclical Teachings from Pius VI–Pius XI (1791-1939)" (Ph.D. dissertation, Catholic University of Louvain, 1985).

48. *Pacem in Terris,* para. 9 (1963), reprinted in Joseph Gremillion, ed., *The Gospel of Peace and Justice: Catholic Social Teaching Since Pope John* (Maryknoll, N.Y.: Orbis, 1976), p. 203.

lary, the Church advocated limited constitutional government, disestablishment of religion, and the separation of Church and state.[49] The vast pluralism of religions and cultures, and the inherent dangers in state endorsement of any religion, in the Church's view, rendered mandatory such democratic forms of government.[50]

Vatican II and its progeny transformed not only the theological attitude but also the social actions of the Catholic Church respecting human rights and democracy. After Vatican II, the Church was less centralized and more socially active. Local bishops and clergy were given greater autonomy and incentive to participate in local and national affairs, to bring the Church's new doctrines to bear on matters political and cultural. Particularly in North America and Western Europe, bishops and bishops' conferences became active in cultivating and advocating a variety of political and legal reforms. Likewise in Latin America, the rise of liberation theologies and base communities helped to translate many of the enduring and evolving rights perspectives of the Church into intensely active social and political programs. The Catholic Church was thereby transformed from a passive accomplice in authoritarian regimes to a powerful advocate of democratic and human rights reform.

The Catholic Church has been a critical force in the new wave of political democratization that has been breaking over the world since the early 1970s, both through the announcements and interventions of the papacy and through the efforts of its local clergy. New democratic and human rights movements in Brazil, Chile, Central America, the Philippines, South Korea, Poland, Hungary, the Czech Republic, Ukraine, and elsewhere owe much of their inspiration to the social teachings and political activism of the Catholic Church.[51]

The Catholic Church has thus come full circle. The Church led the first human rights movement of the West at the opening of the second millennium. It stands ready to lead the first human rights movement of the world at the opening of the third millennium — equipped with a refined

49. *Pacem in Terris,* pp. 203-18.

50. *Dignitatis Humanae,* in *The Documents of Vatican II,* ed. Walter M. Abbott and Joseph Gallagher (New York: Guild, 1967), p. 675.

51. J. Bryan Hehir, "Catholicism and Democracy: Conflict, Change, and Collaboration," in *Christianity and Democracy in Global Context,* ed. John Witte Jr. (Boulder, Colo.: Westview, 1993), pp. 25ff.; George Weigel, *The Final Revolution: The Resistance Church and the Collapse of Communism* (New York: Oxford University Press, 1992), pp. 16, 77-102, 191-209.

theology and law of human rights and some one billion members world-wide. The Catholic Church offers a unique combination of local and global, confessional and universal human rights strategies for the next century. Within the internal forum and the canon law, the Church has a distinctly Catholic human rights framework that protects especially the rights of family, education, charity, and health care within a sacramental and sacerdotal context. Within the external forum of the world and its secular law, however, the Church has a decidedly universal human rights framework that advocates especially personal, civil, and political rights for all.

Human Rights and Protestantism

One of the ironies of the contemporary human rights movement is the relative silence of the modern Protestant Churches. Historically, Protestant Churches produced some of the most refined theories and laws of human rights, and catalyzed a number of the early modern revolutions fought in the name of human rights and democratization for all. Today, many Protestant Churches have been content simply to confirm human rights norms and to condemn human rights abuses without deep corporate theological reflection. Where modern Protestant Churches have been politically active, they have often been narrowly preoccupied with single issues — abortion, prayer in schools, same-sex marriage, and the like. To be sure, some leading Protestant lights have taken up the subject more comprehensively in their writings.[52] A number of Protestant groups within the Church, particularly new liberationist and feminist groups, have developed important new themes.[53] The American civil rights movement found some of its strongest support among Baptist, Methodist, and other Free Churches who have continued to be active in certain quarters. The ecumenical movement, especially the World Council of Churches, helped to consolidate the human rights efforts of many Protestant denominations and to combine their efforts with other religious communities.[54] But, to date, no compre-

52. E.g., Hans Dombois, *Das Recht der Gnade*, 3 vols. (Witten: Luther-Verlag, 1969); Huber and Tödt, *Menschenrechte*; Stackhouse, *Creeds, Society, and Human Rights*; Johan D. van der Vyver, *Seven Lectures on Human Rights* (Cape Town: Juta, 1976).

53. Villa-Vicencio, *A Theology of Reconstruction*.

54. Allen O. Miller, ed., *A Christian Declaration on Human Rights: Theological Studies of the World Alliance of Reformed Churches* (Grand Rapids: Eerdmans, 1977); World Council of Churches, *Human Rights and Christian Responsibility*; National Council

hensive and systematic human rights theory or program has taken the Protestant field. Modern Protestantism has produced no John Courtney Murray and no Vatican II. Indeed, several quarters of modern Protestantism — Reformed, Evangelical, and Anabaptist alike — have become theologically predisposed to oppose human rights as the dangerous teaching of Enlightenment liberalism.

The great irony of all this is that the Protestant Reformation was, in effect, the second great human rights movement of the West. Prior to the sixteenth century, there was one universal Catholic faith and Church, one universal system of canon law and sacramental life, one universal hierarchy of courts and administrators centered in Rome that ruled throughout much of the West. Martin Luther (1483-1546), John Calvin (1509-1564), Menno Simons (1496-1561), Thomas Cranmer (1489-1556), and other leading sixteenth-century Reformers all began their movements with a call for freedom from this ecclesiastical regime — freedom of the individual conscience from intrusive canon laws and clerical controls, freedom of political officials from ecclesiastical power and privileges, freedom of the local clergy from central papal rule and oppressive princely controls.

The Protestant Reformation permanently broke the unity of Western Christendom, and thereby introduced the foundations for the modern constitutional system of confessional pluralism.

The Lutheran Reformation territorialized the faith through the principle of *cuius regio, eius religio* (whosever region, his religion), established by the Peace of Augsburg[55] in 1555. Under this principle, princes or city councils were authorized to prescribe the appropriate forms of Evangelical or Catholic doctrine, liturgy, and education for their polities. Religious dissenters were granted the right to worship privately in their homes or to emigrate peaceably from the polity. After decades of bitter civil war, the Peace of Westphalia[56] in 1648 extended this privilege to Reformed Calvinists as well, rendering Germany and beyond a veritable honeycomb of religious plurality for the next two centuries.

The Anglican Reformation nationalized the faith through the famous Supremacy Acts and the Acts of Uniformity passed from 1534 to 1559.[57] Citizens of the Commonwealth of England were required to be communicants of

---

of Churches, *Life in All Its Fullness: The Word of God and Human Rights* (New York: National Council of Churches, Human Rights Office, 1992).

55. In Ehler and Morrall, pp. 164-73.
56. In Ehler and Morrall, pp. 189-92.
57. In Stephenson and Markham, pp. 303-21.

the Church of England, subject to the final ecclesiastical and political authority of the monarch. The Toleration Act of 1689 extended a modicum of rights
to some Protestant dissenters.[58] But it was not until the Catholic and Jewish
Emancipation Acts of 1829 and 1833 that the national identity of the Church
and Commonwealth of England was finally formally broken.[59]

The Anabaptist Reformation communalized the faith by introducing
what Menno Simons once called the *Scheidingsmaurer* — the wall of separation between the redeemed realm of religion and the fallen realm of the
world. Anabaptist religious communities were ascetically withdrawn from
the world into small, self-sufficient, intensely democratic communities,
governed internally by biblical principles of discipleship, simplicity, charity, and Christian obedience. When such communities grew too large or too
divided, they deliberately colonized themselves, eventually spreading the
Anabaptist communities from Russia to Ireland to the furthest frontiers of
North America.[60]

The Calvinist Reformation congregationalized the faith by introducing rule by a democratically elected consistory of pastors, elders, and deacons. In John Calvin's day, the Geneva consistory was still appointed and
held broad personal and subject matter jurisdiction over all members of the
city. By the seventeenth century, most Calvinist communities in Europe and
North America reduced the consistory to an elected, representative system
of government within each Church. These consistories featured separation
among the offices of preaching, discipline, and charity, and a fluid,
dialogical form of religious polity and policing centered around collective
worship and the congregational meeting.[61]

The Protestant Reformation also broke the primacy of corporate
Christianity and gave new emphasis to the role of the individual believer in
the economy of salvation. The Protestant Reformation did not invent the
individual, as too many exuberant commentators still maintain. But
sixteenth-century Protestant Reformers, more than their Catholic contem-
poraries, gave new emphasis to the (religious) rights and liberties of individuals at both religious law and civil law.

58. In Stephenson and Markham, pp. 607-8. See also Joseph Lecler, *Toleration and
the Reformation*, 4 vols., trans. T. L. Westow (New York: Association, 1960).

59. In Ehler and Morrall, pp. 254-71.

60. Walter Klaassen, ed., *Anabaptism in Outline: Selected Primary Sources*
(Scottdale, Pa.: Herald, 1973); Robert M. Friedmann, *The Theology of Anabaptism*
(Scottdale, Pa.: Herald, 1973).

61. See RR and Chapter 5 herein.

This new emphasis on the individual was true even in the more intensely communitarian traditions of Anglicanism and Anabaptism. The Anglican *Book of Common Prayer* was designed, in Thomas Cranmer's words, as a "textbook of liberty."[62] The daily office of the lectionary, together with the vernacular Bible, encouraged the exercise of private worship and devotion outside the Church, particularly in the home. The choices among liturgical rites and prayers within the Prayer Book encouraged the exercise of at least some clerical innovation within the Church, with such opportunities for variation and innovation increasing with the 1662 and 1789 editions of the Prayer Book.

The Anabaptist doctrine of adult baptism gave new emphasis to a voluntarist understanding of religion, as opposed to conventional notions of a birthright or predestined faith. The adult individual was now called to make a conscientious choice to accept the faith — metaphorically, to scale the wall of separation between the fallen world and the realm of religion to come within the perfection of Christ. Later Free Church followers converted this cardinal image into a powerful platform of liberty of conscience and free exercise of religion not only for Christians but also eventually for all peaceable believers. The Great Awakening (ca. 1720-1780) added further strength to this notion. The various Evangelical denominations and movements that emerged from the Great Awakening emphasized Christian conversion, the necessary spiritual rebirth of each sinful individual. On that basis, they strongly advocated the liberty of conscience of each individual and the free speech and press rights and duties of the missionary to proselytize, both on the American frontier and abroad. Evangelicals had a high view of the Christian Bible as the infallible textbook for human living. On that basis, they celebrated the use of the Bible in chapels, classrooms, prisons, and elsewhere. Evangelicals emphasized sanctification, the process of each individual becoming holier before God, neighbor, and self. On that basis, they underscored a robust ethic of spiritual and moral progress, education, and improvement of all. These views eventually had a great influence on the formation of constitutional protections of religious liberty in eighteenth- and nineteenth-century America.

The Lutheran and Calvinist branches of the Reformation laid the anthropological basis for an even more expansive theory and law of rights. As we saw in earlier chapters, Protestant theology teaches that a person is both

---

62. John E. Booty, ed., *The Book of Common Prayer, 1559* (Charlottesville, Va.: University of Virginia Press, 1976), preface.

saint and sinner.[63] On the one hand, a person is created in the image of God and justified by faith in God. The person is called to a distinct vocation, which stands equal in dignity and sanctity to all others. The person is prophet, priest, and king who is responsible to exhort, minister, and rule in the community. Every person, therefore, stands equal before God and before his or her neighbor. Every person is vested with a natural liberty to live, to believe, and to serve God and neighbor. Every person is entitled to the vernacular Scripture, to education, and to work in a vocation. On the other hand, the person is sinful and prone to evil and egoism. He needs the restraint of the law to deter him from evil and to drive him to repentance. He needs the association of others to exhort, minister, and rule him with law and with love. Every person, therefore, is inherently a communal creature. Every person belongs to a family, a Church, and a political community.

These social institutions of family, Church, and state, Protestants believe, are divine in origin and human in organization. They are created by God and governed by godly ordinances. They stand equal before God and are called to discharge distinctive godly functions in the community. The family is called to rear and nurture children, to educate and discipline them, and to exemplify love and cooperation. The Church is called to preach the Word, administer the sacraments, educate the young, and aid the needy. The state is called to protect order, punish crime, and promote community. Though divine in origin, these institutions are formed through human covenants. Such covenants confirm the divine functions — the created offices — of these institutions. Such covenants also organize these offices so that they are protected from the sinful excesses of officials who occupy them. Family, Church, and state are thus organized so far as possible as public institutions, accessible and accountable to each other and to their members. Specifically, the Church is to be organized as a democratic congregational polity, with a separation of ecclesiastical powers among pastors, elders, and deacons, election of officers to limited tenures, and ready participation of the congregation in the life and leadership of the Church.[64]

Protestant groups in Europe and America cast these theological doctrines into democratic forms designed to protect human rights. Protestant doctrines of the person and society were cast into democratic social forms. Given that all persons stand equal before God, they must stand equal before God's political agents in the state. Given that God vested all persons

63. See Chapters 1 and 2 herein.
64. See further Chapter 5 herein.

with natural liberties of life and belief, the state must ensure them of similar civil liberties. Given that God has called all persons to be prophets, priests, and kings, the state must protect their freedoms to speak, to preach, and to rule in the community. Given that God has created persons as social creatures, the state must promote and protect a plurality of social institutions, particularly the Church and the family.

Protestant doctrines of sin were cast into democratic political forms. The political office must be protected against the sinfulness of the political official. Political power, like ecclesiastical power, must be distributed among self-checking executive, legislative, and judicial branches. Officials must be elected to limited terms of office. Laws must be clearly codified and discretion closely guarded. If officials abuse their offices, they must be disobeyed; if they persist in their abuse, they must be removed, even if by force.

These Protestant teachings helped to inspire many of the early modern revolutions fought in the name of human rights and democracy.[65] They were the driving ideological forces behind the revolts of the French Huguenots, Dutch Pietists, and Scottish Presbyterians against their monarchical oppressors in the later sixteenth and seventeenth centuries. They were critical weapons in the arsenal of the revolutionaries in England, America, and France. They were important sources of the great age of democratic construction in later eighteenth- and nineteenth-century America and Western Europe. In this century, Protestant ideas of human rights and democracy helped to drive the constitutional reformation of Europe in the post-War period, as well as many of the human rights and democratic movements against colonial autocracy in Africa and fascist revival in Latin America.

The role of Protestant missionaries in nineteenth- and twentieth-century Africa is particularly notable. Protestant mission Churches sometimes served as "zones of liberty" in African society.[66] They were organized democratically, with ecclesiastical authority distributed among pastors, elders, deacons, and teachers. Communicant members elected the clergy to their offices and had ready access to those who were elected. Churches served as centers of poor relief, education, health care, and social welfare in the community. Churches catalyzed the formation of voluntary associa-

65. See Harold J. Berman, *Faith and Order: The Reconciliation of Law and Religion* (Grand Rapids: Eerdmans, 1993), pp. 83-139.

66. The phrase is from Richard Joseph, "The Christian Churches and Democracy in Contemporary Africa," in *Christianity and Democracy in Global Context*, ed. Witte, pp. 231-48.

tions such as youth groups, women's groups, and business associations. Churches provided a sanctuary for political dissidents and a sanction for movements of political reform and renewal. By so doing, Churches provided both models of democracy and bulwarks against autocracy in Africa.

Their Christian teachings helped to "lower" political officials and to "elevate" political subjects in African cultures. Many traditional African religions, Kwame Bediako has argued, "sacralized" political rulers, viewing them not only as preeminent authorities in the present but also as preeminent interpreters of the past, of an ancestral tradition that had to be obeyed. Christianity "desacralized" politics by showing that all human authorities are subordinate to and empowered by divine authority. Christianity also "dignified" political subjects by giving each person access to the ancestral wisdom of the vernacular Scripture.[67] The Scripture liberated Africans from both their political rulers and their Christian missionaries. It gave the Africans a common point of departure and reference to create a new belief system that combined Scripture with native traditions and a new political system that combined Christian political doctrines with indigenous lore.

These cardinal Protestant teachings and practices have much to offer the regime of human rights still today. Protestant theology avoids the reductionist extremes of libertarianism, which sacrifices the community for the individual, and totalitarianism, which sacrifices the individual for the community. It avoids the limitless expansion of human rights claims by grounding these norms in the creation order, divine callings, and covenant relationships. And it avoids uncritical adoption of human rights by judging their civil, theological, and educational uses in the lives of both individuals and communities. On this foundation, Protestant theology strikes unique balances between liberty and responsibility, dignity and depravity, individuality and community, politics and pluralism.

To translate these theological principles into human rights practices is the great challenge facing the Protestant Churches in the immediate future. The Protestant tradition needs to have its own Vatican II, its own comprehensive and collective assessment of its future role in the human rights drama. Of course, Protestant congregationalism militates against such collective action, as do the many ancient animosities among Prot-

---

67. Kwame Bediako, "Unmasking the Powers: Christianity, Authority, and Desacralization in Modern African Politics," in *Christianity and Democracy in Global Context*, ed. Witte, pp. 207-30. See the monumental work of Lamin Sanneh, *Translating the Message: The Missionary Impact on Culture* (Maryknoll, N.Y.: Orbis, 1989).

estant denominations. But this is no time, and no matter, for denomina-tional snobbery or sniping. Protestants need to sow their own distinct seeds of human rights while the field is still open. Else, there will be little to harvest, and little room to complain, in this new century.

Human Rights and the Orthodox Tradition[68]

The Orthodox Churches, rooted in Eastern Christianity and the Byzantine Empire, ground their human rights theology less in the dignity of the person and more in the integrity of natural law and the human community. To be sure, some of the earliest Church Fathers have sounded familiar Western themes of liberty of conscience, human dignity, and free exercise of religion. For example, Lactantius (ca. 240–ca. 320), whose views were popular among some of the later Greek Fathers, wrote, "[I]t is only in religion that liberty has chosen to dwell. For nothing is so much a matter of free will as religion, and no one can be required to worship what he does not will to worship."[69] Such sentiments have echoed in the Orthodox tradition ever since — particularly in the modern transplanted Orthodox communities of Western Europe and North America that have cultivated a neo-patristic renaissance.[70]

What has rendered the Orthodox human rights understanding unique, however, is its distinct natural law foundations.[71] As Stanley Harakas has shown, a number of Orthodox communities emphasize that

68. See further Chapter 5 herein.

69. J. P. Migne, *Patrologia Latina* (Paris, 1844-91), 6:516-54.

70. See Paul Valliere, "Introduction to the Modern Orthodox Tradition," in *The Teachings of Modern Christianity on Law, Politics, and Human Nature,* ed. John Witte Jr. and Frank S. Alexander, 2 vols. (New York: Columbia University Press, 2005), 1:503-32; Paul Valliere, *Modern Russian Theology: Bukharev, Soloviev, Bulgakov* (Grand Rapids: Eerdmans, 2000).

71. S. L. Frank, *The Light Shineth in Darkness: An Essay in Christian Ethics and So-cial Philosophy,* trans. Boris Jakim (Athens, Ohio: Ohio University Press, 1989), pp. 112-89; Stanley S. Harakas, *Let Mercy Abound: Social Concern in the Greek Orthodox Church* (Brookline, Mass.: Holy Cross Orthodox Press, 1983); Ion Bria, "Evangelism, Proselytism, and Religious Freedom in Romania: An Orthodox Point of View," *Journal of Ecumenical Studies* 36 (1999): 163-83; Stanley Harakas, "Christian Ethics in Ecumenical Perspective," *Journal of Ecumenical Studies* 15 (1978): 631-46; Stanley Harakas, "Human Rights: An Eastern Orthodox Perspective," *Journal of Ecumenical Studies* 19 (1982): 13-24; Anastasios Yannoulatos, "Eastern Orthodoxy and Human Rights," *International Review of Mission* 73 (1984): 454-66.

God has written his natural law on the hearts of all persons and rewritten it on the pages of Scripture. This natural law, which finds its most sublime source and summary in the Ten Commandments, prescribes a series of duties that each person owes to others and to God, such as not to kill, not to steal, not to bear false witness, not to swear falsely, not to serve other gods.[72] Humanity's fall into sin has rendered adherence to such moral duties imperative to the survival of the human community. God has called Church and state alike to assume responsibility for enforcing by law those moral duties that are essential to such survival.

According to classic Orthodox theology, human rights are the reciprocals of these divinely ordained moral duties. One person's moral duties not to kill, steal, or bear false witness give rise to another person's rights to life, property, and dignity. A person's moral duties not to serve other gods or swear falsely give rise to his right to serve the right god and to swear properly. For every moral duty taught by natural law, there is a reciprocal moral right. On the strength of this ancient biblical ethic, Orthodox Churches endorse a three-tiered system of rights and duties: (1) a Christian or "evangelical" system of rights and duties based on the natural law principles of Scripture, which are enforced by the canon law and sacramental theology of the Church; (2) a "common moral" system of rights and duties based on universal natural law principles accepted by rational persons in all times and places, which are enforced by moral agents within the community; and (3) a legal system of rights and duties based on the constitutional laws and social needs of the community, which are enforced by the positive laws of the state. The Church has a responsibility not only to maintain the highest standards of moral right and duty among its subjects, but also to serve as a moral agent in the community, to cultivate an understanding of "common morality," and to admonish pastorally and prophetically those who violate this common morality.[73]

Particularly during the long winter of Marxist-Leninist rule, Orthodox Churches throughout the world let their pastoral and prophetic voices be heard in endorsement of human rights and in condemnation of their violation.[74] The World Congress of Orthodox Bishops (1978), for example, greeted the thirtieth anniversary of the United Nations *Universal Declaration of Human Rights* with the call:

72. Harakas, "Human Rights," pp. 18-19; Harakas, "Christian Ethics in Ecumenical Perspective," pp. 640-41.

73. Harakas, "Christian Ethics in Ecumenical Perspective," pp. 631-46; Harakas, "Human Rights," pp. 18-19.

74. Harakas, "Human Rights," p. 20.

We urge all Orthodox Christians to mark this occasion with prayers for those whose human rights are being denied and/or violated; for those who are harassed and persecuted because of their religious beliefs, Orthodox and non-Orthodox alike, in many parts of the world; for those whose rightful demands and persistence are met with greater oppression and ignominy; and for those whose agony for justice, food, shelter, health care and education is accelerated with each passing day.[75]

In 1980, the Twenty-Fifth Clergy-Laity Congress of the Greek Orthodox Archdiocese of North and South America pronounced:

[H]uman rights consist of those conditions of life that allow us fully to develop and use our human qualities of intelligence and conscience to their fullest extent and to satisfy our spiritual, social, and political needs, including freedom of expression, freedom from fear, harassment, intimidation and discrimination, and freedom to participate in the function of government and to have the guarantee of the equal protection of the law.[76]

They further called upon "totalitarian and oppressive regimes to restore respect for the rights and dignity of the individual and to insure the free and unhindered exercise of these vital rights by all citizens, regardless of racial and ethnic origin, or political or religious espousal."[77] "All people," the Orthodox Congress later declared, "have the God-given right to be free from interference by government or others in (1) freely determining their faith by conscience, (2) freely associating and organizing with others for religious purposes, (3) expressing their religious beliefs in worship, teaching and practice, (4) pursuing the implications of their beliefs in the social and political community."[78]

---

75. Statement by Standing Conference of Canonical Orthodox Bishops in the Americas, *Archdiocesan Archives* (Dec. 1978), quoted in Harakas, "Human Rights," p. 21.

76. Minutes, Decisions, Resolutions and Statements of the Twenty-Fifth Clergy-Laity Congress of the Greek Orthodox Archdiocese of North and South America in Atlanta, Georgia (June 27–July 5, 1980), pp. 114-15, quoted in Harakas, "Human Rights," p. 26.

77. Minutes, Decisions, Resolutions and Statements, in Harakas, "Human Rights," p. 26.

78. Quoted in Alexander F. C. Webster, *The Price of Prophecy: Orthodox Churches on Peace, Freedom, and Security* (Grand Rapids: Eerdmans, 1995), p. 148.

The Orthodox Churches have also begun to move gradually toward a greater separation of Church and state — though seemingly more out of sheer political necessity than out of changed theological conviction. Classically, the Orthodox Church had no concept akin to the political dualisms that prevailed in the West — no Augustinian division between the City of God and the City of Man, no medieval Catholic doctrine of two powers or two swords, no Protestant understandings of two kingdoms or two realms, no American understanding of a wall of separation between Church and state.[79] After the fourth century, the prevailing Orthodox view was that Church and state are part of an organic religious and political community, bonded by blood, soil, and confession.[80]

This symbiosis of Church and state subjected the Orthodox Church to substantial state control over its polities and properties, and substantial restrictions on its religious ministry and prophecy. But this arrangement also gave the Orthodox clergy a strong and singular spiritual voice in civil society. It allowed the clergy to teach the community through Orthodox schools and monasteries, Orthodox literature and preaching, often supported by generous state patronage. It allowed them to nurture the community through the power and pathos of the Orthodox liturgy, icons, artwork, prayers, and music. It allowed them to advise officials on the moral dimensions of positive law.[81]

This symbiotic relationship between Church and state worked well enough when state authorities were themselves Orthodox, or at least openly supportive of Orthodoxy. Such was the case for much of the history of Russia, and other parts of Central Eurasia before the Bolshevik Revolution of 1917.[82] This relationship did not work well, however, when political authorities had no Orthodox allegiances. Such was the case for most other Orthodox communities after the fifteenth century.[83] With the Islamic conquest of the Byzantine Empire in the 1450s and the expansion

79. See Chapter 7 herein on these various dualistic frameworks.

80. See Ernest Barker, ed. and trans., *Social and Political Thought in Byzantium* (Oxford: Clarendon, 1957).

81. See Harold J. Berman, "Freedom of Religion in Russia: An Amicus Brief for the Defendant," in POR, pp. 270-71.

82. See Firuz Kazemzadeh, "Reflections on Church and State in Russian History," in POR, pp. 227-38; Philip Walters, "The Russian Orthodox Church and Foreign Christianity: The Legacy of the Past," in POR, pp. 32-41.

83. Vigen Guroian, "Evangelism and Mission in the Orthodox Tradition," in SB, pp. 231-46.

of the Ottoman Empire thereafter, the Orthodox Church could no longer readily depend upon the state for protection and support. Often consigned to restricted millets, local Orthodox communities turned to the increasingly stretched Patriarchate of Constantinople for their principal support. After the great wars of nationalist liberation in Greece, Bulgaria, Romania, and the Balkans in the eighteenth and nineteenth centuries, the depleted Patriarchate of Constantinople finally broke the Church into autocephalous national Churches, which cooperated with local governments as best they could. Many of these new Orthodox Churches saw separation from state control and state support as the safest policy, even if not necessarily the best theology. Similarly, after the great emigrations of Orthodox believers to North America at the turn of the twentieth century, the transplanted autocephalous Orthodox communities were forced to survive with little support from local state officials. Here, too, separation of Church and state became an expedient principle of ecclesiastical living.[84] Similarly, after the Bolshevik Revolution of 1917 and the gradual Soviet control of Eastern Europe, the Church came to endorse the Marxist-Leninist doctrine of separation of Church and state, mostly out of a sheer need to survive.[85] Although individual theologians have sought to draw a new theology of separation of Church and state from these disparate experiences of Orthodox Churches, no such systematic theory seems to have yet captured the field.[86]

Today, the Orthodox Church's commitment to human rights and democratic principles is being tested more severely than ever before, particularly in Russia and parts of Eastern Europe. The remarkable democratic revolution of the Soviet bloc in the past two decades has brought not only new liberty to these long-closed societies but also new license. These societies now face moral degradation, economic dislocation, and human suffering of massive proportions. They face the renewal of ancient animosities among religious and cultural rivals previously kept at bay by the Communist Party. They face an enormous influx of foreigners, whether religious,

---

84. See further Chapter 8 herein on the growing oppression of Orthodox immigrants and other new religious minorities in the early twentieth century in America. Important Supreme Court protections, in the name of separation of Church and state, came in *Kedroff v. St. Nicholas Cathedral,* 344 U.S. 94 (1952), and *Serbian Orthodox Diocese v. Milivojevich,* 426 U.S. 696 (1976). See further RCE, chap. 8.

85. See Chapter 4 herein.

86. See examples of the writings of Soloviev, Berdiaev, and Lossky in *The Teachings of Modern Christianity,* ed. Witte and Alexander, chaps. 19, 20, 22.

cultural, or economic, who offer beliefs and practices radically different from those held by either the fallen socialist state or the struggling Orthodox Churches.

The leadership of the Orthodox Church of late, while continuing to endorse democratic and human rights principles, has bitterly condemned the corrosive libertarian values that often accompany these principles.[87] Aleksii II, Patriarch of Moscow and All Russia, put the matter crisply in 1996:

> Orthodox consciousness is currently being eroded away by extreme liberalism, capable of leading to tragic consequences for the Church — to schism, division in the church, the undermining of Orthodox beliefs and to ultimate destruction. We must stand against this destructive process by our constancy in faith and belief in the traditions and living Orthodox religious experience of Christian love and concern for each individual believer and for Russia as a whole.[88]

"[F]reedom does not mean general license," Patriarch Aleksii pronounced a few months later.

> The truth of Christ which sets us free (John 8:32) also places upon us a great responsibility, to respect and preserve the freedom of others. However, the aggressive imposition [on Russia] of views and principles which come from a religious and cultural environment which is strange to us, is in fact a violation of both religious and civil rights.[89]

Bartholomew, Orthodox Ecumenical Patriarch of Constantinople, has pressed this critique further, suggesting that Western Catholics and Protestants have fallen under "the shadow of the Enlightenment." The Enlightenment, the Patriarch declared, provides too little room for faith and too much room for freedom.

87. See detailed discussion in Chapter 5 herein.

88. Aleksii II, "Address of the Patriarch to the Councils of the Moscow Parishes at the Episcopal Gathering," December 12, 1996, 6 *Tserkovno-Obschestvennyi Vestnik*, p. 7, col. 1.

89. Aleksii II, "The Report to the Bishops Council in Moscow, 18-23 February 1997, Section 11: Interconfessional and Inter-faith Relations; Participation in the Activity of International Christian Organizations," *Pravoslavnaya Moskva* 103, no. 7 (March 1997): 4.

Since the Enlightenment, the spiritual bedrock of Western civilization has been eroded and undermined. Intelligent, well intentioned people sincerely believed that the wonders of science could replace the miracles of faith. But these great minds missed one vital truth — that faith is not a garment to be slipped on and off; it is a quality of the human spirit, from which it is inseparable.[90]

"There are a few things America [and the rest of the Christian West] can learn from the Orthodox Church," the Patriarch declared. Foremost is the lesson "that, paradoxically, faith can endure without freedom, but freedom cannot long abide without faith." A better balance must be struck between freedom and faith, as the transplanted Orthodox Churches of the West have only recently come to realize.[91]

Where such a critical stand on human rights will lead the Orthodox Church is very much an open question. Orthodoxy has a strong, millennium-old foundation for an alternative Christian theology of duty-based rights and rights-based social action that holds great intellectual and institutional promise. Moreover, as James Billington has brilliantly shown, the Orthodox Church has immense spiritual resources, whose implications for human rights are only now beginning to be seen. These spiritual resources lie, in part, in Orthodox worship — the passion of the liturgy, the pathos of the icons, and the power of spiritual silence. They lie, in part, in Orthodox Church life — the distinct balancing between hierarchy and congregationalism through autocephaly; between uniform worship and liturgical freedom through alternative vernacular rites; between community and individuality through a Trinitarian communalism, which is centered on the parish, on the extended family, on the wizened grandmother (the "babushka" in Russia). These spiritual resources lie, in part, in the massive martyrdom of millions of Orthodox faithful in the twentieth century — whether suffered by Russian Orthodox under the Communist Party, by Greek and Armenian Orthodox under Turkish and Iranian radicals, by Middle Eastern Copts at the hands of religious extremists, or by North African Orthodox under all manner of fascist autocrats.[92]

These deep spiritual resources of the Orthodox Church have no exact

---

90. Quoted in POR, p. 20.

91. In POR, p. 20.

92. James H. Billington, "Orthodox Christianity and the Russian Transformation," in POR, pp. 51-65.

parallels in modern Catholicism and Protestantism. How the Orthodox Church can apply them to the nurture of human rights is one of the great challenges, and opportunities, of this new century. At minimum, it would be wise for us Westerners to lay aside our simple caricatures of the Orthodox Church as a politically corrupted body that is too prone to clerical indiscipline, mystical idolatry, and nominal piety to have much to offer to a human rights regime. A Church with more than 250 million members scattered throughout the world defies such a glib description. It would be wise to hear what an ancient Church, newly charred and chastened by decades of oppression and martyrdom, considers essential to the regime of religious rights. It would be enlightening to watch how ancient Orthodox communities, still largely centered on the parish and the family, will reconstruct social and economic rights. It would be prudent to see whether a culture more prone to beautifying than to analyzing might transform our understanding of cultural rights. It would be instructive to listen to how a tradition that still celebrates spiritual silence as its highest virtue might recast the meaning of freedom of speech and expression. It would be illuminating to feel how a people that have long cherished and celebrated the role of the woman — the wizened babushka of the home, the faithful remnant in the parish pews, the living icon of the Assumption of the Mother of God — might elaborate the meaning of women's rights.

The Problems of International Religious Rights Today

Thus far, I have pressed the twin theses that religion must have a greater role in the cultivation of human rights and that human rights must have a larger place in the calculations of religious bodies. This greater interaction between religion and human rights, I submit, will ultimately strengthen both the regime of human rights and the protection of religious bodies. But this greater interaction with religion will also challenge and complicate some of the current formulations of international human rights.[93] I

93. The fullest formulations are in (1) the *International Covenant on Civil and Political Rights* (1966) (hereafter "1966 Covenant"); (2) the *United Nations Declaration on the Elimination of All Forms of Intolerance and of Discrimination Based on Religion or Belief* (1981) (hereafter "1981 Declaration"); and (3) the *Concluding Document of the Vienna Follow-up Meeting of Representatives of the Participating States of the Conference on Security and Co-operation in Europe* (1989) (hereafter "Vienna Concluding Document") in *Religion and Human Rights,* at pp. 69-82, 102-4, 154-56.

touched on some of these complications in the opening of this chapter. I return to them here.

Defining Religion

The most difficult, and most ironic, problem of all is that the more religion is included in the regime of human rights, the more important it will be to set limits to the regime of religious rights. If religion is to be assigned a special place in the human rights pantheon — if religion is in need of special protections and privileges not afforded by other rights provisions — some means of distinguishing religious rights claims from all others must be offered. Fairness commands as broad a definition as possible, so that no legitimate religious claim is excluded. Prudence counsels a narrower definition, so that not every claim becomes religious and thus no claim becomes deserving of special religious rights protection. To define "religion" too closely is to place too much trust in the capacity of the lexicon or the legislature. To leave the term undefined is to place too much faith in the self-declarations of the claimant or the discernment of local judges and administrators.

International human rights instruments provide very broad definitions of "religion." Article 18 of the 1948 *Universal Declaration of Human Rights* makes a sweeping guarantee: "Everyone has the right to freedom of thought, conscience, and religion; this right includes freedom to change his religion or belief, and freedom, either alone or in community with others and in public or private, to manifest his religion or belief in teaching, practice, worship, and observance."[94] The *Declaration*'s conflation of the terms "religion," "thought," "conscience," and "belief" continues in subsequent instruments — most notably in the 1966 *International Covenant on Civil and Political Rights* and the 1981 *Declaration on the Elimination of All Forms of Intolerance and of Discrimination Based on Religion or Belief.*[95] The *Declaration*'s recognition of religion as individual and communal, internal and external, private and public, permanent and transient likewise persists.

This capacious definition of religion at international law has left it largely to individual nations and individual claimants to define the bound-

94. 1966 Covenant, art. 18.
95. 1981 Declaration, art. 1.1.

aries of the regime of religious rights.[96] No common definition or uniform method has been forthcoming. Indeed, the statutes, cases, and regulations of many nations embrace a bewildering array of definitions of "religion" which neither local officials nor legal commentators have been able to integrate. Some courts and legislatures make a simple "common sense" inquiry as to the existence of religion. Others defer to the good-faith self-declarations of religion by the claimant. Others seek to find sufficient analogies between existing religions and new religious claimants. Others insist on evidence of a god or something transcendent that stands in the same position as a god. Yet others analyze the motives for formation of the religious organization or adoption of a religious belief, the presence and sophistication of a set of doctrines explicating the beliefs, the practice and celebration of religious rites and liturgies, the degree of formal training required for the religious leaders, the strictures on the ability of members to practice other religions, the presence and internal enforcement of a set of ethical rules of conduct, as well as other factors.

These are not idle academic exercises in religious taxonomy. The answer to the threshold legal question of "What is religion?" determines whether a particular claim or claimant, person or group, is entitled to a range of special rights and liberties that are reserved for religion alone. It is a question of particular importance to newly arrived religious minorities (such as Santerians or Scientologists), to growing breakaway faiths (such as the Baha'is, the Ahmadis, or the Mormons), or to the many traditional religions and new sects that are emerging throughout the world.

In my view, the functional and institutional dimensions of religion deserve the strongest emphasis in defining the boundaries of religious rights. Of course, religion viewed in its broadest terms embraces all beliefs and actions that concern the ultimate origin, meaning, and purpose of life, of existence. It involves the responses of the human heart, soul, mind, conscience, intuition, and reason to revelation, to transcendent values, to fundamental questions. But such wide definitions of religion applied at law would render everything (and thus nothing) deserving of religious rights protection. Viewed in a narrower institutional and functional sense, religion embraces what Leonard Swidler has called a creed, a cult, a code of conduct, and a confessional community.[97] A creed defines the accepted cadre of beliefs and

---

96. See Dinah Shelton and Alexandre Kiss, "A Draft Model Law on Freedom of Religion, with Commentary," in RHR II, pp. 568-72.

97. Leonard Swidler, "Introduction to Human Rights and Religious Liberty —

values concerning the ultimate origin, meaning, and purpose of life. A cult defines the appropriate rituals, liturgies, and patterns of worship and devotion that give expression to those beliefs. A code of conduct defines the appropriate individual and social habits of those who profess the creed and practice the cult. A confessional community defines the group of individuals who embrace and live out this creed, cult, and code of conduct, both on their own and with fellow believers.[98] By this definition, a religion can be traditional or very new, closely confining or loosely structured, world-avertive or world-affirmative. Religious claims and claimants that meet this definition, in my view, deserve the closest religious rights consideration.

This is also part of the reason that I stand by the phrase "religious (human) rights" — despite the well-meaning and well-taken criticisms of some that this term is idiosyncratic and too restrictive.[99] It must be said that the phrase "religious rights" is not my idiosyncratic invention. It is a rather common traditional term — used in Europe since the fifteenth century, and in America since the seventeenth century — to describe the body of special liberties, entitlements, immunities, and exemptions that a person or a group can claim on the basis of religion alone and that go beyond the generic freedoms of speech, press, or assembly and the general guarantees of equal protection and due process of law.[100] To be sure, it was unduly churlish in earlier centuries to restrict these claims only to members of one established religion. Many legitimate religious claims and claimants were thereby foreclosed from legal recourse in state courts.[101] But it is un-

---

From the Past to the Future," in *Religious Liberty and Human Rights in Nations and in Religions,* ed. Leonard Swidler (New York: Hippocrene, 1986), p. vii.

98. The former United Nations Special Rapporteur, Elizabeth Odio-Benito, has written similarly that religion is "an explanation of the meaning of life and how to live accordingly. Every religion has at least a creed, a code of action, and a cult." Elizabeth Odio-Benito, *Study of the Current Dimensions of the Problems of Intolerance and of Discrimination on Grounds of Religion and Belief,* UN Doc. E/CN.4/Sub.2/1987/26, p. 4.

99. See David Little, "Studying 'Religious Human Rights': Methodological Foundations," in RHR II, pp. 49-52; David Little, "Religion and Human Rights: A Review Essay on Religion, Relativism, and Other Matters," *Journal of Religious Ethics* 27 (1999): 154 n. 1; Malcolm D. Evans, Book Review, *International and Comparative Law Quarterly* 46 (1997): 728-29.

100. For European sources, see Karl Schwarz, "Der Begriff Exercitium Religionis Privatum," *Zeitschrift der Savigny-Stiftung (Kan. Ab.)* 105 (1988): 495; for American sources, see RCE, chaps. 1-3.

101. See, e.g., Brian Tierney, "Religious Rights: A Historical Perspective," in RHR I, pp. 17-46.

duly charitable today to allow religious claims to be predicated on the almost boundless basis of thought, conscience, or belief. Many legitimate claims of thought, conscience, or belief that are not "religious," as defined above, are amply protected by other rights norms. Claimants should be encouraged to seek their legal recourse there, rather than allowed to stretch the pale of religious rights ever more widely to cover themselves. In the abstract, this may sound elitist and traditionalist. But, unless some clear limit is assigned to the ambit of, and the access to, the regime of religious rights, such rights will be in danger of becoming open to everyone, but protective of nothing.

Religion is special: it has been, and must continue to be, accorded special protection in a human rights regime.[102] Religion is more than simply another form of speech and assembly, privacy, and autonomy. It requires more than simply the freedoms of speech and assembly, equality and nondiscrimination to be effectively protected. Religion is a unique source of individual and personal identity and activity, involving "duties that we owe to our Creator, and the manner of discharging them," as James Madison once put it.[103] Religion is also a unique form of public and social identity, involving a vast plurality of sanctuaries, schools, charities, missions, and other forms and forums of faith. Both individual and corporate, private and public entities and exercises of religion — in all their self-defined varieties — deserve the protection of a human rights regime. Generic human rights guarantees are not protective enough. Even generously defined, freedom of speech cannot protect many forms of individual and corporate religious exercise — from the silent meditations of the sages to the noisy pilgrimages of the saints, from the corporate consecration of the sanctuary to the ecclesiastical discipline of the clergy. Even expansively interpreted, guarantees of equality and nondiscrimination cannot protect the special needs of religious individuals and religious groups to be exempted from certain state prescriptions or proscriptions that run afoul of the core claims of conscience or the central commandments of the faith. Hence the necessity for a special category and concept called religious rights.

---

102. See further Chapters 6-8 herein.

103. James Madison, "Memorial and Remonstrance against Religious Assessments (1785)," in *The Papers of James Madison,* ed. Robert A. Rutland et al., 9 vols. (Chicago: University of Chicago Press, 1973), 8:299.

The Problem of Conversion

A second international human rights problem to be exacerbated by the greater attention to religion concerns the right to change one's religion.[104] How does one craft a legal rule that at once respects and protects the sharply competing understandings of conversion among the Religions of the Book? Most Western Christians have easy conversion into and out of the faith.[105] Most Jews have difficult conversion into and out of the faith. Most Muslims have easy conversion into the faith, but allow for no conversion out of it.[106] Whose rites get rights? Moreover, how does one craft a legal rule that respects Orthodox, Hindu, Jewish, or Traditional groups that tie religious identity not to voluntary choice but to birth and caste, blood and soil, language and ethnicity, sites and sights of divinity?[107]

International human rights instruments initially masked over these conflicts, despite the objections of some Muslim delegations. The 1948 *Universal Declaration* included an unequivocal guarantee: "Everyone has the right to freedom of thought, conscience, and religion; this right includes the right to change his religion or belief. . . ."[108] The 1966 *Covenant,* whose preparation was more highly contested on this issue, became more tentative: "This right shall include to have or adopt a religion or belief of his choice. . . ."[109] The 1981 *Declaration* repeated this same more tentative language. The dispute over the right to conversion, however, contributed greatly to the long delay in the production of this instrument, and to the

---

104. See Natan Lerner, "Proselytism, Change of Religion, and International Human Rights," *Emory International Law Review* 12 (1998): 477-561, updated in Lerner's *Religion, Beliefs, and International Human Rights,* pp. 80-118.

105. But cf. Eastern Orthodox understandings of the permanent effects of baptism and theosis discussed in Chapter 4 herein.

106. See Donna E. Arzt, "The Treatment of Religious Dissidents Under Classical and Contemporary Islamic Law," in RHR I, pp. 406-8; David Novak, "Proselytism in Judaism," in SB, pp. 17-44; Joel A. Nichols, "Mission, Evangelism, and Proselytism in Christianity: Mainline Conceptions As Reflected in Church Documents," *Emory International Law Review* 12 (1998): 563.

107. See, e.g., Michael J. Sandel, "Freedom of Conscience or Freedom of Choice?" in *Articles of Faith, Articles of Peace: The Religious Liberty Clauses and the American Public Philosophy,* ed. James Davison Hunter and Os Guinness (Washington, D.C.: Brookings Institution, 1990), pp. 74-92.

108. 1948 Declaration, art. 18, in *Religion and Human Rights,* ed. Stahnke and Martin, p. 59.

109. 1966 Covenant, art. 18.1.

number of dissenters to it.[110] The 1989 *Vienna Concluding Document* did not touch the issue at all, but simply confirmed "the freedom of the individual to profess and practice religion or belief" before turning to a robust rendition of religious group rights.[111] Today, the issue has become more divisive than ever as various soul wars have broken out between and within Christian and Muslim communities around the globe.

"A page of history is worth a volume of logic," Oliver Wendell Holmes Jr. (1841-1935) once said.[112] And, on an intractable legal issue such as this, recollection might be more illuminating than ratiocination. It is discomforting, but enlightening, for Western Christians to remember that the right to enter and exit the religion of one's choice was born in the West only after centuries of cruel experience and stalwart resistance. To be sure, a number of the early Church Fathers considered the right to change religion an essential element of the notion of liberty of conscience. Such sentiments have been repeated and glossed continuously until today. In practice, however, the Christian Church largely ignored these sentiments for centuries. As the medieval Church refined its rights structures in the twelfth and thirteenth centuries, it also routinized its religious discrimination, reserving its harshest sanctions for heretics. The communicant faithful enjoyed full rights. Jews and Muslims enjoyed fewer rights, but full rights if they converted to Christianity. Heretics — those who voluntarily chose to leave the faith — enjoyed still fewer rights and had little opportunity to recover them, even after full confession. Indeed, in the heyday of the Inquisition, heretics faced not only severe restrictions on their persons, properties, and professions, but also sometimes unspeakably cruel forms of torture and punishment. Similarly, as the Lutheran, Calvinist, and Anglican Churches routinized their establishments in the sixteenth and seventeenth centuries, they inflicted all manner of repressive civil and ecclesiastical censures on those who chose to deviate from established doctrine — savage torture and execution in a number of instances and also unspeakably cruel forms of religious warfare.

It was, in part, the recovery and elaboration of earlier patristic concepts of liberty of conscience as well as the slow expansion of new Protestant theologies of religious voluntarism that helped to end this practice. But it was also the new possibilities created by the frontier and by the

110. 1981 Declaration, art. 1.1.
111. Vienna Concluding Document, art. 16.
112. *New York Trust Co. v. Eisner,* 256 U.S. 345, 349 (1921).

colony that helped to forge the Western understanding of the right to change religion. Rather than stay at home and fight for one's faith, it became easier for the dissenter to move away quietly to the frontier, or later to the colony, to be alone with his conscience and his co-religionists.[113] Rather than tie the heretic to the rack or the stake, it became easier for the establishment to banish him quickly from the community with a strict order not to return. Such pragmatic tempering of the treatment of heretics and dissenters eventually found theological justification. By the later sixteenth century, it became common in the West to read of the right, and the duty, of the religious dissenter to emigrate physically from the community whose faith he or she no longer shared.[114] In the course of the next century, this right of physical emigration from a religious community was slowly transformed into a general right of voluntary exit from a religious faith. Particularly American writers, many of whom had voluntarily left their European faiths and territories to gain their freedom, embraced the right to leave — to change their faith; to abandon their blood, soil, and confession; to reestablish their lives, beliefs, and identities afresh — as a veritable sine qua non of religious freedom. This understanding of the right to choose and change religion — patristic, pragmatic, and Protestant in initial inspiration — has now become an almost universal feature of Western understandings of religious rights.

To tell this peculiar Western tale is not to resolve current legal conflicts over conversion. Rather, it is to suggest that even hard and hardened religious traditions can and do change over time, in part out of pragmatism, in part out of fresh appeals to ancient principles long forgotten. Even those schools of jurisprudence within Shi'ite and Sunni communities that have been the sternest in their opposition to a right of conversion from Islam have resources in the Qur'an, in the early development of Shari'a, and in the more benign policies of other contemporary Muslim communities, to rethink their theological positions.

Moreover, the Western story suggests that there are halfway measures, at least in banishment and emigration, that help to blunt the worst tensions between a religious group's right to maintain its standards of en-

---

113. On faith, freedom, and the frontier, see further Chapter 8 herein.

114. The most famous formulation of the right (and duty) of the dissenter to emigrate peaceably from the territory whose religious establishment he or she could not abide came in the Peace of Augsburg (1555), and its provisions are repeated in the Edict of Nantes (1598) and the Religious Peace of Westphalia (1648). See Ehler and Morrall, pp. 164-73, 183-93.

trance and exit and an individual's liberty of conscience to come and go. Not every heretic needs to be executed. Not every heretic needs to be indulged. It is one thing for a religious tradition to insist on executing its charges of heresy when a mature adult, fully aware of the consequences of his or her choice, voluntarily enters a faith, and then later seeks to leave or to insist on a right to maintain a heretical position. In that instance, group religious rights must trump individual religious rights — with the limitation that the religious group, which has no coercive power parallel to that of the state, has no right to violate or to solicit violation of the life and limb of the wayward member. It is quite another thing for a religious tradition to press the same charges of heresy against someone who was born into, married into, or coerced into the faith and now, upon opportunity for mature reflection, voluntarily chooses to leave. In that case, individual religious rights trump group religious rights.

Where a religious group exercises its trump by banishment or shunning and the apostate voluntarily chooses to return, he does so at his peril. He should find little protection in state law when subject to harsh religious sanctions, unless the religious group threatens or violates his life or limb. Where a religious individual exercises her trump by emigration, and the group chooses to pursue her, it does so at its peril. It should find little protection from the state when charged with a tort or crime against the individual.

There are numerous analogous tensions — generally with lower stakes — between the religious rights claims of a group and its individual members. These will become more acute as religion and human rights become more entangled. Particularly volatile will be tensions over discrimination against women and children within religious groups; enforcement of traditional religious laws of marriage, family, and sexuality in defiance of state domestic laws; and maintenance of religious property, contract, and inheritance norms that defy state private laws. On such issues, the current categorical formulations of both religious group rights and religious individual rights simply restate the problems, rather than resolve them. It will take new arguments from history and experience and new appeals to internal religious principles and practices, along the lines just illustrated, to blunt, if not resolve, these tensions.

The Problem of Proselytism

The corollary to the modern problem of conversion is the modern problem of proselytism — of the efforts taken by individuals or groups to seek the conversion of another. How does the state balance one person's or community's right to exercise and expand its faith versus another person's or community's right to be left alone to its own traditions? How does the state protect the juxtaposed rights claims of majority and minority religions, or of foreign and indigenous religions? These are not new questions. They confronted the drafters of the international bill of rights from the very beginning. On this issue, the international human rights instruments provide somewhat more nuanced direction.[115]

Article 18 of the 1966 *International Covenant on Civil and Political Rights* protects a person's "freedom, individually or in community with others and in public or private, *to manifest his religion or belief in worship, observance, practice, and teaching.*"[116] But the same article allows such manifestation of religion to be subject to limitations that "are prescribed by law and are necessary to protect public safety, order, health, or morals, or the fundamental rights and freedoms of others."[117] It prohibits outright any "coercion" that would impair another's right "to have or adopt a religion or belief of [his or her] choice."[118] It also requires state parties and individuals to have "respect for the liberty of parents . . . to ensure the religious and moral education of their children in conformity with [the parents'] convictions" — a provision underscored and amplified in more recent instruments and cases on the rights of parents and children.[119]

Similarly, Article 19 of the same 1966 covenant protects the "*freedom to seek, receive, and impart information and ideas of all kinds,* regardless of frontiers, either orally, in writing, or in print, in the form of art, or through any other media of his choice."[120] But Article 19, too, allows legal restric-

---

115. See Lerner, *Religion, Beliefs, and International Human Rights*, pp. 80-118; Tad Stahnke, "Proselytism and the Freedom to Change Religion in International Human Rights Law," *Brigham Young University Law Review* (1999): 251-350.

116. 1966 Covenant, art. 18.1 (emphasis added).

117. 1966 Covenant, art. 18.3.

118. 1966 Covenant, art. 18.2.

119. 1966 Covenant, art. 18.4; see also United Nations, *Convention on the Rights of the Child*, [28 I.L.M. 1448] November 20, 1989, in *Religion and Human Rights*, ed. Stahnke and Martin, p. 128.

120. 1966 Covenant, art. 19.2 (emphasis added).

tions that are necessary for "respect of the rights and reputation of others; for the protection of national security or of public order (*ordre public*) or of public health or morals."[121] As a further limitation on the rights of religion and (religious) expression guaranteed in Articles 18 and 19, Article 26 of the 1966 *Covenant* prohibits any discrimination on grounds of religion. And Article 27 guarantees to religious minorities "the right to enjoy their own culture" and "to profess and practise their own religion."[122]

The literal language of the mandatory 1966 *Covenant* (and its amplification in more recent instruments and cases) certainly protects the general right to proselytize — understood as the right to "manifest," "teach," "express," and "impart" religious ideas for the sake, among other things, of seeking the conversion of another. The *Covenant* provides no protection for coercive proselytism; at minimum this bars physical or material manipulation of the would-be convert, and in some contexts even more subtle forms of deception, enticement, and inducement to convert. The *Covenant* also casts serious suspicion on any proselytism among children or among adherents to minority religions. But, outside of these contexts, the religious expression inherent in proselytism is no more suspect than political, economic, artistic, or other forms of expression, and should have at minimum the same rights.

Such rights to religion and religious expression, of course, are not absolute. The 1966 *Covenant* and its progeny allow for legal protections of "public safety, order, health, or morals," "national security," and "the rights and reputation of others," particularly minors and minorities. But all such legal restrictions on religious expression must always be imposed without discrimination against any religion, and with due regard for the general mandates of "necessity and proportionality" — the rough international analogues to the "compelling state interest" and "least restrictive alternative" prongs of the strict scrutiny test of American constitutional law.[123] General "time, place, and manner" restrictions on all proselytizers, applied without discrimination against any religion, might thus well be apt. But categorical criminal bans on proselytism, or patently discriminatory licensing or registration provisions, are *prima facie* a violation of the religious rights of the

---

121. 1966 Covenant, art. 19.3.

122. 1966 Covenant, art. 27; see also United Nations, *Declaration on the Rights of Persons Belonging to National or Ethnic, Religious, and Linguistic Minorities*, [A/RES/47/135] December 18, 1992, Article 2.1, in *Religion, Beliefs, and International Human Rights*, by Lerner, p. 140.

123. See detailed discussion of this "strict scrutiny" standard in RCE, chap. 7.

proselytizer — as has been clear in the United States since *Cantwell v. Connecticut* (1940)[124] and in the European community since *Kokkinakis v. Greece* (1993).[125]

To my mind, the preferred solution to the modern problem of proselytism is not so much further state restriction as further self-restraint on the part of both local and foreign religious groups. Again, the 1966 *Covenant on Civil and Political Rights* provides some useful cues.

Article 27 of the *Covenant* reminds us of the special right of local religious groups, particularly minorities, "to enjoy their own culture, and to profess and practise their own religion."[126] Such language might well empower and encourage vulnerable minority traditions to seek protection from aggressive and insensitive proselytism by missionary mavericks and "drive-by" crusaders who have emerged with alacrity in the past two decades. It might even have supported a moratorium on proselytism for a few years in places like post-Communist Russia so that local religions, even the majority Russian Orthodox Church, had some time to recover from nearly a century of harsh oppression that destroyed most of its clergy, seminaries, monasteries, literature, and icons. But Article 27 cannot permanently insulate local religious groups from interaction with other religions. No religious and cultural tradition can remain frozen. For local traditions to seek blanket protections against foreign proselytism, even while inevitably interacting with other dimensions of foreign cultures, is ultimately a self-defeating policy. It stands in sharp contrast to cardinal human rights principles of openness, development, and choice. Even more, it belies the very meaning of being a religious tradition. As Jaroslav Pelikan reminds us, "Tradition is the living faith of the dead; traditionalism is the dead faith of the living."[127]

Article 19 of the *Covenant* reminds us further that the right to expression, including religious expression, carries with it "special duties and responsibilities."[128] One such duty, it would seem, is to respect the religious dignity and autonomy of the other, and to expect the same respect for one's own dignity and autonomy. This is the heart of the Golden Rule. It encour-

124. 310 U.S. 296 (1940).

125. 260-A European Court of Human Rights (ser. A) (1993). For a detailed analysis, see Gunn, "Adjudicating Rights," in RHR II, pp. 305-30.

126. 1966 Covenant, art. 27.

127. Jaroslav Pelikan, *The Vindication of Tradition* (New Haven: Yale University Press, 1984), p. 65.

128. 1966 Covenant, art. 19.3.

ages all parties, especially foreign proselytizing groups, to negotiate and adopt voluntary codes of conduct, restraint, and respect of the other. This requires not only continued cultivation of interreligious dialogue and co-operation — the happy hallmarks of the modern ecumenical movement and of the growing emphasis on comparative religion and globalization in our seminaries. It also requires guidelines of prudence and restraint that every foreign mission board would do well to adopt and enforce: Proselytizers would do well to know and appreciate the history, culture, and language of those being proselytized; to avoid Westernization of the Gospel and "First Amendmentization" of politics; to deal honestly and respectfully with theological and liturgical differences; to respect and advocate the religious rights of all peoples; to be Good Samaritans as much as good preachers; to proclaim their Gospel both in word and in deed.[129] Moratoria on proselytism might provide temporary relief, but moderation by proselytizers and proselytizees is the more enduring course.

Concluding Reflections

A number of distinguished commentators have recently encouraged the abandonment of the human rights paradigm altogether — as a tried and tired experiment that is no longer effective, even a fictional faith whose folly has now been fully exposed.[130] Others have bolstered this claim with cultural critiques — that human rights are instruments of neo-colonization which the West uses to impose its values on the rest, even toxic compounds that are exported abroad to breed cultural conflict, social instability, religious warfare, and thus dependence on the West.[131] Others have added philosophical critiques — that rights talk is the wrong talk for mean-

129. See Anita Deyneka, "Guidelines for Foreign Missionaries in the Former Soviet Union," in POR, pp. 332-33; Lawrence A. Uzzell, "Guidelines for American Missionaries in Russia," in POR, pp. 323-30; M. Thomas Thangaraj, "Evangelism *sans* Proselytism: A Possibility?" in SB, pp. 335-52.

130. See, e.g., Alasdair MacIntyre, *After Virtue: A Study in Moral Theory* (Notre Dame, Ind.: University of Notre Dame Press, 1984), pp. 69-70, who writes: "[T]he truth is plain: there are no such rights, and belief in them is one with belief in witches and in unicorns. . . . Natural or human rights . . . are fictions." See critical analysis in Max L. Stackhouse and Stephen E. Healey, "Religion and Human Rights: A Theological Apologetic," in RHR I, pp. 485-516.

131. See critical discussion in Little, "Religion and Human Rights: A Review Essay."

ingful debate about deep questions of justice, peace, and the common good.[132] Still others have added theological critiques — that the secular beliefs in individualism, rationalism, and contractarianism inherent to the human rights paradigm cannot be squared with cardinal biblical beliefs in creation, redemption, and covenant.[133]

Such criticisms properly soften the overly bright optimism of some human rights advocates. They properly curb the modern appetite for the limitless expansion and even monopolization of human rights in the quest for toleration, peace, and security.[134] And they properly criticize the libertarian accents that still too often dominate our rights talk today. But such criticisms do not support the conclusion that we must abandon the human rights paradigm altogether — particularly when no viable alternative global forum and no viable alternative universal faith is yet at hand. Instead, these criticisms support the proposition that the religious sources and dimensions of human rights need to be more robustly engaged and extended. Human rights norms are not a transient libertarian invention, or an ornamental diplomatic convention. Human rights norms have grown out of millennium-long religious and cultural traditions. They have traditionally provided a forum and focus for subtle and sophisticated philosophical, theological, and political reflections on the common good and our common lives. And they have emerged today as part of the common law of the emerging world order. We should abandon these ancient principles and practices only with trepidation, only with explanation, only with articulation of viable alternatives. For modern academics to stand on their tenured liberties to deconstruct human rights without posing real global alternatives is to insult the genius and the sacrifice of their many creators. For now, the human rights paradigm must stand — if nothing else as the "null hypothesis." It must be constantly challenged to improve. It should be discarded, however, only on cogent proof of a better global norm and practice.

A number of other distinguished commentators have argued that religion can have no place in a modern regime of human rights. Religions might well have been the mothers of human rights in earlier eras, perhaps

132. See Mary Ann Glendon, *Rights Talk: The Impoverishment of Political Discourse* (New York: Free Press, 1991).

133. See Joan Lockwood O'Donovan, "The Concept of Rights in Christian Moral Discourse," in *A Preserving Grace,* ed. Cromartie, pp. 143-56; David M. Smolin, "Church, State, and International Human Rights: A Theological Appraisal," *Notre Dame Law Review* 73 (1998): 1515-46.

134. See further critique in Chapter 1 herein.

even the midwives of the modern human rights revolution. Religion has now, however, outlived its utility. Indeed, the continued insistence on special roles and rights for religion is precisely what has introduced the Dickensian paradoxes that now befuddle us. Religion is, by its nature, too expansionistic and monopolistic, too patriarchal and hierarchical, too antithetical to the very ideals of pluralism, toleration, and equality inherent in a human rights regime. Purge religion entirely, this argument concludes, and the human rights paradigm will thrive.[135]

This argument proves too much to be practicable. In the course of the twentieth century, religion defied the wistful assumptions of the Western academy that the spread of Enlightenment reason and science would slowly eclipse the sense of the sacred and the sensibility of the superstitious.[136] Religion defied the evil assumptions of Nazis, Fascists, and Communists alike that gulags and death camps, iconoclasm and book burnings, propaganda and mind controls would inevitably drive religion into extinction. Yet another great awakening of religion is upon us — now global in its sweep and frightening in its power.

It is undeniable that religion has been, and still is, a formidable force for both political good and political evil, that it has fostered both benevolence and belligerence, peace and pathos of untold dimensions. But the proper response to religious belligerence and pathos cannot be to deny that religion exists or to dismiss it to the private sphere and sanctuary. The proper response is to castigate the vices and to cultivate the virtues of religion, to confirm those religious teachings and practices that are most conducive to human rights, democracy, and rule of law.

Religion is an ineradicable condition of human lives and human communities. As Patriarch Bartholomew reminds, "faith is not a garment to be slipped on and off; it is a quality of the human spirit, from which it is inseparable."[137] Religion will invariably figure in legal and political life — however forcefully the community might seek to repress or deny its value or validity, however cogently the academy might logically bracket it from its political and legal calculus. Religion must be dealt with because it exists — perennially, profoundly, pervasively — in every community. It must be drawn into a constructive alliance with a regime of law, democracy, and human rights.

135. See critical analysis in Max L. Stackhouse, "The Intellectual Crisis of a Good Idea," *Journal of Religious Ethics* 26 (1998): 263-68.
136. See Martin E. Marty, "Religious Dimensions of Human Rights," in RHR I, pp. 1-2.
137. POR, p. 20.

The regime of law, democracy, and human rights needs religion to survive, for this regime is an inherently relative system of ideas and institutions. It presupposes the existence of a body of beliefs and values that will constantly shape and reshape it, that will constantly challenge it to improve. "Politicians at international forums may reiterate a thousand times that the basis of the new world order must be universal respect for human rights" and democracy, Czech President Václav Havel declared in 1994 after receiving the Liberty Medal in Philadelphia. "[B]ut it will mean nothing as long as this imperative does not derive from the respect of the miracle of being, the miracle of the universe, the miracle of nature, the miracle of our own existence. Only someone who submits in the authority of the universal order and of creation, who values the right to be a part of it, and a participant in it, can genuinely value himself and his neighbors, and thus honor their rights as well."[138]

138. Václav Havel, "Speech on July 4, 1994 in Philadelphia, on Receipt of the Liberty Medal," reported and excerpted in *Philadelphia Inquirer* (July 5, 1994): A08; *Buffalo News* (July 10, 1994): F8; *Newsweek* (July 18, 1994): 66. See also Václav Havel et al., "Civil Society after Communism," *Journal of Democracy* 7 (1996): 11, 13-14, where Havel calls for a focus on "the roots, spirit and direction of democracy [and] . . . a clear recognition of the moral and spiritual precepts upon which our democracy rests," and applauds that in the transition from communism "such values as solidarity, a spiritual dimension of life, 'love thy neighbor' tolerance, and civil society experience[d] some kind of renaissance."

Soul Wars in Russia:
The Clash of Eastern and Western Christianity over Religion and Liberty

It is our obligation to battle [for] people's souls by all legal means available, rather than allowing them to perish. [We must] react to the continuing intensive proselytizing activity by some Catholic circles and various Protestant groups . . . [and] to the growing activity of sects, including those of a totalitarian nature . . . for it is largely our own brothers and sisters who fall victim to these sects.

Patriarch Aleksii II (1996)[1]

The Promises and Problems of Religious Liberty

A new war for souls has broken out in Russia — a war to reclaim the traditional spiritual and moral soul of the Russian people, and a war to retain adherence and adherents to the Russian Orthodox Church. In part, this is a *theological* war — as the Moscow Patriarchate of the Russian Orthodox Church has sought to reestablish itself as the spiritual leader of the Russian people, and as rival religious communities from Russia and abroad have begun actively to defame and demonize each other. In part, this is a *legal* war — as local and national legislatures have passed laws severely restricting the rights of many religious persons and peoples of Russia.

In the late 1980s, Russia embraced religious liberty for all. President Mikhail Gorbachev's revolutionary ideals of *glasnost* and *perestroika* broke

1. Aleksii II, Patriarch of Moscow and All Russia, "Address of the Patriarch to the Councils of the Moscow Parishes at the Episcopal Gathering, 12 December 1996," *Tserkovno-Obschestvennyi Vestnik*, no. 6 (December 26, 1996): 7, col. 1.

the harsh establishment of Marxist-Leninist atheism, and awakened the sundry traditional faiths of Russia. The 1990s saw the revival not only of Russian Orthodoxy but also of an array of traditional Adventist, Armenian Apostolic, Baptist, Buddhist, Georgian Orthodox, Greek Catholic, Jewish, Lutheran, Roman Catholic, Shi'ite and Sunni Muslim, Ukrainian Autocephalous Orthodox, and other groups.[2] Many of these religious groups had been driven underground by Communist purges and reprisals, and kept alive through countless sacrifices and martyrdoms of four generations of the faithful. Gorbachev established an ambitious campaign of restitution for those religious groups, particularly the Russian Orthodox Church that had suffered massive losses of clergy, property, literature, and art since the 1917 Bolshevik Revolution.[3] These religious groups, in turn, provided moral and material support to the tender and volatile movements of *glasnost* and *perestroika*.[4] Foreign religious groups — particularly Protestants and Catholics from Europe and North America — began to receive visas to enter Russia in order to reconvene with their co-religionists, to offer their charity, and to spread their faiths. Russian Jews, Christians, and Muslims, in turn, were granted visas to travel to holy sites in Jerusalem, Rome, Mecca, and elsewhere.

These favorable policies toward religion were soon translated into strong legal terms. On October 1, 1990, Gorbachev signed a comprehensive new law, "On Freedom of Conscience and On Religious Organizations," for the USSR.[5] On October 25, 1990, the Russian Soviet Federative Socialist Republic (RSFSR) passed its own law on "Freedom of Worship," which repeated and strengthened many of the provisions of the USSR law, and survived the breakup of the USSR in December, 1991.[6] Both the USSR

2. See detailed religious case studies in POR. See also Igor Troyanovsky, *Religion in the Soviet Republics: A Guide to Christianity, Judaism, Islam, Buddhism, and Other Religions* (San Francisco: Harper and Row, 1991); Juliet Johnson, Marietta Stephaniants, and Benjamin Forest, eds., *Religion and Identity in Modern Russia: The Revival of Orthodoxy and Islam* (Burlington, Vt.: Ashgate, 2005); Zoe Katrina Knox, *Russian Society and the Orthodox Church: Religion in Russia After Communism* (London: Routledge, 2005).

3. Sabrina P. Ramet, ed., *Religious Policy in the Soviet Union* (Cambridge: Cambridge University Press, 1993); Sabrina P. Ramet, *Nihil Obstat: Religion, Politics, and Change in East-Central Europe and Russia* (Durham, N.C.: Duke University Press, 1998).

4. Michael Bourdeaux, *Gorbachev, Glasnost and the Gospel* (London: Hodder and Stoughton, 1990).

5. Translated in Troyanovsky, *Religion in the Soviet Republics*, at pp. 23-30 (hereafter "1990 USSR Law").

6. Translated in Troyanovsky, *Religion in the Soviet Republics*, pp. 31-37 (hereafter "1990 RSFSR Law").

and RSFSR laws set forth sweeping guarantees of liberty of conscience and freedom of exercise for all citizens. Both laws included strong prohibitions against religious discrimination, stigmatizing, abuse, and coercion.[7] The RSFSR law insisted that "freedom of worship is an inalienable right of the citizens of the RSFSR, guaranteed by the Constitution and international obligations of the RSFSR" and includes "the right to select and hold religious beliefs and to freely change them."[8]

These 1990 laws guaranteed the religious liberty not only of individuals but also of properly registered groups. "All religions and denominations shall be equal before the law," reads the USSR law. "The institution of any form of privileges or restrictions for one religion or denomination in comparison to others shall be prohibited."[9] Both 1990 laws insisted that state and religious organizations be as separate as possible. Religious groups were not to finance, staff, or interfere in state elections, secular public education, or other political affairs. The state, in turn, was not to finance, tax, control, or interfere in the worship, order, festivals, discipline, education, or charity of religious groups. The RSFSR law included within the "inalienable right to freedom of worship" the right to "establish and maintain international communication and direct contacts" with co-religionists outside Russia.[10] It also included the "right to promotion of a faith," defined as the right to "dissemination of one's beliefs in society directly or via the mass media, missionary work, acts of compassion and charity, religious instruction and education. . . ."[11]

These statutory guarantees for religious liberty were confirmed by the Russian Constitution of 1993. Article 14 of the Constitution provides: "1. The Russian Federation shall be a secular state. No religion may be instituted as [a] state-sponsored or mandatory religion. 2. Religious associations shall be separated from the state, and shall be equal before the law." Article 19 states that "[a]ll people shall be equal before the law and in the court of law" and further that "[t]he state shall guarantee the equality of rights and liberties regardless of . . . [a person's] attitude to religion [or] convictions. . . ." Article 28 provides: "Everyone shall be guaranteed the right to freedom of conscience, to freedom of religious worship, including the right to profess, individually or jointly with others, any religion, or to

7. 1990 USSR Law, arts. 1-4; 1990 RSFSR Law, arts. 1-7, 17, 22, 25, 29.
8. RSFSR Law, Preamble, and elaborated in arts. 3-5, 13, 16.
9. USSR Law, art. 5; see parallels in RSFSR Law, arts. 8-10, 16-19, 23-25.
10. RSFSR Law, art. 25.
11. RSFSR Law, art. 17. See also USSR Law, art. 23.

profess no religion, to freely choose, possess and disseminate religious or other beliefs, and to act in conformity with them." Russia had incorporated some of the most advanced international human rights norms governing religious liberty, proselytism, and change of religion.

These strong legal guarantees helped to usher in what Mikhail Gorbachev proudly proclaimed to be "a golden age of religious liberty" in Russia.[12] Various indigenous Orthodox, Catholic, and Protestant Churches, seminaries, schools, and charities began to be restored or rebuilt — sometimes with the material support of local political leaders. Muslim mosques, Buddhist temples, and Jewish synagogues also began to be restored together with a few of their schools, charities, and publishing houses. Particularly Russian Orthodox religious literature, artwork, icons, candles, vestments, and other materials for worship were imported en masse and, later, produced locally. A host of long dormant Russian animist groups, goddess religions, personality cults, and occultist groups began to revive, especially outside the main cities. Even more startling was the rapid growth of several exotic and well-organized indigenous religions such as the Great White Brotherhood, the Center of the Mother of God, and the Church of the Last Testament.

This religious awakening of Russia came not only from within but also from without. Already in the wake of the 1986 Chernobyl disaster, and the scourge of ominous accidents, earthquakes, and droughts that followed, foreign religious groups had begun to trickle into Russia to offer charitable relief and longer-term care. After passage of the 1990 laws, these foreign religious groups came to Russia in greater numbers. From the West, these included various Evangelicals, Pentecostals, mainline Protestants, Roman Catholics, Mormons, Moonies, Scientologists, and others. From the Middle East, they included Shi'ite, Sunni, and Sufi Muslims, together with some Baha'is. From the East, they included Presbyterians and Methodists from Korea; Hindus, Hare Krishnas, Rastafarians, and Buddhists from the Indian subcontinent; members of the Aum Association, Shri Chinmoy, the Rerikh Movement, and other groups from Japan. Many of these groups preached their beliefs and activities on the streets and door-to-door as well as through distribution of sermons, pamphlets, and texts. Other groups organized crusades, tent meetings, billboard advertising, and mass media events, or rented out stadiums, the-

12. Mikhail Gorbachev, Commencement Address, Emory University, May 11, 1992.

aters, and community halls for religious festivals. Many of these groups also began to establish schools, hospitals, charities, youth groups, old age homes, and other social services.

The few reliable demographic studies available suggest that these foreign religious groups made rather modest gains against the Russian Orthodox Church and other local Russian groups. Mark Elliott and Anita Deyneka have shown that by 1997, the Protestant missionary force in the entire former Soviet Union of over 280 million persons stood at a mere 5,606 persons divided among 561 groups.[13] To be sure, Russian Protestant Churches, indigenous and foreign, more than doubled in number — from a total of 1,002 registered groups in 1993 to 2,280 in 1996. But indigenous Orthodox and Catholic Churches in Russia experienced nearly comparable growth, and their absolute numbers dwarf those of Protestants — from a total of 4,815 registered groups in 1993 to 7,666 in 1996.[14] Indeed, in 1996, there were more registered Muslim groups in Russia (2,494) than all Protestant groups combined (2,280).[15]

The rate of growth of *new* religious groups in Russia in this same period was more impressive, but their absolute numbers remained very small. The plight of the Unification Church in Russia is a case in point. The Unification Church had already begun secretly to enter the Soviet Union in the early 1980s, using tourist and business visas. It was among the first foreign groups to begin actively proselytizing in Russia in the mid 1980s. After Reverend Moon met with President Gorbachev in 1990, the Unification Church sponsored an aggressive campaign of conferences, seminars, textbook distribution, study trips, and the like aimed especially at political leaders and at lower school and university students and their teachers. "Tens of thousands" of Russians participated in these activities, according to Unification Church officials, and by 1994 more than two thousand state schools used the "moral textbooks" furnished gratis by the Unification Church. Despite this massive effort and expense, the Unification Church in Russia at its peak in 1994 attracted only five thousand full members, and since then the numbers have slowly declined.[16]

13. See chapter by Elliott and Deyneka in POR.
14. See chapter by Aleksandr Shchipkov in POR.
15. See chapters by Shchipkov and by Donna Arzt in POR.
16. See chapter by Sergei Filatov in POR.

Storm Signals

Whatever their real numbers and growth rates, the noisy arrival of these foreign religious groups eventually bred considerable resentment in Russia. Indigenous Russian Protestant and Catholic groups began to resent the linguistic deficiencies and the fiscal leveraging of some of their Western and Korean co-religionists. Russian Catholics and Protestants also resented the criticisms from afar of the doctrinal, liturgical, and ecclesiological innovations that they had introduced during their decades of brutal isolation — a resentment doubly acute for Greek Catholics, who had suffered savage abuses in the bitter political struggles between Constantinople and Rome for jurisdiction over them.[17] Russian Muslim leaders, as well as political officials, expressed increasing concern about the politicization of some Muslim groups inspired by "the Ayatollah Khomeini's Iranian messianism and Afghan *mujaheddin* agitation and propaganda."[18] A number of clashes also broke out between competing schools of jurisprudence within and among Shi'ite, Sunni, and Sufi groups — tensions sometimes exacerbated by the sharp ethnic, racial, and linguistic diversity within the Russian Muslim population.

By far the greatest expressions of concern, however, came from the Moscow Patriarchate of the Russian Orthodox Church. Already in 1991, Moscow Patriarch Aleksii II expressed dismay at the "massive influx" of foreign missionaries, both religious and economic, that competed for souls in the new marketplace of religious ideas in Russia. Initially, the Patriarchate's resentment was focused on missionary mavericks. These were culturally and linguistically inept missionaries, inclined toward "a wild West, free spirit, lone ranger approach to ministry" that resulted in "hit and run evangelism, with its neglect of disciplining for new believers and its inattention to respectful partnerships with existing churches."[19] At the same time, officials within the Moscow Patriarchate singled out for special criticism the "totalitarian sects," charging that these groups used "illegitimate material inducements" to win new converts and then turned their converts against "their Russian families, faiths, and cultures."[20]

17. See chapters by James Billington, Lawrence A. Uzzell, and Philip Walters in POR.

18. Donna E. Arzt, "Proselytizing and the Muslim Umma of Russia: Historical Heritage or Ethno-National Threat," in POR, pp. 108-40, at p. 116.

19. See chapters by Elliott and Deyneka and by Uzzell in POR.

20. Comments of Alexandr Dvorkin, Member of the Moscow Patriarchate Depart-

By 1993, the Moscow Patriarchate's resentment was directed more generally at all "well-organized and well-financed" mission groups, particularly from the West. Unwelcome "foreign proselytizing faiths" now included various Roman Catholics, mainline Protestants, and Western Evangelicals, alongside religious mavericks and totalitarian cults.[21] Members of the Patriarchate came to regard these groups collectively, and issued three charges against them. First, all these foreign proselytizing groups were forcing an impoverished and understaffed Russian Orthodox Church into an unfair competition for souls — not only lost souls on the Russian streets, but also saved souls within the Russian Churches. Second, many Western proselytizing groups seemed bent on breaking the soul of the Russian people — by inundating them with a toxic wave of Western materialism, individualism, and pluralism for which Russia was not, and could not be, prepared. Third, many of these foreign proselytizing groups were simply dangerous to the Russian people and to social order — by breaking up families, encouraging civil disobedience, extorting property and money, administering drugs and mind controls, committing battery, rape, and other offenses against recalcitrant members, and even inducing homicide, suicide, and insurrection as acts of faith.

Such charges against foreign proselytizing groups can be seen in dozens of statements issued by the Moscow Patriarchate in the period after 1993.[22] In 1993, Metropolitan Kirill complained of the "dishonorable" actions of "missionaries [who] are making use of . . . the spiritual

---

ment of External Church Relations, at a conference at Oxford, May 29, 1996, which I attended. When I asked him to elaborate, Dvorkin defined "illegitimate material inducements" to include the furnishing of humanitarian aid, English lessons, education, and employment; the inculcation of the public school curriculum with religious texts and rituals; the use of television, newspapers, and other mass media to propagate the faith; and the organization of "loud and insensitive crusading carnivals."

21. Comments by Alexandr Dvorkin at the same conference, who listed among "proselytizing faiths" the following: (1) Roman Catholics "who established dioceses, parishes, and monasteries without Orthodox approval"; (2) "traditional Protestant denominations" including those who are members of the World Council of Churches (Methodists, Finnish and German Lutherans, Free Evangelicals, and Korean Protestants); and (3) "new religious movements" (Hare Krishnas, Baha'is, Moonies, and Jehovah's Witnesses especially).

22. See samples in V. Polosin and G. Yakunin, "Federal Authorities and Freedom of Conscience" (unpublished manuscript, November, 1996), pp. 16-38, and Jane Ellis, "The Moscow Patriarchate's Attitude to Protestant Missionaries: A Decade of Misunderstanding" (unpublished manuscript, June, 1998), pp. 2-7.

vacuum" of post-Soviet Russia.[23] Three years later, he elaborated his criticism:

> As soon as freedom for mission work was allowed, a crusade began against the Russian church even as it began recovering from a prolonged disease, standing on its feet with weakened muscles. Hordes of missionaries dashed in, believing the former Soviet Union to be a vast missionary territory. They behaved as though no local churches existed, no gospel was being proclaimed. They began preaching without even making an effort to familiarize themselves with the Russian cultural heritage or to learn the Russian language. In most cases the intention was not to preach Christ and the gospel but to tear the faithful away from their traditional churches and recruit them into their own communities. Perhaps these missionaries sincerely believed that they were dealing with non-Christian or atheistic communist people, not suspecting that our culture was formed by Christianity and that our Christianity survived through the blood of martyrs and confessors, through the courage of bishops, theologians, and laypeople asserting their faith.

> Missionaries from abroad came with dollars, buying people with so-called humanitarian aid and promises to send them abroad for study or rest. We expected that our fellow Christians would support and help us in our own missionary service. In reality, however, they have started fighting with our church. . . . All this has led to an almost complete rupture of the ecumenical relations developed during the previous decades. An overwhelming majority of the population refused to accept this activity, which offends people's national and religious sentiments by ignoring their spiritual and cultural tradition. Indeed, given the lack of religious education, people tend to make no distinctions between the militant missionaries we are speaking about and ordinary people of their own faiths or confessions. For many of Russia today, "non-Orthodox" means those who have come to destroy the spiritual unity of the people and the Orthodox faith — spiritual colonizers who by fair means or foul try to tear the people away from the church.[24]

23. Interview in *Nezavisimaya gazeta* (June 5, 1993), quoted by Ellis, "The Moscow Patriarchate's Attitude," pp. 2-3. See also Metropolitan Kirill, "The Church and Perestroika (c. 1992)," in Troyanovsky, *Religion in the Soviet Republics*, pp. 82-90.

24. See chapter by Metropolitan Kirill in POR.

The Council of Bishops meeting in Moscow made an even more pointed charge against foreign missionaries:

> We express our concern in connection with the continuing proselytizing activity of Protestant false missionaries in Russia [and] the growth of organized pseudo-Christian and pseudo-religious sects, of neo-pagan communities, occultists and devil worshippers in the CIS and the Baltic States. The Council is extremely troubled by the anti-Orthodox campaign which is being waged by the followers of these pseudo-religious organizations and their protectors. The members of the Council call on the entire church to confront this false missionary activity and sectarianism through religious education and apologetics, by educating both Orthodox parishioners and society as a whole. We acknowledge that the right of each person to freedom of conscience and religion should be respected, but the leaders of these totalitarian sects are in fact depriving their followers of these rights and reacting to any criticism of their activity. Those who attempt to oppose them are subjected to cruel persecution by the sect leaders and their highly-placed protectors, including intimidation, psychological pressure, the gathering of incriminating information, slanders, and repeated searches of their property.[25]

These were not idle words. Officials of the Moscow Patriarchate several times requested restraint, even a one-generation moratorium, on foreign mission activities in Russia. This would allow indigenous Churches to recover from their Communist plight, and enable them to compete fairly.[26] Orthodox theologians, from Russia and abroad, pressed this case with increasing urgency at various ecumenical conferences on mission.[27] Orthodox clergy that fell out of line with these official sentiments faced firm discipline — defrocking and excommunication in extreme cases.[28]

---

25. Resolution of the Council of Bishops in Moscow, February 18-23, 1997, article no. 35, in *Pravoslavnaya Moskva* 103, no. 7 (March 1997): 11.

26. See quotes in Resolution of the Council of Bishops in Moscow, p. 11; see also "Declaration of the Holy Synod of the Russian Orthodox Church, 3 April 1990," in Troyanovsky, *Religion in the Soviet Republics*, pp. 66-72.

27. See Joel A. Nichols, "Mission, Evangelism, and Proselytism in Christianity: Mainline Conceptions As Reflected in Church Documents," *Emory International Law Review* 12 (1998): 563-652, at 622-52.

28. See chapters by Walters and Billington in POR and Polosin and Yakunin, "Federal Authorities."

When such diplomatic and ecumenical entreaties failed, the Moscow Patriarchate turned to the law of the state for its protection. Already in 1993, the Moscow Patriarchate joined with various nationalist groups to pressure the Russian Parliament to amend the 1990 RSFSR law. The proposed amendments gave special protections, subsidies, and rights to "those religious organizations, the activity of which maintains and develops historical traditions and customs, national and cultural originality, art and other cultural heritage of the peoples of the Russian Federation — that is, the traditional confessions of the Russian Federation." The proposed law stated categorically that foreign religious groups "have no right of religious-missionary activity in the Russian Federation." And it instituted a series of cumbersome new registration and property regulations designed to deter and obstruct foreign mission groups already in place. Under severe pressure from indigenous and foreign religious and political groups, the Russian Parliament did not pass this proposed law in 1993, nor a variant on the same, proposed in 1995.[29]

While, initially, the Russian Parliament did little to assuage the problem of proselytism in Russia, a number of local legislatures did. "[M]ore than one third of Russia's 89 provincial governments enacted or considered laws or executive orders shrinking the rights of foreign religious organizations and religious minorities."[30] These local laws, often passed under strong orchestration by the Russian Orthodox clergy, imposed various registration and accreditation requirements as a condition for any religious activity of the non-Orthodox, particularly those who were not Russian citizens. These local laws monitored, restricted, and discriminated against the religious speech, literature, and associations of non-Orthodox believers and groups. They placed limits on the access of non-Orthodox to public forums and media, and restricted their ability to hold corporate property, build religious structures, or gain permits to build and maintain religious schools, charities, and other ministries.[31] A number of Lutheran, Catholic,

29. See details in W. Cole Durham, Lauren B. Homer, Pieter van Dijk, and John Witte Jr., "The Future of Religious Liberty in Russia: Report of the DeBurght Conference on Pending Russian Legislation Restricting Religious Liberty," *Emory International Law Review* 8 (1994): 1-66, at 3-11, updated in W. Cole Durham Jr., Marie Zimmermann, and John Witte Jr., "Liberté, de religion et confessionnalité: Les projets de revision de la loi de 1990 de la Republique de Russie," *Praxis juridique et religion* 14 (1997): 3-81.

30. See chapter by Lauren B. Homer and Lawrence A. Uzzell in POR.

31. Samples of these provincial and municipal laws are translated in Appendix B-E, *Emory International Law Review* 12 (1998): 681-714.

Pentecostal, Jewish, and Adventist groups have suffered miserably under these laws.

The New Law on Freedom of Conscience and on Religious Associations

The promise of Russia's "golden age of religious liberty" ended on September 26, 1997, the day Russian President Boris Yeltsin signed a new law "On Freedom of Conscience and on Religious Associations."[32] This new law — passed after four years of advocacy by the Moscow Patriarchate and various nationalist groups within Russia — institutes a Soviet-style system of severe state registration and restrictions on religion. The 1997 law supersedes the 1990 RSFSR law. It preempts all provincial and municipal laws on religion to the contrary.[33] New administrative regulations, issued in the spring of 1998, have ensured the rapid execution of the 1997 law, which has continued with alacrity to this day.[34]

The 1997 law effectively establishes three classes of religions in Russia: (1) the Russian Orthodox Church and its members, which receive full legal protection and various state benefits; (2) various "traditional" Christian, Muslim, Jewish, and Buddhist groups and persons, which receive full legal protection but fewer state benefits; and (3) all other religious groups and persons, which receive only a pro forma guarantee of freedom of worship and liberty of conscience.

This tripartite classification of religious groups is adumbrated in the preamble to the 1997 law. The preamble "recogniz[es] the special contribution of Orthodoxy to the history of Russia and to the establishment and development of Russia's spirituality and culture." It further "respect[s] Christianity, Islam, Buddhism, Judaism, and other religions and creeds which constitute an inseparable part of the historical heritage of Russia's peoples." For the rest, the preamble provides only that it "consider[s] it important to promote the achievement of mutual understanding, toler-

32. Translated in Appendix A, *Emory International Law Review* 12 (1998): 657-80.

33. "Russian Federation Federal Law on Freedom of Conscience and on Religious Associations" [hereafter "1997 Law"], translated by Lawrence A. Uzzell for the Keston Institute, in *Emory International Law Review* 12 (1998): 657-80, art. 27.6; 2.2.

34. See updated analysis by Forum 18 in Oslo (www.forum18.org), Helsinki Watch (www.csce.gov), and the various reports issued by Keston Institute and International Religious Freedom Watch.

ance, and respect in questions of freedom of conscience and freedom of creed."

This tripartite classification is elaborated in the eighteen articles on religious associations set out in the 1997 law — and in the 1998 regulations in amplification of the same. The 1997 law defines a religious association as a "voluntary association of citizens of the Russian federation and other persons permanently and legally residing [therein] formed with the goals of joint confession and possessing features corresponding to that goal: a creed, the performance of worship services, religious rituals, and ceremonies; the teaching of religion and religious upbringing of its followers."[35]

Religious *associations* are differentiated into (1) religious *organizations,* which receive a wide array of protections and benefits; and (2) religious *groups,* which receive only minimal protections. Religious *organizations,* in turn, are divided into (a) favored *centralized* groups (notably, the Russian Orthodox Church); and (b) less favored *local* groups (mostly other "traditional" Russian religions).

Religious organizations receive "juridical personality" — the basic right to exist as a licit group, from which a number of other rights automatically follow. "Religious organizations can own buildings, plots of land, objects for the purpose of production and for social, charitable, educational, and other purposes, articles of religious significance, financial means and other property which is essential for their activity including that necessary for historical and cultural monuments." Religious organizations can acquire property by purchase or donation and devote it to multiple uses — worship, pilgrimage, hospitals, cemeteries, children's homes, charities, cultural-educational institutions, seminaries, and "business undertakings." Such properties are generally held free from state taxation, and those properties devoted to worship are immune from "proceedings by creditors."[36]

Religious organizations are also assured of various affirmative rights. They have the right to undertake charitable activities, including the administration of chaplaincy and other religious services in state hospitals and "places of detention." "Religious organizations have the right to produce, acquire, export, and distribute religious literature, printed, audio and video material and other articles of religious significance. Religious organizations have the exclusive right to institute enterprises for producing liturgical lit-

---

35. 1997 Law, art. 6.1.
36. Art. 4.3; art. 7.1; art. 16; art. 18; art. 21; art. 23.

erature and articles for religious services." Religious organizations have the right to establish and maintain contacts with co-religionists abroad, and have "the exclusive right to invite foreign citizens for professional purposes, including preaching and religious activity in the said organizations."[37]

Religious organizations are also entitled to certain direct benefits from the state. They have "the right to use for their own needs plots of land, buildings and property provided by state, municipal, social and other organizations . . . free of charge." Moreover, the state "is to provide financial, material, and other aid to religious organizations in the restoration, maintenance, and protection of buildings and objects which are monuments of history and culture, and also in providing instruction in general educational subjects in educational institutions created by religious organizations."[38]

A religious organization's panoply of rights and benefits does not come automatically. Only properly registered religious associations are classified as "religious organizations" and entitled to these rights and benefits. It is here that the 1997 law works its greatest injustice. And it is here that the law in effect establishes what Michael Bourdeaux calls "another Council for Religious Affairs (the name of the hated body which oversaw and controlled the persecution of the Churches, in the days of Communism)."[39]

The law distinguishes between "locally" and "centralized" registered groups. *Local* religious organizations must consist of "ten or more participants who are at least eighteen years of age and who are permanently residing in one locality or in one urban or rural settlement." *Centralized* religious organizations must exist "in accordance with its charter of no fewer than three local religious organizations." Once a religious organization is deemed "centralized," as is the case with the hierarchical Russian Orthodox Church, every new local unit created thereafter is automatically registered as a religious organization. If a religious organization is only "localized," however, as in the case of many Protestant, Mormon, Jewish, and other congregationally organized religious communities, each new local unit must be registered separately.[40]

37. Art. 16.2-3; 17.1-2; art. 18.1; 20.1-2.
38. Art. 4.3; 22.1-2.
39. Michael Bourdeaux, "Religious Freedom Russian-Style," *The Tablet* (September 27, 1997): 1216.
40. 1997 Law, art. 8.1-6; art. 9.1-2.

Only "*centralized* religious organizations which have been active [in Russia] on a *legal basis* for no fewer than 50 years" may use the term "Russian" in their title.[41] In practice, the Russian Orthodox Church is the only group that qualifies. Other traditional religions of Russia, such as Muslims, Jews, and Buddhists, were "illegal" after 1917 and before 1905. And while they were "legal" briefly from 1905 to 1917, they were not "centralized." The Orthodox Church's right to use the term "Russian" is more than honorary. In practice, this is the only religious organization that receives the promised governmental subsidies for the "restoration, maintenance, and protection of buildings and objects which are monuments of history and culture."[42]

Centralized or local religious communities that "existed" in Russia "no less than 15 years" must register only once to be categorized as "religious organizations."[43] Once registered, they are thereafter automatically entitled to the full range of rights and benefits set forth above — save the direct benefits reserved to the Russian Orthodox Church alone. In reality, this "15 year" provision covers only a few "traditional" Russian groups — Muslims, Jews, and some Christians. As Lawrence Uzzell explains,

> These provisions discriminate in favor of those religious organizations that were legally registered under the Soviet state fifteen years ago and against those that were founded more recently or that existed only illegally or semi-legally during the Soviet years. Thus, for example, the favored category included many Baptist congregations — those which were willing during the pre-glasnost era to make the compromises needed to get official registration. . . . [But] the [Roman] Catholics have only two parishes in all of the Russian Federation that were legally registered or functioning fifteen years ago. The other 160 Roman Catholic parishes in Russia, the diocesan administrations in Moscow and Novosibirsk, the Catholic seminary in St. Petersburg, the dozens of Jesuit orders, publishing houses, charities, and other groups affiliated with Rome have now been reduced to second-class status.[44]

This "second-class status" is occupied by all religious communities in Russia that do not meet either the "50 year" or the "15 year" registration pro-

41. Art. 8.5 (emphasis added).
42. Art. 4.3 and 22.1.
43. Art. 9.1.
44. Lawrence A. Uzzell, "Letter from Moscow," *First Things* 79 (January 1998): 17-19.

visions. The 1997 law categorizes all these as "new" religions — regardless of their real vintage. "New" religions are required to register with local and/or centralized authorities — annually. The registration procedures are cumbersome, fraught with delay and discretion, and expensive. Registration can be denied, or a registered group can be dissolved, on any number of stated grounds. Some of the grounds set forth in the 1997 law are reasonable enough — "by decision of their founders"; because of the group's "creation of armed units"; or "in the case of frequent and gross infringement of the norms of the Constitution . . . or federal law."[45] But vaguer, and more expansive, grounds for denial of registration or dissolution of a religious organization have been smuggled into the new regulations implementing this law. These include: "if the founder(s) of the religious organization is (are) incompetent"; if "the organization being established is not recognized as a religious one"; and "on the grounds of a judicial ruling in cases established by law."[46]

Those religious communities that cannot — or for religious or political reasons will not — register themselves are categorized as "religious groups." Religious groups "have the right to carry out worship services, religious rituals, and ceremonies, and also the teaching of religion and religious upbringing of their followers."[47] But nothing more. Religious groups are subject to a number of explicit restrictions and disabilities. Such groups have no right of juridical personality, no right to hold collective property, and no access to state material benefits to religion. Their clergy and members are denied conscientious objection status to military participation. They cannot create or own schools, seminaries, or other educational institutions, nor have their faith taught in local state schools. They may not have "a representative body of a foreign religious organization" in place in Russia. They may not carry out religious rites or services, or furnish chaplain services, in hospitals, health centers, children's homes, homes for the aged or handicapped, or prisons. They may not produce, acquire, export, import, or distribute religious literature, videos, and other articles of religious significance, nor establish local institutions for the production of the same. They may not invite foreign citizens into Russia to preach or carry on religious activities.[48]

45. 1997 Law, art. 14.1.
46. *Regulations for the State Registration of Religious Organizations in the Judicial Bodies of the Russian Federation,* trans. U.S. Department of State Office of Language Services (unpublished ms., 1997), items 24 and 31.
47. 1997 Law, art. 7.2.
48. Art. 27.3, read with arts. 3.4, 5.3, 5.4, 13.5, 16.3, 17.1, 17.2, 18.1, 18.2, 19.

This entire law on religious association contradicts the guarantees of individual and corporate religious liberty set forth elsewhere in the 1997 law. The preamble to the 1997 law, for example, confirms "the right of each to freedom of conscience and freedom of creed, and also to equality before the law regardless of his attitude to religion and his convictions." Article 2.3 states boldly that "Nothing in the law . . . may be interpreted in such a way as to diminish or limit the right of man and citizen to freedom of conscience and freedom of creed." Article 4 provides familiar guarantees of freedom of all from discrimination, abuse, coercion, or other deprivations on religious grounds. It further guarantees to all persons "the right to confess, individually or jointly with others, any religion or not to confess any, and the freedom to choose, change, possess or disseminate religious or other convictions and to act in accordance with them." The 1997 law guarantees that "The Russian federation is a secular state. No religion may be established as a state or compulsory religion. Religious associations are separate from the state and are equal before the law." In amplification of this guarantee, the 1997 law repeats a number of the provisions of the 1990 law on separation of Church and state.[49] Even the most skillful casuistry cannot explain the blatant contradictions between these guarantees of religious liberty for all and the discriminatory regulations on religious associations.

Not only is the 1997 law blatantly self-contradictory but it also violates a number of the most basic human rights guarantees. As Jeremy Gunn demonstrates, the 1997 law must respect the human rights norms of the 1993 Russian Constitution, the 1966 International Covenant on Civil and Political Rights, and the 1950 European Charter of Human Rights, all of which are formally binding on Russia. The 1997 law defies these norms openly and without justification. It violates the rights of equality between citizens and noncitizens, and the prohibitions against nondiscrimination on grounds of religion. It tramples on basic rights of freedom of thought, religion, and belief, freedom of expression, and freedom of association.[50]

The injustice of the 1997 law was not lost on Russia's political and religious leaders when they were crafting it. Many religious groups and human rights advocates in Russia formally protested earlier drafts of the bill — the Baptist Union, the Pentecostal Union, the Seventh Day Adventists, the Union of Councils for Soviet Jews, the Roman Catholic Church, the

---

49. Arts. 3.1-3.7, 4.1-4.2.
50. See analysis in chapter by T. Jeremy Gunn in POR.

Russian Orthodox Free Church, the Russian Orthodox Church Abroad, and the Old Believers. Pope John Paul II sent a personal letter to President Yeltsin protesting the bill. Several Western European heads of state and the Council of Europe registered their stern objections with President Yeltsin, with members of his cabinet, and with members of the Russian Parliament. Presidents Clinton and Carter did likewise, together with 160 Senators and Representatives in the U.S. Congress. Human rights organizations and religious liberty experts from around the world issued a torrent of detailed and devastating criticisms of draft bills, many of which came into the hands of members of the Russian Parliament.[51] But all to no avail.

Ontological Differences

Russia has moved from *glasnost* to soul wars — from the open embrace of religious rights for everyone to tight restrictions on everyone's rights, save those of the Russian Orthodox Church. Today in Russia, the Russian Orthodox Church is free and favored by the state. Indigenous Russian Christians, Muslims, Jews, and Buddhists are largely free, but on their own. Foreign religions, particularly from the West, are neither free nor welcome. None of this religious line-drawing has been done in secret or in ignorance of Russia's human rights obligations. Russian leaders have telegraphed their protectionist intentions for the whole world to see, and have calculated their religious discrimination so carefully that no religious person or group can be confused about where they stand.

There is more at stake in the current war for souls than temporary concerns over unfair religious competition, unsafe religious practices, or unruly religious policies in the provinces. If this were all that was at stake, surely a diplomatic solution could be crafted. Surely, these warring parties could agree more easily to a ten, fifteen, or twenty year moratorium on further foreign missions to Russia, for example — with the interim period used for intense interreligious dialogue and education, for policing of the more belligerent and dangerous groups in Russia, for multilateral negotiations on future Russian visa and import controls that affect religious groups, for aggressive affirmative action programs to shore up beleaguered Russian religions, and the like.

51. Derek Davis, "Editorial: Russia's New Law on Religion: Progress or Regress," *Journal of Church and State* 39 (1997): 643, 647-48.

But there are deeper sources of this war for souls in Russia. Orthodox Ecumenical Patriarch Bartholomew of Constantinople hinted at these sources repeatedly during his lecture tour in the United States in 1997. Responding to American Church overtures for greater cooperation with the Orthodox Churches, and greater respect among them for human rights values, the Patriarch replied: "The Orthodox Christian does not live in a place of theoretical and conceptual conversations but rather in a place of an essential and empirical lifestyle and reality as confirmed by grace in the heart."[52] "The Orthodox Church is not a museum church. . . . It is a living church which, although keeping the old traditions from the very beginning, nevertheless understands very well the message of every new era, and it knows how to adapt itself to the conditions of every period of human history."[53] The Orthodox Church's adaptations in matters of theology, polity, and law over the centuries have differed from those of Western Christianity. "The divergence between us [on these points] continually increases," the Patriarch stated, "and the end points to which our courses are taking us, foreseeably, are indeed different." But the heart of our difference is "something deeper and more substantive. The manner in which we exist has become *ontologically different*."[54]

Western Christianity exists under "the shadow of the Enlightenment," the Patriarch explained. Orthodox Christianity does not. The Enlightenment provides too little room for faith and too much room for freedom. "Since the Enlightenment, the spiritual bedrock of Western civilization has been eroded and undermined. Intelligent, well intentioned people sincerely believed that the wonders of science could replace the miracles of faith. But these great minds missed one vital truth — that faith is not a garment to be slipped on and off; it is a quality of the human spirit, from which it is inseparable."[55] "There are a few things America [and the rest of the West] can learn from the Orthodox Church," the Patriarch declared. Foremost is the lesson "that, paradoxically, faith can endure without freedom, but freedom cannot long abide without faith."[56] A balance must be struck between freedom and faith, as the transplanted Orthodox

---

52. Address of His All Holiness Ecumenical Patriarch Bartholomew, "*Phos Hilaron* (Joyful Light)," Georgetown University, Washington, D.C., October 21, 1997, at http://www.geocities.com/Heartland/5654/orthodox/bartholomew_phos.html.

53. *Washington Post* (October 25, 1997): H12.

54. "*Phos Hilaron* (Joyful Light)" (emphasis added).

55. Quoted in *Washington Post* (October 25, 1997): H12.

56. Quoted in *Washington Post* (October 25, 1997): H12.

Churches of the West have only recently come to realize. "Orthodox Christians, who live in a country where full religious freedom reigns and where adherents of various religions live side by side, . . . constantly see various ways of living and are in danger of being beguiled by certain of them, without examining if their way is consonant with the Orthodox Faith. Already, many of the old and new Orthodox . . . are stressing different, existing deviations from correct Orthodox lives."[57]

"*Ontological differences*" between the Orthodox and the non-Orthodox, between the East and the West: these are deep, and often intractable, sources of the current war for souls in Russia. The Russian people, the Russian Church, and the Russian state are fundamentally different from their counterparts in the West — in their traditions and experiences, in their anthropology and psychology, in their worldviews and visions. These fundamental differences have led to intense mutual misunderstanding between East and West, and between Orthodox and other Christians, in the past few years. They warn against any attempts to craft simple legal, political, or diplomatic solutions to the current war for souls.

Change of Religion, Mission, and Proselytism

These ontological differences between Orthodoxy and Western Christianity are evident in competing understandings of evangelism and proselytism. Natan Lerner puts the matter sagely: "What constitutes the sacred duty of evangelization for one group is seen by another group as improper proselytizing. Some groups would consider a given act a normal exercise of freedom of expression and freedom of teaching or propagating a religion or belief; others would view this same act as an illegitimate intrusion into their intimacy, their group identity, and a violation of their freedom of conscience."[58] This problem of perspective, which Lerner parses carefully in human rights terms, must also be parsed in theological terms.

Russian Orthodox and Western Evangelicals, in particular, have fundamentally different theologies of mission. Some of these missiological differences reflect more general differences in theological emphasis. Russian Orthodox tend to emphasize the altar over the pulpit, the liturgy over the

57. Quoted in *The Jupiter Courier* (November 16, 1997): A17.
58. Natan Lerner, "Proselytism, Change of Religion, and International Human Rights," *Emory International Law Review* 12 (1998): 477-562, at 488.

homily, the mystery of faith over rational disputation on faith, the priestly office of the clergy over the devotional tasks of the laity.[59] Western Evangelicals generally reverse these priorities — and sometimes accuse the Orthodox of idolatry, introversion, and invasion of the believer's personal relationship with God.[60] And, even without such accusations and prejudicial actions, it is these rational, homiletic, and plastic qualities of non-Orthodox faith that sometimes attract converts to Protestantism, as well as to Catholicism, Adventism, and other faiths.

These differences in theological emphasis are exacerbated by conflicting theologies of the nature and purpose of mission. Evangelicals assume that, in order to be saved, every person must make a personal, conscious commitment to Christ — to be born again, to convert. Any person who has not been born again, or who once reborn now leads a nominal Christian life, is a legitimate object of evangelism — regardless of whether the person has already been baptized. The principal means of reaching that person is through proclamation of the Gospel, rational demonstration of its truth, and personal exemplification of its efficacy. Any region of the world that has not been open to the Gospel is a legitimate "mission field" — regardless of whether the region might have another Christian Church in place. Under this definition of mission, Russia and its people are prime targets for Evangelical witness.[61]

The Russian Orthodox Church, too, believes that each person must come into a personal relationship with Christ in order to be saved. But such a relationship comes more through birth than rebirth, and more through regular sacramental living than a one-time conversion. A person who is born into the Church has by definition started *"theosis"* — the process of becoming "acceptable to God" and ultimately "coming into eternal communion with Him." Through infant baptism, and later through the mass, the Eucharist, the icons, and other services of the Church, a person slowly comes into fuller realization of this divine communion.[62] Proclamation of the Gospel is certainly a legitimate means of aiding the process of *theosis* — and is especially effective in reaching those not born into the Russian Orthodox Church. But, for the Russian Orthodox, Joel Nichols writes, "mission does not aim primarily at transmission of moral and intellectual con-

---

59. See chapters by Harold J. Berman and by Billington in POR.
60. See chapter by Elliott and Deyneka in POR.
61. See chapters by Elliott and Deyneka and by Kent Hill in POR.
62. See chapters by Elliott and Deyneka, Hill, Billington, and Walters in POR.

victions and truths, but at the . . . incorporation of persons into the communion that exists in God and in the Church."[63]

This theology leads the Russian Orthodox Church to a quite different understanding of the proper venue and object of evangelism. The territory of Russia is hardly an open "mission field" which Evangelicals are free to harvest. To the contrary, much of the territory and population of Russia is under the "spiritual protectorate" of the Russian Orthodox Church. Any person who has been baptized into the Russian Orthodox Church is no longer a legitimate object of evangelism — regardless of whether that person leads only a nominal Christian life. Indeed, according to some Orthodox, any person who is born in the territory of Russia must first be evangelized by the Russian Orthodox Church; only if he actively spurns the Orthodox Church is he open to the evangelism of others.

This is the theological source of the Patriarchate's repeated complaints about "the proselytizing activity of many Protestant Churches, missionary organizations, and individual preachers . . . on the historical territory of our Church."[64] The Patriarchate is not only complaining about *improper methods* of evangelism — the bribery, blackmail, coercion, and material inducements used by some groups; the garish carnivals, billboards, and media blitzes used by others. The Patriarchate is also complaining about the *improper presence* of missionaries — those who have come not to aid the Orthodox Church in its mission but to compete with the Orthodox Church for its own souls on its own territory. "The Patriarch has quoted, in this connection, the Epistle of St. Paul to the Romans, where the Apostle said: 'It is my ambition to bring the Gospel to places where the very name of Christ has not been heard, for I do not want to build on another man's foundation' (Rom. 15:20). . . . [T]he Moscow Patriarch welcomes friendly visits by Russian Christians of other denominations from other countries, but opposes their proselytism of Russian Christians."[65]

Human rights norms alone will ultimately do little to resolve this fundamental theological difference between Russian Orthodox and Western Christians. "In seeking to limit the incursion of missionary activity we of-

63. Nichols, "Mission, Evangelism, and Proselytism," p. 624.
64. Aleksii II, Patriarch of Moscow and All Russia, "The Report to the Bishops Council in Moscow, 18-23 February 1997, Section 11: Interconfessional and Inter-Faith Relations; Participation in the Activity of International Christian Organizations," *Pravoslavnaya Moskva* 103, no. 7 (March 1997): 4.
65. See chapter by Berman in POR.

ten are accused of violating the right to freedom of conscience and the restriction of individual rights," Patriarch Aleksii II explained. "But freedom
does not mean general license. The truth of Christ which sets us free (John
8:32) also places upon us a great responsibility, to respect and preserve the
freedom of others. However, the aggressive imposition by foreign missionaries of views and principles which come from a religious and cultural environment which is strange to us, is in fact a violation of both [our] religious and civil rights."[66] The Russian Orthodox Church must be as free in
the exercise of its missiology as Western Evangelicals wish to be. Both
groups' rights, when fully exercised, will inevitably clash.

The war for souls in Russia thus requires a theological resolution as
much as a human rights resolution. Interreligious dialogue, education, and
cooperation sound like tried and tired remedies, but these are essential first
steps. Self-imposed guidelines of prudential mission are essential steps as
well: know and appreciate Russian history, culture, and language; avoid
Westernization of the Gospel and "First Amendmentization" of politics;
deal honestly and respectfully with theological and liturgical differences;
respect and advocate the religious rights of all peoples; be Good Samaritans
before good preachers; proclaim the Gospel in word and deed.[67] Such steps
will slowly bring current antagonists beyond caricatures into a greater mutual understanding, and a greater unity in diversity.

The ultimate theological guide to resolve the deeper conflict over
mission and conversion, however, must be a more careful balancing of the
Great Commission and the Golden Rule. Christ called his followers to mission: "Go therefore and make disciples of all nations, baptizing them in the
name of the Father and of the Son and of the Holy Ghost, teaching them to
observe all that I have commanded you."[68] But Christ also called his followers to restraint and respect: "Do unto others, as you would have done
unto you."[69] If both sides in the current war for souls would strive to hold
these principles in better balance, their dogmatism might be tempered and
their conflicts assuaged.

66. Aleksii II, "The Report to the Bishops Council in Moscow," p. 4.
67. See chapters by Michael Bourdeaux, Hill, Elliott and Deyneka, and Uzzell in
POR.
68. Matthew 28:19-20 (RSV).
69. Cf. Matthew 7:12.

Church, State, and Nation

A related, and deeper, ontological difference is reflected in the Russian Orthodox Church's attitude toward the state. The Russian Orthodox Church has no concept akin to the Western dualistic constructions of Church and state — no Augustinian division between the City of God and the City of Man, no medieval Catholic doctrine of two powers or two swords, no Protestant understanding of two kingdoms or two realms, no American understanding of a wall of separation between Church and state.[70] In Russian Orthodoxy — as in many parts of the Orthodox world rooted in the ancient Byzantine Empire — Church and state are viewed as part of an organic religious and political community, united by blood and by soil. Throughout Russian history, there was always a "close connection between the Russian people, the *narod,* the nation, on the one hand, and Russian Orthodox Christianity, on the other."[71] At the same time, there was always a "symbiosis of Church and State."[72] As President Boris Yeltsin once put it,

> For more than 1000 years the Russian Orthodox Church has fulfilled its sacred mission, affirming spiritual and moral values on Russian soil. . . . The Church is an inalienable part of the history of our country and our people. Its selfless activities have deservedly earned [the state's] gratitude and respect.[73]

This organic unity of Church, state, and nation gave the Russian Orthodox clergy a unique spiritual and moral voice among the Russian people, and unique access to the power and privileges of the Russian state. It allowed the Orthodox clergy to lead Russia in times of great crisis, such as the Napoleonic Wars and World War I. It allowed the Orthodox clergy to

---

70. See Chapter 7 herein.

71. See chapter by Berman in POR, p. 266.

72. See chapter by Firuz Kazemzadeh in POR, p. 229.

73. Boris Yeltsin, Christmas Eve Message (January 6, 1998), quoted in Gareth Jones, "Yeltsin Lauds Orthodoxy on Russian Christmas Eve," reprinted at http://www.themoscowtimes.com/stories/2000/01/06/005.html. See also the statement of the Russian Orthodox Church's Council of Bishops meeting in Moscow in March, 1997: "The Russian Orthodox Church has for a thousand years of Russian history formed the spiritual and moral outlook of the Russian people, and that the overwhelming majority of religious believers belong to the Russian Orthodox Church. . . ." Reprinted in *Prasvoslavnaya Moskva* 103, no. 7 (March 1997): 12.

teach Russia, through its schools and monasteries, its literature and preaching. It also allowed the Orthodox clergy to nourish Russia through the power and pathos of its liturgy, icons, prayers, and music.[74]

But this organic unity also subjected the Russian Orthodox Church to substantial state control over its polities and properties, and substantial restrictions on its religious ministry and prophecy. Particularly during and after the reign of Tsar Peter the Great at the turn of the eighteenth century, the Church was effectively reduced to an "arm of the State, teaching obedience to the government, glorifying absolutism, and serving as spiritual police" of the Russian people. The tripartite formula of "Orthodoxy, Autocracy, and Nationality" was eagerly embraced by tsars and patriarchs alike and "became a central element of the Russian official ideology at least until 1905."[75]

In return for their subservience, the Russian Orthodox clergy could turn to the state to protect them against religious outsiders and competition.[76] A poignant and prescient illustration of this is offered by Joachim, the Patriarch of Moscow at the turn of the eighteenth century. In a 1690 testament, the Patriarch implored co-Tsars Ivan and Peter "never to allow any Orthodox Christians in their realm to entertain any close friendly relations with heretics and dissenters — with Latins, Lutherans, Calvinists, and Tatars." He further urged the tsars to pass a decree "that men of foreign creeds who come here to this pious realm shall under no circumstances preach their religion, disparage our faith in any conversations or introduce their alien customs derived from their heresies for the temptation of Christians."[77] "Such was the position of the Muscovite Church at the close of the seventeenth century," Firuz Kazemzadeh concludes, "and such, in essence, it has remained."[78]

To be sure, Russia has, since the days of Peter and Joachim, occasionally experimented with Western ideas of liberalism and religious liberty — only to have the state crush these experiments. In the later nineteenth cen-

---

74. See chapter by Berman in POR and Harold J. Berman, "The Challenge of Christianity and Democracy in the Soviet Union," in *Christianity and Democracy in Global Context,* ed. John Witte Jr. (Boulder, Colo.: Westview, 1993), pp. 287ff.

75. Chapter by Kazemzadeh in POR, p. 238.

76. Robert P. Geraci and Michael Khodarkovsky, eds., *Of Religion and Empire: Missions, Conversion, and Tolerance in Tsarist Russia* (Ithaca, N.Y.: Cornell University Press, 2001).

77. Quoted in chapter by Kazemzadeh in POR, p. 236.

78. Quoted in chapter by Kazemzadeh in POR, p. 237.

tury, for example, Russian elites trained in the West or exposed to Enlightenment literature began pressing for cultural, political, and legal reforms of all kinds. One of the products of this liberal agitation was the Russian Law on Tolerance, signed by the tsar immediately after the 1905 Revolution. The 1905 law gave new rights to Old Believers (who reject the authority of the Moscow Patriarchate) as well as to Christian sects (from within and beyond Russia), to worship, to hold property, to build Churches and schools, and to train children in their faith. The 1905 law also gave parties the right to leave the Russian Orthodox Church, even if they were born and baptized in it. The Bolshevik Revolution of 1917 crushed this experiment. And the Communist Party ultimately outlawed all Churches, besides the Russian Orthodox Church, and all religious expression, save Orthodox worship services. Again, in the heady days of Gorbachev's democratic revolution of the late 1980s, the USSR and Russia in 1990 passed visionary statutes of religious freedom for all. The 1997 law crushed this experiment, again in favor of the Russian Orthodox Church.

We can easily read current developments as the inevitable next act in this Russian drama of Church-state relations. For seven centuries, the Russian tsars ruled and protected the Orthodox Church — sometimes benignly, occasionally belligerently; often restricting other religions, sometimes tolerating them. For the next seven decades, the Communist Party ruled the Orthodox Church — following the same pattern, albeit more harshly. Since 1993, a "constitutional government" has ruled the Orthodox Church — again following the same patterns, but now at an accelerated pace. The Russian state has always indulged and occasionally protected the Orthodox Church, in return for the Church's support and allegiance. The Russian state has always restricted and occasionally crushed non-Orthodox faiths, in response to the Church's needs and requests. In this light, the 1997 law comes as no surprise.

We can also treat current developments as the birth pangs of a new political and legal order struggling to come forth in Russia. Great legal revolutions, Harold Berman reminds us, always pass through phases of radicality and retrenchment before settling down.[79] The 1990 laws reflect the radical phase of this revolution; the 1997 laws reflect the retrenchment phase. Both phases are part of a greater revolutionary soul-searching of Russia for a new vision, indeed a new ontology.

It is often said that Russia did not experience the Enlightenment, and

---

79. Berman, LR I and II.

that this is one reason for its fundamental differences from the West. But the reality is that Russia and the West drew different lessons from the same Enlightenment, which visions Russia is now struggling mightily to integrate. The 1917 Bolshevik Revolution had drawn one lesson from the Enlightenment — that of totalitarian fascism. The 1987 Gorbachevian Revolution drew a second lesson from the same Enlightenment — that of "totalitarian democracy."[80] Neither course has worked in Russia. Ultimately, Russia will settle somewhere between these extremes, or it will direct its collective genius to the creation of a wholly new understanding of Church, state, and nation. A new religious liberty law will follow in this course — settling somewhere between the extremes of 1990 and 1997, or fashioning a wholly new ensemble.

80. See J. L. Talmon, *The Origins of Totalitarian Democracy* (London: Secker and Warburg, 1955).

LAW AND RELIGION
IN AMERICAN HISTORY AND TODAY

How to Govern a City on a Hill:
Puritan Contributions to American
Constitutional Law and Liberty

In his 1765 *Dissertation on the Canon and the Feudal Law,* John Adams
(1735-1826) defended the "sensible" New England Puritans against those
"many modern Gentlemen" of his day who dismissed them as bigoted, narrow, "enthusiastical, superstitious and republican." Such "ridicule" and
"ribaldry" of the Puritans, proffered mainly by the fashionable "new lights"
of philosophy and politics, are "grosly injurious and false," Adams retorted.
Far from being narrow bigots, the Puritans were "illustrious patriots," for
they were the first "to establish a government of the Church more consistent with the scriptures, and a government of the state more agreeable to
the dignity of humane nature than any other seen in Europe: and to transmit such a government down to their posterity."[1]

What impressed Adams most was that the New England Puritans had
created a comprehensive system of ordered liberty and orderly pluralism
within Church, state, and society. The centerpiece of their system was the
idea of covenant, which they used in both theological and sociological
terms. For the Puritans, the idea of covenant described not only the relationships between persons and God but also the multiple relationships
among persons in Church, state, and civil society. These divine and temporal covenants, in turn, defined each person's religious and civil rights and
duties within these various relationships. In his later writings, Adams came
to see this Puritan covenantal theory of ordered liberty and orderly pluralism as a critical antecedent, analogue, and alternative to the Enlightenment
contractarian theories of individual liberty and religious pluralism that

1. *Papers of John Adams,* ed. R. Taylor, M. Kline, and G. Lint, 2 vols. (Cambridge,
Mass.: Belknap, 1977), 1:114-16.

were gaining prominence in eighteenth-century America. Adams eventually worked this early Puritan covenantal theory into the 1780 Massachusetts Constitution, which he drafted and defended at great length.

Liberty of Covenant

The idea of a divine covenant between God and humanity was part of Western Christian theology from the very beginning. The Bible referred to this covenant 310 times — 286 times in the Hebrew Bible (as *b'rit*), 24 more times in the New Testament (as *foedus*). Classically, Western Christian theologians distinguished two biblical covenants: (1) the covenant of works whereby the chosen people of Israel, through obedience to God's law, are promised eternal salvation and blessing; and (2) the covenant of grace whereby the elect, through faith in Christ's incarnation and atonement, are promised eternal salvation and beatitude. The covenant of works was created in Abraham, confirmed in Moses, and consummated with the promulgation and acceptance of the Torah. The covenant of grace was promised to Abraham, created in Christ, confirmed in the Gospel, and consummated with the confession and conversion of the Christian. A few earlier Christian writers had also described the Church as a "covenant community" and the Christian sacraments as "signs" and "symbols" of the covenant of grace. On the whole, however, discussions of covenant in the Christian theological tradition were only incidental and isolated, comprising little more than a footnote to the great doctrines of God and humanity, sin and salvation, law and Gospel.[2]

Puritan writers, first in Europe and then in America, transformed the covenant into one of the cardinal doctrines of their theology. "The whole of God's word," wrote one Puritan theologian already in 1597, "has to do with some covenant. . . ."[3] "All that we teach you from day to day," another Puritan informed his students, "are but conclusions drawn from the covenant."[4] The doctrine of covenant, wrote another leading divine,

2. See detailed sources in Daniel J. Elazar, *Covenant and Commonwealth: From Christian Separation through the Protestant Reformation* (New Brunswick, N.J.: Transaction, 1996); Daniel J. Elazar, *Covenant and Civil Society: The Constitutional Matrix of Modern Democracy* (New Brunswick, N.J.: Transaction, 1998).

3. Robert Rollock, *Tractatus de Vocatione Efficaci* (1597), in *Selected Works of Robert Rollock,* ed. W. Gunn, 2 vols. (Edinburgh: Wodrow Society, 1849), 1:15.

4. John Preston, *The New Covenant or the Saints Portion* (London: n.p., 1629),

"embraces the whole of the catechism. . . . [N]o context of Holy Scripture can be explained solidly, no doctrine of theology can be treated properly, no controversy can be decided accurately" without reference to this doctrine.[5]

The Puritans made two innovations to traditional understandings of God's covenant relationships with persons. First, the Puritans developed a more participatory theory of the covenant of works. Traditionally, the covenant of works was treated as God's special relation with the chosen people of Israel and their representatives, Abraham, Moses, and David. It designated the Israelites as God's elect nation and called them to serve as special agents in God's kingdom. It divulged to them in detail the requirements of God's law — their obligations toward God, neighbor, and self. It demanded of them perfect obedience of God's law, and perfect fulfillment of their divine callings. It promised them, in return, eternal prosperity, blessing, and salvation.

For many Puritan writers, the covenant of works was not so limited in participation or purpose. The covenant of works was not created in Abraham, the representative of the Jews, but in Adam, the representative of all humanity. It was not a privileged relation in which only elect persons participated, but a natural relation, in which all persons participated. The covenant of works was established at the creation of the world, before the fall into sin, the Puritans argued. Through Adam, the "federal head of the human race," all persons were parties to this covenant. Through Adam, all persons received its promises and blessings as well as its threats and curses.

This pre-fall covenant of works, the Puritans believed, was "God's special constitution for mankind," God's "providential plan for creation."[6] The covenant of works defined each person's telos or purpose in life, each person's role in the unfolding of God's providential plan. It instituted basic human relationships of friendship and kinship, authority and submission. It established basic principles of social, political, familial, and moral life and thought. It created the conditions for perfect communion with God and perfect community among persons. To abide by this divine covenant,

p. 351; see David Zaret, *The Heavenly Contract: Ideology and Organization in Pre-Revolutionary Puritanism* (Chicago: University of Chicago Press, 1985), p. 151.

5. Johann Heinrich Alsted, *Catechetical Theology* (1619), quoted by Jaroslav Pelikan, *Reformation of Church and Dogma, 1300-1700* (Chicago: University of Chicago Press, 1984), p. 367.

6. William Ames, *Medulla Sacrae Theologiae Pertita* (Frankener: Uldaricus Balk, 1623), 1.10; John Norton, *Orthodox Evangelist* (London: J. Macock, 1654), pp. 102ff.

in every particular, was to earn eternal life and salvation; to breach the covenant was to receive eternal death and damnation.[7]

Adam and Eve's fall into sin did not abrogate this covenant of works, the Puritans argued. It only altered humanity's relation to it. The created norms set out in this covenant for the ordering and governing of human life remained in effect. All persons still stood in covenant relationship with God. Because of their sin, however, all persons had lost their view of the norms of creation and lost their capacity to earn their salvation. Thus, after the fall, God sent his son, Jesus Christ, as humanity's guarantor and representative. As guarantor, Christ satisfied each person's debt under the covenant of works and absorbed the punishment that each person deserved because of his or her sin. As representative, as the "second Adam," Christ negotiated a second covenant with God, the covenant of grace whereby the elect, despite their sin, could still inherit salvation.[8] This new covenant of grace repeated the terms of the old covenant of works. But, unlike the old covenant, it conditioned a person's salvation on faith in Christ, not on the works demanded by the covenant of works. And this new covenant of grace revealed the terms of the covenant not only in the hearts and consciences of persons, but also in the pages of Scripture. Accordingly, the Puritans frequently referred to the Bible as the Book of the Covenant, the Covenant Register, the Book of Covenant Liberty.

Second, the Puritans reconfigured not only the traditional covenant of works but also the traditional covenant of grace. Traditionally, the covenant of grace was treated primarily as God's merciful gift to his elect. God set the terms and obligations of the covenant and determined its parties and their participation. Persons, in their sin, could not demand God's gracious covenant gift or bind God by it once it was conferred. Persons could simply accept the covenant in gratitude. Many Puritan writers, by contrast, came to describe the covenant of grace as a bargained contract between God and each person. Acts of divine will and human will were required to form this covenant. Through "voluntary condescension" (as the Westminster Confession put it), God offered the terms of salvation and promised to abide by the offer. Through a voluntary act of faith, a person accepted God's offer. Once God and the person had accepted the terms, both parties were contractually bound to the cove-

---

7. Ames, *Medulla Sacrae*, pp. 14-15; *The Works of Thomas Shepard*, 3 vols. (Boston: Doctrinal Tract and Book Society, 1853), 1:17ff., 90ff.

8. Richard Alleine, *Heaven Opened: Or the Riches of God's Covenant of Grace* (London: n.p., 1665), pp. 29ff.

nant. Each could insist upon the faithful compliance of the other. God could demand faithful devotion and service from the person; if the person refused it, God was released from the covenant and free to consign the person to hell. But the person could also demand that God abide by his promise of salvation. "You may sue [God] of his bond written and sealed," wrote one Puritan, "and he cannot deny it." "Take no denyall, though the Lord may defer long, yet he will doe it, he cannot chuse; for it is part of his covenant."[9] What traditionally had been treated as God's gift of faith and salvation to the elect became, in later Puritan covenant theology, a bargained contract. What traditionally had been understood as God's covenant faithfulness to persons became God's contractual obligation to them. What traditionally had been a person's faithful acceptance of God's irresistible call to elected salvation became a person's voluntary formation of a covenant relationship with God.

Both the expansion of the parties and the contractualization of the terms of the covenant of salvation helped to expand Puritan understandings of religious liberty and religious pluralism. Initially, seventeenth-century New England Puritans were notorious for their religious rigidity and illiberality, and banished any and all who deviated even slightly from the orthodox way. Remember Anne Hutchinson (1591-1643) and Roger Williams (1604-1680). For, in this early period, the Puritans still treated the covenant of salvation as something of a "divine adhesion contract."[10] God set the covenantal terms for salvation in the Bible that the community had come to interpret in a distinct way; a person had the freedom only to accept or reject these covenantal terms of salvation. Such sentiments can be seen in a lengthy 1682 tract on "covenant liberty" by Samuel Willard (1640-1707), the great New England systematizer of Puritan doctrine. Willard argued that every person had the "equal right," "title," "claim," "liberty," and "prerogative" "to enter and to enjoy every blessing of the covenant." But, by the time Willard finished spelling out all the standard terms and conditions of the covenant, there seemed to be few at liberty to enter the covenant, and little liberty left for those few who could.[11]

9. John Preston, quoted by Christopher Hill, *Puritanism and Revolution: Studies in Interpretation of the English Revolution of the 17th Century* (London: Secker and Warburg, 1958), p. 246.

10. The term is from Paul Ramsey, *Basic Christian Ethics* (New York: Scribner, 1950), p. 371; see discussion in Robert W. Tuttle, "A Treason of the Clerks: Paul Ramsey on Christian Ethics and the Common Law" (Ph.D. diss., University of Virginia, 1997), pp. 106-7.

11. Samuel Willard, *Covenant-Keeping the Way to Blessedness* (Boston: J. Glen,

By the eighteenth century, however, some Puritan writers began to view this covenantal relationship between God and persons in more open and voluntarist terms. Not only was the covenant made more accessible to parties of various Christian faiths, but the terms of the divine covenant itself were made more open to personal deliberation and innovation. Elisha Williams (1694-1755), the great-grandson of early Puritan stalwart John Cotton (1584-1652), put the matter thus in 1744:

> Every man has an equal right to follow the dictates of his own conscience in the affairs of religion. Every one is under an indispensable obligation to search the Scriptures for himself . . . and to make the best use of it he can for his own information in the will of God, the nature and duties of Christianity. And as every Christian is so bound; so he has the inalienable right to judge of the sense and meaning of it, and to follow his judgment wherever it leads him; even an equal right with any rulers be they civil or ecclesiastical.[12]

Such formulations became increasingly common among Puritan writers in the later eighteenth century. These sentiments helped lead the New England leaders to greater toleration of Baptists, Anglicans, Methodists, and other Christians who abided by the basic terms of the biblical covenants.[13]

It was only a short step from this formulation to the more generic and generous religious liberty guarantee of the 1780 Massachusetts Constitution that John Adams drafted.[14] Freedom of religion was among the first rights that the Constitution protected. We must begin "by setting the con-

---

1682). See further Samuel Willard, *Morality Not to Be Relied on for Life* (Boston: B. Green and J. Allen, 1700); Samuel Willard, *Walking with God, the Great Duty and Privilege of True Christians* (Boston: B. Green and J. Allen, 1701).

12. Elisha Williams, *The Essential Rights and Liberties of Protestants* (Boston: S. Kneeland and T. Green, 1744), pp. 3, 7-8.

13. Despite this liberalization, it took Baptists another fifty years to achieve full equality in New England. William G. McLoughlin, *New England Dissent 1630-1833*, 2 vols. (Cambridge, Mass.: Harvard University Press, 1971); William G. McLoughlin, *Soul Liberty: The Baptists' Struggle in New England, 1630-1833* (Hanover: University Press of New England, 1991).

14. In F. Thorpe, ed., *The Federal and State Constitutions, Colonial Charters, and Other Organic Laws,* 7 vols. (Washington: Government Printing Office, 1909), vol. 3, and analyzed in detail in my "'A Most Mild and Equitable Establishment of Religion': John Adams and the Massachusetts Experiment," *Journal of Church and State* 41 (1999): 213-52.

science free," Adams wrote in presenting his draft Constitution, for the rights of conscience and religion are "indisputable, unalienable, indefeasible, [and] divine."[15] Accordingly, Article II of the Massachusetts Constitution provided:

> It is the right as well as the duty of all men in society, publickly, and at stated seasons to worship the SUPREME BEING, the great Creator and preserver of the Universe. No subject shall be hurt, molested, or restrained, in his person, Liberty, or Estate, for worshipping GOD in the manner and season most agreeable to the Dictates of his own conscience, or for his religious profession or sentiments; provided he doth not Disturb the public peace, or obstruct others in their religious Worship.

Article III, at least tacitly, recognized the right to form religious associations, to select one's own minister, and to pay tithes directly to him. Chapter VI included within the ambit of religious freedom the right of Quakers to claim an exemption from the swearing of oaths to which they were "conscientiously opposed."

Adams regarded the protection of religious pluralism as essential for the protection of religious and other forms of liberty. As he put it in a letter to Thomas Jefferson (1743-1826), "Roman Catholics, English Episcopalians, Scotch and American Presbyterians, Methodists, Moravians, Anbabtists [sic], German Lutherans, German Calvinists, Universalists, Arians, Priestlyians, Socinians, Independents, Congregationalists, Horse Protestants and House Protestants, Deists and Atheists and Protestants *qui ne croyent rien* [who believe nothing] are . . . [n]ever the less all Educated in the general Principles of Christianity: and the general Principles of English and American liberty."[16] "Checks and balances, Jefferson," in the political as well as the religious sphere, "are our only Security, for the progress of Mind, as well as the Security of Body. Every Species of these Christians would persecute Deists, as [much] as either Sect would persecute another, if it had unchecked and unballanced Power. Nay, the Deists would persecute Christians, and Atheists would persecute Deists, with as unrelenting

---

15. Thorpe, *Federal and State Constitutions*, 3:452-56.

16. Letter to Thomas Jefferson (June 28, 1813), in *The Adams-Jefferson Letters*, ed. Lester J. Cappon, 2 vols. (Chapel Hill, N.C.: University of North Carolina Press, 1959), pp. 339-40.

Cruelty, as any Christians would persecute them or one another. Know thyself, Human nature!"[17]

Covenant theology was certainly not the only argument available for the constitutional guarantee of religious liberty of various peaceable religions. But, for the New England Puritans, covenant theology provided a sturdy foundation for a theory of ordered religious liberty and orderly religious pluralism. By expanding the ambit of the covenant of works, the Puritans expanded the realm of religious liberty to all persons, not just the elect. By contractualizing the terms of the covenant of grace, the Puritans expanded the range of religious exercises, no longer privileging established forms. But not all claims of religious liberty could be accepted. Legitimate claims to religious liberty protection had to be anchored in some semblance of a covenant with God, however each person chose to define this God and covenant. Legitimate claimants had to abide by the natural duties of love of God, neighbor, and self taught by the covenant of works, however each community chose to delineate these duties.

Covenants of Liberty

The Puritans regarded themselves not only as covenant persons in their relationship to God, but also as covenant people bound together by covenants with each other. Each of these covenants, they believed, though formed by voluntary human acts, was ultimately founded on the norms and principles set forth in the covenant of works. Each of these covenants had a place in God's providential plan, a purpose for which it existed.

Building on their innovations to traditional covenant theology, the New England Puritans distinguished three such covenants: (1) a social or communal covenant; (2) an ecclesiastical or Church covenant; and (3) a political or governmental covenant. The social covenant created the society or commonwealth as a whole. The political and ecclesiastical covenants created the two chief seats of authority within that society, the Church and the state, whose authority was both separated and pluralized. The social, ecclesiastical, and political covenants confirmed and coordinated the natural, religious, and political liberties of the members of these covenant communities.

---

17. Letter to Thomas Jefferson (June 25, 1813), in *Adams-Jefferson Letters,* p. 334.

Natural Liberty and the Social Covenant

At the creation of the world, the Puritans believed, God had vested all persons with "a natural liberty" and subjected them to "a natural law." The natural person, Massachusetts Governor John Winthrop (1588-1649) declared, "stands in relation to [his fellow] man simply, [and] hath liberty to do what he lists; it is at liberty to [do] evil as well as to [do] good."[18] The vice or virtue of a person's actions is determined by the natural law, which God has written into the covenant of works that is binding on all.[19]

The Puritans believed, however, that "the Voice of Nature plainly declares that Mankind" join together in social covenant and "dwell together in Societies."[20] This calling from a natural state to a social state was born of both human necessity and divine destiny. On the one hand, God had called all persons to form societies in order to provide the order and stability needed to maintain the natural liberty and natural law that God had created. "The exercise and maintaining of [natural] liberty," without social constraints, wrote Winthrop, "makes men grow more evil, and in time to be worse than brute beasts."[21] Persons "prey" upon each other, placing the natural liberty of all into jeopardy. Society helps guarantee such liberty. Moreover, in a natural state, persons suffer from "weakness, impotencie and insufficiency" both in the apprehension of and the obedience to the natural law.[22] Society helps reconfirm and reinforce these natural law principles.

On the other hand, and more importantly, God had called the Puritans in particular to form their society to help fulfill his providential plan in the New World. The Puritans believed that God had entered into a special covenant relationship with them to be his "surrogate Israel," his newly chosen people.[23] By this covenant, they were called to be a "city on the hill," a

18. John Winthrop, *Winthrop's Journal*, ed. James K. Hosmer, 2 vols. (New York: C. Scribner's Sons, 1908), 2:238.

19. John D. Eusden, "Natural Law and Covenant Theology in New England, 1620-1670," *Natural Law Forum* 5 (1960): 1.

20. John Barnard, *The Throne Established By Righteousness* (1734), in *The Puritans*, ed. Perry Miller and Thomas Johnson (New York: American Book Company, 1938), pp. 270-71 [hereafter Miller and Johnson].

21. *Winthrop's Journal*, 2:238.

22. Thomas Hooker, *The Application of Redemption by the Effectual Work of the Word, and Spirit of Christ, for the Bringing Home of Lost Sinners to God* (London: Peter Cole, 1659), p. 43.

23. Cotton Mather, *The Serviceable Man* (1690), in *Puritan Political Ideas*, ed.

"light to the nations," "a model of Christ's kingdom among the hea-
thens."[24] They were commanded to preserve and propagate godly beliefs
and values, to adopt and advocate godly morals and mores, to arouse themselves and all those around them to godly obedience. God had promised
them peace and prosperity if they succeeded in their covenantal task, death
and damnation if they failed.[25]

The Puritan colonists swore allegiance to such social covenants before God and each other when forming their new communities. "We whose
names are underwritten," reads the famous Mayflower Compact of 1620,
"[h]aving under-taken for the glory of God, and advancement of the Christian Faith, . . . a Voyage to plant the first Colony . . . doe by these presents,
solemnly & mutually in the presence of God and one of another, covenant,
and combine our selues together into a civill body politike, for our better
ordering and preservation, and furtherance of the ends aforesaid."[26] The
citizens of the new town of Salem convened in 1629 to swear, "We Covenant with the Lord and one with an other; and doe bynd our selves in the
presence of God, to walke together in all his waies, according as he is
pleased to reveale himself unto us in his Blessed word of truth."[27] The following year John Winthrop declared to the new citizens of Massachusetts
Bay, "Thus stands the cause betweene God and us, wee are entered into
Covenant with him for this worke, wee have taken out a Commission, [and
He] will expect a strickt performance of the Articles contained in it."[28]
Hundreds of such social covenants and compacts are sprinkled throughout
the early New England archives.

Participation in these social covenants had to be wholly voluntary
and consensual. "There can be no necessary tye of mutuall accord and fellowship come, but by free engagement," wrote Thomas Hooker (1586-
1647), the founder of New Haven. "[H]e that will enter must also willingly

---

Edmund S. Morgan (Indianapolis: Bobbs-Merrill, 1965), p. 233 [hereafter Morgan]. See
also J. Higginson, *The Cause of God and His People in New England* (Cambridge, Mass.:
Samuel Green, 1663), p. 18.

24. John Winthrop, *A Model of Christian Charity* (1630), in Morgan, pp. 75, 93.
J. Scottow, *Narrative of the Planting of Massachusetts* (1694), in *Collections of the Massachusetts Historical Society* (4th ser.) (1871), 4:279.

25. Willard, *Covenant-Keeping the Way to Blessedness.*

26. The Agreement Between the Settlers of New Plymouth (1620), in Williston
Walker, *The Creeds and Platforms of Congregationalism* (Boston: Pilgrim, 1960), p. 92.

27. The Covenant of 1629, in Walker, *Creeds and Platforms,* p. 116.

28. Winthrop, *Model of Christian Charity,* p. 92.

binde and ingage himself to each member of that society . . . or else a member actually he is not."[29] The voluntary participation of both the entering individual and the existing community were essential. No person could be forced to join the community whose covenant and culture he or she found objectionable. No community could be forced to accept or retain a person whose convictions or conduct it found objectionable.[30]

Those who voluntarily joined this covenant were subject to both the benevolence and the discipline of the community. The Puritans attached great importance to public benevolence. Charity and public spiritedness were prized. Churlishness and private sumptuousness were scorned. "[W]ee must entertaine each other in brotherly Affeccion," declared Winthrop. "[W]ee must delight in eache other, make others Condicions our owne, rejoyce together, mourne together, labour, and suffer together, allwayes haveing before our eyes our Commission and Community in the worke, our Community as members of the same body."[31] These were not just homiletic platitudes. The New England Puritans prescribed and practiced good samaritanism. They punished citizens who failed to aid their neighbors in need or peril. They set up public trusts, community chests, and work programs for indigents and immigrants. They developed systems of relief for the poor, the elderly, and the handicapped. They established systems of academic and vocational education.[32] This was a very modest social welfare program when viewed by contemporary standards, but rather magnanimous when judged by standards of the day.

The Puritans attached even greater importance to public discipline. The social covenant, the Puritans believed, placed each community "under a solemn divine Probation" and under threat of "eminent [divine] trial."[33] This belief translated the most mundane of human affairs into cosmic terms. The Puritans stressed ambition, austerity, frugality, and other supposed virtues in their lives precisely because the social covenant rendered

29. Thomas Hooker, *A Survey of the Summe of Church-Discipline,* 2 vols. (London: John Bellamy, 1648), 1:47, 50.

30. John Winthrop, "A Defense of an Order of Court Made in the Year 1637," in Miller and Johnson, pp. 200-201.

31. Winthrop, *Model of Christian Charity,* p. 92; Increase Mather, *The Excellency of a Publick Spirit* (Boston: B. Green and J. Allen, 1702).

32. Robert W. Kelso, *The History of Public Poor Relief in Massachusetts, 1620-1920* (Boston: Houghton Mifflin, 1922).

33. W. Stoughton, *New Englands True Interest: Not to Lie* (1670), in Miller and Johnson, p. 243.

them agents of God, instruments of God's providential plan. For them to be lax in zeal, loose in discipline, or sumptuous in living would be a disservice to God, a breach of the social covenant. Such a breach would inevitably bring divine condemnation on the community in the form of war, pestilence, poverty, and other forms of force majeure. This belief that the community lived perennially under "solemn divine probation" is reflected not only in sundry sermons but also in many statutes of the day. A 1675 Massachusetts statute, for example, prefaced its rigid disciplinary code with these words: "Whereas the most wise & holy God, for seuerall yeares past, hath not only warned us in his word, but chastized us with his rods, inflicting upon us many generall (though lesser) judgments, but we haue neither heard the word nor rod as wee ought, so as to be effectually humbled for our sinns, to repent of them, reforme and amend our wayes. . . ."[34]

The Puritans' belief in a "solemn divine probation" rendered the reformation of society a constant priority. They had to ensure that all institutions and all aspects of society comported with the covenantal ideal. Thus Puritan sermonizers urged their listeners to "Reform all places, all persons and all callings. Reform the benches of judgment, the inferior magistrates. . . . Reform the universities, reform the cities, reform the counties, reform inferior schools of learning, reform the Sabbath, reform the ordinances, the worship of God. Every plant which my Father hath not planted shall be rooted up."[35]

Adams wrote a good deal of this traditional theory of the social covenant into the 1780 Massachusetts Constitution. The preamble refers to the constitution repeatedly as "a covenant" or "compact" between the people and God: "[T]he whole people covenants with each Citizen, and each Citizen with the whole people, that all shall be governed by certain Laws for the Common good." And again, "the people of Massachusetts, acknowledging, with grateful hearts, the goodness of the Great Legislator of the Universe, in affording us, in the course of his Providence, an opportunity, deliberately and peaceably, without fraud, violence, or surprize, o[f] entering into an Original, explicit, and Solemn Compact with each other; and of forming a New Constitution of Civil Government for ourselves and Posterity; and devoutly imploring His direction in so interesting a Design, DO

---

34. *Records of the Governor and Company of the Massachusetts Bay in New England,* ed. N. Shurtleff, 5 vols. (Boston: W. White, 1853-1854), 5:59; see also *Election Day Sermons: Plymouth and Connecticut,* facs. ed. (New York: AMS, 1983).

35. Quoted in Harold J. Berman, "Religious Foundations of Law in the West: An Historical Perspective," *Journal of Law and Religion* 1 (1983): 3, 30.

agree upon, ordain and establish the following Declaration of Rights and Frame of Government."

A variant of this covenant ceremony was the oath-swearing ritual of state officials. Adams wrote into Chapter VI of the Frame of Government the requirement that all state officials must swear a full oath to the constitution and the commonwealth — not just privately, but before the people and their representatives in full assembly. "I, A, B, do declare, that I believe the Christian religion, and have a firm persuasion of its truth . . . ; and I do swear, that I will bear true faith and allegiance to the said Commonwealth . . . so help me God." Adams's insistence on such oaths reflected the conventional view that the oath was "a cement of society" and "one of the principal instruments of government," for it invoked and induced "the fear and reverence of God, and the terrors of eternity."[36] This provision also reflected Adams's view that the oath of office was a public confirmation of the covenant among God, the people, and their rulers. These preambulary and oath-swearing provisions were not merely a bit of hortatory throat-clearing that preceded the real business of constitutional government. They established traditional ceremonies of the social covenant.

Adams also wrote the traditional morality of the social covenant into the 1780 Constitution. Article II of the Declaration of Rights stipulated that it was not only the right but also "the Duty of all men in society, publickly, and at stated seasons to worship the SUPREME BEING, the great Creator and preserver of the Universe." Article III follows with the reason for this duty: "the happiness of a people, and good order and preservation of civil government, essentially depend upon piety, religion, and morality; and . . . these cannot be generally diffused through a Community, but by the institution of publick Worship of God, and of public instructions in piety, religion, and morality. . . ." Article XVIII of the Declaration of Rights rendered adherence to these moral duties integral to the character of public offices and public officials:

> A frequent recurrence to the fundamental principles of the constitution, and a constant adherence to those of piety, justice, moderation, temperance, industry, and frugality, are absolutely necessary to pre-

36. See Phillips Payson, "Election Sermon of 1778," reprinted in *American Political Writing during the Founding Era, 1760-1805,* ed. Charles S. Hynemann and Donald S. Lutz, 2 vols. (Indianapolis: Liberty, 1983), 1:529. This was also one reason that Adams wrote into his draft of Chapters I and II that every official must be "of the Christian religion."

serve the advantages of liberty, and to maintain a free government. The people ought, consequently, to have a particular attention to all those principles, in the choice of their Officers and Representatives, and they have a right to require of their lawgivers and magistrates, an exact and constant observance of them, in the formation and execution of the laws necessary for the good administration of the Commonwealth.

For, as Article VII of the Declaration put it, "Government is instituted for the Common good; for the protection, safety, prosperity, and happiness of the people." And, as Chapter V of the Frame of Government provides: "Wisdom, and knowledge, as well as virtue, diffused generally among the body of the people, [are] necessary for the preservation of their rights and liberties."

These twin goals of the social covenant — to maintain natural law and natural liberty and to attain the ideal community of benevolence and discipline — could not be realized without institutions of law and authority. The Church and the state were the two chief instruments of law and authority, the Puritans believed. God had laid the foundations for both these in the covenant of works of creation, on which natural foundation the new covenants of Church and state had to be built.

Religious Liberty and the Church Covenant

Following Calvinist commonplaces, the Puritans believed that God had vested in the Church the spiritual power of the Word. The Church had the power to preach the Gospel, to administer the sacraments, to teach the young, to prophesy against injustice, and to care for the poor and the needy. By such activities, the Church would lead all members of the community to a greater understanding of their covenantal responsibilities of benevolence and love. The Church also had the power to devise its own polity, to define its own doctrine, and to discipline its own members who had sinned — using the spiritual means of instruction, the ban, and excommunication. By such activities, the Church would confirm and reinforce the natural law and the divine authority that undergirded it.[37]

37. *The Cambridge Synod and Platform* (1648), chaps. 1-3, 5, in Walker, *Creeds and Platforms*, pp. 203-10. See also Richard Mather, *Church Government and Church-Covenant Discussed* (1643), in *Church Covenant: Two Tracts*, ed. R. Robey (New York: Arno, 1972), p. 217.

The New England Puritans had a congregationalist understanding of the Church. Each congregational Church was constituted by a voluntary covenant between God and like-minded believers. By this covenant, these believers swore to God and to each other to uphold God's ordinances, to discharge the special calling of the Church, and to be subject to those who came into authority within the Church. "Saints by Calling," reads one Puritan document, "must have a Visible-Political-Union amongst themselves." They must form a "Co[m]pany of professed believers Ecclesiastically Confoederat."[38] "This Form is the Visible Covenant, Agreement, consent wherby they give up themselves unto the Lord, to the observing of the ordinances of Christ together in the same society, which is usually called the Church-Covenant; For wee see not otherwise how members can have Church-power one over another mutually."[39]

Many of the Puritan congregational Churches swore to such covenants both upon initially forming the Church and upon subsequently admitting new members to it. The Watertown Covenant-Creed of 1647 contains typical language:

> We believe that God's people, besides their general covenant with God, . . . ought also to join themselves into a church covenant one with another, and to enter into a particular combination together with some of his people to erect a particular ecclesiastical body, and kingdom, and visible family and household of God, for the managing of discipline and public ordinances of Christ in one place in a dutiful way, there to worship God and Christ, as his visible kingdom and subjects, in that place waiting on him for that blessing of his ordinances and promises of his covenant, by holding communion with him and his people, in the doctrine and discipline of that visible kingdom. . . . We . . . do here bind ourselves, in the presence of men and angels, by his grace assisting us, to choose the Lord, to serve him, and to walk in all his ways, and to keep all his commandments and ordinances. . . .[40]

These Church covenants formed the core of congregational Church constitutions, which defined in detail the form and function of the Church offices and the rights and responsibilities of its parishioners.

---

38. *Cambridge Synod and Platform,* chaps. 4-10.
39. *Cambridge Synod and Platform,* chap. 4.
40. Watertown Covenant-Creed (1647), in Miller and Johnson, pp. 149, 155-56.

Political Liberty and the Political Covenant

While God vested in the Church the spiritual power of the Word, God vested in the state the temporal power of the sword. "Civil Rulers," the Puritans believed, were "Gods Vice regents here upon earth."[41] They were called to reflect and represent God's majesty and authority. They were to exemplify godly justice, mercy, discipline, and benevolence. Political rulers were vested in their offices by a three-party covenant among God, the people, and themselves. By this covenant, the rulers accepted the divine mandate for their political office. The people, in turn, vowed to God and to the rulers to oblige and submit to this rule, to accept and respect the laws.[42]

Political officials took on three specific responsibilities under this political covenant. First, political officials were required to appropriate and apply natural law in the positive law of the state. The Puritans, following Calvinist commonplaces, often equated this natural law with the Decalogue and thus described the magistrate as a custodian of both tables of the Decalogue.[43] The positive law of the state was thus to govern both the relationship between persons and God, based on the First Table of the Decalogue, and the multiple relationships among persons, based on the Second Table. On the authority of the First Table, political officials were to punish all forms of idolatry, witchcraft, blasphemy, false swearing, and Sabbath Day violations.[44] On the authority of the Second Table, they were to punish all forms of disobedience to authority, all violations of the person or property of the other, all adultery, prostitution, and other sexual misconduct, all dishonesty, false testimony, and other fraud against another.[45] Only those positive laws that were rooted in and reflected the natural law, the Puritans believed, had legitimacy and authority.

This concern that political officials preserve the natural law is prominent in many of the early New England law codes of the seventeenth cen-

---

41. Samuel Willard, *The Character of a Good Ruler* (1694), in Miller and Johnson, p. 253. See also Jonathan Todd, *Civil Rulers the Ministers of God for Good to Men* (New London, Conn.: Timothy Green, 1749).

42. Willard, *The Character of a Good Ruler*, p. 253. See also John Winthrop, *On Arbitrary Government*, in Morgan, p. 152; Cotton Mather, *Bonifacious: An Essay upon the Good*, ed. David Levin (Cambridge, Mass.: Belknap, 1966), pp. 91, 94.

43. *Cambridge Synod and Platform*, chap. 17.

44. *Cambridge Synod and Platform*, chap. 17.

45. Letter from John Cotton to Lord Say (1636), in Miller and Johnson, pp. 209-12; Willard, *The Character of a Good Ruler*, pp. 250-56.

tury. The preface to the famous Booke of the Generall Lawes and Liberties of New Plymouth (1685) has typical language: "God being the God of order and not of confusion hath Comaunded in his word; and put man into a capasitie in some measure to obserue and bee guided by good and wholesome lawes which are soe fare good and wholsome; as by how much they are deriued from and agreeable to; the Ancient platforme of Gods lawe . . . [which are] soe exemplary being grounded on principalls of morall equitie as that all men; Christians especially ought alwaies to haue an eye thervnto; in the framing of theire Politique Constitutions."[46]

Second, political officials were required to protect and promote the liberties and rights of their subjects. "A People are not made for Rulers, But Rulers for a People," wrote a leading Puritan.[47] God has set the rulers in authority, and the people have submitted to that authority, in order to gain a "Civil felicity" not available to them in the "natural state."[48] Such "felicity" can exist only "[w]hen men can injoy their Liberties and Rights without molestation or oppression," "when they are secured against Violence, and may be Righted against them that offer them any injury, without fraud; and are encouraged to serve God in their own way."[49]

This concern that political officials preserve the natural liberty of subjects by positive law was prominent even in the early New England law codes which are often lampooned for their biblical legalism. The most famous statement of this principle appears in the opening words of the Laws and Liberties of Massachusetts (1648):

> Forasmuch as the free fruition of such Liberties, Immunities, priviledges as humanitie, civilitie & christianity call for as due to everie man in his place, & proportion, without impeachment & infringement hath ever been, & ever will be the tranquility & stability of Churches & Common-wealths; & the deniall or deprivall thereof the disturbance, if not ruine of both: It is therefore ordered . . . [t]hat no mans life shall be taken away; no mans honour or good name shall be stayned; no mans person shall be arrested, restrained, bannished, dismembred nor any wayes punished; no man shall be deprived of his wife or children; no mans goods or estate shall be taken away from

46. *The Book of the General Laws of the Inhabitants of the Jurisdiction of New-Plimouth* (Boston: Samuel Green, 1685), p. 148.
47. Willard, *The Character of a Good Ruler*, p. 254.
48. Willard, *The Character of a Good Ruler*, p. 254.
49. Willard, *The Character of a Good Ruler*, p. 255.

him; nor any wayes indamaged under colour of Law or countenance of Authoritie unless it be by vertue or equity of some expresse law of this Country warranting the same established by a General Court & sufficiently published; or in case of the defect of a law in any particular case by the word of God.[50]

Third, political officials were to be the catalysts and champions of the perpetual reformation mandated by the social covenant. "[A] work of Reformation," wrote Samuel Willard, "is set about in vain, and to no purpose, if Rulers do not lead in it."[51] Officials were required to compel the community by their example, by their authority, and by their law to reach and retain the covenantal ideals to which the community had subscribed in the social covenant. This mandate often required that the law itself be perpetually emended and amended. "The reformation of the law, and more law for the reformation of the world, is what is mightily called for."[52]

Separation and Cooperation of Church and State

The theological doctrine of separation of Church and state went hand-in-hand with the doctrine of ecclesiastical and political covenants. The Puritans conceived the Church and the state as two separate covenantal associations, two coordinate seats of godly authority and power in society. Each institution had a distinctive calling and responsibility. Each had a distinctive polity and practice. "[O]ur Churches, and civil State have been planted, and growne up (like two tvvinnes)," reads the preamble to the Laws and Liberties of Massachusetts. To conflate these two institutions would be to the "misery (if not ruine) of both."[53]

The Puritans adopted a variety of safeguards to ensure this basic separation of the associations and activities of Church and state. Church officials were prohibited from holding political office, from serving on juries, from in-

50. *The Book of the General Laws and Liberties Concerning the Inhabitants of Massachusetts* (1648), ed. Max Farrand (Cambridge, Mass.: Harvard University Press, 1929), p. 1.

51. Samuel Willard, *A Sermon upon the Death of John Leverett, Esq.* (Boston: John Foster, 1679), p. 6; see also Increase Mather, *The Necessity of Reformation with the Expedients Thereunto Asserted* (Boston: John Foster, 1679), pp. iii-iv.

52. Mather, *Bonifacious,* p. 130.

53. *Book of the General Laws and Liberties of Massachusetts,* p. A2.

terfering in governmental affairs, from endorsing political candidates, or from censuring the official conduct of a statesman who was also a parishioner in the Church. Political officials, in turn, were prohibited from holding ministerial office, from interfering in internal ecclesiastical government, from performing sacerdotal functions of clergy, or from censuring the official conduct of a cleric who was also a citizen of the commonwealth.[54] To permit any such officiousness on the part of the Church or the state, Winthrop averred, "would confounde those Jurisdictions, which Christ hath made distinct."[55]

Although Church and state were not to be confounded, they were still to be "close and compact."[56] For, to the Puritans, these two institutions were inextricably linked in nature and in function. Each was an instrument of godly authority. Each did its part to establish and maintain the covenantal ideals of the community. "I look upon this as a little model of the Gloriou[s] Kingdome of Christ on Earth," wrote Urian Oakes (1631-1681). "Christ Reigns among us in the Common wealth as well as in the Church, and hath his glorious Interest involved and wrapt up in the good of both Societies respectively." Thus "the Interest of Righteousness in the Common wealth, and Holiness in the Churches are inseparable. The prosperity of Church and Common wealth are twisted together. Break one Cord, you weaken and break the other also."[57]

It was on the strength of such arguments that various laws and policies were enacted to facilitate the coordination and cooperation of Church and state in colonial New England, even while keeping the institutions separate from each other in their core form and function. The state provided various forms of material aid to congregational Churches and officials. Public lands were donated to Church groups for the construction of meetinghouses, parsonages, day schools, orphanages, and other structures used in the Church's ministry. Tithes and Church taxes were collected to support congregational ministers and teachers. Tax exemptions and immunities were accorded to some of the religious, educational, and charitable organizations that they operated. Special subsidies and military protections were provided for congregational missionaries.

---

54. *Book of the General Laws and Liberties of Massachusetts*, pp. 18-20; *Cambridge Synod and Platform*, chap. 17. See also Thomas Breen, *The Character of the Good Ruler 1630-1730* (New Haven: Yale University Press, 1970), pp. 37-44.

55. Breen, *The Character of the Good Ruler*, p. 42.

56. Letter from John Cotton to Lord Say (1636), in Miller and Johnson, p. 209.

57. Urian Oakes, *New England Pleaded with, and Pressed to Consider the Things Which Concern Her* (Cambridge, Mass.: Samuel Green, 1673), p. 49.

The state also provided various forms of moral support to ensure that "the people be fed w[i]th wholesome & sound doctrine" and to preserve the "order and comunion of churches."[58] Sabbath-day laws prohibited all forms of unnecessary labor and uncouth leisure on Sundays and holy days; they also required faithful attendance at services. Blasphemy laws prohibited all forms of false swearing, foul language, and irreverence either "toward the Word preached or the Messengers thereof." Idolatry laws sanctioned various forms of sacrilege, witchcraft, sorcery, magic, alchemy, and other invocations of "false gods." Religious incorporation laws required all new Churches to secure "the approbation of the Magistrates," and required all "schismaticall" Churches to submit to the "coercive power" of the magistrates.[59]

Churches, in turn, provided various forms of material aid and accommodation to the state. Church meetinghouses and chapels were used not only to conduct religious services, but also to host town assemblies, political rallies, and public auctions, to hold educational and vocational classes, to house the community library, to maintain census rolls as well as birth, marriage, and death certificates. Parsonages were used not only to house the minister and his family, but also to harbor orphans and widows, the sick and the aged, victims of abuse and disaster, and other wards of the state.

Churches also afforded various forms of moral support to the state. They preached obedience to the authorities and disciplined by spiritual means those parishioners found guilty of "serious" crimes. They encouraged their parishioners to be active in political affairs and each year offered "election day sermons" on Christian political principles. These ministers also offered learned advice on the requirements of godly law, and were often asked to participate in the drafting of new legislation and the resolution of cases that raised particularly trying moral issues.

Checks and Balances

Beyond insisting on this balance of separation and cooperation of Church and state, the New England Puritans were rather pragmatic in developing

58. *Records of the Governor and Company of the Massachusetts Bay in New England*, 5:328.

59. *Records of the Governor and Company of the Massachusetts Bay in New England*, 5:328; *Book of the General Laws and Liberties of Massachusetts*, pp. 18-20; *Cambridge Synod and Platform*, chap. 17.

the appropriate forms of government for each. They made little pretense that their government structures were biblically commanded or divinely inspired. John Adams wrote that those "employed in the service of forming a constitution" cannot pretend that they "had interviews with the gods, or were in any degree under the inspiration of Heaven." "[G]overnments [are] contrived merely by the use of reason and the senses." Constitutions "are merely experiments made on human life and manners, society and government."[60] There will always be "a glorious uncertainty in the law."[61] "I know of no particular Form of . . . Government," wrote another Puritan leader, "that God Himself has, directly, and immediately, appointed, by any clear Revelation of His Mind and Will, to any People whatever. . . . God Almighty has left it to the natural Reason of Mankind, in every Nation and Country, to set up that Form, which, upon a thorow Consideration of the Nature, Temper, Inclinations, Customs, Manners, Business, and other Circumstances of a People, may be thought best for them."[62]

One constant element in the "nature, temper, and inclination" of persons, however, was their sinfulness. Each person, by his or her very nature, the Puritans believed, is a fallen, sinful, and depraved creature. Each person is inherently tempted by egoism, greed, and corruption. "Sin has . . . vitiated the humane Nature," wrote one New England leader, and driven persons to "unruly Lusts," "rampant Passions," and "a constant Endeavour . . . to promote his own, and gratify Self."[63]

This temptation toward self-indulgence and self-gain was particularly strong and dangerous among officials in Church and state. "Power is too intoxicating and liable to abuse," wrote one Puritan leader.[64] Many officials succumb to their corrupt natures and "make no other use of their higher station, than to swagger over their neighbors, and command their obsequious flatteries, and enrich themselves with the spoils of which they are able to pillage them."[65] Such official arbitrariness and abuse would inevitably

60. Adams, *Works,* 4:297.

61. Letter to Josiah Quincy (February 9, 1811), in Adams, *Works,* 9:629-32, at 630.

62. John Barnard, *The Throne Established by Righteousness* (1734), in Miller and Johnson, p. 273.

63. Barnard, *The Throne Established,* in Miller and Johnson, p. 272.

64. Peter Whitney, *The Transgression of a Land Punished by a Multitude of Rulers* (Boston: John Boyle, 1774), p. 21; John Cotton, *An Exposition on the Thirteenth Chapter of the Revelation* (1655), in Morgan, p. 175.

65. Mather, *Bonifacious,* p. 92.

lead to both popular insurrection and divine sanction. The New England Puritans therefore advocated and adopted a variety of safeguards against tyranny for the state as well as the church.

First, the Puritans insisted that all officials have as "godly a character" as possible, notwithstanding their inherent sinfulness.[66] Officials were to be models of spirituality and morality for the community. They were to be professing members of a local congregational Church and to swear oaths of allegiance to God upon assuming their office. They were also to be diligent, upright, respectful, authoritative, and free from guile and graft. "Their very Example," wrote Samuel Willard, "will have the force of a Law in it, and win many by a powerful Attraction, to the avoiding of sin, and practising of Righteousness. . . . [T]heir faithful administrations will render them a Terror to Evil Doers, and an Encouragement to them that do well."[67]

Second, the Puritans insisted that both state and Church officials occupy their offices for only limited tenures. Life tenures were too dangerous, the Puritans believed, for they afforded the official the opportunity slowly to convert his office into an instrument of self-gain and self-aggrandizement. It was safer to limit the official's tenure and require periodic rotation of officers.[68]

Third, the Puritans advocated the development of what they called self-limiting "republican" forms of government for both the Church and the state. Rather than consolidate all forms of authority in one person or one office, they insisted on separate forms or branches of authority, each empowered to check the excesses of the other. Without such division and diffusion of authority, one preacher put it, "we shall ultimately find papacy in the Church and monarchy in the state."[69] Church government was thus divided among the offices of pastor, elder, and deacon. Each office held a distinct responsibility in the congregation, and each wielded a measure of authority over the others.[70] Political government was divided into executive (administrative), legislative, and judicial offices. Each office had a distinct responsibility in the commonwealth. Each wielded a measure of authority over the others.

Fourth, the Puritans advocated the development of legal codes and

66. Willard, *The Character of a Good Ruler,* p. 250.

67. Willard, *The Character of a Good Ruler,* p. 254.

68. Breen, *The Character of the Good Ruler,* pp. 74-75.

69. Willard, *The Character of a Good Ruler,* pp. 251-52; see also Hooker, *The Summe of Church-Discipline,* 1:3-5.

70. *Cambridge Synod and Platform,* chaps. 5-7.

clear statutes so that "magistrates might not proceed according to their discretions."[71] Early colonial leaders, such as John Winthrop and John Cotton, had resisted such codification. Codified law was, for them, inequitable because it deprived the magistrate of following "the wisdome and mercy of God as well as his Justice: as occasion shall require."[72] Opponents to discretion, such as Thomas Hooker, found this "a course which wants both safety and warrant, [for] it is a way which leads to tyranny, and so to confusion."[73] Proponents of codification prevailed. The Puritans devised elaborate legal codes and subjected the most minute of daily affairs to close statutory regulation.

Fifth, the Puritans adopted what they called a "federalist" structure of government (from *foedus,* the Latin word for covenant) for both the Church and the state. The Church was divided into semi-autonomous congregations, each with its own internal structures of pastoral, pedagogical, and diaconal authority and discipline but each loosely conjoined by democratically elected synods and assemblies. The state was divided into semi-autonomous town governments, each with its own internal structures of executive, legislative, and judicial authority, but conjoined in a broader colonial and later state government.

Finally, the Puritans advocated the "democraticall election" of both Church and state officials, and periodical congregational and town meetings in between. Early colonial leaders, like Winthrop and Cotton, opposed democracy as vehemently as they opposed codification. "A democratie is . . . accounted the meanest & worst of all formes of Governmt," Winthrop declared.[74] Likewise Cotton argued that democracy is not "a fitt government eyther for Church or commonwealth. If a people be governors, who shall be governed?"[75] Other colonial leaders, however, insisted that "Election is the Foundation of our Government."[76] On the one hand, God uses

71. *Winthrop's Journal,* 2:191.

72. John Cotton, quoted by Breen, *The Character of a Good Ruler,* p. 60.

73. Thomas Hooker, in *Collections of the Connecticut Historical Society* 1 (1860): 11; see also Perry Miller, "Thomas Hooker and the Democracy of Early Connecticut," *New England Quarterly* 4 (1931): 663.

74. *Life and Letters of John Winthrop,* ed. R. Winthrop, 2 vols., repr. ed. (New York: Da Capo, 1971), 2:430.

75. Quoted by Clinton Rossiter, *The First American Revolution: The American Colonies on the Eve of Revolution* (New York: Harcourt Brace, 1956), p. 90.

76. William Hubbard, *The Benefit of a Well-Ordered Conversation* (Boston: Samuel Green, 1684), p. 25.

democratic elections to select those officials who will best maintain the covenantal ideal of the community. Thus "the privilege of election, which belongs to the people," wrote Hooker, "must not be exercised according to their humours, but according to the blessed will and law of God."[77] On the other hand, the people use elections to protect themselves against autocratic, arbitrary, and avaricious rulers. "They who have the power to appoint [or elect] officers and magistrates, it is in their power, also, to set the bounds and limitations of the power and place unto which they call them."[78]

Both Church and state officials came to be democratically elected in the colony. Communicant members of the congregation voted by simple majority rule on the pastors, elders, and deacons who served in the Church.[79] Citizens of the townships and commonwealth voted by simple majority rule for their respective executive, legislative, and judicial officials.[80] Between such democratic elections, the Puritans held periodic popular meetings. Town meetings were convened for officials to give account of their conduct and citizens to give air to their concerns. Congregational meetings were convened for the purpose of the "discussing and resolving of any such doubts & cases of conscience concerning matter of doctrine, or worship, or government of the Church."[81]

A Puritan Seedbed of American Constitutionalism and Religious Liberty

These Puritan teachings on liberties of covenant and covenants of liberty were one fertile seedbed out of which later American constitutionalism grew. Many of the basic constitutional ideas and institutions developed by the Puritans in the seventeenth century remained firmly in place in the eighteenth century. These ideas and institutions were advocated and adopted not only in their original forms by Puritan sermonizers and political conservatives, but also in vestigial forms by those who had claimed no adherence to Puritan beliefs.

77. *Collections of the Connecticut Historical Society,* 1:20; Hooker, *Summe of Church-Discipline,* 1:8-13.
78. *Collections of the Connecticut Historical Society,* 1:20.
79. *Cambridge Synod and Platform,* chap. 8.
80. *Book of the General Laws and Liberties of Massachusetts,* pp. 20-21, 50-51.
81. *Book of the General Laws and Liberties of Massachusetts,* p. 19.

Puritan constitutional ideas lived on among various Enlightenment Liberal and Civic Republican schools of political thought in the later eighteenth and nineteenth centuries. Enlightenment liberals of various sorts found in the Puritan ideas of natural man and natural law important sources and analogies for their ideas of the state of nature and natural liberty. They found in the Puritan ideas of a social covenant and a political covenant pristine prototypes for their theories of a social contract and a governmental contract. They found in the doctrine of separation of Church and state a foundation for their ideas of disestablishment and free exercise of religion.[82] In turn, Civic Republican writers of various sorts transformed the Puritan idea of the elect nation under "solemn divine probation" into a revolutionary theory of American nationalism under divine inspiration. They recast the Puritan ideal of the covenant community into a theory of public virtue, discipline, and order. They translated the Puritans' insistence on spiritual rebirth and reformation into a general call for "moral reformation" and "republican regeneration."[83]

Some Puritan constitutional institutions likewise survived within the new federal and state constitutions of the later eighteenth and early nineteenth centuries — and not just in Massachusetts and other New England states where Puritans dominated the constitutional conventions. In many state constitutions, political rulers were still required to manifest a moral, virtuous, and godly character, and to swear oaths attesting to their theistic, if not Christian, beliefs. Most officials were required to stand for democratic elections to their offices. Political offices had limited tenures of office in many states. Political authority was distributed among executive, legislative, and judicial branches, each with authority to check the others. Liberties of citizens were copiously enumerated. Church and state were separated, yet allowed to cooperate.

In his landmark study, *The American Commonwealth*, James Bryce (1838-1922) wrote: "Someone has said that the American Government and Constitution are based on the theology of Calvin and the philosophy of Hobbes. This at least is true, that there is a hearty Puritanism in the view of human nature which pervades the instrument of 1787. It is the work of men who believed in original sin, and were resolved to leave open

82. See generally Bernard Bailyn, *The Ideological Origins of the American Revolution* (Cambridge, Mass.: Harvard University Press, 1967), pp. 32-34, 161-229, 246-72.
83. See Gordon Wood, *The Creation of the American Republic, 1776-1787* (Chapel Hill, N.C.: University of North Carolina Press, 1969), pp. 107-24.

for transgressors no door which they could possibly shut. Compare this spirit with the enthusiastic optimism of the Frenchman of 1789. It is not merely a difference of race temperaments; it is a difference of fundamental ideas."[84] The "fundamental ideas" of Puritan Calvinism did, indeed, contribute to the genesis and genius of the American experiment in ordered liberty and orderly pluralism. American religious, ecclesiastical, associational, and political liberty were grounded in fundamental Puritan ideas of conscience, confession, community, and commonwealth. American religious, confessional, social, and political pluralism, in turn, were bounded by fundamental Puritan ideas of divine sovereignty and created order.

84. James Bryce, *The American Commonwealth*, 2 vols. (Boston: Little, Brown, 1889), 1:299.

Religious Rights in Eighteenth-Century America: The Original Understanding of the First Amendment

Religious rights were a central concern of the eighteenth-century American founders. Churchmen and statesmen, believers and skeptics alike issued a torrent of writings to define and defend these rights. The founders considered religious rights to be among "the most essential" and "the most sacred of human rights" and regarded their firm constitutional guarantee to be indispensable to the success of the American constitutional experiment.[1]

The American constitutional experiment in religious rights cannot be reduced to the First Amendment religion clauses alone ("Congress shall make no law respecting an establishment of religion or prohibiting the free exercise thereof"). And the "original understanding"[2] of religious rights cannot be determined by simply studying the debates on these religion clauses in the First Session of Congress in 1789. Not only is the record of these congressional debates very slender and unreliable — a mere three pages of uneven notes in modern edition[3] — but the First Amendment reli-

1. See detailed quotations in RCE, chaps. 2-3.
2. See Jack N. Rakove, *Original Meanings: Politics and Ideas in the Making of the Constitution* (New York: A. A. Knopf, 1996), pp. 3-22, 288-338, and Jack N. Rakove, "Fidelity through History (Or to It)," *Fordham Law Review* 65 (1997): 1587-1609 (arguing for a distinction among the original "meaning," "intention," and "understanding" of the Constitution, and urging a use of both "textual" and "contextual" material to understand the "original understanding").
3. *The Debates and Proceedings in the Congress of the United States* [March 3, 1789– May 27, 1824] (Washington, D.C.: Gales and Seaton, 1834-1856), vol. 1, columns 451, 452, 468, 757-59, 778-80, 783-84, 795-96, 808 [hereafter *Annals*]; *Journal of the First Session of the Senate of the United States of America* (New York, 1789) (Evans, First Series, No. 22207), 1:116-17, 129, 145, 148 [hereafter *Journal*]. Both texts are reprinted with commentary in RCE, chap. 4 and Appendix 1.

gion clauses, by design, reflect only a part of the early constitutional experiment and experience. The religion clauses, on their face, define only the outer boundaries of appropriate governmental action respecting religion: Congress may not prescribe ("establish") religion nor proscribe ("prohibit") its exercise. Precisely what governmental conduct short of outright prescription or proscription of religion is constitutionally permissible was left open for debate and development in the Congress and the federal courts.

Moreover, the religion clauses bind only the federal government ("Congress"), rendering prevailing state constitutional provisions, and the sentiments of their drafters and ratifiers, equally vital sources of the original understanding of religious rights. By 1784, eleven of the thirteen original states had enacted constitutional provisions on religion, many of them quite detailed. The two remaining states, Connecticut and Rhode Island, retained their colonial charters on religious liberty but augmented them amply with new legislation.

Six principles recurred regularly in discussions of these federal and state legal guarantees of religious rights: (1) liberty of conscience; (2) free exercise of religion; (3) religious pluralism; (4) religious equality; (5) separation of Church and state; and (6) disestablishment of religion. These six principles, though given widely varying emphases and applications, came in for repeated and heated debate in the state constitutional debates in the 1770s to 1790s. They recurred in some of the surviving debates and draft provisions on religion in the First Congress of 1789 and in the state ratification debates about the same. And they were the subject of many hundreds of sermons, speeches, pamphlets, letters, and other documents in the last half of the eighteenth century.

This chapter explores a cross section of these documents to test the meaning and to take the measure of religious rights in the American founding era. I first summarize the prevailing understanding of each of these six principles and their manifestation in some of the new state constitutions. I then sift through the surviving drafts of the First Amendment to assess the place of these six principles in its final text.

Liberty of Conscience

Liberty of conscience was the general solvent used in the early American constitutional experiment in religious rights. It was almost universally embraced in the young republic — by everyone from conservative Calvinist congregationalists and civic republicans to radical "new light" Evangelicals and exponents of various forms of Enlightenment liberalism. "Liberty of conscience" was an ancient guarantee, rooted in early Roman and Christian sources, and laden with multiple meanings in the traditions of canon law, common law, and civil law alike. The plasticity of the phrase was not lost on the American founders. Like their predecessors, they often conflated or equated "liberty of conscience" with other favorites, such as "free exercise of religion," "religious freedom," "religious liberty," "religious privileges," and "religious rights." James Madison (1751-1836), for example, simply rolled into one linguistic heap "religious freedom" or "the free exercise of religion according to the dictates of conscience."[4] In another passage, he spoke of "liberty of conscience" as the "religious rights and privileges . . . of a multiplicity of sects."[5] Such patterns of interwoven language appear regularly in writings of the day. One term often implicated and connoted several others.[6] To read the original guarantees of liberty of conscience too dogmatically is to ignore their inherent plasticity.

That said, the founders did ascribe distinct content to the phrase "liberty of conscience," which won wide assent in the early republic.

First, for most founders liberty of conscience protected *voluntarism* — "the unalienable right of private judgment in matters of religion," the unencumbered ability to choose and to change one's religious beliefs and adherences.[7] The Puritan jurist Elisha Williams (1694-1755) put the matter strongly already in 1744:

---

4. Virginia Declaration of Rights (1776), art. XVI.

5. Jonathan Elliot, ed., *The Debates in the Several State Conventions, on the Adoption of the Federal Constitution* (Washington, D.C., 1854), 3:113-14 [hereafter *Debates*]; see also *The Papers of James Madison*, ed. W. T. Hutchinson et al., 16 vols. (Chicago: University of Chicago Press, 1962), 11:130-31 [hereafter Madison, *Papers*]. See further Anson P. Stokes and Leo Pfeffer, *Church and State in the United States,* rev. ed. (Westport, Conn.: Greenwood, 1975), p. 61.

6. See, e.g., John Mellen, *The Great and Happy Doctrine of Liberty* (Boston: Samuel Hall, 1795), pp. 17-18; Amos Adams, *Religious Liberty an Invaluable Blessing* (Boston: Kneeland and Adams, 1768), pp. 39-40, 45-46; Benjamin Hoadley, *A Manual of Religious Liberty,* third ed. (New York: Rivington, 1767).

7. Elisha Williams, *The Essential Rights and Liberties of Protestants* (Boston: S. Kneeland and T. Green, 1744), p. 42. See also John Lathrop, *A Discourse on the Peace* (Boston: Peter Edes, 1784), p. 29; Hugh Fisher, *The Divine Right of Private Judgment, Set in a True Light,* repr. ed. (Boston: n.p., 1790).

Every man has an equal right to follow the dictates of his own conscience in the affairs of religion. Every one is under an indispensable
obligation to search the Scripture for himself . . . and to make the best
use of it he can for his own information in the will of God, the nature
and duties of Christianity. And as every Christian is so bound; so he has
the inalienable right to judge of the sense and meaning of it, and to follow his judgment wherever it leads him; even an equal right with any
rulers be they civil or ecclesiastical.[8]

Every person must be "left alone" to worship God "in the manner and season most agreeable to the Dictates of his own conscience," John Adams
(1735-1826) echoed. For the rights of conscience are "indisputable, unalienable, indefeasible, [and] divine."[9] James Madison wrote more generically: "The Religion then of every man must be left to the conviction and
conscience of every man; and it is the right of every man to exercise it as
these may dictate."[10] The Baptist leader John Leland (1754-1841) echoed
these sentiments:

Every man must give an account of himself to God, and therefore every
man ought to be at liberty to serve God in that way that he can reconcile it to his conscience. . . . It would be sinful for a man to surrender to
man [that] which is to be kept sacred for God. A man's mind should be
always open to conviction, and an honest man will receive that doctrine which appears the best demonstrated; and what is more common
[than] for the best of men to change their minds?[11]

While some eighteenth-century American theologians continued the ancient Christian battle over free will and determinism, and over voluntarism
and predestination, the main architects of the constitutional religion
clauses presumed that faith was to be freely chosen.

8. Williams, *Essential Rights,* pp. 7-8.
9. Adams, *Works,* 3:452-56; and Massachusetts Constitution (1780), pt. I, art. II.
10. James Madison, "Memorial and Remonstrance against Religious Assessments"
(1785), para. 1, in Madison, *Papers,* 8:298.
11. See esp. John Leland, "The Rights of Conscience Inalienable (1791)," in *Political Sermons of the American Founding Era, 1730-1805,* ed. Ellis Sandoz (Indianapolis:
Liberty Fund, 1991), pp. 1079-1099, at 1085; see also Israel Evans, "A Sermon Delivered
at Concord, Before the Hon. General Court of the State of New Hampshire at the Annual
Election (1791)," in *Political Sermons,* ed. Sandoz, pp. 1057-1078, at 1063ff.

Second, and closely related, liberty of conscience *prohibited* religiously based *discrimination* against individuals. Persons could not be penalized for the religious choices they made nor swayed to make certain choices because of the civil advantages attached to them. Liberty of conscience, Yale President Ezra Stiles (1727-1795) opined, permits "no bloody tribunals, no cardinal inquisitors-general, to bend the human mind, forcibly to control the understanding, and put out the light of reason, the candle of the Lord in man."[12] Liberty of conscience also prohibits more subtle forms of discrimination, prejudice, and cajolery by state, Church, or even other citizens. "[N]o part of the community shall be permitted to perplex or harass the other for any supposed heresy," wrote a Massachusetts pamphleteer. "[E]ach individual shall be allowed to have and enjoy, profess and maintain his own system of religion."[13]

Third, in the view of some founders, liberty of conscience guaranteed "a freedom and *exemption* from human impositions, and legal restraints, in matters of religion and conscience."[14] Persons of faith were to be "exempt from all those penal, sanguinary laws, that generate vice instead of virtue."[15] Such laws not only included the onerous criminal rules that traditionally encumbered and discriminated against religious nonconformists, and led to fines, whippings, banishments, and occasional executions of dissenting colonists. They also included more facially benign laws that worked injustice to certain religious believers: conscription laws that required religious pacifists to participate in the military, oath-swearing laws that ran afoul of the religious scruples of certain believers, tithing and taxing laws that forced believers to support Churches, religious schools, and other causes that they found religiously otiose, if not odious.[16] Liberty of conscience required that persons be exempt or immune from civil duties and restrictions that they could not, in good conscience,

---

12. Ezra Stiles, *The United States Elevated to Glory and Honor* (New Haven: Thomas and Samuel Green, 1783), p. 56.

13. "Worcestriensis, Number IV (1776)," in *American Political Writing during the Founding Era, 1760-1805,* ed. Charles S. Hynemann and Donald S. Lutz, 2 vols. (Indianapolis: Liberty Fund, 1983), 1:449-50.

14. Mellen, *The Great and Happy Doctrine of Liberty,* p. 17 (emphasis added).

15. Mellen, *The Great and Happy Doctrine of Liberty,* p. 20.

16. See, e.g., Jonathan Parsons, *Freedom from Civil and Ecclesiastical Slavery* (Newburyport, R.I.: I. Thomas and H. W. Tinges, 1774); Isaac Backus, *Appeal to the Public for Religious Liberty against the Oppressions of the Present Day* (Boston: Benjamin Edes and Sons, 1773).

accept or obey.[17] As Evangelical preacher Henry Cumings (1739-1823) put it, "Liberty of conscience requires not [only] that persons are . . . exempt from hierarchical tyranny and domination, from the usurped authority of pope and prelates, and from every species of persecution on account of religion." It also requires that they "stand on equal ground, and behaving as good members of society, may equally enjoy their religious opinions, and without molestation, or being exposed to fines or forfeitures, or any other temporal disadvantages."[18]

It was commonly assumed in the eighteenth century that the laws of conscientious magistrates would not often tread on the religious scruples of their subjects. George Washington (1732-1799) put it thus in a letter to a group of Quakers: "In my opinion the conscientious scruples of all men should be treated with great delicacy and tenderness: and it is my wish and desire, that the laws may always be as extensively accommodated to them, as a due regard for the protection and essential interests of the nation may justify and permit."[19] It was also commonly understood that the growing pluralization of American religious life might make such inherent accommodation of all religions increasingly difficult. Where general laws and policies did intrude on the religious scruples of an individual or group, liberty of conscience demanded protection of religious minorities through exemptions from such laws and policies. Whether such exemptions should be accorded by the legislature or by the judiciary and whether they were per se a constitutional right or simply a rule of equity — the principal bones of contention among a raft of recent commentators — the eighteenth-century sources do not dispositively say.

All the early state constitutions included a guarantee of liberty of conscience for all.[20] The Delaware Constitution had typical language:

17. Henry Cumings, *A Sermon Preached at Billerica* (Boston: Thomas Fleet, Jun. Cornhill, 1797), pp. 12-13.

18. Cumings, *A Sermon Preached at Billerica*, pp. 12-13.

19. Letter to the Religious Society Called Quakers, October, 1789, in *The Writings of George Washington from the Original Manuscript Sources, 1745-1799*, ed. J. C. Fitzpatrick (Washington, D.C.: Government Printing Office, 1931), 30:416. See similar sentiments in *George Washington on Religious Liberty and Mutual Understanding: Selections from Washington's Letters*, ed. Edward F. Humphrey (Washington, D.C.: n.p., 1932).

20. For good summaries of these state developments, see Chester Antieau et al., *Religion under the State Constitutions* (Brooklyn: Central Book Company, 1965); Thomas J. Curry, *The First Freedoms: Church and State in America to the Passage of the First Amendment* (New York: Oxford University Press, 1986).

That all men have a natural and inalienable right to worship Almighty God according to the dictates of their own consciences and understandings; and that no man ought or of right can be compelled to attend any religious worship or maintain any religious ministry contrary to or against his own free will and consent, and that no authority can or ought to be vested in, or assumed by any power whatever that shall in any case interfere with, or in any manner controul the right of conscience and free exercise of religious worship.[21]

The Pennsylvania Constitution added a protection against religious discrimination: "Nor can any man, who acknowledges the being of a God, be justly deprived or abridged of any civil right as a citizen, on account of his religious sentiments or peculiar mode of religious worship." It also provided an exemption for conscientious objectors: "Nor can any man who is conscientiously scrupulous of bearing arms, be justly compelled thereto, if he will pay such equivalent."[22] The Constitution of New York addressed both state and Church intrusions on conscience, endeavoring "not only to expel civil tyranny, but also to guard against that spiritual oppression and intolerance . . . wherewith the bigotry and ambition of weak and wicked priests have scourged mankind." It thus declared "that the free exercise and enjoyment of religious profession and worship, without discrimination or preference, shall forever hereafter be allowed, within this State, to all mankind."[23] The Constitution of New Jersey provided exemptions from religious taxes, using typical language: "nor shall any person . . . ever be obliged to pay tithes, taxes, or any other rates, for the purpose of building or repairing any other church, . . . or ministry, contrary to what he believes to be right."[24]

Free Exercise of Religion

Liberty of conscience was a guarantee to be left alone to choose from among the plural religions that were equally available to all. Free exercise of religion was the right to act publicly on the choices of conscience once

21. Delaware Declaration of Rights (1776), sec. 2.
22. Pennsylvania Declaration of Rights (1776), II, VIII.
23. Constitution of New York (1777), art. XXXVIII.
24. Constitution of New Jersey (1776), art. XVIII.

made, without intruding on or obstructing the rights of others or the general peace of the community. This organic tie between religious conscience and religious exercise was well known in the Western tradition and was not lost on English and American writers. In 1670, for example, the Quaker leader William Penn (1644-1718) had linked these two guarantees, insisting that religious liberty entails "not only a mere Liberty of the Mind, in believing or disbelieving . . . but [also] the Exercise of ourselves in a visible Way of Worship."[25] In the next century, this organic linkage was commonplace. Religion, Madison wrote, "must be left to the convictions and conscience of every man; and it is the right of man to exercise it as these may dictate."[26] For most eighteenth-century writers, religious belief and religious action went hand in hand, and each deserved legal protection.

Although the founders offered no universal definition of "free exercise," they generally used the phrase to describe the freedom to engage in various forms of public religious action — religious worship, religious speech, religious assembly, religious publication, and religious education, among others. Free exercise of religion also embraced the right of the individual to join with like-minded believers in religious societies, which were free to devise their own modes of worship, articles of faith, standards of discipline, and patterns of ritual, without undue influence or intrusion by the state.[27] The founders did not speak of "religious group rights" or "corporate free exercise rights" as we do today. But they did regularly call for "ecclesiastical liberty," "the equal liberty of one sect . . . with another," and the right "to have the full enjoyment and free exercise of those purely spiritual powers . . . which, being derived only from CHRIST and His Apostles, are to be maintained, independent of every foreign, or other, jurisdiction, so far as may be consistent with the civil rights of society."[28]

---

25. William Penn, "The Great Case of Liberty of Conscience (1670)," in *A Collection of the Works of William Penn*, 2 vols. (London: J. Sowell, 1726), 1:443, 447.

26. Madison, "Memorial and Remonstrance," sec. 1. See also Levi Hart, *Liberty Described and Recommended* (Hartford, Conn.: E. Watson, 1775), pp. 14-15.

27. See, e.g., Williams, *Essential Rights*, pp. 46ff.; Isaac Backus, *Isaac Backus on Church, State, and Calvinism: Pamphlets, 1754-1789*, ed. William G. McLoughlin (Cambridge, Mass.: Belknap, 1968), pp. 348ff.; Parsons, *Freedom from Civil and Ecclesiastical Slavery*, pp. 14-15; Stiles, *The United States Elevated*, pp. 55ff.; Amos Adams, *Religious Liberty*, pp. 38-46.

28. See, respectively, Hart, *Liberty Described and Recommended*, p. 14; Backus,

Virtually all the early state constitutions guaranteed "free exercise" rights — adding the familiar caveat that such exercise must not violate the public peace or the private rights of others. Most states limited their guarantee to "the free exercise of religious worship" or the "free exercise of religious profession" — thereby leaving the protection of other non-cultic forms of religious expression and action to other constitutional guarantees, if any. A few states provided more generic free exercise guarantees. The Virginia Declaration of Rights, for example, guaranteed "the free exercise of religion, according to the dictates of conscience"[29] — thereby expanding free exercise protection to cultic and non-cultic religious expression and action, provided these were mandated by conscience. The Constitution of Georgia provided even more flatly: "All persons whatever shall have the free exercise of their religion; provided it be not repugnant to the peace and safety of the State."[30]

Religious Pluralism

The founders regarded religious "multiplicity," "diversity," or "plurality" to be an equally essential principle of religious rights. Two kinds of pluralism were distinguished.

Evangelical and Enlightenment writers stressed the protection of *confessional pluralism* — the maintenance and accommodation of a plurality of forms of religious expression and organization in the community. Evangelical writers advanced a theological argument for this principle, emphasizing that it was for God, not the state, to decide which forms of religion should flourish and which should fade. "God always claimed it as his sole prerogative to determine by his own laws what his worship shall be, who shall minister in it, and how they shall be supported," Baptist leader Isaac Backus (1724-1806) wrote.[31] "God's truth is great, and in the end He will

Isaac Backus on Church, State, and Calvinism, pp. 348-49; "A Declaration of Certain Fundamental Rights and Liberties of the Protestant Episcopal Church in Maryland," quoted in Anson P. Stokes, *Church and States in the United States,* 3 vols. (New York: Harper, 1950), 1:741.

29. Virginia Declaration of Rights (1776), sec. 16.

30. Constitution of Georgia (1777), art. LVI.

31. Backus, *Isaac Backus on Church, State, and Calvinism*, p. 317. See also, e.g., *The Freeman's Remonstrance against an Ecclesiastical Establishment* (Boston: T. Green, 1777), p. 13.

allow it to prevail."[32] Confessional pluralism served to respect and reflect this divine prerogative.

Enlightenment writers advanced a rational and utilitarian argument for this same principle of confessional pluralism. "Difference of opinion is advantageous in religion," Thomas Jefferson (1743-1826) wrote. "The several sects perform the office of a *Censor morum* over each other. Is uniformity attainable? Millions of innocent men, women, and children, since the introduction of Christianity, have been burnt, tortured, fined, imprisoned; yet we have not advanced one inch towards uniformity. . . . Reason and persuasion are the only practicable instruments."[33] When Jefferson seemed to be wandering from these early sentiments, John Adams wrote to him: "Checks and balances, Jefferson," in the political as well as the religious sphere, "are our only Security, for the progress of Mind, as well as the Security of Body. Every Species of these Christians would persecute Deists, as [much] as either Sect would persecute another, if it had unchecked and unballanced Power. Nay, the Deists would persecute Christians, and Atheists would persecute Deists, with as unrelenting Cruelty, as any Christians would persecute them or one another. Know thyself, Human nature!"[34] Madison wrote similarly that "freedom arises from the multiplicity of sects, which pervades America, and which is the best and only security for religious liberty in any society. For where there is such a variety of sects, there cannot be a majority of any one sect to oppress and persecute the rest."[35] Other writers added that the maintenance of multiple faiths is the best protection of the core guarantee of liberty of conscience.[36]

---

32. Isaac Backus, *Truth Is Great and Will Prevail* (Boston: Philip Freeman, 1781). For comparable sentiments, see John R. Bolles, *A Brief Account of Persecutions, in Boston and Connecticut Governments* (New London, Conn.: n.p., 1758), pp. 47, 59. See also George Washington, who expressed comparable sentiments to Roman Catholics, Quakers, Jews, and other religious minorities in the young republic. Humphrey, ed., *George Washington on Religious Liberty.*

33. In *The Complete Jefferson, Containing His Major Writings,* ed. Saul K. Padover (Freeport, N.Y.: Duell, Sloan, and Pearce, 1943), pp. 673-76. See also Thomas Paine, *Common Sense* (1776), in *Common Sense and the Crisis* (Garden City, N.J.: Doubleday, 1960), p. 50.

34. John Adams, Letter to Thomas Jefferson, June 25, 1813, in *The Adams-Jefferson Letters,* ed. Lester J. Cappon (Chapel Hill, N.C.: University of North Carolina Press, 1959), p. 334.

35. *Debates,* 3:313. See further Chapter 5 herein.

36. See Williams, *Essential Rights,* pp. 40-42; Stiles, *The United States Elevated,* pp. 55ff.; *Debates,* 3:207-8; Max Farrand, ed., *The Records of the Federal Convention of 1787* (New Haven: Yale University Press, 1911), 3:310.

Congregationalist and civic republican writers, while endorsing confessional pluralism with comparable arguments, also urged the protection of *social pluralism* — the maintenance and accommodation of a plurality of associations to foster and to protect religion. Churches and synagogues were not the only "religious societies" that deserved constitutional protection. Families, schools, charities, and various learned and civic societies were equally vital bastions of religion and equally deserving of the special protections of religious liberty. These diverse social institutions had several redeeming qualities. They provided multiple forums for religious expressions and actions, important bulwarks against state encroachment on natural liberties, particularly religious liberties, and vital sources of theology, morality, charity, and discipline in the state and broader community.[37] John Adams put it thus:

> My opinion of the duties of religion and morality comprehends a very extensive connection with society at large. . . . The benevolence, charity, capacity and industry which, exerted in private life, would make a family, a parish or a town happy, employed upon a larger scale, in support of the great principles of virtue and freedom of political regulations might secure whole nations and generations from misery, want and contempt.[38]

The Scotch Presbyterian Benjamin Rush (1746-1813) concurred:

> Religion is best supported under the patronage of particular societies. . . . Religion could not long be maintained in the world without [these] forms and the distinctions of sects. The weaknesses of human nature require them. The distinction of sects is as necessary to the perfection and government of the whole as regiments and brigades are in an army.[39]

Religious pluralism was thus not just a sociological fact for many of the founders. It was also an essential condition for the guarantee of reli-

37. W. C. McWilliams, *The Idea of Fraternity in America* (Berkeley: University of California Press, 1973), pp. 112-23; Clinton Rossiter, *The Political Thought of the American Revolution* (New York: Harcourt, Brace and World, 1963), p. 204.

38. Letter from John Adams to Abigail Adams (October 29, 1775), quoted in *The Changing Political Thought of John Adams*, by John R. Howe Jr. (Princeton, N.J.: Princeton University Press, 1966), pp. 156-57 (capitalization modernized).

39. Letter from Benjamin Rush to John Armstrong (March 19, 1793), in *The Founders' Constitution*, ed. Philip B. Kurland and Ralph S. Lerner, 5 vols. (Chicago: University of Chicago Press, 1987), 5:78 [hereafter *The Founders' Constitution*].

gious rights. This was a species and application of Madison's argument in the *Federalist Papers* about the virtues of republican pluralism. In a federalist republic, Madison had argued famously in Federalist Paper No. 10:

> The influence of factious leaders may kindle a flame within their particular States but will be unable to spread a general conflagration through the other States. A religious sect may degenerate into a political faction in a part of the Confederacy; but the variety of sects dispersed over the entire face of it must secure the national councils against any danger from that source.[40]

Madison summarized this general point crisply in Federalist Paper No. 51: "In a free government, the security for civil rights must be the same as that for religious rights; it consists in the one case in the multiplicity of interests, and in the other in the multiplicity of sects."[41]

Religious Equality

The efficacy of a religious rights regime also depended on a guarantee of equality of all peaceable religions before the law. For the state to single out one pious person or one form of faith for either preferential benefits or discriminatory burdens would skew the choice of conscience, encumber the exercise of religion, and upset the natural plurality of faiths. Many of the founders therefore insisted on the principle of a presumptive equality of all peaceable religions before the law.

James Madison captured well the prevailing sentiment: "A just Government . . . will be best supported by protecting every Citizen in the enjoyment of his religion, with the same equal hand which protects his person and property; by neither invading the equal rights of any sect, nor suffering any sect to invade those of another."[42] John Adams concurred: "[A]ll men of all religions consistent with morals and property [must] enjoy equal liberty, . . . security of property . . . and an equal chance for honors and power."[43] Isaac Backus

---

40. Clinton Rossiter, ed., *The Federalist Papers: Alexander Hamilton, James Madison, John Jay* (New York: New American Library, 1961), p. 84.

41. Rossiter, ed., *The Federalist Papers*, p. 324.

42. Madison, "Memorial and Remonstrance," secs. 4, 8.

43. Adams, *Works*, 8:232; see further Frank Donovan, ed., *The John Adams Papers* (New York: Dodd Mead, 1965), p. 181; *The Freeman's Remonstrance*, pp. 5, 10-13.

wrote similarly that religious liberty requires that "each person and each [religious] society are equally protected from being injured from others, all enjoying equal liberty to attend the worship which they believe is right."[44]

The founders' argument for religious equality became particularly pointed in their debates over religious test oaths as a condition for holding federal political office and positions of public trust. Oaths were commonly accepted in the early republic as "one of the principal instruments of government." They induce "the fear and reverence of God, and the terrors of eternity," one Puritan preacher put it, and thus impose "the most powerful restraints upon the minds of men."[45] Following colonial custom, eleven of the original thirteen states prescribed such oaths. These ranged in specificity from a general affirmation of belief in God or in (Protestant) Christianity to the Trinitarian confession required by Delaware: "I, A. B., do profess faith in God the Father, and in Jesus Christ His only Son, and in the Holy Ghost, one God, blessed for evermore; and I do acknowledge the holy scriptures of the Old and New Testament to be given by divine inspiration."[46] A number of Quakers, Baptists, and Moravians, before and after the American Revolution, had condemned such oaths as a violation of the liberty of conscience and as an "invading of the essential prerogatives of our Lord Jesus Christ."[47] The few Jewish voices of the day protested oaths as a violation of their liberty of conscience and civil rights.[48] In response, most colonies and states exempted Quakers (and sometimes others with conscientious objections) from the oaths in deference to the principle of liberty of conscience.

The addition of an argument from religious equality proved particularly persuasive in outlawing religious test oaths. The argument first came to

44. Backus, *Isaac Backus on Church, State, and Calvinism,* p. 333.

45. Phillips Payson, "Election Sermon of 1778," in *American Political Writing,* pp. 523, 529. A decade later, Payson apparently changed his mind, arguing in the Massachusetts Ratifying Convention that such religious tests were "attempts to erect human tribunals for the consciences of men, impious encroachments upon the prerogatives of God." *Debates,* 2:120.

46. Delaware Constitution (1776), art. XXII. This oath was outlawed by a 1792 amendment to the Delaware Constitution. See others in Daniel L. Dreisbach, "The Constitution's Forgotten Religion Clause: Reflections on the Article VI Religious Test Ban," *Journal of Church and State* 38 (1996): 263-95, at 264-69.

47. *Debates,* 2:148; *The Founders' Constitution,* 4:633ff.

48. See "Petition of the Philadelphia Synagogue to the Council of Censors of Philadelphia (December 23, 1783)," in *The Founders' Constitution,* 4:635; and "Jonas Phillips to the President and Members of the Convention (September 7, 1789)," in *Records of the Federal Convention,* ed. Farrand, 3:78-79.

prominence in the federal constitutional convention of 1787 and in the ratification debates that followed. Article VI of the Constitution provided that "no religious Test shall ever be required as a Qualification to any office or public Trust under the United States." James Iredell (1751-1799) of North Carolina offered a typical defense of this provision: "This article is calculated to secure universal religious liberty, by putting all sects on a level."[49] Fellow Carolinian Richard Spaight (1758-1802) elaborated the argument: "No sect is preferred to another. Every man has the right to worship the Supreme Being in the manner that he thinks proper. No test is required. All men of equal capacity and integrity are equally eligible to offices."[50]

Such an argument for equality proved persuasive enough to garner state ratification of Article VI of the Constitution in 1789. It also helped to outlaw some of the state religious test oaths: Georgia (1789), Delaware (1792), and Vermont (1793) dropped their test oaths. Pennsylvania (1790) extended its law to include Jews. The new state constitutions of Kentucky (1792) and Tennessee (1796) included no religious test oaths, although they still required that political officials be theists, if not Christians.[51]

Most founders extended the principle of equality before the law to all peaceable religions — though sometimes they only grudgingly conceded its application to Jews and Muslims. A few founders pressed the principle further, arguing for the equality of religions and nonreligions — particularly on issues of test oaths and religious taxes. Luther Martin (1744-1826) of Maryland grumbled about this solicitude for the nonreligious shown during the 1787 constitutional convention debates over religious test oaths:

> The part of the system which provides, that no religious test shall ever be required as a qualification to any office or public trust under the United States, was adopted by a great majority of the convention, and without much debate; however, there were some members so unfashionable as to think, that a belief of the existence of a Deity, and of a state of future rewards and punishments would be some security for the good conduct of our rulers, and that, in a Christian country, it would be *at least decent to hold out some distinction between the professors of Christianity and downright infidelity or paganism*.[52]

---

49. *Records of the Federal Convention*, ed. Farrand, 3:204; see also 3:207.
50. *Debates*, 4:208.
51. Antieau et al., *Religion under the State Constitutions*, pp. 101-7.
52. *Records of the Federal Convention*, ed. Farrand, 3:227 (italics revised).

Similarly, James Madison, in protesting the proposed state tax scheme to support religious teachers in Virginia, wrote:

> Above all are they to be considered as retaining an "equal title to the free exercise of religion according to the dictates of conscience." While we assert for ourselves a freedom to embrace, to profess and to observe the religion which we believe to be of divine origin, *we cannot deny an equal freedom to those whose minds have not yet yielded to the evidence which has convinced us.* If this freedom be abused, it is an offence against God, not against man.[53]

The founders' principal concern, however, concerned equality among religions, not equality between religion and nonreligion. Benjamin Huntington indicated during the House debate over the First Amendment that "he hoped the amendment would be made in such a way to secure the rights of conscience, and a free exercise of the rights of religion *but not to patronize those who professed no religion at all.*"[54] Likewise, in the House debates about including conscientious objection to military service among the rights of conscience, Representative Scott stated firmly, without rejoinder: "There are many sects I know, who are religiously scrupulous in this respect; I do not mean to deprive them of any indulgence.... *[M]y design is to guard against those who are of no religion.*"[55]

This principle of equality of all peaceable religious persons and bodies before the law found its way into a number of early state constitutions. New Jersey insisted that "there shall be no establishment of any one religious sect in ... preference to another."[56] Delaware guaranteed Christians "equal rights and privileges" — a guarantee soon extended to all religions.[57] Maryland insisted that Christians "are equally entitled to protection in their religious liberty."[58] Virginia guaranteed that "all men are equally entitled to the free exercise of religion."[59] New York guaranteed all persons "free exercise and enjoyment of religious profession and worship, without discrimination or preference."[60] Even

---

53. Madison, "Memorial and Remonstrance," sec. 4 (emphasis added).
54. *Annals*, 1:758 (emphasis added).
55. *Annals*, 1:796 (emphasis added).
56. Constitution of New Jersey (1776), art. XIX.
57. Delaware Declaration of Rights (1776), sec. 3.
58. Maryland Declaration of Rights (1776), sec. 33.
59. Virginia Declaration of Rights (1776), art. XVI.
60. Constitution of New York (1777), art. XXXVIII.

Massachusetts, which maintained what John Adams called "a mild and equitable establishment of religion,"[61] nonetheless guaranteed that "all religious sects and denominations, demeaning themselves peaceably, and as good citizens of the commonwealth, shall be equally under the protection of the law; and no subordination of one sect or denomination to another shall ever be established by law."[62]

Separation of Church and State

"Separation of Church and state" was a familiar Western principle, as we shall detail in the next chapter. The most influential formulations in the founding era were Protestant in inspiration. Building on biblical and traditional formulations, early modern European Protestants had used these biblical passages to press for all manner of separations — between Church and state, religion and politics, faith and government, cleric and magistrate, ecclesiastical power and political power, spiritual law and temporal law, Church counsel and state coercion, and more. And, in a time where walled towns and cities were commonplace, they often drew on the biblical images of walls of separation to illustrate what distinctions were appropriate and inappropriate. The German reformer Martin Luther (1483-1546), for example, had spoken of "a paper wall . . . between the spiritual estate [and] the temporal estate" and built thereon his intricate theory of the two kingdoms.[63] The Genevan Reformer John Calvin (1509-1564) repeatedly invoked St. Paul's image of a "wall of separation" to argue that the "political kingdom" and "spiritual kingdom" must always be "considered separately." For there is "a great difference between the ecclesiastical and civil power," and it would be "unwise to mingle these two which have a completely different nature."[64] Such early Protestant views were repeated in a number of Puritan writings and laws in both England and New England.[65] The early Anabaptist leader Menno Simons (1496-1561) had called for a "wall of separation" between the redeemed realm of religion and the fallen realm of the world, and urged Christians to remain faithful within the religious realm. Such views recurred

---

61. Adams, *Works*, 2:399.

62. Constitution of Massachusetts (1780), part I, art. III, as amended by art. XI.

63. LP, pp. 87-117.

64. Institutes (1559), bk. 3, chap. 19.15; bk. 4, chap. 11.3; bk. 4, chap. 20.1-2; CO 48:277; 39:352.

65. See Chapter 3 herein.

in Roger Williams's (1604-1680) image of "a wall of separation between the garden of the Church and the wilderness of the world" and were repeated by later Evangelical writers in the eighteenth century, notably Isaac Backus.[66]

Such quotes, from both theological and political sources, reflect the central understanding of the principle of separation inherited by the eighteenth-century American founders: The offices and officers of the Churches and states must break their traditional alliances.[67] "Upon no plan, no system," wrote the Jeffersonian Tunis Wortman (d. 1822), "can they become united, without endangering the purity and usefulness of both — the church will corrupt the state, and the state pollute the church."[68] Separation, in this sense, benefited both the Church and the state. On the one hand, it guaranteed purity and liberty of Churches. On the other hand, it guaranteed "political and social stability" — the protection of individual rights and social cohesion. James Madison put this well in discussing Church and state:

> Their jurisdiction is both derivative and limited. It is limited with regard to the co-ordinate departments; more necessarily is it limited with regard to the constituents. The preservation of a free government requires not merely that the metes and bounds which separate each department of power be invariably maintained; but more especially that neither of them be suffered to overleap the great barrier which defends the rights of the people.[69]

Disestablishment of Religion

The term "establishment of religion" was an ambiguous phrase — in the eighteenth century, as much as today. In the dictionaries and common parlance of the eighteenth century, to "establish" meant "to settle firmly," "to fix unalterably," "to settle in any privilege or possession," "to make firm," "to ratify," "to ordain," "to enact," "to set up," to "build firmly."[70] Such was the

---

66. Roger Williams, Letter to John Cotton (1643), in *The Complete Writings of Roger Williams,* 7 vols. (New York: Russell and Russell, 1963), 1:392.

67. For other meanings, see Chapter 7 herein.

68. Tunis Wortman, *A Solemn Address to Christians and Patriots* (1800), in *Political Sermons,* ed. Sandoz, p. 1488.

69. Madison, "Memorial and Remonstrance," sec. 2.

70. See entries under "establish" and "establishment" in John Andrews, *A Complete Dictionary of the English Language,* fourth ed. (Philadelphia: William Young, 1789);

basic meaning of the term, for example, when used in the 1787 Constitution — "We the people of the United States, in order to form a more perfect Union, to *establish* justice . . . do ordain and *establish* this Constitution" (preamble); Congress shall have power "[t]o *establish* an uniform rule of naturalization" and "[t]o *establish* post offices" (art. I.8); Governmental offices "shall be *established* by law" (art. II.2); Congress may "ordain and *establish* . . . inferior courts" (art. III.1); the ratification of nine states "shall be sufficient for the *establishment* of this Constitution" (art. VI).[71]

Following this basic sense of the term, the founders understood the *establishment* of religion to mean the actions of government to "settle," "fix," "define," "ordain," "enact," or "set up" the religion of the community — its religious doctrines and liturgies, its religious texts and traditions, its clergy and property. The most notorious example of this, to their minds, was the establishment by law of Anglicanism.[72] English ecclesiastical law formally required use of the Authorized (King James) Version of the Bible and of the liturgies, rites, prayers, and lectionaries of the *Book of Common Prayer.* It demanded subscription to the Thirty-Nine Articles of Faith and the swearing of loyalty oaths to the Church, Crown, and Commonwealth of England. When such ecclesiastical laws were rigorously applied — as they were in England in the early Stuart period of the 1610s to 1630s, and again in the Restoration of the 1660s to 1670s, and intermittently in the American colonies — they led to all manner of state controls of the internal affairs of the established Church, and all manner of state repression and coercion of religious dissenters.

Those founders who called for the disestablishment of religion sought to outlaw at least this traditional form of religious establishment and so protect the foregoing first principles of religious liberty.

Disestablishment of religion thus served to protect the principle of liberty of conscience and free exercise of religion by foreclosing government from coercively prescribing mandatory forms of religious belief, doctrine, and practice. As both the Delaware and Pennsylvania constitutions put it, "[N]o authority can or ought to be vested in, or assumed by any

---

John Ash, *The New and Complete Dictionary of the English Language* (London: E. and C. Dilly, 1775); Samuel Johnson, *A Dictionary of the English Language,* fourth ed. (London: W. Strahan, 1773); William Perry, *The Royal Standard English Dictionary,* first Am. ed. (Worcester: n.p., 1788); Thomas Sheridan, *A Complete Dictionary of the English Language,* fifth ed. (Philadelphia: William Young, 1789).

71. See T. Jeremy Gunn, *A Standard for Repair: The Establishment Clause, Equality, and Natural Rights* (New York: Garland, 1992), pp. 46-47, 71-73.

72. See further Introduction and Chapter 6 herein.

power whatever, that shall in any case interfere with, or in any manner control, the right of conscience in the free exercise of religious worship."[73]

Disestablishment of religion further protected the principles of religious equality and religious pluralism by preventing government from singling out certain religious beliefs and bodies for preferential treatment. This concept of disestablishment came through repeatedly in both state and federal debates. In the Virginia Ratification Convention, for example, both Madison and Edmund Randolph (1753-1813) stressed that religious pluralism would "prevent the establishment of any one sect in prejudice, to the rest, and will forever oppose all attempts to infringe religious liberty."[74] South Carolina conventioneer Francis Cummins (1752-1832) likewise stated that it was "his duty and honor to oppose the ideas of religious establishments; or of states giving preference to any religious denomination."[75] The New Jersey Constitution provided "there shall be no establishment of any one religious sect . . . in preference to another."[76] Both the New York and the Rhode Island Ratifying Conventions suggested amendments to the Constitution that "no religious sect or society ought to be favored or established by law in preference to others."[77]

Disestablishment of religion also served to protect the principle of separation of Church and state. It prohibited government, as Jefferson put it, "from intermeddling with religious institutions, their doctrines, discipline, or exercises" and from "the power of effecting any uniformity of time or matter among them. Fasting & prayer are religious exercises. The enjoining them is an act of discipline. Every religious society has a right to determine for itself the times for these exercises, & the objects proper for them, according to their own peculiar tenets."[78] To allow such governmental intermeddling in the affairs of religious bodies would inflate the competence of government. As Madison wrote, it "implies either that the Civil

73. Delaware Declaration of Rights (1776), sec. 3; Pennsylvania Declaration of Rights (1776), II.

74. *Debates*, 3:208, 313, 431.

75. Quoted in Chester J. Antieau et al., *Freedom from Federal Establishment: Formation and Early History of the First Amendment Religion Clauses* (Milwaukee, Wis.: Bruce, 1964), p. 106. Cummins went on to say, "It would be impolite for a state to give preference to one religious order over any others in matters of state, and to dictate and prescribe in points of religion, in which men . . . from different modes of education and circumstances of one kind or other, will and must split in opinion" (p. 106).

76. Art. XIX.

77. *Debates*, 1:328, 334.

78. In *The Founders' Constitution*, 5:98-99.

Magistrate is a competent judge of religious truth; or that he may employ religion as an engine of civil policy. The first is an arrogant pretension falsified by the contradictory opinions of rulers in all ages, and throughout the world, the second an unhallowed perversion of the means of salvation."[79] Governmental interference in religious affairs also compromises the pacific ideals of most religions. Thomas Paine (1737-1809), who is usually branded as a religious skeptic, put this well:

> All religions are in their nature mild and benign, and united with principles of morality. They could not have made proselytes at first, by professing anything that was vicious, cruel, persecuting or immoral. . . . Persecution is not an original feature in any religion; but it is always the strongly marked feature of all law-religions, or religions established by law. Take away the law-establishment, and every religion reassumes its original benignity.[80]

The question that remained controversial — in the eighteenth century as much as today — was whether more gentle and generic forms of governmental support for religion could be countenanced. Did disestablishment of religion prohibit governmental support for religion altogether, or did it simply require that such governmental support be distributed nonpreferentially among religions?

It takes a bit of historical imagination to appreciate this question in eighteenth-century terms. In eighteenth-century America, government typically patronized religion in a variety of ways. Officials donated land and personalty for the building of Churches, religious schools, and charities. They collected taxes and tithes to support ministers and missionaries. They exempted Church property from taxation. They incorporated religious bodies. They outlawed blasphemy and sacrilege, unnecessary labor on the Sabbath and on religious holidays. They administered religious test oaths. They made regular political use of the Bible, of religious imagery, of the services and facilities of religious institutions.

Historically, such forms of state patronage of religion had been reserved to the established Church alone. All other faiths, if tolerated at all, were left to depend on their own resources. In the course of the eighteenth century, the growth of religious freedom often entailed the gradual extension of these

---

79. Madison, "Memorial and Remonstrance," sec. 5.
80. Thomas Paine, in *The Founders' Constitution,* 5:95-96.

forms of state privilege and patronage to other faiths. Often this was done in a piecemeal fashion: benefit by benefit, congregation by congregation, county by county. By the later eighteenth century, the hard constitutional questions became this: Should state patronage for religion end altogether? Or should state patronage be extended to all religions nonpreferentially, rather than granted only in this piecemeal fashion? Given the overwhelmingly Christian, indeed Protestant, character of the new nation, a policy of nonpreferential governmental support for virtually all religions could be quite realistically envisioned — particularly if some accommodation were made for Jewish sabbatarian beliefs and Quaker aversions to religious oaths and military service. (No founder seriously thought of having to accommodate the African religions of the slaves or the traditional religions of the Native Americans.)

The question of whether disestablishment of religion outlaws all governmental support for religion or only preferential governmental support for some religions was not resolved in the eighteenth century. The founders were divided on the question. A number of Evangelical and Enlightenment writers viewed the principle of disestablishment as a firm bar on state support, particularly financial support, of religious beliefs, believers, and bodies.[81] James Madison, for example, wrote late in his life that "Every new & successful example . . . of a perfect separation between ecclesiastical and civil matters, is of importance. And I have no doubt that every new example, will succeed, as every past one has done, in shewing that religion & Govt. will both exist in greater purity, the less they are mixed together."[82] Similar sentiments can be found in contemporaneous Baptist tracts, particularly those of Isaac Backus and John Leland.[83] Puritan and Civic Republican writers often viewed the principle of separation of Church and state only as a prohibition against direct financial support for the religious worship or exercise of one particular religious group. General governmen-

81. See Leo Pfeffer, *Church, State, and Freedom,* rev. ed. (Boston: Beacon, 1967); Leonard W. Levy, *The Establishment Clause: Religion and the First Amendment* (New York: Oxford University Press, 1986).

82. *The Founders' Constitution,* 5:105-6. See also Madison, "Memorial and Remonstrance," sec. 9: "Distant as it may be in its present form from the Inquisition, it [i.e., the general assessment for religion] differs from it only in degree. The one is the first step, the other the last step in the career of intolerance."

83. See, e.g., *The Freeman's Remonstrance,* pp. 5-11; Isaac Backus, *The Infinite Importance of the Obedience of Faith, and of a Separation from the World, Opened and Demonstrated,* second ed. (Boston: Samuel Hall, 1791), pp. 15-31; Isaac Backus, *Policy As Well As Honesty Forbids the Use of Secular Force in Religious Affairs* (Boston: Draper and Folsom, 1779).

tal support for religion of all sorts — in the form of tax exemptions to religious properties, land grants and tax subsidies to religious schools and charities, tax appropriations for missionaries and military chaplains, and similar general causes — were considered not only licit but necessary for good governance.

The state constitutions were likewise divided on the question. A number of states explicitly authorized such support in their original constitutions. The Constitution of Maryland (1776) was quite typical. It included strong guarantees of religious liberty that touched each of the principles of religious liberty we have rehearsed. "[A]ll persons, professing the Christian religion, are equally entitled to protection in their religious liberty." This includes freedom from "molestation" "on account of his religious persuasion or profession, or for his religious practice"; "nor ought any person to be compelled to frequent or maintain, or contribute, unless on contract [i.e., by agreement] to maintain any particular place of worship, or any particular ministry." But, the Maryland Constitution continues, without pause, to provide that "the Legislature may, in their discretion, lay a general and equal tax, for the support of the Christian religion; leaving to each individual the power of appointing the payment over of the money, collected from him, to the support of any particular place of worship or minister, or for the benefit of the poor of his own denomination, or the poor in general of any particular county."[84] Similar provisions were included in the original constitutions of Massachusetts, New Hampshire, and Connecticut.[85] The other original state constitutions simply repeated the general principles of religious liberty, without touching the issue of whether government could support religion(s).

Drafts of the First Amendment Religion Clauses

It is in the context of this plurality of opinions and panoply of principles of religious rights that the First Amendment religion clauses should, in my view, be understood. Many of the representatives and senators gathered in the First Session of Congress of 1789 had participated in the formation of

84. Declaration of Rights, XXXIII. This was outlawed by amendment, art. XIII (1810). See F. Thorpe, ed., *The Federal and State Constitutions, Colonial Charters, and Other Organic Laws,* 7 vols. (Washington: Government Printing Office, 1909), 3:1189, 1705.

85. See my "A Most Mild and Equitable Establishment of Religion: John Adams and the Massachusetts Experiment," *Journal of Church and State* 41 (1999): 213.

state constitutional laws of religious rights. A good number of them had also written detailed pamphlets, sermons, and letters on the subject. Even those uninitiated members of this First Congress could take instruction on the meaning of religious rights from the four drafts of the religion clauses that were submitted by the state ratification conventions.

The states sent in four proposed drafts of the religion clauses for the First Congress to consider:[86]

1. *"Congress shall make no laws touching religion, or to infringe the rights of conscience."* New Hampshire Proposal, June 21, 1788.

2. *"That religion, or the duty which we owe to our creator, and the manner of discharging it, can be directed only by reason and conviction, not by force or violence, and therefore all men have an equal, natural and unalienable right to the free exercise of religion according to the dictates of conscience, and that no particular religious sect or society ought to be favored or established by law in preference to others."* Virginia Proposal, June 26, 1788.

3. *"That the people have an equal, natural, and unalienable right freely and peaceably to exercise their religion, according to the dictates of conscience; and that no religious sect or society ought to be favored or established by law in preference to others."* New York Proposal, July 26, 1788.

4. *"That any person religiously scrupulous of bearing arms ought to be exempted, upon payment of an equivalent to employ another to bear arms in his stead. That religion, or the duty which we owe to our Creator, and the manner of discharging it, can be directed only by reason and conviction, not by force or violence; and therefore all men have an equal, natural, and unalienable right to the free exercise of religion according to the dictates of conscience, and that no particular religious sect or society ought to be favored or established by law in preference to others."* North Carolina Proposal, August 1, 1788; Repeated by Rhode Island, June 16, 1790.

Ten drafts of the religion clauses were ultimately debated in the House in the summer of 1789.[87] They read thus in the order that they were proposed and debated:

5. *"The civil rights of none shall be abridged on account of religious belief or worship, nor shall any national religion be established, nor shall the full and equal rights of conscience be in any manner, or any pretext infringed."* Draft proposed to the House by James Madison, June 8, 1789.

---

86. These are documented in detail in RCE, chap. 4 and Appendix 3.

87. The full record of the House debates, and the *Journal* of the Senate, is reproduced and discussed in RCE, chap. 4.

6. *"No state shall violate the equal rights of conscience, or the freedom of the press, or the trial by jury in criminal cases."* Draft proposed to House by James Madison, June 8, 1789.

7. *"[N]o religion shall be established by law, nor shall the equal rights of conscience be infringed."* Draft proposed to House by Committee of Eleven, July 28, 1789.

8. *"[N]o person religiously scrupulous shall be compelled to bear arms."* Draft proposed to House by Committee of Eleven, July 28, 1789.

9. *"[N]o State shall infringe the equal rights of conscience, nor the freedom of speech or of the press, nor of the right of trial by jury in criminal cases."* Draft proposed to House by Committee of Eleven, July 28, 1789.

10. *"Congress shall make no laws touching religion, or infringing the rights of conscience."* Draft proposed by Charles Livermore on August 15, 1789; passed by the House.

11. *"[T]he equal rights of conscience, the freedom of speech or of the press, and the right of trial by jury in criminal cases, shall not be infringed by any State."* Draft proposed by Charles Livermore on August 17, 1789; passed by the House.

12. *"Congress shall make no law establishing religion, or to prevent the free exercise thereof, or to infringe the rights of conscience."* Revised Draft proposed by Fisher Ames on August 20, 1789; passed by the House.

13. *"No person religiously scrupulous shall be compelled to bear arms in person."* Revised Draft passed by the House, August 20, 1789.

14. *"Congress shall make no law establishing religion, or prohibiting the free exercise thereof, nor shall the rights of conscience be infringed."* Final Draft proposed by the Style Committee, passed by the House, and sent to the Senate, August 25, 1789.[88]

Five more drafts of the religion clauses were considered in the Senate:

15. *"Congress shall make no law establishing One Religious Sect or Society in preference to others, nor shall the rights of conscience be infringed."* Draft proposed and defeated in the Senate, September 3, 1789.

16. *"Congress shall not make any law, infringing the rights of conscience, or establishing any Religious Sect or Society."* Draft proposed and defeated in the Senate, September 3, 1789.

17. *"Congress shall make no law establishing any particular denomination of religion in preference to another, or prohibiting the free exercise thereof,*

---

88. *Annals*, 1:451-52, 757-59, 778-89, 783-84, 795-96, 808. The full debate on these drafts is reproduced in RCE, pp. 64-71.

nor shall the rights of conscience be infringed." Draft proposed and defeated in the Senate, September 3, 1789.

18. *"Congress shall make no law establishing religion, or prohibiting the free exercise thereof."* Draft proposed and passed by the Senate, September 3, 1789.

19. *"Congress shall make no law establishing articles of faith or a mode of worship, or prohibiting the free exercise of religion."* Draft proposed and passed by the Senate, and sent to the House, September 9, 1789.[89]

What ultimately passed both Houses was a draft proposed by a joint House-Senate Committee:

20. *"Congress shall make no Law respecting an establishment of Religion, or prohibiting the free exercise thereof."* Proposed on September 24, 1789, and passed by House and Senate on September 25, 1789.[90]

The Original Understandings of the First Amendment

Determining the original understanding of the First Amendment has been the perennial challenge of the American experiment ever since. The final text of the First Amendment has no plain meaning. The congressional record holds no Rosetta stone for easy interpretation. Twenty separate drafts of the religion clauses came under Congress's consideration. The congressional record holds no dispositive argument against any one of the nineteen interim drafts, and few clear clues on why the sixteen words that comprise the final text were chosen.

It is worth pondering the possible original understandings of these sixteen words, based on what survives of the House debates, and what was consistent with the more general opinions on religious rights that prevailed in the later eighteenth century.

"Congress"

The First Amendment's specification of "Congress" underscored the founders' general agreement that the religion clauses were binding not on the states but on the most dangerous branch of the new federal government.

89. *Journal,* 1:116, 117, 129.
90. *Journal,* 1:145, 148; *Annals,* 1:948.

This was the strong sentiment of the 1787 constitutional convention and the state ratification debates. It was repeated in several of the surviving speeches in the House.

The first draft of the religion clauses, submitted by New Hampshire, had specified "Congress" (No. 1). The three other state drafts submitted in the summer of 1788 included general guarantees of religious liberty that could be read to bind both federal and state governments. In his June 8, 1789, consolidated draft, Madison had sought to accommodate both readings — by outlawing a "national" establishment and by prohibiting states from infringing on conscience (Nos. 5, 6). This construction failed, despite Madison's two arguments for it in the August 15 debate. The original New Hampshire focus on "Congress" became the norm.

In his same June 8 draft, Madison had also included generic guarantees of religious liberty without specifying the government entity bound thereby — "the full and equal rights of conscience shall not be infringed" and "the civil rights of none shall be abridged on account of religion" (No. 5). Such provisions, too, died without explanation. By August 20, Massachusetts Representative Fisher Ames's (1758-1808) draft (No. 12) specified Congress alone, and the Senate held to this.

"Shall Make"

The phrase "*shall make* no law" is rather distinctive — written in a future active imperative voice. In eighteenth-century parlance, "shall," as opposed to "will," is an imperative; it is an order, rather than a prediction, about what Congress does in the future. "Shall" is so used fifteen times in the Bill of Rights alone. But why the construction "shall make no law," which is a phrasing unique to the First Amendment? Could it be that Congress could make no new laws on religion, but could confirm laws that had already been made — before the First Amendment was passed, or by the Continental Congress before it?

Such a reading seems fanciful until one notes the exchange in the House, on September 25, 1789, the very day the House approved the final text of the religion clauses. Elias Boudinot (1740-1821) of New Jersey, who chaired the recorded House debates on the religion clauses, announced that "he could not think of letting the session pass over without offering an opportunity to all the citizens of the United States of joining, with one voice, in returning to Almighty God their sincere thanks for the many blessings he had poured down upon them." He then moved that both houses of Congress request the president to set aside a day of "public thanksgiving and prayer, to be observed by acknowledging . . . the many signal favors of Almighty God." Aedanus Burke (1743-1802) of South Carolina thought this too redolent of a military European custom which made "a mere mockery of thanksgiving." Thomas Tucker (1745-1828), also of South Carolina, objected that "it is a business with which Congress ha[s] nothing to do; it is a religious matter, and, as such, is proscribed to us. If a day of thanksgiving must take place, let it be done by the authority of the several States; they know best what reason their constituents have to be pleased with the establishment of the Constitution." Roger Sherman (1721-1793) of Connecticut countered that the tradition of offering such public prayers was "laudable," and, after citing a few biblical precedents for it, declared the practice "worthy of Christian imitation on the present occasion." Boudinot defended his motion on grounds that it was "a measure both prudent and just" and quoted "further precedents from the practice of the late Congress" to drive home his point. The motion passed in the House, and later also in the Senate.[91] President Washington set aside a Thanksgiving Day, and gave a robust proclamation on October 3, 1789. This Thanksgiving Day proclamation tradition, regularized by Abraham Lincoln (1809-1865), has continued virtually uninterrupted ever since.

This was not the only such inherited tradition touching religion that the First Congress confirmed and continued. On April 15, 1789, before deliberating on the religion clauses, the Congress voted to appoint "two Chaplains of different denominations" to serve Congress, one in each house.[92] On April 27, the Congress ordered, relevant to the pending inauguration of President Washington, "That after the oath shall have been administered to the President, he, attended by the Vice President, and members of the Senate, and House of Representatives, proceed to St. Paul's Chapel, to hear divine service, to be performed by the Chaplain of Congress already appointed."[93] These chaplains served the Congress throughout the period of the debates on the religion clauses. On September 22, 1789, just as the joint committee was polishing the final draft of the religion clauses, Congress passed an act confirming their appointment and stipulating that the chaplains were to be paid a salary of five hundred dol-

91. *Annals,* 1:949-50, 958-59.
92. *Annals,* 1:18-19, 233; *Journal,* 1:16.
93. *Annals,* 1:25, 241.

lars per annum.[94] Similarly, on August 7, 1789, after the committee of eleven had put to the House its three proposed religion clauses, the Congress reenacted without issue the Northwest Ordinance, with its two religion clauses: "No person, demeaning himself in a peaceable and orderly manner, shall ever be molested on account of his mode of worship, or religious sentiments"; and "Religion, morality and knowledge, being necessary to good government and happiness of mankind, schools and other means of education shall forever be encouraged. . . ."[95]

It is rather clear that the First Session of Congress had little compunction about confirming and continuing the Continental Congress's tradition of supporting chaplains, prayers, Thanksgiving Day proclamations, and religious education. And, in later sessions in the 1790s and 1800s, the Congress also continued the Continental Congress's practice of including religion clauses in its treaties, condoning the American edition of the Bible, funding chaplains in the military, and celebrating religious services officiated by congressional chaplains — all with very little dissent or debate. The ease with which Congress passed such laws does give some guidance on what forms of religious support the First Congress condoned within the constraints of the religion clauses.

"Respecting an Establishment"

The phrase "respecting an establishment of religion" has long been the most hotly contested phrase of the First Amendment. We certainly cannot resolve all the modern contests on a reading of the congressional record alone. But at least three plausible lines of interpretation, that speak to perennial questions of the relationship of religion and government, can be made out.

Thirteen of the nineteen drafts of the religion clauses included disestablishment clauses. The only recorded debate is that of August 15 on the formulation, "no religion shall be established by law" (No. 7), but there is nothing in what survives that is dispositive. While all the words of the final text of the disestablishment clause appear and recur in earlier drafts, the word "respecting" is new. It is a studiously ambiguous term, variously de-

94. *Annals,* 2:2237.

95. Statutes 1789, C. VIII, in *Documents of American History,* Henry Steele Commager, fifth ed. (New York: Appleton-Century-Crofts, 1949), pp. 130, 131.

fined in the day as: "to look at, regard, or consider"; to "heed or pay attention to"; "to regard with deference, esteem, or honor"; to "expect, anticipate, look toward."[96]

One plausible reading of the final text is that Congress shall make no laws "respecting" a state establishment of religion. In 1789, six states still had some form of religious establishment, which both their state legislatures and constitutional conventions defined and defended, often against strong opposition from religious dissenters. Moreover, Virginia had just passed Jefferson's bill "for the establishment of religious freedom," also against firm opposition by defenders of the traditional establishment of Anglicanism. Having just defended their state establishments at home, the new members of Congress were not about to relinquish control of them to the new federal government. There was special concern to prevent Congress, the law-making body, from passing laws that might interfere in such religious matters — particularly through the "necessary and proper clause" of Article I, which Madison in the August 15 debate signaled as the danger point.[97]

To be sure, the First Congress had already quite explicitly rejected those drafts of the religion clauses that bound the states directly, or were cast in general terms and thus were potentially binding on the states. And to be sure, the Tenth Amendment guaranteed generally that "The powers not delegated to the United States by the Constitution . . . are reserved to the States respectively, or to the people." But, perhaps on so sensitive an issue as religion, it was best to be triply sure — and explicitly outlaw any congressional interference in the states' religious establishments. Perhaps, in the final House-Senate committee of six, it was the hard political issue of federal versus state power that was resolved by adding the curious phrase "respecting an establishment." Congress could simply make no law that "looked at," "regarded," or "paid attention to" a state establishment of religion — whether benignly or unfavorably.

This reading of the disestablishment clause would be considerably easier to press if the final draft said "a state establishment," rather than "an establishment." But since reference to "state establishments" had not appeared before in the drafts, perhaps the final committee thought it prudent to avoid introducing a new contested term so late in the debate — particu-

---

96. See dictionaries cited above in n. 71 (s.v. "respect," "respecting").
97. *Annals,* 1:757-59.

larly given the squabbling over the term "national establishment" in the August 15 House debate.

A second plausible reading is that Congress could neither establish religion outright nor make laws that would "point toward," "anticipate," or "reflect" such an establishment. On this reading, Congress could not pass a comprehensive new religion law defining the texts, doctrines, and liturgies of the nation's faith and/or governing religious polity, clergy, and property. Such a law, reminiscent of prevailing English ecclesiastical laws, would clearly be unconstitutional. But that was not the founders' only fear, according to this reading. Congress could also not make more discrete laws that might "respect" — that is, point toward, anticipate, or reflect — such an establishment. The First Congress's concern was to prevent not only a comprehensive new law that established a national religion, but also piecemeal laws that would move incrementally toward the same.

The disestablishment clause, on this reading, was not necessarily a prohibition against all laws "touching" religion, as some earlier drafts had indicated. After all, Congress had already passed several such laws (supporting chaplains, prayers, religious education, and the like). Such laws presumably did not point toward or reflect an established religion, but simply reflected commonplaces of the day about what was proper for the young nation. But the disestablishment clause was a rather firm barrier against a large number of laws touching religion that might move toward an establishment.

This reading turns on a crucial judgment about why the First Congress had rejected earlier drafts that were more specific about defining a religious establishment. On August 15, the House debated whether to outlaw "religious establishment" per se (No. 7). There seemed to be consensus on this, as Roger Sherman said early in the debate.[98] The moment that the Representatives began to specify what they meant by religious establishment, however, the conversation broke down: Representative Gerry was concerned about establishing religious doctrines, Representative Huntington about forced payments of religious tithes, Representative Madison about compulsory worship of God and giving preeminence to one sect — all of which were features of a traditional establishment of religion. The initial compromise was Charles Livermore's clause that sought "no law touching religion" at all (No. 10). By August 20, the House had returned to the language that opened the August 15 debate: "no law establishing religion"

98. *Annals*, 1:757-59.

(No. 12). That was the language sent to the Senate. The Senate also could not nuance this "no establishment" formulation — failing to reach agreement on clauses that would outlaw the establishment of "one Religious Sect or Society" or "articles of faith or a mode of worship" or that would outlaw the preference of one religious sect, society, or denomination (Nos. 15-17, 19). On this second reading of the disestablishment clause, the word "respecting," therefore, becomes something of an umbrella term for these and other features of a religious establishment. Congress could not agree on what specifics of a religious establishment to outlaw — and so they simply outlawed the establishment of religion altogether, and anything that "pointed to" or "moved toward" the same.

On the first reading, the disestablishment clause is a limited prohibition against congressional interference with state controls of religion. This leaves little guidance for what Congress might do at the federal level respecting (an establishment of) religion. On the second reading, the establishment is a comprehensive prohibition against any congressional inclination toward establishing religion. This leaves a little room for Congress to pass laws "touching religion," but not much. Between these two readings of "respecting an establishment" of religion, one can find in the literature a whole host of alternatives.

Among the more popular of such intermediate readings is that of "non-preferentialism." The disestablishment clause, on this reading, simply outlaws preferential support for a "national religion," but allows for "non-preferential" support for multiple religions. On this reading, the feature of "establishment" that concerned Congress most was not a grand scheme of ecclesiastical law as prevailed in England; that was clearly beyond the pale, and no one was seriously advocating this for America in the 1780s. Congress's real concern was to avoid official "preferences" for certain religious sects, denominations, doctrines, or modes of worship. Six drafts, including the penultimate one, sought to formulate this directly by outlawing various types of "preferential" establishments by name (Nos. 2, 3, 15-17, 19). None of these drafts passed muster. But Congress accomplished its goal of outlawing preferential support more efficiently by simply prohibiting laws against "an" establishment of this sort — rather than prohibiting laws against "the" establishment of religion altogether. On this formulation, Congress could certainly "touch religion" — rather generously, in fact — so long as it did so in a way that would not prefer one religious sect or society above another. And Congress demonstrated what such non-preferential support meant by appointing and funding chaplains from different denominations, supporting general "religious education," and condoning pious but ecumenical prayers and Thanksgiving Day proclamations.

This "non-preferential" reading of the disestablishment clause, while certainly plausible, relies heavily on Madison's rejected concern about "national establishment." It does rather little to explain the insertion of the curious word "respecting." It also relies heavily on a clever distinction between "an" and "the" establishment of religion — words on which the sloppy Congressional record slipped more than once.[99]

"Prohibiting Free Exercise"

While the origins of the disestablishment clause have long occupied commentators, the origins of the free exercise clause have only recently come into prominent discussion. A modern controversy has driven much of the new interest — the weakening of the free exercise clause, culminating in the Supreme Court case of *Employment Division v. Smith* (1990)[100] and Congress's (ultimately failed) attempt in the Religious Freedom Restoration Act (1993) to restore a more rigorous free exercise test. Here, too, as in the case of the disestablishment clause, the record does not resolve all modern questions. Indeed, in the case of the free exercise clause, the congressional record raises as many questions as it answers.

First, the free exercise clause merely outlaws congressional acts that "prohibit" the free exercise of religion. Earlier drafts had included much more embracive protections, outlawing laws that would "touch," "infringe," "abridge," "violate," "compel," or "prevent" the same. All this is replaced by the seemingly minimalist guarantee that Congress not "prohibit" the free exercise of religion.

Second, the free exercise clause is not matched by a liberty of conscience clause. The first seventeen drafts of the religion clauses had included a provision protecting the liberty or rights of conscience, sometimes generally, sometimes specifically with respect to religious scruples against

99. See, e.g., *Annals*, 1:948 transcribing the final Senate version of the free exercise clause: "prohibiting *a* free exercise thereof." See also *Annals*, 1:451, 778-80, variously quoting Madison's call for disestablishment of *"any"* and *"a"* religion. On the sloppiness of the record, see generally James H. Hutson, "The Creation of the Constitution: The Integrity of the Documentary Record," *Texas Law Review* 65 (1986): 1.

100. 494 U.S. 872 (1990).

bearing arms. The final recorded House debates on August 20 show agreement on both such protections: "Congress shall make no law establishing religion, or to prevent the free exercise thereof, or to infringe the rights of conscience" (No. 12). And again, "no person religiously scrupulous shall be compelled to bear arms in person" (No. 13). The Senate included such a guarantee in its first three drafts, but then abruptly dropped it for good at the end of September 3 (No. 18). We are left with the final spare free exercise clause.

Third, it must be remembered that while formulating the free exercise clause, Congress was also formulating the free speech, free press, and free assembly clauses. The House had combined the speech, press, and religion clauses already on July 28 (Nos. 9, 11). The Senate combined these and the assembly clause on September 9 (No. 19), and thereafter, they were considered together. The surviving House debates on these other First Amendment provisions make rather clear that religious speech, religious press, and religious assembly were covered by these three clauses.[101] The free exercise clause could not be merely redundant of these attendant clauses of the First Amendment. So what is protected by the free exercise clause beyond free religious speech, free religious press, and free religious assembly?

To read the free exercise clause too minimally is hard to square with the widespread solicitude for rights of conscience and free exercise reflected in the First Congress's debates. All four drafts of the religion clauses proposed by the states included strong protections of free exercise. The House debates that have survived show equal solicitude. Daniel Carroll (1756-1829) of Maryland, for example, spoke eloquently that "the rights of conscience are, in their nature of such peculiar delicacy, and will little bear the gentlest touch of government."[102] Benjamin Huntington (1736-1800) warned against anything "hurtful to religion" and hoped the amendment would be made in such a way as "to secure the rights of conscience and a free exercise of the right of religion. . . ."[103] Elias Boudinot gave the final resounding word of the House on August 20: "I hope that in establishing this Government, we may show the world that proper care is taken that the Government may not interfere with the religious sentiments of any person."[104]

---

101. See debates in *The Founders' Constitution*, 5:111-208.
102. *Annals*, 1:757.
103. *Annals*, 1:757-58.
104. *Annals*, 1:796.

How does all this enthusiasm in the First Congress for the rights of conscience and freedom of exercise square with the seemingly crabbed guarantee that "Congress shall make no law . . . prohibiting the free exercise" of religion?

The free exercise clause is somewhat less crabbed when read in eighteenth-century terms, rather than ours. The word "prohibiting," in eighteenth-century parlance, was as much a synonym as a substitute for the terms "infringing," "restraining," or "abridging." Both dictionaries and political tracts of the day conflated these terms. To flip from one to the other, particularly in the charged political rhetoric of the First Congress, might well have been driven more by aesthetics and taste than by substantive calculation.[105]

One can see this conflation of terms in the original draft submitted by the Virginia Ratification Convention in the summer of 1788. In the preface to its proffered amendments, the convention cites its main concern — "that essential rights, the liberty of conscience, and of the press, cannot be cancelled, abridged, restrained, or modified, by any authority. . . ." Commenting on this passage in 1800, Madison argued that the point of listing all these verbs was simply to underscore "that the liberty of conscience and the freedom of press were equally and completely exempted from all authority whatever of the United States." And such rights, in Madison's view, were equally and completely protected by the First Amendment, despite its use of the alternative terms "prohibiting" and "abridging." To read the First Amendment otherwise would lead to silly results. As James Madison put it:

> [I]f Congress may regulate the freedom of the press, provided they do not abridge it, because it is said only "they shall not abridge it," and is not said, "they shall make no law respecting it," the analogy of reasoning is conclusive that Congress may regulate and even abridge the free exercise of religion, provided they do not prohibit it; because it is said only "they shall not prohibit it," and is not said "they shall make no law respecting, or no law abridging it."[106]

One cannot lean too heavily on this construction, since the primary meaning of "prohibit" in the eighteenth century was still to "forbid," "prevent,"

---

105. See Michael W. McConnell, "The Origins and Historical Understanding of Free Exercise of Religion," *Harvard Law Review* 103 (1990): 1409, 1486-88.

106. *The Founders' Constitution*, 5:146-47.

or "preclude." But awareness both of the elasticity of the term in the day and of the inexactitude of the congressional record helps to explain what the First Congress may have been about.

Moreover, the words "free exercise," in eighteenth-century parlance, were both a source and a summary of a whole range of principles of religious rights and liberties. "Free exercise" did have a distinct meaning in the eighteenth century, as we saw. It was conventionally understood to protect the religious speech, press, assembly, and other activities of individuals, and the actions respecting the religious property, polity, discipline, and clergy of religious groups. But "free exercise" was just as much an umbrella term that connoted protections of liberty of conscience, religious equality and pluralism, and (in some formulations) separation of Church and state. In earlier drafts of the religion clauses, Congress sought to spell out these various principles separately — listing liberty of conscience fifteen times, free exercise and religious equality nine times each, and religious pluralism six times. Perhaps in an attempt to avoid giving priority to any particular construction, Congress thought it best to use the generic term "free exercise," and leave its specific province open to ongoing constitutional development and application. This is a speculative reading, but plausible even on the thin congressional record.

The record of the First Congress does give a better indication of why the clause on conscientious objection to bearing arms might have been excluded. The North Carolina ratification convention had introduced this provision in 1788 (No. 4). The House committee of eleven had repeated it on July 28 (No. 8). The House debated the clause on August 17 and 20. It was clearly controversial — passing only 24 to 22 in the full House on August 20, before being silently dropped by the House style committee four days later. In the House debates, both Representatives Gerry and Scott had objected because such an open-ended clause might well be abused, with the military and the nation thereby imperiled. Both Representatives Scott and Jackson thought it unfair that "one part" of the nation "would have to defend the other in case of invasion." Chairman Boudinot, however, ultimately carried the slender majority with an impassioned speech: "what justice can there be in compelling them to bear arms, when, according to their religious principles, they would rather die than use them?"[107]

But three of the Representatives had suggested a legislative alternative that may have ultimately led to the quiet disappearance of this clause

107. *Annals*, 1:778-80, 796.

after August 20. Sherman hinted at this by saying the clause was not "absolutely necessary." Scott said more explicitly that conscientious objection status was not a constitutional but a "legislative right." Benson elaborated this view, advising that such questions be left "to the benevolence of the Legislature," to the "discretion of the Government." "If this stands part of the constitution," Benson reasoned, "it will be before the Judiciary on every regulation you make with respect to the organization of the militia."[108] Such a reading has proved prophetic. The contentious issue of conscientious objection status in the military has remained almost consistently subconstitutional ever since — handled by statute and regulation, rather than by direct free exercise inquiry.

"Religion"

"What is religion?" is today a recurrent refrain that echoes through much First Amendment law. The issue is as intractable at modern law as it is in modern theology, philosophy, sociology, and anthropology. At law, a claim or claimant must be deemed religious to seek the protection of the free exercise clause. A government action must be deemed religious to trigger the remedies of the disestablishment clause. With the remarkable pluralism of modern America, featuring more than one thousand denominations, charting the course between religion and nonreligion is often a hazardous exercise.

The issue was a good bit simpler in the eighteenth century. The founders recognized and celebrated a plurality of Protestant Christian faiths. The issue was how much further to extend the pale of recognized religion, and thus of constitutional protection. Some set the legal line at Protestantism. Others set the legal line at Christianity, thereby including Catholics and Eastern Orthodox. Others set the legal line at theism, thereby including Jews, Muslims, and Deists. No founders writing on religious rights and liberties argued seriously about setting the line any further — to include African or Native American religions, let alone nontheistic faiths from the East, such as Buddhism.

The First Congress did little more than repeat this conventional lore. The House debates repeated the general endorsement of a plurality of sects, societies, and denominations, but touched by name only Quakers and

---

108. *Annals*, 1:778-80, 796.

Moravians. They also alluded to a distinction between religion and nonreligion, seeking to reserve the protections of constitutional religious rights to the former. In the House debates, Representative Sylvester expressed concern about "abolishing religion altogether" by crafting too broad a disestablishment clause.[109] Representative Huntington wished "to secure the rights of conscience, and a free exercise of the rights of religion, but not to patronize those who professed no religion at all."[110] Representative Scott wanted to prevent misuse of the conscientious objection clause by "those who are of no religion." But precisely what constituted religion and nonreligion, and where the line was to be drawn between them, the congressional record simply does not say.

Summary and Conclusions

Six principles lay at the heart of the new American constitutional experiment in religious rights — liberty of conscience, free exercise of religion, religious equality, religious pluralism, separation of Church and state, and disestablishment of religion.

These principles came to fullest expression and experimentation in the eleven new state constitutions forged between 1776 and 1784. No state constitution, however, embraced all six of these principles equally. Nor did they institute them without the kind of qualifications we would regard as improper, if not unconstitutional, today. Most states still retained some semblance of a traditional religious establishment — usually by favoring certain religious ceremonies and moral codes; sometimes by instituting religious tithes, taxes, and test oaths; occasionally by condoning only certain modes and manners of religious worship and organization. Most of the states still retained ample constraints on the free exercise of religion — usually by prohibiting breaches of the peace and public morality; sometimes by curbing religious speech that was deemed blasphemous, religious assemblies that were considered dangerous, or religious allegiances that were judged unpatriotic, if not treasonous.

These principles of religious rights were also incorporated into the First Amendment to the United States Constitution. The religion clauses bound only the national government ("Congress"). They set only outer

109. *Annals,* 1:757.
110. *Annals,* 1:758-59.

boundaries to constitutional congressional conduct respecting religion. These religion clauses were designed in part to legitimate, and to live off, the state constitutional guarantees of religious rights and liberties. The twin guarantees of disestablishment and free exercise depended for their efficacy both on each other and on other religious rights that the founders regarded as essential. The guarantees of disestablishment and free exercise of religion standing alone — as they came to be during the 1940s when the Supreme Court "incorporated" these two guarantees into the due process clause of the Fourteenth Amendment — could legitimately be read to have multiple principles incorporated within them.

Indeed, it might not be too strong to say that the "first incorporation" of religious rights was engineered not by the Supreme Court in the 1940s but by the First Congress in 1789 when it drafted the First Amendment religion clauses. This "first incorporation" — if it can be so called — had two dimensions. First, the pregnant language that "Congress shall make no law respecting an establishment of religion" can be read as a confirmation and incorporation of prevailing state constitutional precepts and practices. Such state practices included "the slender establishments" of religion in New England, Maryland, and the Carolinas, which nonetheless included ample guarantees of liberty of conscience, free exercise, religious equality, religious pluralism, and separation of Church and state. Such practices also included the "establishment of religious freedom" that had prevailed in Virginia since 1786. The First Amendment drafters seem to have contemplated and confirmed a plurality of constitutional constructions "respecting" religion and its establishment.

Second, the embracive terms "free exercise" and "establishment" can be read to incorporate the full range of "essential rights and liberties" discussed in the eighteenth century. The founders often used the term "free exercise" synonymously with liberty of conscience, religious equality, religious pluralism, and separation of Church and state. They similarly regarded "non-" or "disestablishment" as a generic guarantee of liberty of conscience, religious equality, and separation of Church and state. Read in historical context, therefore, the cryptic religion clauses of the First Amendment can be seen to "embody" — to "incorporate" — multiple expressions of the essential rights of religion.

That Serpentine Wall of Separation
Between Church and State

"The task of separating the secular from the religious in education is one of magnitude, intricacy, and delicacy," Justice Jackson wrote, concurring in *McCollum v. Board of Education* (1948), the Supreme Court's first case on the place of religion in public schools. "To lay down a sweeping constitutional doctrine" of absolute separation of Church and state "is to decree a uniform . . . unchanging standard for countless school boards representing and serving highly localized groups which not only differ from each other but which themselves from time to time change attitudes." If we persist in this experiment, Justice Jackson warned his brethren, "we are likely to make the legal 'wall of separation between church and state' as winding as the famous serpentine wall designed by Mr. Jefferson for the University he founded."[1]

While a majority of the United States Supreme Court embarked on a four-decade project of building this "serpentine wall,"[2] Justice Jackson took little further part in the effort. He continued to regard the separation of Church and state as essential to the protection of religious liberty, along with the freedoms of conscience, exercise, and speech.[3] But he had no patience with unilateral or extreme applications of any of these First Amendment

1. *McCollum v. Board of Education*, 333 U.S. 203, 237-38 (1948) (Jackson, J., concurring).

2. The most recent Supreme Court cases where the separationist principle dominated the Court's reasoning were *Texas Monthly Inc. v. Bullock*, 489 U.S. 1 (1989); *Aguilar v. Felton*, 473 U.S. 402 (1985); and *Larkin v. Grendel's Den Inc.*, 459 U.S. 116 (1982).

3. Paul A. Freund, "Mr. Justice Jackson and Individual Rights," in *Mr. Justice Jackson: Four Lectures in His Honor*, ed. Robert H. Jackson and Charles S. Desmond (New York: Columbia University Press, 1969), pp. 36-43 (summarizing cases).

principles, not least the principle of separation of Church and state. Imprudent application of separationism, he wrote, would draw the Court into "passionate dialectics" about "nonessential details" that were often better left to state and local governments to resolve.[4] In his last years on the bench, Jackson thus led the Court in a case that denied standing to a party who argued that religious instruction in a local public school violated the separation of Church and state.[5] He was the sole dissenter in a Church property dispute case, where the Court read the principle of separation to require a state to defer to the internal religious law of the Church disputants rather than apply its own state laws.[6] He dissented again from the Court's decision to uphold a public school program that gave students release time to participate in religious events off site. Arguing that this was precisely the kind of case where the principle of separation did apply, he complained: "The wall which the Court was professing to erect between Church and State has become even more warped and twisted than I expected."[7]

For all his growing misgivings about separationism, however, even this bold dissenter on the Court,[8] well trained in legal history, never once questioned the historical foundation or constitutional imperative of a strict separation between Church and state. In *Everson v. Board of Education,* the Supreme Court for the first time applied the First Amendment disestablishment guarantee to the states. Justice Black, Jackson's nemesis,[9] wrote for the *Everson* majority. After a lengthy historical recitation, Black quoted Thomas Jefferson's famous 1802 Letter to the Danbury Baptist Association as dispositive evidence that the "First Amendment has erected a wall of separation between church and state" that "must be kept high and impregnable."[10] Though Jackson dissented from the *Everson* holding, he accepted the Court's account of the history and meaning of the First Amendment guarantee of no establishment of religion. Jackson was concerned about the

4. *Zorach v. Clauson,* 343 U.S. 306, 325 (1952) (Jackson, J., dissenting).

5. *Doremus v. Board of Education,* 342 U.S. 429 (1952).

6. *Kedroff v. St. Nicholas Cathedral,* 344 U.S. 94, 126-32 (1952) (Jackson, J., dissenting).

7. *Zorach,* 343 U.S. at 323-25.

8. Of Justice Jackson's 324 Supreme Court opinions, 109 were dissents, 63 concurrences. "Bibliography: The Judicial Opinions of Justice Robert H. Jackson in the Supreme Court of the United States October 6, 1941–October 9, 1954," *Stanford Law Review* 8 (1955): 60-71.

9. Dennis J. Hutchinson, "The Black-Jackson Feud," *Supreme Court Review* (1988): 203-43.

10. *Everson v. Board of Education,* 330 U.S. 1, 18 (1947).

rhetorical "undertones" of "advocating complete and uncompromising separation of Church from state."[11] He was not concerned about the historical underpinnings of separationism itself. Indeed, Jackson thought his views to be in full accord with the intent of his hero President Thomas Jefferson, whose novel separationist theories, in Jackson's view, had finally come into their constitutional inheritance.[12]

The history of the separation of Church and state, however, has proved far more "serpentine" — far more "warped and twisted" — than the *Everson* Court would have us believe. After two generations of careful historical scholarship, we now know that separation of Church and state was not an invention of nineteenth-century Jeffersonianism and was not simply a mandate for the privatization of religion and the secularization of politics. Separation of Church and state was, rather, an ancient Western principle of religious liberty, rooted in the Bible and subject to all manner of complex theological and political interpretations in the two millennia before the First Amendment was forged. The American founders drew from this tradition at least five distinct understandings of separation of Church and state. All five of these understandings found a place in eighteenth-century American laws of religious liberty, along with such other principles as liberty of conscience, free exercise of religion, and equality of plural faiths before the law.

Moreover, the wall-of-separation metaphor has proved far more "serpentine" than Justice Jackson could have imagined — now in the sense of the ancient serpent in the Garden of Eden, who offered access to enduring wisdom by means of a seductively simple formula.[13] "Metaphors in law are to be narrowly watched," Benjamin Cardozo once warned, "for starting as devices to liberate thought, they end often by enslaving it."[14] So it has been with the metaphor of a wall of separation. What started in the eighteenth century as one of several useful principles of religious liberty eventually became a mechanical and monopolistic test that courts applied bluntly, even slavishly, in a whole series of cases. What started as one of many images[15]

11. *Everson,* 330 U.S. at 19 (Jackson, J., dissenting).

12. Robert H. Jackson, *The Struggle for Judicial Supremacy* (New York: A. A. Knopf, 1941), p. 315.

13. Genesis 3:1-7.

14. *Berkley v. Third Ave. Railway Company,* 155 N.E. 58, 61 (N.Y. 1926).

15. For other images that were current in the eighteenth century, including "barriers," "fences," and "lines" of separation, see Daniel L. Dreisbach, *Thomas Jefferson and the Wall of Separation* (New York: New York University Press, 2002), pp. 83-89.

of a budding new national law of religious liberty has become for many the mandate and measure of the First Amendment itself.

While the United States Supreme Court has, of late, abandoned much of its earlier separationism and overruled some of its harshest applications in earlier cases,[16] the wall of separation metaphor has lived on in popular imagination as the salutary source and summary of American religious liberty. Popular imagination, too, might begin to change if we can get our history right. This chapter is offered in that spirit. It surveys a few of the high points of the long Western story of the genesis, exodus, and deuteronomy of the principle of separation of Church and state: (1) its genesis or origins in biblical and apostolic and patristic texts; (2) its exodus or migration through the next 1500 years of the Western Christian tradition and in the first 150 years of American law and culture; and (3) its deuteronomy or second legal life ("deutero-nomos") in *Everson* and its progeny. The chapter concludes by seeking to harvest from this history the most enduring lessons about separation of Church and state that modern constitutional law still needs to heed, a theme which the following chapter takes up in more detail.

Genesis: The Roots of American Separationism

Separation of Church and state is often regarded as a distinctly American and relatively modern invention. In reality, separationism is an ancient Western teaching rooted in the Bible. In the Hebrew Bible, the chosen people of ancient Israel were repeatedly enjoined to remain separate from the Gentile world around them[17] and to separate the Levites and other temple officials from the rest of the people.[18] The Hebrew Bible also made much of building and rebuilding "fortified walls"[19] to protect the city of Jerusalem from the outside world and to separate the temple and its priests from the commons

---

16. *Mitchell v. Helms,* 530 U.S. 793, 808 (2001), overruling *Meek v. Pittenger,* 421 U.S. 329 (1975) and *Wolman v. Walter,* 433 U.S. 229 (1977); *Agostini v. Felton,* 521 U.S. 203, 235 (1997), overruling *Aguilar v. Felton,* 473 U.S. 402 (1985). See further Chapter 8 herein.

17. Exodus 34:11-16; Leviticus 20:24-25; 2 Samuel 22:26-27; 1 Kings 8:53; Ezra 6:21; 10:1; Nehemiah 9:1-15; 10:28-31; 13:1-3; 1 Esdras 7–9.

18. Leviticus 21:1–22:16; Numbers 8:14; 16:9; Deuteronomy 10:8; 32:8; 1 Chronicles 23:13; Ezekiel 40–42.

19. Jeremiah 1:18; 15:20.

and its people[20] — an ancient tradition still recognized and symbolized in the Jewish rituals and prayers that take place at the Western (Wailing) Wall.

The New Testament commanded believers to "render to Caesar the things that are Caesar's and to God the things that are God's,"[21] and reminded them that "two swords" were enough to govern the world.[22] Christians were warned that they should "be not conformed to this world"[23] but remain "separate" from the world and its temptations,[24] maintaining themselves in purity and piety. Echoing the Hebrew Bible, St. Paul spoke literally of a "wall of separation" *(paries maceriae)* between Christians and non-Christians interposed by the law.[25] Interspersed among these various political dualisms, the Bible included many other dualisms — between spirit and flesh, soul and body, faith and works, heaven and hell, grace and nature, the kingdom of God and the kingdom of Satan, and much more.[26]

Early Catholic Views

These various biblical dualisms were repeated in some of the early Church constitutions. Among the earliest was the *Didache* (ca. 120 C.E.), which opened with a call for believers to separate from the world around them: "There are two Ways, one of Life and one of Death; but there is a great separation between the two Ways."[27] The Way of Life follows the commandments of law and love. The Way of Death succumbs to sins and temptations. The two ways must remain utterly separate, and those who stray from the Way of Life must be cast out. *The Epistle of Barnabas* (ca. 100-120 C.E.) provided similarly:

20. 1 Kings 3:1; Nehemiah 3:1-32; 4:15-20; 12:27-43; Jeremiah 1:18-19; 15:19-21; Ezekiel 42:1.

21. Matthew 22:21; Mark 12:17; Luke 20:25.

22. Luke 22:38.

23. Romans 12:2.

24. 2 Corinthians 6:14-18.

25. Ephesians 2:14. See historical interpretation of this text in Markus Barth, *The Anchor Bible: Ephesians* (Garden City, N.Y.: Doubleday, 1974), pp. 263-65, 283-87.

26. Oliver O'Donovan, *The Desire of the Nations: Rediscovering the Roots of Political Theology* (Cambridge: Cambridge University Press, 1996), pp. 82-119, 193-211.

27. In Philip Schaff, *The Teaching of the Twelve Apostles* (New York: Funk and Wagnalls, 1889), pp. 162-63 (my translation). Several comparable formulae from the apostolic sources are quoted in Schaff, p. 163, n. 1. See comparable language in Deuteronomy 30:15; Jeremiah 21:8; Matthew 7:13-14; and 2 Peter 2:2.

There are two ways of teaching and of authority, one of light and one of darkness. And there is a great difference between the two ways. For over one are set light-bearing angels of God, but over the other angels of Satan. And the one is Lord from eternity to eternity, but the other is prince of the present time of darkness.[28]

These dualistic adages and images recurred in scores of later apostolic and patristic writings of the second through fifth centuries — both in the East and in the West.[29] They became the basis for one persistent model of separationism in the Christian West — the separation of the pure Christian life and community governed by religious authorities from the sinful and sometimes hostile world governed by political authorities. This apostolic ideal of separationism found its strongest and most enduring institutional form in monasticism, which produced a vast archipelago of communities of spiritual brothers and sisters, each walled off from the world around them.[30] But separationism in this sense also remained a recurrent spiritual ideal in Christian theology and homiletics — a perennial call to Christians to keep the Way of Life in the community of Christ separate from the Way of Death in the company of the Devil.

By the fifth century, Western Christianity had distilled these early biblical teachings into other models of separationism. The most famous was the image of two cities within one world, developed by St. Augustine, Bishop of Hippo (354-430). In his *City of God* (ca. 413-427),[31] Augustine contrasted the City of God with the city of man. The City of God consisted of all those who were predestined to salvation, bound by the love of God,

28. In Schaff, *Teaching of the Twelve Apostles,* pp. 227-28.

29. Schaff, *Teaching of the Twelve Apostles,* p. 18; Gerard E. Caspary, *Politics and Exegesis: Origen and the Two Swords* (Berkeley: University of California Press, 1979); Lester L. Field Jr., *Liberty, Dominion, and the Two Swords: On the Origins of Western Political Theology* (Notre Dame, Ind.: University of Notre Dame Press, 1998), pp. 180-398; Adolf Harnack, *The Constitution and Law of the Church in the First Two Centuries,* trans. F. L. Pogson, ed. H. D. A. Major (New York: G. P. Putnam's Sons, 1910).

30. Gerd Tellenbach, *Church, State and Christian Society at the Time of the Investiture Culture,* trans. R. F. Bennett (Oxford: Blackwell, 1959), pp. 25-29. See Marilyn Dunn, *The Emergence of Monasticism: From the Desert Fathers to the Early Middle Ages* (Oxford: Blackwell, 2000); David Knowles, *Christian Monasticism* (New York: McGraw-Hill, 1969); and C. H. Lawrence, *Medieval Monasticism: Forms of Religious Life in Western Europe in the Middle Ages* (New York: Longman, 2001).

31. Augustine of Hippo, *City of God,* trans. Gerald G. Walsh et al., ed. Vernon J. Bourke (Garden City, N.Y.: Image, 1958), pp. 84-89, 460-73, 483-506.

and devoted to a life of Christian piety, morality, and worship led by the Christian clergy. The city of man consisted of all the things of this sinful world, and the political and social institutions that God had created to maintain a modicum of order and peace.[32] Augustine sometimes depicted this dualism as two walled cities separated from each other[33] — particularly when he was describing the sequestered life and discipline of monasticism or the earlier plight of the Christian Churches under Roman persecution.[34] But Augustine's more dominant teaching was that dual citizenship in both cities would be the norm until these two cities were fully and finally separated at the Last Judgment of God.[35] For Augustine, it was ultimately impossible to achieve complete separation of the City of God and the city of man in this world. A Christian remained bound by the sinful habits of the world, even if he aspired to greater purity of the Gospel. A Christian remained subject to the authority of both cities, even if she aspired to be a citizen of the City of God alone.

It was crucial, however, that the spiritual and temporal powers that prevailed in these two cities remain separate in function. Even though Christianity became the one established religion of the Roman Empire, patronized and protected by the Roman state, Augustine and other Church Fathers insisted that state power remain separate from Church power. All magistrates, even the Roman emperors, were not ordained clergy but laity. They had no power to administer the sacraments or to mete out religious discipline. They were bound by the teachings of the Bible, the decrees of the ecumenical councils, and the traditions of their predecessors. They also had to accept the Church's instruction, judgment, and spiritual discipline. Pope Gelasius (d. 496) put the matter famously in 494 in a letter rebuking Emperor Anastasius:

> There are indeed, most august Emperor, two powers by which this world is chiefly ruled: the sacred authority of the Popes and the royal

32. Augustine, *City of God*, pp. 494-506.

33. Augustine, *City of God*, pp. 466-72; Henry Paolucci, ed., *The Political Writings of St. Augustine* (South Bend, Ind.: Gateway, 1962), pp. 241-75, 305-17.

34. Jean Bethke Elshtain, *Augustine and the Limits of Politics* (Notre Dame, Ind.: University of Notre Dame Press, 1995); J. van Oort, *Jerusalem and Babylon: A Study into Augustine's City of God and the Sources of His Doctrine of the Two Cities* (New York: E. J. Brill, 1991); and Eugene TeSelle, *Living in Two Cities: Augustinian Trajectories in Political Thought* (Scranton: University of Scranton Press, 1998).

35. Augustine, *City of God*, pp. 481-93.

power. Of these the priestly power is much more important, because it has to render account for the kings of men themselves at [the Last Judgment]. For you know, our very clement son, that although you have the chief place in dignity over the human race, yet you must submit yourself faithfully to those who have charge of Divine things, and look to them for the means of your salvation.[36]

This "two powers" passage became a locus classicus for many later theories of a basic separation between pope and emperor, clergy and laity, regnum and sacerdotium.[37]

In the course of the Papal Revolution of the eleventh to thirteenth centuries, this model of two separate powers operating within the extended Christian empire was transformed into a model of two swords ruling a unified Christendom by law.[38] In the name of "freedom of the Church" (libertas ecclesiae), Pope Gregory VII (1015-1085) and his successors threw off their political patrons and protectors and established the Catholic Church itself as the superior legal and political authority of Western Christendom. The Church now claimed more than a spiritual and sacramental power over its own affairs, a spiritual office within the Christian empire. It claimed a vast new jurisdiction, a political authority to make and enforce laws for all of Christendom. The pope and the clergy claimed exclusive personal jurisdiction over clerics, pilgrims, students, heretics, Jews, and Muslims. They claimed subject matter jurisdiction over doctrine, liturgy, patronage, education, charity, inheritance, marriage, oaths, oral promises, and moral crimes. And they claimed concurrent jurisdiction with state authorities over secular subjects that required the Church's special forms of Christian equity.[39]

This late medieval system of Church government and law was

36. In Ehler and Morrall, pp. 10-11.

37. See, e.g., Ernst H. Kantorowicz, The King's Two Bodies: A Study in Mediaeval Political Theology (Princeton, N.J.: Princeton University Press, 1957); Karl Frederick Morrison, The Two Kingdoms: Ecclesiology in Carolingian Political Thought (Princeton, N.J.: Princeton University Press, 1964).

38. For the transmutation of the two powers image to two swords, see Brian Tierney, The Crisis of Church and State, 1050-1300: With Selected Documents (Englewood Cliffs, N.J.: Prentice-Hall, 1964), p. 53.

39. Berman, LR I, pp. 85-119, 165-200; Udo Wolter, "Amt und Officium in mittelalterlichen Quellen vom 13. bis 15. Jahrhundert," Zeitschrift der Savigny-Stiftung (Kan. Ab.) 105 (1988): 246-80.

grounded in part in the two-swords theory. This theory taught that the pope is the vicar of Christ, in whom Christ has vested his whole authority.[40] This authority was symbolized in the "two swords" discussed in the Bible,[41] a spiritual sword and a temporal sword. Christ had metaphorically handed these two swords to the highest being in the human world — the pope, the vicar of Christ. The pope and lower clergy wielded the spiritual sword, in part by establishing canon law rules for the governance of all Christendom. The clergy, however, generally delegated the temporal sword to those authorities below the spiritual realm — emperors, kings, dukes, and their civil retinues, who held their swords "of" and "for" the Church. These civil magistrates were to promulgate and enforce civil laws in a manner consistent with canon law. Under this two-swords theory, civil law was by its nature preempted by canon law. Civil jurisdiction was subordinate to ecclesiastical jurisdiction. The state answered to the Church.[42] Pope Boniface VIII (d. 1303) put this two-swords theory famously and forcefully in 1302:

> We are taught by the words of the Gospel that in this Church and in its power there are two swords, a spiritual, to wit, and a temporal. . . . [B]oth are in the power of the Church, namely the spiritual and [temporal] swords; the one, indeed, to be wielded for the Church, the other by the Church; the former by the priest, the latter by the hand of kings and knights, but at the will and sufferance of the priest. For it is necessary that one sword should be under another and that the temporal authority should be subjected to the spiritual. . . . If, therefore, the earthly power err, it shall be judged by the spiritual power; if the lesser spiritual power err, it shall be judged by the higher, competent spiritual power; but if the supreme spiritual power [i.e., the pope] err, it could be judged solely by God, not by man.[43]

Two communities, two cities, two powers, two swords: these were four main models of separationism that obtained in the Western Catholic

40. Brian Tierney, *The Origins of Papal Infallibility, 1150-1350* (Leiden: E. J. Brill, 1972), pp. 39-45, 82-121.

41. Luke 22:38.

42. Otto von Gierke, *Political Theories of the Middle Age,* trans. Frederic William Maitland (Cambridge: Cambridge University Press, 1958), pp. 7-21; Ewart Lewis, *Medieval Political Ideas,* 2 vols. (New York: Knopf, 1954), 2:506-38.

43. In Ehler and Morrall, pp. 91-92; see others in Tierney, *The Crisis of Church and State,* p. 180.

tradition in the first 1500 years. Each model emphasized different biblical texts. Each started with a different theory of the Church. But each was designed ultimately to separate the Church from the state. On one extreme, the apostolic model of two communities was a separationism of survival — a means to protect the Church from a hostile state and pagan world. On the other extreme, the late medieval model of two swords was a separation of preemption — a means to protect the Church in its superior legal rule within a unified world of Christendom.

Early Protestant Views

The sixteenth-century Protestant Reformation began as a call for freedom from the late medieval "two swords" regime — freedom of the Church from the tyranny of the pope, freedom of the individual conscience from canon law and clerical control, freedom of state officials from Church power and privilege. "Freedom of the Christian" was the rallying cry of the early Reformation.[44] Catalyzed by Martin Luther's (1483-1546) posting of the Ninety-Five Theses in 1517 and his burning of the canon law books in 1520, early Protestants denounced Church laws and authorities in violent and vitriolic terms, and urged radical reforms of Church and state on the strength of the Bible.[45]

After a generation of experimentation, however, the four branches of the Protestant Reformation returned to variations of the same four models of separationism that the earlier Catholic tradition had forged — two communities, two cities, two powers, two swords — adding new accents and applications.

The Anabaptist tradition — Amish, Hutterites, Mennonites, Swiss Brethren, German Brethren, and others — returned to a variation of the apostolic model of two communities. Most Anabaptist communities separated themselves into small, self-sufficient, intensely democratic communities, cordoned off from the world by what they called a "wall of separation."[46] These separated communities governed themselves by bibli-

---

44. LW 31:327-77. See further Chapter 2 herein.

45. See sources and discussion in LP, pp. 33-64.

46. The phrase is from Menno Simons, quoted in Dreisbach, *Thomas Jefferson and the Wall of Separation,* p. 73. See comparable sentiments in *The Complete Writings of Menno Simons, c. 1496-1561,* trans. L. Verduin, ed. J. C. Wenger (Scottdale, Pa.: Herald, 1984), pp. 29, 117-20, 158-59, 190-206. See also the call for "separation" in the

cal principles of discipleship, simplicity, charity, and nonresistance. They set their own internal standards of worship, liturgy, diet, discipline, dress, and education. They handled their own internal affairs of property, contracts, commerce, marriage, and inheritance, without appeal to the state or to secular law.[47]

The state, most Anabaptists believed, was part of the fallen world, and was to be avoided so far as possible. Though once the perfect creation of God, the world was now a sinful regime "beyond the perfection of Christ"[48] and beyond the daily concern of the Christian believer. God had allowed the world to survive by appointing magistrates who used the coercion of the sword to maintain a modicum of order and peace. Christians should thus obey the state, so far as Scripture enjoined, such as in paying their taxes or registering their properties. But Christians were to avoid active participation in and interaction with the state and the world. Most early-modern Anabaptists were pacifists, preferring derision, exile, or martyrdom to active participation in war. Most Anabaptists also refused to swear oaths, or to participate in political elections, civil litigation, or civic feasts and functions.[49]

This early Anabaptist separationism was echoed in the seventeenth century by Rhode Island founder Roger Williams (1604-1680), who in 1643 called for a "hedge or wall of Separation between the Garden of the Church and the Wilderness of the world."[50] It was elaborated by American Baptist and other Evangelical groups born of the Great Awakening (ca. 1720-1780). These latter American groups were principally concerned to protect their Churches from state interference. They strove for freedom from state control of their assembly and worship, state regulations of their property and polity, state incorporation of their society and clergy, state in-

---

Schleitheim Confession (1527), art. 4, in *One Lord, One Church, One Hope, and One God: Mennonite Confessions of Faith in North America,* by Howard J. Loewen (Elkhart, Ind.: Institute of Mennonite Studies, 1985), pp. 79-84. For the biblical roots of this Anabaptist separationism, see *Biblical Concordance of the Swiss Brethren, 1540,* trans. Gilbert Fast and Galen A. Peters, ed. C. Arnold Synder (Kitchener, Ont.: Pandora, 2001), pp. 56-60.

47. Walter Klaassen, ed., *Anabaptism in Outline* (Scottdale, Pa.: Herald, 1981), pp. 101-14, 211-32.

48. *Schleitheim Confession* (1527), art. 6, in *One Lord,* by Loewen, pp. 80-81.

49. Klaassen, *Anabaptism in Outline,* pp. 244-63.

50. Roger Williams, "Letter from Roger Williams to John Cotton (1643)," in *The Complete Writings of Roger Williams,* 7 vols. (New York: Russell and Russell, 1963), 1:392.

terference in their discipline and government, state collection of religious tithes and taxes, and more. Some American Baptist groups went further to argue against tax exemptions, civil immunities, and property donations as well. Religious bodies that received state benefits, they feared, would become too beholden to the state and too dependent on its patronage for survival.[51]

The Lutheran tradition returned to a variation on Augustine's two-cities theory. The fullest formulation came in Martin Luther's (1483-1546) complex two kingdoms theory, which provided what Luther called a "paper wall" between the spiritual and temporal estates.[52] God has ordained two kingdoms or realms in which humanity is destined to live, Luther argued, the earthly kingdom and the heavenly kingdom. The earthly kingdom is the realm of creation, of natural and civic life, where a person operates primarily by reason and law. The heavenly kingdom is the realm of redemption, of spiritual and eternal life, where a person operates primarily by faith and love. These two kingdoms embrace parallel forms of righteousness and justice, government and order, truth and knowledge. They interact and depend upon each other in a variety of ways. But these two kingdoms ultimately remain distinct. The earthly kingdom is distorted by sin and governed by the law. The heavenly kingdom is renewed by grace and guided by the Gospel. A Christian is a citizen of both kingdoms at once and invariably comes under the distinctive government of each. As a heavenly citizen, the Christian remains free in his or her conscience, called to live fully by the light of the Word of God. But as an earthly citizen, the Christian is bound by law, and called to obey the natural orders and offices of household, state, and visible Church that God has ordained and maintained for the governance of this earthly kingdom.

In Luther's view, the Church was not a political or legal authority. The Church has no sword, no jurisdiction, no daily responsibility for law. The Church and its leadership were to separate themselves from legal affairs and attend to the principal callings of preaching the Word, administering the sacraments, catechizing the young, and helping the needy. While the

51. See sources in William G. McLoughlin, *New England Dissent, 1630-1833: The Baptists and the Separation of Church and State,* 2 vols. (Cambridge: Harvard University Press, 1971); William G. McLoughlin, *Soul Liberty: The Baptists' Struggle in New England, 1630-1833* (Hanover: University Press of New England, 1991); Isaac Backus, *Isaac Backus on Church, State, and Calvinism: Pamphlets, 1754-1789,* ed. William G. McLoughlin (Cambridge, Mass.: Belknap, 1968).

52. See further Chapter 2 herein and LP, pp. 87-117.

Church should cooperate in implementing laws, and its clergy and professors were to preach against injustice and advise the magistrates when called upon, formal legal authority lay with the state. The local magistrate was God's vice-regent called to elaborate natural law and to reflect divine justice in his local domain.[53]

The Calvinist Reformation returned to a variation on the two powers model, in which both Church and state exercised separate but coordinate powers within a unitary local Christian commonwealth. Calvinists insisted on the basic separation of the offices and operations of Church and state. Adverting frequently to St. Paul's image of a "wall of separation," John Calvin (1509-1564) insisted that the "political kingdom" and "spiritual kingdom" must always be "examined separately." For there is "a great difference . . . between ecclesiastical and civil power," and it would be unwise to "mingle these two, which have a completely different nature."[54] But Calvin and his followers insisted that the Church play a role in governing the local Christian commonwealth. In Calvin's Geneva, this role fell largely to the consistory, an elected body of civil and religious officials, with original jurisdiction over cases of marriage and family, charity and social welfare, worship and public morality. Among most later Calvinists — French Huguenots, Dutch Pietists, Scottish Presbyterians, German Reformed, and English Puritans — the Genevan-style consistory was transformed into the body of pastors, elders, deacons, and teachers that governed each local Church congregation without state interference and cooperated with state officials in defining and enforcing public morals.[55] These early Calvinist views on separationism came to especially prominent expression in the New England colonies and states.[56]

The Anglican tradition returned to a variation on the two swords theory, but now with the English Crown, not the pope, holding the superior sword within the unitary Christian commonwealth of England.[57] In a series of acts passed in the 1530s, King Henry VIII (1491-1547) severed all legal

53. LP, pp. 108-15, 129-40, 147-64.

54. Calvin, Institutes (1559), bk. 3, ch. 19.15; bk. 4, ch. 11.3; bk. 4, ch. 20.1-2; CO 32:352; 48:277.

55. See Josef Bohatec, *Calvin und das Recht* (Graz: H. Böhlaus, 1934); Richard C. Gamble, ed., *Calvin's Thought on Economic and Social Issues and the Relationship of Church and State* (New York: Garland, 1992).

56. See Chapter 5 herein.

57. Philip Edgecumbe Hughes, *The Theology of the English Reformers* (London: Hodder and Stoughton, 1965), pp. 235-53.

and political ties between the Church in England and the pope. The Supremacy Act of 1534 declared the English monarch to be "the only supreme head" of the Church and Commonwealth of England, with final spiritual and temporal authority.[58] The English monarchs and Parliaments thus established a uniform doctrine, liturgy, and canon by issuing the *Book of Common Prayer* (1559), the Thirty-Nine Articles (1563/71), and the Authorized (King James) Version of the Bible (1611). They also assumed jurisdiction over poor relief, marriage, education, and other activities, delegating some of this responsibility back to Convocation, the Church courts, or parish clergy. Clergy were appointed, supervised, and removed by the Crown and its delegates. Communicant status in the Church of England was rendered a condition for citizenship status in the Commonwealth of England. Contraventions of royal religious policy were punishable both as heresy and as treason.

A whole battery of apologists rose to the defense of this alliance of Church and state, most notably Richard Hooker (ca. 1553-1600). Hooker's lengthy apologia for the Anglican establishment included a sustained rebuke to English separationists. In the later sixteenth and seventeenth centuries various non-Anglican Protestant groups in England — Puritans, Brownists, Independents, and other self-styled "Separatists"[59] — had called the English Church and state to a greater separation from each other and from the Church of Rome. They also had called their own faithful to a greater separation from the Church and Commonwealth of England. Hooker had no patience with any of this. In his massive eight-

---

58. In Stephenson and Markham, p. 311.

59. On various English and New England "separatists" see Norman Allen Baxter, *History of the Freewill Baptists: A Study in New England Separatism* (Rochester, N.Y.: American Baptist Historical Society, 1957); Edward H. Bloomfield, *The Opposition to the English Separatists, 1570-1625* (Washington, D.C.: University Press of America, 1981); Stephen Brachlow, *The Communion of Saints: Radical Puritan and Separatist Ecclesiology 1570-1625* (Oxford: Oxford University Press, 1988); Champlin Burrage, *The Early English Dissenters in the Light of Recent Research (1550-1641)* (Cambridge: Cambridge University Press, 1912); James Robert Coggins, *John Smyth's Congregation: English Separatism, Mennonite Influence, and the Elect Nation* (Scottdale, Pa.: Herald, 1991), pp. 29-68, 128-32; Timothy George, *John Robinson and the English Separatist Tradition* (Macon, Ga.: Mercer University Press, 1982); C. C. Goen, *Revivalism and Separatism in New England, 1740-1800* (New Haven: Yale University Press, 1962); B. R. White, *The English Separatist Tradition: From the Marian Martyrs to the Pilgrim Fathers* (London: Oxford University Press, 1971); and Verne Dale Morey, *The Brownist Churches: A Study in English Separatism, 1553-1630* (Ph.D. diss., Harvard University, 1954).

book *Laws of Ecclesiastical Polity* (ca. 1593-1600), Hooker recognized a "natural separation" between the Church and the Commonwealth of England. But he insisted that these two bodies had to be "under one chief Governor."[60] For Hooker, Separatists who sought to erect "a wall of separation" between Church and Commonwealth would destroy English unity and deprive its Church of the natural and necessary patronage and protection of the Crown. It was a short step from this argument to the bitter campaigns of persecution in the early seventeenth century that drove many thousands of Separatists from England to Holland and to North America.

Early Enlightenment Views

The principle of separation of Church and state also had solid grounding in early Enlightenment sources. One of the earliest and most influential sources was John Locke's (1632-1704) famous *Letter Concerning Toleration* (1689), which had a great influence on several American founders, notably Thomas Jefferson (1743-1826). In this tract, Locke had distilled the liberal English and Dutch learning of the seventeenth century into an elegant plea for Church and state to end their corrosive alliances and to end their corrupt abridgments of the liberty of conscience.[61] "[A]bove all things," Locke pleaded, it is "necessary to distinguish exactly the business of civil government from that of religion, and to settle the just bounds that lie between the one and the other." The Church, Locke wrote, must be "absolutely separate and distinct from the commonwealth." For the Church is simply "a voluntary society of men, joining themselves together of their own accord in order to the public worshipping of God in such manner as they judge acceptable to Him, and effectual for the salvation of their souls." Church members are free to enter and free to exit this society. They are free to determine its order and organization and to arrange its discipline and worship in a manner they consider most conducive to eternal life. "Nothing ought nor can be trans-

60. Richard Hooker, *Of the Laws of Ecclesiastical Polity*, ed. Arthur Stephen McGrade (Cambridge: Cambridge University Press, 1989), pp. 129-38.

61. John Locke, *Letter Concerning Toleration* (1689), in *The Works of John Locke*, twelfth ed., 9 vols. (1824), 5:1-58. Locke wrote two subsequent such letters and had a fragment of a fourth letter underway on his death in 1704. It was the first letter of 1689 that was best known in America.

acted in this society relating to the possession of civil and worldly power. No force is to be made use of upon any occasion whatsoever. For force belongs wholly to the civil magistrate."

State force, in turn, cannot touch religion, Locke argued. The state exists merely to protect persons in their outward lives, in their enjoyment of life, liberty, and property. "True and saving religion consists in the inward persuasion of the mind," which only God can touch and tend. A person cannot be compelled to true belief of anything by outward force — whether through "confiscation of estate, imprisonments, [or] torments" or through mandatory compliance with "articles of faith or forms of worship" established by law. "For laws are of no force without penalties, and penalties in this case are absolutely impertinent, because they are not proper to convince the mind." "It is only light and evidence that can work a change in men's [religious] opinions: which light can in no manner proceed from corporal sufferings, or any other outward penalties" inflicted by the state. Every person "has the supreme and absolute authority of judging for himself" in matters of faith.

Locke did not press this thesis to radical conclusions. His *Letter Concerning Toleration* presupposed a magistracy and community committed to a common Christianity. State laws directed to the common good, he believed, would only "seldom . . . appear unlawful to the conscience of a private person" and would only seldom run afoul of conventional Christian beliefs and practices. Catholics, Muslims, and other believers "who deliver themselves up to the service and protection of another prince" have no place in this community. Moreover, "those are not at all tolerated who deny the being of a God" — for "promises, covenants, and oaths which are the bonds of human society, can have no hold upon an atheist." Locke strengthened these qualifications even more in his theological writings — arguing in his volumes *The Reasonableness of Christianity, Essays on the Law of Nature,* and *Thoughts on Education* for the cogency of a simple biblical natural law and endorsing in his several commentaries on St. Paul's epistles the utility of a moderate Christian republicanism.[62]

62. John Locke, *The Reasonableness of Christianity,* in *Works of John Locke,* 6:1-158, at 140-43; John Locke, *Essays on the Law of Nature,* ed. W. von Leyden [ca. 1662] (Oxford: Oxford University Press, 1954); *The Educational Writings of John Locke,* ed. James L. Axtell (London: Cambridge University Press, 1968). See Nicholas P. Wolterstorff, *John Locke and the Ethics of Belief* (Cambridge: Cambridge University Press, 1996); Jeremy Waldron, *God, Locke, and Equality: Christian Foundations of John Locke's Political Thought* (Cambridge: Cambridge University Press, 2002); John Perry, "Locke's

James Burgh (1714-1775), a Scottish Whig who was popular among several American founders, notably James Madison (1751-1836), was less equivocal in advocating the principle of separation of Church and state. In his influential writings of the 1760s and 1770s,[63] Burgh lamented the "ill consequences" of the traditional "mixed-mungrel-spiritual-secular-ecclesiastical establishment." Such conflations of Church and state, said Burgh, lead to "follies and knaveries," and make "the dispensers of religion despicable and odious to all men of sense, and will destroy the spirituality, in which consists the whole value, of religion." "Build an impenetrable wall of separation between sacred and civil," Burgh enjoined. "Do not send the graceless officer, reeking from the arms of his trull [i.e., prostitute], to the performance of a holy rite of religion, as a test for his holding the command of a regiment. To profane, in such a manner, a religion, which you pretend to reverence, is an impiety sufficient to bring down upon your heads, the roof of the sacred building you thus defile."[64]

The French revolutionary Marquis de Condorcet (1743-1794), who influenced Thomas Paine (1737-1809) and others, put his case "to separate religion from the State" in the shriller anti-Catholic terms that would dominate the French Revolution. While it was important "to leave to the priests the freedom of sacraments, censures, [and] ecclesiastical functions," Condorcet conceded, the state must take steps to remove the traditional influence and privileges of the Catholic Church and clergy in society. The state was "not to give any civil effect to any of their decisions, not to give any influence over marriages or over birth or death certificates; not to allow them to intervene in any civil or political act; and to judge the lawsuits which would arise, between them and their citizens, for the temporal rights relating to their functions, as one would decide the similar lawsuits that would arise between the members of a free association, or between this association and private individuals."[65] Such anti-clerical and anti-Catholic separationist sentiments were quite typical of the French revolutionaries.

Accidental Church: The Letter Concerning Toleration and the Church's Witness to the State," *Journal of Church and State* 47 (2005): 269-88.

63. Dreisbach, *Thomas Jefferson and the Wall of Separation*, pp. 79-82.

64. James Burgh, *Crito, or Essays on Various Subjects*, 2 vols. (London: Messrs. Dodsley, 1767), 2:117-19 (emphasis removed).

65. Condorcet's notes on Voltaire, in *Oeuvres Completes de Voltaire* (Kehl: De L'Imprimerie de la Société Littéraire-Typographique, 1784), 18:476, using translation in *Separation of Church and State*, by Philip A. Hamburger (Cambridge, Mass.: Harvard University Press, 2002), p. 60.

And, in the following decades, these kinds of sentiments inspired a devastating political and popular attack on the clergy and property of the Catholic Church.[66]

Exodus: The Routes of American Separationism

The eighteenth-century American founders called on this European and colonial legacy to press at least five concerns in the name of separation of Church and state.

First, the founders invoked separationism to protect the Church from the state. This had been a common Christian understanding of separation of Church and state since the first century. It was captured in the Christian clergy's perennial call in subsequent centuries for "freedom of the Church" — or what the Edict of Milan of 313 had called the "free exercise and practice of religious groups."[67] This understanding of separation of Church and state was prominent in eighteenth-century America. The American founders' principal concern was to protect Church affairs from state intrusion, the clergy from the magistracy, Church properties from state interference, ecclesiastical rules and rites from political coercion and control. Elisha Williams (1694-1755), the New England Puritan jurist, spoke for many churchmen when he wrote in 1744: "[E]very church has [the] right to judge in what manner God is to be worshipped by them, and what form of discipline ought to be observed by them," and what clergy are to be "elected by them," from all of which the state must be "utterly separate."[68] George Washington (1732-1799) wrote in 1785 of the need "to establish effectual barriers" so that there was no threat "to the religious rights of any ecclesiastical Society," including particularly beleaguered minorities like Jews, Catholics, and Quakers, to whom he wrote several tender letters.[69] Thomas Jefferson called for government to resist what he called "inter-

---

66. Russell Hittinger, "Introduction to Catholicism," in *The Teachings of Modern Christianity on Law, Politics and Human Nature,* ed. John Witte Jr. and Frank S. Alexander (New York: Columbia University Press, 2005), chap. 1.

67. In Lactantius, *De Mortibus Persecutorum* [c. 315], 48.2-12, ed. and trans. J. L. Creed (Cambridge: Cambridge University Press, 1984), pp. 71-73.

68. Elisha Williams, *The Essential Rights and Liberties of Protestants* (Boston: S. Kneeland and T. Green, 1744), p. 46.

69. Quoted by Dreisbach, *Thomas Jefferson and the Wall of Separation Beween Church and State,* pp. 84-85.

meddling with religious institutions, their doctrines, discipline, or exercises." "Every religious society has a right to determine for itself the times for these exercises, & the objects proper for them, according to their own peculiar tenets," Jefferson wrote. And none of this can "concern or involve" the state.[70] A decade later, Tunis Wortman (d. 1822), a Jeffersonian, wrote:

> It is your duty, as Christians, to maintain the purity and independence of the church, to keep religion separate from politics, to prevent an union between the church and the state, and to preserve the clergy from temptation, corruption and reproach. . . . Unless you maintain the pure and primitive spirit of Christianity, and prevent the cunning and intrigue of statesmen from mingling with its institutions, you will become exposed to a renewal of the same dreadful and enormous scenes which have not only disgraced the annals of the church, but destroyed the peace, and sacrificed the lives of millions.[71]

This first understanding of separation of Church and state was captured especially in state constitutional guarantees of the free exercise rights of peaceable religious groups — the right of religious bodies to incorporate and to hold property, to appoint and remove clergy and other officials, to have sites and rites of worship, education, charity, mission, and burial, to maintain standards of entrance and exit for their members, and more — all of which were specified in state constitutions and implementing legislation.[72]

This understanding of separationism was also implicit in the First Amendment free exercise guarantee. Earlier drafts of the First Amendment, and the cryptic House debates that have survived about these drafts, spoke repeatedly of the need to protect religious sects, denominations, groups, or societies, to guarantee their rights to worship, property, and practice.[73] None of this concern for the detailed rights of religious groups was rejected

70. Thomas Jefferson, Letter to Rev. Samuel Miller (1808), in *The Founders' Constitution*, ed. Philip B. Kurland and Ralph S. Lerner, 5 vols. (Chicago: University of Chicago Press, 1987), 5:98-99.

71. Tunis Wortman, "A Solemn Address to Christians and Patriots (1800)," in *Political Sermons in the American Founding Era, 1730-1805,* ed. Ellis Sandoz (Indianapolis: Liberty, 1991), pp. 1477, 1482, 1487-88.

72. See esp. Chester J. Antieau, Phillip Mark Carroll, and Thomas Carroll Burke, *Religion under the State Constitutions* (Brooklyn: Central Book, 1965).

73. See details in Chapter 6 herein.

in the House debates — and can at least be plausibly read into the generic free exercise guarantee that was ultimately passed.[74]

Second, the founders invoked the principle of separationism to protect the state from the Church. This was a more recent Western understanding but it became increasingly prominent in the seventeenth and eighteenth centuries. "The sorest tyrannies have been those, who have united the royalty and priesthood in one person," wrote the authors of *Cato's Letters* in 1723. "Churchmen when they ruled states, had not only double authority but also double insolence and remarkably less mercy and regard to conscience, property," and the domains and demands of statecraft.[75] In the same vein, John Adams (1735-1826) devoted much of his 1774 *Dissertation on the Canon and the Feudal Law* to documenting what he called the "tyrannous outrages" that the medieval Catholic Church and early modern Protestant Churches had inflicted through their control of the state. This was "a wicked confederacy between two systems of tyranny," Adams wrote with ample bitterness.[76] Drawing on these same historical lessons, John Jay (1745-1829) urged his fellow constitutional conveners in New York "not only to expel civil tyranny, but also to guard against that spiritual oppression and intolerance wherewith the bigotry and ambition of weak and wicked priests and princes have scourged mankind."[77]

This second understanding of separation of Church and state helped to inform the movement in some states to exclude ministers and other religious officials from participating in political office. Such exclusions had been commonplace among seventeenth-century American Puritans and Anabaptists. But arguments for such clerical exclusions became more commonplace in eighteenth-century America. Ministers in political office, it was commonly argued, could use the threat of spiritual reprisal to force their congregants, including fellow politicians who sat in their pews, to acquiesce in their political positions. Ministers could be conflicted over whose interests to represent and serve — the interests of their congregants or their constituents. Ministers could have disproportionate influence on the political process since they represented both religious congregants and

74. See drafts and debates in RCE, pp. 80-105, 261-63.

75. John Trenchard and Thomas Gordon, *Cato's Letters, or Essays on Liberty, Civil and Religious, and Other Important Subjects* (1720-23), 2 vols., ed. Ronald Hamowy (Indianapolis: Liberty, 1995), 2:467-68.

76. Adams, Works, 3:447.

77. Jay, quoted by Hamburger, *Separation of Church and State*, pp. 81-82; New York Constitution (1777), arts. XXXVIII-XXXIX.

political constituents. Ministers who tried to serve both God and the state could be distracted from their fundamental callings of preaching and teaching, and tempted to train their religious messages toward political causes. Ministers could not enjoy both the benefit of exemption of taxation for themselves and the power to impose taxation on all others; this was even more odious than the great offense of taxation without representation.[78]

These kinds of arguments led seven of the original thirteen states, and fifteen later states, to ban ministers from serving in political office.[79] The South Carolina Constitution (1778) contained typical language:

> And whereas, ministers of the Gospel are by their profession dedicated to the service of God and the cure of souls, and ought not to be diverted from their great duties of their function, therefore no minister of the Gospel or public preacher of any religious persuasion, while he continues in the exercise of his pastoral function, and for two years after, shall be eligible either as governor, lieutenant-governor, a member of the senate, house representative, or privy council in this State.[80]

Third, the founders sometimes invoked the principle of separation of Church and state as a means to protect the individual's liberty of conscience from the intrusions of either Church or state, or both conspiring together. This had been an early and enduring understanding of separationism among colonial Anabaptists and Quakers. In eighteenth-century America, this argument became more prominent. "Every man has an equal right to follow the dictates of his own conscience in the affairs of religion," Elisha Williams wrote. This is "an equal right with any rulers be they civil or ecclesiastical."[81] James Madison put this case in his 1785 *Memorial and Re-*

---

78. John Witte Jr., "'A Most Mild and Equitable Establishment of Religion': John Adams and the 1780 Massachusetts Constitution," *Journal of Church and State* 41 (1999): 242ff.; Hamburger, *Separation of Church and State,* pp. 79-88.

79. Daniel L. Dreisbach, "The Constitution's Forgotten Religion Clause: Reflections on the Article VI Religious Test Ban," *Journal of Church and State* 38 (1996): 261-95; Derek Davis, *Religion and the Continental Congress 1774-1789: Contributions to Original Intent* (Oxford: Oxford University Press, 2000), pp. 50-51, 73-94.

80. South Carolina Constitution (1778), art. XXI. See also New York Constitution (1777), arts. XXXVIII-XXXIX; Delaware Constitution (1776), art. XXIX; Maryland Constitution (1776), art. XXXVII; North Carolina Constitution (1776), art. XXXI. Among later constitutions, see Tennessee Constitution (1796), art. 8, struck down in *McDaniel v. Paty,* 436 U.S. 618 (1978).

81. Williams, *Essential Rights and Liberties,* pp. 7-8.

monstrance, calling for what he termed "a great barrier" between Church and state to defend the religious rights of the individual. Thomas Jefferson's famous 1802 letter to the Danbury Baptist Association also tied the principle of separation of Church and state directly to the principle of liberty of conscience. After his opening salutation, Jefferson's letter reads thus:

> Believing with you that *religion is a matter which lies solely between a man and his God,* that he owes account to none other for his faith or his worship, that the [legitimate] powers of government reach actions only, and not opinions, I contemplate with sovereign reverence that [ ] act of the whole American people which declared that their legislature should "make no law respecting an establishment of religion, or prohibiting the free exercise thereof," *thus building a wall of separation between church and State.* Adhering to this expression of the supreme will of the nation *in behalf of the rights of conscience,* I shall see with sincere satisfaction the progress of those sentiments which tend to *restore to man all his natural rights,* convinced he has no natural right in opposition to his social duties.[82]

In Jefferson's formulation here, separation of Church and state assured individuals of their natural right of conscience, which could be exercised freely and fully to the point of breaching or shirking social duties. Jefferson is not talking of separating politics and religion altogether. Indeed, in the very next paragraph of his letter, President Jefferson performed an avowedly religious act of offering prayers on behalf of his Baptist correspondents. He wrote, "I reciprocate your kind prayers for the protection and blessing of the common Father and Creator of man."

Fourth, the founders occasionally used the principle of separation of Church and state to argue for the protection of individual states from interference by the federal government in governing local religious affairs. As Daniel Dreisbach has shown, Jefferson pressed this federalist jurisdictional sense of separation as well. He said many times that the federal government had no jurisdiction over religion; religion was entirely a state and local matter, in his view. As he put it in his Second Inaugural: "In matters of religion, I have considered that its free exercise is placed by the constitution independent of the [federal] government. I have therefore undertaken, on

82. In Dreisbach, *Thomas Jefferson and the Wall of Separation,* p. 148 (emphasis added).

no occasion, to prescribe the religious exercises suited to it; but have left them, as the constitution found them, under the direction and discipline of State or Church authorities."[83] The separation that Jefferson had in mind here was between local Church-state relations and the federal government. The federal government could not interfere in the affairs of local Churches. And the federal government could not interfere in the affairs of local states vis-à-vis these local Churches. Under this federalist jurisdictional reading of separationism, state governments were free to patronize and protect religion, or to prohibit or abridge religion, as their own state constitutions dictated. But the federal government was entirely foreclosed from the same.

As I noted in the previous chapter, some scholars have imputed this fourth understanding of separation of Church and state into the First Amendment provision that "Congress shall make no law *respecting* an establishment of religion." The argument is that Congress shall make no laws respecting any *state establishment* of religion. In 1789, when the First Amendment was being drafted, several of the original thirteen states still had some form of religious establishment, which both their state legislatures and constitutional conventions defined and defended, often against strong opposition. Moreover, Virginia had just passed Jefferson's bill for the "*establishment* of religious freedom," also against firm opposition. Having just defended their state establishments (of whatever sort) at home, the new members of Congress had no intention of handing over control of them to the new federal government. This is a plausible reading of the "respecting" language in the First Amendment, though the evidence for this reading is very thin. This federalist reading of the establishment clause is becoming more prominent in the literature today, and has recently captured the imagination of Justice Clarence Thomas.[84]

Fifth, the founders invoked the principle of separation of Church and state as a means to protect society and its members from unwelcome participation in and support for religion. Already in later colonial America, several religious groups used separationism to argue against the established Church poli-

83. Quoted and discussed in Dreisbach, *Thomas Jefferson and the Wall of Separation*, p. 152.

84. See *Elk Grove Unified School District v. Newdow*, 542 U.S. 1, 46 (2004) (Thomas, J., concurring); *Zelman v. Simmons-Harris*, 536 U.S. 639, 677-80 (2002) (Thomas, J., concurring); *Van Orden v. Perry*, 125 S. Ct. 2854, 2867 (2005) (Thomas, J., concurring). See Steven K. Green, "Federalism and the Establishment Clause: A Reassessment," *Creighton Law Review* 38 (2005): 761; Symposium, "Interactive Federalism," *Emory Law Journal* (forthcoming).

cies of mandatory payments of tithes, required participation in swearing oaths, forced attendance at religious services, compulsory registration of Church properties, and more. At the turn of nineteenth century, the language of separation of Church and state also began to fuel broader campaigns to remove traditional forms and forums of religion in law, politics, and society altogether, and of special state protection, patronage, and participation in religion.

This was the most novel, and most controversial, understanding of separation of Church and state in the young American republic. But it began to gain rhetorical currency in the nineteenth century, as Philip Hamburger has shown. The first notorious instance came in 1800 during the heated election debates between Thomas Jefferson's Republican party and John Adams's Federalist party. Adams's party accused Jefferson of being "the anti-Christ" and the new "whore of Babylon," a "Jacobin infidel" and secularist bent on destruction of the necessary religious foundations of law and necessary alliances of Church and state. Jefferson's party accused Adams of being a "Puritan pope" and "religious tyrant" bent on subjecting the whole nation to his suffocating beliefs and to his smug, self-serving ministers who stood "foursquare against liberty and progress."[85]

These proved to be only the opening shots in a century-long American battle over the meaning and means of separating Church and state. The battles broke out thereafter over dueling, freemasonry, lotteries, drunkenness, Sunday laws, slavery, marriage, divorce, women's property rights, women's suffrage, religious education, blasphemy prosecutions, enforcement of Christian morals, and more. These were battles fought in Congress and in the courts, in states and on the frontier, in Churches and in the schools, in clubs and at the ballot box. They were largely wars of words, occasionally wars of arms. The battles included many familiar foes — Republicans and Federalists, the north and the south, native Americans and new immigrants. They also included a host of newly established political groups: the Know-Nothing Party, the American Protective Association, the National Liberal League, the American Secular Union, the Ku Klux Klan, and dozens of other new groups.

Let me just focus on one running episode in this great nineteenth-century battle, namely, the repeated clashes between Protestants and Catholics over separationism. The long and sad story of the anti-Catholicism of nineteenth-century American Protestants is well known. Around 1800, American Protestants and Catholics had seemed ready to put their bitter

---

85. Hamburger, *Separation of Church and State,* pp. 111-43.

and bloody battles behind them. But with the swelling tide of Catholic émigrés into America after the 1820s — all demanding work, building schools, establishing charities, converting souls, and gaining influence — native-born Protestants and patriots began to protest. Catholic bashing became a favorite sport of preachers and pamphleteers. Then rioting and Church-burnings broke out in the 1830s and 1840s, followed by even more vicious verbal pillorying and repressive actions against Catholics.

What several recent studies have made clear is that the principle of separation of Church and state became one of the strong new weapons in the anti-Catholic arsenal. Foreign Catholics were for the union of Church and state, the propagandists claimed. American Protestants were for the separation of Church and state. To be a Catholic was to oppose separationism and American-style liberties. To be a Protestant was to defend separationism and American-style liberties. To bash a Catholic was thus not a manifestation of religious bigotry but a demonstration of American patriotism. Protestants and patriots began to run closely together, often tripping over each other to defend separationism and to decry and deny Catholics for their failure to do so. All this is a proper corrective that students of American religious liberty need to hear.[86]

But it is important that the corrected story not now be read as a simple dialectic of Protestant separationist hawks versus Catholic unionist doves. And it is important to be clear that the Protestant-Catholic battle over separation of Church and state had two sides, with Catholics giving as well as taking, winning as well as losing.

First, many American Catholic clergy in antebellum America were themselves separationists, building their views in part on ancient patristic models of two communities, two cities, and two powers. Moreover, a good number of American Catholic clergy saw separation of Church and state as an essential principle of religious liberty and embraced the doctrine without evident cavil or concern. Alexis de Tocqueville (1805-1859), for one, noted this in his *Democracy in America* (1835):

> In France I had seen the spirits of religion and of freedom almost always marching in opposite directions. In America I found them intimately linked together in joint reign over the same land. My longing to

---

86. Including my own unduly pro-Protestant reading. See criticisms in Richard W. Garnett, "Francis Bacon Takes on the Ghouls: The 'First Principles' of Religious Freedom," *Green Bag* 3 (2000): 453-54.

understand the reason for this phenomenon increased daily. To find this out, I questioned the faithful of all communions; I particularly sought the society of clergymen, who are the depositaries of the various creeds and have a personal interest in their survival. As a practicing Catholic I was particularly close to the Catholic priests, with some of whom I soon established a certain intimacy. I expressed my astonishment and revealed my doubts to each of them; I found that they all agreed with each other except about details; all thought that the main reason for the quiet sway of religion over their country was the complete separation of church and state. I have no hesitation in stating that throughout my stay in America I met nobody, lay or cleric, who did not agree about that.[87]

Second, many Protestant anti-Catholic writings started not so much as attacks upon American Catholics but as counterattacks to several blistering papal condemnations of Protestantism, democracy, religious liberty, and separation of Church and state. In *Mirari vos* (1832), for example, Pope Gregory XVI (d. 1846) condemned in no uncertain terms all Churches that deviated from the Church of Rome, and all states that granted liberty of conscience, free exercise, and free speech to their citizens. For the pope it was an "absurd and erroneous proposition which claims that liberty of conscience must be maintained for everyone."[88] The pope "denounced freedom to publish any writings whatever and disseminate them to the people. . . . The Church has always taken action to destroy the plague of bad books."[89] He declared anathema against the "detestable insolence and probity" of Luther and other Protestant "sons of Belial" (i.e., the Devil), those "sores and disgraces of the human race" who "joyfully deem themselves 'free of all.'"[90] Even worse, the pope averred, were "the plans of those who desire vehemently to separate the Church from the state, and to break the mutual concord between temporal authority and the priesthood."[91] The reality, the pope insisted, was that state officials "re-

---

87. Alexis de Tocqueville, *Democracy in America*, trans. George Lawrence, ed. J. P. Mayer (Garden City, N.Y.: Anchor, 1969), p. 295 (paragraph breaks removed).

88. Gregory XVI, *Mirari vos (On Liberalism and Religious Indifferentism)* (1832), para. 14.

89. *Mirari vos*, paras. 15-16.

90. *Mirari vos*, para. 19. "Belial" means the "spirit of evil personified" or "fallen angel." "Belial," *Oxford English Dictionary* (Oxford: Oxford University Press, 1971).

91. *Mirari vos*, para. 20.

ceived their authority not only for the government of the world, but especially for the defense of the Church."[92]

In the blistering *Syllabus of Errors* (1864), the papacy condemned as cardinal errors the propositions that:

18. Protestantism is nothing more than another form of the same true Christian religion, in which it is possible to be equally pleasing to God as in the Catholic Church.

19. The Church is not a true, and perfect, and entirely free society, nor does she enjoy peculiar and perpetual rights conferred upon her by her Divine Founder, but it appertains to the civil power to define what are the rights and limits with which the Church may exercise authority. . . .

24. The Church has not the power of availing herself of force, or any direct or indirect temporal power. . . .

55. The Church ought to be separate from the State, and the State from the Church.[93]

In place of these cardinal errors, the papacy declared that the Catholic Church was the only true Church, which must, as in medieval centuries past, enjoy power in both spiritual and temporal affairs, unhindered by the state.[94] Six years later, the Vatican Council declared the pope's teachings to be infallible and again condemned Protestants as "heretics" who dared subordinate the "divine magisterium of the Church" to the "judgment of each individual."[95]

It is perhaps no surprise that American Protestants repaid such alarming comments in kind — and then with interest. The pope, as Americans heard him, had condemned the very existence of Protestantism and the very fundamentals of American democracy and liberty — effectively calling the swelling population of American Catholics to arms. Many Protestants saw in the papacy's favorable references to its past medieval

92. *Mirari vos*, para. 23.

93. Pius IX, *The Papal Syllabus of Errors* (1864), in *Creeds of Christendom with a History and Critical Notes,* by Philip Schaff, 3 vols. (New York: Harper, 1877), 2:213, 217-19, 227.

94. *The Papal Syllabus of Errors*, 2:218-33, esp. paras. 20, 24-35, 41-44, 53-54, 75-80.

95. *The Dogmatic Decrees of the Vatican Council Concerning the Catholic Faith and the Church of Christ* (1870), in *Creeds of Christendom,* by Schaff, 2:234, 236.

powers[96] specters of the two swords theory by which the papacy had claimed supreme rule in a unified Christendom. This simply could not be for Protestants. Conveniently armed with new editions of the writings of Martin Luther,[97] John Calvin,[98] and others,[99] American Protestants repeated much of the vitriolic anti-Catholic and anti-clerical rhetoric that had clattered so loudly throughout the sixteenth century.

At least initially, the loud commendation of America's separation of Church and state and loud condemnation of the Catholic union of Church and state was more of a rhetorical quid pro quo to the papacy than a political low blow to American Catholics. Inevitably, there was plenty of political imitation and plenty of cheap shots taken at the American Catholic clergy, particularly those who echoed the papacy. And inevitably, this rhetoric brought anti-Catholicism and pro-separationism into close association — particularly when the issue was taken up by secular political groups, few of whom spoke for mainstream Protestants.

A third and final caveat is that when local anti-Catholic measures did pass, as they too often did in the later nineteenth and twentieth centuries, both the United States Supreme Court and Congress did sometimes provide Catholics with relief, often using separation of Church and state as their guiding principle. Thus in *Cummings v. Missouri* (1866), the Court held that a state may not deprive a Catholic priest of the right to preach for failure to take a mandatory oath disavowing his support for the confederate states.[100] In *Watson v. Jones* (1871) and three later cases, the Court required civil courts to defer to the judgment of the highest religious authorities in resolving intra-Church disputes, explicitly extending that principle to Catholics.[101] In *Church of the Holy Trinity v. United States* (1892), the Court refused to uphold a new federal law forbidding contracts with foreign clergy, a vital issue for Catholic clergy.[102] In *Bradfield v. Roberts* (1899), the

96. *Dogmatic Decrees of the Vatican Council,* 2:221, para. 34.

97. See Eric W. Gritsch, *A History of Lutheranism* (Minneapolis: Fortress, 2002), pp. 179-216; Eric W. Gritsch and Robert W. Jenson, *Lutheranism: The Theological Movement and Its Confessional Writings* (Philadelphia: Fortress, 1976).

98. See Wulfert de Greef, *The Writings of John Calvin,* trans. Lyle D. Bierma (Grand Rapids: Baker, 1993).

99. See, e.g., John Adams, *A Dissertation on the Canon and the Feudal Law* (1774), in Adams, Works, 3:447 (denouncing Catholic canon law and papal authority for its intrusions on liberty).

100. 71 U.S. (4 Wall.) 277 (1866).

101. 80 U.S. (13 Wall.) 679 (1871).

102. 143 U.S. 457 (1892).

Court upheld, against establishment clause challenge, a federal grant to build a Catholic hospital in the District of Columbia.[103] In *Quick Bear v. Leupp* (1908), the Court upheld the federal distribution of funds to Catholic schools that offered education to Native Americans.[104] In *Order of Benedict v. Steinhauser* (1914), the Court upheld a monastery's communal ownership of property against claims by relatives of a deceased monk.[105] In *Pierce v. Society of Sisters* (1925), the Court invalidated a state law making public school attendance mandatory, thereby protecting the rights of Catholic parents and schools to educate children in a religious school environment.[106] A good number of these Supreme Court holdings were, in part, expressions of the principle of separation of Church and state. And there were more such Catholic victories in state courts, in cases where separation was again used as a means to protect religious consciences, clergy, and corporations from state interference.[107]

This is not to say that anti-Catholic and broader anti-religious measures were always struck down, and it is not to say that separation of Church and state was not sometimes put to blatantly discriminatory purposes. In the last half of the nineteenth century, a number of state constitutions adopted the spirit of separation of Church and state (though not the language) in the context of education and state funding. Thirty-five state constitutions ultimately insisted that state and local governments grant no funds to religious schools. Fifteen state constitutions insisted that state schools remain free from "sectarian influence" or from the control of religious officials and institutions. These provisions were certainly motivated, in part, by the growing bias against emerging Catholic primary and secondary schools in the nineteenth century.[108] But these provisions also testified to the growing number and power of Baptists and Methodists who, following their eighteenth-century forebearers, urged a greater separation of Church and state for their own theological reasons and not out of Catholic bias.

103. 175 U.S. 291 (1899).
104. 210 U.S. 50 (1908).
105. 234 U.S. 640 (1914).
106. 268 U.S. 510 (1925).
107. See Carl Zollman, *American Church Law*, repr. ed. (St. Paul, Minn.: West, 1933); W. Torpey, *Judicial Doctrines of Religious Rights in America* (Chapel Hill, N.C.: University of North Carolina Press, 1948).
108. See John C. Jeffries Jr. and James E. Ryan, "A Political History of the Establishment Clause," *Michigan Law Review* 100 (2001): 279, 297ff.; Hamburger, *Separation of Church and State*, pp. 219-29, 321-22, 340-41, 412-18.

In the later nineteenth and early twentieth centuries, twenty-nine state constitutions broadened their rule of no-state-funding-for-religion to apply not only to religious schools but to all religious causes and institutions. The Nevada Constitution (1864), for example, provided briefly: "No public funds of any kind or character whatever, State, county, or municipal, shall be used for sectarian purpose[s]."[109] Several states echoed the strong language of the 1870 Illinois Constitution:

> Neither the General Assembly nor any county, city, town, township, school district or other public corporation shall ever make any appropriation or pay from any public fund whatever, anything in aid of any church or sectarian purpose, or to help support or sustain any school, academy, seminary, college, university or other literary or scientific institution, controlled by any church or sectarian denomination whatever; nor shall any grant or donation of land, money or other personal property ever be made by the State or any such public corporation to any church or for any sectarian or religious purpose.[110]

Today, these state constitutional provisions against funding of religion and religious education are often called "state-Blaine" or "mini-Blaine" amendments, in reference to Representative Blaine's proposed amendment to the Constitution that was narrowly defeated in the Congress in 1875.[111] The anti-Catholic and sometimes anti-religious and anti-clerical prejudices that Blaine championed certainly figured in some states — particularly new Western states on whose new state constitutions Congress imposed its prejudices as a condition for granting the rights of statehood.

But again this evidence should not be over-read. A number of the state constitutional provisions against religious funding antedated Blaine's efforts by more than a decade. The language they used was often very different

109. Constitution of Nevada (1864), art. XI.10.

110. Constitution of Illinois (1870), art. VIII.3.

111. 4 Congressional Record 5190 (1876); Alfred W. Meyer, "The Blaine Amendment and the Bill of Rights," *Harvard Law Review* 64 (1951): 939; F. William O'Brien, "The Blaine Amendment, 1875-1876," *University of Detroit Law Journal* 41 (1963): 137-205; F. William O'Brien, "The States and 'No Establishment': Proposed Amendments to the Constitution Since 1789," *Washburn Law Journal* 4 (1965): 183-210; Steven K. Green, "The Blaine Amendment Reconsidered," *American Journal of Legal History* 36 (1992): 38.

from Blaine's proposed federal amendment. A good number of the state constitutional delegates who sought to outlaw government aid to religion were themselves clerics, who used familiar seventeenth- and eighteenth-century Protestant and Enlightenment arguments for separation of Church and state that had little to do with anti-Catholicism or anti-clericalism.[112] Moreover, these separationist arguments against government funding of some religions were often coupled with separationist arguments for religious tax exemptions for all religions. Thirty-three state constitutions ultimately included new provisions exempting from property taxation all properties devoted to religious worship, religious charity, and religious education.[113] These new tax exemption provisions were not just Pyrrhic victories — attempts by religious bodies to seize indirect funding now that they lacked the political power to command direct funding. Tax exemption provisions were presented as a better way to ensure nonpreferential state support to all religious organizations, rather than continuing to give preferential status to those religious groups who had majoritarian power to extract funding from the legislatures.[114]

Deuteronomy: What Legal Place for Separationism Today?

All this changed rather dramatically with the Supreme Court case of *Everson v. Board of Education* (1947), as we shall see in more detail in the following chapter. This case made two major moves at once. First, the Court applied the First Amendment establishment clause to the states: "Congress shall make no law . . . ," now became, in effect, "Governments of any kind shall make no law respecting an establishment of religion" — a re-

112. See examples in Thomas E. Buckley, "After Disestablishment: Thomas Jefferson's Wall of Separation in Antebellum Virginia," *Journal of Southern History* LXI (1995): 445; Thomas E. Buckley, "The Use and Abuse of Jefferson's Statute: Separating Church and State in Nineteenth-Century Virginia," in *Religion and the New Republic: Faith in the Founding of America*, ed. James H. Hutson (Lanham, Md.: Rowman and Littlefield, 2000), pp. 41-64; Thomas E. Buckley, "'A Great Religious Octopus': Church and State at Virginia's Constitutional Convention, 1901-1902," *Church History* 72 (2003): 333.

113. Twenty-seven of the thirty-three state constitutions that explicitly outlawed state funding of religion also explicitly authorized such exemptions, and the remaining seven states had strong statutory provisions in effect providing for the same. See RCE, Appendix 2.

114. John Witte Jr., "Tax Exemption of Church Property: Historical Anomaly or Valid Constitutional Precept," *Southern California Law Review* 64 (1991): 363-415.

jection of the original federalist understanding of separation of Church and state. Second, Justice Black read into the establishment clause a strict separationist logic that was amply coated and coded with the anti-clerical sentiments that Black had absorbed as a former member of the Ku Klux Klan. The anti-Catholic and sometimes anti-religious sentiments of the later nineteenth century were suddenly lifted to a constitutional mandate for the entire nation.

The First Amendment establishment clause "means at least this," Justice Black wrote for the *Everson* court:

> Neither a state nor the federal government can set up a church. Neither can pass laws which aid one religion, aid all religions, or prefer one religion over another. . . . No tax in any amount, large or small, can be levied to support any religious activities or institutions, whatever they may be called. Neither a state nor the federal government can, openly or secretly, participate in the affairs of any religious organizations or groups, or vice versa. In the words of Jefferson, the clause against establishment of religion by law was intended to erect "a wall of separation between church and state."[115]

In later cases, Justice Black stressed that "a union of government and religion tends to destroy government and to degrade religion." "Religion is too personal, too sacred, [and] too holy, to permit its 'unhallowed perversion' by a civil magistrate."[116] Religion is also too powerful, too sinister, and too greedy to permit its unhindered pervasion of a civil magistracy. "[T]he same powerful religious propagandists" who are allowed to succeed in making one inroad on the state and its laws, Justice Black wrote, "doubtless will continue their propaganda, looking toward complete domination and supremacy of their particular brand of religion. And it is nearly always by insidious approaches that the citadels of [religious] liberty are more successfully attacked."[117] "The First Amendment has erected a wall of separation between Church and state. That wall must be kept high and impregnable. We could not approve the slightest breach."[118]

The Supreme Court applied its strict separationist logic with special

115. *Everson*, 330 U.S. at 15-16.
116. *Engel v. Vitale*, 370 U.S. 421, 430-32 (1962).
117. *Board of Education v. Allen*, 392 U.S. 236, 251-52 (1968) (Black, J., dissenting).
118. *Everson*, 330 U.S. at 18.

vigor in cases challenging the traditional state patronage and protection of religious education. In more than two dozen cases after *Everson,* the Court held that public schools could not offer prayers or moments of silence, could not read Scripture or religious texts, could not house Bibles or prayerbooks, could not teach theology or creationism, could not display Decalogues or crèches, could not use the services or facilities of religious bodies. At the same time, states could not provide salary and service supplements to religious schools, could not reimburse them for administering standardized tests, could not lend them state-prescribed textbooks, supplies, films, or counseling services, could not allow tax deductions or credits for religious school tuition. The Court purged religion from the public school and removed religious schools from many traditional forms of state support.

In *Lemon v. Kurtzman* (1971), the Court distilled the separationist logic of its early cases into a general test to be used in all establishment clause cases. Henceforth every law challenged under the establishment clause would pass constitutional muster only if it could be shown (1) to have a secular purpose; (2) to have a primary effect that neither advances nor inhibits religion; and (3) to foster no excessive entanglement between Church and state.[119] The *Lemon* test rendered the establishment clause a formidable obstacle to many traditional forms and forums of Church-state cooperation. Particularly the lower courts used this *Lemon* test to outlaw all manner of government subsidies for religious charities, social services, and mission works; government use of religious services, facilities, and publications; and much more.

Some of these establishment clause cases in the name of separation of Church and state helped to extend the ambit of religious liberty, particularly for minority faiths. But some of these cases also helped to erode the province of religious liberty by effectively empowering a single secular party to veto popular laws touching religion that caused him or her only the most tangential constitutional injury. It must be remembered that separation of Church and state is only one principle that the establishment clause embraces, and that the establishment clause is only one guarantee the First Amendment embraces for the protection of religious liberty, the other being the free exercise clause.[120] The First Amendment says, "Congress shall make no law respecting an establishment of religion or prohibiting the free exercise

119. 403 U.S. 602 (1971).
120. See Chapter 6 herein.

thereof." These two religion clauses hold complementary guarantees of religious freedom. The free exercise clause outlaws government proscriptions of religion — actions that unduly burden the conscience, restrict religious expression, discriminate against religion, or invade the autonomy of Churches and other religious bodies. The establishment clause outlaws government prescriptions of religion — actions that coerce the conscience, mandate forms of religious expression, discriminate in favor of religion, or improperly ally the state with Churches or other religious bodies. No burden on, no coercion of conscience. No undue restrictions on, no undue mandating of religious expression. No discrimination against, no discrimination for religion. No government intrusions within, no government alliances with religious bodies. Read together this way, the First Amendment free exercise and establishment clauses afford reciprocal and complementary protections to liberty of conscience, freedom of religious expression, religious equality, and separation of Church and state.

When viewed in isolation, the principle of separation of Church and state serves religious liberty best when it is used prudentially, not categorically. Separationism needs to be retained, particularly for its ancient insight of protecting religious bodies from the state and for its more recent insight of protecting the consciences of religious believers from violations by government or religious bodies. Today, as much as in the past, government officials have no constitutional business interfering in the internal affairs of religious groups. Religious officials have no constitutional business converting the offices of government into instruments of their mission and ministry. Government has no business funding, sponsoring, or actively involving itself in the religious exercises of a particular religious group or religious official alone. Religious groups have no business drawing on government sponsorship or funding for their core religious exercises. All such conduct violates the core principle of separation of Church and state and should be outlawed.

The principle of separation of Church and state, however, also needs to be contained, and not used as an anti-religious weapon in the culture wars of the public square, public school, or public court. Separationism must be viewed as a shield rather than a sword in the great struggle to achieve religious liberty for all. A categorical insistence on the principle of separation of Church and state avails us rather little. James Madison warned already in 1833 that "it may not be easy, in every possible case, to trace the line of separation between the rights of Religion and the Civil authority, with such distinctness, as to avoid collisions & doubts on unessential points."[121] This caveat has become even more salient today, when the modern welfare state, for better or worse, reaches deeply into virtually all aspects of modern life — through its network of education, charity, welfare, child care, health care, construction, zoning, workplace, taxation, and sundry other regulations. Madison's solution to the separation issue was "an entire abstinence of the Government from interference [with religion] in any way whatever, beyond the necessity of preserving public order, & protecting each sect against trespasses on its legal rights by others."[122] But this traditional understanding of a minimal state role in the life of society in general, and of religious bodies in particular — however alluring it may be in theory — is no longer realistic in practice.

It is thus even more imperative today than it was in Madison's day that the principle of separation of Church and state not be pressed to reach what Madison called the "unessentials." It is one thing for the Court to outlaw daily Christian prayers and broadcasted Bible readings from the public school, quite another thing to ban moments of silence and private displays of the Decalogue in the same schools. It is one thing to bar direct tax support for religious education, quite another thing to bar tax deductions for parents who wish to educate their children in the faith. It is one thing to prevent government officials from delegating their core police powers to religious bodies, quite another thing to prevent them from facilitating the charitable services of voluntary religious and nonreligious associations alike. It is one thing to outlaw governmental prescriptions of prayers, ceremonies, and symbols in public forums, quite another thing to outlaw governmental accommodations of private prayers, ceremonies, and symbols in public forums. To press separationist logic too deeply into "unessentials" not only "trivializes" the place of religion in public and private life, as Stephen Carter argues.[123] It also trivializes the power of the constitution, converting it from a coda of cardinal principles of national law into a codex of petty precepts of local life.

Too zealous an interpretation of the principle of separation of Church and state also runs afoul of other constitutive principles of the First Amendment — particularly the principles of liberty of conscience and reli-

---

121. Letter to Rev. Jasper Adams (1833), in *Religion and Politics in the Early Republic: Jasper Adams and the Church-State Debate*, ed. Daniel L. Dreisbach (Lexington: University Press of Kentucky, 1996), pp. 117-21, at 120 (emphasis added).

122. Quoted by Dreisbach, *Religion and Politics*, p. 120.

123. Stephen L. Carter, *The Culture of Disbelief: How American Law and Politics Trivializes Religious Devotion* (New York: Basic, 1993).

gious equality. The Court must be at least as zealous in protecting religious conscience from secular coercion as in protecting secular conscience from religious coercion. The Court should be at least as concerned to ensure the equal treatment of religion as to ensure the equality of religion and nonreligion. It is no violation of the principle of separation of Church and state when a legislature or court accommodates judiciously the conscientious scruples of a religious individual or the cardinal callings of a religious body. It is also no violation of this principle when government grants religious individuals and institutions equal access to state benefits, public forums, or tax disbursements that are open to nonreligionists similarly situated. To do otherwise is, indeed, to move toward what Justice Stewart once called "the establishment of a religion of secularism."[124]

124. *Abington School District v. Schempp,* 374 U.S. 203, 313 (Stewart, J., dissenting).

8

Adams versus Jefferson:
From Establishment to Freedom of Public Religion

The civic catechisms and canticles of our day still celebrate Thomas Jefferson's experiment in religious liberty. To end a millennium of repressive religious establishments, we are taught, Thomas Jefferson (1743-1826) sought liberty in the twin formulas of privatizing religion and secularizing politics. Religion must be "a concern purely between our God and our consciences," he wrote. Politics must be conducted with "a wall of separation between Church and state."[1] "Public Religion"[2] is a threat to private religion, and must thus be discouraged. "Political ministry" is a menace to political integrity and must thus be outlawed.

These Jeffersonian maxims remain for many today the cardinal axioms of a unique American logic of religious freedom to which every patriotic individual and institution should yield. Every public school student learns the virtues of keeping his Bible at home and her prayers in the closet. Every Church knows the tax-law advantages of high cultural conformity and low political temperature. Every politician understands the calculus of courting religious favors without subvening religious causes. Religious privatization is the bargain we must strike to attain religious freedom for all. A wall of separation is the barrier we must build to contain religious bigotry for good. If only those right-wing killjoys of our day would learn proper

1. H. Washington, ed., *The Writings of Thomas Jefferson*, 10 vols. (Washington, D.C.: Taylor and Maury, 1853-1854), 8:113.

2. A popular source of this phrase in American history is Benjamin Franklin, "Proposals Relating to the Education of Youth in Pensilvania (1749)," in *Benjamin Franklin: Representative Selections*, ed. C. Jorgenson and F. Mott (New York: Hill and Wang, 1962), p. 203. See Martin E. Marty, "On a Medial Moraine: Religious Dimensions of American Constitutionalism," *Emory Law Journal* 39 (1990): 1, 16-17.

patriotism, instead of pestering us with their Decalogues and faith-based initiatives!

"A page of history is worth a volume of logic," Oliver Wendell Holmes Jr. (1841-1935) once said.[3] And careful historical work in the past two decades has begun to call a good deal of this popular Jeffersonian logic into question. Not only are Jefferson's views on disestablishment and free exercise considerably more delphic than was once imagined,[4] but the fuller account now available of the genesis and exodus of the American experiment in religious liberty suggests that Jefferson's views were hardly conventional in his own day — or in the century to follow. Indeed, the Jeffersonian model of religious liberty came to constitutional prominence only in the 1940s, and then largely at the behest of the United States Supreme Court.[5] During much of the time before that, the American experiment was devoted not so much to privatizing religion and to secularizing politics, as to balancing the freedoms of all private religions against the establishment of one public religion.

The implications of these new historical insights have only begun to be worked out. The hard religious right has woven these historical insights into a crusade to reclaim the nation's Christian roots and to reestablish its Christian traditions in place of the current establishment of secularism. The hard religious left has converted them into a new appreciation for the bold prescience of the United States Supreme Court to anticipate the needs of our fragmented postmodern and post-Christian polity. The Supreme Court itself, however, has quietly abandoned much of its earlier separationist logic in recent years, and moved gradually toward the recognition that both private and public forms of religion deserve constitutional freedom.

To relate this story and its implications a bit more fully, permit me to revisit Jefferson's model of religious liberty, now viewed in juxtaposition with the model of religious liberty developed by John Adams (1735-1826), his life-long friendly rival. It was Adams's model, more than Jefferson's, I shall argue, that dominated American constitutional law for the first 150 years of the republic. It was Jefferson's model that the Supreme Court revived in the 1940s to overcome the abuses and limitations that Adams's

3. *New York Trust Co. v. Eisner,* 256 U.S. 345, 349 (1921).

4. See, e.g., Daniel L. Dreisbach, *Thomas Jefferson and the Wall of Separation between Church and State* (New York: New York University Press, 2002); Philip A. Hamburger, *Separation of Church and State* (Cambridge: Harvard University Press, 2002).

5. See further Chapter 7 herein.

model had betrayed. Today, I shall conclude, neither model standing alone is adequate, but the insights of both models can be combined into a new understanding of the freedom of public religion.

Jefferson versus Adams on Religious Liberty

As our civic catechism has taught us, Thomas Jefferson did regard his 1779 Bill for the Establishment of Religious Freedom in Virginia as a "fair" and "novel experiment."[6] This law, declared Jefferson, defied the ancient assumptions of the West: that one form of Christianity must be established in a community, and that the state must protect and support it against all other religions. Virginia would no longer suffer such state prescriptions or proscriptions of religion. All forms of Christianity must now stand on their own feet and on an equal footing with the faiths of "the Jew and the Gentile, . . . the Mahometan, the Hindu, and [the] Infidel of every denomination."[7] Their survival and growth must turn on the cogency of their word, not the coercion of the sword, on the faith of their members, not the force of the law.

True religious liberty, Jefferson argued, requires both the free exercise and the disestablishment of religion. On the one hand, the state should protect the liberty of conscience and free exercise of all its subjects — however impious or impish their religious beliefs and customs might appear. "Almighty God hath created the mind free," Jefferson wrote, and thus "no man shall be compelled to frequent or support any religious worship, place, or ministry whatsoever, nor shall be enforced, restrained, molested, or burthened in his body or goods, nor shall otherwise suffer on account of his religious opinions or belief; but that all men shall be free to profess, and by argument to maintain, their opinion in matters of religion, and that the same shall in no wise diminish, enlarge, or affect their civil capacities."[8]

On the other hand, the state should disestablish all religion. The state should not give special aid, support, privilege, or protection to religious doctrines or groups — through special tax appropriations and exemptions, special donations of goods and realty, or special laws of incorporation and

6. Saul K. Padover, ed., *The Complete Jefferson, Containing His Major Writings* (Freeport, N.Y.: Duell, Sloan, and Pearce, 1943), p. 538.
7. Padover, *The Complete Jefferson*, p. 1147.
8. Padover, *The Complete Jefferson*, pp. 946-47.

criminal protection. The state should not direct its laws to religious purposes. The state should not draw on the services of religious associations, nor seek to interfere in their order, organization, or orthodoxy. As Jefferson put it in his famous 1802 letter to the Danbury Baptist Association, "Believing with you that religion is a matter which lies solely between a man and his God, that he owes account to none other for his faith or his worship, that the [legitimate] powers of government reach actions only, and not opinions, I contemplate . . . a wall of separation between church and State."[9]

Clerics as much as politicians were to respect this wall of separation. They need to stick to their specialty of soulcraft rather than interfere in the specialty of statecraft. Religion is merely "a separate department of knowledge," Jefferson wrote, alongside other specialized disciplines like physics, biology, law, politics, and medicine. Preachers are the specialists in religion, and are hired to devote their time and energy to this specialty. "Whenever, therefore, preachers, instead of a lesson in religion, put them off with a discourse on the Copernican system, on chemical affinities, on the construction of government, or the characters of those administering it, it is a breach of contract, depriving their audience of the kind of service for which they were salaried."[10]

Jefferson's life-long friendly rival, John Adams, wrote an equally spirited defense of the Massachusetts "experiment" in religious liberty. "It can no longer be called in question," Adams wrote, that "authority in magistrates and obedience of citizens can be grounded on reason, morality, and the Christian religion," without succumbing to "the monkery of priests or the knavery of politicians."[11] The 1780 Massachusetts Constitution, which Adams largely drafted, guarantees the liberty of conscience and free exercise of all its citizens. But it also institutes a "mild and equitable establishment of religion," featuring special state protections and privileges for preferred forms of Christian piety, morality, and charity.[12]

---

9. Padover, *The Complete Jefferson*, pp. 518-19, 673-76, 946-47, 957-58. See further Edwin S. Gaustad, *Sworn on the Altar of God: A Religious Biography of Thomas Jefferson* (Grand Rapids: Eerdmans, 1996).

10. Letter from Thomas Jefferson to P. H. Wendover (Mar. 13, 1815), quoted and discussed in Hamburger, *Separation of Church and State*, pp. 152-54.

11. Adams, Works, 4:290, 293.

12. Adams, Works, 2:399; 3:451; 4:290-97; 8:232. See further Chapter 5 herein and John Witte Jr., "'A Most Mild and Equitable Establishment of Religion': John Adams and the Massachusetts Experiment," *Journal of Church and State* 41 (1999): 213-52.

True religious liberty, Adams argued, requires the state to balance the freedom of many private religions with the establishment of one public religion. On the one hand, every civil society must protect a plurality of private religions — whose rights are limited only by the parallel rights of juxtaposed religions and the duties of the established public religion. The notion that a state could coerce all persons to become adherents of a common public religion alone was for Adams a philosophical fiction. Persons would make their own private judgments in matters of faith. Any attempt to coerce their consciences would only breed hypocrisy and resentment. Moreover, the maintenance of religious plurality was essential for the protection of civil society and civil liberties. Adams's letter to Jefferson, quoted in Chapter 5 and Chapter 6, is worth recalling: "Checks and balances," Adams wrote, in the political as well as the religious sphere, "are our only Security, for the progress of Mind, as well as the Security of Body. Every Species of Christians would persecute Deists, as either Sect would persecute another, if it had unchecked and unballanced Power. Nay, the Deists would persecute Christians, and Atheists would persecute Deists, with as unrelenting Cruelty, as any Christians would persecute them or one another. Know thyself, Human nature!"[13]

On the other hand, every polity must establish by law some form of public religion, some image and ideal of itself, some common values and beliefs to undergird and support the plurality of protected private religions. The notion that a state could remain neutral and purged of any public religion was, for Adams, equally a philosophical fiction. Absent a commonly adopted set of values and beliefs, politicians would invariably hold out their private convictions as public ones. It was thus essential for each community to define and defend the basics of a public religion. In Adams's view, its creed was honesty, diligence, devotion, obedience, virtue, and love of God, neighbor, and self. Its icons were the Bible, the bells of liberty, the memorials of patriots, the Constitution. Its clergy were public-spirited ministers and religiously committed politicians. Its liturgy was the public proclamation of oaths, prayers, songs, and election and Thanksgiving Day sermons. Its policy was state appointment of chaplains for the legislature, military, and prison, state sanctions against blasphemy, sacrilege, and iconoclasm, state administration of tithe collections, test oaths, and clerical appointments, state sponsorship of religious societies, schools, and charities.

13. Lester J. Cappon, ed., *The Adams-Jefferson Letters* (Chapel Hill, N.C.: University of North Carolina Press, 1959), pp. 333-35.

"Statesmen may plan and speculate for liberty," Adams wrote in defense of his views, "but it is religion and morality alone which can establish the principles upon which freedom can securely stand." A "Publick Religion" sets "the foundation, not only of republicanism and of all free government, but of social felicity under all governments and in all the combinations of human society."[14]

Here are two models of religious liberty offered by two of the greatest luminaries of the American founding era. There were many other models available in their day — some more theological, some more philosophical in tone.[15] But these two models, given the eminence of their authors and the importance of their home states of Virginia and Massachusetts, were of central importance. Both Jefferson and Adams were self-consciously engaged in a new experiment in religious liberty. Both started with the credo of the American Declaration of Independence which they drafted: that "all men are created equal" and that they have "certain unalienable rights." Both insisted upon bringing within the mantle of constitutional protection every peaceable private religious belief and believer of their day.

But while Jefferson advocated a robust freedom of exercise, Adams condoned only a "tempered" religious freedom. While Jefferson urged the separation of Church and state, Adams urged only a division of religious and political offices. While Jefferson advocated the disestablishment of all religions, Adams insisted on the "mild and equitable" establishment of one public religion.

For Jefferson, to establish one public religion was to threaten all private religions. To encourage religious uniformity was to jeopardize religious sincerity. To limit religious exercise was to stymie religious development. To enlist the Church's ministry was to impugn the state's integrity. Religion was thus best left to the private sphere and sanctuary; Church and state were best left separated from each other.

Adams agreed that too little religious freedom was a recipe for hypocrisy and impiety. But too much religious freedom, he argued, was an invitation to depravity and license. Too firm a religious establishment would certainly breed coercion and corruption. But too little a religious establishment

14. Adams, Works, 9:636. See also Adams, Works, 2:399; 3:448-64; 4:193-209, 227-28, 290-97; 8:232; 9:419-20; 10:253-54, 415-16; John A. Schutz and Douglass Adair, eds., *The Spur of Fame: Dialogues of John Adams and Benjamin Rush, 1805-1813* (San Marino, Calif.: Huntington Library, 1966), pp. 75-77, 191-95, 224-26, 238-39.

15. See discussion of various theological and political models in Chapter 6 herein and further in RCE, chap. 2.

would convert private prejudices into constitutional prerogatives. Somewhere between these extremes a society must strike its balance.

Adams's Model in Action: 1776-1940

For the first century and a half of the republic, it was Adams's model of religious liberty more than Jefferson's that dominated the nation — even, ironically, in nineteenth-century Virginia.[16] Before 1940, principal governance of the American experiment lay with the states, not with the federal government. The First Amendment applied, by its terms, only to "Congress."[17] Its provisions were rarely invoked and only lightly enforced by the federal courts. Most questions of religious liberty were left to the states to resolve, each in accordance with its own state constitution.[18]

The dominant pattern was that states sought to balance the general freedom of all private religions with the general patronage of one common public religion — increasingly relying on the frontier as a release valve for the tensions between this private religious freedom and public religious patronage. On the one hand, state and local governments granted basic freedoms of conscience, exercise, and equality to most religious groups and religious practices, at least those that conformed with common culture and average temperament. Most religious individuals were granted rights to assemble, speak, publish, parent, educate, travel, and the like on the basis of their religious beliefs. Most religious groups were generally afforded the rights to incorporate, to hold property, to receive private donations, to enforce religious laws, and to maintain buildings, schools, and charities for their voluntary members.

Many states, however, still dealt discriminately with religious minori-

16. See three works by Thomas E. Buckley: "After Disestablishment: Thomas Jefferson's Wall of Separation in Antebellum Virginia," *Journal of Southern History* LXI (1995): 445; "The Use and Abuse of Jefferson's Statute: Separating Church and State in Nineteenth-Century Virginia," in *Religion and the New Republic: Faith in the Founding of America*, ed. James H. Hutson (Lanham, Md.: Rowman and Littlefield, 2000), pp. 41-64; and "'A Great Religious Octopus': Church and State at Virginia's Constitutional Convention, 1901-1902," *Church History* 72 (2003): 333.

17. United States Constitution, Amendment I: "Congress shall make no law respecting an establishment of religion, or prohibiting the free exercise thereof. . . ." See further Chapter 6 herein.

18. See sources for this section in RCE, pp. 107-24.

ties, particularly those of high religious temperature or low cultural conformity. The New England states, for example, continued to resist the missionizing efforts of Catholics, Baptists, and Methodists, routinely delaying delivery of their corporate charters, tax exemptions, and educational licenses. New York, New Jersey, and Pennsylvania were similarly churlish with Unitarians and Seventh-Day Adventists, often turning a blind eye to private abuses against them. Virginia and the Carolinas tended to be hard on conservative Episcopalians and upstart Evangelicals alike. Many of the southern states were notorious in their resistance to Catholic Churches, schools, missions, and literature. Few legislatures and courts, outside of the main cities on the Eastern seaboard, showed much respect for the religious rights of the few Jews or Muslims about, let alone the religious rights of Native Americans or enslaved African-Americans.

On the other hand, state and local governments patronized a "public" religion that was generally Christian, if not Protestant, in character. A "mass of organic utterances," as the Supreme Court later put it, attest to the typical features of this system.[19] State and local governments endorsed religious symbols and ceremonies. "In God We Trust" and similar confessions appeared on governmental seals and stationery. The Ten Commandments and favorite Bible verses were inscribed on the walls of court houses, public schools, and other public buildings. Crucifixes were erected in state parks and on state house grounds. Flags flew at half mast on Good Friday. Christmas, Easter, and other holy days were official holidays. Sundays remained official days of rest. Government-sponsored chaplains were appointed to the state legislatures, military groups, and state prisons, asylums, and hospitals. Prayers were offered at the commencement of each session of many state legislatures and at city council meetings. Thanksgiving Day prayers were offered by governors, mayors, and local officials. Election day sermons were offered, especially in rural and town Churches, throughout the nineteenth century.

State and local governments also afforded various forms of aid to religious groups. Subsidies were given to Christian missionaries on the frontier. States and municipalities occasionally underwrote the costs of Bibles and liturgical books for poorer Churches and donated land and services to them. Property grants and tax subsidies were furnished to Christian schools and charities. Special criminal laws protected the property, clergy, and worship services of the Churches. Tax exemptions were accorded to

19. *Church of the Holy Trinity v. United States,* 143 U.S. 457, 471 (1892).

the real and personal properties of many Churches, clerics, and charities. Tax revenues supported the acquisition of religious art and statuary for state museums and other public buildings.

State and local governments predicated some of their laws and policies on biblical teachings. Many of the first public schools and state universities had mandatory courses in the Bible and religion and compulsory attendance in daily chapel and Sunday worship services. Employees in state prisons, reformatories, orphanages, and asylums were required to know and to teach basic Christian beliefs and values. Polygamy, prostitution, pornography, and other sexual offenses against Christian morals and mores were prohibited. Blasphemy and sacrilege were still prosecuted. Gambling, lotteries, fortune-telling, and other activities that depended on fate or magic were forbidden. In many jurisdictions, these and other laws were predicated on explicitly religious grounds. It was a commonplace of nineteenth-century American legal thought that "Christianity is a part of the common law."[20]

This prevalent pattern of balancing the freedom of all private religions with the patronage of one public religion worked well enough for the more religiously homogeneous times and towns of the early republic. The established public religion confirmed and celebrated each community's civic unity and confessional identity. It also set natural limits to both political action and individual freedom — limits that were enforced more by communal reprobation than by constitutional litigation.

One of the saving assumptions of this system was the presence of the frontier, and the right to emigrate thereto. Religious minorities who could not abide a community's religious restrictions or accept its religious patronage were not expected to stay long to fight the local establishment as their European counterparts had done. They moved — sometimes at gunpoint — to establish their own communities on the frontier, often on the heels of missionaries and schoolmasters who had preceded them. Mormons moved from New York to Ohio, to Missouri, to Illinois, before finally settling in Utah and in neighboring states. Catholics moved to California, the Dakotas, Illinois, Louisiana, Montana, Nevada, and New Mexico. Baptists and Methodists poured into the southern states from Georgia and Tennessee to

---

20. The phrase was coined by Sir Matthew Hale in Taylor's Case (1676), 1 Vent. 293, 86 English Reports 189, and became an American commonplace. Stuart Banner, "When Christianity Was Part of the Common Law," *Law and History Review* 16 (1998): 27-62.

Mississippi and Louisiana. Free spirits escaped to the mountainous frontiers of Wyoming, Montana, Washington, and Oregon.[21]

The right and the duty to emigrate was a basic assumption of the early American experiment in religious liberty. Many first-generation Americans had left their European faiths and territories to gain their freedom. Accordingly, they embraced the right to leave — to exit their faith, to abandon their blood and soil, to reestablish their lives, beliefs, and identities afresh — as a cardinal axiom of religious freedom. Escape to the frontier provided the release valve for the common nineteenth-century pattern of balancing freedom for all private religions with patronage of one public religion.[22]

As the American populace became more pluralized and the American frontier more populated, however, this system became harder to maintain. The Second Great Awakening of circa 1810 to 1860 introduced to the American scene a host of newly minted faiths — Adventists, Christian Scientists, Disciples, Holiness Churches, Jehovah's Witnesses, Mormons, Pentecostals, Unitarians, Universalists, and more. The Second Great Awakening also fueled what Edwin S. Gaustad has aptly called "the reconquest" of the original Eastern seaboard states by Evangelical Baptists and Methodists as well as by Roman Catholics.[23] The American Civil War (1861-1865) permanently divided Lutherans, Presbyterians, and other denominations into northern and southern branches. The Thirteenth, Fourteenth, and Fifteenth Amendments (1865-1870) not only outlawed slavery but also liberated a host of long-cloaked African beliefs and rituals, some in pure African forms, many inculturated with various Christian and Islamic traditions. After the 1860s, the great waves of European immigration brought new concentrations and forms of Catholicism and Protestantism from Ireland, Germany, and Great Britain, joined by a number of Catholic immigrants from Mexico and Latin America. After the 1880s, fresh waves of immigrants from Eastern Europe and Russia brought new forms and concentrations of Catholicism, Judaism, and Orthodox Christianity. At the same time, a growing number of immigrants from across the Pacific introduced Buddhism, Confucianism, Hinduism, and other Eastern religions to the Western states.

---

21. For detailed religious demography, see Edwin S. Gaustad and Philip L. Barlow, *New Historical Atlas of Religion in America* (New York: Oxford University Press, 2001).

22. See further Chapter 3 herein.

23. Gaustad and Barlow, *New Historical Atlas*, p. 23.

These movements of new inspiration, immigration, and invention radically recast the American religious map in the course of the nineteenth century — with the traditional Calvinist and Anglican strongholds of the early republic giving way especially to precocious new forms of Evangelical Baptists and Methodists. This radical reconfiguration of the American religious map in the later nineteenth century eventually challenged state constitutional patterns of religious liberty. In particular, state policies of patronizing a preferred form of public religion became increasingly difficult to maintain with the growing plurality of the populace and the growing political strength of groups who opposed such policies. Many Evangelical Churches, both Baptist and Methodist, insisted that states adhere more firmly to principles of disestablishment and separatism; in a number of states, they gained the political power to revise the constitutions accordingly.[24] Religious minorities in many communities — whether Protestant, Catholic, Orthodox, Jewish, Adventist, or Mormon — also began to ally themselves in opposition to this system, particularly the patronage of a common Protestantism within the public schools. Some of these minority religious communities refused to conform or to assimilate. Others refused to live or leave quietly. Still others began to crusade actively against the system.

When neither assimilation nor accommodation policies proved effective, state and local legislatures began to clamp down on these dissenters. At the turn of the twentieth century and increasingly thereafter, local officials began routinely to deny Roman Catholics their school charters, Jehovah's Witnesses their preaching permits, Eastern Orthodox their canonical freedoms, Jews and Adventists their Sabbath-day accommodations, non-Christian pacifists their conscientious objection status. As state courts and legislatures turned an increasingly blind eye to their plight, religious dissenters began to turn to the federal courts for relief.

Jefferson's Model in Action: 1940-1985

The United States Supreme Court responded forcefully to the plight of these religious minorities — first by applying the First Amendment to the states, then by applying Jefferson's model to the First Amendment. Both moves brought fundamental change to the American experiment.

24. See further Chapter 7 herein.

In the landmark cases of *Cantwell v. Connecticut* (1940)[25] and *Everson v. Board of Education* (1947),[26] the Court read the First Amendment religion clauses into the due process clause of the Fourteenth Amendment. On its face, the Court said, the First Amendment binds the federal government: "Congress shall make no law respecting an establishment of religion, or prohibiting the free exercise thereof." As a general statement of religious liberty, the Court continued, the First Amendment also binds state and local governments. For religious liberty is part of the body, the corpus, of fundamental liberties in the Fourteenth Amendment guarantee that "no state shall deprive any person of . . . liberty . . . without due process of law."[27] By so incorporating the First Amendment religion clauses into the Fourteenth Amendment due process clause, the Court accomplished what sixteen failed amendments to the Constitution could not accomplish — to create a national law on religious liberty, governed by the federal courts, and enforceable against state and local governments.

In its early application of the free exercise clause, the Court simply adjusted the American experiment by protecting the rights of newly emergent religious groups against recalcitrant local officials. Jehovah's Witnesses, the Court held repeatedly, could not be denied licenses to preach, parade, or pamphleteer just because they were unpopular.[28] Public school students could not be compelled to salute the flag or recite the pledge if they were conscientiously opposed.[29] Other parties, with scruples of conscience, could not be forced to swear oaths before receiving citizenship status, property tax exemptions, state bureaucratic positions, social welfare benefits, or standing in courts.[30] Such free exercise remedies can be read as an effort to make the traditional state establishments of a public religion more "mild and equitable" for the many new private religions on the American scene.

In its early application of the establishment clause, however, the

25. 310 U.S. 296 (1940).

26. 330 U.S. 1 (1947).

27. United States Constitution (1789), Amend. XIV, sec. 1.

28. *Cantwell v. Connecticut,* 310 U.S. 296 (1940); *Cox v. New Hampshire,* 312 U.S. 569 (1941); *Murdock v. Pennsylvania* 319 U.S. 105 (1943); *Follet v. McCormick,* 321 U.S. 573 (1944); *Fowler v. Rhode Island,* 345 U.S. 67 (1953); *Poulos v. New Hampshire,* 345 U.S. 395 (1953).

29. *West Virginia State Board of Education v. Barnette,* 319 U.S. 624 (1943).

30. *In re Summers,* 325 U.S. 561 (1945); *Girouard v. United States,* 328 U.S. 61 (1946); *First Unitarian Church v. County of Los Angeles,* 357 U.S. 545 (1958).

Court radically reconfigured the American experiment by outlawing state establishments of public religion altogether. State patronage of a public religion, the Court held, was not only a threat to an individual's free exercise rights. It was also a violation of the government's non-establishment duties. It was Thomas Jefferson who had first seen the virtues of combining a strong free exercise clause with a strong disestablishment clause. It was Thomas Jefferson who had hit upon the formula for enforcing both clauses with equal vigor — by consigning religion to the private sphere and sanctuary, and by separating Church from state. Jefferson's views henceforth would be the law of the nation.[31]

Everson was an open invitation to litigation. A long tradition of state and local policies that patronized a public religion was now open to challenge. The new application of the First Amendment religion clauses to the states encouraged such extensive litigation. The *Everson* Court's adoption of the Jeffersonian separationist model of religious liberty demanded it. Hundreds of establishment clause cases poured into the lower federal courts after the 1940s.

The Supreme Court applied its newly minted Jeffersonian logic primarily in cases challenging the traditional state patronage of religious education, devoting nearly three quarters of its establishment clause cases to this issue. As we saw in Chapter 7, the Court removed religion from the public school. Public schools could not offer prayers or moments of silence, could not read Scripture or religious texts, could not house Bibles or prayer books, could not teach theology or creationism, could not display Decalogues or crèches, and could not use the services or facilities of religious bodies.[32] The Court also removed religious schools from much traditional state support. States could not provide salary and service supplements to religious schools, could not reimburse them for administering standardized tests, could not lend them state-prescribed textbooks, supplies, films, or counseling services, could not allow tax deductions or credits for religious school tuition, and more.[33]

---

31. See further Chapter 7 herein.

32. *McCollum v. Board of Education*, 333 U.S. 203 (1948); *Engel v. Vitale*, 370 U.S. 421 (1962); *Abington School District v. Schempp*, 374 U.S. 203 (1963); *Epperson v. Arkansas*, 393 U.S. 97 (1968); *Stone v. Graham*, 449 U.S. 39 (1980); *Wallace v. Jaffree*, 472 U.S. 38 (1985).

33. *Lemon v. Kurtzman*, 403 U.S. 602 (1971); *Sloan v. Lemon*, 413 U.S. 825 (1973); *Meek v. Pittenger*, 421 U.S. 349 (1975); overruled by *Mitchell v. Helms*, 530 U.S. 793 (2000); *Wolman v. Walter*, 433 U.S. 229 (1977); overruled by *Mitchell v. Helms*, 530

In *Lemon v. Kurtzman* (1971), the Court distilled the Jeffersonian logic of its early cases into a general test to be used in all establishment clause cases.[34] We saw in Chapter 7 that the three-part test required that laws challenged under the establishment clause would now pass constitutional muster only if they (1) had a secular purpose; (2) had a primary effect that neither advances nor inhibits religion; and (3) fostered no excessive entanglement between Church and state. Incidental religious "effects" or modest "entanglements" of Church and state could be tolerated, but defiance of any of these criteria would be constitutionally fatal.

This constitutional reification of Jeffersonian logic rendered the establishment clause a formidable obstacle to many traditional forms of state patronage of public religion. The lower courts in particular used this test to outlaw a wide variety of government subsidies for religious charities, social services, and mission works, government use of religious services, facilities, and publications, government protections of Sundays and Holy Days, government enforcement of blasphemy and sacrilege laws, government participation in religious rituals and religious displays. It must be emphasized that it often did not take lawsuits to effectuate these reforms. Local governments in particular, sensitive to the political and fiscal costs of constitutional litigation, often voluntarily ended their prayers, removed their Decalogues, and closed their coffers to religion long before any case was filed against them. The Jeffersonian logic of the establishment clause seemed to demand this.

Toward the New Freedom of Public Religion?

While many local officials and private citizens have remained faithful to this Jeffersonian logic, the Supreme Court has been quietly defying it and has recently reversed some of its harshest separationist precedents.[35] The Court has not yet crafted a coherent new logic, let alone consistent new test, to resolve these disputes, and has been properly pilloried for some of

U.S. 793 (2000); *Grand Rapids School District v. Ball,* 473 U.S. 373 (1985); overruled by *Agostini v. Felton,* 521 U.S. 203 (1997); *Aguilar v. Felton,* 473 U.S. 402 (1985); overruled by *Agostini v. Felton,* 521 U.S. 203 (1997).

34. *Lemon v. Kurtzman,* 403 U.S. 602, 612-13 (1971).

35. *Mitchell v. Helms,* 530 U.S. 793, 808 (2001), overruling *Meek v. Pittenger,* 421 U.S. 329 (1975) and *Wolman v. Walter,* 433 U.S. 229 (1977); *Agostini v. Felton,* 521 U.S. 203, 235 (1997), overruling *Aguilar v. Felton,* 473 U.S. 402 (1985).

its blundering and badly fractured opinions. But these cases hold signposts of a new way to define and defend the legal place of public religion.

Tradition has become one strong vector in some of the Court's more recent First Amendment cases. The Court had used arguments from tradition a few times before, as part of broader rationales for upholding religious tax exemptions and Sabbath Day laws. But in *Marsh v. Chambers* (1983), the argument from tradition became the exclusive basis for upholding a state legislature's century-long practice of funding a chaplain and opening its sessions with his prayers. Writing for the Court, Chief Justice Burger defended such practices as a noble survival of the traditional public role of religion in American life and law:

> In light of the unambiguous and unbroken history of more than 200 years, there can be no doubt that the practice of opening legislative sessions with prayer has become part of the fabric of our society. To invoke Divine guidance on a public body entrusted with making the laws is not, in these circumstances, an "establishment" of religion [but] simply a tolerable acknowledgement of beliefs widely held among the people of this country. . . . "[W]e are a religious people whose institutions presuppose a Supreme Being."[36]

Arguments from tradition, while by themselves rarely convincing, can sometimes bolster a broader rationale for upholding traditional features of a public religion and a religious public. Tradition can sometimes serve effectively as something of a null hypothesis — to be overcome by strong constitutional arguments rather than discarded by simple invocations of principle. As Justice Holmes once put it: "If a thing has been practised for two hundred years by common consent, it will need a strong case for the Fourteenth Amendment to affect it."[37] Innocuous long-standing practices, therefore, such as religious tax exemptions, military chaplains, prison prayer books, and public displays of Decalogues and of other religious symbols might well be justified.[38]

There are limits and dangers to arguments from tradition, which the Court itself betrayed the following year. In *Lynch v. Donnelly* (1984)

---

36. *Marsh v. Chambers*, 463 U.S. 783 (1983), quoting, in part, *Zorach v. Clauson*, 343 U.S. 306 (1952).

37. *Jackman v. Rosenbaum*, 260 U.S. 22, 31 (1922).

38. See *Van Orden v. Perry*, 125 S. Ct. 2854 (2005); *Elk Grove Unified School District v. Newdow*, 124 S. Ct. 2301, 2311 (2004) (Rehnquist, C. J., concurring).

the Court upheld a municipality's traditional practice of maintaining a manger scene (a crèche) on a public park as part of a large holiday display in a downtown shopping area. "There is an unbroken history of official acknowledgment by all three branches of government of the role of religion in American life," Chief Justice Burger wrote, repeating his *Marsh* argument and now giving an ample list of illustrations. There is another reason to uphold this display, however, Burger continued. Crèches, while of undoubted religious significance to Christians, are merely "passive" parts of "purely secular displays extant at Christmas."[39] They "engender a friendly community spirit of good will" that "brings people into the central city and serves commercial interests and benefits merchants."[40] The prayers that are occasionally offered at the crèche, Justice O'Connor wrote in concurrence, merely "solemnize public occasions, express confidence in the future, and encourage the recognition of what is worthy of appreciation in society."[41] Governmental participation in and support of such "ceremonial deism," the Court concluded, cannot be assessed by "mechanical logic" or "absolutist tests" of establishment. "It is far too late in the day to impose a crabbed reading of the [Disestablishment] Clause on the country."[42]

A crabbed reading of establishment would have been better than such a crass rendering of religion. For the Court to suggest that crèches are mere advertisements, prayers mere ceremony, and piety mere nostalgia is to create an empty "American Shinto"[43] — a public religion that is perhaps purged enough of its confessional identity to pass constitutional muster,

39. *Lynch v. Donnelly*, 465 U.S. 668, 674-75 (1984).

40. *Lynch*, 465 U.S. at 685.

41. *Lynch*, 465 U.S. at 693 (O'Connor, J., concurring). Twenty years after *Lynch*, concurring in *Elk Grove Unified School District v. Newdow*, 124 S. Ct. at 2317, Justice O'Connor elaborated her theory of "ceremonial deism": "I believe that government can, in a discrete category of cases, acknowledge or refer to the divine without offending the Constitution. This category of 'ceremonial deism' most clearly encompasses such things as the national motto ('In God We Trust'), religious references in traditional patriotic songs such as the Star-Spangled Banner, and the words with which the Marshal of this Court opens each of its sessions ('God save the United States and this honorable Court'). These references are not minor trespasses upon the Establishment Clause to which I turn a blind eye. Instead, their history, character, and context prevent them from being constitutional violations at all."

42. *Lynch*, 465 U.S. at 678.

43. John T. Noonan Jr., *The Lustre of Our Country: The American Experience of Religious Freedom* (Berkeley: University of California Press, 1998), pp. 230-31.

but too bleached and too bland to be religiously efficacious, let alone civilly effective.

Arguments from tradition, while helpful, are thus inherently limited in their ability to define and defend the public place of religion today. Such arguments perforce assume a traditional definition of what a public religion is — namely, a common system of beliefs, values, and practices drawn eclectically from the multiple denominations within a community. In the religiously homogeneous environment of John Adams's day, a public religion of the common denominator and common denomination still had the doctrinal rigor, liturgical specificity, and moral suasion to be effective. In the religiously heterogeneous environment of our day — with more than one thousand incorporated denominations on the books — no such effective common religion can be readily devised or defended.

More recent cases suggest a budding new way of defining and defending the legal place of public religion. The Court has numerous times upheld government policies that support the public access and activities of religious individuals and groups — so long as these religious parties act voluntarily, and so long as nonreligious parties also benefit from the same government support. Under this logic, Christian clergy were just as entitled to run for state political office as nonreligious candidates.[44] Church-affiliated pregnancy counseling centers could be funded as part of a broader federal family counseling program.[45] Religious student groups could have equal access to state university and public school classrooms that were open to nonreligious student groups.[46] Religious school students were just as entitled to avail themselves of general scholarships, remedial, and disability services as public school students.[47] Religious groups were given equal access to public facilities or civic education programs that were already opened to other civic groups.[48] Religious parties were just as entitled as nonreligious parties to display their symbols in public forums.[49] Reli-

---

44. *McDaniel v. Paty*, 435 U.S. 618, 629 (1978).

45. *Bowen v. Kendrick*, 487 U.S. 589, 617 (1988).

46. *Widmar v. Vincent*, 454 U.S. 263, 277 (1981); *Board of Education of the Westside Community Schools v. Mergens*, 496 U.S. 226, 236 (1990).

47. *Witters v. Washington Department of Services for the Blind*, 474 U.S. 481, 489 (1986); *Zobrest v. Catalina Foothills School District*, 509 U.S. 1, 10 (1993). But cf. *Locke v. Davey*, 124 S. Ct. 1307 (2004).

48. *Lamb's Chapel v. Center Moriches Union Free School District*, 508 U.S. 384, 395 (1993); *Good News Club v. Milford Central School District*, 533 U.S. 98, 112 (2001).

49. *Capitol Square Review and Advisory Board*, 515 U.S. 753, 770 (1995).

gious student newspapers were just as entitled to public university funding as those of nonreligious student groups.[50] Religious schools were just as entitled as other private schools to participate in a state-sponsored educational improvement or school voucher or educational program.[51]

The Court has defended these holdings on wide-ranging constitutional grounds — as a proper accommodation of religion under the disestablishment clause, as a necessary protection of religion under the free speech or free exercise clauses, as a simple application of the equal protection clause, among other arguments.

One theme common to many of these cases, however, is that public religion must be as free as private religion. Not because the religious groups in these cases are really nonreligious.[52] Not because their public activities are really nonsectarian. And not because their public expressions are really part of the cultural mainstream. To the contrary, these public groups and activities deserve to be free, just because they are religious, just because they engage in sectarian practices, just because they sometimes take their stands above, beyond, and against the mainstream. They provide leaven and leverage for the polity to improve.

A second theme common to these cases is that the freedom of public religion sometimes requires the support of the state. Today's state is not the distant, quiet sovereign of Jefferson's day from whom separation was both natural and easy. Today's modern welfare state, whether for good or ill, is an intensely active sovereign from whom complete separation is impossible. Few religious bodies can now avoid contact with the state's pervasive network of education, charity, welfare, child care, health care, family, construction, zoning, workplace, taxation, security, and other regulations. Both confrontation and cooperation with the modern welfare state are almost inevitable for any religion. When a state's regulation imposes too heavy a burden on a particular religion, the free exercise clause should provide a pathway to relief. When a state's appropriation imparts too generous a benefit to religion alone, the establishment clause should provide a pathway to dissent. But when a general government scheme provides public re-

---

50. *Rosenberger v. University of Virginia,* 515 U.S. 819, 843-44 (1995).

51. *Mitchell v. Helms,* 530 U.S. 793, 829 (2000); *Zelman v. Simmons-Harris,* 536 U.S. 639, 662-63 (2002).

52. See esp. *Van Orden v. Perry,* 125 S. Ct. 2854 (2005), where Chief Justice Rehnquist emphasizes that the Decalogue displayed on government property is indeed a religious text and symbol (not just a moral code, as supporters had argued), but that it can be displayed properly alongside various nonreligious texts and symbols.

ligious groups and activities with the same benefits afforded to all other eligible recipients, disestablishment clause objections are not only "crabbed" but corrosive.

A third theme common to these cases is that a public religion cannot be a common religion. If the religious gerrymandering of *Lynch v. Donnelly* and its progeny had not already made this clear, these more recent cases underscore the point. Today, our public religion must be a collection of particular religions, not the combination of religious particulars. It must be a process of open religious discourse, not a product of ecumenical distillation. All religious voices, visions, and values must be heard and deliberated in the public square. All public religious services and activities, unless criminal or tortious, must be given a chance to come forth and compete, in all their denominational particularity.

Some conservative Evangelical and Catholic groups today have seen and seized on this insight better than most. Their rise to prominence in the public square in recent years should not be met with glib talk of censorship or habitual incantation of Jefferson's mythical wall of separation.[53] The rise of the so-called Christian right should be met with the equally strong rise of the Christian left, of the Christian middle, and of many other Jewish, Muslim, and other religious groups who test and contest its premises, prescriptions, and policies. That is how a healthy democracy works. The real challenge of the new Christian right is not to the integrity of American politics but to the apathy of American religions. It is a challenge for peoples of all faiths and of no faiths to take their place in the marketplace.

A fourth teaching of these cases is that freedom *of* public religion also requires freedom *from* public religion. Government must strike a balance between coercion and freedom. The state cannot coerce citizens to participate in religious ceremonies and subsidies that they find odious.[54] But the state cannot prevent citizens from participation in public ceremonies and programs just because they are religious, as we saw in the last chapter.

Individuals should exercise a comparable prudence in seeking protection from public religion. In the public religion schemes of nineteenth-century America, it was not so much the courts as the frontier that provided this freedom — a place away from it all, where one could escape with one's conscience and co-religionists. Today, the frontier still provides this

53. See further Chapter 7 herein.
54. *Lee v. Weisman,* 505 U.S. 577, 596 (1991); *Santa Fe Independent School District v. Doe,* 530 U.S. 290, 312 (2000).

freedom — if not physically in small towns and wild mountains, then virtually in our ability to sift out and shut out the public voices of religion that we do not wish to hear.

Both modern technology and modern privacy make escape to the frontier considerably easier than in the days of covered wagons and mule trains. Just turn off Pat Roberston or Jerry Falwell. Turn away the missionary at your door. Close your eyes to the city crucifix that offends. Cover your ears to the public prayer that you can't abide. Forgo the military chaplain's pastoral counseling. Skip the legislative chaplain's prayers. Walk by the town hall's menorah and star. Don't read the Decalogue on the classroom wall. Don't join the religious student group. Don't vote for the collared candidate. Don't browse the Evangelicals' newspapers. Avoid the services of the Catholic counselors. Shun the readings of the Scientologists. Turn down the trinkets of the colporteurs. Turn back the ministries of the hate-mongers. All these escapes to the virtual frontier, the law does and will protect — with force if necessary. Such voluntary self-protections from religion will ultimately provide far greater religious freedom for all than pressing yet another tired constitutional case.

9

The Three Uses of the Law:
A Protestant Source of the Purposes
of Criminal Punishment?

The foregoing chapters in this section have focused on various Christian sources and dimensions of American understandings of law, constitutional authority, and religious liberty. This chapter focuses on the role of a distinctive Protestant theological doctrine in the evolution of English and American criminal law, namely, the doctrine of the "uses of the law." I argue (1) that the sixteenth-century Protestant theological doctrine of the three uses of moral law provided a critical analogue, if not antecedent, to the classic Anglo-American doctrine of the three purposes of criminal law and punishment; and (2) that this theological doctrine provides important signposts to the development of a more integrated moral theory of criminal law and punishment still today.

The first part of this chapter sets out the theological doctrine of the "civil," "theological," and "educational" uses of the moral law, as formulated by sixteenth-century Lutherans and Calvinists, and elaborated by later Protestant writers on both sides of the Atlantic. The second part analyzes the analogous "deterrent," "retributive," and "rehabilitative" purposes of criminal law, as articulated by early modern Anglo-American jurists and moralists, and explores the historical cross-fertilization between these theological and legal doctrines. Part Three reflects on contemporary American criminal law developments in light of this three uses doctrine.

The Theological Doctrine of the Uses of Moral Law

The theological doctrine of the uses of law was forged in the Protestant Reformation.[1] It was a popular doctrine, particularly among Lutheran and Calvinist Reformers. Martin Luther (1483-1546), Philip Melanchthon (1497-1560), John Calvin (1509-1564), and other Protestant Reformers gave the doctrine a considerable place in their monographs and sermons,[2] as well as in their catechisms and confessional writings.[3] It was also a pivotal doctrine, for it provided the Reformers with something of a middle way between radical Catholic legalism, on the one hand, and radical Anabaptist antinomianism, on the other. It allowed the Reformers to reject the claims of certain Catholics that salvation can be achieved by works of the law as well as the claims of certain Anabaptists that those who are saved have no further need of the law.

The Reformers focused their uses doctrine primarily on the natural or moral law — that compendium of moral rights and duties that transcend the positive laws of the state. God, they believed, has written a moral law on the hearts of all persons, rewritten it in the pages of Scripture, and summarized it in the Ten Commandments. A person comes to know the meaning and measure of this moral law both through the counsel of reason and conscience and, more completely, through the commandments of Scripture

1. Patristic and scholastic theologians had, of course, recognized the idea that the natural or moral law has different functions in the life of the individual and community. The Protestant Reformers, however, were the first to develop a systematic theological doctrine of the "uses of the law" *(usus legis)*. Luther was the first to give prominence to the doctrine. In his 1522 Commentary on Galatians 3, Luther spoke of the "three-fold use of the law" *(drey wysse am brauch des gesetz)*, though in this tract as well as his 1531 Commentary on Galatians, he focused on only the civil and theological uses of the law. WA 10/1:457. Martin Bucer, in his 1525 Latin translation of Luther's sermon, rendered Luther's German phrase as *triplex usus legis,* a Latin phrase which other Reformers adopted. WA 10/1:457, note 2. Philip Melanchthon, in his 1535 *Loci communes,* and Calvin, writing independently in his 1536 *Institutes,* were the first to expound systematically all three uses of the moral law. CR 21:405-6; Institutes (1536), pp. 48-50. See further Gerhard Ebeling, *Word and Faith,* trans. J. N. Leitch (London: SCM, 1963), pp. 62-78.

2. For Luther, WA 10/1:454ff.; 16:363ff., 40:481ff. For Melanchthon, CR1:706ff.; 11:66ff.; 21:405ff., 716ff.; 22:248ff. For Calvin, Institutes (1559), bk. 2, chap. 7; CO 24:725-27.

3. Philip Melanchthon, *Catechesis puerilis* (1558), in CR 23:176-77; John Calvin, "The Geneva Catechism," in CO 6:80; "Formula of Concord (1577), part 6," in *Triglott Concordia: The Symbolic Books of the Ev. Lutheran Church German-Latin-English* (St. Louis: Concordia, 1921), p. 805.

and the Spirit.[4] Though a person can be saved if he obeys the moral law perfectly, his inherently sinful nature renders him incapable of such perfect obedience. This human incapacity does not render the moral law useless. The moral law retains three important uses or functions in a person's life, which the Reformers variously called (1) a civil or political use; (2) a theological or spiritual use; and (3) an educational or didactic use.

First, the moral law has a *civil* use to restrain persons from sinful conduct by threat of divine punishment. "[T]he law is like a halter," Calvin wrote, "to check the raging and otherwise limitlessly ranging lusts of the flesh. . . . Hindered by fright or shame, [persons] dare neither execute what they have conceived in their minds, nor openly breathe forth the rage of their lust."[5] The law thus imposes upon saints and sinners alike what Calvin called a "constrained and forced righteousness" or what Melanchthon called "an external or public morality."[6] Threatened by divine sanctions, persons obey the basic commandments of the moral law — to obey authorities, to respect their neighbor's person and property, to remain sexually continent, to speak truthfully of themselves and their neighbors.

Although "such public morality does not merit forgiveness of sin,"[7] it benefits sinners and saints alike. On the one hand, it allows for a modicum of peace and stability in this sin-ridden world. "Unless there is some restraint," Calvin wrote, "the condition of wild beasts would be better and more desirable than ours. [Natural] liberty would always bring ruin with it if it were not bridled by the moderation" born of the moral law.[8] On the other hand, such public morality enables persons who later become Christians to know at least the rudiments of Christian morality and to fulfill the vocations to which God has called them. "Even the children of God before they are called and while they are destitute of the spirit of sanctification become partly broken in by bearing the yoke of coerced righteousness. Thus, when they are later called, they are not entirely untutored and uninitiated in discipline as if it were something foreign."[9]

Second, the moral law has a *theological* use to condemn sinful persons for their violations of the law. Such condemnation ensures both the integrity of the law and the humility of the sinner. On the one hand, the vio-

---

4. See further Chapter 2 herein.
5. Institutes (1559), 2.7.10.
6. Institutes (1559), 2.7.10, 4.20.3.; CO 52:255; CR 1:706-8.
7. CR 22:151, 250.
8. CO 39:66.
9. Institutes (1559), 2.7.10.

lation of the law is avenged, and the integrity — the balance — of the law is restored by the condemnation of those who violate it. On the other hand, the violator of the law is appropriately chastened. In Luther's hard words, the law serves as a mirror "to reveal to man his sin, blindness, misery, wickedness, ignorance, hate, contempt of God. . . . When the law is being used correctly, it does nothing but reveal sin, work wrath, accuse, terrify, and reduce consciences to the point of despair."[10] "In short," Calvin writes, "it is as if someone's face were all marked up so that everybody who saw him might laugh at him. Yet he himself is completely unaware of his condition. But if they bring him a mirror, he will be ashamed of himself, and will hide and wash himself when he sees how filthy he is."[11] Such despair, the Reformers believed, was a necessary precondition for the sinner both to seek God's help and to have faith in God's grace. "For man, blinded and drunk with self-love, must be compelled to know and confess his own feebleness and iniquity. . . . [A]fter he is compelled to weigh his life in the scales of the law, he is compelled to seek God's grace."[12]

Third, the moral law has an *educational* use of enhancing the spiritual development of believers, of teaching those who have already been justified "the works that please God."[13] Even the most devout saints, Calvin wrote, still need the law "to learn more thoroughly . . . the Lord's will [and] to be aroused to obedience."[14] The law teaches them not only the "public" or "external" morality that is common to all persons, but also the "private" or "internal" morality that is becoming only of Christians. As a teacher, the law not only coerces them against violence and violation, but also cultivates in them charity and love. It not only punishes harmful acts of murder, theft, and fornication, but also prohibits evil thoughts of hatred, covetousness, and lust.[15] Through the exercise of this private morality, the saints glorify God, exemplify God's law, and impel other sinners to seek God's grace.

This theological doctrine of the three uses of the moral law was rooted in the Protestant theology of salvation. Following St. Paul, the Reformers recognized various dimensions (if not stages) of the spiritual life (if not formation) of the Christian — from predestination to justification to

10. WA 40:481-86.
11. CO 50:535.
12. Institutes (1559), 2.7.6.
13. CR 21:406.
14. Institutes (1559), 2.7.12
15. Institutes (1559), 2.8.6; CR 1:706-8; Martin Bucer, *Deutsche Schriften,* ed. Robert Stupperich (Gütersloh: Gutersloher Verlagshaus C. Mohn, 1960-), 1:36ff.

sanctification.[16] The moral law, they believed, plays a part in all three steps of the soteriological process. It coerces sinners so that they can be preserved. It condemns them so that they can be justified. It counsels them so that they can be sanctified. The doctrine was also rooted in the Protestant theology of the person. Following Luther, the Reformers emphasized that a person is *simul iustus et peccatur*, at once saint and sinner, spirit and flesh.[17] The moral law caters to both the spiritual and the carnal dimensions of a person's character. The person of the flesh is coerced to develop at least a minimal public or external morality; the person of the spirit is counseled to develop a more holistic private or internal morality.

Although rooted in the intricacies of Protestant theology, the uses doctrine had broad appeal among sixteenth-century Protestants. The doctrine found its way into a number of popular pamphlets, diaries, and handbooks. It is an instructive anecdote that one of the most popular formulations of the uses doctrine was provided by a German jurist, Christoph Hegendorf (1500-1540), who was a friend of Luther and Melanchthon. Hegendorf, who is known to legal historians as a legal humanist and civilian,[18] was, seemingly, best known in his day for his *Domestic or Household Sermons for a Godly Householder to his Children and Family*. Hegendorf's sermons, written in Latin, and quickly translated into German, English, and French,[19] set out the uses doctrine in clear, accessible terms. He describes the moral law as "those precepts divinely engraven on our minds," and "comprehended in a compendious summary . . . in the Ten Commandments." "[A]lthough there are many things contained in those precepts and commandments which are impossible to be done in our carnal nature," Hegendorf wrote, "the law is still good, whole, and useful." It ensures "that our untrained lusts shall be bridled

16. Romans 8:28-30 and Galatians 3:21-29 and the Reformers' commentaries thereon in CR 15:654-78; LW 25:371-78; 26:327-58. Calvin also follows this sequencing from predestination to justification to sanctification in the arrangement of Books II and III of his Institutes (1559).

17. WA 7:50.

18. Roderich von Stintzing, *Geschichte der deutschen Rechtswissenschaft*, Erste Abteilung (München: R. Oldenbourg, 1880), pp. 249-50.

19. See Christoph Hegendorf, *Die zehen Gepot der Glaub, und das Vater unser, fuer die Kinder ausgelegt* (1527). An expanded version of this tract, which I have not been able to locate, was published in Latin in the early 1530s, and translated as *Domestycal or housholde Sermons, for a godly housholder, to his children and famyly, compiled by the godlye learned man Christopher Hegendorffyne, doctor*, trans. Henry Reiginalde (Ippiswich: J. Oswen, 1548).

. . . not so that we are justified, but so that we should escape temporal punishment." It reminds us "oftentimes of [our] imbecility and the weakness of [our] nature . . . so that we should flee unto Christ our Savior, who was the only one to observe and to keep all his Father's commandments." It exists so that "we shall be instructed to lead an honest life and perform [good] works."[20]

The theological doctrine of the three uses of the moral law was not merely an anachronism of the early Reformation that died with the magisterial Reformers.[21] The doctrine remained a staple of Protestant dogma after the early Reformation. The classic texts of Luther, Melanchthon, Calvin, and others, which expounded the uses doctrine, were constantly reprinted and translated and circulated widely in Protestant circles. Some Protestant editions of the Bible, particularly the Geneva Bible, set out the uses doctrine in marginal glosses on the relevant texts of St. Paul. A steady stream of references to the doctrine can be found in Protestant monographs, sermons, catechisms, and confessional writings from the seventeenth century onward. A number of distinguished Protestant theologians in the twentieth century — Dietrich Bonhoeffer, Emil Brunner, and Alec Vidler, among others — included the doctrine in their theological systems.[22] One could multiply examples to demonstrate the continuity of this uses doctrine in the Protestant tradition — a worthy exercise, given the paucity of studies available. For our purposes of discovering an intellectual analogue or antecedent to Anglo-American theories of criminal punishment, however, we need cite

20. Hegendorf, *Die zehen Gepot der Glaub,* Sermon 1, "Prooemium."

21. That position has been argued most forcefully by Karl Barth and his student Hermann Diem. See Hermann Diem, *Dogmatik: ihr Weg zwischen Historismus und Existentialismus* (Munich: Chr. Kaiser Verlag, 1955), arguing that the three uses doctrine died after the Reformation because it gives the law priority over the Gospel, suggests stages of justification, and is a sort of "Trojan horse" for smuggling natural law into theology. See further discussion in Coslett Quin, *The Ten Commandments: A Theological Exposition* (London: Lutterworth, 1951), p. 32. Even sympathetic accounts of the uses doctrine generally focus only on the early Reformation era.

22. See, e.g., Dietrich Bonhoeffer, *Ethics,* ed. Eberhard Bethge, trans. Neville H. Smith (New York: Macmillan, 1955), pp. 303ff.; Emil Brunner, *Dogmatik,* 3 vols. (Zürich: Zwingli-Verlag, 1960), 2:131ff.; 3:306ff.; Emil Brunner, *The Mediator: A Study of the Central Doctrine of the Christian Faith,* trans. O. Wyon (London: Lutterworth, 1934), pp. 441ff. For other modern accounts, see, e.g., Ebeling, *Word and Faith,* pp. 62-78; Alec R. Vidler, *Christ's Strange Work: An Exposition of the Three Uses of God's Law* (London: SCM, 1963); Quin, *Ten Commandments,* pp. 31ff.

only a few texts to illustrate the wide acceptance of the uses doctrine among Anglican, Calvinist, and Free Church groups in England and America.

Leading Anglican divines of the later Tudor Reformation embraced the uses doctrine. John Hooper (d. 1555), for example, offered a brisk rendition of the doctrine before launching into his famous exposition on the Decalogue:

> Seeing that the works of the law cannot deserve remission of sin, nor save man, and yet God requireth our diligence and obedience unto the law, it is necessary to know the use of the law, and why it is given us. The first use is civil and external, forbidding and punishing the trangression of politic and civil ordinance. . . . The second use of the law is to inform and instruct man aright, what sin is, to accuse us, to fear us, and damn us. . . . These two uses of the law appertain as well unto infideles, as to the fideles. . . . The third use of the law is to shew unto the Christians what works God requireth of them.[23]

Thomas Becon (1512-1567), chaplain to Archbishop Cranmer and a scholar well-steeped in Lutheran theology, offered a powerful description of the uses doctrine, parts of which found their way into Anglican sermons for centuries thereafter:

> [First,] Christ calleth the law of God "a light." For as the light doth shew to him that walketh in darkness the way perfectly, and how he may safely walk, and without jeopardy; so likewise the law of God sheweth a christian man how he ought to direct his ways. . . . St. James compareth the law of God to a glass. For as in a glass we see what is fair and foul in our face, so likewise when we look in the law of God, we easily see and perceive what is well or evil in our doings; so that through the benefit of this glass, I mean that law of God, we are provoked to amend those things that are amiss, which otherwise should remain and continue in us unto our damnation.
>
> Second, forasmuch as man of himself is nothing else than a very lump of pride, and soon forgetteth his vileness, nakedness, corrupt and sinful nature . . . God, willing to paint, shew, and set forth man to him-

---

23. *Early Writings of John Hooper, D.D.* (Cambridge: University Press, 1843), pp. 281-82.

self as it were in his native colours, gave unto himself his law, that by the consideration thereof he might learn to know himself, his misery, weakness, impiety, sin, and his unableness to fulfill the law of God, seeing that law is spiritual, and we are carnal. . . . [W]ithout this knowledge, we esteem of ourselves, of our strengths, of our own free will, might, and power, more than becometh us; yet we think ourselves through our own good works and merits worthy of the favour of God, remission of sins, the gift of the Holy Ghost, and everlasting life, when we be least of all worthy of those things. But the law uttereth and sheweth us unto ourselves, and maketh evident, plain, and open before our eyes, our own wickedness, misery, and wretchedness [and] accuseth, condemneth, killeth, and casteth us down headlong into hell-fire. . . .

Thirdly, God hath given us his law unto this end that, after we have perfectly learned of the law our corruption, our wicked nature, our impiety, our pronity unto sin, our slackness unto all goodness, and finally our feebleness . . . [the law] should be unto us a schoolmaster to point and lead us unto Christ, which is "the end and perfect fulfilling of the law to make righteous so many as believe on him;" that we, apprehending and laying hand through strong faith on his perfection and fulfilling of the law, might be counted righteous before God, and so become heirs of everlasting glory.[24]

Heinrich Bullinger's (1504-1575) formulations of the uses doctrine enjoyed perhaps the widest authority among Anglican and Anglo-Puritan divines. Like Luther, Bullinger viewed the theological use as "the chief and proper office of the law" — "a certain looking-glass, wherein we behold our own corruption, frailness, imbecility, imperfection" — and he waxed eloquently on the doctrine for several pages. He also insisted, however, that the moral law has a vital civil use to teach the unregenerate "the first principles and rudiments of righteousness" and an educational use to teach the redeemed "the very and absolute righteousness" that becomes Christians.[25] By the end of the sixteenth century, Bullinger's printed sermon on the topic became a standard classroom text for budding Anglican

---

24. John Ayre, ed., *The Catechism of Thomas Becon, S.T.P.* (Cambridge: University Press, 1844).

25. *The Decades of Henry Bullinger,* 4 vols. (Cambridge: University Press, 1849-1852), 2:235-45.

clergy.[26] Comparable sentiments on the uses doctrine are peppered throughout Richard Hooker's (ca. 1553-1600) classic eight-volume *Laws of Ecclesiastical Polity*.[27]

The uses doctrine did not remain confined to the Anglican academy. An early liturgical handbook from Waldegrave, for example, put a crisp distillation of the doctrine in the hands of the parishioner. The "godly order and discipline" born of adherence to the moral law, the handbook reads, "is, as it were, sinews in the body, which knit and join the members together with decent order and comeliness. It is a bridle to stay the wicked from their mischiefs; it is a spur to prick forward such as be slow and negligent: yea, and for all men it is the Father's rod, ever in a readiness to chastise gently the faults committed, and to cause them afterward to live in more godly fear and reverence."[28] The famous prayers of Chaplain Becon, which enjoyed broad circulation in the English and American Anglican Churches, are filled with invocations that God allow his commandments to work their three uses in the lives of individuals and the community.[29] Anglican sermons and catechisms of the seventeenth and eighteenth centuries, in England and America, also propounded the doctrine, both in their exegesis of Moses and St. Paul and in their elaborations of the cryptic statements on law in the Thirty-Nine Articles.[30]

Calvinist groups in England and America — Puritans, Pilgrims, Hu-

26. See H. A. Wilson, *Episcopacy and Unity* (London: Longmans, Green, 1912), p. 39; Vidler, *Christ's Strange Work*, p. 34, noting that, in 1586, Convocation and Archbishop Whitgift directed the lower clergy in England to procure and study Bullinger's tract.

27. See references in Vidler, *Christ's Strange Work*. For a suggestive tabular summary of the three types and offices of law set out by Hooker, see Francis Paget, *An Introduction to the Fifth Book of Hooker's Treatise on the Laws of Ecclesiastical Polity* (Oxford: Clarendon, 1899), p. 99.

28. Quoted by Horton Davies, *The Worship of the English Puritans* (Oxford: Oxford University Press, 1948), pp. 232-33.

29. See, e.g., *Prayers and Other Pieces of Thomas Becon, S.T.P.*, pp. 56-63, a series of prayers against idolatry, swearing, pride, whoredom, covetousness, gluttony, idleness, slandering, and other general offenses arising out of the Decalogue.

30. See, e.g., John Smalley, *The Perfection of the Divine Law; And Its Usefulness for the Conversion of Souls: A Sermon Delivered in the College Chapel in New-Haven . . . in 1787* (New Haven, Conn.: Josiah Meigs, 1787), pp. 16-28; C. E. De Coetlogon, *The Harmony Between Religion and Policy, or Divine and Human Legislation* (London: J. F. Riverton, 1790), pp. 24ff.; Ezekial Hopkins, *An Exposition of the Ten Commandments* (London: G. Whitfield, 1799).

guenots, Presbyterians, Congregationalists, Independents, Brownists, and others — embraced the uses doctrine, both in its classic form and with a distinctive covenantal cast. Classic formulations of the uses doctrine recur repeatedly in Calvinist sermons, catechisms, and theological handbooks from the early seventeenth century onward. A short catechism, prepared by the seventeenth-century Scottish lawyer and theologian Samuel Rutherford (ca. 1600-1661), for example, has typical language on the theological and educational uses of the moral law:

> Q. What is the use of the law if we can not obteane salvatione by it? A. It encloseth us under condemnation as a citie beseiged with a garrisone of souldiers that we may seek to Christ for mercie. Q. What is the use of the law after we are com to Christ? A. After Christ has made agreement betwixt us and the law, we delight to walk in it for the love of Christ.[31]

An American catechism, prepared a century later, has a similar entry on the use of law:

> Q. Of what use, then, is the law unto men, since righteousness and life cannot be attained by it? A. It is of manifold use. . . . [T]o unregenerate sinners, it is of use to discover to them their utter impotence and inability to attain justification and salvation by the works thereof. . . . [T]o believers, it is of use to excite them to express their gratitude and thankfulness to Christ.[32]

Both catechisms also devoted several pages to exegesis of the Decalogue, which included ample discussion of the civil use of the moral law.

Puritan Calvinists in England and New England cast the uses doctrine in a distinctive covenantal mode. The broad contours of Puritan covenant theology are well known.[33] Like other Protestants, the Puritans recog-

---

31. "Ane Catachisme Conteining The Soume of Christian Religion by Mr. Samuell Rutherford (c. 1644)," chap. 33, in *Catechisms of the Second Reformation*, ed. Alexander F. Mitchell (London: James Nesbit, 1886), p. 226 (citations and question numbers omitted).

32. James Fisher and Ebenezer Erskine, *The Westminster Assembly's Shorter Catechism Explained, By Way of Question and Answer, Part II* (Philadelphia: J. Towar and D. M. Hogan, 1831), QQ. 40.25, 28 (citations and question numbers omitted).

33. See sources in John Witte Jr., "Blest Be the Ties That Bind: Covenant and

nized a divine covenant or agreement between God and humanity. They recognized two distinct biblical covenants: the Old Testament covenant of works whereby the chosen people of Israel, through obedience to God's law, are promised eternal salvation and blessings; and the New Testament covenant of grace, whereby the elect through faith in Christ's incarnation and atonement are promised eternal salvation and beatitude. Unlike other Protestants, however, a number of Puritans conceived these covenants largely in legalistic terms — viewing the moral law as a summary of the provisions of the covenant which God made binding on man. These Puritans further conceived that both the covenant of works and the covenant of grace have continued to operate since biblical times. The covenant of works binds the unregenerate — all those who are without faith, and beyond the realm of salvation. The covenant of grace binds the redeemed — all those who are with faith and are fully justified. Both covenants bind the predestined — those who are elected to salvation but still without faith; their compliance with the covenant of works ultimately leads them to enter the covenant of grace.[34]

This doctrine of the covenant informed the Puritan doctrine of the three uses of the law.[35] The Westminster Confession of Faith (1647) provided a classic early statement, which was often glossed in sermons and commentaries:

> Although true believers be not under the [moral] law as a covenant of works, to be thereby justified or condemned; yet is it of great use to them, as well as to others; in that, as a rule of life, informing them of the will of God and their duty, it directs them and binds them to walk accordingly; discovering also the sinful pollution of their nature, hearts, and lives; so as, examining themselves thereby, they may come to further conviction of, humiliation for, and hatred against sin; to-

Community in Puritan Thought," *Emory Law Journal* 36 (1987): 579-601, and Chapters 5 and 12 herein.

34. See, e.g., Thomas Hooker, *The Faithful Covenanter* (London: Christopher Meredith, 1644); Peter Bulkeley, *The Gospel-Covenant; Or the Covenant of Grace Opened* (London: Matthew Simmons, 1651); John Cotton, *The Covenant of God's Free Grace* (London: Matthew Simmons, 1645).

35. See especially E. Brooks Holifield, *The Era of Persuasion: American Thought and Culture, 1521-1680* (Boston: Twayne, 1989), pp. 98-99, arguing that the Puritan description of man's positions under the covenant of works and covenant of grace simply restated Calvin's three uses doctrine.

gether with a clearer insight of the need they have of Christ and the perfection of his obedience. It is likewise of use to the regenerate, to restrain their corruptions, in that it forbids sin; and the threatenings of it serve to show what even their sins deserve, and what afflictions in this life they may expect for them. . . .[36]

Half a century later, Samuel Willard (1604-1707), the grand systematizer of American Puritan theology, linked explicitly the three states of covenantal existence and the three uses of the moral law. Effectively, both the covenant and the moral law which it embraces have distinctive uses, which Willard spelled out in some detail:

As for natural men that are without the Gospel, the [moral] law is serviceable to them on such accounts as these. (1) to keep them in awe and prompt them to duty. . . . (2) for the maintenance and preservation of civil societies from ruin. . . . (3) to direct in the ordering of the civil government of mankind . . . [and] (4) to dispose them to entertain the Gospel, when it should be offered to them. With respect to natural men that are under the Gospel dispensations, [b]esides what they have in common with others in the forecited benefits, . . . it serves, (1) to convince men of sin, which is the first step to conversion. . . . (2) to discover in them their woeful misery by sin. . . . (3) to slay them as to any expectation of help by any righteousness or strength of their own. . . . (4) to awaken in them, an apprehension of their absolute need of help from abroad. . . . (5) to make the glad tidings of Christ and salvation by him welcome. As to those that are under grace, the law is no more a covenant of works to them . . . [nor] a covenant of life to them, having life secured to their personal obedience, yet it is a rule according to which God expects that they should order their life and conversation. This is denied by some, practically abused by others, and not rightly understood by many. And may therefore be made clear and evident in the following conclusions, (1) that God's people have a life and conversation to lead in this

36. "Westminster Confession of Faith (1647)," art. 19, in *The Creeds of Christendom with a History and Critical Notes,* by Philip Schaff, 3 vols. (New York: Harper and Brothers, 1882), 3:640-42 (citations and subpart designations omitted). See also "The Savoy Declaration of 1658," a classic congregational confession, which tracks the Westminster formulations closely, in *The Creeds and Platforms of Congregationalism,* ed. Williston Walker (Boston: Pilgrim, 1960), p. 387.

world. . . . (2) that it is not at the liberty of God's people to live as they list, nor ought they to live as other men. . . . (3) there must therefore be a rule for their direction in leading such a [redeemed] life. . . . (4) the children of God are therefore sanctified, that they may be fitted for compliance with this rule. . . . (6) this rule is not made known to everyone, by immediate inspiration, but is laid down in the Gospel. . . . (7) it is the moral law which is reinforced in the Gospel, as a rule for the children of God to order their lives by.[37]

Willard's formulations of the civil, theological, and educational uses of the law, and of the covenants, became the prevailing Puritan understanding of the uses doctrine, which was repeated among American Calvinists until well into the nineteenth century.[38]

The Free Churches, especially those born of the Great Awakening in America (1720-1780), occasionally included the uses doctrine in their literature and sermons as well.[39] Among their leaders, John Wesley (1703-1791), the father of Methodism, devoted ample attention to the uses doctrine, both in his writings on law and in his sermons on salvation and sanctification.[40] His formulations resonate rather closely with those of

---

37. Samuel Willard, "Sermon 149, Question 40 (January 14, 1700)," in *A Compleat Body of Divinity [of 1726]*, by Samuel Willard (New York: Johnson Reprint Company, 1968), pp. 568-72 (spelling modernized and citations and numbering omitted). Similar sentiments on Question 40 appear in Thomas Watson's weighty seventeenth-century volume *A Body of Divinity*, reprinted several times in England and in America. See, for example, a later American edition published in Philadelphia, Thomas Watson, *A Body of Practical Divinity* (Philadelphia: T. Wardle, 1833), and a London version, Thomas Watson, *A Body of Divinity Contained in Sermons upon the Assembly's Catechism* (London: Passmore, 1881).

38. See, for example, Thomas Ridgeley, *A Body of Divinity: Wherein the Doctrines of Christian Religion Are Explained and Defended*, 2 vols., ed. John M. Wilson (New York: R. Carter, 1855), 2:300-307.

39. The adherence of the American Free Churches to the uses doctrine is consistent with the teachings of one of their earliest leaders, Menno Simons, who embraced at least the civil and theological uses of the law. See *The Complete Writings of Menno Simons* (Scottdale, Pa.: Herald, 1956), p. 718: "This is the real function and end of law: To reveal unto us the will of God, to discover sin unto us, to threaten with the wrath and punishment of the Lord, to announce death and to point us from it to Christ, so that we, crushed in spirit, may before the eyes of God die unto sin, and seek and find the only eternal medicine, and remedy for our souls, Jesus Christ."

40. See discussion in Harald Lindström, *Wesley and Sanctification* (Grand Rapids: Francis Asbury, 1980), pp. 75-83.

Melanchthon and Luther. In his circa 1749 sermon, *The Original, Nature, Property, and Use of the Law,* for example, Wesley declared:

> The first use of the law [is] to slay the sinner, . . . to destroy the life and strength wherein he trusts, and convince him that he is dead while he liveth; not only under the sentence of death, but actually dead unto God, void of all spiritual life, "dead in trespasses and sins." The second use of it is, to bring him unto life, unto Christ, that he may live. . . . The third use of the law is, to keep us alive. It is the grand means whereby the blessed spirit prepares the believer for larger communications of the life of God.[41]

Similar statements appear occasionally in Methodist sermons and handbooks of the nineteenth and twentieth centuries.[42]

The uses doctrine was thus well known in English and American Protestant circles, both academic and lay. To be sure, the doctrine was no centerpiece of Protestant dogma: it never won universal assent or uniform articulation, and it always remained in the shadow of the grand Protestant doctrines of man and God, sin and salvation, law and Gospel. Yet the doctrine had ample enough coherence and adherence to provide a common theological touchstone for members of fiercely competing sects. It also provided a common intellectual framework in which to situate a distinctive understanding of the purposes of criminal law and punishment, to which we now turn.

The Legal Doctrine of the Purposes of Criminal Law

The new theological doctrine of the uses of moral law that emerged out of the Reformation had a close conceptual cousin in the new legal doctrine of the purposes of criminal law that came to prevail in early modern England and America. The early Protestant Reformers themselves occasionally touched on this legal doctrine in their discussions of ecclesiastical

41. Reprinted in Edward H. Sugden, ed., *Wesley's Standard Sermons,* 2 vols. (London: Epworth, 1964), 2:52-53.

42. See, e.g., Adam Clarke, "Life, the Gift of the Gospel; Law, the Ministration of Death [Sermon on Galatians 3]," in *Discourses on Various Subjects Relative to the Being and Attributes of God,* by Adam Clarke, 2 vols. (New York: M'Elrath and Bangs, 1830), 1:156-72.

discipline[43] and in their asides on criminal law.[44] Philip Melanchthon, for example, whose writings inspired European jurists for more than two centuries thereafter, explicitly linked the uses of moral law and divine punishment with the purposes of criminal law and punishment. "All punishments by the state and others should remind us of God's wrath against our sin, and should warn us to reform and better ourselves," he writes. God has ordained "four very important reasons for criminal punishment":

> (1) God is a wise and righteous being, who out of his great and proper goodness created rational creatures to be like him. Therefore, if they strive against him the order of justice [requires that] he destroy them. The first reason for punishment then is the order of justice in God. (2) The need of other peaceful persons. If murderers, adulterers, robbers, and thieves, were not removed, nobody would be safe. (3) [To set an e]xample. When some are punished, others are reminded to take account of God's wrath and to fear his punishment and thus to reduce the causes of punishment. (4) The importance of divine judgment and external punishment, in which all remain who in this life are not converted to God. As God in these temporal punishments shows that he distinguishes between virtue and vice, and that he is a righteous judge, we are reminded more of this example that also after this life all sinners who are not converted to God will be punished.[45]

The Strasbourg Reformer Martin Bucer (1491-1551), in his *De Regno*

---

43. See LP, chap. 5; Josef Bohatec, *Calvin und das Recht* (Graz: H. Böhlaus, 1934); Walter Köhler, *Zürcher Ehegericht und Genfer Konsistorium*, 2 vols. (Leipzig, 1942); John Witte Jr. and Robert M. Kingdon, *Sex, Marriage, and Family Life in John Calvin's Geneva*, 3 vols. (Grand Rapids: Eerdmans, 2005-).

44. See, e.g., WA 6:267ff.; 19:626ff.; 32:394ff.; CR 22:224ff., 615ff. and discussion in H. Mayer, "Die Strafrechtstheorie bei Luther und Melanchthon," in *Rechtsidee und Staatsgedanke: Beiträge zur Rechtsphilosophie und zur politischen Ideengeschichte: Festgabe für Julius Binder* (Berlin: Junker and Dünnhaupt, 1930), p. 771; Wolfgang Naucke, "Christliche, aufklärerische, und wissenschaftstheoretische Begründung des Strafrechts (Luther-Beccaria-Kant)," in *Christentum, Säkularisation und modernes Recht*, 2 vols., ed. Luigi L. Vallauri and Gerhard Dilcher (Baden-Baden: Nomos Verlagsgesellschaft, 1981), 2:1201. See further Institutes (1559), 4.12.4-6, 20.3, 9, and discussion in E. William Monter, "Crime and Punishment in Calvin's Geneva, 1562," *Archiv für Reformationsgeschichte* 64 (1973): 281; Robert M. Kingdon, *Adultery and Divorce in John Calvin's Geneva* (Cambridge, Mass.: Harvard University Press, 1995).

45. CR 22:224.

Christi prepared for King Edward VI, wrote similarly of the functions of criminal law and punishment: "For the nature of all men is so corrupt from birth and has such a propensity for crimes and wickedness that it has to be called away and deterred from vices, and invited and forced to virtues, not only by teaching and exhortation, admonition and reprimand, which are accomplished by words, but also by the learning and correction that accompany force and authority and the imposition of punishments."[46]

A long tradition of Anglo-American jurists and moralists, from the early seventeenth century onward, expounded and expanded the legal doctrine of the purposes of criminal law in an array of treatises,[47] pamphlets,

46. Martin Bucer, "De Regno Christi (1550)," translated in *Melanchthon and Bucer,* ed. William Pauck (Philadelphia: Westminster, 1969), p. 383.

47. Among the numerous relevant treatises in the seventeenth and eighteenth centuries that had influence on the criminal law of England and America, see, e.g., William Blackstone, *Commentaries on the Laws of England,* ed. Robert M. Kerr (Boston: Beacon, 1962 [1765]), bk. 4, chap. 1; Hugo Grotius, *On the Law of War and Peace,* trans. Francis W. Kelsey (Indianapolis: Bobbs-Merrill, 1962 [1625]), bk. 2, chaps. 20, 21; Thomas Hobbes, *De Cive,* ed. Sterling P. Lamprecht (New York: Appleton-Century Crofts, 1949 [1642]), chap. 14; Thomas Hobbes, *Leviathan,* ed. C. B. McPherson (Baltimore: Penguin, 1968 [1651]), chap. 28; Samuel von Pufendorf, *The Law of Nature and Nations,* ed. W. A. Oldfather (New York: Oceana, 1964 [1688]), bk. 8, chap. 3; Thomas Rutherforth, *Institutes of Natural Law, Being the Substance of a Course of Lectures on Grotius De Jure Belli et Pacis* (Whitehead: William Young, 1799), bk. 1, chap. 18; Robert Sanderson, *Bishop Sanderson's Lectures on Conscience and Human Law* (Lincoln: Williamson, 1877 [1647]), Lect. 8.10-25; John Selden, *De Jure Naturali et Gentium juxta disciplinam Ebraeorum libri septem* (Lipsiae et Francofurti: Apud Jeremiam Schrey, 1695), bk. 1, chap. 4; bk. 4, chap. 11; James Wilson, "Lectures on Law (1790-1792)," in *The Works of James Wilson,* 2 vols., ed. James D. Andrews (Chicago: Callaghan, 1896), 2:337-482. Excerpts from these and many other early modern sources are included in Basil Montagu, compiler, *The Opinions of Different Authors upon the Punishment of Death,* 3 vols. (Buffalo, N.Y.: W. S. Hein, 1984).

Among the writings of the later eighteenth and nineteenth centuries most critical for the development of Anglo-American criminal law are those by Beccaria, Voltaire, Bentham, Romilly, Eden, and others excerpted in Gertrude Ezorsky, ed., *Philosophical Perspectives on Punishment* (Albany: State University of New York Press, 1973), and discussed in J. M. Beattie, *Crime and the Courts in England, 1660-1800* (Princeton, N.J.: Princeton University Press, 1986); Leon Radzinowicz, *A History of English Criminal Law and Its Administration from 1750,* 5 vols. (New York: Macmillan, 1948-1986). For discussion of contemporaneous American writers and developments, see, for example, Edwin Powers, *Crime and Punishment in Early Massachusetts, 1620-1692* (Boston: Beacon, 1966); William E. Nelson, "Emerging Notions of Criminal Law in the Revolutionary Era," *New York University Law Review* 42 (1967): 450-83.

and sermons[48] — in some instances, writing under the direct inspiration of Protestant theologians.[49]

The legal doctrine of the purposes of criminal law was similarly formulated but differently focused than its theological cousin. Like the theologians, early modern jurists accepted a general moral theory of government and criminal law. God has created a moral or natural law. He has vested in this moral law three distinctive uses. He imposes divine punishments to ensure that each use is fulfilled. State magistrates are God's vice-regents in the world. They must represent and reflect God's authority and majesty on earth. The laws which they promulgate must encapsulate and elaborate the principles of God's moral law, particularly as it is set out in the Ten Commandments. The provisions of the criminal law, therefore, must perforce parallel the provisions of the moral law.[50] The purposes of criminal punish-

48. The most valuable such sermons were the so-called "execution sermons" delivered by eminent ministers and/or jurists on the occasion of public executions. See J. A. Sharpe, "'Last Dying Speeches': Religion, Ideology, and Public Execution in England," *Past and Present* 107 (1985): 144-67; Ronald A. Bosco, "Lectures at the Pillory: The Early American Execution Sermon," *American Quarterly* 30 (1978): 156-76; David Edwards, *Sermons to the Condemned* (London: R. Hawes, 1775); Richard W. Hamilton, *A Sermon Preached at Leeds . . . on Occasion of the Execution of Mr. Joseph Blackburn, Attorney at Law, for Forgery* (London: Longman, Hurst, Rees, Orme, and Brown, 1815); Increase Mather, *The Wicked Mans Portion, or A Sermon Preached at the Lecture in Boston in New England . . . 1674* (Boston: John Foster, 1675); Increase Mather, *A Sermon Occasioned by the Execution of a Man Found Guilty of Murder* (Boston: J. Brunning, 1687); Nathan Strong, *A Sermon Preached in Hartford . . . At the Execution of Richard Doane* (Hartford: Elisha Babcock, 1797).

49. Not only the writings of sixteenth-century Protestant jurists, but even those of later civilian and common law writers on criminal law, draw on the Magisterial Reformers. A standard mid-eighteenth-century handbook on crimes by Antonius Matthaeus, for example, includes several citations to Melanchthon, Calvin, and the English Protestants William Ames, Peter Martyr, and William Perkins. See Antonius Matthaeus, *On Crimes: A Commentary on Books XLVII and XLVIII of the Digest,* ed. and trans. M. L. Hewett (Cape Town: Juta, 1987 [1761]), pp. 61-64.

50. It was common, particularly in colonial America, to draw criminal law provisions directly from the Bible, and to classify criminal laws in accordance with the commandments in the Decalogue. See, for example, the section of capital crimes in *The Book of the General Lauues and Libertyes Concerning the Inhabitants of the Massachusets* (Cambridge: Hezekiah Usher, 1648) and the extensive commentary on crime and sin against the Ten Commandments in Willard, *A Compleat Body of Divinity,* pp. 563-784. See further David Flaherty, "Law and the Enforcement of Morals in Early America," in *Law in American History,* ed. Donald Fleming and Bernard Bailyn (Boston: Little, Brown, 1971), pp. 203-53; Lawrence M. Friedman, *Crime and Punishment in American History* (New York: Basic, 1993), pp. 1-58.

ment must perforce parallel the purposes of divine punishment.[51] As William Blackstone (1723-1780) put it, "the state's criminal law plays the same role in man's social life that God's moral law plays in man's spiritual life."[52]

From these premises, the English and American jurists argued that the criminal law serves three uses or purposes in the lives of the criminal and the community. These they variously called: (1) deterrence or prevention; (2) retribution or restitution; and (3) rehabilitation or reformation — the classic purposes of criminal law and punishment that every law student learns still today. The precise definition of these three purposes, and the relative priority and propriety of them, were subjects of endless debate among jurists and judges. Individual jurists, particularly those inspired by later Enlightenment and utilitarian sentiments, championed deterrence theories alone. But all three purposes were widely accepted at English and American criminal law until the end of the nineteenth century. The definition of the deterrent, retributive, and rehabilitative purposes of criminal law bears a striking resemblance to the definition of the civil, theological, and educational uses of the moral law.

First, the jurists believed, criminal law has a *deterrent* function. The criminal law prohibits a variety of harmful and immoral acts — murder, rape, battery, and other violations of the person; arson, theft, burglary, and other violations of property; riot, tumult, nuisance, and other violations of public peace and order. A person who violates these prohibitions must be punished.

51. See, e.g., Mather, *A Sermon Occasioned by the Execution of a Man* (1687), p. 13: "[The Magistrate] is a minister of God, a Revenger to execute wrath upon him that does Evil. Rom. 13.4. Private Reveng[e] is evil; but publick Revenge on those that violate Laws of God, is good. The Magistrate is God's Vice-gerent. As none can give life but God; so none may take it away but God, and such as He has appointed" (italics deleted); Thomas Hancock, *He is the Minister of God to Thee for Good* (Maidstone: T. Edlin, 1735), p. 12: "The magistrate . . . must exercise this power [of punishment], in imitation of God, for the good of man"; George Stonestreet, *The Especial Importance of Religious Principles in the Judges and the Advocates of the Courts of Law* (London: J. Rowden, 1822), pp. 28-29: "The justice men seek at an earthly tribunal is, when impartially and mercifully administered, both an emblem and an emanation of that essential attribute which we adore in the Almighty. . . . [T]he punishments, which at your hands await the workers of iniquity, while they preserve the order of society, serve also to vindicate the moral government of God over His creatures, and to warn men of that heavier vengeance which must hereafter await the impenitent sinner." See summary in Willard, *A Compleat Body of Divinity,* pp. 617-42.

52. Quoted by Adolf Bodenheimer, *Recht und Rechtfertigung* (Tübingen: Mohr, 1907), p. 118.

Criminal punishment is designed to deter both the individual defendant (special deterrence) and other members of the community (general deterrence) from committing such violations. The punishment imposed must be sufficiently onerous and automatic to deter the individual defendant from repeating the violation. It must also be sufficiently grave and public so that others will see the defendant's plight and be deterred from similar conduct.[53] This accounts in part for the traditional publicity of the criminal justice system — with its public trials, public confessions, public pillories, public brandings, and public executions. Criminal punishments, particularly executions, Samuel Johnson (1709-1784) quipped, "are intended to draw spectators; if they do not, they don't answer their purpose."[54] Most jurists and moralists had little compunction about using the punishment of one individual to serve the ends of both the criminal and the community.[55] "When a man has been proved to have committed a crime," the American moralist Sydney Smith (1771-1845) put it, "it is expedient that society should make use of that man for the diminution of crime; he belongs to them for that purpose."[56]

Through these prohibitions and punishments, the jurists believed, the criminal law coerces persons to adopt what they called an external, public, or civic morality — the very same terms the theologians had used. This, to be sure, is only what Justice Joseph Story (1779-1845) once called a "minimal morality," and what Lon Fuller later called "a morality of duty," rather than a "morality of aspiration."[57] It consists only of "thou shalt not"

---

53. See, for example, Pufendorf, *The Law of Nature and Nations,* bk. 8, chap. 3.9, 11, 12; Grotius, *On the Law of War and Peace,* bk. 2, chap. 20.7-9.

54. Quoted in James Boswell, *Boswell's Life of Samuel Johnson,* 2 vols. (New York: A. S. Barnes, 1916), 2:447. See also Pufendorf, *The Law of Nature and Nations,* bk. 8, chap. 3.11.

55. But cf. Immanuel Kant, *The Metaphysical Elements of Justice,* trans. John Ladd (Indianapolis: Bobbs-Merrill, 1965 [1785]), p. 100: "Judicial punishment *(poenis forensis)* is entirely distinct from natural punishment *(poenis naturalis).* In natural punishment, vice punishes itself, and this fact is not taken into account by the legislator. Judicial punishment can never be administered merely as a means to promote some other good for the criminal himself or for civil society, but instead it must in all cases be imposed on him only on the ground that he has committed a crime; for a human being can never be manipulated merely as a means to the purposes of someone else."

56. Sydney Smith, *Elementary Sketches of Moral Philosophy* (New York: Harper and Brothers, 1856), p. 252.

57. Lon L. Fuller, *The Morality of Law* (New Haven, Conn.: Yale University Press, 1964), pp. 3-9.

commands, not "thou shouldst do" commands. It defines only the outer boundaries of propriety and civility. It provides only the barest modicum of civil order and stability. Yet the jurists believed that, given the inherent depravity of all persons and given the inevitable presence of some persons who yield to their depravity, such a deterrent function of criminal law is indispensable.

The deterrent function of criminal law runs closely parallel to the civil use of the moral law. The theologians stressed the "wrath of God against all unrighteousness" to coerce persons against following their natural inclination to sin, and adduced ample biblical examples of the ill plight of the sinner to bring home their point.[58] The jurists stressed the "severity of the magistrate against all uncivil conduct" and used examples of the law's harsh public sanctions to deter persons from all such "uncivil" conduct.[59]

Second, many jurists believed, criminal law has a *retributive* function.[60] Retribution, like deterrence, has both a communal and an individual dimension. On the one hand, the criminal law provides a formal procedure for the community to avenge a defendant's violation of both its morality and its security. Criminal conduct, Henry Fielding (1707-1754) put it, "tears both the moral fiber and the social fabric of the community; criminal punishment serves to mend that tear."[61] If punishment is not imposed, both the moral fiber and the social fabric of the community will eventually unravel — and, in the view of some early moralists, God's vengeance will be visited on the whole community.[62] This is a second reason

58. See particularly Strong, *A Sermon Preached in Hartford*, pp. 66ff.

59. Cotton Mather, *The Call of the Gospel Applied unto all Men in General, and unto a Condemned Malefactor in Particular* (Boston: Richard Pierce, 1687), p. 58.

60. A number of early modern jurists spurned retribution as a purpose of punishment on the argument that this was the function of moral law and divine punishment. See, e.g., Grotius, *On the Law of War and Peace*, bk. 2, chap. 20.4.2; Blackstone, *Commentaries*, bk. 4, chap. 1.2; Beccaria, *On Crimes and Punishments*, p. 28; Hobbes, *De Cive*, chap. 3.11; Francis Bacon, "On Revenge," in *Essays or Counsels Civil or Moral, by Francis Bacon* (New York: Dutton, 1906 [1597]), p. 11.

61. Henry Fielding, quoted by Bodenheimer, *Recht und Rechtfertigung*, p. 177. See also J. Welland, *Difficulties Connected with Punishment As Part of the Divine System of Government* (Calcutta: R. C. LePage, 1864), p. 12: "[P]unishment may be inflicted for some benefit [of] pointing out that sin is not to be regarded as a solitary act, beginning and ending in ourselves, but as an offence and injury to the supreme Law, and so to all, for the law is the life of the community."

62. See, for example, Mather, *A Sermon Occasioned by the Execution of a Man*, pp. 10-13, and discussions in Powers, *Crime and Punishment in Early Massachusetts*, p. 517. Likewise, Kant argues that a criminal must be punished so that "the bloodguiltiness may

for the publicity of the prosecution and punishment of criminals — not only so that others may be deterred from crime, but also so that the community can avenge the violation of itself and its law. In James Fitzjames Stephen's (1829-1884) famous words,

> [T]he sentence of the law is to the moral sentiment of the public in relation to any offence what a seal is to hot wax. It converts into a permanent final judgment what might otherwise be a transient sentiment. . . . [T]he infliction of punishment by law gives definite expression and a solemn ratification and justification of the hatred which is excited by the commission of the offence, and which constitutes the moral or popular as distinguished from the conscientious sanction of that part of morality which is also sanctioned by the criminal law.[63]

On the other hand, criminal punishment induces the individual criminal to reconcile himself or herself to God. Though the state itself cannot forgive the sinner, it can induce the sinner to repent from his evil, confess his sin, and seek God's forgiveness.[64] This was one of the principal early rationales for the establishment of penitentiaries in England and America — to give prisoners the solitude and serenity necessary to reflect on their crime and seek forgiveness for it.[65] This was one of the principal rationales for infliction of hard labor and harsh suffering on criminals in

---

not remain upon the people." Quoted by Graeme R. Newman, *The Punishment Response* (Philadelphia: Lippincott, 1978), p. 193.

63. James Fitzjames Stephen, *A History of the Criminal Law of England,* 3 vols. (London: Macmillan, 1883), 2:81. See also A. L. Goodhart, *English Law and the Moral Law* (London: Stevens, 1953), p. 93: "[I]f this retribution is not given recognition, then the disapproval may also disappear. A community which is too ready to forgive the wrongdoer may end up condoning the crime."

64. See, e.g., Selden, *De Jure Naturali,* bk. 1, chap. 4: In addition to the purposes of deterrence and reformation, "we should set another called the end of satisfaction, or purgation, or expiation, as though a deviation from law were made up, as it were, and the consequent inequality of action corrected." This agitation for confession was a constant refrain of the execution sermons. See examples in Sharpe, "Last Dying Speeches"; Bosco, "Lectures at the Pillory."

65. See Montagu, *The Opinions of Different Authors upon the Punishment of Death,* vols. 2 and 3. On the history of the penitentiary in England and America, see Beattie, *Crime and the Courts in England, 1660-1800,* pp. 520ff.; Radzinowicz, *A History of English Criminal Law and Its Administration from 1750,* vol. 5; Michael Ignatieff, *A Just Measure of Pain: The Penitentiary in the Industrial Revolution* (New York: Pantheon, 1978); W. J. Forsythe, *The Reform of Prisoners 1830-1900* (London: Croom Helm, 1987).

workhouses and labor gangs — "to soften the hardened soul the way fire softens hardened steel."[66] This was one of the principal rationales for delaying the execution of a criminal for a time after he is convicted for a capital crime, and furnishing him with chaplain services and execution sermons — to give him the opportunity to reconcile himself to God before he meets his end.[67]

This retributive function of the criminal law runs closely parallel to the theological use of the moral law, though the emphases are different. The theologians emphasized the need to avenge violations of the moral law and to impel a sinner to seek grace. The jurists emphasized the need for the community to participate in such avenging of its law and emphasized the responsibility of the state to induce the sinner to seek God's grace.

Third, criminal law has the function of *rehabilitation* or reformation. This function, like retribution and deterrence, has both a communal and an individual dimension. On the one hand, criminal law serves to restore in the community a knowledge of and respect for the requirements of moral law. In the view of many early modern jurists, the criminal law must not only teach citizens a minimal "public" morality of avoiding harm and threats to others. It must also teach them a more expansive "private" morality of avoiding fault and evil. Thus, historically, the criminal law established one Christian religion and punished heresy, blasphemy, idolatry, false swearing, and violations of the Sabbath. It prescribed various acts of charity and good samaritanism and punished sharp dealing, unfair bargaining, and ignorance of the poor and needy. It prescribed sexual propriety and restraint and punished sodomy, homosexuality, bestiality, buggery, pornography, prostitution, concubinage, and other types of sexual misconduct.[68]

66. Lance Falconer, quoted in Walter Moberly, *The Ethics of Punishment* (Hamden, Conn.: Archon, 1968), p. 124. See also the discussion of the penitentiary as "moral hospital" in Isaac Kramnick, "Eighteenth-Century Science and Radical Social Theory: The Case of Joseph Priestly's Scientific Liberalism," *Journal of British Studies* 25 (1986): 1-30.

67. See Sharpe, "Last Dying Speeches"; Bosco, "Lectures at the Pillory."

68. See Blackstone, *Commentaries*, bk. 4, chaps. 4-17, which begins with "Offenses against God and Religion," a scheme followed by the many English and American writers on criminal law, who modeled their analysis on Blackstone's. In the seventeenth and eighteenth centuries, a number of English and American societies for the reformation of manners and morals emerged, both to promote legislation against various forms of public and private immorality and to catalyze judicial enforcement of these provisions. Radzinowicz, *A History of English Criminal Law and Its Administration from 1750*, 2:1-15; Friedman, *Crime and Punishment in American History*, pp. 31-48; Da-

On the other hand, the criminal law serves to reform and reeducate criminals who have violated the moral law. Criminals are punished not only to induce them to seek God's grace, but also to instruct them on godly virtue. This was the second principal rationale for the penitentiary and the workhouse. They served, in the words of an early English statute of penitentiaries, "by sobriety . . . solitary confinement, . . . labour, [and] due religious instruction . . . to accustom [prisoners] to serious reflection and to teach them both the principles and practices of every Christian and moral duty."[69]

There are striking analogies between this rehabilitative function of criminal law and the educational use of moral law, though here, too, the emphases are different. The theologians emphasized the moral reeducation of justified sinners alone; the jurists emphasized the moral reeducation of all persons, including convicted criminals. The theologians recognized that the moral education and rehabilitation, even of Christians, would remain incomplete until the life hereafter. The jurists recognized that the criminal law was inherently limited in its ability to educate and rehabilitate morally the recalcitrant. In Alexis de Tocqueville's (1805-1859) words,

> The moral reformation of . . . a depraved person is only an accidental instead of being a natural consequence of the penitentiary system[;] it is nevertheless true that there is another kind of reformation, less thorough than the former, but yet useful for society, and which the system we treat of seems to produce in a natural way. We have no doubt, but that the habits of order to which the prisoner is subjected for several years, influence very considerably his moral conduct after his return to society. The necessity of labor which overcomes his disposition to idleness; the obligation of silence which makes him reflect; the isolation which places him alone in presence of his crime and suffering; the religious instruction which enlightens and comforts him. . . . Without loving virtue, he may detest the crime of which he has suffered the cruel consequences; and if he is not more virtuous he has become at least more judicious; his morality is not honour, but interest. His religious

---

vid Flaherty, *Privacy in Colonial New England* (Charlottesville, Va.: University Press of Virginia, 1972).

69. 18 Geo 3, c. 17. Similar sentiments were part of American theories of the penitentiary. See, for example, "Report of the Board of Inspectors of the Prison for the City and County of Philadelphia (1791)," in *The Opinions of Different Authors upon the Punishment of Death,* compiled by Montagu, 3:284-85.

faith is perhaps neither lively nor deep; but even supposing that religion has not touched his heart, his mind has contracted habits of order, and he possesses rules for his conduct in life; without having a powerful religious conviction, he has acquired a taste for moral principles which religion affords.[70]

The theological doctrine of the uses of moral law and the legal doctrine of the purposes of criminal law are closely analogous not only in their formulation but also in their foundation. Like the theologians, the jurists believed that persons and societies are at once sinful and saintly. They thus tailored the criminal law as a whole to both types of persons and the criminal punishment of any individual to both dimensions of his or her character. Also like the theologians, the jurists subsumed and integrated their "uses" doctrine in a more general theory. The theologians subsumed their uses doctrine in a more general theology of salvation. For them, the moral law played an indispensable role in the process from predestination to justification to sanctification. The jurists subsumed their uses doctrine in a moral theory of government. For them, the criminal law played an indispensable role in discharging the divinely ordained tasks of the state to coerce, discipline, and nurture its citizens.

It would be too strong, of course, to say that the Protestant theological doctrine of the three uses of moral law was *the* source of the modern Anglo-American legal doctrine of the purposes of criminal law. Western writers since Plato have reflected on the purposes of criminal law,[71] and early modern Anglo-American jurists certainly drew on these writings as much as those of Protestant theology. Yet the Protestant theological "uses" doctrine seems to have provided an important source of integration and instruction for the jurists. The uses doctrine was a commonplace of Protestant theology and ethics from the sixteenth century onward — well known to both learned theologians and lay parishioners. Several sixteenth-century Protestant writers explicitly linked the theological and legal "uses" doc-

---

70. Gustave de Beaumont and Alexis de Tocqueville, *On the Penitentiary System in the United States and Its Application in France* (1833), trans. Francis Lieber (New York: Augustus M. Kelley, 1970), pp. 58-59. See also Zephaniah Swift, *A Digest of the Laws of the State of Connecticut* (New Haven, Conn.: S. Converse, 1823), pp. 260-61: "[I]t is vain to attempt to reform those who have committed crimes which evidence a total destitution of those moral principles that are the basis of reformation."

71. M. McKenzie, *Plato on Punishment* (Berkeley: University of California Press, 1981).

trines, and their writings were constantly reprinted and studied by later Protestants in England and America. Protestant jurists and Protestant theologians thereafter regularly collaborated in formulating criminal doctrines and inflicting criminal punishment. The archives we have consulted harbor no "smoking gun" — no classic legal monograph that systematically pours the theological "uses" doctrine into the theory of criminal law — though there may well be such evidence in the proceedings and opinions of lay ecclesiastical, marriage, and consistory courts that we have yet to explore. But the close analogies between the structure and content of these theological and legal doctrines reflect ample doctrinal cross-fertilization between them.

The Uses Doctrine in Contemporary Law

Even today, vestiges of this traditional understanding of the three purposes of criminal law and punishment remain evident. Consistent with traditional formulations, modern American criminal law still includes deterrence, retribution, and rehabilitation among the principal purposes of punishment. Late-nineteenth- and early-twentieth-century experiments at reducing the purposes of criminal punishment to deterrence or rehabilitation alone have proved to be unpersuasive in theory and unworkable in practice.[72] The 1984 Federal Sentencing Act, for example, indicates that criminal punishments must be imposed on criminals "(A) to reflect the seriousness of the offense, to promote respect for the law, and to provide just punishment for the offense; (B) to afford adequate deterrence to criminal conduct; (C) to protect the public from further crimes of the defendant; and (D) to provide the defendant with needed educational or vocational training, medical care, or other correctional treatment in the most effective manner."[73] A few modern jurists, like Johannes Andenaes, Lon Fuller, and Joel Feinberg, retain a rather traditional Protestant tone and terminology in

---

72. Earlier in the twentieth century, retribution had fallen into disfavor — as "a disguised form of vengeance" and a "vestige of man's instinctual past." Jerome Hall, "Justice in the 20th Century," *California Law Review* 59 (1971): 753-54; Jerome Hall, *Studies in Jurisprudence and Criminal Theory* (New York: Oceana, 1958), pp. 242ff. Today it has returned as a valid purpose of punishment. See, e.g., George Fletcher, *Rethinking Criminal Law* (Boston: Little, Brown, 1978), pp. 416-18; Herbert Packer, *The Limits of the Criminal Sanction* (Stanford, Calif.: Stanford University Press, 1968), pp. 38ff.; Jeffrie Murphy, *Retribution Reconsidered* (Dordrecht: Kluwer Academic, 1992).

73. 18 USCA § 3553(a) (2) (1988).

describing these functions — arguing that criminal law and punishment must induce respect for formal law and social norms, confirm moral inhibitions and habits of citizens, and "shape the framework of moral education."[74] Most contemporary jurists, however, define these three purposes in less moralistic and more utilitarian terms. They define deterrence as making the crime too costly to risk, retribution as making the criminal pay what he owes, rehabilitation as returning the criminal to an acceptable level of social conformity and functionality.

Also consistent with traditional formulations, contemporary criminal law continues to inculcate various "levels of morality" in citizens.[75] The criminal law still proscribes conduct that harms others. Homicide, rape, battery, and other personal offenses; arson, theft, trespass, and other property offenses; tumult, riot, nuisance, and other public offenses are still prohibited and punished. Through such prohibitions and punishments, the criminal law supports a basic "public" or "civic" morality. The criminal law also continues to outlaw polygamy, obscenity, bestiality, and similar actions that, though not directly harmful to other persons, are nonetheless considered morally and socially unacceptable. Through such punishment, the criminal law supports at least a "quasi-private" form of morality. Certain specialized bodies of criminal law, notably juvenile law, go even further and seek to inculcate in certain citizens charity, piety, sobriety, and other purely private virtues. Whether accidental or deliberate, modern criminal law perforce still defines and enforces moral values in American society.

Most contemporary jurists, however, seem to have abandoned at least three of the cardinal premises upon which the traditional Protestant understanding of the purposes of criminal law and punishment was founded. They have thus lost a vital source of unity and integration inherent in the traditional doctrine.

74. See Johannes Andenaes, *Punishment and Deterrence* (Ann Arbor: University of Michigan Press, 1974), pp. 110ff.; Fuller, *The Morality of Law;* Joel Feinberg, "The Expressive Function of Punishment," *The Monist* 49 (1965): 397-423; see also Walter Moberly, *The Ethics of Punishment* (Hamden, Conn.: Archon, 1968), pp. 78ff.; Walter Moberly, *Legal Responsibility and Moral Responsibility* (Philadelphia: Fortress, 1965).

75. Morris R. Cohen, "Moral Aspects of the Criminal Law," *Yale Law Journal* 49 (1940): 987-1026; Patrick Devlin, *The Enforcement of Morals* (London: Oxford University Press, 1965); Joel Feinberg, *The Moral Limits of the Criminal Law* (New York: Oxford University Press, 1984); Thomas C. Grey, *The Legal Enforcement of Morality* (New York: Knopf, 1983); Basil Mitchell, *Law, Morality and Religion in a Secular Society* (London: Oxford University Press, 1970); Lloyd L. Weinreb, *Natural Law and Justice* (Cambridge, Mass.: Harvard University Press, 1987).

First, most contemporary jurists have abandoned the theory of natural or moral law, which traditionally inspired both the form and the content of criminal law. Arguments from moral relativism, cultural pluralism, separation of Church and state, and the rights of privacy have all contributed to this change. The Supreme Court has reified this erosion through its broad interpretation of various constitutional freedoms. Traditional criminal laws against blasphemy or false swearing, for example, though once widely enforced, have today been eclipsed by the expansion of free speech protections of the First Amendment. Traditional laws against Sabbath-breaking, heresy, idolatry, or religious nonconformity have been eclipsed by the expansion of the free exercise and establishment clause protections of the First Amendment. Traditional laws that restricted sexual exercise and relationships have been eclipsed by a new privacy right imputed to the due process and equal protection clauses of the federal and state constitutions.

Second, most contemporary writers have abandoned the traditional anthropological assumption that human beings and human communities are at once saintly and sinful, *simul iustus et peccator.* Some stress the inherent goodness of the person and consider crime as aberrational and correctable. They have, accordingly, emphasized the rehabilitative purpose of criminal law and have deprecated particularly its retributive purpose. Others stress the inherent depravity of the person and consider crime inevitable. They have, accordingly, stressed the deterrent and retributive functions of criminal law, and have deprecated the rehabilitative function.

Third, most contemporary writers have abandoned the traditional moral theory of government which helped to integrate the three purposes of criminal law and punishment. Today the state is seen solely as a representative of the people, not a vice-regent of God. Its laws must effectuate the will of the majority, not appropriate the will of God.[76] The notion that the three functions of criminal law can thus be integrated into the divinely ordained tasks of the state to coerce, discipline, and nurture its citizens is foreign to our modern understanding.

This modern understanding is derived from liberal individualism, the regnant political philosophy of our age. The cardinal teaching of liberalism, whether the social welfare version of John Rawls[77] or the libertarian variety of Robert Nozick,[78] is that government should be morally neutral, showing

76. See further introduction herein.
77. John Rawls, *A Theory of Justice* (Cambridge: Belknap, 1971).
78. Robert Nozick, *Anarchy, State, and Utopia* (New York: Basic, 1974).

no preference among competing concepts of the good. Government has no higher role to play than to mediate among the conflicting private desires and selfish interests of its citizens. It has no legitimate role in shaping those desires.[79] In Justice Frankfurter's words, "Law is concerned with external behavior and not with the inner life of man."[80] Even as to that, the only justification for government control of individual behavior, in John Stuart Mill's (1806-1873) famous words, "is to prevent harm to others. His own good, either physical or moral, is not a sufficient warrant. . . . Over himself, over his own body and mind, the individual is sovereign."[81] These attitudes are expressed less elegantly in the contemporary nostrums that private morality cannot be legislated and, indeed, its lack cannot even be criticized, lest we be "judgmental."

Liberalism, of course, has many great virtues, which are evident when liberal societies like ours are compared to those which reject its core values of tolerance, liberty, and equality. But liberalism also has its vices, for which we have paid dearly. On the one hand, we have become, in the words of Leonard Levy, "not only a free society, but a numb society. We are beyond outrage."[82] On the other hand, we are beset by appalling levels of violence, crime, drug addiction, illegitimacy, and the like, all products at least in part of a moral climate in which the satisfaction of private desires is the highest good.[83] The moral relativism underlying liberalism's neutrality tends to corrode all values, even liberalism's own values of individual dignity and rights.

This moral relativism especially erodes the criminal law. Traditionally, criminal law and punishment were sharply distinguished from private law and legal and equitable remedies. Criminal law expressed a society's collective moral vision and values; criminal punishment expressed a society's moral condemnation of the criminal act.[84] Citizens felt morally

---

79. See, e.g., Arnold Brecht, *Political Theory: The Foundations of Twentieth-Century Political Thought* (Princeton, N.J.: Princeton University Press, 1959), pp. 117-70, 231-60, 302-66.

80. *West Virginia State Board of Education v. Barnette*, 319 U.S. 624, 655 (1943) (Frankfurter, J., dissenting).

81. John Stuart Mill, *On Liberty* (New York: Norton, 1975 [1859]), p. 11.

82. Leonard W. Levy, *Blasphemy: Verbal Offenses against the Sacred from Moses to Salman Rushdie* (New York: Knopf, 1993), pp. 568-79.

83. See further Chapters 10 and 14 herein.

84. Feinberg, "The Expressive Function of Punishment"; Henry M. Hart, "The Aims of the Criminal Law," *Law and Contemporary Problems* 23 (1958): 404-5. For a good early American expression of this point, see James Wilson, "Lectures on Law (1790-1792)," pp. 341ff.

bound to obey the criminal law because they identified its commands with those of morality. Such a moral duty is lacking when laws prohibit conduct that citizens do not deem immoral. Yet without a feeling of moral compulsion to obey among citizens, the criminal law cannot succeed.

This crucial point is missed by theories which view criminal punishment as just another form of deterrence, with criminal penalties differing from civil penalties only in their severity, in order to prevent especially harmful behavior that monetary compensation cannot remedy.[85] These theories rest on a view of human conduct as motivated solely by the selfish calculation of personal advantage. In this view, all persons act like Oliver Wendell Holmes's famous "bad man" who "cares nothing for an ethical rule" but is "likely nevertheless to care a good deal to avoid being made to pay money, and will want to keep out of jail if he can."[86] These theories are not just flawed, they are impractical. Deterrence alone clearly cannot compel obedience, as the historic example of prohibition and the current failures of the war on drugs or of the fifty-five-mile-per-hour speed limit demonstrate. Deterrence works only as a reinforcement of the voluntary inclination of the mass of society to obey laws that they could successfully evade to their profit. Holmes himself understood the importance of morality to law. In the same essay in which his "bad man" appears, Holmes also asserted that the "law is the witness and external deposit of our moral life" which "tends to make good citizens and good men."[87]

Thus, if criminal law is to succeed, ordinary citizens must voluntarily avoid criminal activity as morally abhorrent. As both the Protestant Reformers and classical jurists understood, the retributive function of criminal punishment underscores and reinforces the societal condemnation of morally abhorrent behavior, especially when the punishment fits the crime, when serious offenses are met with serious punishments. Conversely, the failure to impose suitable punishments for serious violations undermines and corrodes the moral beliefs of citizens by suggesting that their moral beliefs are wrong, that this conduct must not be so bad after all.[88] By permitting wrongdoers to profit by their wrongs, the failure to punish demoralizes the law-abiding.

---

85. See, e.g., Richard A. Posner, *Economic Analysis of Law* (Boston: Little, Brown, 1992), pp. 217-47; Robert Cooter and Thomas Ulen, *Law and Economics* (Glenview, Ill.: Scott, Foresman, 1988), pp. 507-84.

86. Oliver Wendell Holmes Jr., "The Path of the Law" (1890), in *Collected Legal Papers,* ed. Harold J. Laski (New York: Harcourt, Brace and Co., 1920), p. 170.

87. Holmes, "The Path of the Law," p. 170.

88. See generally Feinberg, "The Expressive Function of Punishment."

To bring to light a Protestant source of modern Anglo-American theories of criminal law and punishment is not to offer a panacea. One cannot readily transpose the moral concepts and criminal institutions of the sixteenth century into contemporary culture. But the Protestant tradition offers important insights even for our day. Protestant writers recognized that a system of criminal law depends upon a transcendent moral source for its structure, content, and efficacy, that any measure of criminal punishment must balance the values of deterrence, retribution, and rehabilitation, and that through punishment the state serves at once as disciplinarian, counselor, and teacher of its citizens. Protestant writers also recognized that criminal law is inherently limited in its capacities, and cannot operate alone. Other social institutions alongside the state, like the family, the school, the Church, and other voluntary associations, must play complementary roles.[89] Each of these social institutions, too, bears the responsibility of encapsulating and elaborating moral principles. Each of these social institutions, too, must participate in the deterrence and retribution of crime, and in the rehabilitation and reformation of the criminal and the community. These time-tested insights provide important signposts along the way to the development of a more integrated understanding of criminal law and punishment for contemporary America.

---

89. See further Chapters 2, 10-12, and 15 herein.

LAW, RELIGION, AND THE FAMILY

10

An Apt and Cheerful Conversation on Marriage

"The apt and cheerful conversation of man with woman is the chief and noblest purpose of marriage," wrote the English poet and philosopher John Milton (1608-1674). "Where loving [conversation] cannot be, there can be left of wedlock nothing but the empty husk of an outside matrimony" — dry, shrivelled, and dispensable. Aptness can strain cheerfulness: candid conversations between spouses can be very painful. Cheerfulness can strain aptness: blissful domestic ignorance can be very tempting. But aptness and cheerfulness properly belong together in a marriage, Milton tells us. Where they fail, the marriage fails.[1]

An apt and cheerful conversation *about* marriage must be part of our dialogue today. For marriage is one of the great mediators of individuality and community, revelation and reason, tradition and modernity. Marriage is at once a harbor of the self and a harbinger of the community, a symbol of divine love and a structure of reasoned consent, an enduring ancient mystery and a constantly modern invention.

To be "apt," our conversation cannot wax nostalgic about a prior golden age of marriage and the family, nor wax myopic about modern ideals of liberty, privacy, and autonomy. We cannot be blind to the patriarchy, paternalism, and plain prudishness of the past. Nor can we be blind to the massive social, psychological, and spiritual costs of the modern sexual revolution. To be apt, participants in the conversation on marriage must seek to understand both traditional morals and contemporary mores on their

---

1. John Milton, *The Doctrine and Discipline of Divorce*, second ed. (London, 1644), in *The Complete Prose Works of John Milton* (New Haven: Yale University Press, 1959), 2:235-56 (spelling modernized).

own terms and in their own context — without deprecating or privileging either form or norm. Traditionalists must heed the maxim of Jaroslav Pelikan that "[t]radition is the living faith of the dead; traditionalism is the dead faith of the living."[2] Wooden antiquarianism, a dogmatic indifference to the changing needs of marriages and families, is not apt. Modernists must heed the instruction of Harold Berman that "we must walk into the future with an eye on the past."[3] Chronological snobbery, a calculated disregard for the wisdom of the past, also is not apt.

To be "cheerful," our conversation must proceed with the faith that the crisis of modern American marriage and family life can be overcome. Marriage and the family are in trouble today. Statistics tell the bald American story. From 1975 to 2000, roughly one quarter of all pregnancies were aborted. One third of all children were born to single mothers. One half of all marriages ended in divorce. Three quarters of all African-American children were raised without fathers. The number of "no parent" households rose exponentially. Children from broken homes proved two to three times more likely to have behavioral and learning problems as teenagers than children from two-parent homes. More than two-thirds of juveniles and young adults convicted of major felonies from 1970 to 1995 came from single- or no-parent homes. So much is well known.[4] It brings little cheer.

What is less well known, and what brings more cheer, is that the Western tradition has faced family crises on this scale before. And apocalyptic jeremiads about the end of civil society have been uttered many times before. What brings cheer is that the Western tradition of marriage has always found the resources to heal and reinvent itself, to strike new balances between orthodoxy and innovation, order and liberty, with regard to our enduring and evolving sexual, marital, and familial norms and habits. The prospect of healing and reinvention is no less likely today — so long as academics, activists, and advocates, political, religious, and civic leaders ponder these problems in good faith and direct their resources to good works.

This chapter makes a small start at such an apt and cheerful conversation on marriage. My argument is that modern Anglo-American marriage law was formed out of two traditions — one rooted in Christianity, a second

2. Jaroslav Pelikan, *The Vindication of Tradition* (New Haven: Yale University Press, 1984), p. 65.

3. Berman, LR I, pp. v, vii.

4. See sources in Chapter 12 herein.

in the Enlightenment. Each of these traditions has contributed a variety of familiar legal ideas and institutions — some overlapping, some conflicting. It is in the overlapping and creatively juxtaposed legal contributions of the Christian and Enlightenment traditions that one sees some of the ingredients of a third way respecting marriage. These are outlined in the latter part of the chapter.

Marriage in the Christian Tradition

The Western tradition has, from its beginnings, viewed marriage in at least four perspectives.[5] Marriage is a *contract,* formed by the mutual consent of the marital couple, and subject to their wills and preferences. Marriage is a *spiritual association,* subject to the creed, code, cult, and canons of the religious community. Marriage is a *social estate,* subject to special state laws of property, inheritance, and evidence, and to the expectations and exactions of the local community. And marriage is a *natural institution,* subject to the natural laws taught by reason and conscience, nature and custom.

These four perspectives are in one sense complementary, for they each emphasize one aspect of this institution — its voluntary formation, its religious sanction, its social legitimation, and its natural origin, respectively. These four perspectives have also come to stand in considerable tension, however, for they are linked to competing claims of ultimate authority over the form and function of marriage — claims by the couple, by the Church, by the state, and by nature and nature's God. Some of the deepest fault lines in the historical formation and the current transformations of Western marriage ultimately break out from this central tension of perspective. Which perspective of marriage dominates a culture, or at least prevails in an instance of dispute — the contractual, the spiritual, the social, or the natural? Which authority wields preeminent, or at least peremptory, power over marriage and family questions — the couple, the Church, the state, or God and nature operating through one of these parties?

Catholics, Protestants, and Enlightenment exponents alike have constructed elaborate models to address these cardinal questions. Each group recognizes multiple perspectives on marriage but gives priority to one of them. Catholics emphasize the spiritual (or sacramental) perspective of marriage. Protestants emphasize the social (or public) perspective. Enlight-

5. FSC, pp. 1-22, and further Chapter 12 herein.

enment exponents emphasize the contractual (or private) perspective. In broad outline, the Catholic model dominated Western marriage law until the sixteenth century. From the mid sixteenth to the mid nineteenth centuries, Catholic and Protestant models, in distinct and hybrid forms, dominated Western family law. In the past century, the Enlightenment model has emerged, in many instances eclipsing the theology and law of Christian models. A brief snapshot of each of these traditions follows, to come to terms with a bit of the theological and legal pedigree of modern marriage.

The Catholic Inheritance[6]

The Roman Catholic Church first systematized its theology and law of marriage in the course of the Papal Revolution of the twelfth and thirteenth centuries. For the first time in that era, the Church came to treat marriage systematically as a natural, contractual, and sacramental unit. First, the Church taught, marriage is a *natural association,* created by God to enable man and woman to "be fruitful and multiply" and to raise children in the service and love of God. Since the fall into sin, marriage has also become a remedy for lust, a channel to direct one's natural passion to the service of the community and the Church. Second, marriage is a *contractual unit,* formed by the mutual consent of the parties. This contract prescribes for couples a lifelong relation of love, service, and devotion to each other and proscribes unwarranted breach or relaxation of their connubial and parental duties. Third, marriage, when properly contracted between Christians, rises to the dignity of a *sacrament.* The temporal union of body, soul, and mind within the marital estate symbolizes the eternal union between Christ and his Church. Participation in this sacrament confers sanctifying grace upon the couple and the community. Couples can perform this sacrament privately, provided they are capable of marriage and comply with the rules for marriage formation.

This sacramental theology placed marriage squarely within the social hierarchy of the Church. The Church claimed jurisdiction over marriage formation, maintenance, and dissolution. It exercised this jurisdiction through both the penitential rules of the internal forum and the canon law rules of the external forum.

---

6. FSC, pp. 16-41, 221-26; Brundage; Theodor Mackin, *Marriage in the Catholic Church,* 2 vols. (New York: Paulist, 1982-1984); George Hayward Joyce, *Christian Marriage: An Historical Doctrinal Study,* 2nd enl. ed. (London: Sheed and Ward, 1948).

The Church did not regard marriage and the family as its most exalted estate, however. Though a sacrament and a sound way of Christian living, marriage was not considered to be so spiritually edifying. Marriage was a remedy for sin, not a recipe for righteousness. Marriage was considered subordinate to celibacy, propagation less virtuous than contemplation, marital love less wholesome than spiritual love. Clerics, monastics, and other servants of the Church were to forgo marriage as a condition for ecclesiastical service. Those who could not were not worthy of the Church's holy orders and offices.

The medieval Catholic Church built upon this conceptual foundation a comprehensive canon law of sex, marriage, and family life that was enforced by a hierarchy of Church courts throughout Christendom. Until the sixteenth-century Protestant Reformation, the Church's canon law of marriage was the preeminent marriage law of the West. A civil law or common law of marriage, where it existed, was usually supplemental and subordinate.

Consistent with the naturalist perspective on marriage, the canon law punished contraception, abortion, infanticide, and child abuse as violations of the natural marital functions of propagation and childrearing. It proscribed unnatural relations, such as incest and polygamy, and unnatural acts such as bestiality and buggery. Consistent with the contractual perspective, the canon law ensured voluntary unions by annulling marriages formed through mistake, duress, fraud, or coercion. It granted husband and wife alike equal rights to enforce conjugal debts that had been voluntarily assumed, and emphasized the importance of mutual love among the couple and their children. Consistent with the sacramental perspective, the Church protected the sanctity and sanctifying purpose of marriage by declaring valid marital bonds to be indissoluble, and by annulling invalid unions between Christians and non-Christians or between parties related by various legal, spiritual, blood, or familial ties. It supported celibacy by annulling unconsummated vows of marriage if one party made a vow of chastity and by prohibiting clerics or monastics from marriage and concubinage.

The medieval canon law of marriage was a watershed in the history of Western law. On the one hand, it distilled the most enduring teachings of the Bible and the Church Fathers and the most salient rules of earlier Jewish, Greek, and Roman laws. On the other hand, it set out many of the basic concepts and rules of marriage and family life that have persisted to this day — in Catholic, Protestant, and secular polities alike. Particularly, the great decree *Tametsi,* issued by the Council of Trent in 1563, codified and refined this medieval law of marriage, adding the rules that marriage formation requires parental consent, two witnesses, civil registration, and Church consecration. A 1566 Catechism commissioned by the same Council, and widely disseminated in the Catholic world in multiple translations, rendered the underlying sacramental theology of marriage clear and accessible to clergy and laity alike.

The Protestant Inheritance[7]

The Protestant Reformers of the sixteenth and seventeenth centuries supplanted the Catholic sacramental model of marriage and the family with a social model. Like Catholics, Protestants retained the *naturalist perspective* of the family as an association created for procreation and mutual protection. They retained the *contractual perspective* of marriage as a voluntary association formed by the mutual consent of the couple. Unlike Catholics, however, Protestants rejected the subordination of marriage to celibacy and the celebration of marriage as a sacrament. According to common Protestant lore, the person was too tempted by sinful passion to forgo God's remedy of marriage. The celibate life had no superior virtue and was no prerequisite for clerical service. It led too easily to concubinage and homosexuality and impeded too often the access and activities of the clerical office. Moreover, marriage was not a sacrament. It was an independent *social institution* ordained by God, and equal in dignity and social responsibility with the Church, state, and other social units. Participation in marriage required no prerequisite faith or purity and conferred no sanctifying grace, as did true sacraments.

Calvinist Protestants emphasized that marriage was not a sacramental institution of the Church, but a covenantal association of the entire community. A variety of parties played a part in the formation of the marriage covenant. The marital couple themselves swore their betrothals and espousals before each other and God — rendering all marriages tripartite agreements with God as party, witness, and judge. The couple's parents, as God's bishops for children, gave their consent to the union. Two witnesses, as God's priests to their peers, served as witnesses to the marriage. The minister, holding the spiritual power of the Word, blessed the couple and

7. FSC, pp. 42-193, 226-68.

admonished them in their spiritual duties. The magistrate, holding the temporal power of the sword, registered the parties and their properties and ensured the legality of their union.

This involvement of parents, peers, ministers, and magistrates in the formation of a marriage was not an idle or dispensable ceremony. These four parties represented different dimensions of God's involvement in the marriage covenant, and were thus essential to the legitimacy of the marriage itself. To omit any of these parties was, in effect, to omit God from the marriage covenant. Protestant covenant theology thus helped to integrate what became universal requirements of valid marriage in the West after the mid sixteenth century — mutual consent of the couple, parental consent, two witnesses, civil registration, and Church consecration.[8]

As a social estate, Protestants taught, marriage was no longer subject to the Church and its canon law, but to the state and its civil law. To be sure, Church officials should continue to communicate biblical moral principles respecting sexuality and parenthood. Church consistories could serve as state agents to register marriages and to discipline infidelity and abuse within the household. All Church members, as priests, should counsel those who seek marriage and divorce, and cultivate the moral and material welfare of baptized children, as their congregational vows in the sacrament of baptism required. But principal legal authority over marriage, most Protestants taught, lay with the state, not with the Church.

Despite the bitter invectives against the Catholic canon law by early Protestant theologians — symbolized poignantly in Luther's burning of the canon law and confessional books in 1520 — Protestant rulers and jurists appropriated much of the traditional canon law of marriage and the family. Traditional canon law prohibitions against unnatural sexual relations and acts and against infringements of the procreative functions of marriage remained in effect. Canon law procedures treating wife and child abuse, paternal delinquency, child custody, and the like continued. Canon law impediments that protected free consent, that implemented biblical prohibitions against marriage of relatives, and that governed the relations of husband and wife and parent and child within the household were largely retained. These and many other time-tested canon law rules and procedures were as consistent with Protestant theology as with Catholic theology, and were transplanted directly into the new state laws of marriage of Protestant Europe.

8. See further Chapter 12 herein.

The new Protestant theology of marriage, however, also yielded critical changes in this new civil law of marriage. Because the Reformers rejected the subordination of marriage to celibacy, they rejected laws that forbade clerical and monastic marriage and that permitted vows of chastity to annul vows of marriage. Because they rejected the sacramental concept of marriage as an eternal enduring bond, the Reformers introduced divorce in the modern sense, on grounds of adultery, desertion, cruelty, or frigidity, with a subsequent right to remarry at least for the innocent party. Because persons by their lustful nature were in need of God's soothing remedy of marriage, the Reformers rejected numerous canon law impediments to marriage not countenanced by Scripture.

After the sixteenth century, these two Christian models of marriage lay at the heart of Western marriage law. The medieval Catholic model, confirmed and elaborated by the Council of Trent, flourished in southern Europe, Spain, Portugal, and France, and their many trans-Atlantic colonies. A Protestant social model rooted in the Lutheran two kingdoms theory dominated portions of Germany, Austria, Switzerland, and Scandinavia together with their colonies. A Protestant social model rooted in Calvinist covenant theology came to strong expression in Calvinist Geneva, and in portions of Huguenot France, the Pietist Netherlands, Presbyterian Scotland, and Puritan England and New England. A Protestant social model rooted in an Anglican theology of the overlapping domestic, ecclesiastical, and political commonwealths dominated England and its many colonies all along the Atlantic seaboard.

The Early American Distillation

These European Christian models of marriage were transmitted across the Atlantic to America during the great waves of colonization and immigration in the sixteenth to eighteenth centuries. They provided much of the theological foundation for the American law of marriage until well into the nineteenth century.

Catholic models of marriage, while not prominent in early America, came to direct application in parts of the colonial American south and southwest.[9] Before the United States acquired the territories of Louisiana

---

9. Hans W. Baade, "The Form of Marriage in Spanish North America," *Cornell Law Review* 61 (1975): 1-89.

(1803), the Floridas (1819), Texas (1836), New Mexico (1848), and California (1848), these colonies were under the formal authority of Spain, and under the formal jurisdiction of the Catholic Church. Most of the areas east of the Mississippi River came within the ecclesiastical provinces of San Domingo or Havana; most of those west came within the ecclesiastical province of Mexico. The Catholic clergy and missionaries taught the sacramental theology of marriage. The ecclesiastical hierarchy sought to enforce the canon laws of marriage, particularly the Decree *Tametsi* issued by the Council of Trent in 1563.[10]

To be sure, there was ample disparity between the law on the books and the law in action, particularly on the vast and sparsely populated American frontier. Religious and political authorities alike often had to recognize the validity of private marriages formed simply by mutual consent, particularly if the union had brought forth children. Yet the Church hierarchy sought to enforce the marital formation rules of *Tametsi* — mutual consent of the couple, parental consent on both sides, two witnesses to betrothals and espousals, and priestly consecration in the face of the Church (or, in the absence of a priest, which was not uncommon, a substitute "marital bond" pending later consecration). Privately or putatively married couples that had defied these rules sometimes faced sanctions. Intermarriage between Catholics and non-Catholics, in open defiance of the sacrament, led to involuntary annulment of the union and the illegitimating of children born of the same. Ecclesiastical authorities also grudgingly acceded to the reality of divorce and remarriage, particularly in distant regions to the north and west that lay beyond their practical reach. Yet their persistent teaching was that a marriage, once properly contracted, was an indissoluble union to be maintained until the death of one of the parties.

With the formal acquisition of these territories by the United States in

---

10. This was not true of American Catholic communities, outside of Spanish territory, that came within the ecclesiastical provinces of Baltimore, Philadelphia, New York, and Boston, and, later, ecclesiastical provinces in the West. The original settlers in these non-Spanish communities were from Britain, Scotland, or other parts of northern Europe where the Decree *Tametsi* was not in effect. They thus continued to recognize the pre-Tridentine Catholic canon law that a secret marriage formed by mutual consent was valid, even without priestly consecration. This disparity continued among some American Catholics until the Tridentine legislation was written into the 1918 Code of Canon Law. See Baade, "Marriage in Spanish North America," pp. 19-24, 36-38; John T. Noonan, *The Power to Dissolve: Lawyers and Marriages in the Courts of the Roman Curia* (Cambridge: Belknap, 1972), pp. 255-56.

the nineteenth century, jurisdiction over marriage shifted to the American Congress and, after statehood, to local state governments. These new civil governments at first rejected roundly portions of the inherited Catholic tradition of marriage, introducing a persistent streak of anti-Catholicism in American marriage law tracts for the next century and more.[11] Particularly the Church's administration of marriage laws and the canonical prohibitions on religious intermarriage and on divorce and remarriage were written out of the new state laws almost immediately. But the Catholic clergy in these territories were generally left free to teach the doctrines and retain the canons of marriage for their own parishioners. Marriages contracted and consecrated before Catholic priests were eventually recognized in all former Spanish colonies in America. The Catholic hierarchy was generally free to pass and enforce new rules for sex, marriage, and family life to guide their own faithful and to advocate state adoption of these rules. Many basic Christian marital norms thereby found their way into American common law, particularly with the exponential growth of America Catholicism in the later nineteenth century.

Protestant models of marriage were much more influential in shaping early American marriage law. By the American Revolution of 1776, the Atlantic seaboard was a veritable checkerboard of Protestant pluralism. Lutheran settlements were scattered throughout Delaware, Maryland, Pennsylvania, and New York. Calvinist communities (Puritan, Presbyterian, Reformed, and Huguenot) were strong in New England, and in parts of New York, New Jersey, Pennsylvania, and the coastal Carolinas and Georgia. Evangelical and Free Church communities (Baptists, Methodists, and Quakers especially) found strongholds in Rhode Island and Pennsylvania and were scattered throughout the new states and far onto the frontier. Anglican communities (after 1780 called Episcopalian) were strongest in Virginia, Maryland, Georgia, and the Carolinas, but had ample representation throughout the original thirteen states and beyond.

These plural Protestant polities, though hardly uniform in their marital norms and habits, were largely united in their adherence to basic Protestant teachings. While adhering to many of the same basic Christian norms of sex, marriage, and domestic life taught by Catholics, they rejected Catholic sacramental views of marriage and ecclesiastical jurisdiction over

11. See, e.g., James Shouler, *A Treatise on the Law of Marriage, Divorce, Separation, and Domestic Relations*, sixth ed., 2 vols. (Albany, N.Y.: Matthew Bender, 1921), 1:19; John Bouvier, *Institutes of American Law*, 2 vols. (Philadelphia: Robert E. Peterson, 1851), 1:101.

marital formation, maintenance, and dissolution. They encouraged ministers to be married. They permitted religious intermarriage. They truncated the law of impediments. They allowed for divorce on proof of fault. They encouraged remarriage of those divorced or widowed.

One issue, however, divided these Protestant communities rather sharply — jurisdictional conflicts over marriage and divorce. New England Calvinist communities, from the beginning of the colonial period, allowed eligible couples to choose to marry before a justice of the peace or a religious official. Anglican communities, following the *Book of Common Prayer,* insisted that such marriages be contracted "in the face of the church" and be consecrated by a properly licensed religious official. Calvinist communities in the north granted local civil courts jurisdiction over issues of divorce, annulment, child custody, and division of the marital estate. Anglican communities in the South insisted that only the legislature should hear and decide such cases.[12] These jurisdictional differences between north and south were eventually smoothed over in the nineteenth century — with the Mid-Atlantic and Midwestern states often providing examples of a middle way between them. The New England way ultimately prevailed.

Aside from these jurisdictional differences, however, a common "Protestant temperament" attended much of the American legal understanding of marriage in the nineteenth and early twentieth centuries.[13] Most common law authorities accepted Protestant social models of marriage that placed special emphasis on the personal felicity, social utility, and moral civility of this godly institution.[14] They also accepted the basic law of marriage inherited from earlier Protestant models. With ample variations across state jurisdictions, a typical state statute in the nineteenth century defined marriage as a permanent monogamous union between a fit man and a fit woman of the age of consent, designed for mutual love and support and for mutual procreation and protection. The common law required that betrothals be formal, and, in some states, that formal banns be published for three weeks before the wedding. It required that marriages of minors be contracted with parental consent on both sides, and that all marriages be contracted in the company of two or more witnesses. It required

12. See detailed study in George Elliott Howard, *A History of Matrimonial Institutions,* 3 vols. (Chicago: University of Chicago Press, 1904).

13. The phrase is from Philip Greven, *The Protestant Temperament: Patterns of Child-Rearing, Religious Experience, and the Self in Early America* (Chicago: University of Chicago Press, 1977).

14. See examples in Chapters 11 and 12 herein.

marriage licenses and registration and solemnization before civil and/or religious authorities. It prohibited marriages between couples related by various blood or family ties identified in the Mosaic law. The common law discouraged — and, in some states, annulled — marriage where one party was impotent, sterile, or had a contagious disease that precluded procreation or gravely endangered the health of the other spouse. Couples who sought to divorce had to publicize their intentions, to petition a court, to show adequate cause or fault, to make permanent provision for the dependent spouse and children. Criminal laws outlawed fornication, adultery, sodomy, polygamy, incest, contraception, abortion, and other perceived sexual offenses against the natural goods and goals of sex and marriage. Tort laws held third parties subject to suit for seduction, enticement, loss of consortium, or alienation of the affections of one's spouse.[15]

Marriage in the Enlightenment Tradition

The Contract Model of Marriage

The Enlightenment contractarian model of marriage was adumbrated in the seventeenth and eighteenth centuries, elaborated theoretically in the nineteenth century, and implemented legally in the twentieth century.[16] Exponents of the Enlightenment introduced a theology of marriage that gave new, and sometimes exclusive, priority to the contractual perspective. The essence of marriage, they argued, was neither its sacramental symbolism, nor its covenantal association, nor its social utility for the community and commonwealth. The essence of marriage was the voluntary bargain struck between the two married parties. The terms of their marital bargain were not preset by God or nature, Church or state, tradition or community. These terms were set by the parties themselves, in accordance with general rules of contract formation and general norms of civil society. Such rules and norms demanded respect for the life, liberty, and property interests of other parties, and compliance with general standards of health, safety, and welfare in the community. But the form and function and the length and limits of the mari-

---

15. See a comprehensive summary of laws in Chester Vernier, *American Family Laws: A Comparative Study of the Family Law of the Forty-Eight States,* 5 vols. (Stanford, Calif.: Stanford University Press, 1931-1938).

16. See sources and discussion in FSC, pp. 194-215, 268-73.

tal relationship were to be left to the private bargain of the parties — each of whom enjoyed full equality and liberty, both with each other and within the broader civil society. Couples should now be able to make their own marriage beds, and lie in them or leave them as they saw fit.

This contractarian model of marriage, already adumbrated ambivalently by John Locke (1632-1704) in his *Two Treatises of Government* (1690), was elaborated in endless varieties and combinations in the eighteenth and nineteenth centuries.[17] The Enlightenment was no single, unified movement, but a series of diverse ideological movements, in various academic disciplines and social circles throughout Europe and North America. For all the variations on its basic themes, however, the Enlightenment was quite consistent in its formulation of marriage as contract and quite insistent on the reformation of traditional marriage laws along contractarian lines.

It must be emphasized that the inspiration for this model was not simply ideological fiat. The Enlightenment model was aimed at the abuses that sometimes attended traditional Christian doctrines of marriage in action. The traditional doctrine of parental consent to marriage, for example, gave parents a strong hand in the marital decisions of their children. Some enterprising parents used this as a means to coerce their children into arranged marriages born of their own commercial or diplomatic convenience, or to sell their consent to the highest bidder for their children's affections. The traditional doctrine of Church consecration of marriage gave clergy an effective instrument to probe deeply into the intimacies of their parishioners. Some enterprising clergy used this as a means to extract huge sums for their marital consecration, or to play the role of officious matchmaker in callous defiance of the wills of the marital parties or their parents. The traditional doctrine of common law coverture, which folded the person and property of the wife into that of her husband, gave husbands the premier place in the governance of the household. Some enterprising husbands used this as a license to control closely the conduct and careers of their wives, or, worse, to visit all manner of savage abuses upon them and upon their children, often with legal impunity. The traditional doctrine of adultery imposed upon innocent children the highest costs of their parents' extra-marital experimentation. Children conceived of such dalliances were sometimes aborted *in vitro* or smothered on birth. If they survived, they

---

17. John Locke, *Two Treatises of Government,* ed. Peter Laslett (Cambridge: Cambridge University Press, 1960 [1690]), I.9, I.47, I.98, II.2, II.77-83.

were declared illegitimate bastards with severely truncated civil, political, and property rights. It was, in part, these and other kinds of abuses manifest in the Christian models of marriage in action that compelled Enlightenment exponents to strip marriage and its law to its contractual core.

Exponents of the Enlightenment advocated the abolition of much that was considered sound and sacred in the Western legal tradition of marriage. They urged the abolition of the requirements of parental consent, Church consecration, and formal witnesses for marriage. They questioned the exalted status of heterosexual monogamy, suggesting that such matters be left to private negotiation. They called for the absolute equality of husband and wife to receive, hold, and alienate property, to enter into contracts and commerce, to participate on equal terms in the workplace and public square. They castigated the state for leaving annulment practice to the Church, and urged that the laws of annulment and divorce be both merged and expanded under exclusive state jurisdiction. They urged that paternal abuse of children be severely punished and that the state ensure the proper nurture and education of all children, legitimate and illegitimate alike.

This contractarian Gospel for the reformation of marriage was too radical to transform much of American law in the nineteenth century. But it anticipated much of the agenda for the reform of American marriage law in the twentieth century. The reform proceeded in two waves. The first wave of reform, which crested from 1910 to 1940, was designed to bring greater equality and equity to the traditional family and civil society, without denying the basic values of the inherited Western tradition of marriage. The second wave of reform, which crested from 1965 to 1990, seemed calculated to break the preeminence of traditional marriage, and the basic values of the Western tradition which have sustained it.

First Wave of Legal Reforms[18]

In the early part of the twentieth century, sweeping new laws eventually broke the legal bonds of coverture which bound the person and property of

---

18. Max Rheinstein, *Marriage Stability, Divorce, and the Law* (Chicago: University of Chicago Press, 1972); Carl E. Schneider, "Moral Discourse and the Transformation of American Family Law," *Michigan Law Review* 83 (1985): 1803; Mary Ann Glendon, *The New Family and the New Property* (Toronto: Butterworths, 1981); Elaine Tyler May, *Great Expectations: Marriage and Divorce in Post-Victorian America* (Chicago: University of Chicago Press, 1980).

a married woman. A married woman eventually gained the right to hold independent title and control of, and exercise independent contractual and testimonial rights over, the property she brought into the marriage or acquired thereafter. She also gained the capacity to litigate in respect of her property, without interference from her husband. As their rights to property were enhanced, (married) women slowly gained broader rights to higher education, learned societies, trade and commercial guilds and unions, and various professions, occupations, and societies, and ultimately to the right to vote in political elections — all of which had been largely closed to them, by custom or by statute.

Other new laws provided that, in cases of annulment or divorce, courts had discretion to place minor children in the custody of that parent who was best suited to care for them. This reversed the traditional presumption that child custody automatically belonged to the father, regardless of whether he was at fault in breaking the marriage. The wife could now gain custody after divorce, particularly when children were of tender years or when the husband was found to be cruel, abusive, or unfit as a caretaker. Courts retained the traditional power to order guilty husbands to pay alimony to innocent wives; they also gained new powers to make other "reasonable" allocations of marital property to the innocent wife for child support.

Other new laws granted greater protection to minor children, within and without the household. Firm new laws against assault and abuse of children offered substantive and procedural protections to children, particularly those who suffered under intemperate parents or guardians. Ample new tax appropriations were made available to orphanages and other charities catering to children. Abortion and infanticide were subject to strong new criminal prohibitions. Child labor was strictly outlawed. Educational opportunities for children, boys and girls alike, were substantially enhanced through the expansion of public schools. Illegitimate children could be more easily legitimated through subsequent marriage of their natural parents, and eventually also through adoption by any fit parent, even if not a blood relative. Annulments no longer automatically illegitimated children born of a putative marriage, particularly if the child remained in the custody of one of the two parents.

This first wave of legal reforms sought to improve traditional marriage and family life more than to abandon it. Most legal writers in the first half of the twentieth century still accepted the traditional Western ideal of marriage as a permanent union of a fit man and fit woman of the age of consent. Most accepted the classic Augustinian definition of the marital goods of *fides, proles, et sacramentum* — sacrificial love of the couple, benevolent procreation of children, and structural stability of marriage as a pillar of civil society. The primary goal of these early reforms was to purge the traditional household and community of its paternalism and patriarchy and thus render the ideals of marriage and family life a greater potential reality for all.

Second Wave of Legal Reforms

The same judgment cannot be so easily cast for the second wave of legal reforms, which crested from 1965 to 1995. From the later 1960s onward, American writers have been pressing the Enlightenment contractarian model of marriage to more radical conclusions. The same Enlightenment ideals of freedom, equality, and privacy which had earlier driven reforms of traditional marriage laws are now being increasingly used to reject traditional marriage laws altogether. The early Enlightenment ideal of marriage as a presumptively permanent contractual union designed for the sake of mutual love, procreation, and protection is slowly giving way to a new reality of marriage as a "terminal sexual contract" designed for the gratification of the individual parties.[19]

The Uniform Marriage and Divorce Act (1987) — both a barometer of enlightened legal opinion and a mirror of conventional custom on marriage — reflects these legal changes. The Uniform Act defines marriage simply as "a personal relationship between a man and a woman arising out of a civil contract to which the consent of the parties is essential."[20] Historically, valid marriage contracts required the consent of parents or guardians, the attestation of two witnesses, Church consecration, and civil licensing and registration. The Uniform Act requires only the minimal formalities of licensing and registration for all marriages, and parental consent for children under the age of majority. Marriages contracted in violation even of these minimal formation requirements, however, are still presumptively valid and immune from independent legal attack, unless the parties themselves petition for dis-

19. Carole Pateman, *The Sexual Contract* (Stanford, Calif.: Stanford University Press, 1988).

20. See, e.g., Uniform Marriage and Divorce Act, 9 U.L.A. 147 (1987), sec. 201 [hereafter UMDA]. The Act is duplicated in Walter Weyrauch, Sanford N. Katz, and Frances Olsen, *Cases and Materials on Family Law* (St. Paul: West, 1994), pp. 1092-1110.

solution within ninety days of contracting marriage.[21] Historically, impediments of infancy, incapacity, inebriation, consanguinity, affinity, sterility, frigidity, and bigamy, among several others, would nullify the marriage or render it voidable and subject to attack from various parties. It would also expose parties who married in knowing violation of these impediments to civil and criminal sanctions. The Uniform Act makes no provision for sanctions, and leaves the choice of nullification to the parties alone. The Act does confirm the traditional impediments protecting consent — granting parties standing to dissolve marriages where they lacked the capacity to contract by reason of infirmity, mental incapacity, alcohol, drugs, or other incapacitating substances, or where there was force, duress, fraud, or coercion into entering a marriage contract.[22] But the Act limits the other impediments to prohibitions against bigamy and marriages between "half or whole blood relatives" or parties related by adoption.[23] And, in many states that have adopted the Uniform Act, all impediments, save the prohibition against bigamy, are regularly waived in individual cases.

These provisions of the Uniform Marriage and Divorce Act reflect a basic principle of modern American constitutional law, first articulated clearly by the United States Supreme Court in *Loving v. Virginia* (1967): "The freedom to marry has long been recognized as one of the vital personal rights essential to the orderly pursuit of happiness by free men. Marriage is one of the 'basic civil rights of man', fundamental to our very existence and survival. . . ."[24] Using that principle, the Court has struck down, as undue burdens on the right to marry, a state prohibition against interracial marriage, a requirement that noncustodial parents obligated to pay child support must receive judicial permission to marry, and a requirement that a prisoner must receive a warden's permission to marry.[25] This same principle of freedom of marital contract, the drafters of the Uniform Act report, has led state courts and legislatures to peel away most of the traditional formalities for marriage formation.

The Supreme Court has expanded this principle of freedom of mari-

---

21. UMDA, secs. 202-6. Parents or guardians may seek dissolution of the marriage of their minor child or ward, provided the action is brought before the child reaches the age of majority. UMDA, sec. 208.

22. UMDA, secs. 207-8.

23. UMDA, sec. 207.

24. *Loving v. Virginia,* 388 U.S. 1, 12 (1967).

25. Respectively *Loving v. Virginia; Zablocki v. Redhail,* 434 U.S. 374 (1978); *Turner v. Safley,* 482 U.S. 78 (1987).

tal contract into a more general right of sexual privacy within the household.[26] In *Griswold v. Connecticut* (1965), for example, the Supreme Court struck down a state law banning the use of contraceptives by a married couple as a violation of their freedom to choose whether to have or to forgo children.[27] In a 1972 case, the Court stated its rationale clearly: "The marital couple is not an independent entity with a mind and heart of its own, but an association of two individuals, each with a separate emotional and intellectual makeup. If the right of privacy means anything, it is the right of the *individual,* married or single, to be free from unwanted governmental intrusion into matters so fundamentally affecting the person as the decision whether to bear or beget a child."[28] In *Roe v. Wade* (1973), the Court extended this privacy principle to cover the right of abortion by a married or unmarried woman during the first trimester of pregnancy — without interference by the state, her husband, parent, or other third party. Still today, a married woman cannot be required to obtain permission from her husband to have an abortion.[29] In *Moore v. East Cleveland* (1978), the Court struck down a municipal zoning ordinance that impaired members of an extended family from living together in the same household.[30] In all such cases, the private contractual calculus of the parties was considered superior to the general state interest in the health, safety, and welfare of its citizens.

State legislatures and courts have extended these principles of freedom of contract and sexual privacy to other aspects of marriage. Many states, for example, have abandoned their traditional reticence about enforcing prenuptial and marital contracts. The Uniform Premarital Agreement Act, adopted in nearly half the states today, allows parties to contract, in advance of their marriage, all rights pertaining to their individual and common property and "any other matter, including their personal rights

26. See analysis, from different perspectives, in E. R. Rubin, *The Supreme Court and the American Family* (Westport, Conn.: Greenwood, 1986); David J. Garrow, *Sexuality and Liberty: The Right to Privacy and the Making of Roe v. Wade,* rev. ed. (Berkeley: University of California Press, 1998).

27. 381 U.S. 479 (1965). The same principle has been extended to protect access of unmarried couples, and minors, to contraceptives. See *Eisenstadt v. Baird,* 405 U.S. 438 (1972); *Carey v. Population Services International,* 431 U.S. 678 (1977).

28. *Eistenstadt,* 405 U.S. at 453.

29. 410 U.S. 113 (1973). In *Planned Parenthood v. Casey,* 112 S. Ct. 2791 (1992), the Court upheld the right of abortion, and struck down a state requirement of notification of one's spouse or the natural father as an "undue burden" upon this right.

30. 431 U.S. 494 (1977).

and obligations, not in violation of public policy or a statute imposing a criminal penalty."[31] The Uniform Premarital Agreement Act does prohibit courts from enforcing premarital contracts that are involuntary, unconscionable, or based on less than full disclosure by both parties. But, within these broad strictures, marital parties are left free to define in advance their own personal and property rights during marriage or in the event of separation, dissolution, or divorce.

Similarly, many states have left marital parties free to contract agreements on their own, or with a private mediator, in the event of temporary or permanent separation. The Uniform Marriage and Divorce Act provides that "parties may enter into a written separation agreement containing provisions for disposition of property owned by either of them, maintenance of either of them, and support, custody, and visitation of their children." Such agreements are presumptively binding on a court. Absent a finding of unconscionability, courts will enforce these agreements on their own terms, reserving the right to alter those contract provisions that bear adversely on the couple's children. If the separation ripens into divorce, courts will also often incorporate these separation agreements into the divorce decree, again with little scrutiny of the contents of the agreement.

The same principles of freedom of contract and sexual privacy dominate contemporary American laws of divorce. Until the mid 1960s, a suit for divorce required proof of the fault of one's spouse (such as adultery, desertion, or cruelty), and no evidence of collusion, connivance, condonation, or provocation by the other spouse. Today, this law of divorce has been abandoned. Every state has promulgated a "no-fault divorce" statute, and virtually all states allow for divorce on the motion of only one party. Even if the innocent spouse forgives the fault and objects to the divorce, courts must grant the divorce if the plaintiff insists. The Uniform Act and fifteen states have eliminated altogether consideration of the fault of either spouse — even if the fault rises to the level of criminal conduct. The remaining states consider fault only for questions of child custody, not for questions of the divorce itself.

Virtually all states have also ordered a one-time division of marital property between the divorced parties. Parties may determine their own property division through prenuptial or separation agreements, which the courts will enforce if the agreements are not unconscionable. But, absent

31. Uniform Premarital Agreement Act, sec. 3. The act is duplicated in Weyrauch et al., *Cases and Materials on Family Law,* pp. 1111-13.

such agreements, courts will simply pool the entire assets of the marital household and make an equitable division of the collective property. These one-time divisions of property have largely replaced traditional forms of alimony and other forms of ongoing support — regardless of the fault, expectations, or needs of either party.

These two reforms of the modern law of divorce served to protect both the privacy and the contractual freedom of the marital parties. No-fault divorces freed marital parties from exposing their marital discords or infidelities to judicial scrutiny and public record. One-time marital property divisions gave parties a clean break from each other and the freedom to marry another. Both changes, together, allowed parties to terminate their marriages as easily and efficiently as they were able to contract them, without much interference from the state or from the other spouse.

These principles of contractual freedom are qualified in divorce cases involving minor children. The fault of the marital party does still figure modestly in current decisions about child custody. The traditional rule was that custody of children was presumptively granted to the mother, unless she was found guilty of serious marital fault or maternal incompetence. Proof of marital fault by the husband, particularly adultery, homosexuality, prostitution, or sexual immorality, virtually eliminated his chances of gaining custody, even if the wife was also at fault. Today, the court's custodial decisions are guided by the proverbial principle of the "best interests of the child." According to the Uniform Marriage and Divorce Act, courts must consider at once the child's custodial preferences, the parents' custodial interests, "the interrelationship of the child with his [or her] parent or parents," "the child's adjustment to his [or her] home, school, or community," and "the mental and physical health of all parties involved."[32] "The court shall not consider the conduct of a proposed custodian that does not affect his relationship to the child," the Uniform Act concludes, setting a high burden of proof for the party who wishes to make their spouse's marital fault an issue in a contested custody case. Under this new standard, the presumption of maternal custody is quickly softening, and joint and shared custody arrangements are becoming increasingly common.

32. UMDA, sec. 402.

Signposts of a Third Way

A Hegelian might well be happy with this dialectical story — Christian models of marriage that prioritized religious norms and ecclesiastical strictures squared off against Enlightenment models of marriage that prioritized private choice and contractual strictures. Christianity was exposed for its penchant for paternalism and patriarchy, and lost. The Enlightenment was embraced for its promise of liberty and equality, and won. Thesis gives way to anti-thesis. Such is the way of progress.

The story is not so simple. It is true that the Enlightenment ideal of marriage as a privately bargained contract between husband and wife about all their rights, goods, and interests has largely become a legal reality in America. The strong presumption today is that adult parties have free entrance into marital contracts, free exercise of marital relationships, and free exit from marriages once their contractual obligations are discharged. Parties are still bound to continue to support their minor children, within and without marriage. But this merely expresses another basic principle of contract law — that parties respect the reliance and expectation interests of their children, who are third-party beneficiaries of their marital or sexual contracts.[33]

It is equally true, however, that undue contractualization of marriage has brought ruin to many women and children, as many nineteenth-century conservatives had warned.[34] Premarital, marital, separation, and divorce contracts too often are not arm's-length transactions, and too often are not driven by rational calculus alone. In the heady romance of budding nuptials, parties are often blind to the full consequences of their bargain. In the emotional anguish of separation and divorce, parties are often driven more by the desire for short-term relief from the other spouse than by the concern for long-term welfare of themselves or their children. The economically stronger and more calculating spouse triumphs in these con-

---

33. See Lenore J. Weitzman, *The Marriage Contract: Spouses, Lovers, and the Law* (New York: Free Press, 1991).

34. See, for example, James Fitzjames Stephen, *Liberty, Equality, and Fraternity,* ed. Stuart D. Warner (Indianapolis: Liberty Fund, 1993 [1857]), pp. 138-41, 150-53, arguing that to allow marriage to become "a simple bargained-for contract," without oversight by parents and peers and by Church and state, "will inevitably expose women to great abuse." They will have no protection in forming the bargain with naturally superior men, nor protection from men who dismiss them when "barren, old, unattractive, troubled, or destitute."

texts. And in the majority of cases today, that party is still the man — despite the tempting egalitarian rhetoric to the contrary.

"Underneath the mantle of equality [and freedom] that has been draped over the ongoing family, the state of nature flourishes," Mary Ann Glendon writes.[35] In this state of nature, contractual freedom and sexual privacy reign supreme. But also in this state of nature, married life is becoming increasingly "brutish, nasty, and short," with women and children bearing the primary costs. The very contractarian Gospel that first promised salvation from the abuses of earlier Christian models of marriage now threatens with even graver abuse.[36]

What is the way out of this dilemma? Surely, part of the way forward is to look backward — back to the sources of our marriage traditions, but now newly enlightened! The achievements of the Enlightenment in reforming the traditional theology and law of marriage cannot be lost on us. It took the contractual radicalism of the Enlightenment to force the Western tradition to reform itself — to grant greater respect to the rights of women and children, to break the monopoly and monotony of outmoded moral and religious forms and forums respecting sexuality, marriage, and the family. It took the bold step of stripping marriage and its law to its contractual core for the Western tradition to see the need to reform its basic doctrines of parental consent, Church consecration, male headship, child illegitimation, and others. While some religious traditions may have retrieved or conceived their own resources to achieve these reforms, it was the Enlightenment critique that forced these traditions to reform themselves and the state to reform its laws. This was no small achievement.

Just as the Enlightenment tradition still has much to teach us today, so do the earlier Catholic and Protestant traditions of the West.

First, these Western Christian traditions have seen that a marriage is at once a contractual, religious, social, and natural association, and that in order to survive and flourish, this institution must be governed both exter-

---

35. Mary Ann Glendon, *The Transformation of Family Law: State, Law, and Family in the United States and Western Europe* (Chicago: University of Chicago Press, 1989), p. 146.

36. See, from different perspectives, Lenore J. Weitzman, *The Divorce Revolution: The Unexpected Social and Economic Consequences for Women and Children* (New York: Free Press, 1985); Barbara Dafoe Whitehead, *The Divorce Culture: How Divorce Became an Entitlement and How It Is Blighting the Lives of Our Children* (New York: Alfred A. Knopf, 1997); Paul R. Amato and Alan Booth, *A Generation at Risk: Growing Up in an Era of Family Upheaval* (Cambridge, Mass.: Harvard University Press, 1997).

nally by legal authorities and internally by moral authorities. From different perspectives, Catholic and Protestant traditions have seen that marriage is an inherently communal enterprise, in which marital couples, magistrates, and ministers must all inevitably cooperate. After all, marital contracts are of little value without courts to enforce them. Marital properties are of little use without laws to validate them. Marital laws are of little consequence without canons to inspire them. Marital customs are of little cogency without natural norms and narratives to ground them.

The modern lesson in this is that we must resist the temptation to reduce marriage to a single perspective, or to a single forum. A single perspective on marriage — whether religious, social, or contractual — does not capture the full nuance of this institution. A single forum — whether the Church, state, or the household itself — is not fully competent to govern all marital questions. Marriage demands multiple forums and multiple laws to be governed adequately. American religious communities must think more seriously about restoring and reforming their own bodies of religious law on marriage, divorce, and sexuality, instead of simply acquiescing in state laws. American states must think more seriously about granting greater deference to the marital laws and customs of legitimate religious and cultural groups that cannot accept a marriage law of the common denominator or denomination. Other sophisticated legal cultures — Denmark, England, India, and South Africa — grant semi-autonomy to Catholic, Hindu, Jewish, Muslim, and Traditional groups to conduct their subjects' domestic affairs in accordance with their own laws and customs, with the state setting only minimum conditions and limits. It might well be time for America likewise to translate its growing cultural pluralism into a more concrete legal pluralism on marriage and family life.[37]

Second, the Western tradition has learned to distinguish between betrothals and espousals, engagements and weddings. Betrothals were defined as a future promise to marry, to be announced publicly in the local community and to be fulfilled after a suitable waiting period. Espousals were defined as the present promise to marry, to be celebrated in a public ceremony before civil and/or religious officials. The point of a public betrothal and waiting period was to allow couples to weigh the depth and du-

---

37. Joel A. Nichols, "Louisiana's Covenant Marriage Law: A First Step Toward a More Robust Pluralism in Marriage and Divorce Law," *Emory Law Journal* 47 (1998): 929-1001; John Witte Jr. and Eliza Ellison, eds., *Covenant Marriage in Comparative Perspective* (Grand Rapids: Eerdmans, 2005).

rability of their mutual love. It was also to invite others to weigh in on the maturity and compatibility of the couple, to offer them counsel and commodities, and to prepare for the celebration of their union and their life together thereafter. Too long an engagement would encourage the couple to fornication. But too short an engagement would discourage them from introspection. Too secret and private a marriage would deprive couples of the essential counsel and gifts of their families and friends. But too public and routinized a marriage would deprive couples of the indispensable privacy and intimacy needed to tailor their nuptials to their own preferences. Hence the traditional balance of engagement and wedding, of publicity and privacy, of waiting and consummating.

The modern lesson in this is that we must resist collapsing the steps of engagement and marriage, and restore reasonable waiting periods between them, especially for younger couples. Today, in most states, marriage requires only the acquisition of a license from the state registry followed by solemnization before a licensed official — without banns, with little waiting, with no public celebration, without notification of others. So sublime and serious a step in life seems to demand a good deal more prudent regulation than this. It may well not be apt in every case to invite parents and peers, ministers and magistrates to evaluate the maturity and compatibility of the couple. Our modern doctrines of privacy and disestablishment of religion militate against this. But, especially in the absence of such third parties, the state should require marital parties themselves to spend some time weighing their present maturity and prospective commitment. A presumptive waiting period of at least ninety days between formal engagement and wedding day seems to be reasonable, given the stakes involved — particularly if the parties are under twenty-five years of age. Probationary waiting periods, particularly for younger parties, are routinely required to enter a contract for a home mortgage, or to procure a license to operate a motor vehicle or handgun. Given the much higher stakes involved, marital contracts should be subject to at least comparable conditions.

Third, the Western tradition has learned to distinguish between annulment and divorce. Annulment is a decision that a putative marriage was void from the start, by reason of some impediment that lay undiscovered or undisclosed at the time of the wedding. Divorce is a decision that a marriage once properly contracted must now be dissolved by reason of the fault of one of the parties after their wedding. The spiritual and psychological calculus and costs are different in these decisions. In annulment cases, a party may discover features of their marriage or spouse that need not, and sometimes cannot, be forgiven — that they were manipulated or coerced into marriage; that the parties are improperly related by blood or family ties; that the spouse will not or cannot perform expected connubial duties; that the spouse misrepresented a fundamental part of his or her faith, character, or history. Annulment in such instances is prudent, sometimes mandatory, even if painful. In divorce cases, by contrast, the moral inclination (and, for some, the moral imperative) is to forgive a spouse's infidelity, desertion, cruelty, or crime. Divorce, in such instances, might be licit, even prudent, but it often feels like, and is treated as, a personal failure even for the innocent spouse. The historical remedy was often calculated patience; early death by one spouse was the most common cure for broken marriages. In the modern age of fitness and longevity, this remedy is usually less apt.

The modern lesson in this is that not all marital dissolutions are equal. Today, most states have simply collapsed annulment and divorce into a single action, with little procedural or substantive distinction between them. This is one (largely forgotten) source of our exponentially increased divorce rates; historically, annulment rates were counted separately. This is one reason that religious bodies have become largely excluded from the marital dissolution process; historically, annulment decisions were often made by religious bodies and then enforced by state courts. And this is one reason that "no-fault" divorce has become so attractive; parties often have neither the statutory mechanism nor the procedural incentive to plead a legitimate impediment. Parties seeking dissolution are thus herded together in one legal process of divorce — subject to the same generic rules respecting children and property, and prone to the same generic stigmatizing by self and others.

Fourth, the Western tradition has learned, through centuries of hard experience, to balance the norms of marital formation and dissolution. There was something cruel, for example, in a medieval Catholic canon law that countenanced easy contracting of marriage but provided for no escape from a marriage once properly contracted. The Council of Trent responded to this inequity in the *Tametsi* decree of 1563 by establishing several safeguards to the legitimate contracting of marriage — parental consent, peer witness, civil registration, and Church consecration — so that an inapt or immature couple would be less likely to marry. There was something equally cruel in the rigid insistence of some early Protestants on reconciliation of all married couples at all costs — save those few who could successfully sue for divorce. Later Protestants responded to this inequity by reinstituting the traditional remedy of separation from bed and board for miserable couples incapable of either reconciliation or divorce.

The modern lesson in this is that rules governing marriage formation and dissolution must be balanced in their stringency — and separation must be maintained as a release valve. Stern rules of marital dissolution require stern rules of marital formation. Loose formation rules demand loose dissolution rules, as we see today. To fix the modern problem of broken marriages requires reforms of rules at both ends of the marital process. Today, more than twenty states have bills under discussion seeking to tighten the rules of divorce, without corresponding attention to the rules of marital formation and separation. Such efforts, standing alone, are misguided. The cause of escalating divorce rates is not only no-fault divorce, as is so often said, but also no-faith marriage.

Fifth, the Western tradition has recognized that the household has multiple forms, that it can change over time and across cultures. The celebrated nuclear family of husband and wife, daughter and son is only one model that the Western tradition has cherished. It was common in the past to extend the theological and legal concept of the family to other kinds of units — the single household with one parent alongside children, stepchildren, adopted children, or grandchildren; the extended household embracing servants, students, and sojourners or embracing three or four generations of relatives with obligations of mutual care and nurture among them; the communal household of siblings or friends, single or widowed, with or without children; the spiritual household of brothers and sisters joined in the cloister, chantry, or charity, and dedicated to service of God, neighbor, and each other.

The modern lesson in this is that we must not cling too dogmatically to an ideal form of household. It was common in the recent past for the establishment to look askance on the commune but approvingly on the community home, to look churlishly at the divorcee but charitably on the widow, to look suspiciously on the spinster but benevolently on the spurned. Today, we accept, sometimes even admire, communes, divorcees, and spinsters — and make provision for them in our laws of taxation, property, and zoning as well as in our pastoral, diaconal, and pedagogical ministries. We now have other targets of suspicion — homosexuals and polygamists prominently among them.

Finally, the Western tradition has recognized that marriage and the family have multiple goods and goals. This institution might well be rooted in the natural order and in the will of the parties. Participation in it might well not be vital, or even conducive, to a person's salvation. But the Western tradition has seen that the marriage and family are indispensable to the integrity of the individual and the preservation of the social order.

In Catholic and Anglican parlance, marriage has three inherent goods, which St. Augustine identified as *fides, proles, et sacramentum.*[38] Marriage is an institution of *fides* — faith, trust, and love between husband and wife, and parent and child, that goes beyond the faith demanded of any other temporal relationship. Marriage is a source of *proles* — children who carry on the family name and tradition, perpetuate the human species, and fill God's Church with the next generation of saints. Marriage is a form of *sacramentum* — a symbolic expression of Christ's love for his Church, even a channel of God's grace to sanctify the couple, their children, and the broader community.

In Lutheran and Calvinist parlance, marriage has both civil and spiritual uses in this life. On the one hand, the family has general "civil uses" for all persons, regardless of their faith. Marriage deters vice by furnishing preferred options to prostitution, promiscuity, pornography, and other forms of sexual pathos. Marriage cultivates virtue by offering love, care, and nurture to its members, and holding out a model of charity, education, and sacrifice to the broader community. Ideally, marriage enhances the life of a man and a woman by providing them with a community of caring and sharing, of stability and support, of nurture and welfare. Ideally, marriage also enhances the life of the child, by providing it with a chrysalis of nurture and love, with a highly individualized form of socialization and education. It might take a village to raise a child properly, but it takes a marriage to make one.

On the other hand, the family has specific "spiritual uses" for believers — ways of sustaining and strengthening them in their faith. The love of wife and husband can be among the strongest symbols we can experience of Yahweh's love for his elect, of Christ's love for his Church. The sacrifices we make for spouses and children can be among the best reflections we can offer of the perfect sacrifice of Golgotha. The procreation of children can be among the most important Words we have to utter.[39]

---

38. Augustine, *On Original Sin,* chap. 39 [xxxix], in *A Select Library of Nicene and Post-Nicene Fathers of the Christian Church,* ed. Philip Schaff and Henry Wace, Second Series, repr. ed. (Grand Rapids: Eerdmans, 1952), 5:251.

39. Cf. John E. Coons, "The Religious Rights of Children," in RHR I, p. 172: "In a faint echo of the divine, children are the most important Word most of us will utter."

The Goods and Goals of Marriage
in the Western Tradition

In the past decade, a substantial new body of social science and public health literature has emerged seeking to make the statistical case that marriage is a good institution. The central thesis of this new literature is that, on the whole, it is healthier (1) to be married or remarried than to remain single, widowed, or divorced; (2) to have two parents raising a child rather than one or none; and (3) to have marital cohabitation rather than nonmarital cohabitation for couples who are planning to be together for the long term. On average, a number of recent studies show, married adults are less likely than nonmarried adults to abuse alcohol, drugs, and other addictive substances. Married parties take fewer mortal and moral risks, even fewer when they have children. They live longer by several years. They are less likely to attempt or to commit suicide. They enjoy more regular, safe, and satisfying sex. They amass and transmit greater per capita wealth. They receive better personal health care and hygiene. They provide and receive more effective co-insurance and sharing of labor. They are more efficient in discharging essential domestic tasks. They enjoy greater overall satisfaction with life measured in a variety of ways. Men, on average, enjoy more of these health benefits of marriage than women. The presence of children in the household decreases the short-term benefits but increases the long-term benefits of marriage for both spouses. Most children reared in two-parent households perform better in their socialization, education, and development than their peers reared in single- or no-parent homes.[1]

1. See Centers for Disease Control and Prevention per Charlotte A. Schoenborn, "Vital and Health Statistics Number 351" (December 15, 2004); Steven M. Tipton and John Witte Jr., eds., *The Family Transformed: Religion, Values, and Society in American Life*

These general data on the health benefits of marriage do not pretend to describe all particular cases. There are plenty of happy singles. Sometimes widow(er)s and divorcees thrive after surviving or escaping miserable marriages. There are plenty of successful single parents. Sometimes their children thrive in the absence of perennial parental abuse or conflict and/or upon negotiation of a suitable joint custody or visitation arrangement. There are plenty of committed couples that transfer smoothly from nonmarital to marital cohabitation. Sometimes such experiments convince couples to forgo marriage and to spare themselves and their prospective children the painful costs of divorce. But the recent social science data suggest strongly that these exceptions, though ample and diverse in number, do not overcome the basic presumptions about the superior utility and healthiness of monogamous marital unions and intact two-parent families.[2]

I read these new social science data on the health benefits of marriage as a historian. In my view, these data help to corroborate and to elaborate a number of ancient and enduring teachings on the goods and goals of marriage that have undergirded the classic professions of the West — especially the professions of law and theology. The aim of this chapter is (1) to compare these new social science data with some of the traditional Western legal and theological formulations of the goods and goals of marriage; and (2) to explore the role of law in defining and defending these marital goods and goals.

The Goods and Goals of Marriage: Classical Formulations

It has long been common in the Western Christian tradition to speak of the end (*finis*) of marriage. The Latin term *finis* is a term both of ontology and

---

(Washington, D.C.: Georgetown University Press, 2005); Don S. Browning, *Marriage and Modernization: How Globalization Threatens Modern Marriage and What to Do about It* (Grand Rapids: Eerdmans, 2003); John Wall, Don Browning, William J. Doherty, and Stephen Post, eds., *Marriage, Health and the Professions* (Grand Rapids: Eerdmans, 2002); Linda J. Waite and Maggie Gallagher, *The Case for Marriage* (New York: Doubleday, 2000); Stephen G. Post, *More Lasting Unions: Christianity, the Family and Society* (Grand Rapids: Eerdmans, 2000).

2. What have apparently not yet been closely studied by social scientists are the comparative health benefits of (1) monogamous v. polygamous unions; (2) committed married lives v. committed monastic lives; or (3) committed heterosexual v. committed homosexual unions.

of teleology. It describes both the *goods* of marriage (its virtue, its reason for being, its intrinsic worth) and the *goals* of marriage (its purposes, its expected consequences, its instrumental value). To signal this distinction, early Catholic canonists and moralists sometimes spoke of the purpose (*causa*) and effect (*effectus*) of marriage, or its inherent goods (*fines operis*) and its actualized goals (*fines operantis*).[3] Early Protestant jurists and theologians repeated these distinctions but also spoke of the reason (*ratio*) and use (*usus*) of marriage. Most Western Christian writers — patristic, Catholic, and Protestant alike — spoke to both the goods and the goals, the intrinsic and the instrumental values, of marital institutions and activities. But Catholics have tended to emphasize the intrinsic goods of marriage, its ontology.[4] Protestants have tended to emphasize the instrumental goals of marriage, its teleology.[5]

The Western Christian tradition inherited this idea of marital goods and goals from classical Greece and Rome.[6] A number of Greek and Roman writers regarded marriage as a natural institution that served the couple, the children, and the community at once. In a suggestive passage in *The Republic,* for example, Plato (ca. 428–ca. 347 B.C.E.) said it was "obvious" that a "just republic" "must arrange [for] marriages, sacramental so far as may be. And the most sacred marriages would be those that were the most beneficial."[7] In his *Laws,* when advising young men on how to choose a wife, Plato wrote: "A man should 'court the tie' that is for the city's good, not that

3. See sources and discussion in Francis W. Carney, *The Purposes of Christian Marriage* (Washington, D.C.: Catholic University of America Press, 1950); Theodor Mackin, *What Is Marriage?* (New York: Paulist, 1982); Dietrich von Hildebrand, *Marriage* (New York: Longmans Green, 1942).

4. See, e.g., Germain Grisez, *The Way of the Lord Jesus: Living a Christian Life* (Quincy, Ill.: Franciscan, 1993), pp. 556-659; Robert P. George and Gerard V. Bradley, "Marriage and the Liberal Imagination," *Georgetown Law Journal* 84 (1995): 305ff.

5. See sources and discussion in FSC, pp. 42-193.

6. I have not addressed the use of Judaic sources in the early Church, ably and amply discussed in Michael J. Broyde and Michael Asubel, eds., *Marriage, Sex, and Family in Judaism* (Lanham, Md.: Rowman and Littlefield, 2005); Leo G. Perdue et al., *Families in Ancient Israel* (Louisville, Ky.: Westminster John Knox, 1997); Carolyn L. Osiek and David Balch, eds., *Families in the New Testament World: Households and House Churches* (Louisville, Ky.: Westminster John Knox, 1997); David L. Balch and Carolyn Osiek, eds., *Early Christian Families in Context* (Grand Rapids: Eerdmans, 2003).

7. Plato, *Republic,* V.458e, in *The Collected Dialogues of Plato, Including the Letters,* ed. Edith Hamilton and Huntington Cairns (Princeton, N.J.: Princeton University Press, 1961), p. 698.

which most takes his own fancy."[8] Once married, the man should restrict "procreative intercourse to its natural function," for such "moderation" will bring "untold good. It is dictated, to begin with, by nature's own voice, leads to the suppression of the mad frenzy of sex, as well as marriage breaches of all kinds, and all manner of excess in meats and drinks, and wins men to affection of their wedded wives. There are also numerous other blessings which will follow. . . ."[9]

Aristotle (384-321 B.C.E.) viewed marriage as the foundation of the republic and the prototype of friendship. "[M]an is a political animal" who forms states and other associations "for the purpose of attaining some good," Aristotle wrote famously in his *Politics*: "[E]very state is composed of households." Every household, in turn, is composed of "a union or pairing of those who cannot exist without one another. A man and woman must unite for the reproduction of the species — not from deliberate intention, but from the natural impulse . . . to leave behind something of the same nature as themselves."[10]

Aristotle extended this insight in his *Ethics*, now emphasizing goods of marriage beyond its political and social expediency:

> The love between husband and wife is evidently a natural feeling, for nature has made man even more of a pairing than a political animal in so far as the family is an older and more fundamental thing than the state, and the instinct to form communities is less widespread among animals than the habit of procreation. Among the generality of animals male and female come together for this sole purpose [of procreation]. But human beings cohabit not only to get children but also to provide whatever is necessary to a fully lived life. From the outset, the partners perform distinct duties, the man having one set, the woman another. So by pooling their individual contributions [into a common stock] they help each other out. Accordingly there is general agreement that marital affection combines the useful and the pleasant. But it may also embody a moral ideal, when husband and wife are virtuous persons. For man and woman have each their own special excellence, and this may

8. Plato, *Laws*, VI.773b., in *Collected Dialogues of Plato*, p. 1350. Cf. Genesis 6:2 (complaining that "the sons of God saw that the daughters of men were fair and took to wife such of them as they chose").

9. Plato, *Laws*, VIII.839a-b, in *Collected Dialogues of Plato*, p. 1404.

10. Aristotle, *The Politics of Aristotle*, trans. Ernest Barker (New York: Oxford University Press, 1962), I.1.1; I.2.2; I.2.9.

be a source of pleasure to most. Children, too, it is agreed, are a bond between the parents — which explains why childless unions are more likely to be dissolved. The children do not belong to one parent more than to another, and it is the joint ownership of something valuable that keeps people from separating.[11]

To ensure that marital couples would remain bonded together for the sake of their children, Aristotle (emulating some of Plato's teachings) prescribed a whole series of laws on the ideal ages, qualities, and duties of husband and wife to each other and to their children.[12]

The Roman Stoics repeated and glossed these classical Greek views about marriage, even while many of them celebrated celibacy as the higher ideal. Cicero (106-34 B.C.E.), for example, the leading jurist and moralist of his day, called marriage a "natural sharing" of the person and property of husband and wife that served for the procreation of children, for companionship, and ultimately for the broader cultivation of "dutifulness, goodness, liberality, kindness, courtesy, and similar virtues."[13] Musonius Rufus (b. ca. 30 C.E.), an influential moralist, described marriage in robust companionate terms, anticipating by many centuries the familiar language of the Christian marriage liturgy:

> The husband and wife . . . should come together for the purpose of making a life in common and of procreating children, and furthermore of regarding all things in common between them, and nothing peculiar or private to one or the other, not even their own bodies. The birth of a human being which results from such a union is to be sure something marvelous, but it is not yet enough for the relation of husband and wife, inasmuch as, quite apart from marriage, it could result from any

11. Aristotle, *The Ethics of Aristotle,* trans. J. A. K. Thomson (Baltimore, Md.: Penguin, 1965), VIII.12. The interpolation "into a common stock" is an alternative translation that appears in several other English editions of the *Ethics.*

12. Aristotle, *Politics,* VII.16-17; see also Plato, *Republic,* V.457d, 459-61, 696-97, 698-701; Plato, *Laws,* VIII.772d-e, 774a-b, 1349-1351. See further Sarah Pomeroy, *Families in Classical and Hellenistic Greece: Representations and Realities* (Oxford: Oxford University Press, 1997); Cynthia B. Patterson, *The Family in Greek History* (Cambridge, Mass.: Harvard University Press, 1998); and the discussions of comparable sentiments in Xenophon in *Xenophon Oeconomicus: A Social and Historical Commentary,* by Sarah Pomeroy (Oxford: Oxford University Press, 1994).

13. Cicero, *De Finibus,* III.23, 65; Cicero, *De Republica,* I.5, V.5; Cicero, *De Officiis,* I.27, 54.

other sexual union, just as in the case of animals. But in marriage there must be above all perfect companionship and mutual love of husband and wife, both in health and in sickness and under all conditions, since it was with desire for this as well as for having children that both entered upon marriage.[14]

Musonius further insisted that sexual intercourse was "justified only when it occurs in marriage and is indulged in for the purpose of begetting children," and he praised those lawgivers who "consider the increase of the homes of the citizens [through procreation] the most fortunate thing for the cities and the decrease of them [through infanticide] the most shameful thing."[15] Indeed, he wrote, "whoever destroys human marriage destroys the home, the city, and the whole human race."[16]

Musonius's student, Hierocles, argued more strongly than his teacher that it was incumbent upon all men, even philosophers seeking quiet contemplation, to marry and to maintain a household, since "marriage is the basis of the household, and the household is essential to civilization."[17] While procreation remained the ultimate ideal of marriage, in Hierocles's view, the consistent companionship and mutual care of husband and wife were no less important, even in the absence of children:

[T]he beauty of the household consists in the yoking together of a husband and wife who are united together by fate, are consecrated by the gods who preside over weddings, births and houses, agree with each other and have all things in common, including their bodies, or rather their souls, and who exercise appropriate rule over their household and servants, take care in rearing their children, and pay attention to the necessities of life.[18]

14. Musonius Rufus, Fragment 13A, "What is the Chief End of Marriage?" reprinted and translated in *Musonius Rufus: The Roman Socrates*, ed. Cora E. Lutz (New Haven: Yale University Press, 1947), p. 88.

15. Musonius Rufus, Fragment 12, "On Aphrodisia," and Fragment 15, "Should Every Child That Is Born Be Raised?" in *Musonius Rufus*, pp. 86, 96. See further Roy B. Ward, "Musonius and Paul on Marriage," *New Testament Studies* 36 (1990): 281-89.

16. Musonius Rufus, Fragment 14, "Is Marriage a Handicap to the Pursuit of Philosophy?" in *Musonius Rufus*, p. 92.

17. Judith Evans Grubb, *Law and Family in Late Antiquity: The Emperor Constantine's Marriage Legislation* (Oxford: Clarendon, 1995), p. 59.

18. Quoted in Grubb, *Law and Family in Late Antiquity*, pp. 59-60.

The great Roman historian and moralist Plutarch (46-120 C.E.), though a critic of Stoicism on many points, wrote much like a Stoic on the pleasures of love, intimacy, and friendship within the marital household. The ideal marriage, he wrote, is "a union for life between a man and a woman for the delights of love and the getting of children." "In the case of lawful wives, physical union is the beginning of friendship, a sharing as it were, in great mysteries. The pleasure [of sexual intercourse] is short, but the respect and kindness and mutual affection and loyalty that daily spring from it . . . [render] such a [marital] union a 'friendship'."[19] And again: "No mutual pleasures are greater, no mutual services more constant, no form of affection is more enviable and estimable for its sheer beauty than 'when man and wife in harmony of mind keep house together.'"[20]

The ideal marital household, Plutarch continued in his *Advice to the Bride and Groom,* is a sharing of the person, property, and pursuits of its members, under the gentle leadership of the paterfamilias. Plutarch piled metaphor upon metaphor to drive home his point:

> When two notes are struck together, the melody belongs to the lower note. Similarly, every action performed in a good household is done by the agreement of the partners, but displays the leadership and decision of the husband. . . .
>
> Plato says that the happy and blessed city is one in which the words "mine" and "not mine" are least to be heard, because the citizens treat everything of importance, so far as possible, as their common property. Even more firmly should these words be banished from a marriage. Doctors tell us that an injury on the left side refers the sensation to the

19. Plutarch, *Life of Solon,* 20.4, in *Plutarch's Lives,* 11 vols., ed. G. P. Goold, trans. Bernadette Perrin (Cambridge: Harvard University Press, 1982), 1:459; Plutarch, *Erotikos* 769, in *Plutarch's Moralia,* trans. Edwin L. Minar Jr. et al. (Cambridge: Harvard University Press, 1961), 9:427. See John Finnis, "Law, Morality, and Sexual Orientation," *Notre Dame Law Review* 69 (1994): 1063-64; John Finnis, "Is Natural Law Theory Compatible with Limited Government?" in *Natural Law, Liberalism, and Morality,* ed. Robert P. George (Oxford: Clarendon, 1996), pp. 12-17.

20. Plutarch, *Erotikos* 770A, in *Plutarch's Moralia,* 9:459, quoting in part Homer, *Odyssey,* 6.183. See Lisette Goessler, "Advice to the Bride and the Groom: Plutarch Gives a Detailed Account of His Views of Marriage," in *Plutarch's Advice to the Bride and Groom and A Consolation to his Wife,* ed. Sarah B. Pomeroy (Oxford: Oxford University Press, 1999), pp. 112-14. See also Plutarch, *Erotikos* 769E, in *Plutarch's Moralia,* 9:431: "In marriage, to love is a greater boon than to be loved: it rescues us from many errors — or rather from all errors that wreck or impair wedlock."

right. Similarly, it is good for a wife to share her husband's feelings, and a husband his wife's, so that, just as ropes gain strength from the twisting of the strands, so their communion may be the better preserved by their joint effort, through mutual exchanges of goodwill. Nature joins you together in your bodies, so that she may take a part of each, and mixing them together give you a child that belongs to you both, such that neither of you can say what is his or her own, and what the other's. Community of resources also is particularly appropriate for the married; they should pour everything into one fund, mix it all together, and not think of one part as belonging to one and another to the other, but of the whole as their own, and none of it anyone else's.[21]

Plutarch also wrote at length on the natural affinity and affection of parents, especially mothers, to their children. Among "the first mothers and fathers, there was no law ordering them to have families, no expectation of advantages or return to be got out of them." "But the love of one's offspring, implanted by nature, moves and influences" parents even then to have and nurture children, much as it moves many other animals. "[T]here is no power or advantage to be got from children, but that the love of them, alike in mankind as among the animals, proceeds entirely from nature."[22] Nature also teaches that mothers should nurse and nurture their own infant children, and that both mother and father should cooperate in the upbringing, discipline, and education of their children.[23]

Some of these views about marriage entered classical Roman law, well before the conversion to Christianity of the Roman emperor and empire in the fourth century. For example, two mid-third-century legal texts define marriage thus: "Marriage is a union of a man and a woman, and a sharing for the whole of their life [or a sharing for their whole life; *consortium omnis vitae*], in accordance with divine and human law." And again: "Marriage, or matrimony, is a union of a man and a woman that involves a continuous or undivided sharing of life."[24] Other second- and third-century

---

21. Plutarch, *Advice to the Bride and Groom*, Precepts 11, 20, reprinted and translated in *Plutarch's Advice*, ed. Pomeroy, pp. 6, 8. See also Precept 34, p. 10, and Plutarch, *Erotikos* 770, in *Plutarch's Moralia*, 9:419.

22. Plutarch, "Affection for One's Offspring," in *The Complete Works of Plutarch*, 6 vols. (New York: Kelmscott Society, 1909), 5:25, 27.

23. Plutarch, "The Training of Children," in *The Complete Works of Plutarch*, 5:1-20.

24. Justinian, *Digest*, 23.2.1, quoting Modestinus (ca. 224): "Nuptiae sunt

Roman law texts emphasized that marriage was a "sacred and enduring" union, voluntarily contracted for the sake of "marital affection" and the propagation of offspring.[25]

Such were some of the sentiments about marriage among pre-Christian writers. These classical sources illustrate that the West has long recognized that marriage has natural goods and benefits for the couple, their children, and the broader community. Particularly perceptive were Aristotle's insights that marriage is a natural institution fundamental and foundational to any republic; that marriage is at once "useful," "pleasant," and "moral" in its own right; that it provides efficient pooling and division of specialized labor and resources within the household; and that it serves both for the fulfillment and happiness of spouses and for the procreation and nurture of children. Also influential was the Stoic and Roman natural law idea that marriage is a "sacred and enduring union" that entails a complete sharing of the persons, properties, and pursuits of husband and wife in service of marital affection and friendship, mutual caring and protection, and mutual procreation and education of children.

These classical sources also illustrate that the Christian tradition, from the beginning, had at its disposal an ample natural logic and language about the goods and goals of marriage. To be sure, when compared to the modern social science data about the health benefits of marriage, these classical reflections are more avuncular than statistical, more anecdotal than inductive, more prudential than scientific. And, to be sure, these classical reflections are only very small fragments within a vast Graeco-Roman literature that also condoned sexual norms and habits that the Christian tradition would later condemn — prostitution, concubinage, pedophilia, homosexuality, polygamy, mixed bathing, communal propagation, anonymous parentage, casual consortium with slaves, and more.[26] But in these vast classical sources,

---

coniunctio maris et feminae et consortium omnis vitae, divine et humani iuris communicatio." Justinian, *Institutes,* I.9.1, quoting Ulpian (d. ca. 228): "Nuptiae autem sive matrimonium est viri et mulieris coniunctio, individuam consuetudinem vitae continens."

25. See Gaius, *Institutes,* 1.56ff.; Justinian, *Digest,* 24.1.32; 35.1.15; 25.1.3; Justinian, *Institutes,* 1.10.pr. For a full study of Roman law texts, before and after Christianization, see Susan Treggiari, *Roman Marriage: Iusti Conjuges from the Time of Cicero to the Time of Ulpian* (Oxford: Clarendon, 1991), pp. 1-13, 183-319; Grubb, *Law and Family in Late Antiquity,* pp. 54-102; Jane F. Gardner, *Family and Familia in Roman Law and Life* (Oxford: Clarendon, 1998), pp. 47-55.

26. See Philip L. Reynolds, *Marriage in the Western Church: The Christianization of*

the Christian tradition could pluck out a number of touchstones about the natural goods and goals of marriage that would prove helpful to their broader theological formulations about marriage. Natural arguments about marriage could not provide the Christian tradition with a complete theology of marriage. But a theology of marriage could not be complete, or cogent, without some natural foundation and corroboration.

Early Christian Formulations

Thus the Western Christian tradition has always included a natural perspective in its theology of marriage. To be sure, marriage is more than a natural institution. The Christian tradition has also understood it as a spiritual, social, economic, and contractual association — subject to the Church, state, community, and couple at once.[27] But, at its foundation, marriage is also a natural institution, subject to the laws of nature communicated in Scripture, reason, and conscience, and reflected in tradition, custom, and experience.

Patristic, Catholic, and Protestant writers alike taught that marriage was created and ordered by God. Already in Paradise, God had brought the first man and the first woman together, and commanded them to "be fruitful and multiply." God had created them as social creatures, naturally inclined and attracted to each other. God had given them the physical capacity to join together and to beget children. God had commanded them to love, help, and nurture each other and to inculcate in each other and in their children the love of God, neighbor, and self. These duties and qualities of marriage, the Christian tradition has long taught, continued after the fall into sin. After the fall, however, marriages also became a remedy for lust, a balm to incontinence. Rather than allowing sinful persons to burn with lust, God provided the remedy of marriage, in order for parties to direct their natural drives and passions to the service and love of the spouse, the child, and the broader community.

On this common foundation about the created origin and natural order of marriage, Christian writers over the centuries devised various formulas to define the goods and goals of marriage. The most famous and enduring formulation came from St. Augustine, the Bishop of Hippo (354-430).

Marriage during the Patristic and Early Modern Periods (Leiden: E. J. Brill, 1994), pp. 38-40, 156-72; Brundage, pp. 10-50.

27. See further Chapter 10 herein.

Like his classical predecessors, Augustine called marriage a "true and loyal partnership," the "seedbed of the city," the "first step in the organization of men."[28] He also quoted his Greek contemporary, St. John Chrysostom (345-407), about the political and social utility of marriage: "The love of husband and wife is the force that welds society together. Because when harmony prevails, the children are raised well, the household is kept in order, and neighbors and relatives praise the result. Great benefits, both for families and states, are thus produced."[29]

In its essence, however, Augustine wrote, marriage has three goods (*bona*). Marriage "is the ordained means of procreation (*proles*), the guarantee of chastity (*fides*), and the bond of permanent union (*sacramentum*)."[30] As a created, natural means of procreation, Christian marriage rendered sexual intercourse licit. As a contract of fidelity, marriage gave husband and wife an equal power over the other's body, an equal right to demand that the other spouse avoid adultery, and an equal claim to the "service, in a certain measure, of sustaining each other's weakness, for the avoidance of illicit intercourse."[31] As a "certain sacramental bond," marriage was a source and symbol of permanent union between Christians.[32] "[M]arriage bears a kind of sacred bond," Augustine wrote; "it can be dissolved in no way except by the death of one of the parties. The bond of marriage remains, even if offspring for which the marriage was entered upon, should not follow because of a clear case of sterility, so that it is not lawful for married people who know they will not have any children to separate and to unite with others even for the sake of having children."[33]

Procreation, fidelity, and sacrament: These were the three goods of marriage, in Augustine's view. They were the reason that the institution of marriage was good. They were why participation in marriage was good. They were the goods and goals that a person could hope and expect to real-

28. Augustine, *City of God*, XIV.10, 21, 22; XV.16; XIX.7, 14.

29. John Chrysostom, "Homily 20 on Ephesians 5:22-33," in *St. John Chrysostom on Marriage and Family Life*, trans. Catharine Roth and David Anderson (Crestwood, N.Y.: St. Vladimir's Seminary Press, 1986), pp. 43-44.

30. Augustine, *On Original Sin*, chap. 39, in *A Select Library of Nicene and Post-Nicene Fathers of the Christian Church*, ed. Philip Schaff and Henry Wace, vol. 5 (Grand Rapids: Eerdmans, 1978), p. 251.

31. Augustine, *The Good of Marriage*, in *St. Augustine: Treatises on Marriage and Other Subjects*, ed. R. J. Deferrari (New York: Fathers of the Church, 1955), p. 17.

32. Augustine, *On Marriage and Concupiscence*, in *Nicene and Post-Nicene Fathers*, ed. Schaff and Wace, 5:271.

33. Augustine, *The Good of Marriage*, pp. 31-32.

ize upon marrying. Augustine usually listed the goods of marriage in this order, giving first place to the good of procreation. At least twice, he underscored this priority by writing that "the institution of marriage exists for the sake of procreation; for this reason did our forbearers enter into the union of marriage and lawfully take to themselves their wives, *only* because of the duty to beget children."[34]

Augustine, however, did not call procreation the primary good of marriage, and the others secondary. He sometimes changed the order of his list of marital goods to "fidelity, procreation, and sacrament" — passages that inspired later canonists and theologians to develop theories of "marital affection" as the primary marital good.[35] Even when he listed procreation as the first marital good, Augustine made clear that spousal fidelity and sacramental stability were essential for a marriage to be good — and sufficient when married couples were childless or their children had left the household. And in doing so, he followed the classic authors in highlighting some of the benefits of marriage to the couple themselves:

> [Marriage] does not seem to me to be a good solely because of the procreation of children, but also because of the natural companionship (*societas*) between the two sexes. Otherwise, we could not speak of marriage in the case of old people, especially if they had lost their children or had begotten none at all. But, in a good marriage, although one of many years, even if the ardor of youth has cooled between man and woman, the order of chastity still flourishes between husband and wife. . . . there is observed that promise of respect and of services due to each other by either sex, even though both members weaken in health and become moribund, the chastity of souls rightly joined together continues the purer, the more it has been proved, the more secure, the more it has been calmed.[36]

34. Augustine, *Adulterous Marriages,* in *St. Augustine: Treatises on Marriage and Other Subjects,* ed. Deferrari, p. 116 (emphasized added). See also Augustine, *Contra Faustum Manichaeum,* XIX.26.

35. Augustine, *Commentary on the Literal Meaning of Genesis,* 9.7.12, in *Ancient Christian Writers: The Works of the Fathers in Translation,* ed. Johannes Quasten et al., trans. John Hammond Taylor, 54 vols. (New York: Newman, 1982), 42:78. See later medieval theories in John T. Noonan Jr., "Marital Affection among the Canonists," *Studia Gratiana* 14 (1967): 489-99; Jean Leclerq, *Monks on Marriage: A Twelfth Century View* (New York: Seabury, 1982), pp. 11-38, 71-81.

36. Augustine, *The Good of Marriage,* pp. 12-13. See further John J. Hugo, *St. Au-*

Augustine's account of the goods of marriage was more positive than most early Christian formulations. Many other Church Fathers, before and after him, not only treated marriage as less virtuous than chastity and celibacy, but also spoke of marriage and of sexual intercourse even within marriage in increasingly deprecatory and discouraging terms. Augustine's views ultimately proved more enduring in the Western tradition. Both Catholic and Protestant writers took Augustine as their touchstone, and his formulation of the goods of marriage was subject to endless repetition and elaboration.

Roman Catholic Formulations

One of the most important transmissions and elaborations of St. Augustine's views of marital goods came during the Papal Revolution of circa 1075-1300. This was the era when the Roman Catholic Church developed a systematic theology and law of marriage. From the twelfth century forward, the Church's doctrine of marriage was categorized, systematized, and refined, notably in Hugh of St. Victor's *On the Sacraments of the Christian Faith* (ca. 1143), Peter Lombard's *Book of Sentences* (1150), and Thomas Aquinas's *Summa Theologiae* (ca. 1265-1273) — and the scores of thick glosses and commentaries on these texts published in subsequent centuries. From the twelfth century forward, the Church's canon law of marriage was also systematized, first in Gratian's *Decretum* (ca. 1140), then in a welter of later legal commentaries and new papal and conciliar laws that eventually would form the *Corpus Iuris Canonici*. These core theological and legal texts of medieval Catholicism repeated St. Augustine's formulation of the marital goods of procreation, faith, and sacrament. Each of them gave Augustine's formulations a new accent and application — medieval canonists and civilians often adducing Roman law texts in so doing, medieval theologians and philosophers often adducing Aristotle and the Stoics.

Thomas Aquinas's (1225-1274) formulations of the three marital goods, which systematized more than a century of high medieval legal and theological thought, provide a good illustration of emerging Roman Catholic teaching. Thomas wrote at great length on the theology and law of mar-

---

riage. Especially important were his commentaries on Peter Lombard and Aristotle.[37] He included in the former commentary a long discussion of marital goods, in the latter a number of glosses on Aristotle's notions of marriage as an institution of nature and a prototype of friendship. These latter themes also recurred in his *Summa Contra Gentiles*.[38]

Thomas first dealt with objections that Augustine's list of faith, children, and sacramentality (*fides, proles, et sacramentum*)[39] might be "insufficiently enumerated." After all, critics of the day argued, Augustine had not taken into sufficient account Aristotle's insights that marriage is not only for procreation but also for spouses to enjoy a common life, a common stock, and companionship. Maybe love, charity, and sacrifice between spouses would be a better understanding of a "marital good" than *fides*. Maybe *proles* should be considered a derivative good, since children are not essential to marriage, and many married parties do not have them. Maybe *sacramentum* is not really a marital good at all, since Augustine is referring to the indissolubility of marriage, and indissolubility does not seem to be an essential feature of a sacrament. Maybe marriage should also have a good of justice, since it involves the discharge of marital rights and conjugal debts. Maybe the goods of marriage would be better if they were listed as those qualities of marriage that are "useful" rather than "virtuous."[40]

Thomas defended Augustine's three goods as a sufficient and complete account: "The goods which justify marriage belongs to the nature of marriage, which consequently needs them, not as extrinsic causes of its rectitude, but as causing in it that rectitude which belongs to it by nature." "From the very fact that marriage is intended as an office or as a remedy [from sexual sin] it has the aspect of something useful and right; neverthe-

---

37. Thomas Aquinas, *Scriptum super Libros Sententiarum Petri Lombardiensis*, in *Opera Omnia Sancti Thomae Aquinatis Doctoris Angelici* (Rome, 1882), vol. 7/2 [hereafter Aquinas, Sent.]; this commentary recurs almost verbatim in Thomas Aquinas, Supplement to *The Summa Theologica*, trans. English Dominican Fathers, repr. ed. (New York: Benzinger Brothers, 1948) [hereafter ST Supp.]. Thomas's commentary on Aristotle's *Ethics* and *Politics* appears in *Opera Omnia*, vols. 47 and 48, but the commentary on the *Ethics* breaks off at chapter 6, just before Aristotle's crucial passage on marital love. See discussion in Mackin, *What Is Marriage?* pp. 176-91; John Finnis, *Aquinas: Moral, Political, and Legal Theory* (Oxford: Oxford University Press, 1998), pp. 143-54.

38. Thomas Aquinas, *Summa contra Gentiles*, trans. V. J. Bourke (Notre Dame, Ind.: University of Notre Dame Press, 1975), III.122-26 [hereafter Aquinas, SCG].

39. Thomas generally renders the list in this order. See Aquinas, Sent. IV.31, q. 1; Aquinas, ST Supp., q. 49, art. 2.

40. Aquinas, Sent. IV.31.2, q. 1; Aquinas, ST Supp., q. 49, art. 2, obj. 1-7.

less both aspects belong to it from the fact that it has these goods by which it fulfills the office and affords a remedy to concupiscence."[41] "Matrimony is instituted both as an office of nature and as a sacrament of the church. As an office of nature it is directed by two things, like every other virtuous act. One of these is required on the part of the agent and is the intention of the due end, and thus the offspring *(proles)* is accounted a good of marriage; the other is required on the part of the act, which is good generically through being about a due matter; and thus we have faith *(fides)*, where a man has intercourse with his wife and with no other woman. Besides this it has a certain goodness as a sacrament, and this is signified by the word sacrament *(sacramentum)*."[42]

Thomas elaborated these three Augustinian goods of marriage, however, in a way that both integrated them more fully than Augustine had done and resolved more clearly the question of their priority. While his views were not fully developed, he argued effectively that marriage is a three-dimensional institution and that each of the marital goods anchors one of these three dimensions.

If marriage is viewed as a natural institution, Aquinas argued, procreation *(proles)* is the primary good. Building on both Augustine and Aristotle, Aquinas argued that man and woman are naturally inclined to come together for the sake of having children, and that nature teaches the licit means of doing so is through a voluntary act of marriage.[43] Procreation, however, means more than just conceiving children. It also means rearing and educating them for spiritual and temporal living — a common Stoic sentiment. The good of procreation cannot be achieved in this fuller sense simply through the licit union of husband and wife in sexual intercourse. It also requires maintenance of a faithful, stable, and permanent union of husband and wife, so that both mother and father may participate in the education and rearing of their children. In this natural sense, the primary good of marriage is procreation; the secondary goods are faith and sacramental stability.[44]

41. Aquinas, ST Supp., q. 49, art. 1; Aquinas, Sent. IV.26.1, 2.

42. Aquinas, ST Supp., q. 49, art. 2.

43. Aquinas, Sent. IV.26.1; 33.1; Mackin, *What Is Marriage?* pp. 182-83; Grisez, *The Way of the Lord Jesus,* pp. 558-60.

44. Aquinas, Sent. IV.26.1; Aquinas, ST Supp., q. 49, art. 2-3, 5; Aquinas, SCG, III.123.1-10; 124.3. In ST Supp., q. 49, art. 3, Thomas writes: "[F]aith and offspring may be considered as in their principles so that offspring denote the intention of having children and faith the duty of remaining faithful, and there can be no matrimony without these also,

If marriage is viewed as a contractual association, faith (*fides*) is the primary good. Marital faith is not a spiritual faith, but a faith of justice, Aquinas argued. It means keeping faith, being faithful, holding faithfully to one's promises made in the contract of marriage. Marital faith requires, as Augustine had said, forgoing sexual intercourse with another and honoring the connubial debt (that is, yielding to the reasonable sexual advances of one's spouse). But marital faith also involves, as Aristotle and the Stoics had said, the commitment to be indissolubly united with one's spouse in body and mind, to be the "greatest of friends," to be willing to share fully and equally in the person, property, lineage, and reputation — indeed, in the "whole life" — of one's spouse. It is to be and bear with each other in youth and in old age, in sickness and in health, in prosperity and adversity. Marital faith, in this richer understanding, is a good in itself, Aquinas insisted. It need not necessarily be expected or intended for the procreation of children; indeed, a marriage promise need not even be consummated to be valid and binding. If it is consummated faithfully, sexual intercourse is a good act in itself, even if procreation is a natural impossibility.[45] In this contractual sense, the primary good of marriage is faith (*fides*); the secondary goods are sacrament and procreation.[46]

---

since they are caused in matrimony by the marriage compact itself, so that if anything contrary to these were expressed in the consent which makes a marriage, the marriage would be invalid. Taking faith and offspring in this sense, it is clear that offspring is the most essential thing in marriage, secondly faith, and thirdly sacrament; even as to man it is more essential to be in nature than to be in grace, although it is more excellent to be in grace." See further Don S. Browning et al., *From Culture Wars to Common Ground: Religion and the American Family Debate* (Louisville, Ky.: Westminster John Knox, 1997), pp. 113-24; Don S. Browning, "Altruism and Christian Love," *Zygon* 27 (1992): 421-36.

45. Aquinas, Sent. IV.26.2; 27.1; 31.1; 33.1; 41.1; Aquinas, ST Supp., q. 42, 47, 49; Aquinas, SCG, III.123.3, 4, 8; 124.4-5; 125.6; 126.1-6. See Finnis, *Aquinas*, pp. 143-48.

46. While Thomas spoke explicitly of ways in which *proles* and *sacramentum* could be viewed as primary and the other goods secondary, he never, so far as I have found, spoke explicitly of *fides* as the primary end. But this is a natural implication of his argument about the faith of the marriage contract, and the friendship of the marital institution. Thomas comes close to saying this in his argument that the marriage of Mary and Joseph was "perfect" even though not consummated. See Aquinas, ST Supp., q. 29, art. 2: "Marriage or wedlock is said to be true by reason of its attaining its perfection. Now perfection of anything is two-fold. The perfection of a thing consists in its very form from which it receives its species; while the second perfection of a thing consists in its operation, by which in some way a thing attains its end. Now the form of matrimony consists in a certain inseparable union of souls, by which husband and wife are pledged by a bond of mutual affection that cannot be sundered. And the end of marriage is the

If marriage is viewed as a spiritual institution, *sacramentum* is the primary good. Marriage between baptized Christians is a sacrament of grace, Aquinas argued citing Lombard — much like the sacraments of baptism, Eucharist, penance, and others. The temporal union of body, soul, and mind within the marital estate at once symbolizes the eternal union between Christ and the Church and confers sanctifying grace upon the couple, their children, and the community. Viewed as a spiritual institution, Aquinas wrote, "sacrament is in every way the most important of the three marriage goods, since it belongs to marriage considered as a sacrament of grace; while the other two belong to it as an office of nature; and a perfection of grace is more excellent than a perfection of nature."[47]

A sacramental marriage, once properly contracted between Christians in accordance with the laws of nature and of the Church, is an indissoluble union, Aquinas insisted, a permanently open channel of grace. For marriage partakes of the quality that it symbolizes, namely, the indissoluble bond between Christ and the Church:

[S]ince the sacraments effect what they figure, it is to be believed that grace is conferred through this sacrament on the spouses, whereby they might belong to the union of Christ and the Church. And this is very necessary to them so that as they concern themselves with carnal and earthly matters, they do not become detached from Christ and the Church. Now since the union of husband and wife designates the union of Christ and the Church, the figure must correspond with that which it signifies. Now the union of Christ and the Church is a union of one to another, and it is to last in perpetuity. For there is only one Church, . . . and Christ will never be separated from his Church. As he himself says in the last chapter of Matthew, "Behold I am with you even unto the end of the world. . . ." It follows necessarily then that a marriage, in so far as it is a sacrament of the Church, must be one holding to another indivisibly.[48]

---

begetting and upbringing of children, the first of which is attained by conjugal intercourse; the second by the other duties of husband and wife, by which they help one another in rearing their offspring. Thus we may say, as to the first perfection, that the marriage of the Virgin Mother of God and Joseph was absolutely true, because both consented to the nuptial bond but not to the bond of flesh."

47. Aquinas, Sent. IV.31.2; Aquinas, ST Supp., q. 49, art. 3.
48. Aquinas, SCG, IV.78.

Aquinas's understanding of the good of *sacramentum* went well beyond the formulations of Augustine. Augustine called marriage a sacrament to demonstrate its symbolic stability. Aquinas called marriage a sacrament to demonstrate its spiritual efficacy. Augustine said that marriage as a perennial symbol of Christ's bond to the Church should not be dissolved. Aquinas said that marriage as a permanent channel of sacramental grace could not be dissolved. Augustine called marriage a sacrament because it was indissoluble. Aquinas called marriage indissoluble because it was a sacrament.

This understanding of the good of *sacramentum* also elevated and integrated the goods of procreation and faith. On the one hand, the sacramental quality of Christian marriage helped to elevate the natural acts of marriage to spiritual significance. At minimum, it helped to remove the stigma of sin in sexual intercourse and to elevate the procreation and nurture of children into an act useful for the Church. More fully conceived, the sacramental quality effectively placed the natural institution of marriage into the hierarchy of Church orders as something of an institution and instrument of grace — though one clearly subordinate to the celibate clerical and monastic orders. On the other hand, the sacramental quality of Christian marriage helped to elevate the marriage contract into more than just a bargained-for exchange between two parties. At minimum, it rendered marriage an "adhesion contract" that was indissoluble: the terms of the marital bargain were already set by nature, and as a symbol of Christ's bond with the Church, the marital bond was per force indissoluble. More fully conceived, the exchange of consent between the couple also signified an exchange of consent of the couple with God and the Church. In essence, the parties consented to bind themselves to each other and to God and the Church and thus to accept God's sacramental grace and the Church's spiritual nurture for their marriage.

Thomas Aquinas's elegant integration of the three goods of marriage found a growing team of champions in the fourteenth through sixteenth centuries. The fresh rise and extension of Thomism among such sixteenth-century Spanish luminaries as Francisco de Vitoria (c. 1486-1546), Francisco Suárez (1548-1617), and Thomas Sanchez (1550-1610) eventually helped to transmit Aquinas's understanding of marriage and its goods very widely, not only in Catholic and Protestant Europe, but also among the many new Latin American colonies.

These views also entered the canon law and catechism of the Catholic Church. The great Council of Trent (1545-1563) took Thomas's and related medieval views of marriage as dispositive, and reflected them in a series of canons under the decree *Tametsi* of 1563.[49] The Catechism, commissioned by the Council and issued in 1566, spoke directly to the goods of marriage.[50] Citing the "general opinion of the theologians," the Catechism defined marriage much as Aquinas had done — "as a natural union, since it was not invented by man but instituted by nature" and "as a Sacrament, the efficacy of which transcends the order of nature." As a natural union, created by God in Paradise, marriage has "three reasons" *(causae)* for its existence — (1) the "companionship" of husband and wife," (2) "an antidote to avoid sins of lust," and (3) "the desire of family, not so much, however, with a view to leave after us heirs to inherit our property and fortune, as to bring up children in the true faith and service of God." As a sacramental union, marriage "is far superior . . . and aims at an incomparably higher end." "For as marriage, as a natural union, was instituted from the beginning to propagate the human race; so was the sacramental dignity subsequently conferred upon it in order that a people might be begotten and brought up for the service and worship of the true God and of Christ our Savior."

Marriage brings "three goods" *(bona)* to the couple, the 1566 Catechism states: (1) "offspring, if it is the Lord's will"; (2) faith, which is "a special, holy, and pure love"; and (3) "sacrament," now used in the Augustinian sense of stability and permanence. God confers those blessings where couples abide by his duties for marriage — set out in the natural law and elaborated in the Bible. "It is the duty of the husband to treat his wife generously and honorably," to be "constantly occupied in some honest pursuit with a view to provide necessaries for his family and to avoid idleness, the root of almost every vice." Wives, in turn, must "never forget that next to God they are to love their husbands, to esteem them above all others, yielding to them in all things not inconsistent with Christian piety, a willing and ready obedience."

Both the nuance and the balance of these medieval and Tridentine formulations of marital goods were increasingly lost on the Church after the sixteenth century. By the later nineteenth century, many of the Church's doctrinal statements and legal texts treated procreation as the primary

49. In *The Canons and Decrees of the Council of Trent,* trans. H. J. Schroeder (St. Louis: B. Herder, 1941).

50. All quotes are from John A. McHugh and Charles J. Callan, trans., *Catechism of the Council of Trent for Parish Priests* (Rockford, Ill.: Tan Books and Publishers, 1982), pp. 338-55.

good, sometimes even the exclusive good, of marriage, and outlawed with increasing sternness contraception, abortion, and other actions that obstructed or compromised the good of procreation.[51] The good of marital faith, in the full sense that Thomas and others had described it, was reduced to a dispensable means to the end of procreation.[52] The good of the marital sacrament, in the rich integrating sense that medieval and Tridentine theology had defined it, was reduced to simple platitudes about grace and the Church's jurisdiction over its instruments.

The 1917 *Code of Canon Law* sealed this shift in perspective, stating repeatedly the priority of the good of procreation: "The primary good or end [*finis*] of marriage is procreation and the nurture of children; its secondary end is mutual help and the remedying of concupiscence." "Marital consent is an act of the will by which each party gives and accepts a perpetual and exclusive right over the body for acts which are of themselves suitable for the generation of children." And again: "[M]arriage is a permanent society for the procreation of children."[53]

Pope Pius XI's (1857-1939) encyclical letter *Casti Connubi* (1930) underscored this shift in perspective: "Among the blessings of marriage, offspring holds the first place," Pius wrote, citing (selectively) from Augustine. "The conjugal act is of its very nature designed for the procreation of offspring" and any acts to the contrary are condemned.[54] Pius also confirmed a ruling of the Holy Office that condemned "certain modern writers" who gave priority to marital love and companionship in expression of new European personalist and phenomenological theories. Such views were considered anathema, for they "either deny that the primary end of marriage is the generation and education of children, or teach that the secondary ends are not essential to the primary end."[55] Marital love

51. See generally John T. Noonan Jr., *Contraception: A History of Its Treatment by the Catholic Theologians and Canonists* (Cambridge: Harvard University Press, 1965).

52. Grisez, *The Way of the Lord Jesus*, p. 561; Germain Grisez, *Contraception and the Natural Law* (Milwaukee: Bruce, 1964).

53. *1917 Code of Canon Law,* Canons 1013, 1081.2, 1082.1, reprinted in *Canon Law: A Text and Commentary,* trans. T. Lincoln Bouscaren et al. (Milwaukee: Bruce, 1966), pp. 466, 565-67.

54. Pius XI, *Casti Connubi,* in *Matrimony,* trans. M. J. Byrnes (Boston: St. Paul Editions, 1963), pp. 224-25.

55. Quoted and critically discussed in Lisa Sowle Cahill, "Marriage: Institution, Relationship, Sacrament," in *One Hundred Years of Catholic Social Thought,* ed. John A. Coleman (Maryknoll, N.Y.: Orbis, 1991), p. 108. The most influential of these European writers, whose work was censored, was Herbert Doms, *Vom Sinn und Zweck der Ehe*

must be viewed as a means to the end (or good) of procreation, not as an end in itself.

At the end of *Casti Connubi,* however, Pius XI offered several pastoral sentiments about marital love that would help to return the Church to the more nuanced position of the Council of Trent, and indeed to go beyond it: "The action in the home is not confined to mutual help," Pius wrote; "it must have as its higher and indeed its chief objective that of shaping and perfecting the interior life of husband and wife. Their life partnership must help them to increase daily in the practice of virtue, and above all to grow in the true love of God and their neighbor. . . ." And then, more generously still: "This mutual interior formation of husband and wife, this persevering endeavor to bring each other to the state of perfection, may in a true sense be called, as the Roman Catechism calls it, the primary cause and reason of marriage, so long as marriage is considered not in the stricter sense as the institution designed for the creation and education of children, but in the wider sense as a complete and intimate life-partnership and association."[56]

Pius XI's pastoral aside eventually became a doctrinal priority. The Second Vatican Council (1962-1965), after anguished and angry debate, returned to the fuller formulation of the goods of *fides, proles, et sacramentum* that had been adumbrated by Augustine and elaborated by St. Thomas and the Tridentine Reformers. In its pastoral constitution, *Gaudium et Spes,* the Council declared:

> God himself is the author of matrimony, endowed as it is with various goods *(bona)* and ends *(fines).* All of these have a very decisive bearing on the continuation of the human race, on the personal development and eternal destiny of the individual members of a family, and on the dignity, stability, peace, and prosperity of the family itself and human society as a whole.[57]

(Breslau: Ostdeutsche Verlagsanstalt, 1935), translated (imprecisely) as Herbert Doms, *The Meaning of Marriage* (New York: Sheed and Ward, 1939).

56. Pius XI, *Casti Connubi,* p. 231.

57. *Gaudium et Spes,* para. 48, translated in *The Documents of Vatican II,* ed. Walter M. Abbott and Joseph Gallagher (Chicago: Follet, 1966), p. 250. The Council cites, inter alia, the passages from Augustine, Aquinas, and *Casti Connubi* quoted above. *Gaudium et Spes,* p. 250, n. 154. The translation renders the phrase "bona et fines" as "benefits and purposes"; I have rendered it "goods" and "ends."

The Second Vatican Council amplified this latter concern for the role of the family within broader society, elaborating, as no Catholic Church Council before had done, the social and political goods of marriage. "The well being of . . . human and Christian society is intimately linked with the healthy condition of that community produced by marriage and family."[58] "The family is a kind of school of deeper humanity," holding out a model of love, charity, stewardship, authority, dignity, faithfulness, education, nurture, discipline, and care for each new generation of children to learn, and for other institutions to emulate. "Thus the family is the foundation of society. In it the various generations come together and help one another to grow wiser and to harmonize personal rights with the other requirements of social life. All those, therefore, who exercise influence over communities and social groups should work effectively for the welfare of marriage and the family. Public authority should regard it as a sacred duty to recognize, protect, and promote their authentic nature, to shield public morality, and to favor the prosperity of domestic life."[59] In *Lumen et Gentium,* the Council pronounced famously: "The family is, so to speak, the domestic Church." The parents are "the first preachers" who nurture the faith not only of their children but of broader society as well.[60]

Gaudium et Spes was even more expansive in its treatment of marital love and affection as indispensable to the "well being of the individual person."[61] In Vatican II's formulation, marital love was no longer simply a form and function of marital faith, as was traditional. It was the good that permeated and integrated all three of the classic goods of faith, children, and sacrament:

> The intimate partnership of married life and love has been established by the Creator and qualified by His laws. It is rooted in the marriage covenant of irrevocable personal consent. . . . [A] man and a woman, who by the marriage covenant of conjugal love "are no longer two but one flesh" (Mt. 19:6), render mutual help and service to each other through an intimate union of their persons and of their actions. Through this union they experience the meaning of their oneness and attain to it with growing perfection day by day. As a mutual gift of two

58. *Gaudium et Spes,* para. 47.
59. *Gaudium et Spes,* para. 48, 49, 52.
60. *Lumen et Gentium,* para. 11 in *Documents of Vatican II,* p. 29.
61. *Gaudium et Spes,* para. 47.

persons, this intimate union, as well as the good of children, imposes total fidelity on the spouses, and argues for an unbreakable oneness between them. Christ the Lord abundantly blessed this many-faceted love, welling up as it does from the fountain of divine love and structured as it is on the model of His union with the Church. For as God of old made himself present to His people through a covenant of love and fidelity, so now the Savior of men and the Spouse of the Church comes into the lives of married Christians through the sacrament of matrimony.[62]

Marital love involves "the good of the whole person," *Gaudium et Spes* continued. It "ennobles" those "special ingredients and signs of the friendship distinctive of marriage." It impels spouses to make "a free and mutual gift of themselves, a gift proving itself by gentle affection and by deed." It expresses itself in sexual intercourse, which is "good," "noble and worthy" regardless of any procreative promise, intent, outcome. It is structured through the "equal personal dignity of husband and wife, a dignity acknowledged by mutual and total love." Marital love brings to the couple "the cultural, psychological, and social renewal" that they need daily to survive, flourish, and indeed to perfect themselves.[63]

In an Appendix to *Gaudium et Spes*, the Council again underscored that marriage was "a covenant of love" formed voluntarily. "Marital consent of its essence intends the unity of this covenant, its indissolubility and the love that is devoted to the service of life. The stronger and purer the marital love, the more strongly and perseveringly will the spouses accept and realize marriage's specific traits and its essential goods. . . . No one is aware of how seriously necessary it is that love be fully present in the act of consent, and increase throughout the married life. For love will fulfill, and cause to be fulfilled what the consent has said and has promised."[64]

A number of subsequent doctrinal and canonical documents have repeated Vatican II's integrative theory of the three goods of the covenant of marriage.[65] But several subsequent Church statements, particularly on

62. *Gaudium et Spes*, para. 48.
63. *Gaudium et Spes*, para. 49.
64. Quoted in Mackin, *What Is Marriage?* p. 261.
65. See, e.g., *1983 Code of Canon Law*, Canon 1055, translated in *The Code of Canon Law* (London: Collins Liturgical Publications, 1983), p. 189: "The matrimonial covenant, by which a man and a woman establish between themselves a partnership of the whole of life, is by its nature ordered toward the good of the spouses and the procre-

abortion and contraception, emphasized anew the marital good of procreation.[66] In his encyclical *Humanae Vitae* (1968), for example, Pope Paul VI spoke favorably of "total, faithful, and exclusive" conjugal love and mutual self-giving and self-perfection in and through marriage.[67] But these familiar refrains from Vatican II seemed almost drowned out in the robust new orchestrations on procreation. Marital union and procreation are "inseparable," *Humanae Vitae* reads, and it "is necessary that each matrimonial function (*matrimonii usus*) remain ordained in itself to the procreating of human life." "[C]onjugal love requires that spouses be fully aware of their mission (*manus*) of responsible parenthood." Through marital union "the spouses perfect each other so that they might share with God the task of procreating and educating new living beings."[68] There followed a series of pronouncements against abortion, contraception, sterilization, and other interruptions of the natural "generative" and "procreative process." Critics have viewed *Humanae Vitae* and its ample progeny as a retreat from the integrative theory of marital love developed by Vatican II. In particular, they see in these documents a tacit reassertion of an instrumentalist view of marriage and of the primacy of the good of procreation over that of marital faith and love — a trend underscored, in their view, by the Church's many recent pronouncements against committed homosexual unions.[69] Defenders view this language as further confirmation of the Church's new understanding of the covenant of marriage as a basic or intrinsic human good ordained by God for the mutual blessing of the couple, their children, and the broader communities of which they are a part.

---

ation and education of offspring; this covenant between baptized persons has been raised by Christ to the dignity of a sacrament." See also John Paul II, "Familiaris Consortio," *Acta Apostolicae Sedis* 74 (1982): 92; *L'Osservatore Romano,* December 21-28, 1981, p. 3, discussing the plan of God for marriage and the family. Also see discussion in Michael J. Wrenn, ed., *Pope John Paul II and the Family* (Chicago: Franciscan Herald, 1983).

66. For various interpretations, see Janet E. Smith, *Humanae Vitae: A Generation Later* (Washington, D.C.: Catholic University Press, 1991), pp. 267-95; Janet E. Smith, ed., *Why* Humanae Vitae *Was Right: A Reader* (San Francisco: Ignatius, 1993); Germain Grisez et al., *The Teachings of Humanae Vitae: A Defense* (San Francisco: Ignatius, 1988).

67. Paul VI, "Humane Vitae," nos. 8, 9, translated in *The Papal Encyclicals, 1958-1981,* ed. Claudia Carlen (Ann Arbor, Mich.: Pierian, 1990), pp. 223, 225.

68. Paul VI, "Humane Vitae," nos. 8, 11, 12.

69. See, e.g., articles in Smith, *Humanae Vitae* and Smith, ed., *Why* Humanae Vitae *Was Right;* Mark D. Jordan, *The Silence of Sodom: Homosexuality in Modern Catholicism* (Chicago: University of Chicago Press, 2000), pp. 21-82.

Protestant Formulations

The recent emphasis among Roman Catholics on love and companionship within the covenant of marriage and on the individual and social utility of marriage was a dominant theme of Protestant theology and law from the very beginning. The leading sixteenth-century Protestant Reformers — Martin Luther (1483-1546) and Philip Melanchthon (1497-1560), John Calvin (1509-1564) and Martin Bucer (1491-1551), Thomas Cranmer (1489-1556) and Heinrich Bullinger (1504-1575) — all wrote at length on marriage. In their view, God had created and ordered marriage to achieve three purposes (*causae*) or goals (*fines*): (1) the mutual love and support of husband and wife; (2) the mutual procreation and nurture of children; and (3) the mutual protection of both spouses from sexual sin — usually put in that order of priority.[70]

This early Protestant formulation of the marital goods of love, procreation, and protection was no invention of the sixteenth century. This trilogy had already appeared more than a millennium before in Roman law and in Isidore of Seville's (d. 636) *Etymologies* (though Isidore made procreation the first good).[71] By the sixteenth century, it had also become a standard formula among Catholic canonists and theologians to describe the purposes or reasons for marrying (*causae*), as opposed to the inherent goods (*bona*) of marriage itself. Most early Protestants rejected this medieval distinction between the purposes and goods of marriage. From God's point of view, they argued, marriage has built-in purposes that God wishes to see achieved among his creatures. From humanity's point of view, these are the created goods that we need to realize. To make fine distinctions between the goods and purposes, causes and effects, ends and means, motivations and measures of marriage, most early Protestants believed, is ultimately to engage in idle casuistry. For most Protestants, love, procreation, and protection was the essential formula.

This formula overlapped with Augustine's formula of faith, children, and sacramentality, but amended it in critical ways. Like Augustine, Protes-

---

70. See sources in FSC, pp. 96-108, 143-50, and the copiously documented interplay of the theology and practice of marital and familial love in Steven Ozment, *Ancestors: The Loving Family in Old Europe* (Cambridge: Harvard University Press, 2001); Steven E. Ozment, *Flesh and Spirit: Private Life in Early Modern Germany* (New York: Viking, 1999); Steven E. Ozment, *When Fathers Ruled: Family Life in Reformation Europe* (Cambridge: Harvard University Press, 1983).

71. Isidore, *Etymologiae*, 9.7.27.

tants emphasized the good of marital faithfulness (*fides*). But they cast this good in increasingly overt terms of marital love, affection, friendship, and companionship, sometimes adducing Stoic and Roman sources in so doing. Also like Augustine, Protestants emphasized the good of procreating children (*proles*). But they amended this good with the familiar medieval gloss that procreation included the Christian nurture and education of children. They underscored this amendment by insisting on the creation of schools for the religious and civic education of all children, and by producing a welter of catechisms, textbooks, and household manuals to assist in the same.[72]

Unlike Augustine, however, the early Protestant Reformers emphasized protection from sexual sin as a good in itself, not just a function of *fides*. Since the fall into sin, humankind has become totally depraved, the Reformers insisted. Lust has pervaded the conscience of every person. Participation in marriage has become an absolute necessity. For without marriage, the person's distorted sexuality becomes a force capable of overthrowing the most devout conscience. A person is enticed by nature to prostitution, masturbation, voyeurism, and other sexual sins. The "good gift" of marriage, Luther wrote, should thus be declined only by those who have received God's gift of continence. "Such persons are rare, not one in a thousand, for they are a special miracle of God." The apostle Paul has identified this group as the permanently impotent and the eunuchs; few others can claim such a unique gift.[73]

Also unlike Augustine, Protestants gave no place to the marital good of *sacramentum* — either in the Augustinian sense of symbolic stability, or in the medieval Catholic sense of a permanent channel of sanctifying grace. For most early Protestants, marriage was neither a sacrament of the Church on the order of baptism or the Eucharist, nor a permanent union dissolvable only upon death of one of the parties. To be sure, Protestants like Catholics believed that marriages should be stable and presumptively indissoluble. But this presumption could be overcome if one of the other marital goods were frustrated. If there was a breach of marital love by one of the parties — by reason of adultery, desertion, or cruelty — the marriage was broken. The innocent spouse who could not forgive this breach could sue for divorce and remarry. If there was a failure of procreation — by reason of sterility, incapacity, or disease discovered shortly after the wedding

72. See LW 45:11-49, 46:259-320; LP, chaps. 6-7.
73. LW 45:18-22; 28:9-12, 27-31.

— the marriage was also broken. Those spouses who could not reconcile themselves to this condition could seek an annulment and at least the healthy spouse could marry another. And if there was a failure of protection from sin — by reason of frigidity, separation, or cruelty — the marriage was again broken. If the parties could not be reconciled to regular cohabitation and consortium, they could divorce and seek another marriage.

Most early Protestants, especially Lutherans and Calvinists, thus tended to view the goods of marriage in more teleological terms than their Catholic brethren. Marriage was a means to love, to children, and to protection. Where such goods failed, the marriage failed, and such goods should be sought in a second marriage. Martin Bucer, the Strasbourg Reformer who influenced Lutherans, Calvinists, and Anglicans alike, put the matter more flatly than most of his co-religionists: "A proper and useful" marriage, Bucer wrote, has "four necessary properties": "1. That the [couple] should live together. . . . 2. That they should love one another in the height of dearness. . . . 3. That the husband bear himself as the head and preserver of the wife instructing her to all godliness and integrity of life; that the wife also be to her husband a help, according to her place, especially furthering him in the true worship of God, and next in all the occasions of civil life. And 4. That they not defraud each other of conjugal benevolence." Marriages that exhibit these four properties must be maintained and celebrated. But even "where only one [property] be wanting in both or either party . . . it cannot then be said that the covenant of matrimony holds good between such." To perpetuate the formal structure of marriage after a necessary property is lost, Bucer argued, is not only a destructive custom but an unbiblical practice. "[T]he Lord did not only permit, but also expressly and earnestly commanded his people, by whom he would that all holiness and faith of the marriage covenant be observed, that he [who] could not induce his mind to love his wife with a true conjugal love, might dismiss her that she might marry to another" who is more meet and good.[74]

This more teleological view of marriage is also reflected in the tendency of early Protestants to introduce alternative formulations of the goods of marriage to those inherited from the tradition. Aquinas and other medieval writers had considered, but then rejected, the notion that marriage might have additional or alternative goods beyond the Augustinian

---

74. Martin Bucer, *De Regno Christi* (1550), 2.26, 38, 39, in *Melanchthon and Bucer,* ed. Wilhelm Pauck (Philadelphia: Westminster, 1969).

goods of faith, children, and sacramentality. The Protestant Reformers showed no such reticence. They held out all manner of personal, social, and political goods that marriage could offer — in part, on the basis of a fresh reading of biblical and classical sources, in part in support of their relentless arguments against celibacy and monasticism.

One common Protestant formulation was that marriage had civil and spiritual "uses" in this life — a variant on the Protestant theory of the "uses of the moral law."[75] Both Luther and Calvin sometimes spoke in these terms. On the one hand, they argued, marriage has general *civil uses* for all persons, regardless of their faith. Marriage deters vice by furnishing preferred options to prostitution, promiscuity, pornography, and other forms of sexual pathos. Marriage cultivates virtue by offering love, care, and nurture to its members, and holding out a model of charity, education, and sacrifice to the broader community. Marriage enhances the life of a man and a woman by providing them with a community of caring and sharing, of stability and support, of nurture and welfare. Marriage enhances the life of the child, by providing it with a chrysalis of nurture and love, with a highly individualized form of socialization and education. On the other hand, marriage has specific *spiritual uses* for believers — ways of sustaining and strengthening them in the Christian faith. The love of wife and husband is among the strongest symbols Christians can experience of Yahweh's love for the elect, of Christ's love for the Church. The sacrifices one makes for spouse and child can be among the best expressions of Christian charity and agape. For Christian believers, Calvin wrote, marriage can thus be "a sacred bond," "a holy fellowship," a "divine partnership," "a heavenly calling," "the fountainhead of life," "the holiest kind of company in all the world," "the principal and most sacred . . . of all the offices pertaining to human society." "God reigns in a little household, even one in dire poverty, when the husband and the wife dedicate themselves to their duties to each other. Here there is a holiness greater and nearer the kingdom of God than there is even in a cloister."[76]

Other Protestants emphasized not only the civil and spiritual uses of marriage but also its social and political goods. Building especially on Aristotelian and Roman law antecedents, Lutheran, Calvinist, and Anglican

---

75. See Chapter 9 herein.

76. Comm. Gen. 2:18, 21, 24, 6:2; Serm. Deut. 21:10-14; Comm. Mal. 2:14, 16; Comm. Harmony of the Gospels, Matt. 19:11; Comm. 1 Cor. 7:14, 9:11; Serm. 1 Tim. 5. See John Witte Jr. and Robert M. Kingdon, *Sex, Marriage, and Family in John Calvin's Geneva*, 3 vols. (Grand Rapids: Eerdmans, 2005-).

writers alike treated marriage as the created, natural foundation of civil society and political authority.

For example, Philip Melanchthon, Luther's eminent co-worker in
Wittenberg, opened a long discussion of political authority thus:

> The earthly life has orders (*Stände*) and works (*Werke*) which serve to
> keep the human race, and are ordained by God with certain limits and
> means. By this order we should know that this human nature is not cre-
> ated without the distinct counsel of God, and that God in this way lets
> his goodness shine on us to sustain and provide for us.
>
> Matrimony is first, for God does not want human nature simply to
> run its course as cattle do. Therefore God ordained marriage (Gen. 2;
> Matt. 19; 1 Cor. 7) as an eternal, inseparable fellowship of one husband
> and one wife. . . . [M]atrimony is a very lovely, beautiful fellowship and
> church of God, if two people in true faith and obedience toward God
> cheerfully live together, together invoke God, and rear children in the
> knowledge of God and virtue.[77]

Elsewhere, Melanchthon, like Luther, emphasized that marriage was
one of the three great estates (*drei Stände*), along with the Church and the
state, that God had appointed for the governance of the earthly kingdom.
The estate of marriage was to teach all persons, particularly children, Christian values, morals, and mores. It was to exemplify for a sinful society a
community of love and cooperation, meditation and discussion, song and
prayer. It was to hold out for the Church and the state an example of firm
but benign parental discipline, rule, and authority. It was to take in and care
for wayfarers, widows, and destitute persons — a responsibility previously
assumed largely by monasteries and cloisters. Marriage was thus as indispensable an agent in God's redemption plan as the Church. It was as indispensable an agent of social order and communal cohesion as the state.[78]

Johannes Althusius (1557-1638), a distinguished Protestant jurist
and political theorist, drew on sundry Christian and classical sources to
construct a comprehensive covenantal theory of the state and society —
again with marriage at its foundation.[79] "Politics is the art of associating

---

77. Philip Melanchthon, "Loci Communes," in *Melanchthon on Christian Doctrine*,
trans. Clyde Manschreck (New York: Oxford University Press, 1965 [1555]), p. 323.

78. See sources in FSC, pp. 42-73; LP, pp. 214-32.

79. Johannes Althusius, *Politica: Methodice digesta atque exemplis sacris et profanis*

men for the purpose of establishing, cultivating, and conserving social life among them," Althusius wrote, citing Aristotle. "The goal of political man is a holy, just, comfortable, and happy symbiosis, a life lacking nothing either necessary or useful."[80] All such political associations are formed by "individual men covenanting among themselves to communicate whatever is necessary and useful for organizing and living in private life."[81] At the base of every such association is marriage, which is a "natural, necessary, economic, and domestic society that is contracted permanently. . . . Therefore it is rightly called the most intense society, friendship, relationship, and union, the seedbed of every other symbiotic association."[82]

Althusius went on to elaborate the relations and functions of husband and wife, adducing scores of classical, biblical, and early Christian sources to support the early modern patriarchal ideal of a hierarchical household under the benign authority of the *paterfamilias*:

> Husband and wife, who are bound to each other, communicate the advantages and responsibilities of married life. The director and governor of the common affairs of the marital association is the husband. The wife and family are obedient, and do what he commands. The advantages and responsibilities are either proper to one of the spouses, or common to both. Proper advantages and duties are either those the husband communicates to his wife, or those the wife communicates to her husband. The husband communicates to his wife his name, family, reputation, station in life, and economic condition. He also provides her with guidance, legal protection, and defense against violence and injury [and] supplies her with all other necessities, such as management, solicitude, food, and clothing. . . . The wife extends to her husband obedience, subjection, trust, compliance, services, aid, honor, reverence, modesty, and respect. She brings forth children for him, and nurses and trains them. She joins and consoles him in misery and calamity. She accommodates herself to his customs, and without his counsel and consent she does nothing. And thus she renders to her husband an agreeable and peaceful life. There are common advantages and responsibilities that are provided and communicated by both

---

illustrate, ed. Carl J. Friedrich (Cambridge, Mass.: Harvard University Press, 1932 [1614]).

80. Althusius, *Politica,* I.1-3, 17.

81. Althusius, *Politica,* II.2, 27.

82. Althusius, *Politica,* II.14-15, 28 (citations omitted).

spouses, such as kindness, use of the body for avoiding harlotry and for procreating children, mutual habitation except when absence may be necessary, intimate and familiar companionship, mutual love, fidelity, patience, mutual service, communication of all goods and right . . . management of the family, administration of household duties, education of children in the true religion, protection against and liberation from perils, and mourning of the dead.[83]

Anglican and Anglo-Puritan writers argued even more expansively than Continental Protestants that marriage at once served and symbolized the commonwealth (literally the "common good") of the couple, the children, the Church, and the state. William Perkins (1558-1602) put it thus in 1590: "[M]arriage was made and appointed by God himself to be the foundation and seminary of all sorts and kinds of life in the commonwealth and the church. . . . [T]hose families wherein the service of God is performed are, as it were, little churches; yea, even a kind of paradise on earth."[84] Robert Cleaver (c. 1561-1625) opened his famous 1598 tract, *A Godly Form of Householde Gouernment,* with an oft-repeated maxim: "A household is as it were a little commonwealth, by the good government whereof, God's glory may be advanced, the commonwealth which stands of several families, benefited, and all that live in that family, may receive much comfort and commodity."[85] William Gouge (1578-1653) premised his massive 800-page *Domestic Duties* (1622) on the same belief that "the family is a seminary of the Church and the Commonwealth," and is indeed in its own right "a little church, and a little commonwealth, whereby a trial may be made of such as are fit for any place of authority, or subjection in Church or commonwealth."[86]

Like the political and ecclesiastical commonwealths, Anglican divines argued, the domestic commonwealth was created as a hierarchical structure. God had created Eve as "a help meet" for Adam. He had called

---

83. Althusius, *Politica,* II.38-49, 29-30 (citations omitted).

84. William Perkins, *Christian Oeconomy or a Short Survey of the Right Manner of Erecting and Ordering a Family according to the Scriptures,* in *The Work of William Perkins,* ed. Ian Breward (Abbingdon: Sutton Courtenay, 1970), pp. 418-19. I have modernized the spelling and punctuation in this and the next five quotations.

85. Robert Cleaver, *A Godly Forme of Householde Gouernment* (London: Thomas Creed, 1598), p. 1.

86. William Gouge, *Of Domesticall Duties: Eight Treatises* (London: J. Haviland, 1622), pp. 17-18.

Adam and Eve to mutual society among themselves and mutual procreation of children (Gen. 1:28; 2:18). After the fall, he had commanded that Adam "shall rule over" Eve (Gen. 3:16). As heir of Adam, the modern husband was thus the head of his wife. As heir of Eve, the modern wife was his subject, his "help meet." Together husband and wife were the heads of their children and the rest of the household. Each of these offices in the family hierarchy was bound by a series of duties, rooted in the Bible and natural law, which dozens of thick household manuals and catechisms of the day elaborated.[87]

Faithful maintenance of domestic duties and offices, Anglican divines believed, was the best guarantee of individual flourishing and social order within the broader commonwealths of Church and state. Robert Cleaver put it thus: "[I]f masters of families do not practice catechizing and discipline in their houses and thereby join their helping hands to Magistrates, and Ministers, social order and stability will soon give way to chaos and anarchy."[88] "A conscionable performance of household duties . . . may be accounted a public work," William Gouge echoed. For "good members of a family are likely to make good members of church and commonwealth."[89] Daniel Rogers (1573-1652) concurred, arguing that a stable marriage and household served as "the right hand of providence, supporter of laws, states, orders, offices, gifts, and services, the glory of peace, . . . the foundation of Countries, Cities, Universities, . . . Crowns and Kingdoms."[90] Dozens of Anglican and Anglo-Puritan writers, from 1600 onward, expounded this "commonwealth model" of marriage.[91]

87. See sources in FSC, pp. 130-93, and Chapter 15 herein.

88. Cleaver, *Householde Gouernment,* p. A3.

89. Gouge, *Domesticall Duties,* pp. 17, 27.

90. Daniel Rogers, *Matrimoniall Honour* (London: Philip Nevil, 1642), p. 17.

91. See, e.g., Gordon J. Schochet, *Patriarchalism in Political Thought: The Authoritarian Family and Political Speculation and Attitudes Especially in Seventeenth Century England* (New York: Basic, 1975), pp. 179-91; Mary Lynn Shanley, "Marriage Contract and Social Contract in Seventeenth-Century English Political Thought," *Western Political Quarterly* 32 (1979): 187-89; Beatrice Gottlieb, *The Family in the Western World from the Black Death to the Industrial Age* (Oxford: Oxford University Press, 1993), pp. 89-109.

Early American Formulations

These classical and Christian formulations of the goods and goals of marriage did not remain confined to Western Europe. They were also transmitted across the Atlantic to America during the great waves of colonization in the seventeenth and eighteenth centuries, and the great waves of immigration in the nineteenth and early twentieth. Even a brief sampling of the vast American literature allows us to see how commonplace these traditional Western sentiments became in American theology and law.

Roman Catholic formulations of marriage and its goods, while not so prominent in early America, were present from the colonial beginnings, not only in Lord Baltimore's Maryland founded in 1649, but also and especially in the colonial south and southwest.[92] As we noted in the previous chapter, the territories of Louisiana (1803), the Floridas (1819), Texas (1836), New Mexico (1848), and California (1848) were under the formal authority of Spain until they were acquired by the United States, and were under the formal jurisdiction of Catholic bishops in San Domingo, Havana, and Mexico. The clergy taught the sacramental theology of marriage, particularly as set out in the Roman Catechism of 1566. Both Church and state authorities sought to enforce the Church's canon laws of marriage, particularly the decree *Tametsi* of 1563 that required parental consent, two witnesses, civil registration, and Church consecration for the formation of marriage and that prohibited clerical marriage, intermarriage with non-Catholics, and divorce and remarriage.[93]

In the nineteenth century, when these Spanish territories were formally acquired by the United States, jurisdiction over marriage shifted to the American Congress and, after statehood, to local state governments. But the Catholic clergy in these vast former Spanish territories were generally left free to teach the doctrines and retain the canons of marriage for their own parishioners — a prerogative which had already been extended to the growing numbers of American Catholic bishoprics along the Atlantic seaboard and in the Midwest.[94]

92. See esp. Hans W. Baade, "The Form of Marriage in Spanish North America," *Cornell Law Review* 61 (1975): 1-89.

93. But see explanation and sources in note 10 on p. 303 herein for an explanation of why this was not true of American Catholic communities that came within the ecclesiastical provinces of Baltimore, Philadelphia, New York, and Boston, and, later, ecclesiastical provinces in the West.

94. John T. Noonan, *The Power to Dissolve: Lawyers and Marriages in the Courts of the Roman Curia* (Cambridge: Belknap, 1972), pp. 302-40; Brundage, pp. 608-17.

In the nineteenth and early twentieth centuries, American Catholic bishops issued hundreds of sermons and pastoral letters that reflected traditional Catholic formulations on the goods of marriage.[95] They repeated and glossed endlessly the traditional formula of *proles, fides, et sacramentum* — emphasizing, like their fellow European bishops, the goods of procreation and education, the ills of contraception and prostitution, and the mortal perils of intermarriage and divorce.[96]

More than a few American Catholic bishops, however, also emphasized the unique psychological, social, and political goods of marriage — anticipating by a century and more the formulations of Vatican II. An 1863 Lenten pastoral of Bishop Augustin Verot (1805-1876) of Savannah, Georgia, provides a good example. Lamenting the breakdown of the family born of the budding urbanization, industrialization, and modernization of his day, newly exacerbated by the Civil War, Verot declared that the intact marital household "is at the bottom of all the good that can be done among men."

> The Family is a society instituted and appointed by God himself, for nature is but a borrowed name to express the Maker and Author of this universe, and of all the laws which govern it. It is God who instituted and blessed marriage, and from the laws of marriage husband, wife, and children form a perfect and close society, sacred on account of its author, and indissoluble by the very nature of the ties which unite the members of it together. Hence the domestic society, because it is directly and immediately the work of God, is or ought to be a mirror, reflecting the supreme law of heaven, order, peace, and holiness, more exquisitely and perfectly than civil or political societies, which are more or less of human origin.[97]

95. A number of these American pastoral letters were prompted by the promulgation of Pius IX's *Syllabus of Errors* (1864), which included a list of ten errors about marriage.

96. See, e.g., the collection in Hugh J. Nolan, ed., *Pastoral Letters of the American Hierarchy, 1792-1970* (Huntington, Ind.: Our Sunday Visitor, 1971). See discussion of shifting (American) Catholic views of marriage in Christine Firer Hinze, "Catholic: Family Unity and Diversity within the Body of Christ," in *Faith Traditions and the Family,* ed. Phyllis D. Airhart and Margaret Lambert Bendroth (Louisville, Ky.: Westminster John Knox, 1996), pp. 53-72.

97. Augustin Verot, *Lenten Pastoral of Right Rev. A. Verot, Bishop of Savannah and Administrator Apostolic of Florida for 1863* (Savannah, Ga.: Diocese of Savannah, 1863), p. 4.

Verot then waxed at length about the social and political utility of the family — sounding very much like the Protestant Reformers before him and the Vatican II Reformers after him: "The Family is the first school where we learn good or evil. It is the source and fountainhead of morality or immorality, of a Christian or an infidel life, of virtue or vice, of good behavior or profligacy. . . . Oh! that this paramount importance of early impressions and of domestic training were well understood, felt, and acted upon. This would at once bring about the most salutary reformation in society, in church and state." Properly viewed, Verot continued, marriage is "*a domestic church . . .* a society bound by the ties of religion, faith, and virtue, yet more than by the bonds of a common origin and identity of blood." The Christian family is "the first step in virtue, the foundation of solid merit, a school of morality and piety, a centre of union, love, and peace, an unfailing element of future usefulness and greatness, a terrestrial paradise, an image of the blessed City of God, where order and happiness prevail undisturbed and unalterable."[98]

As we noted in the previous chapter, Protestant formulations of marriage and its goods were more prominent in early American writings and more influential in American law. By the turn of the nineteenth century, the Atlantic coast was covered with representatives from a wide variety of Protestant faiths — Anglican, Lutheran, Puritan, Presbyterian, Reformed, Huguenot, Baptist, Methodist, Moravian, and more — and this Protestant pluralism only increased with the Second Great Awakening of 1800-1860.[99] Although these plural Protestant polities were far from uniform in their marital norms and habits, they were largely united in their adherence to basic Protestant teachings about marriage inherited from Western Europe.[100] While adhering to many of the same basic Christian norms of sex,

---

98. Verot, *Lenten Pastoral*, pp. 4-5, 9. See comparable views in Third Plenary Council of Baltimore, "Pastoral Letter (1884)," in *Pastoral Letters,* ed. Nolan, pp. 175-76; Joseph Farrell, *Pastoral Letter of the Right Reverend Michael Joseph O'Farrell, Bishop of Trenton, on Christian Marriage* (New York: Benziger Brothers, 1883), pp. 4-7; "Pastoral Letter Issued by the Roman Catholic Hierarchy of the United States (1919)," in *Pastoral Letters,* ed. Nolan, pp. 309-11. These views were elaborated in various Catholic household manuals and catechetical texts. See, e.g., Bernard O'Reilly, *The Mirror of True Womanhood* (New York: Peter F. Collier, 1878), a 466-page women's manual premised on the assumption that the household is "a little Eden."

99. Edwin S. Gaustad and Philip Barlow, *New Historical Atlas of Religion in America* (Oxford: Oxford University Press, 2001).

100. The most important difference among these colonies and early American states was over whether marriages could be contracted before a civil official only, as New

marriage, and domestic life taught by Catholics, they rejected sacramental views of marriage and ecclesiastical jurisdiction over marital formation, maintenance, and dissolution. They encouraged ministers to be married. They permitted religious intermarriage. They truncated the law of impediments. They allowed for divorce on proof of fault. They encouraged remarriage of those divorced or widowed.

Protestant theologians, of various denominations, repeated the familiar Protestant trilogy of marital goods. Many Anglican and Methodist writers — following the Anglican *Book of Common Prayer* of 1662 and its Episcopalian revision of 1789 — rendered this trilogy as "procreation, love, and protection," and expressed ample reticence about the propriety of divorce and remarriage.[101] Most other Protestant writers — following Lutheran and Calvinist confessions and conventions — rendered this as "love, protection, and procreation," and countenanced divorce and remarriage if one or more of these goods of marriage was irreconcilably compromised by the fault of one of the parties.[102]

These variations on traditional formulations of marital goods did not prevent American Protestant theologians from underscoring the health benefits of marriage to the couple — particularly to the husband. John Bayley, for example, an influential Methodist preacher, wrote a lengthy volume in 1857 expounding the ideal nature, structure, and purpose of marriage. His central thesis was that "prudent marriages are favorable to health, long life, and prosperity."[103] He defended this proposition with some twenty pages of quotations from classical and Christian authors. Among his favorites was the Anglican divine Jeremy Taylor (1613-1667), who had rhapsodized: "If you are for pleasure, marry; if you prize rosy health, marry. A good wife is heaven's last best gift to man — his angel and minister of graces innumerable — his gem of many virtues — his casket of jewels. . . ."[104] Bayley then defended at length the conventional legal requirements of marital formation

England Puritans allowed, or required Church consecration, as Anglican communities required. See further Chapter 10 herein.

101. See, e.g., George Bourne, *Marriage Indissoluble and Divorce Unscriptural* (Harrisonburg, Va.: Davidson and Bourne, 1813), pp. 9-14, 23-35; Bufford W. Coe, *John Wesley and Marriage* (Bethlehem, Pa.: Lehigh University Press, 1996), pp. 52ff.

102. See, e.g., Howard Malcom, *The Christian's Rule of Marriage* (Boston: James Loring, 1834), pp. 48-75.

103. John Bayley, *Marriage As It Is, and As It Should Be* (New York: M. W. Dodd, 1857), p. 13.

104. Quoted in Bayley, *Marriage As It Is*, p. 26.

— formal betrothals, public banns, parental consent, two witnesses, civil registration, and Church consecration — and set out the respective "duties of love" between husband and wife, parent and child.

George Bourne (1780-1845) of Virginia, in his oft-reprinted tome, voiced comparable sentiments about the emotional and moral benefits of married life. God has created marriage to be "sacred and honorable, of high Distinction, and nearly combined with the dignity and fruition of human nature," Bourne wrote. When marriage is properly entered into, it provides "every blessing which man can enjoy during his abode in this pilgrimage state; it diminishes his pain, excites his sympathies, purifies his desires, invigorates his exertions, unfolds his usefulness, duplicates his enjoyments, counteracts his vicious propensities, exalts his character, animates his devotional principles for present rectitude and future bliss everlasting. . . ."[105] Scores of other theological tracts and sermons on marriage are at hand to document this common "Protestant temperament" about the individual goods and benefits of marriage.[106]

It was the American jurists, more than the American Protestant theologians, who expounded the social and political goods of marriage and family — adducing Anglican moralists, Roman jurists, and Greek philosophers alike to drive home the legal priorities of marriage. For example, Chancellor James Kent (1763-1847), one of the great early systematizers of American law, wrote about the spiritual and social utility of marriage:

> The primary and most important of the domestic relations is that of husband and wife. It has its foundations in nature, and is the only lawful relation by which Providence has permitted the continuance of the human race. In every age it has had a propitious influence on the moral improvement and happiness of mankind. It is one of the chief foundations of social order. We may justly place to the credit of the institution of marriage a great share of the blessings which flow from the refinement of manners, the education of children, the sense of justice, and cultivation of the liberal arts.[107]

105. Bourne, *Marriage Indissoluble*, pp. 9, 12, 113. See also p. 18: "Early marriages combine advantages so numerous, personal sanctity, relative comfort, social utility, and national stability."

106. Philip Greven, *The Protestant Temperament: Patterns of Child-Rearing, Religious Experience, and the Self in Early America* (New York: Knopf, 1977).

107. James Kent, *Commentaries on American Law*, ed. O. W. Holmes Jr., 2 vols. (Boston: Little, Brown, 1896), 2:76.

W. C. Rogers, a leading jurist at the end of the nineteenth century, opened his oft-reprinted treatise on the law of domestic relations with a veritable homily on marriage:

> In a sense it is a consummation of the Divine Command to "multiply and replenish the earth." It is the state of existence ordained by the Creator, who has fashioned man and woman expressly for the society and enjoyment incident to mutual companionship. This Divine plan is supported and promoted by natural instinct, as it were, on the part of both for the society of each other. It is the highest state of existence, . . . the only stable substructure of our social, civil, and religious institutions. Religion, government, morals, progress, enlightened learning, and domestic happiness must all fall into most certain and inevitable decay when the married state ceases to be recognized or respected. Accordingly, we have in this state of man and woman the most essential foundation of religion, social purity, and domestic happiness.[108]

Other standard legal texts spoke of marriage as "the highest state of existence," "a public institution of universal concern," "the very basis of the whole fabric of civilized society," "a spiritual association . . . transcendent in its importance both to individuals and to society."[109]

Likewise, the United States Supreme Court spoke repeatedly of marriage as "more than a mere contract," "a Godly ordinance," "a sacred obligation."[110] In *Murphy v. Ramsey* (1885), one of a series of Supreme Court cases upholding the constitutionality of anti-polygamy laws, Justice Field declared for the Court:

---

108. W. C. Rogers, *A Treatise on the Law of Domestic Relations* (Chicago: T. H. Flood, 1899), sec. 2, 2.

109. James Schouler, *A Treatise on the Law of Marriage, Divorce, Separation, and Domestic Relations*, 3 vols. (Albany, N.Y.: Matthew Bender, 1921), 1:17-19; Joel Bishop, *New Commentaries on Marriage, Divorce, and Separation*, 2 vols. (Chicago: T. H. Flood, 1891), 1:4-15, 2:217; Joseph Story, *Commentaries on the Conflict of Laws* (Boston: Hillard, Gray, 1834), sec. 109; Chester Vernier, *American Family Laws*, 5 vols. (Stanford, Calif.: Stanford University Press, 1931-1938), 1:45.

110. *Maynard v. Hill*, 125 U.S. 190, 210-11 (1888); *Reynolds v. United States*, 98 U.S. 145, 165 (1879); *Murphy v. Ramsey*, 114 U.S. 15, 45 (1885); *Davis v. Beason*, 133 U.S. 333, 341-42 (1890).

For, certainly, no legislation can be supposed more wholesome and necessary in the founding of a free, self-governing commonwealth . . . than that which seeks to establish it on the basis of the idea of the family, as consisting in and springing from the union for life of one man and one woman in the holy estate of matrimony; the sure foundation of all that is stable and noble in our civilization; the best guarantee of that reverent morality which is the source of all beneficent progress in social and political improvement.[111]

The Supreme Court elaborated these sentiments in *Maynard v. Hill* (1888), in another opinion by Justice Field:

[W]hilst marriage is often termed . . . a civil contract — generally to indicate that it must be founded upon the agreement of the parties, and does not require any religious ceremony for its solemnization — it is something more than a mere contract. The consent of the parties is of course essential to its existence, but when the contract to marry is executed by marriage, a relation between the parties is created which they cannot change. Other contracts may be modified, restricted, or enlarged, or entirely released upon the consent of the parties. Not so with marriage. The relation once formed, the law steps in and holds the parties to various obligations and liabilities. It is an institution, in the maintenance of which in its purity the public is deeply interested, for it is the foundation of the family and society, without which there would be neither civilization nor progress.[112]

Summary and Conclusions

The health paradigm of marriage is both very new and very old. What is new is the wealth of recent statistical evidence demonstrating that, for most adult parties most of the time, married life is better than single life, marital cohabitation is better than nonmarital cohabitation, married parents do better than single parents in raising their children. According to several recent studies, married folks on average live longer, happier, and safer lives. They are more satisfied, prosperous, and efficient. They receive better hy-

---

111. *Murphy*, 114 U.S. at 45.
112. *Maynard*, 125 U.S. at 210-11.

giene, health care, and co-insurance. Their children develop better emotional, social, and moral skills. These data on the health benefits of marriage are now emerging with increasing alacrity within a variety of modern professions, including very recently in public health recommendations. They have enormous implications for our professional responsibilities to couples and children, and to the institution of marriage itself.

The health paradigm of marriage is also very old. It repeats and refines a number of ancient and enduring Western ideas about the goods and goals of marriage. Already in the centuries before Christ and before the Christianization of the West, classical Greek and Roman writers taught that marriage is a natural institution to which most men and women are naturally inclined; that marriage is a useful, pleasant, moral, and even sacred institution; that it provides an efficient pooling of property and division of labor and resources within the household; that it provides mutual care, protection, and compensation to couples; that it serves both for the fulfillment, companionship, and happiness of spouses and for the procreation, nurture, and education of children.

The Roman Catholic tradition, building on Augustine and Aquinas, wove these classical insights into the famous theory that marriage has three inherent goods: (1) *fides* — a faithfulness and friendship between husband and wife that goes beyond that demanded of any other temporal relationship; (2) *proles* — children, who are to be nurtured and educated to perpetuate the human species and to transmit and live out the proper norms and habits of spiritual and temporal life; and (3) *sacramentum* — an enduring expression of Christ's love for his Church, an indissoluble channel of God's grace to sanctify the couple, their children, and the broader community. Particularly, in the Second Vatican Council (1962-1965), the Catholic Church has emphasized the need to keep these three marital goods in balance, and has held out the covenant of marital love as the new organizing idiom of the goods of marriage. The Church has also recently emphasized that marriage serves for the physical, emotional, moral, and spiritual "perfection" of a man and woman, and that the household is a "domestic Church" and a model of love, charity, stewardship, authority, dignity, faithfulness, discipline, and care for each new generation of children to learn.

The Protestant tradition, from its sixteenth-century beginnings, placed emphasis not only on the intrinsic goods but also on the instrumental goals of the covenant or estate of marriage. Marriage was created by God to foster love, to deter sin, and to produce children. If one or more of these created marital goals was permanently frustrated, those parties who could not reconcile themselves to this condition could seek divorce and remarry. Particularly Luther and Calvin emphasized further that marriage has "uses" in this life. Marriage deters vice by furnishing preferred options to prostitution, promiscuity, pornography, and other forms of sexual pathos. It cultivates virtue by offering love, care, and nurture to its members, and by holding out a model of charity, education, and sacrifice to the broader community. It enhances the life of a man and a woman by providing them with a community of caring and sharing, of stability and support, of nurture and welfare. It enhances the life of the child, by providing it with a chrysalis of nurture and love, with a highly individualized form of socialization and education. Such views echoed loudly in the theological and legal literature of the American colonies and the early American republic.

For all of its theological and philosophical diversity, therefore, the West has had a long and thick overlapping consensus that marriage is good, does good, and has goods both for the couple and for the children. Classical, patristic, Catholic, and Protestant writers alike have all recognized the natural teleology and utility of marriage: (1) the natural drive on the part of most adults toward the institution of marriage because of the inherent goods of individual survival, flourishing, happiness, and even perfectibility that it provides; and (2) the natural capacity on the part of most adults to engage in the expected performance of marriage — the unique combination of sexual, physical, economic, emotional, charitable, moral, and spiritual performances that become marriage. Obviously, there are ample exceptions to this natural norm of marriage that the tradition has long recognized. Some are called to celibacy or to the single or widowed life. Some lack the physical capacity or emotional temperament to engage in marriage. Some who get married should not, and need to be removed from the institution through annulment or divorce. But the general inclination and instruction of nature, of the human body, of the human psyche, of the human heart, is for marriage, the Western tradition teaches.

The new social science data can thus be viewed as the start to a new chapter in a long and familiar Western story about the goods and goals of marriage. This new social science chapter supplements and supports somewhat the many, more theologically explicit and expansive chapters that have been written and continue to be written. The new social science data present older prudential insights about marriage with more statistical precision. They present ancient avuncular observations about marital benefits with more inductive generalization. They reduce common Western observations about marital health into more precise and measurable categories.

These new social science data thus offer something of a neutral apologetic for marriage. They provide a start to a useful bilingual vocabulary that allows us to move more easily between traditional and contemporary, theological and natural, spiritual and civil, confessional and professional terms and concepts of marriage.

What is still largely missing from this new social science chapter of marriage is a careful demonstration and documentation of the second core insight of the Western tradition — that marriage is good not only for the couple and their children but also for the broader civic communities of which they are a part. The ancient Greeks and Roman Stoics called marriage "the foundation of the republic," "the private font of public virtue." The Church Fathers called marital and familial love "the seedbed of the city," "the force that welds society together." Catholics called the family "a domestic Church," "a kind of school of deeper humanity." Protestants called the household a "little Church," a "little state," a "little seminary," a "little commonwealth." American jurists and theologians taught that marriage is both private and public, individual and social, temporal and transcendent in quality — a natural if not a spiritual estate, a useful if not an essential association, a pillar if not the foundation of civil society.

At the core of all these metaphors is a perennial Western ideal that stable marriages and families are essential to the survival, flourishing, and happiness of the greater commonwealths of Church, state, and civil society, and that a breakdown of marriage and the family will eventually have devastating consequences on these larger social institutions. To date, we have ample anecdotal evidence of the social pathos that sometimes follows the breakdown of the family, and ample political manipulation of the same, particularly in election years. But a careful measuring and mapping of the health benefits of marriage and the family for Church, state, and civil society alike would be an apt conclusion to this latest chapter in the long Western story of the goods and goals of marriage.

12

More Than a Mere Contract:
Marriage As Contract and Covenant
in Law and Theology

Covenant Marriage v. Contract Marriage

On August 15, 1997, the state of Louisiana put in place the nation's first modern covenant marriage law. The law creates a two-tiered system of marriage. Couples may choose a contract marriage, with minimal formalities of formation and attendant rights to no-fault divorce. Or couples may choose a covenant marriage, with more stringent formation and dissolution rules. The licensing costs for either form of marriage are the same. But in order to form a covenant marriage, the parties must receive detailed counseling about marriage from a professional marriage counselor or a religious official, and then swear an oath, pledging "full knowledge of the nature, purposes, and responsibilities of marriage" and promising "to love, honor, and care for one another as husband and wife for the rest of our lives." Divorce is allowed such covenanted couples only on grounds of serious fault (adultery, capital felony, malicious desertion, and/or physical or sexual abuse of the spouse or one of the children) or after two years of separation. Separation from bed and board is allowed on any of these same fault grounds as well as on proof of habitual intemperance, cruel treatment, or outrages of the other spouse. Comparable covenant marriage statutes are now in place in Arizona and Arkansas as well.[1] Twenty-seven other states have covenant marriage alternatives to contract marriage under consideration.[2]

---

1. Louisiana (1997): La. R.S. 9:272 et seq. (2003); Arizona: Ariz. R.S. 25-901 et seq.; Arkansas: Ark. Code § 9-11-801 et seq.
2. Alabama, California, Colorado, Georgia, Indiana, Iowa, Kansas, Maine, Maryland, Michigan, Minnesota, Mississippi, Missouri, Nebraska, New Jersey, New Mexico,

These new covenant marriages laws are designed, in part, to help off-set the corrosive effects of America's experiment with a private contractual model of marriage. Historically, in America and in much of the West, mar-riages were presumptively permanent commitments, and marriage forma-tion and dissolution were serious public events. Marriage formation re-quired the consent of parents and peers, the procurement of a state certificate, the publication of banns, and a public ceremony and celebration after a period of waiting and discernment. Marriage dissolution required public hearings, proof of serious fault by one party, alimony payments to the innocent dependent spouse, and ongoing support payments for minor children.[3]

In the last third of the twentieth century, many of these traditional rules gave way to a private contractual model of marriage grounded in new cultural and constitutional norms of sexual liberty and privacy. In virtually all states, marriage formation rules were simplified to require only the ac-quisition of a license from the state registry followed by solemnization be-fore a licensed official — without banns, with little or no waiting, with no public celebration, without notification of others. Marriage dissolution rules were simplified through the introduction of unilateral no-fault di-vorce. New streamlined and inexpensive marital dissolution procedures aimed to release miserable couples from the shackles of unwanted mar-riages and to relieve swollen court dockets from the prospects of protracted litigation. Either the husband or the wife could now file a simple suit for di-vorce. No fault by either party would need to be proved — or staged. Courts would dissolve the union, often making a one-time division of mar-ital property to give each party a clean break to start life anew.[4]

America's experiment with the private contractual model of marriage has failed on many counts and accounts — with children and women bear-ing the primary costs.[5] The statistics are worth repeating: From 1975 to

---

Ohio, Oklahoma, Oregon, South Carolina, Tennessee, Texas, Utah, Virginia, Washing-ton, West Virginia, Wisconsin.

3. For a comprehensive survey of these earlier American marriage laws, see Chester Vernier, *American Family Laws,* 5 vols. (Stanford: Stanford University Press, 1931-1938). See also Chapters 10-11 and 15 herein.

4. See FSC, chap. 5.

5. Don S. Browning, *Marriage and Modernization* (Grand Rapids: Eerdmans, 2003); Katherine Shaw Spaht, "For the Sake of the Children: Recapturing the Meaning of Marriage," *Notre Dame Law Review* 73 (1998): 1547; Linda J. Waite, *Does Divorce Make People Happy? Findings from a Study of Unhappy Marriages* (New York: Institute for

2000, a quarter of all children were raised in single-parent households. One quarter of all pregnancies were aborted. One third of all children were born to single mothers. One half of all marriages ended in divorce. Two-thirds of all African-American children were raised without a father. Mother-only homes had less than a third of the median income of homes with a regular male present, and four times the rates of foreclosure and eviction. Teenagers who grew up in broken homes proved two to three times more likely to have behavioral, learning, and socialization problems than teenagers from two-parent homes. More than two-thirds of juveniles and young adults convicted of major felonies from 1970 to 1995 came from single- or no-parent homes.[6]

Covenant marriage laws have been one of several legal responses to these mounting social and psychological costs of America's experiment with easy-in/easy-out marriage. Covenant marriage laws capture the traditional ideal that marriage is "more than just a piece of paper," more than just a transient and terminal private contract for sexual intimacy.[7] The foundation of covenant marriage is a pledge of presumptive permanent sacrifice — "to love, care, and honor one another as husband and wife for the rest of our lives." The formation of covenant marriage is a public and deliberative event — requiring a waiting period and at least the consent of the couples' parents or guardians and the counseling of therapists or clerics, and by implication the communities whom those third parties represent. The dissolution of covenant marriage comes only upon betrayal of the fundamental goods of this institution or after a suitable period of separation and careful deliberation.

American Values, 2002); Judith Wallerstein, *Second Chances: Men, Women, and Children a Decade After Divorce,* fifteenth ann. ed. (Boston: Houghton Mifflin, 2004); Judith Wallerstein, Julia Lewis, and Sandra Blakeslee, *The Unexpected Legacy of Divorce* (New York: Hyperion, 2000); Barbara Dafoe Whitehead, *The Divorce Culture* (New York: Alfred A. Knopf, 1996).

6. Joel A. Nichols, "Louisiana's Covenant Marriage Law: A First Step toward a More Robust Pluralism in Marriage and Divorce Law," *Emory Law Journal* 47 (1998): 920. More recent studies, some with more encouraging recent statistics, include: Mary Ann Mason, Arlene Skolnick, Stephen D. Sugarman, *All Our Families: New Policies for a New Century* (New York: Oxford University Press, 1998); Milton C. Regan Jr., *Alone Together: Law and the Meanings of Marriage* (New York: Oxford University Press, 1999); Steven M. Tipton and John Witte Jr., eds., *The Family Transformed: Religion, Values, and Family Life in America* (Washington, D.C.: Georgetown University Press, 2005).

7. Katherine Anderson, Don Browning, and Brian Boyer, eds., *Marriage: Just a Piece of Paper?* (Grand Rapids: Eerdmans, 2002).

Covenant marriage laws reflect the historical lesson that rules governing marital formation and marital dissolution must be balanced in their stringency — and that separation must be maintained as a release valve. Stern rules of marital dissolution require stern rules of marital formation. Loose formation rules demand loose dissolution rules. To fix the modern problem of transient marriages, covenant marriage proponents have insisted, requires reforms at both ends of the marital process.[8] A number of states have recently responded to the problem of transient marriage simply by tightening their rules of no-fault divorce, but without corresponding attention to the rules of marital formation and separation. Such efforts, standing alone, are misguided. No-fault divorce is not the only cause of escalating marital breakdown, as is so often claimed; no-fault marriage is to blame as well.

Covenant marriage laws allow prospective marital couples to contract out of the state's laws of marriage contract by choosing a covenant marriage. Couples who consider covenant marriage must fully apprise themselves of the costs and benefits of protracting the process of marital formation and waiving their rights to no-fault divorce. But the choice of marital form is theirs. Having this choice encourages inaptly matched couples to discover their incompatibility before marriage, rather than after it. If one engaged party wants a contract marriage and the other a covenant marriage, the disparity in prospective commitment should, for many couples, be too plain to ignore. Couples should delay their wedding until their mutual commitment has deepened, or cancel their wedding if their respective commitments remain disparate. Better to prepare well for a marriage than to rush into it. Better to cancel a wedding than to divorce shortly after it. Such is the theory of the new covenant marriage laws.

These covenant marriage laws seek to respect both the virtues of marriage contracts and the values of enduring marriages. These laws have been attacked as an undue encroachment on sexual liberty and on the rights of women and children; as a "Trojan horse" designed to smuggle biblical principles back into American law; as an improper delegation of state responsibilities to religious officials; and as a reversion to the days of staged and spurious charges of marital fault which no-fault laws had sought to overcome. But, given the religiously neutral language of these laws; their ex-

8. See chapter by Katherine Shaw Spaht, one of the principal drafters of the Louisiana covenant marriage statute, in *Covenant Marriage in Comparative Perspective*, ed. John Witte Jr. and Eliza Ellison (Grand Rapids: Eerdmans, 2005) [hereafter CM].

plicit protections of both voluntary entrance and exit from the covenant union; their insistence that religious counselors be restricted in the marriage counseling they can offer on behalf of the state; and the overriding commitment of these laws to the freedom of contract of both parties, such constitutional objections seem largely unavailing.[9]

Marriage As More Than a Mere Contract

Covenant marriage laws are not only a new form of social engineering, designed to counter the rise of privatized marriage and no-fault divorce. They are also a new forum for the expression of traditional common law teachings that marriage is "more than a mere contract." In the American common law tradition, marriage has long been regarded as a natural if not a spiritual estate, a useful if not an essential association, a pillar if not the foundation of civil society.[10] Marriage has required more than the general rules of private contract — of offer and acceptance, consideration and rescission, reformation and remedy. It has drawn to itself special rules and rituals of betrothal and espousal, of registration and consecration, of consent and celebration. It has also provided the basis for a long series of special rights and duties of husband and wife, parent and child that are respected at both public and private law. As the American jurist Joseph Story (1779-1845) put it in 1834,

> Marriage is treated by all civilized societies as a peculiar and favored contract. It is in its origin a contract of natural law. . . . It is the parent, and not the child of society; the source of civility and a sort of seminary of the republic. In civil society it becomes a civil contract, regulated and prescribed by law, and endowed with civil consequences. In most civilized countries, acting under a sense of the force of sacred obligations, it has had the sanctions of religion superadded. It then becomes a religious, as well as a natural and civil contract; . . . it is a great mistake to suppose that because it is the one, therefore it may not be the other.[11]

9. See Spaht's chapter in CM and chapter by Margaret Brinig and Stephen Nock in CM.

10. See further Chapters 10 and 11 herein.

11. Joseph Story, *Commentaries on the Conflict of Laws, Foreign and Domestic, in Regard to Contracts, Rights, and Remedies* (Boston: Little, Brown, 1834), p. 100 (sec. 108). In his second edition, Story added this note to the quoted passage: "It appears to me

These traditional common law teachings that marriage is both a contract and something more were rooted in ancient Christian teachings. These Christian teachings, in turn, had antecedents and analogues in ancient Jewish and Islamic teachings. Jewish, Christian, and Islamic traditions alike have long taught that marriage is a contract — called the *ketubah* in Judaism, the *pactum* in Christianity, the *kitab* in Islam. But these traditions have also long taught that marriage is more than a mere contract — more than simply a private bargain to be formed, maintained, and dissolved as the two marital parties see fit. For all three traditions, marriage is an institution that is both private and public, individual and social, temporal and transcendent in quality. Its origin, nature, and purpose lie beyond and beneath the terms of the marriage contract itself.[12]

Marriage As Contract

It is important to recognize that, while the three traditions of Judaism, Christianity, and Islam have long taught that marriage is more than a contract, they have also insisted that marriage is not less than a contract.

Nearly two millennia ago, Jewish rabbis created the *ketubah,* the premarital contract in which the husband and the wife spelled out the terms and conditions of their relationship before, during, and after the marriage, and the rights and duties of husband, wife, and child in the event of marital dissolution or death of one of the parties. The Talmudic rabbis regarded these marriage contracts as essential protections for wives and children who were otherwise subject to the unilateral right of divorce granted to men by the Mosaic law (Deut. 24:1-4). While the terms of the *ketubah* could be privately contracted, both the couple's families and the rabbinic authorities were often actively involved in their formation and enforcement.[13]

---

something more than a mere contract. It is rather to be deemed an institution of society founded upon the consent and contract of the parties; and in this view it has some peculiarities in its nature, character, operation, and extent of operation, different from what belongs to ordinary contracts."

12. See analysis and primary texts on the theological, ethical, and legal teachings on marriage in these three traditions and others in Don S. Browning, M. Christian Green, and John Witte Jr., eds., *Sex, Marriage and Family in the World Religions* (New York: Columbia University Press, 2006).

13. See chapters by David Novak and Michael J. Broyde in CM; Ze'ev W. Falk, *Jewish Matrimonial Law in the Middle Ages* (Oxford: Oxford University Press, 1966).

More than a millennium and a half ago, Christian theologians adopted the marriage pact or bond.[14] These contracts forged a new relationship between husband and wife and their respective families. They adopted and adapted a number of the marital and familial rights and duties set out in the household codes of the New Testament, in the apostolic Church constitutions, and in Jewish, Greek, Roman, and patristic writings.[15] The early rules governing these marriage contracts, as well as related contracts respecting dowries and other marital property, were later systematized and elaborated by Christian jurists and theologians — in the eighth and ninth centuries by Eastern Orthodox, in the twelfth and thirteen centuries by Catholics, in the sixteenth and seventeenth centuries by Protestants.

More than a millennium ago, Muslim jurists and theologians created the *kitab,* a special form of contract (*'adq*) that a devout Muslim was religiously bound to uphold in imitation and implementation of the Prophet's example and teaching. The *kitab* ideally established a distinctive relationship of "affection, tranquility, and mercy" between husband and wife. It defined their respective rights, duties, and identities vis-à-vis each other, their parents and children, and the broader communities of which they were part. The signing of the *kitab* was a solemn religious event involving a cleric who instructed the couple on their marital rights and duties as set out in the Qur'an. While the Qur'an and the Prophet's teaching in the Hadith set out basic norms of marriage life and liturgy, it was particularly the Shari'a, the religious laws developed in the centuries after the Prophet, which crystallized much of this tradition of marital contracts, with ample variation among the Islamic schools of jurisprudence.[16]

14. See examples and analysis in Philip L. Reynolds and John Witte Jr., eds., *To Have and to Hold: Marrying and Its Documentation in Western Christendom, 400-1600* (Cambridge: Cambridge University Press, 2007); Philip L. Reynolds, *Marriage in the Western Church: The Christianization of Marriage during the Patristic and Early Medieval Periods* (Leiden: E. J. Brill, 1994).

15. Eph. 5:21–6:9; Col. 3:18–4:1; 1 Tim. 2:8-15; 5:1-2; 6:1-2; Titus 2:1-10; 3:1; 1 Peter 2:11–3:12. See sources and discussion in David Balch and Carolyn Osiek, *Marriage in the New Testament* (Louisville: Westminster John Knox, 1997); Don S. Browning et al., *From Culture Wars to Common Ground,* second ed. (Louisville: Westminster John Knox, 2000); David Balch and Carolyn Osiek, *Early Christian Families in Context: An Interdisciplinary Dialogue* (Grand Rapids: Eerdmans, 2003).

16. See chapter by Azizah al-Hibri in CM; Abdullahi A. An-Na'im, ed., *Islamic Family in a Changing World: A Global Resource Book* (London: Zed, 2002).

An exception to the usual rules of Islamic jurisprudence was the *muta'a,* a temporary marriage contract traditionally recognized by some Shi'ite Muslims and now be-

While these marriage contracts differed markedly within and among these three Abrahamic traditions, several broad features were common.

First, Jewish, Christian, and Islamic traditions alike made provision for two contracts — betrothals or future promises to marry and espousals or present promises to marry — with a mandatory waiting period between them. The point of this waiting period was to allow couples to weigh the depth and durability of their mutual love. It was also to invite others to weigh in on the maturity and compatibility of the couple, to offer them counsel and commodities, and to prepare for the celebration of their union and their life together thereafter.

Second, all three traditions insisted that marriage depended in its essence on the mutual consent of the man and the woman. Even if the man and woman were represented by parents or guardians during the contract negotiation, their own consent was essential to the validity of their marriage. Jewish and Muslim jurists came to this insight early in the development of their law of marriage contracts. The Catholic tradition reached this insight canonically only in the twelfth century, after which it was absorbed in Orthodox and later in Protestant teachings. All three traditions continued to tolerate the practice of arranged marriages and child marriages, particularly when those were politically or commercially advantageous. But the theory was that both the young man and the young woman reserved the right to dissent from the arrangement upon reaching the age of consent.

Third, while all three traditions taught that every person of the age of consent was free to choose a marital partner, persons were not free to choose just anyone. God and nature set a first limit to the freedom of marital contract. Parties could not marry those who were related to them by blood or by marriage — by bonds of consanguinity and affinity, as these relations were called in Scripture. Custom and culture set a second limit. The parties had to be of suitable piety and modesty, of comparable social and

---

coming newly popular among the majority Shi'ite populations in Iraq. The *muta'a* was traditionally reserved to circumstances when men were involved in protracted absences from home or on dangerous pilgrimages and became a way of not only channeling his incontinence but also devising some of his property to his temporary wife. Today, the *muta'a* is also becoming a convenient form of effectively legalizing prostitution and concubinage, with *muta'a* contracts as short as an hour being upheld by Shi'ite clerics. See Shala Haeri, *The Law of Desire: Temporary Marriage in Shi'i Iran* (Syracuse, N.Y.: Syracuse University Press, 1989); Abu al Qasim Gurji, *Temporary Marriage (Mut'ah) in Islamic Law*, trans. Sachicho Murata (Qum: Ansariyan Publications, 1986); "'Pleasure Marriages' Regain Popularity in Iraq," *USA Today* (May 12, 2005): 4A.

economic status, and ideally (and, in some communities, indispensably) of the same faith. The general law of contracts set a third limit. Both parties had to have the capacity and freedom to enter contracts, and had to follow proper contractual forms and ceremonies. Parents and guardians set a fourth limit. A valid marriage (at least for minors) required the consent of both sets of parents or guardians — and sometimes as well the consent of political and/or spiritual authorities who stood *in loco parentis*.

Fourth, all three traditions often accompanied marriage promises with elaborate exchanges of property, which sometimes gave rise to their own marital property contracts. The prospective husband gave to his fiancée (and, sometimes, to her father or family as well) a betrothal gift, sometimes a very elaborate and expensive gift. In some cultures, husbands followed this by giving a wedding gift to the wife. The wife, in turn, brought into the marriage her dowry, which was at minimum her basic living articles, sometimes a great deal more. These property exchanges were not an absolute condition to the validity of a marriage. But breach of a contract to deliver property in consideration of marriage could often result in dissolution at least of the engagement contract.

Fifth, all three traditions eventually developed a marriage liturgy. In the Jewish tradition, the Talmud provided detailed liturgies and prayers for both the betrothal and the marriage, building in part on prototypes in the book of Tobit. In the Jewish tradition, weddings were essential community events, presided over by the rabbi, and involving the entire local community.[17] The Christian tradition celebrated wedding liturgies of some sort from the start, but the earliest surviving marriage liturgies are from the eighth century.[18] Particularly among the Eastern Orthodox, these liturgies became extraordinary visual and verbal symphonies of prayers, blessings, oaths, and rituals, including the Eucharist. These liturgies grew more slowly in the Christian West, not becoming mandatory among Catholics until 1563, and subject to wide and perennial variation and disputation among Protestants. The Islamic tradition mandated an engagement ceremony, which was a private, religious occasion involving the couple, their families, a cleric, and two or more witnesses. It began with readings from the Qur'an and marital instruction followed by final negotiation of the

17. Kenneth Stevenson, *Nuptial Blessing* (New York: Oxford University Press, 1982), pp. 3-8.

18. Stevenson, *Nuptial Blessing*, pp. 33-122, with samples in Mark Searle and Kenneth W. Stevenson, *Documents of the Marriage Liturgy* (Collegeville, Minn.: Liturgical Press, 1992), pp. 3ff.

terms of the marriage contract, and execution and attestation by the parties. The wedding was a separate and joyous celebration, entirely secular in nature and significance, and optional.[19]

Finally, all three traditions gave husband and wife standing before their religious tribunals to press for the vindication of their marital rights. The rights to support, protection, sexual intercourse, and care for the couple's children were the most commonly litigated claims in all three traditions. But any number of other conjugal rights stipulated in the marriage contract or guaranteed by general religious law could be litigated. Included in all three traditions was the right of the parties to seek dissolution of the marriage on discovery of an absolute impediment to its validity (such as incest) or on grounds of a fundamental breach of the marriage commitment (such as adultery).

Marriage As More Than Contract

The insistence on a marriage liturgy, with its solemn rituals, prayers, blessings, and oaths, is one important indication that, for Jews, Christians, and Muslims, marriage was more than a simple bilateral contract. It was also a fundamental public institution and religious practice. Other media complemented the liturgies in reflecting these higher dimensions of marriage — the beautiful artwork, ornate iconography, and lofty religious language of the marriage contracts themselves; the elaborate rituals and etiquette of courtship, consent, and communal involvement in establishing the new marital household; the impressive production of poems, household manuals, and books of etiquette detailing the proper norms and habits of love, marriage, and parentage of a faithful religious believer. All these media, and the ample theological writings on them, helped to confirm and celebrate the deeper origin, nature, and purpose of marriage in Judaism, Christianity, and Islam.

First, all three traditions recognized that marriage has its ultimate origin in the creation and commandments of God. The Jewish and Christian traditions shared the teaching of Genesis that, already in Paradise, God had brought the first man and the first woman together and commanded them to "be fruitful and multiply" (Gen. 1:28). God had created them as social creatures, naturally inclined and attracted to each other. God had given them the physical capacity to join together and to beget children. God had

19. See chapter by al-Hibri in CM.

commanded them to love, help, and nurture each other and to inculcate in each other and in their children the love of God, neighbor, and self. "Therefore a man leaves his father and mother and cleaves to his wife, and the two become one flesh," Genesis 2:24 concludes. Both the Jewish tradition and the Christian tradition eventually built on this primeval commandment, and its later biblical echoes, many of the basic norms of heterosexual monogamous marriage and sexual ethics.[20]

The Muslim tradition rooted marriage not only in the teachings of the Qur'an but also in the example of Mohammed. The Qur'an speaks of marriage as a "solemn covenant" (mithaquan) (Q. 4.20), indeed a form of worship ('ibadat) and religious observance enjoined upon each Muslim as a way of keeping faith with the tradition of Islam. In the Hadith, the Prophet provided that "marriage is my Sunnah, so the one who turns away from my Sunnah, turns away from me."[21] Also in the Hadith, the Prophet set out in great detail the principles of proper marriage for a Muslim that were elaborated in later books of Islamic law and etiquette.[22] A number of these teachings emulated, if not echoed, Jewish and Christian rules — the requirement of monogamy notably excepted.

Second, all three traditions recognized that marriage is by nature a multidimensional institution, whose formation, maintenance, and dissolution involve a variety of parties besides the couple themselves. Yes, marriage is a contract, formed by the mutual consent of the marital couple, and subject to their wills and preferences. But in all three traditions, marriage is also a spiritual association, subject to the creed, code, cult, and canons of the religious community. Marriage is a social estate, subject to special laws of property and association, and to the expectations and exactions of the local community. Marriage is an economic institution, involving the creation and merger of properties, and triggering obligations of mutual care, nurture, and sacrifice between husband and wife, parent and child. And marriage is a ritual institution, formed through liturgical prayers, oaths, and blessings, and functioning thereafter as a vital site of religious instruction, piety, and worship alongside the synagogue, Church, or mosque.

Third, all three traditions recognized that marriage has inherent goods that lie beyond the preferences of the couple, or the terms of their

20. See illustrative texts from all three traditions in *Eve and Adam: Jewish, Christian, and Muslim Readings on Genesis and Gender*, ed. Kristen E. Kvam, Linda S. Shearing, Valarie H. Zeigler (Bloomington: Indiana University Press, 1999).

21. Quoted in chapter by al-Hibri in CM, at n. 80.

22. See detailed study in chapter by Richard Martin in CM.

marriage contract. Fundamental to all three traditions is the ideal of marriage as the divinely sanctioned means of perpetuating the faith — not only by the couple maintaining their own household rites as vital sites of confessional identity, but also by the couple's procreation and teaching of children who will form the next *Schul,* the next Church, the next *Umma.* Hence the emphasis in all three traditions on avoiding marriage with a nonbeliever.

The emphasis on the procreation and nurture of children in the faith and the corresponding prohibition on interreligious marriage were particularly prominent themes in biblical and diaspora Judaism. These rules were not only fundamental safeguards against assimilation into (an often hostile) gentile culture. They were also essential conditions for the Jewish community to continue to flourish and grow despite its aversion to proselytism.[23] These same emphases on procreation and against intermarriage also emerged among some later Christian and Islamic communities, particularly when they were placed in minority contexts. Think of Catholics in nineteenth-century America, and Muslims and Orthodox in twentieth-century America.

The Christian tradition devised the most elaborate lists of the inherent goods and goals of marriage, beyond the good of producing the next generation of the faithful.[24] Among the most famous formulations was St. Augustine's fifth-century discourse on the marital goods of *fides, proles, et sacramentum.*[25] Marriage, said Augustine, is an institution of *fides* — faith, trust, and love between husband and wife, and between parent and child, that goes beyond the faith demanded of any other temporal relationship. Marriage is a source of *proles* — children who carry on the family name and tradition, perpetuate the human species, and fill God's Church with the next generation of saints. And marriage is a form of *sacramentum* — a symbolic expression of Christ's love for his Church, even a channel of God's grace to sanctify the couple, their children, and the broader community. This trilogy of marital goods became axiomatic in later medieval Catholic theology, and remains at the core of Catholic marriage teaching to this day.

An overlapping formulation, drawn from Roman law and patristic lore, was captured by the early-seventh-century encyclopedist, St. Isidore of

23. See chapters by David Novak and Michael J. Broyde in CM, and also chapters by Novak, Broyde, and Jocelyn Hellig in SB, pp. 17-78.

24. See further Chapter 11 herein.

25. See further Chapters 10 and 11 herein.

Seville. Marriage, Isidore argued, provides husbands and wives with (1) mutual love and support; (2) the mutual procreation and nurture of children; and (3) the mutual protection from sexual sin and temptation. This formula of marital goods confirmed the divine origins of marriage without ascribing to it sacramental status. It also placed greater emphasis on the virtues of marital love and the need for protection from sexual sin alongside the emphasis on procreation. Isidore's trilogy of marital goods eventually became a popular formulation of marital goods among both Orthodox and Protestant Christians, and has strong analogues if not echoes in contemporaneous Islamic tracts on marriage.[26] The Christian tradition, building on Graeco-Roman sources, also emphasized the broader social goods of marriage — teaching that marriage is good not only for the couple and their children, but also for the broader civic communities of which they are a part.[27]

Marriage As Covenant

The idea of covenant is emerging in Western law, theology, and ethics today as a common trope to capture some of these higher dimensions of marriage.[28] It is also emerging as a common term to connect the interreligious dialogue among Jews, Christians, and Muslims and the interdisciplinary dialogue among jurists, theologians, and ethicists about marriage. The connections between these layers of dialogue about marriage and covenant are still developing. But it is no coincidence that the covenant marriage movement in American law has been orchestrated, in ample part, by proponents of a covenantal theology and ethics of marriage.

"Covenant" is a common scriptural term for Jews, Christians, and Muslims alike. It appears 286 times in the Hebrew Bible (as *berit*), 24 times in the New Testament (as *foedus*), 26 times in the Qur'an (as *mithaquan*). "Covenant" has multiple meanings and purposes in these three sacred

---

26. Among the most famous formulations was that developed by the great eleventh-century medieval jurist and theologian, Abu Hamid al-Ghazali (1058-1111), who listed as marital goods: (1) procreation; (2) proper satisfaction of natural sexual desires; (3) love and companionship; (4) efficient ordering of the household; and (5) disciplining oneself. See chapter by Martin in CM.

27. See further Chapter 11 herein.

28. See, e.g., William Johnson Everett, *Religion, Federalism, and the Struggle for Public Life* (New York: Oxford University Press, 1997); Max L. Stackhouse, *Covenant and Commitments: Faith, Family, and Economic Life* (Louisville: Westminster John Knox, 1997).

Scriptures. But it is used most importantly and most frequently to describe the special relationship between Yahweh and Israel, God and his elect, Allah and his chosen ones.

In each of these three Scriptures, "covenant" is also occasionally used to describe marriage. In the Hebrew Bible, Yahweh's special covenantal relationship with Israel is analogized to the special relationship between husband and wife. Israel's disobedience to Yahweh, in turn, particularly its proclivity to worship false gods, is frequently described as a form of "playing the harlot." Idolatry, like adultery, can lead to divorce, and Yahweh threatens this many times, even while calling his chosen to reconciliation. This image comes through repeatedly in the writings of the Prophets: Hosea (2:2-23), Isaiah (1:21-22; 54:5-8; 57:3-10; 61:10-11; 62:4-5), Jeremiah (2:2-3; 3:1-5, 6-25; 13:27; 23:10; 31:32), and Ezekiel (16:1-63; 23:1-49).[29]

The Hebrew Bible also speaks about marriage as a covenant in its own right (Prov. 2:17; Mal. 2:14-16). The Prophet Malachi's formulation is the fullest:

> You cover the LORD's altar with tears, with weeping and groaning because he no longer regards the offering or accepts it with favor at your hand. You ask, "Why does he not?" Because the LORD was witness to the covenant between you and the wife of your youth, to whom you have been faithless, though she is your companion and your wife by covenant. Has not the one God made and sustained for us the spirit of life? And what does he desire? Godly offspring. So take heed to yourselves, and let none be faithless to the wife of his youth. "For I hate divorce, says the LORD the God of Israel, and covering one's garment with violence, says the LORD of hosts. So take heed to yourselves and do not be faithless." (Mal. 2:13-16).

The Qur'an has comparable verses about marriage as a "solemn covenant" *(mithaquan ghalithan)* that cannot be easily broken:

> But if you decide to take one wife in place of another, even if you have given the latter a quintal for dowry, take not the least amount of it back; would you take it by slander and a manifest wrong? And how could

29. See detailed study in Gordon P. Hugenberger, *Marriage As Covenant: A Study of Biblical Law and Ethics Governing Marriage Developed from the Perspective of Malachi* (Leiden: E. J. Brill, 1994).

you take it when you have gone into one another, and they have taken from you a solemn covenant? (Q. 4:20-21).

Jews, Christians, and Muslims alike have long used these kinds of scriptural verses to speak of marriage, inter alia, as a covenant and to encourage the procreation of children and to discourage the practice of easy divorce. This comes through in many theological, pastoral, and liturgical texts already in the first millennium of the common era.[30] What has not been common in these three traditions until more recently is to link explicitly the divine covenant between God and humanity and the marital covenant of husband and wife — in effect to make God a third party to the marriage covenant, and in turn to make marriage a forum for the expression of the divine-human covenant. What also has not been common until recently is to develop a theology and jurisprudence of covenant marriage, a way of describing the higher dimensions of marriage in concrete covenantal terms, and linking those terms to the concrete contractual terms of marriage that all three traditions have long had in place.

In the Jewish and Muslim traditions, the development of a covenant model of marriage is very recent, indeed. David Novak and David Hartman are pioneering the creation of a new covenantal theology, ethic, and law of marriage within Judaism.[31] Azizah al-Hibri is doing the same in the Islamic tradition.[32] What makes their respective efforts so promising is their insistence on grounding their covenantal models of marriage in long-neglected texts of the Hebrew Bible and Talmud and of the Qur'an and Hadith respectively, and rereading and rethinking their own traditions in light of these original canonical texts.

Covenant marriage has a longer pedigree in the Christian tradition. The emerging scholarly consensus is that John Calvin (1509-1564), the

---

30. See examples in the chapters by David Novak, Max Stackhouse, Michael G. Lawler, Stanley Harakas, and James Turner Johnson in CM. See also Stackhouse, *Covenant and Commitments*; Daniel J. Elazar, *Covenant and Commonwealth: From Christian Separation through the Protestant Reformation* (New Brunswick, N.J.: Transaction, 1996); Daniel J. Elazar, *Covenant and Civil Society: The Constitutional Matrix of Modern Democracy* (New Brunswick, N.J.: Transaction, 1998).

31. See chapter by Novak in CM; David Novak, *Covenantal Rights: A Study in Jewish Biblical Theology* (Princeton, N.J.: Princeton University Press, 2000); David Hartman, *A Living Covenant: The Innovative Spirit of Traditional Judaism* (New York: Free Press, 1985); David Hartman, *Mi-Sinai le-Tsiyon: hithadshutah shel berit* (Tel Aviv: 'Am 'oved, 1992).

32. See her chapters in CM and in *Sex, Marriage and Family in the World Religions*.

sixteenth-century Protestant Reformer of Geneva, was the first to develop a detailed covenant model of marriage in place of the prevailing Catholic sacramental theology and canon law of marriage.[33] Much of Calvin's general covenant theology was not new. Calvin expounded the traditional biblical idea of a divine covenant or agreement between God and humanity. He followed conventional Christian teachings in distinguishing two interlocking biblical covenants: (1) the covenant of works whereby the chosen people of Israel, through obedience to God's law, are promised eternal salvation and blessing; and (2) the covenant of grace whereby the elect, through faith in Christ's incarnation and atonement, are promised eternal salvation and beatitude.

Calvin went beyond the tradition, however, in using the doctrine of covenant to describe not only the vertical relationships between God and humanity, but also the horizontal relationships between husband and wife. Just as God draws the elect believer into a covenant relationship with him, Calvin argued, so God draws husband and wife into a covenant relationship with each other. Just as God expects constant faith and good works in our relationship with him, so he expects connubial faithfulness and sacrificial works in our relationship with our spouses.[34] As Calvin put it:

> God is the founder of marriage. When a marriage takes place between a man and a woman, God presides and requires a mutual pledge from both. Hence Solomon in Proverbs 2:17 calls marriage the covenant of God, for it is superior to all human contracts. So also Malachi [2:14-16] declares that God is, as it were, the guarantor [of marriage] who by his authority joins the man to the woman, and sanctions the alliance.[35]

We discussed briefly in Chapter 10 Calvin's belief that God participates in the formation of the covenant of marriage through his chosen

---

33. See sources and discussion in the chapters by Lawler, Martin, and Stackhouse in CM. See elaboration of this thesis in FSC, chap. 3, and in John Witte Jr. and Robert M. Kingdon, *Sex, Marriage, and Family in John Calvin's Geneva*, vol. 1: *Courtship, Engagement, and Marriage* (Grand Rapids: Eerdmans, 2005).

34. See the following writings of Calvin: Comm. Isaiah 1:21-22; 54:5-8; 57:3-10; 61:10-11; 62:4-5 (1551); Serm. Deut. 5:18; 22:22 (1555); Comm. Harm. Gospel Luke 1:34-38 (1555); Comm. Ps. 16:4; 45:8-12; 82:1 (1557); Lect. Hosea 1:1-4; 2:19-20; 3:1-2; 4:13-14; 7:3, 9-10 (1557); Lect. Zech. 2:11; 8:1-2 (ca. 1560); Lect. Mal. 2:13-16 (ca. 1560); Lect. Jer. 2:2-3, 25; 3:1-5, 6-25; 13:27; 23:10; 31:32, 51:4 (1563); Comm. Harm. Law Deut. 11:26-32 (1563); and Lect. Ezek. 6:9, 16:1-63 (1564).

35. Calvin, Lect. Mal. 2:14.

agents on earth. The couple's parents, as God's "lieutenants" for children, instruct the young couple in the mores and morals of Christian marriage and give their consent to the union. Two witnesses, as "God's priests to their peers," testify to the sincerity and solemnity of the couple's promises and attest to the marriage event. The minister, holding "God's spiritual power of the Word," blesses the union and admonishes the couple and the community of their respective biblical duties and rights. The magistrate, holding "God's temporal power of the sword," registers the parties, ensures the legality of their union, and protects them in their conjoined persons and properties. This involvement of parents, peers, ministers, and magistrates in the formation of marriage was not an idle or dispensable ceremony. Because these four parties represented different dimensions of God's involvement in the marriage covenant, they were essential to the legitimacy of the marriage itself. To omit any such party in the formation of the marriage was, in effect, to omit God from the marriage covenant. On this foundation, Calvin worked out in great detail a covenantal theology of the origin, nature, and purpose of marriage and a covenantal law of marital formation, maintenance, and dissolution; spousal rights, roles, and responsibilities; child care, custody, and control; and much more. This was the first comprehensive covenantal model of marriage in the Christian tradition, and it informed the policies of the Genevan Church and state alike.

Calvin may have developed the first covenantal model of marriage, but his was by no means the last. An analogous covenantal model of marriage emerged from the hand of contemporary Zurich Reformer Heinrich Bullinger (1504-1575), whose work was tremendously influential both on the Continent and in England. By the later sixteenth century, the writings of Calvin and Bullinger, separately and together, catalyzed a veritable industry of Protestant covenant theology, jurisprudence, and ethics. These writings on covenant, which crested in seventeenth- and eighteenth-century England and New England, provided a detailed integrated understanding not only of marriage per se, but also of the place of marriage in Church, state, and the broader society.[36] In the last two centuries, covenantal language has also become prominent in Protestant marriage and wedding liturgies. Indeed, today, Protestant liturgies more than Protestant theologies are strongholds for covenant marriage lore.

36. See Chapter 9 herein and David A. Weir, *Early New England: A Covenanted Society* (Grand Rapids: Eerdmans, 2005).

In the Catholic tradition, the Council of Trent closed the door firmly on covenant marriage language in 1563. In its decree *Tametsi,* the Council declared canonical the pervasive medieval teaching that marriage is a sacrament. Heretical Protestant teachings on marriage, including the emerging teaching on covenant marriage in Reformed circles, could henceforth have no place in the Catholic tradition.[37] Four centuries later, however, the Second Vatican Council reopened this door, using the language of covenant as an organizing idiom to describe the origins, nature, and purpose of marriage. In *Gaudium et Spes,* one of the Council's most influential documents, the Vatican Fathers put it thus:

> The intimate partnership of married life and love has been established by the Creator and qualified by His laws. It is rooted in the marriage covenant of irrevocable personal consent. . . . [A] man and a woman, who by the marriage covenant of conjugal love "are no longer two but one flesh" (Mt. 19:6), render mutual help and service to each other through an intimate union of their persons and of their actions. . . . For as God of old made himself present to His people through a covenant of love and fidelity, so now the Savior of men and the Spouse of the Church comes into the lives of married Christians through the sacrament of matrimony.[38]

Since Vatican II, a number of Catholic ethicists, jurists, theologians, and catechists have come to adopt the language of covenant marriage, alongside the traditional language of marriage as sacrament. A number of these same Catholic scholars have used the language of covenant to engage in rigorous ecumenical discussions of the higher dimensions of marriage and to find common cause with Protestants, Jews, and others in pressing reforms of state marriage law.

37. See "Doctrine of the Sacrament of Matrimony," Twenty-Fourth Session (November 11, 1563), in *The Canons and Decrees of the Council of Trent,* trans. H. J. Schroeder (St. Louis: B. Herder, 1941), pp. 180ff.; *Catechism of the Council of Trent for Parish Priests,* trans. John A. McHugh and Charles J. Callan (Rockford, Ill.: Tan, 1982), pp. 338ff. See discussion of occasional pre-Tridentine Catholic references to marriage as covenant in chapter by Lawler in CM.

38. Second Vatican Council, *Gaudium et Spes,* para. 48, in *The Documents of Vatican II,* ed. and trans. Walter M. Abbott and Joseph Gallagher (New York: Guild, 1966). See fuller exposition in Chapter 11 herein.

Concluding Reflections

The Jewish, Christian, and Muslim traditions have long taught that marriage is a contract. Marriage is predicated on the mutual consent of the man and the woman. It is recorded in written instruments. It is celebrated in formal rituals. It triggers exchanges of property. It creates a new legal entity, the marital household, with a complex of new rights and duties between husband and wife, parent and child, couple and state. It grants husband and wife alike the right to press lawsuits to vindicate their marital rights. Contract is the backbone of marriage. It gives marriage its legal structure, stature, and strength.

The Jewish, Christian, and Muslim traditions have also long taught, however, that marriage is more than a mere contract. Marriage is also one of the great mediators of individuality and community, revelation and reason, tradition and modernity. It is at once a harbor of the self and a harbinger of the community, a symbol of divine love and a structure of reasoned consent, an enduring ancient mystery and a constantly modern invention. Marriage is rooted in primeval commands and prophetic examples. It is reflected in religious, ceremonial, social, economic, political, and cultural norms and forms. It is at once private and public, contractual and spiritual, voluntary and natural, psychological and civilizational in origin, nature, and function.

The term "covenant" is emerging today as a convenient and cogent means to capture these higher dimensions of marriage — though this is by no means the only language available. "Covenant" is an ancient trope, with deep roots in Jewish, Christian, and Muslim canonical texts and with ample and diverse expression in the legal traditions that emerged under the influence of these religious traditions. In contemporary American law, "covenant" has the kind of neutrality and plasticity needed to signal that marriage has higher dimensions, even while leaving the definition of these higher dimensions to individual choice and community accent.

While, historically, the Jewish, Christian, and Muslim traditions found ways to reconcile the contractual and covenantal dimensions of marriage, American law today juxtaposes them. In all but three states, parties who wish to marry must choose the state's contract marriage option. Contract marriage has minimal rules of formation and dissolution and hundreds of built-in state and federal rights and duties for the couple and their children. Couples may add rights and duties beyond those defined by the state's contract marriage law. These can be set out in prenuptial contracts negotiated between the parties, or they can be set out in the religious laws and customs of the community of which these marital parties are voluntary members. But, even here, the contractual dimensions of marriage are preferred. Private prenuptial contracts will be enforced by state courts. Religious laws of marriage and divorce will not be enforced — even if the couple's prenuptial contract stipulates that religious law should govern their contract in the event of dispute. New York's *get* statute — which allows an Orthodox Jewish couple to divorce only if their rabbis first give them a Jewish divorce — is a rare and remarkable exception to the usual rules.[39] State courts usually will not enforce religious laws of marriage and divorce, particularly if those religious laws differ from state laws. Religious authorities are thus largely powerless to enforce their religious rulings on marriage against one of their members who sues in state court. They may apply spiritual pressure and sanctions to get a party to comply with their internal religious norms — even shun or excommunicate that party for defying their authority.[40] But if the party persists in the civil suit, the state court will enforce its own state marriage and divorce laws, not those of the religious community. Religious norms and forms of marriage and divorce are subordinate to the state's contract laws of marriage.

This is not altogether true in Louisiana, Arkansas, and Arizona today. In these three states, parties who wish to marry may choose either contract marriage or covenant marriage. The contract marriage option in these three states is largely the same as that available in any other state. The covenant marriage option, however, is unique in that it tightens marital formation and dissolution rules considerably. In particular, covenant marriage requires parties to involve third-party counselors, including the parties' own religious authorities if they are licensed to be counselors. It also requires parties to waive their rights to unilateral no-fault divorce and to accept rules of marital dissolution that are closer to the grounds and procedures traditionally recognized by Jewish, Christian, and Muslim authorities. Covenant marriage laws thus go further than contract marriage laws in reflecting and protecting some of the higher dimensions of marriage. Covenant

---

39. See Michael J. Broyde, *Marriage, Divorce, and the Abandoned Wife in Jewish Law* (New York: Ktav, 2001).

40. See Michael J. Broyde, "Forming Religious Communities and Respecting Dissenters' Rights: A Jewish Tradition for a Modern Society," in RHR I, p. 203.

marriage statutes serve a particularly valuable teaching function — instructing the community on the higher regard that the state has for marriage, instructing the couple of the higher rigor that marriage has for them, instructing religious communities that marriage is more than a mere contract.

It is the state authorities, however, not the religious authorities, who enforce covenant marriages in these three states. As with contract marriage, so with covenant marriage, parties may supplement the rights and duties set out by state law with voluntarily chosen or religiously mandated norms. But the same limitations on the enforceability of these supplementary norms by religious authorities will apply in these three covenant marriage states as prevail in contract marriage states. State formulations of what marriage entails in the individual case will still trump countervailing religious formulations — even if the state is interpreting the meaning of a "covenant" marriage.

Moreover, outside of Louisiana, Arkansas, and Arizona, the state will not even recognize a covenant marriage, only a contract marriage. An estranged spouse can thus escape a covenant marriage simply by moving to and filing for divorce in any of the forty-seven American states or any number of foreign countries without covenant marriage options. Current conflict of laws rules, both domestic and international, do not favor the enforcement of covenant marriage laws over the contract marriage laws of the forum state where the divorce case is litigated. And the trend in many no-covenant states and many foreign nations in the past decade has been to weaken, rather than strengthen, traditional forms and norms of marriage.[41] These unfavorable conflicts rules, though not yet strongly tested through litigation, underscore the reality that covenant marriage laws are an important, but only a partial, legal response to the fallout of the modern revolution of marriage and divorce.

A fuller legal response requires additional strategies of reform and engagement, particularly on the part of religious communities.[42] The first step is for America's religious communities to get their legal and theological houses on marriage and the family in order. They must think more seriously about restoring and reforming their own bodies of religious law on

41. See detailed analysis and sources in chapter by Peter Hay in CM.

42. See various options outlined in Don S. Browning and David Clairmont, introduction to *Families and American Religion: Comparative Family Ethics and Strategies of the Major American Faiths* (New York: Columbia University Press, 2006).

marriage, divorce, and sexuality, instead of simply acquiescing in state laws and culture. American states, in turn, must think more seriously about granting greater deference to the marital laws and customs of legitimate religious and cultural groups that cannot accept a marriage law of the common denominator or denomination. As we have noted, other sophisticated legal cultures — England, India, and South Africa — grant semi-autonomy to Catholic, Hindu, Jewish, Muslim, and other groups to conduct their subjects' domestic affairs in accordance with their own laws and customs, with the state setting only minimum conditions and limits. It might well be time for America likewise to translate its growing cultural pluralism into a more concrete legal pluralism on marriage and family life.[43]

43. See further Chapter 10 herein.

13

The Perils of Clerical Celibacy

The contemporary battles over clerical celibacy and its abuses are nothing new. When mandatory celibacy was first universally imposed on the Catholic clergy in 1123, clergy and laity alike broke into riotous rebellion for more than two generations, and a good number of bishops and priests flouted these laws for several generations more. When the Protestant Reformation broke out in 1517, clerical celibacy and marriage produced some of the most bitter grievances over which the Western Church ultimately splintered. Today, the exposure of child abuse by some Catholic clergy have renewed these ancient battles within Catholicism and between Catholics and Protestants — and triggered all manner of media exposés, private lawsuits, and criminal prosecutions.

In this little chapter, I would like to revisit the original Protestant case against clerical celibacy and for clerical marriage as it emerged in the sixteenth-century Lutheran Reformation. I shall then draw out a few implications of the significance of these historical battles for the theology and law of clerical celibacy and marriage today.

The Case of Johann Apel[1]

We begin with a concrete case. Our case comes from 1523. This is six years after Luther posted his Ninety-Five Theses in Wittenberg, three years after

1. The case is recounted in Theodore Muther, *Doctor Johann Apell. Ein Beitrag zur Geschichte der deutschen Jurisprudenz* (Königsberg: Universitäts- Buch- und Stein-druckerei, 1861), pp. 14ff., 72ff. Excerpts from the pleadings and court records are in-

Luther's excommunication from the Church, and two years after the Diet of Worms. At the time of the case, Luther was back in Wittenberg from the Wartburg Castle. The Lutheran Reformation was gaining real revolutionary momentum in Germany and beyond.

Our case involves a priest and canon lawyer named Johann Apel (1486-1536). Apel was born and raised in Nürnberg, an important German city, still faithful to Rome at the time of the case. In 1514, Apel had enrolled for theological studies at the brand new University of Wittenberg, where he had passing acquaintance with a new professor of theology there, an Augustinian monk named Martin Luther (1483-1546). In 1516, Apel went to the University of Leipzig for legal studies. He was awarded the doctorate of canon law and civil law in 1519. After a brief apprenticeship, Apel took holy orders and swore the requisite oath of clerical celibacy. One of the strong prince-bishops of the day, Conrad, the Bishop of Würzburg and Duke of Francken, appointed Apel as a cathedral canon in 1523. Conrad also licensed Apel as an advocate in all courts in his domain. Apel settled into his pastoral and legal duties.

Shortly after his clerical appointment, Apel began romancing a nun at the nearby St. Marr cloister. (Her name is not revealed in the records.) The couple saw each other secretly for several weeks. They carried on a brisk correspondence. They began a romance. She apparently became pregnant. Ultimately, the nun forsook the cloister and her vows and secretly moved in with Apel. A few weeks later, they were secretly married and cohabited openly as a married couple.

This was an outrage. Clerical concubinage was one thing. The records show that at least three other priests in Conrad's diocese kept concubines and paid Conrad the standard concubinage tax for that privilege. Earlier that very same year of 1523, another priest had fathered a child and paid the Bishop the standard cradle tax and oblated the infant in the very same St. Marr's cloister that Mrs. Apel had just forsaken. Clerical concubinage and even fatherhood were known and were tolerated by some obliging bishops of the day. But clerical marriage was an outrage, particularly when it involved both a priest and a nun — a prima facie case of double spiritual incest.

cluded in *Politische Reichshandel. Das ist allerhand gemeine Acten Regimentssachen und weltlichen Discursen* (Frankfurt am Main: Johan Bringern, 1614), pp. 785-95, and in Johann Apel, *Defensio Johannis Apelli ad Episcopum Herbipolensem pro svo conivgio* (Wittemberge, 1523). The quotes that follow in this section are from these two sources. See also Martin Luther's correspondence about the case in *D. Martin Luthers Werke: Briefwechsel,* 17 vols. (Weimar: H. Böhlaus, 1930-1983), 2:353, 354, 357.

Upon hearing of Apel's enterprising, Bishop Conrad annulled the marriage and admonished Apel to confess his sin, to return his putative wife to her cloister, and to resume his clerical duties. Apel refused, insisting that his marriage, though secretly contracted, was valid. Unconvinced, the Bishop indicted Apel for his crime and temporarily suspended him from office. Apel offered a spirited defense of his conduct in a frank letter to the Bishop.

Bishop Conrad, in response, had Apel indicted in his own bishop's court — for breach of holy orders and the oath of celibacy and for defiance of his episcopal dispensation and injunction. In a written response, Apel adduced conscience and Scripture in his defense, much like Luther had done two years before at the Diet of Worms. "I have sought only to follow the dictates of conscience and the Gospel," Apel insisted, not to defy episcopal authority and canon law. Scripture and conscience condone marriage for fit adults as "a dispensation and remedy against lust and fornication." My wife and I have availed ourselves of these godly gifts and entered and consummated our marriage "in chasteness and love."

Contrary to Scripture, Apel continued, the Church's canon law commands celibacy for clerics and monastics. This introduces all manner of impurity among them. "Don't you see the fornication and the concubinage" in your bishopric, Apel implored Conrad. "Don't you see the defilement and the adultery . . . with brothers spilling their seed upon the ground, upon each other, and upon many a maiden whether single or married?" My alleged sin and crime of breaking "this little man-made rule of celibacy," Apel insisted, "is very slight when compared to these sins of fornication" which you, "excellent father," "cover and condone if the payment is high enough." "The Word of the Lord is what will judge between you and me," Apel declared to the Bishop, "and such Word commands my acquittal."

Bishop Conrad took the case under advisement. Apel took his cause to the budding Lutheran community. He sought support for his claims from Luther, Philip Melanchthon (1497-1560), Martin Bucer (1491-1551), and other Evangelical leaders who had already spoken against celibacy and monasticism. He published his remarks at trial adorned with a robust preface by Luther, and they became an instant best-seller.

Shortly after publication of the tract, Bishop Conrad had Apel arrested and put in the tower, pending further proceedings. Apel's family pleaded in vain with the Bishop to release him. The local civil magistrate twice mandated that Apel be released. Jurists and councilmen wrote letters of support. Even Emperor Charles V (1500-1558) sent a brief letter urging the Bishop not to protract Apel's harsh imprisonment in violation of impe-rial law, but to try him and release him if found innocent. Apel was finally tried. He was found guilty of several violations of the canon law and of he-retically participating in "Luther's damned teachings." He was defrocked and was excommunicated and evicted from the community. Thereafter Apel made his way to Wittenberg, where, at the urging of Luther and oth-ers, he was appointed to the law faculty at the University. Two years later, Apel served as one of the four witnesses to the marriage of ex-monk Martin Luther to ex-nun Katherine von Bora.

This was a sensational, but not an atypical, case in Reformation Ger-many in the 1520s. Among the earliest Protestant leaders were ex-priests and ex-monastics who had forsaken their orders and vows, and often mar-ried shortly thereafter. Indeed, one of the acts of solidarity with the new Protestant cause was to marry or divorce in open violation of the Church's canon law and in open contempt of episcopal instruction. As the Church courts began to prosecute these offenses of canon law, Protestant theolo-gians and jurists rose to the defense of their budding co-religionists.

Classic Arguments for Clerical Celibacy[2]

Bishop Conrad's position in the Apel case was in full compliance with the prevailing Catholic theology and canon law of marriage and celibacy. Prior to the sixteenth century, the Church regarded marriage as "a duty for the sound and a remedy for the sick," in St. Augustine's (354-430) famous phrase. Marriage was a creation of God allowing man and woman to "be fruitful and multiply." Since the fall into sin, marriage had also become a remedy for lust, a channel to direct one's natural passion to the service of the community and the Church. When contracted between Christians, marriage was also a sacrament, a symbol of the indissoluble union between Christ and his Church. As a sacrament, marriage fell within the social hier-archy of the Church and was subject to its jurisdiction.

The Church did not regard marriage as its most exalted estate, how-

2. On this topic, see discussion and sources in Brundage; Roman Cholij, *Clerical Celibacy in East and West* (Leominster: Fowler-Wright, 1989); Elizabeth L. Abbott, *A History of Celibacy* (Toronto: HarperCollins, 1999); Will Deming, *Paul on Marriage and Celibacy: The Hellenistic Background of 1 Corinthians 7* (Cambridge: Cambridge University Press, 1995); Michael Frassetto, ed., *Medieval Purity and Piety: Essays on Medieval Cleri-cal Celibacy and Religious Reform* (New York: Garland, 1998).

ever. Though a sacrament and a sound way of Christian living, marriage was not considered to be so spiritually edifying. Marriage was a remedy for sin, not a recipe for righteousness. Marriage was considered subordinate to celibacy, propagation less virtuous than contemplation, marital love less wholesome than spiritual love. Clerics, monastics, and other servants of the Church were to forgo marriage as a condition for service.

This prohibition on marriage, first universally imposed on clerics and monastics by the First Lateran Council of 1123, was defended with a whole arsenal of complex arguments.[3] The most common arguments were based on St. Paul's statements in 1 Corinthians 7. In this famous passage, Paul did allow that it was better to marry than to burn with lust. But Paul also said that it was better to remain single than to marry or remarry. "It is well for a man not to touch a woman," he wrote. For those who are married "will have worldly troubles." It is best for you to remain without marriage "to secure your undivided attention to the Lord."[4] These biblical passages, heavily glossed by the early Church Fathers, provided endless medieval commentaries on and commendations of celibacy. They were buttressed by newly discovered classical Greek and Roman writings extolling celibacy for the contemplative as well as by the growing medieval celebration of the virginity of Mary as a model for pious Christian living.

Various philosophical arguments underscored the superiority of the celibate clergy to the married laity. It was a commonplace of medieval philosophy to describe God's creation as hierarchical in structure — a vast chain of being emanating from God and descending through various levels and layers of reality down to the smallest particulars. In this great chain of being, each creature found its place and its purpose. Each institution found its natural order and hierarchy. It was thus simply the nature of things that some persons and institutions were higher on this chain of being, some lower. It was the nature of things that some were closer and had more ready access to God, and some were further away and in need of mediation in their relationship with God. Readers of Dante's *Divine Comedy* will recognize this chain of being theory at work in Dante's vast hierarchies of hell, purgatory, and paradise. Students of medieval political theory will recognize this same theory at work in the many arguments of the superiority of the spiritual sword to the temporal sword, of the pope to the emperor, of the Church to the state.[5]

3. Brundage, pp. 221-23.
4. 1 Corinthians 7:1, 28, 32-35.
5. See Chapter 7 herein.

This chain of being theory was one basis for medieval arguments for the superiority of the clergy to the laity. Clergy were simply higher on this chain of being, laity lower. The clergy were called to higher spiritual activities in the realm of grace, the laity to lower temporal activities in the realm of nature. The clergy were thus distinct from the laity in their dress, in their language, and in their livings. They were exempt from earthly obligations, such as paying civil taxes or serving in the military. They were immune from the jurisdiction of civil courts. And they were foreclosed from the natural activities of the laity, such as sex, marriage, and family life. These natural, corporal activities were literally beneath the clergy in ontological status and thus formally foreclosed. For a cleric or monastic to marry or to have sex was thus in a real sense to act against nature *(contra naturam)*.

The Lutheran Position on Celibacy and Marriage[6]

Johann Apel's arguments with Bishop Conrad anticipated a good deal of the Lutheran critique of this traditional teaching of marriage and celibacy. Like their Catholic brethren, the Lutheran Reformers taught that marriage was created by God for the procreation of children and for the protection of couples from sexual sin. But, unlike their Catholic brethren, the Reformers rejected the subordination of marriage to celibacy. We are all sinful creatures, Luther and his followers argued. Lust has pervaded the conscience of everyone. Marriage is not just an option, it is a necessity for sinful humanity. Without it, a person's distorted sexuality becomes a force capable of overthrowing the most devout conscience. A person is enticed by nature to concubinage, prostitution, masturbation, voyeurism, and sundry other sinful acts. "You cannot be without a [spouse] and remain without sin," Luther thundered from his Wittenberg pulpit. You will test your neighbor's bed unless your own marital bed is happily occupied and well used.[7]

"To spurn marriage is to act against God's calling . . . and against nature's urging," Luther continued. The calling of marriage should be declined only by those who have received God's special gift of continence. "Such persons are rare, not one in a thousand [later he said one hundred

6. See discussion and detailed sources in LP, pp. 214ff.; FSC, pp. 47ff.
7. LW 54:31.

thousand] for they are a special miracle of God."[8] The apostle Paul identified this group as the permanently impotent and the eunuchs, Luther
averred; very few others can claim such a unique gift.

This understanding of marriage as a protection against sin undergirded the Reformers' bitter attack on traditional rules of mandatory celibacy. To require celibacy of clerics, monks, and nuns, the Reformers believed, was beyond the authority of the Church and ultimately a source of
great sin. Celibacy was a gift for God to give, not a duty for the Church to
impose. It was for each individual, not for the Church, to decide whether
he or she had received this gift. By demanding monastic vows of chastity
and clerical vows of celibacy, the Church was seen to be intruding on
Christian freedom and contradicting Scripture, nature, and common sense.
By institutionalizing and encouraging celibacy the Church was seen to prey
on the immature and the uncertain. By holding out food, shelter, security,
and economic opportunity, the monasteries enticed poor and needy parents
to oblate their minor children to a life of celibacy, regardless of whether it
suited their natures. Mandatory celibacy, Luther taught, was hardly a prerequisite to true clerical service of God. Instead it led to "great whoredom
and all manner of fleshly impurity and . . . hearts filled with thoughts of
women day and night."[9]

Furthermore, to impute higher spirituality and holier virtue to the
celibate contemplative life was, for the Reformers, contradicted by the Bible. The Bible teaches that each person must perform his or her calling with
the gifts that God provides. The gifts of continence and contemplation are
but two among many, and are by no means superior to the gifts of marriage
and child-rearing. Each calling plays an equally important, holy, and virtuous role in the drama of redemption, and its fulfillment is a service to God.
Luther concurred with the apostle Paul that the celibate person "may better
be able to preach and care for God's word." But, he immediately added, "It
is God's word and the preaching which makes celibacy — such as that of
Christ and of Paul — better than the estate of marriage. In itself, however,
the celibate life is far inferior."[10]

Not only is celibacy no better than marriage, Luther insisted; clergy
are no better than laity. To make this argument cogent, Luther had to counter the medieval chain of being theory that naturally placed celibate clergy

8. LW 28:912, 27-31; LW 45:18-22.
9. LW 12:98.
10. LW 45:47.

above married laity. Luther's answer was his complex theory of the separation of the earthly kingdom and the heavenly kingdom.[11] Luther's teachings, described in Chapter 2, bear repetition here: God has ordained two
kingdoms or realms in which humanity is destined to live, the earthly kingdom and the heavenly kingdom. The earthly kingdom is the realm of creation, of natural and civic life, where a person operates primarily by reason
and law. The heavenly kingdom is the realm of redemption, of spiritual and
eternal life, where a person operates primarily by faith and love. These two
kingdoms embrace parallel forms of righteousness and justice, government
and order, truth and knowledge. They interact and depend upon each other
in a variety of ways. But these two kingdoms ultimately remain distinct.
The earthly kingdom is distorted by sin, and governed by the law. The
heavenly kingdom is renewed by grace and guided by the Gospel. A Christian is a citizen of both kingdoms at once and invariably comes under the
distinctive government of each. As a heavenly citizen, the Christian remains free in his or her conscience, called to live fully by the light of the
Word of God. But as an earthly citizen, the Christian is bound by law, and
called to obey the natural orders and offices of household, state, and
Church that God has ordained and maintained for the governance of this
earthly kingdom.

For Luther, the fall into sin destroyed the original continuity and
communion between the Creator and the creation, the natural tie between
the heavenly kingdom and the earthly kingdom. There was no series of em-
anations of being from God to humanity. There was no stairway of merit
from humanity to God. There was no purgatory. There was no heavenly hierarchy. God is present in the heavenly kingdom, and is revealed in the
earthly kingdom primarily through "masks." Persons are born into the
earthly kingdom, and have access to the heavenly kingdom only through
faith.

Luther did not deny the traditional view that the earthly kingdom
retains its natural order, despite the fall into sin. There remained, in effect, a chain of being, an order of creation that gave each creature, especially each human creature and each social institution, its proper place
and purpose in this life. But, for Luther, this chain of being was horizontal, not hierarchical. Before God, all persons and all institutions in the
earthly kingdom were by nature equal. Luther's earthly kingdom was a
flat regime, a horizontal realm of being, with no person and no institu-

---

11. See LP, pp. 87-117.

tion obstructed or mediated by any other in access to and accountability before God.

Luther thus rejected traditional teachings that the clergy were higher beings with readier access to God and God's mysteries. He rejected the notion that clergy mediated the channel of grace between the laity and God — dispensing God's grace through the sacraments and preaching, and interceding for God's grace by hearing confessions, receiving charity, and offering prayers on behalf of the laity.

Clergy and laity were fundamentally equal before God and before all others, Luther argued, sounding his famous doctrine of the priesthood of all believers.[12] All persons were called to be priests. Luther at once lowered the clergy and elevated the laity, treating the traditional "clerical" office of preaching and teaching as just one of many vocations a Christian could properly choose. He treated all traditional "lay" offices as forms of divine calling and priestly vocation, each providing unique opportunities for service to one's peers. Preachers and teachers in the Church were not exempt from their share of civic duties and civil taxes. And they should participate in earthly activities such as marriage and family life just like everyone else.

This same two kingdoms theory also provided Luther with a new understanding of the place of marriage within this earthly life. For Luther, marriage was one of the three natural estates of the earthly kingdom, alongside the Church and the state, and was essential to the governance of the earthly kingdom. The marital household was to teach all persons, particularly children, Christian values, morals, and mores. It was to exemplify for a sinful society a community of love and cooperation, meditation and discussion, song and prayer. It was to hold out for the Church and the state an example of firm but benign parental discipline, rule, and authority. It was to take in and care for wayfarers, widows, and destitute persons — a responsibility previously assumed largely by monasteries and cloisters.

The marital estate was thus as indispensable an agent in God's redemption plan as the Church. It no longer stood within the orders of the Church but alongside it. Moreover, the marital estate of marriage was as indispensable an agent of social order and communal cohesion as the state. It was not simply a creation of the civil law, but a godly creation designed to aid the state in discharging its divine mandate.

The best example of such an idealized marital household was the lo-

---

12. See further Chapter 2 herein.

cal parsonage, the home of the married Lutheran minister. The Reformers had already argued that pastors, like everyone else, should be married — lest they be tempted by sexual sin, deprived of the joys of marital love, and precluded from the great act of divine and human creativity in having children. Here was an even stronger argument for clerical marriage. The clergy were to be exemplars of marriage. The minister's household was to be a source and model for the right order and government of the local Church, state, and broader community. As Adolf von Harnack once put it, "The Evangelical parsonage, founded by Luther, became the model and blessing of the entire German nation, a nursery of piety and education, a place of social welfare and social equality. Without the German parsonage, the history of Germany since the sixteenth century is inconceivable."[13]

Contemporary Reflections

In one sense, these ancient battles over clerical and monastic celibacy and marriage are a world away from our common experience today. In another sense, they are the stuff of the very latest headlines. The recent media exposure of child abuse by selected Catholic clergy and of clumsy cover-ups by some of their episcopal superiors has resurrected many of these old issues, and redrawn many of the old battle lines between Protestants and Catholics.

It is, of course, easy for us Protestants today to sit back, content with the knowledge that we pointed out the perils of celibacy five hundred years ago, and replaced this odious institution with a happy system of marriage and family life for all. Just turn on CBN, tune in Sunday sermons, or read some Protestant periodicals, and you cannot help but sniff a thick new air of Protestant smugness, sometimes even triumphalism, about our great reforms of marriage and family life. If only those Catholics would follow us.

Before we Protestants become too content with ourselves, however, it is worth remembering that some of these early Protestant marital reforms, however meritorious, were not without their own enduring problems. Yes, the Protestant Reformers did outlaw monasteries and cloisters. But these reforms also ended the vocations of many single women and men, placing a

13. Quoted by Carter Lindberg, "The Future of a Tradition: Luther and the Family," in *All Theology Is Christology: Essays in Honor of David P. Scaer*, ed. Dean O. Wenthe (Fort Wayne, Ind.: Concordia Theological Seminary Press, 2000), pp. 133, 141.

new premium on the vocation of marriage. Ever since, Protestant single women and men have chafed in a sort of pastoral and theological limbo, objects of curiosity and pity, sometimes even suspicion and contempt. These are stigmata which singles still feel today in more conservative Protestant Churches, despite the avalanche of new ministries to help them. Yes, the Protestant Reformers did remove clerics as mediators between God and the laity, in expression of St. Peter's teaching of the priesthood of all believers. But they ultimately interposed husbands between God and their wives, in expression of St. Paul's teaching of male headship within the home. Ever since, Protestant married women have been locked in a bitter struggle to gain fundamental equality both within the marital household and without — a struggle that has still not ended in more conservative Protestant communities today.[14] Add to this the ample evidence of wife and child abuse within traditional Protestant homes — Protestant ministers' homes notably included — and the story is more sober than might be imagined. We Protestants are not without our own institutional sins and shortcomings on matters of sex and marriage. We would do well to stop throwing stones at Catholics and to start bringing bricks to help in the reconstruction of a better Christian understanding of sex, marriage, and family life.

That said, it must also be said that there seems to be something gravely amiss with the American Catholic Church's insistence on maintaining mandatory clerical celibacy — despite the mounting evidence of homosexual and heterosexual abuses among its clergy, and despite the rapid dwindling of eligible novates within its seminaries. There is something strangely anomalous with a hierarchy that will ordain married Anglican and Orthodox priests who convert to Catholicism to fill its vacant parishes, yet deny Catholic priests and novates any such marital option.

To be sure, the First Amendment free exercise clause mandates that the Catholic hierarchy be free to conduct its internal affairs without interference by the state. And to be sure, this constitutional protection frees the Church to find its own internal resources to repeat, repair, or replace its rules of clerical celibacy as it sees fit. The First Amendment is one of our most cherished freedoms, which protects popular and unpopular religious practices alike.

But the First Amendment does not license violations of the life and

---

14. See David Blankenhorn, Don S. Browning, Mary Stewart van Leeuwen, eds., *Does Christianity Teach Male Headship? The Equal Regard Marriage and Its Critics* (Grand Rapids: Eerdmans, 2004).

limb of another, and does not protect corporate complicity and conspiracy. Child abuse is a very serious felony that the modern criminal law now punishes severely. And even mutually consensual sexual contact with a minor is a strict liability offense called statutory rape. Religious and secular clergy who engage in such sexual acts with minors must be aggressively prosecuted and must be severely punished if found guilty after receiving full due process. Bishops who harbor and hide such sex felons are accomplices after the fact and are just as guilty under modern criminal law as the sexual perpetrator himself. Church corporations who conspire in such subterfuge invite serious charges of corporate criminality and corruption.

The American Church hierarchy today needs to stop hiding behind constitutional walls and sacramental veils and take firm public responsibility for its actions and omissions — ministering first and foremost to the abused victims and their families, exposing and evicting the clerical sex felons and accomplices within their midst, and getting on with their cardinal callings of preaching the Word, administering the sacraments, catechizing the young, and caring for the needy. In medieval centuries past, the Church and its clergy may have been above the law of the state, and thus privileged to deal with such clerical abuses by their own means, in their own courts, at their own pace. No longer. "Privilege of forum" and "benefit of clergy" have been dead letters in this country for more than a century. Clergy are not above the law. They should exemplify its letter and its spirit. The Church is not above the state. It should set a model of justice and equity.

Few issues are as sublime and serious today as those involving sex and sexuality. Few crimes are as scarring as rape and child abuse. To rape a child is to destroy a child. To abuse a child is to forfeit one's office. No cleric found guilty of child abuse can continue in office. No Christian Church found complicit in child abuse is worthy of its name. Bureaucratic wrangling and political lobbying are no way for the Church to respond to recent events. Repentance, restitution, and reformation are the better course.

14

Ishmael's Bane:
The Sin and Crime of Illegitimacy Reconsidered

Sex has long excited an intimate union between law and religion in the Christian West. Western Churches and states have long collaborated in setting private laws to define and facilitate licit sex — rules and procedures for sexual etiquette, courtship, and betrothal, for marital formation, maintenance, and dissolution, for conjugal duties, debts, and desires, for parental roles, rights, and responsibilities, and much more. Western Churches and states have also long collaborated in setting criminal laws to deter and punish illicit sex. For many centuries, these two powers kept overlapping rolls of sexual sin and crime — adultery and fornication, sodomy and buggery, incest and bestiality, bigamy and polygamy, prostitution and pornography, abortion and contraception, and more. They also operated interlocking tribunals to enforce these rules on sex. The Church guarded the internal forum through its canons, confessionals, and consistory courts. The state guarded the external forum through its policing, prosecution, and punishment of sexual crimes. To be sure, Church and state officials clashed frequently over sexual jurisdiction. And their respective private and criminal laws of sex did change a great deal — dramatically in the fourth, twelfth, and sixteenth centuries. But for all this rivalry and change, Christianity, and the Hebrew, Greek, and Roman sources on which it drew, had a formative influence on Western laws of sex.[1]

Most of these classic laws have now been eclipsed in America and the rest of the West by the dramatic rise of new public laws and popular customs of sexual liberty. Courtship, cohabitation, betrothal, and marriage are now mostly private sexual contracts with few roles for Church and state to

---

1. See further Chapters 10 and 11 herein.

play and few restrictions on freedoms of entrance, exercise, and exit. Classic crimes of contraception and abortion have been found to violate Fourteenth Amendment liberties. Classic prohibitions on adultery and fornication have become dead or discarded letters on most statute books. Free speech laws protect all manner of sexual expression, short of outrageous obscenity. Constitutional privacy laws protect all manner of sexual conduct, short of exploitation of children or abuse of others. Only the classic prohibitions on incest, polygamy, and homosexuality remain on most law books — now the subjects of bitter constitutional battles and culture wars.

One tender sexual subject has hovered perennially on the margins of law and religion scholarship and on the boundaries of criminal, private, and public law. That is the subject of illegitimacy or bastardy. In the Western tradition, the bastard was defined as a child born out of lawful wedlock — a product of fornication, adultery, concubinage, incest, or other sexual crime and sin. A bastard was at once a child of no one (*filius nullius*) and a child of everyone (*filius populi*) — born without name and without home, the perennial object of both pity and scorn, charity and abuse, romance and ribaldry. Absent successful legitimation, bastards bore the permanent stigma of their sinful and criminal status, signaled on certificates of baptism, confirmation, marriage, and death. They lived in a sort of legal limbo — with some claims to charity and support but with severely truncated rights to inherit or devise property, to hold high clerical, political, or military office, to sue or testify in certain courts, and more. These formal legal disabilities on bastards were often compounded by chronic poverty, neglect, and abuse — assuming that the infants had escaped the not uncommon historical practice of being secretly smothered or exposed upon birth, or put out to nurse or lease with modest odds of survival.[2]

Illegitimacy doctrine has been a common feature of most legal and religious traditions of the world. It has long been part of a common effort to regulate the scope of the paterfamilias's power and responsibility within the household, and to regularize inheritance of property, title, lineage, and (in

---

2. Mark Jackson, *New-Born Child Murder: Women, Illegitimacy, and the Courts in Eighteenth-Century England* (Manchester: Manchester University Press, 1996), pp. 29-48; T. E. James, "The Illegitimate and Deprived Child: Legitimation and Adoption," in *A Century of Family Law: 1857-1957*, ed. Ronald H. Graveson and F. R. Crane (London: Sweet and Maxwell, 1957), pp. 39-55; Lionel Rose, *The Massacre of the Innocents: Infanticide in Britain 1800-1939* (London: Routledge and Kegan Paul, 1986); Mason P. Thomas, "Child Abuse and Neglect. Part I: Historical Overview, Legal Matrix, and Social Perspectives," *North Carolina Law Review* 50 (1972): 293-349.

some cultures) control of the household religion or the family's ancestral rites.[3]

In the Western tradition, illegitimacy was given special support by Christian theology. Illegitimacy doctrine was a natural concomitant of the Church's attempts to shore up marriage as the only licit forum for sex and procreation. Illegitimacy doctrine was also viewed as an apt illustration and application of the biblical adage that "the sins of the fathers [and mothers] shall be visited upon their children."[4] The Bible itself seemed to condone this reading in its story of Ishmael, the illegitimate son of Abraham who was condemned already in the womb as a "wild man" and was ultimately cast out of his home with minimal prospects of survival. Later biblical laws banned bastards and their seed from the house of the Lord if not from the community altogether. The New Testament equated bastards with those stubborn souls who refused to accept the life and liberty of the Gospel. Christian theologians and jurists alike found in these biblical passages ample new legitimacy for the doctrine of illegitimacy. The doctrine found a prominent place in canon law, civil law, and common law alike from the twelfth to the twentieth centuries.

Illegitimacy doctrine, however, runs counter to a number of standard criminal law doctrines that Christian theology also helped to cultivate. Illegitimacy is an unusual kind of status offense that, by definition, forgoes required proof of actus reus, mens rea, and causation. Illegitimacy doctrine is an unusual form of deterrence that threatens harm to an innocent third party in order to dissuade a couple from committing various sexual crimes. And illegitimacy is a peculiar species of vicarious liability, a sort of *respondeat inferior* doctrine that imposes upon innocent children some of the costs of their parents' extramarital experimentation.

To be sure, a good deal of the classic law of illegitimacy is now falling aside in the United States. Most states have removed the most chronic disabilities on the illegitimate's rights to property, support, and standing. Several remaining legal disabilities on illegitimates have been struck down in a

---

3. See generally John C. Ayer Jr., "Legitimacy and Marriage," *Harvard Law Review* 16 (1902): 22-42; Shirley Hartley, *Illegitimacy* (Berkeley: University of California Press, 1975); Peter Laslett et al., eds., *Bastardy and Its Comparative History: Studies in the History of Illegitimacy and Marital Non-Conformism in Britain, France, Germany, Sweden, North America, Jamaica, and Japan* (Cambridge, Mass.: Harvard University Press, 1980); Bronislaw Malinowski, *Sex, Culture, and Myth* (New York: Harcourt, Brace and World, 1962).

4. Cf. Exodus 20:5; 34:7; Numbers 14:18; Deuteronomy 5:9.

series of cases since 1968 as violations of the equal protection clause of the Fourteenth Amendment.

But what the Fourteenth Amendment gives with one clause it takes back with another. The Fourteenth Amendment equal protection clause does spare illegitimates from vicarious liability for their parents' extramarital experimentation. But the Fourteenth Amendment due process clause spares sexually active adults criminal liability for engaging in extramarital experimentation. With the legal stigma of both illegitimacy and promiscuity removed, it is perhaps no accident that illegitimacy rates in this country have soared. While illegitimate children no longer suffer many formal legal disabilities, they continue to suffer ample social disabilities in the form of higher rates of poverty and poor education, deprivation and child abuse, juvenile delinquency and criminal conduct. Moreover, I shall argue, a new species of *in utero* illegitimates has emerged in the past three decades, condemned even more severely by the very same Fourteenth Amendment that protects the rights of their mothers.

This chapter offers some preliminary research and reflection on the theology and law of illegitimacy. The first part of the chapter sketches a bit of the biblical context and sanction for this doctrine. The second part summarizes the classic canon law and common law on the subject, and some of the recent legal reforms in the United States. The final section offers some critical theological reflections on the doctrine of illegitimacy, and suggests a few historically informed remedies that might be applied to better the plight of the illegitimate today.

Biblical Sources and Sanctions of Illegitimacy

The Christian doctrine of illegitimacy was born in the biblical story of Ishmael, the bastard son of the great patriarch Abraham. The facts, as recorded in the Book of Genesis, are these: At seventy-five years of age, Abraham, a rich and powerful man, grew concerned about his lineage and legacy. He complained to God that he and his wife Sarah were without child. God promised him an heir and countless descendents.[5] But for ten years thereafter he had no children.[6] A concerned Sarah urged Abraham to take her slave maid Hagar as a concubine, and have children by her. Abraham obliged. Hagar conceived.

5. Genesis 15:1-6.
6. Genesis 16:3, 16.

Newly pregnant, Hagar "looked with contempt" upon Sarah, her barren mistress.[7] Sarah was livid. She "dealt harshly" with Hagar, who fled.

An angel enjoined Hagar to return. The angel promised that her child would survive and indeed have many descendents. But the angel also spoke ominously of the bane that would befall her bastard child: "Behold, you are with child, and shall bear a son; you shall call his name Ishmael [meaning "God hears"]; because the LORD has given heed to your affliction. [But] [h]e shall be a wild ass of a man, his hand against every man and every man's hand against him; and he shall dwell over against all his kinsmen."[8]

Ishmael was born and raised in Abraham's household. Abraham embraced him as his first-born son, and circumcised him to signify him as one of God's own.[9] Fifteen years later, however, Abraham and Sarah were miraculously blessed with the birth of their own son Isaac.[10] Sarah grew jealous of the adolescent Ishmael playing with her newly weaned son Isaac. She grew concerned about Isaac's claims to Abraham's vast wealth. "Cast out this slave woman with her son," she enjoined Abraham; "for the son of this slave woman will not be heir with my son Isaac."[11] After anguished reflection and prayer, Abraham obliged Sarah, contrary to his own affection for Ishmael and to the custom of the day that a master care for his slaves and their children, however conceived.

Abraham sent Hagar and Ishmael away into the desert, meagerly armed with food and water. Their provisions ran out. Ishmael grew weak. His mother cast him under a bush, walked away, and sat with her back to him, not wishing to hear or see him die. Ishmael cried. The angel returned to Hagar, his mother, and proclaimed: "Fear not; for God has heard the voice of the lad where he is. Arise, lift up the lad, and hold him fast with your hand; for I will make him a great nation."[12] Miraculously, Hagar found a water well and saved Ishmael. Ishmael grew up to be a skilled huntsman and warrior. His mother later found him a wife from among her kin. Ishmael fathered twelve (legitimate) sons who became princes of the tribes of the ancient Middle East.[13] He received no inheritance, but joined his

---

7. Genesis 16:4. All biblical quotations in this essay are taken from the Revised Standard Version of the Bible.

8. Genesis 16:11-12.

9. Genesis 17:23.

10. Genesis 17:1; 21:5.

11. Genesis 21:8-10.

12. Genesis 21:17-18.

13. Genesis 25:12-18; cf. Galatians 4:24-25.

half-brother Isaac in burying their father Abraham.[14] Ishmael lived a full life and died at 137 years.[15] Thus far the facts as reported in the Book of Genesis.

The ambiguous moral lessons of this story of Ishmael are echoed later in the Christian Bible and Apocrypha. On the one hand, both the Old and New Testaments describe God as One who hears the cries and tends the needs of the "poor" and "fatherless," just as he heard and tended Ishmael. God's people are repeatedly enjoined to do likewise for the bastards and orphans in their midst.[16]

But these quiet biblical refrains on charity are almost drowned out by the robust biblical orchestrations denouncing bastards and bastardy. The Mosaic law precluded illegitimates and their progeny from the priesthood, if not from corporate worship altogether: "No bastard *[mamzer]* shall enter the assembly of the LORD," Deuteronomy provides; "even to the tenth generation none of his descendants shall enter the assembly of the LORD."[17] The Book of Ecclesiasticus imposed on the children of the adulteress vicarious liability for the sins of their mother: "She herself will be brought before the assembly, and punishment will fall on her children. Her children will not take root, and her branches will not bear fruit. She will leave her memory for a curse, and her disgrace will not be blotted out."[18] The Wisdom of Solomon struck an even more threatening tone for illegitimates: "[C]hildren of adulterers will not come to maturity, and the offspring of an unlawful union will perish. Even if they live long they will be held of no account, and finally their old age will be without honor. . . . For children born of unlawful unions are witnesses of evil against their parents when God examines them."[19]

The New Testament went further and labeled as bastards *(nothos)* all those who reject the Gospel's promise of Christian freedom from the law and sin. The legitimate children of Abraham are those who accept the Gospel. The illegitimate children of Abraham are those who stubbornly cling to the law, notably the Jews.[20] Legitimates are free Christians whose lives are filled with promise. Bastards are enslaved non-Christians whose lives are without hope — and who accordingly live as the "wild man"

14. Genesis 25:9.
15. Genesis 25:17.
16. Job 29:12; Isaiah 1:17; Jeremiah 5:28; James 1:27.
17. Deuteronomy 23:2.
18. Sirach 23:24-26.
19. Wisdom of Solomon 3:16-17; 4:6.
20. John 8:31-59; Hebrews 12:8.

Ishmael and need to be curtailed if not cast out. St. Paul captured this new variation on the Ishmael story in a jarring message to the new Christians in Galatia who insisted on continued adherence to the Mosaic law:

> Tell me, you who desire to be under law, do you not hear the law? For it is written that Abraham had two sons, one by a slave [Hagar] and one by a free woman [Sarah]. But the son of the slave was born according to the flesh, the son of the free woman through promise. Now this is an allegory: these women are two covenants. One is from Mount Sinai, bearing children for slavery; she is Hagar. Now Hagar is Mount Sinai in Arabia; she corresponds to the present Jerusalem, for she is in slavery with her children. But the Jerusalem above is free. . . . Now we, brethren, like Isaac, are children of promise. But as at that time he who was born according to the flesh persecuted him who was born according to the Spirit, so it is now. But what does the Scripture say? "Cast out the slave and her son; for the son of the slave shall not inherit with the son of the free woman." So, brethren, we are not children of the slave, but of the free woman.[21]

This passage would become a *locus classicus* for all manner of later Christian theories and practices of illegitimacy, as well as anti-Semitism.

A Primer on the Western Law of Illegitimacy

While the Western Christian doctrine of illegitimacy was born in the Bible, it was raised in Christian theology and jurisprudence. The juxtaposed biblical passages on illegitimacy have inspired nearly two millennia of biblical commentaries, and their basic moral judgments have passed into the canon law of the Church, the civil law of the Continent, and the common law of England and America.

Classic Canon Law

On the one hand, Christian theologians and jurists have long sought to heed the cries of the Ishmaels of the world and to offer them comfort, char-

---

21. Galatians 4:21-31.

ity, and kindness.[22] For example, the early Church Fathers and Church councils condemned the classic Roman law that gave the paterfamilias the power of life and death over his offspring, and that paid little heed to the smothering and abandonment of bastards born in his household — practices which later Christian emperors outlawed, at least with respect to children of wives and concubines. By the fifth century, the Church's canon law grouped bastards with widows, orphans, and the poor as those *personae miserabiles* who deserved special care and charity from the Church.[23] By the twelfth century, bastards were given special standing in Church courts to sue for paternal support from indifferent or recalcitrant fathers.[24] Bastards were also common oblates in medieval Catholic monasteries, ecclesiastical guilds, foundling houses, and cathedral schools.[25] From the sixteenth century onward, they were also among those especially eligible for gratis matriculation in Protestant schools and guilds where they received room, board, education, and vocational training.[26]

On the other hand, medieval Christian theologians and moralists treated illegitimacy as a particularly good case for effectuating the biblical maxim that "the sins of the fathers [and mothers] shall be visited upon their children." The sins of Abraham were adultery and concubinage. The sins of Sarah were contempt for God's promises and complicity in Abraham's adultery, as well as jealousy, cruelty, and greed. Ishmael bore vicarious liability for both sets of sins. There were many sins like those of Abraham and Sarah that should be treated comparably when they produced illegitimate fruit, medieval writers insisted. These included: (1) bodily sins, such as fornication, concubinage, prostitution, and incest; (2) faithless sins, such as breaches of vows of abstinence, chastity, betrothal, or marriage; or (3) spiritual sins of marrying one outside the faith or in viola-

22. John Boswell, *The Kindness of Strangers: The Abandonment of Children in Western Europe from Late Antiquity to the Renaissance* (New York: Pantheon, 1988), pp. 58-59, 72-73, 145, 150-53.

23. Brian Tierney, *Medieval Poor Law: A Sketch of Canonical Theory and Its Application in England* (Berkeley: University of California Press, 1959); Gilles Couvreur, *Les pauvres ont-ils des droits?* (Rome: Libraria editrice dell'Universita Gregoriana, 1961), pp. 37-39.

24. R. H. Helmholz, "Bastardy Litigation in Medieval England," *American Journal of Legal History* 13 (1969): 360-83; R. H. Helmholz, "Support Orders, Church Courts, and the Rule of Filius Nullius: A Reassessment of the Common Law," *Virginia Law Review* 63 (1977): 431-48.

25. Boswell, *The Kindness of Strangers,* pp. 222-23, 302-4.

26. LP, chap. 7.

tion of the Church's rules for marital formation. Children born of all such sins were presumptively the new Ishmaels of the world, and presumptively subject to the same stigma and disabilities imposed on the Ishmael of old.[27]

The Church refined its law of bastardy as it refined its law of marriage. The formative era was the twelfth through fifteenth centuries when the Church reached the height of its political and legal power, and established Church courts through Western Christendom to implement its canon laws.[28] In this formative period, the canon law came to treat marriage systematically as at once a natural, contractual, and spiritual institution, created by God to produce children, to foster faithfulness among spouses, and to sanctify the couple, their children, and the broader Christian community. As a natural association, marriage was created by God to enable man and woman to "be fruitful and multiply" and to raise children together in the service and love of God. As a contract, marriage was a binding contractual unit, formed by the mutual consent of the parties. This contract prescribed for couples a life-long relation of love, service, and devotion to each other and to their natural children. As a sacrament, marriage symbolized the eternal union between Christ and his Church. Participation in this sacrament conferred sanctifying grace upon the couple and their children. Children born of such Christian unions were the saints of the next generation, to be baptized, catechized, and confirmed in the Christian Church, and nurtured, educated, and socialized in the Christian home.[29]

The canon law of illegitimacy was grounded in this newly systematized understanding of marriage. Marriage was the proper and licit place for a Christian to pursue sex and procreation. Sexual intercourse outside of marriage was a serious crime and sin. The natural father and mother were best suited by nature to care for their own children, and in turn to be cared for by them when they grew old and weak. Unnatural relations between parents and children often would not endure nor produce the enduring mutual care that was essential to stable domestic welfare. Blood ties between parents and children were an essential natural foundation for an enduring Christian family.

From these premises, the canon lawyers created a hierarchy of illegit-

27. Ludwig Schmugge et al., eds., *Illegitimität im Spätmittelalter* (Munich: R. Oldenbourg Verlag, 1994).

28. Brundage; Charles J. Reid Jr., *Power over the Body, Equality in the Family: Rights and Domestic Relations in Medieval Canon Law* (Grand Rapids: Eerdmans, 2004).

29. FSC, chap. 1, and Chapters 10 and 11 herein.

imate children.[30] The first and least stigmatized class consisted of "natural illegitimates" born of concubinage or prenuptial sex between fiancées, or, somewhat worse, born of fornication or prostitution by their parents. These children could be legitimated by the subsequent marriage of their parents — though their parents could face severe sanctions for their sexual sin, particularly if they were recidivists.

The second class was those "unnatural illegitimates" born of the innocent sexual crimes of their parents. These were usually children born of a Christian couple who had married in good faith, then had sex and children, but later discovered a blood or family tie between them that rendered their marriage incestuous. Such children could be legitimated if the impediment to their parents' marriage was dispensed.

The third, and worst off, class was those "intentionally unnatural illegitimates" born to parents who had knowingly committed incest or adultery. Such children were permanently condemned to illegitimacy because they were born "not only against the positive law, but against the express natural law."[31] Their parents could never marry, given the continued ties of incest between them or the prior indissoluble marriage that their adultery had betrayed. Also irredeemable from bastardy were children born of bigamy or breached oaths of chastity or celibacy. In each of these cases, one or both parents had precontracted to another marriage or to a life of chastity. Such parents, too, could never be married and thereby legitimate their now illegitimate children. Having made one set of unbreakable vows, they could not make another in a new marriage. Their children were permanently condemned as bastards.

At canon law, bastards were generally barred from the Church's higher religious orders and offices, in emulation of the Deuteronomic law. In firmer decades and dioceses, bastards were also barred from sexual and marital relations, so that their dishonorable seed would die out as Ecclesiasticus and Wisdom had foretold. Canon law did allow for a child's legitimation through papal dispensation, but this was a rare prize reserved principally for well-heeled and well-connected royals and aristocrats.[32]

---

30. Robert Généstal, *Histoire de la légitimation des infantes naturales en droit canonique* (Paris: E. Lourex, 1905); R. H. Helmholz, "Bastardy Litigation in Medieval England."

31. Thomas Aquinas, ST, Supp. q. 68, art 1.

32. See Généstal, *Histoire de la légitimation.*

Classic Common Law

A parallel law of illegitimacy emerged at English common law. The canon law dealt with spiritual sanctions for the sexual sin of the parents and the pastoral care and control of their illegitimate child. The common law dealt with criminal punishment of the parents' sexual crime and the civil status and sanctions of their illegitimate child. Before the sixteenth century, these two laws of illegitimacy remained separate — jealously so in cases involving paternity and family property disputes. After the sixteenth-century Protestant Reformation, the two laws of illegitimacy began to merge slowly in England. Much of the canon law on the subject was ultimately absorbed into the early modern common law. It was the merged system taught by the English common lawyers that came to prevail in the American colonies and the young American states, often amply adapted to local conditions and customs.

At classic common law, a child was considered illegitimate if "born out of lawful wedlock." Illegitimate were children born where there was no wedlock altogether — products of the crimes of fornication *(filii)*, concubinage *(spurii)*, prostitution *(mamzeres)*, or adultery *(nothi)*.[33] Illegitimate, too, were children born of putative marriages that were subsequently found to be unlawful and were annulled by reason of innocent or knowing bigamy or intentional incest.[34] Both English and American common law dropped the category of illegitimates born of breached vows of chastity or celibacy. American common law added a category of illegitimates born of miscegenation (sex between whites and blacks).

The common law, like the canon law, devised endless subclassifications among these illegitimate children. The most important distinctions turned on the severity of the sexual crime of the parents. Children born of adultery, or of intentional incest or bigamy (and, in America before 1865, miscegenation), were the worst off, for these children were products of serious felonies. They faced the most stringent treatment, and their parents faced criminal sanctions of fine, imprisonment, or banishment — and, in

---

33. John Brydall, *Lex Spuriorum, or the Law Relating to Bastardy* (London: Atkins, 1703), pp. 4-14. For detailed discussion of early modern English common law categories and Deuteronomic and Jewish law, see John Selden, *De Successionibus ad leges Ebraeorum in bona defunctorum* (Frankfurt an Oder, 1673), pp. 10-17.

34. Matthew Bacon, *A New Abridgement of the Law* (London: A. Strathan, 1798), s.v. "Bastardy"; Richard Adair, *Courtship, Illegitimacy and Marriage in Early Modern England* (Manchester: Manchester University Press, 1996).

serious cases of recidivism, execution. The common law, like the English canon law, rejected the civil law of adoption as a means of legitimating one's own or another's illegitimate children.[35] At the same time, common law made escape from bastardy nearly impossible, save through procurement of a private act of Parliament or, in America, of the colonial or state legislature.

The common law diverged from the canon law at two crucial points, however, both to the further detriment of the bastard. First, at canon law, the post hoc marriage of the parents of a "natural illegitimate" child automatically legitimated the child, rendering it subject to its father's support, protection, authority, education, and inheritance.[36] At common law, no such legitimation could occur. A child born before his parents married remained illegitimate even if his parents subsequently married.[37] "Shotgun" weddings between conception and birth legitimated the child, but post-birth weddings were of no avail.

Second, at canon law, illegitimate children could sue in Church courts for the support of their mothers and fathers, particularly if the parents were well-heeled. At common law, illegitimate children had no right to their parents' support, and their parents had no duty to deliver the same.[38] This harsh common law rule was slowly changed by the new English poor law of 1576 that empowered local justices of the peace to compel parents to support their illegitimate children who lived in the local parish and were dependent upon the parish Church's charity.[39] But this English poor law reform was of no use for religious dissenters in England and had little place in America. Indeed, the harsh common law of no parental support for bastards persisted on the American law books until well into the twentieth century.

Illegitimate children faced several other disabilities at both English

35. James, "The Illegitimate and Deprived Child"; Jamil S. Zainaldin, "The Emergence of a Modern American Family Law: Child Custody, Adoption, and the Courts, 1796-1851," *Northwestern Law Review* 73 (1979): 1038-89.

36. Helmholz, "Bastardy Litigation in Medieval England," pp. 362-65; Bacon, *A New Abridgement of the Law,* s.v. "Bastardy."

37. William Blackstone, *Commentaries on the Law of England,* ed. Thomas H. Cooley (Chicago: Callaghan, 1884), bk. 1, chap. 16, p. 460.

38. James Kent, *Commentaries on American Law,* 2 vols. (New York: O. Halsted, 1827), 2:173-79; Richard Burn, *Ecclesiastical Law,* sixth ed., 4 vols. (London: A. Strathan, 1797), 1:242-50.

39. Helmholz, "Support Orders, Church Courts, and the Rule of Filius Nullius," pp. 446-48.

and American common law. Lacking the honor of legitimate birth, they were formally precluded from various honorable positions, particularly high political, military, admiralty, and judicial offices, as well as service as coroners, jurors, prison wardens, Church wardens, parish vestrymen, or comparable positions of social visibility and responsibility. However well-propertied they became, bastards were also often denied access to local polls, clubs, schools, learned societies, and licensed professions. However well qualified they might be, they were also formally precluded from ordination in the established Church of England.[40]

While most of these social disabilities had fallen into desuetude by the turn of the nineteenth century, various testamentary disabilities persisted firmly at common law. As a "child of everyone" (filius populi), the bastard could receive alms and other forms of public charity. But as a "child of no one" (filius nullius), the bastard had no inheritable and devisable blood that the common law would recognize. Bastards could thus inherit nothing from parents, siblings, or from anyone else — whether name, property, title, honor, business, license, charter, or other devisable private or public claim or good.[41] American state laws extended this disability specifically to prohibit bastards from claiming wrongful death damages in tort, life or residual disability insurance proceeds, social security benefits, military benefits, and other such proceeds that were earmarked generically for the children of a deceased or disabled parent. Several states further prohibited or taxed private inter vivos gifts to bastards, and denied or impeded their standing in probate courts to sue for legacies from their intestate natural parents.[42]

Illegitimate children, in turn, were limited in their capacities to alienate or devise their own property. The estates of childless bastards, or of those who died intestate or with defective wills, were seized by officials upon their deaths. Even those illegitimates who donated or devised their property to surviving spouses or children by proper instruments were sometimes subject to special gift and inheritance taxes imposed by authorities on both sides of the Atlantic.[43]

40. Brydall, Lex Spuriorum, pp. 15-34; John Godolphin, Reportorium Canonicum (London: Assigns of R. and E. Atkins, 1687), pp. 86-87, 279-80; Burn, Ecclesiastical Law, pp. 244-45; John Selden, Opera Omnia tam edita quam inedita, 3 vols. (London: Guil. Bower, 1726), 3:209, 1335-36.

41. Blackstone, Commentaries, bk. 1, chap. 16.

42. Chester Garfield Vernier, American Family Laws, 5 vols. (Stanford: Stanford University Press, 1938), s.v. "Bastardy or Illegitimacy."

43. Bacon, A New Abridgement of the Law, s.v. "Bastardy."

These common law disabilities on illegitimates were considered necessary to protect licit marriage and to deter illicit sex. It was a commonplace of Anglo-American common law until the twentieth century that traditional marriage was a "Godly ordinance," "a sacred obligation," "a public institution of universal concern," "the very basis of the whole fabric of civilized society."[44] It was an equal commonplace that Christianity — including the Bible's commandments not to commit adultery, fornication, prostitution, incest, and other sexual sins and crimes — was part of the common law. Illegitimacy doctrine was part and product of these Christian common law beliefs — a way for the law to symbolize proper family values and to scapegoat sexual sin at once. An Ohio judge put it thus in a 1961 case: "It might perhaps be mentioned that the Decalog, which is the basis of our moral code, specifically states that the sins of the father may be visited upon the children unto the third and fourth generation, so that the argument against making the children suffer for the mother's wrong can be attacked on ethical grounds."[45] Another authority defended the formal legal disabilities on illegitimates with these words in 1939: "The bastard, like the prostitute, thief, and beggar, belongs to that motley crowd of disreputable social types which society has generally resented, always endured. He is a living symbol of social irregularity, and undeniable evidence of contramoral forces."[46]

Modern American Reforms

Neither moral stigmatization nor legal disability, however, proved enough to deter the conception of illegitimate children. Illegitimacy rates in Europe and America — while subjects of endless debate among demographers — have, by all accounts, risen steadily since the first systematic records were kept in the sixteenth century. Illegitimacy rates stood at 2 to 5 percent in the sixteenth and seventeenth centuries in Europe — with little discernible difference among Catholic and Protestant polities, and surprisingly little demonstrable increase when polities raised the age of marriage or tightened marriage formation rules.[47] With growing liberalization, urbanization, and

44. Quoted in FSC, p. 194.

45. Quoted in Harry D. Krause, *Illegitimacy: Law and Social Policy* (Indianapolis: Bobbs-Merrill, 1971), p. 9.

46. Quoted in Krause, *Illegitimacy: Law and Social Policy*, p. 1.

47. Peter Laslett, *The Family and Illicit Love in Early Generations* (Cambridge: Cambridge University Press, 1977), pp. 102ff.

emigration in the eighteenth and nineteenth centuries, illegitimacy rose to median levels of 5 to 10 percent in Europe and America, often well over 10 percent in some of the larger cities. These rates gradually moved up a percentage point or two from around 1850 to 1950, with larger cities and more liberal communities sometimes reaching rates over 15 percent.[48]

Both the growing numbers of illegitimates and the growing visibility of their poverty and exploitation in cities at the turn of the twentieth century led to a growing campaign to ameliorate their plight.[49] Especially during and after the New Deal, many American states reformed their criminal laws and private laws to give new protection to illegitimate (and legitimate) children. Firm new laws against assault and abuse of children offered substantive and procedural protections, particularly for those who suffered under intemperate parents and guardians. New criminal laws punished more firmly abortion and infanticide. Ample new federal and state tax appropriations were made available to support orphanages and other children's charities, and to establish new children's aid and social welfare societies. Child labor, particularly the cruel industrial exploitation of illegitimate children in factories and workhouses, was firmly outlawed by both federal and state laws. Educational opportunities for children were substantially enhanced through the expansion of public schools. The modern welfare state came increasingly to stand *in loco parentis* for needy children, offering them care, protection, and nurture, regardless of the legitimacy of their birth.[50]

Modern American states also facilitated the legitimation of children. Abandoning a seven-hundred-year-old common law rule, many states in the first half of the twentieth century began to allow for legitimation of children through the subsequent marriage of their natural mother and natural father. More recently, most states extended this to allow for legitimation upon marriage of the natural mother to any man, not necessarily the father of the illegitimate children.

Modern American states further facilitated legitimation by adopting

---

48. Laslett, *The Family and Illicit Love in Early Generations;* Laslett et al., eds., *Bastardy and Its Comparative History,* pp. 48-64; Crane Brinton, *The French Revolutionary Legislation on Illegitimacy* (Cambridge, Mass.: Harvard University Press, 1936), pp. 10-12, 72-76.

49. Gail Reekie, *Measuring Immorality: Social Inquiry and the Problem of Legitimacy* (Cambridge: Cambridge University Press, 1998), pp. 22-36.

50. Thomas, "Child Abuse and Neglect"; Krause, *Illegitimacy: Law and Social Policy.*

the ancient doctrine of adoption.[51] Both medieval canon law and early modern common law had firmly rejected the Roman and civil law of adoption. Classic canon law had treated natural blood ties between parent and child as essential to the formation of a stable Christian family. Classic common law had made blood ties the absolute condition for vesting the father's right and duty to control and support the child and to transfer family property to him or her. This left "unnatural" illegitimates without much prospect for legitimation. It also left childless couples without much hope for perpetuating their name and legacy, unless they could legitimate a child through a private act of Parliament or of the state legislature.

Massachusetts was the first common law jurisdiction to adopt adoption. An 1851 statute allowed for the permanent transfer of parental power to a third-party adopting adult who was biologically unrelated to the child. And, in turn, it automatically legitimated the adopted child as the adopting parent's own, providing it with a name, support, and all the rights and privileges of a legitimate child during and after the adopting parent's lifetime.[52] A century later this was the norm throughout the United States, as well as in England.[53]

Even where children were not or could not be legitimated, modern American states removed a good number of the common law disabilities against them. Most importantly, illegitimate children gained firmer standing in courts and surer footing through agencies to file paternity suits, and to sue their father for support during his lifetime. The growing presumption now in most states is that a father owes a duty of support to his natural children and can be subject to mandatory paternity tests in suspicious cases and to criminal sanctions in cases where he fails to furnish mandated child support. Moreover, a good number of the traditional prohibitions against gifts and devises to illegitimates have fallen aside. In all states, mothers are entirely free to give their illegitimate children property by gift or testament. Illegitimate children, in turn, are freely entitled to receive property from mothers who have died testate or intestate. In most states, this same rule applies to inheritance between fathers and illegitimate children, though several states still impose restrictions on receipt of such paternal legacies, particularly in cases of the father's intestacy. Several states

51. Timothy P. Jackson, *The Morality of Adoption: Social-Psychological, Theological, and Legal Perspectives* (Grand Rapids: Eerdmans, 2005).

52. Zainaldin, "The Emergence of a Modern American Family Law."

53. Vernier, *American Family Laws*; Homer H. Clark Jr., *The Law of Domestic Relations in the United States*, 2nd ed. (St. Paul: West, 1987); James, "The Illegitimate and Deprived Child."

also give priority to legitimate children in cases of inheriting from grandparents or claiming reversionary or remainder property interests,[54] though these traditional preferences, too, are falling aside rapidly.

The plight of illegitimate children has been still further relieved through recent United States Supreme Court interpretations of the equal protection clause of the Fourteenth Amendment (and, in federal cases, the equal protection reading of the Fifth Amendment due process clause). In nearly two dozen cases since 1968, the Court has slowly drawn much of the remaining sting and stigma from illegitimacy — though the formal legal category of illegitimacy still remains licit under the equal protection clause. Illegitimate children are now equally entitled with legitimate children to recover tort damages or workman's compensation benefits for the wrongful death of their parents. They are equally entitled to make claims on the properties and estates of their fathers. They are equally entitled to draw residual social security benefits, residual disability benefits, and life insurance proceeds from their deceased parents.[55]

There is ample irony in the protection afforded by the Fourteenth Amendment, however. The Fourteenth Amendment equal protection clause does remove much of the legal stigma from illegitimate birth. But the Fourteenth Amendment due process clause removes most of the legal sanction from extramarital sex. With the illegal consequences of both illegitimacy and promiscuity largely removed, the number of illegitimates has exploded. In the past two decades, nearly one-third of all American children — and more than one-half of all African-American children — were born illegitimate.[56] While many of these children thrive in single, blended, and adoptive households, a good number more do not. Illegitimate children still suffer roughly three times the rates of poverty and penury, poor education and health care, juvenile delinquency and truancy, and criminal conduct and conviction when compared to their legitimate peers. Illegitimate

54. Douglas E. Abrams and Sarah H. Ramsey, *Children and the Law: Doctrine, Policy, and Practice* (St. Paul, Minn.: West, 2000).

55. Martha T. Zingo and Kevin E. Early, *Nameless Persons: Legal Discrimination against Non-Marital Children in the United States* (Westport, Conn.: Praeger, 1994); Abrams and Ramsey, *Children and the Law*.

56. Mark Abrahamson, *Out of Wedlock Birth: The United States in Comparative Perspective* (Westport, Conn.: Praeger, 1998); David Popenoe and Barbara Dafoe Whitehead, *The State of Our Unions* (Rutgers, N.J.: National Marriage Project, 1998-2000); David Blankenhorn, *Fatherless America: Confronting Our Most Urgent Social Problem* (New York: Basic, 1995).

children and their mothers also drew considerably more heavily upon federal and state welfare programs, with all the stigmatizing by self and others that such dependence often induces.[57] While the legal and moral stigma of illegitimacy may no longer sting much, the social and psychological burdens of illegitimacy remain rather heavy.

There is an even greater irony to the protection afforded by the Fourteenth Amendment. The extension of its guarantee of sexual liberty to include the right of abortion has sanctioned a whole new class of "illegitimates" in the past three decades. These new illegitimates are not those unwanted innocents who are born out of wedlock, but those unwanted innocents who are aborted before their birth. These unwanted innocents pay not with a sort of a civil death as in the past, but with an actual physical death without hope of a future.

This is not to suggest that children conceived out of wedlock are the only or even the majority of those being aborted. Nor is it to say that we must return to a system of criminalizing abortion and thus exposing unwanted innocents and their mothers to more desperate and dangerous measures. But I dare say that it is worth pondering the analogies between the current plight of the innocent being *in utero* and the historical plight of the innocent youngster in limbo. Indeed, if the historical doctrine of illegitimacy was a Christian theology of original sin pressed to untutored extremes (as I shall argue below), this new form of illegitimacy is a constitutional theory of sexual liberty pressed to equally untoward extremes.

Theological and Legal Reflections

Given the shaping historical influence of Christian theology on the Western law of illegitimacy, perhaps it would be useful in conclusion to inquire a bit about what contemporary theology can still say about this doctrine and about its further reform.

It must be remembered that, despite all the recent changes in American law and culture, many religious communities, within and beyond the Abrahamic tradition, continue to maintain a theological doctrine of illegitimacy today. Some of these religious communities continue to predicate this

---

57. Reekie, *Measuring Immorality;* Lewellyn Hendrix, *Illegitimacy and Social Structures* (Westport, Conn.: Bergin and Garvey, 1996); Zingo and Early, *Nameless Persons.*

doctrine on explicit theological and moral grounds of deterring extramarital sex, maintaining marital sanctity, and supporting the natural nuclear family. Illegitimate children born in these religious communities sometimes still continue to bear severe sanctions and disabilities imposed on them by internal religious law: indeed, "honor killings" of bastards and their mothers have recently risen in some religious communities around the world.

The First Amendment lawyer in me cannot resist saying a few words about this. The free exercise clause mandates that religious communities in this country be left free to preach and practice their theology and law of illegitimacy, without undue interference from the state. This corporate free exercise right does not license religious communities to threaten or harm the life and limb of any of their members, whether legitimate or illegitimate. Honor killings or anything remotely resembling the same have no place or protection. Nor does the free exercise clause license the community to impede any party's right to leave that religious community if it finds its preaching and practice on illegitimacy unacceptable. But the free exercise clause should protect the religious community's right to preach and practice peaceably against illegitimacy, and to sanction and shun illegitimates in their midst up to the point that they threaten or commit violence against them. Neither the voluntary members of that religious community nor anyone else should have recourse to state legislatures or courts to enjoin or punish the same. Both popular and unpopular religious beliefs and practices deserve constitutional protection. That is the price we pay for religious freedom for all.

Theological Reflections

The amateur theologian in me, however, cannot resist saying a few more words to challenge the traditional Christian doctrine of illegitimacy, which many conservative Christian Churches still teach today. In my view, the Christian theological doctrine of illegitimacy is theologically illegitimate. It is a misreading of basic biblical texts. It is a misunderstanding of the doctrine of original sin. It is a missed insight into the true meaning and possibility of Christian families.

The biblical story of Abraham and Ishmael is just that — a story, which must be read as part of the full biblical *nomos* and narrative. It is a powerful, troubling, and sobering tale. It is, to my mind, best seen as an injunction to faithfulness and patience, a warning against concubinage and adultery, a testament to divine mercy and miracle, all of which lessons are underscored many times over later in the Bible. But Abraham's harsh treatment of Ishmael is no more to be emulated and implemented today than the later story of Abraham carrying his legitimate son Isaac to the top of a mountain to sacrifice him on an altar.[58]

Illegitimacy doctrine can find no firm anchorage in the familiar biblical adage that "the sins of the fathers shall be visited upon their children." Four times that passage recurs in the Bible. Twice, it appears in the Decalogue as a gloss on the commandment prohibiting idol worship. "You shall not make for yourself a graven image . . . you shall not bow down to them or serve them; for I the LORD your God am a jealous God, visiting the iniquity of the fathers upon the children to the third and the fourth generation of those who hate me, but showing steadfast love to thousands of those who love me and keep my commandments."[59] The sin at issue is idolatry, not adultery. And nothing is said here to distinguish among legitimate or illegitimate children of the next generations. The threat of vicarious liability is clear for any subsequent generations of children who continue to "hate God" or perpetuate idol worship. But "steadfast love" is promised to those who love God and keep his commandments. Exactly the same promise is repeated in the other two passages that repeat this phrase of "visiting iniquity upon children." Legitimate or illegitimate children of sinners who perpetuate their parents' sin are condemned. But those children of sinners who are righteous receive God's steadfast love.[60] These passages do not teach a doctrine of double original sin for illegitimates. They preach the need for all to repent and be righteous.

Later biblical passages support this reading. In Deuteronomy, for example, Moses lays out various laws of crime and tort, and then explicitly rejects the law of vicarious liability for capital offenses within the family: "The fathers shall not be put to death for the children, nor shall the children be put to death for the fathers; every man shall be put to death for his own sin."[61] In the next verse he adds, "You shall not pervert the justice due to the sojourner or to the fatherless."[62] The prophet Ezekiel says clearly

58. Genesis 22:1-14.
59. Exodus 20:4-6; cf. Deuteronomy 5:8-10.
60. Exodus 34:7; Numbers 14:18.
61. Deuteronomy 24:16.
62. Deuteronomy 24:17; see also Deuteronomy 27:19; Psalm 94:6; Isaiah 9:17; Lamentations 5:3.

that in a community dedicated to "Godly justice," children should not bear vicarious liability for their parents' sin:

> "You say, 'Why should not the son suffer for the iniquity of the father?' [I say:] When the son has done what is lawful and right, and has been careful to observe all my statutes, he shall surely live. The soul that sins shall die. The son shall not suffer for the iniquity of the father, nor the father suffer for the iniquity of the son; the righteousness of the righteous shall be upon himself, and the wickedness of the wicked shall be upon himself."[63]

This biblical teaching of individual accountability and liability is further underscored by New Testament teaching. If Christ's atonement for sin means anything for Christians, it means that no one, not least unborn or newborn children, need be scapegoats for the sins of their parents. In Christian theology, one Scapegoat for others' sins was enough — God's own Son. The New Testament says repeatedly that each individual soul will stand directly before the judgment seat of God to answer for what he or she has done in this life, and to receive final divine judgment and mercy.[64] Before the judgment seat of God, there will be no class-action lawsuits, and no joint or vicarious liability for which the individual soul must answer.

Equally exaggerated, in my view, is the conventional theological teaching that blood ties are a sine qua non of faithful and stable family life and love. Kin altruism, of course, is an ancient classical insight, which came most famously into Christian theology via Thomas Aquinas's appropriation of Aristotle.[65] There is something fundamentally sound and sensible in the notion that a parent, particularly a father, will be naturally inclined to invest in the care of a child who carries his blood and name, who looks and acts like him, and who needs him in those tender years to survive.

But it is easy to press this naturalist argument for kin altruism too far. After all, the same Christian theology that insists on blood ties between parent and child insists on no blood ties between husband and wife. Indeed, to marry within the prohibited degrees of consanguinity is to commit

---

63. Ezekiel 18:19-20; cf. Isa. 3:10-11.

64. See especially Matthew 25:31-46.

65. See Don S. Browning, "Adoption and the Moral Significance of Kin Altruism," in *The Morality of Adoption,* ed. Jackson, pp. 52-77.

the crime of incest, a serious offense if it is done with mens rea. But why should the legitimacy of parental love turn essentially on the presence of blood ties, but the legitimacy of marital love turn essentially on the absence of blood ties? The sacrificial love and charity demanded of a parent and a spouse are not the same, but they are certainly very comparable, and they must be discharged concurrently. Why is a blood tie so essential to one and not to the other relationship? This strikes me as a peculiar form of social transubstantiation doctrine gone logically awry.

This is not to argue, as some do today, that the crime of incest must be dropped and that siblings and blood relatives must be left free to marry. It is instead to argue that natural blood ties between parent and child are not essential to stable families. Parental love, like marital love, is in its essence not only an instinct but also a virtue, not only a bodily inclination but also a spiritual intuition.[66] Blood ties between parents and children should not be easily severed. But parental ties to children should not be predicated on blood ties alone. Real family kinship goes beyond "birth, biology, and blood."[67] Adoption of children is an option that must always be considered by some and applauded by all.

Adoption still remains a theologically tender topic today. Until a few generations ago, it was still forbidden or at least severely frowned on in many Christian quarters. But adoption is one of the deepest forms and examples of Christian charity. A Christian need only look so far as the example of the first Christian family: Joseph, after all, adopted Jesus, the purportedly illegitimate child of Mary, and raised him in a stable family despite the absence of a blood tie with him.[68] A Christian might further look at how the New Testament describes God's mechanism for dispensing grace: Christians are adopted as heirs of salvation, despite the sins that they inherit.[69] That is the real point of Paul's jarring passage to the Galatians that we saw earlier. Adoption by grace is the theological means by which God removes the stigma of sin and the punishment it deserves.

66. Timothy P. Jackson, *Love Disconsoled: Meditations on Christian Charity* (Cambridge: Cambridge University Press, 1999); Timothy P. Jackson, *The Priority of Love: Christian Charity and Social Justice* (Princeton, N.J.: Princeton University Press, 2002).

67. Stephen G. Post, *More Lasting Unions: Christianity, the Family, and Society* (Grand Rapids: Eerdmans, 2000), p. 124.

68. Jane Schaberg, *The Illegitimacy of Jesus* (San Francisco: Harper and Row, 1987).

69. Romans 8:15, 23; 9:4; Galatians 4:5; Ephesians 1:5.

Legal Reflections

To castigate the traditional doctrine of illegitimacy, however, does nothing to ameliorate the current plight of outcast children. If theology no longer should support a doctrine of illegitimacy, and the law no longer should stigmatize the incidence of illegitimacy, what can be done about the current problem of so many children born out of wedlock, with all the predictions of social pathos and problems, dependency and delinquency that await them? The ancient angel's description of Ishmael's bane still seems altogether too apt a prediction of the plight of the modern illegitimate: "He will be a wild ass of a man, his hand against every man and every man's hand against him; and he shall dwell over against all his kinsmen."

One obvious legal measure is to assign further responsibility where it is due: on both the mother and the father of the unwanted child. Historically, adulterers, fornicators, and other sexual criminals paid dearly for their crimes — by fine, prison, or banishment, by execution in extreme cases. But this remedy often only exacerbated the plight of their illegitimate child, who in extreme cases was now often left with no or little natural network of family resources and support. Today, adulterers and fornicators pay little if at all for their sexual behavior — protected in part by new cultural mores and constitutional laws of sexual privacy. Even if one wanted to pursue a neo-Puritan path — I, for one, do not! — it is highly unlikely that a new criminalization of adultery or fornication could pass constitutional or cultural muster.

But the elimination of criminal punishment for promiscuity should, to my mind, be coupled with a much firmer imposition of ongoing civil responsibility for the care and support of an innocent child born of such conduct. After all, the same constitutional text that exonerates promiscuity also licenses contraception, which is widely and cheaply available now, indeed free in many quarters. Those who choose to have children out of wedlock notwithstanding these options need to pay dearly for their children's support. I am no fan of shotgun marriages or forced cohabitation of a couple suddenly confronted with the prospect of a new child. But I am a fan of aggressive paternity and maternity suits, now amply aided by the growing availability of cheap genetic technology. I am also a fan of firm laws that compel stiff payments of child support for noncustodial parents, and that garnish the wages, put liens on the properties, and seek reformation of insurance contracts and testamentary instruments of those parents, particularly fathers, who choose to ignore their dependent minor children. I am equally a fan of tort suits by illegitimate children who can seek compensatory and punitive damages from their parents or their parents' estates in instances where these children have been cavalierly abandoned or notoriously abused. These and a good number of comparable provisions are happily becoming more common in many American states today, with several federal laws providing interstate support and enforcement, and criminal law standing ready with sanctions when civil orders are chronically breached.

A second obvious legal measure is a much more robust engagement of the doctrine of adoption. For all the pro- and anti-abortion lobbying and litigation that has emerged in the post–*Roe v. Wade* era, there has been relatively little attention paid to the alternative of adoption. Historically, adoption legitimated illegitimate children, removing the cultural stigma and civil shadow that attended their birth. Today, adoption provides not only this protection, but also one of the best hopes and remedies to the new illegitimates who are condemned *in utero*. Adoption should, to my mind, be much more aggressively advocated and actively facilitated — and amply celebrated and rewarded when a natural mother chooses to make this heroic sacrifice.

The law of adoption has improved somewhat in recent years, and both state and federal laws and appropriations have made it easier and cheaper than in past decades. But adoption is still a clumsy and expensive procedure to pursue in this country, and thus remains reserved primarily for the substantially well to do. It is made worse by the continued insistence of many states that natural fathers and mothers have an effective veto over adoptions — however irresponsible they may have been in conceiving the child and however notorious they may have been in neglecting or abusing it *in utero* or upon birth. It is too easy to say that blood ties should mean nothing and that children should be placed only with the fittest parents. That is a dangerous step along the way to the bleak anonymous parentage contemplated coldly in Plato's *Republic* and B. F. Skinner's *Walden Two*. But a more generously funded, administered, and applied law of adoption would do much to alleviate the plight of the modern illegitimates.

Bastards, like the poor, will doubtless always be with us — subjects of pity and scorn, romance and ribaldry at once. Bastards may now have passed largely beyond the province of religion and criminal law. But they live on in our language and literature, with all the ambivalences of the first story of Ishmael. Contrast the sound still today (in movies or street talk) of the pitying phrase, "Oh, you poor bastard," with the angry retort, "You

Damned Bastard!!" Read still today of the checkered career of the illegitimate love-child in Hawthorne's *The Scarlet Letter* or Shakespeare's plays. Shakespeare's *King Lear* perhaps put the puzzlement and protest over the illegitimate's plight best in the words of Edmund, the scheming bastard, who nonetheless could speak to the injustice of his status:

> Thou, Nature, art my goddess; to thy law
> My services are bound. Wherefore should I
> Stand in the plague of custom, and permit
> The curiosity of nations to deprive me,
> For that I am some twelve or fourteen moonshines
> Lag of a brother? Why bastard? Wherefore base,
> When my dimensions are as well compact,
> My mind as generous, my shape as true,
> As honest madam's issue? Why brand they us
> With base? with baseness? Bastardy base? Base?
> Who, in the lusty stealth of nature, take
> More composition and fierce quality
> Than doth within a dull, stale, tired bed,
> Go to th' creating a whole tribe of fops
> Got 'tween sleep and wake? Well then,
> Legitimate Edgar, I must have your land.
> Our father's love is to the bastard Edmund
> As to the legitimate. Fine word, "legitimate."
> Well, my legitimate, if this letter speed,
> And my invention thrive, Edmund the base
> Shall top the legitimate. I grow. I prosper.
> Now, gods, stand up for bastards.[70]

---

70. William Shakespeare, *King Lear,* I.2.1-22.

The Duties of Love:
The Vocation of the Child
in the Household Manual Tradition

In his *Commentaries on the Laws of England* (1765), William Blackstone (1723-1780) wrote:

> The duties of children to their parents arise from a principle of natural justice and retribution. For to those who gave us existence, we naturally owe subjection and obedience during our minority, and honour and reverence ever after; they, who protected the weakness of our infancy, are entitled to our protection in the infirmity of their age; they who by sustenance and education have enabled their offspring to prosper, ought in return to be supported by that offspring, in case they stand in need of assistance. Upon this principle proceed all the duties of children to their parents, which are enjoined by positive laws.[1]

The contemporaneous *Book of Common Prayer* (American Version, 1789) described the child's vocation thus: "To love, honour, and succour my father and mother: To honour and obey the civil authority: To submit myself to all my governors, teachers, spiritual pastors and masters: To order myself lowly and reverently to all my betters."[2] Hundreds of comparable sentiments can be found in standard textbooks of law and theology in early modern times — both Catholic and Protestant, European and American.

The common source for many of these traditional legal and theologi-

---

1. William Blackstone, *Commentaries on the Laws of England,* 4 vols. (Oxford: Clarendon, 1765), book 1, chap. 16.
2. The Protestant Episcopal Church, *The Book of Common Prayer* (New York, 1789), p. x.

cal sentiments was the Bible, particularly the commandment, "Honor your father and your mother, that your days may be long in the land which the Lord your God gives you" (Exod. 20:12; cf. Lev. 19:3; Deut. 5:16) and its various New Testament echoes (Matt. 15:4; Mark 7:10; Eph. 6:1-2). Also important were the Bible's repeated admonitions to believers to "be subject to the governing authorities" (Rom. 13:1-7; Titus 3:1; 1 Peter 2:13). But what precisely did it mean for a Christian child at various stages of development to "love, honor, and obey" or to "serve, succor, and sustain" parents, guardians, teachers, and other authorities? And what did "natural justice" (as Blackstone put it) add to these obligations of "biblical righteousness"? The answers to these questions came in sundry texts — in sermons, catechisms, and confessional manuals as well as in a growing early modern industry of legal texts on domestic relations.

This chapter samples an interesting, but largely neglected, historical medium for teaching the duties and vocation of the child — the household manuals. These manuals were something of the spiritual "Dr. Spocks" of their day — pious "how to" manuals, usually written in the vernacular (unlike the Latin confessional manuals), sometimes highly illustrated (for the young child's benefit), and used regularly by priests and teachers, parents and guardians, tutors and catechists to instruct children at various stages of their development as budding communicants in the Church and budding citizens of the state. These household manuals sometimes grew out of or merged into catechisms and religious teaching manuals, on the one hand, and books of etiquette, manners, and deportment, on the other. By the later sixteenth and seventeenth centuries, household manuals were increasingly recognized as their own distinct genre of literature, with the duties of love by and to children broken out in separate sections.

The earliest surviving household manuals in English that I have found are from the fourteenth century. The most famous, penned by the early English Reformer John Wycliffe (1324?-1384), was *Of Weddid Men and Wifis and of Here Children Also* (1390). With the advent of the printing press in the fifteenth century, these manuals became more common, finding their way into myriad Church, school, city, and home libraries, Catholic and Protestant alike. They also became more complex and comprehensive, reaching their apex in the massive eight-hundred-page tome of Anglo-Puritan divine William Gouge (1578-1653) published in 1622. Scores of these household manuals have come down to us. They provide an illuminating window on what a late medieval or early modern child was taught was his or her vocation in life, what rights and freedoms the child must enjoy in exercise of these duties, and what rights and duties the child's parents, guardians, teachers, and tutors had in helping the child achieve his or her vocation. These manuals helped to bridge law and theology, practice and theory, belief and action in Catholic and Protestant Europe and North America.

This chapter provides a brief tour of the highpoints of nearly one hundred manuals from the fourteenth to the nineteenth centuries that have survived in English. I focus especially on the common and enduring Western formulations of the vocation of the child set out in these manuals — a rich latticework of virtues, values, and vocations that boys and girls respectively should consider at various stages in life.

The vocation of the child as revealed in these manuals consists of two main types of duties: (1) the duty of the child to love God, neighbor, and self and thereby to become beloved to others; and (2) the duty of the child to *be* loved by parents, guardians, and others. This latter duty was sometimes also cast as the child's right to be loved — though talk of a child's rights remained controversial in the manuals. While the child's basic duties to love did not change much over the five centuries of manuals that I have sampled, the child's duties and rights to be loved and to be beloved did change significantly in substance and form, as noted in the final section of this chapter.

The Child's Duty to Love

Love of God

The household manuals make clear that that the first and most essential duty of the child is to love, revere, and worship God. The German Reformer Martin Luther (1483-1546) put it thus in 1531: "[Y]ou must continually have God's Word in your heart, upon your lips and in your ears. Where the heart is unoccupied and the Word does not sound, Satan breaks in and has done the damage before we are aware."[3] For the first commandment of the Decalogue is "that we are to trust, fear and love [God] with our whole hearts all the days of our lives."[4] An influential Catholic pamphlet, *L'Instruction des*

---

3. Martin Luther, *Large Catechism* (1529), in *Luther on Education, Including a Historical Introduction and a Translation of the Reformer's Two Most Important Educational Treatises*, ed. and trans. F. V. N. Painter (St. Louis: Concordia, 1928), p. 64.

4. Luther, *Large Catechism*, p. 65.

Enfans (1543), stated that the primary command for every child is to "love the Lord God with all your heart" and that the first responsibility of parents and siblings alike is to teach the child to obey that primal command.[5] Richard Baxter's *Rules and Directions for Family Duties* (1681) encouraged parents to "[w]isely break [children] of their own wills, and let them know that they must obey and like God's will" first and foremost.[6] Eleazer Moody's (d. 1720) comprehensive manual *The School of Good Manners* (1775) listed as the first duty of a child the duty to "fear and reverence God."[7] The duty to face God daily with fearful and loving reverence, the vast majority of the manuals made clear, is the foundation of the Christian child's life.

The manuals often invoked the duty to love God in order to compel the child to fulfill his or her other duties, especially the duty to love parents, who are regularly described as God's "priests," "bishops," "kings," and "queens" to their children.[8] Of the duty to love parents, the Catholic *Christian Instructions for Youth* (1821) stated: "You cannot manifest your gratitude towards your parents by any other means but by loving them; this love must not be a natural affection only; it must be a rational love, and according to God; that is to say you must love them, because such is God's will, and you must give proofs of this love."[9] Thomas Becon (1512-1567), the sixteenth-century Anglican divine and confessor to Thomas Cranmer (1489-1556), wrote similarly that children must see their parents as gifts "by the singular providence and good-will of God," and that they must love their parents "not feignedly, but from the very bottom of the heart and in wishing unto them all good things from God."[10] It is the child's duty "to honorably esteem them, godly to think of them, heartily to love them, humbly to obey them, [and] diligently to pray for them."[11]

5. Anonymous, *L'Instruction des Enfans* (London: John Le Roux, 1543), folios 1-2.

6. Richard Baxter, *Rules and Directions for Family Duties* (London: Printed by H. Brugis for J. Conyers, 1681), p. 1.

7. Eleazer Moody, *The School of Good Manners* (Boston: John Boyle, 1775); see also William Smith, *Universal Love* (London: n.p., 1668), pp. 41-56.

8. See examples in FSC, passim.

9. Anonymous, *Christian Instructions for Youth,* second rev. ed., trans. from French (London: Keating and Brown, 1821), p. 34; see also Richard Whitford, *The Werke for Householders* (London: John Waylande, 1537), folios Ei-Fiii; Thomas Cobbett, *A Fruitful and Useful Discourse Touching the Honor Due from Children to Parents* (London: Printed by S. G. for John Rothwell, 1656), pp. 9-68.

10. Thomas Becon, *The Catechism of Thomas Becon* (Cambridge: Cambridge University Press, 1844 [c. 1560]), p. 358.

11. Becon, *Catechism of Thomas Becon,* p. 85.

While love of God and love of parents are conjoined, love of God is the primary commandment. Many of the household manuals make clear that when a parental command and a biblical command conflict, the child must follow the Bible. The manuals limited examples of such "wicked" commands of parents to obvious rejections of God or God's laws, such as a parental command that a child "forsake the true living God and his pure religion and . . . follow strange gods" or where parents, seeing a lucrative and evil opportunity, encourage their daughter "to play the whore."[12] God commands children to obey parents, and the corollary is that in obeying parents a child obeys God. However, "in a matter clearly contrary to the law of God, and to your conscience . . . you do not owe [parents] obedience; but be cautious on such occasions; and when in doubt of the justness of their commands, take the advice of prudent and discreet persons."[13] Later American Protestants made comments like that of Samuel Phillips (b. 1823) in his manual *The Christian Home* (1860): "the authority of God supersedes that of the parent. Obey God rather than man," but obey parents in "all things lawful and Christian."[14]

Honor and Obey Parents

Except in these cases of absolute conflict with divine law and conscience, the manuals stress the child's duty of showing "unhesitating obedience"[15] to her parents, often invoking the commandment to "Honor your father and mother" and its elaborations in later biblical passages. The manuals required children to "obey your parents . . . do what they command, and do it cheerfully. For your own hearts will tell you that this is a most natural extension of honor and love."[16] One manual went so far as to say that children "should have no other will" than the will of their parents, and thus,

12. Becon, *Catechism of Thomas Becon*, p. 87.

13. *Christian Instructions for Youth*, p. 34.

14. Samuel Phillips, *The Christian Home As It Is in the Sphere of Nature and the Church* (New York, 1860), p. 218.

15. Francis Wayland, "Early Training of Children," in *The Fireside Miscellany; and Young People's Encyclopedia* (February, 1864), pp. 60-61.

16. W. E. Channing, *The Duties of Children* (Boston: n.p., 1807), p. 5; see also Cobbett, *A Fruitful and Useful Discourse,* pp. 69-127; W.C., *A School of Nurture for Children: The Duty of Children in Honoring Their Parents* (London: Printed for Simon Miller, 1656), pp. 1-62.

even those things that are good and righteous should not be undertaken without the consent of the parents.[17] Luther explained the duty of love to parents thus:

> God has exalted fatherhood and motherhood above all other relations under his scepter. This appears from the fact that he does not command merely to love the parents, but to honor them. As to our brothers, sisters, and neighbors, God generally commands nothing higher than that we love them. He thus distinguishes father and mother above all other persons upon earth and places them next to himself. It is a much greater thing to honor than to love.[18]

Thomas Becon nicely summed up the parameters of the duty of obedience: "Not only to give them outward reverence, to rise up unto them, to give them place, to put off our caps, to kneel unto them, to ask them blessing . . . but also . . . charitably to conceal and hide their faults, in all honest things to gratify them, in their need to help and succor them, and . . . at all times to do all good things for them, whatsoever lieth in our power."[19]

For most manualists, the one-sentence commandment to "honor your father and mother" was the foundation for a whole range of forbidden activities from the obvious to the tenuously related: striking or kicking parents; desiring a parent's death; hating, mocking, or deriding parents; angering parents; failing to help parents who are in poverty; paying offerings to the Church; keeping fasting days; nonconformity with the divine rights of rulers; fostering unrest or treason against their own rulers or against their city; and depriving someone of an honor or a favor and keeping him from something he is entitled to out of "brotherly love."[20] As this list of proscriptions makes clear, the manuals extended the duty to honor and obey parents to all other earthly authority figures. As the German Catholic Dietrich Kolde (1435-1515) put it in *A Fruitful Mirror* (1470), this commandment "requires and teaches us to assist and serve our parents with a loving heart,

---

17. William Fleetwood, *The Relative Duties of Parents and Children* (London: Printed for John Hooke, 1716), pp. 2-3.

18. Luther, *Large Catechism*, p. 66.

19. Becon, *Catechism of Thomas Becon*, p. 85.

20. Kolde, *A Fruitful Mirror* (1470), in *Three Reformation Catechisms: Catholic, Anabaptist, Lutheran*, ed. and trans. Denis Janz (New York: E. Mellen, 1982), pp. 55-56.

a polite mouth, and a respectful body. This applies not only to our natural parents, but also to spiritual and earthly authorities."[21]

Obedience to parents requires submission to Christian correction. Children have a duty to submit to punishment when it is deserved and must not resent their parents for punishing them.[22] One manual warned: "Forget not, young people, that your parents and masters have a right to correct you. They are bound to correct you, when you deserve it; should a slight correction in this case be not sufficient, it is their duty to use more severity." Children are expected to love parents for correcting them because "they correct you solely for your good, and to make you discreet and virtuous."[23] Some manuals took this duty further: "Should you not perchance have deserved that correction, suffer it patiently, remembering that it is less than your sins deserve; and that Jesus Christ, though innocent, suffered without complaint the torment of the cross, and death itself."[24] As we shall note further below, this duty of obedience even in the face of abuse was dangerous instruction in a world where children were abused, tortured, and sometimes fell to "death itself" at the hands of their parents. The danger of children thinking that their Christian duty required them to suffer at the hands of tyrannical parents is further complicated by instructions throughout the manuals "charitably to conceal and hide" their parents' "faults."[25]

Obedience also requires that a child attend school and aim constantly for excellence in both spiritual and secular education. The manuals frequently admonished children, for their parents' sake, to work at school and aim at high standards of intellectual power and attainment. In the early manuals, this duty was simply one derived from obedience and the obligation to learn about God. Later manuals, however, tied the need for good education to the child's duty to fulfill her social responsibility as well as to her duty to find a calling, which would help her recompense her parents should they fall into poverty or need aid in old age.

21. Kolde, *A Fruitful Mirror,* pp. 55-56.

22. Henry Dixon, *The English Instructor* (Boston: Printed for D. Henchman, 1746), p. 55; see also Baxter, *Rules and Directions for Family Duties;* Anonymous, *True and Faithful Discharge of Relative Duties* (London: Printed for Awnsham Churchill, 1683); John Gother, *Instructions for Children* (n.p.: n.p., 1698); Benjamin Wadsworth, *The Well-Ordered Family* (Boston: B. Green, 1712), pp. 90-102; *Christian Instructions for Youth,* pp. 51-55.

23. *Christian Instructions for Youth,* p. 36.

24. *Christian Instructions for Youth,* p. 37.

25. Becon, *Catechism of Thomas Becon,* p. 85.

The duty to obey requires a child to seek the consent of his or her parents to court and marry another. Marriages without parental consent violate the law of God, both Catholic and Protestant manuals insisted repeatedly.[26] The ultimate authority for choosing at least a minor child's spouse rests with the parents. The child's wishes must be considered, Anglican preacher William Fleetwood (1656-1723) advised in *The Relative Duties of Parents and Children* (1716), for children must have a say "with whom they are to live and die" and "with whom they are to venture being happy or unhappy all their days."[27] But, while parents are encouraged to respect their child's wishes, the parents' decision is absolute, and an obedient Christian child is ultimately bound by their decision.

Respect

The heart of the duty to honor and obey is to have respect for one's parents and other superiors — to develop what the popular American manualist William Ellery Channing (1780-1842) called a "submissive deportment."[28] Channing explained in *The Duties of Children* (1807) that "[y]our tender, inexperienced age requires that you think of yourselves with humility . . . that you respect the superior age and wisdom and improvements of your parents" and "express your respect for [parents] in your manner and conversation. Do not neglect those outward signs of dependence and inferiority which suit your age." Such outward signs include a requirement to "ask instead of demand what you desire," and because children "have much to learn" they should "hear instead of seeking to be heard." Channing was not arguing for a "slavish fear" of parents: "Love them and love them ardently; but mingle a sense of their superiority with your love. Feel a confidence in their kindness; but let not this confidence make you rude and presumptuous, and lead to indecent familiarity. Talk to them with openness and freedom; but never contradict with violence; never answer with passion or contempt."[29]

Learning parental respect is a foundational duty of the child because respecting parents eventually translates into learning the good manners, re-

---

26. Fleetwood, *Relative Duties*, pp. 32-33.
27. Fleetwood, *Relative Duties*, p. 35.
28. Channing, *Duties of Children*, p. 3.
29. Channing, *Duties of Children*, pp. 3-4.

straint, and decorum that are essential for later success in Church, state, and society. To cultivate this respect, the manuals sometimes went to great lengths to dictate every aspect of the child's manners and accompanying emotions, preparing the child for the norms and habits of adult life. In many of these manuals, the litany of duties is almost overwhelming: be pious, work in school with all your heart, beware of being beaten and corrected, do not offend the schoolmaster or schoolmates in word or deed, read continually, be eloquent in speech and writing, go hastily home from school each day without tarrying, learn the catechisms, pray often, honor the Sabbath, do household chores, set the table for dinner, keep yourself upright and proper at the table, walk modestly, avoid "unchaste women," dress neither too sumptuously nor too poorly, study diligently, avoid evil persons — and the list goes on.

Eleazer Moody's wildly popular *The School of Good Manners*, first published in the United States in 1715, outlines 163 rules for children's behavior — 14 rules for behavior at home, 43 for the table, 10 for Church, 41 for company or in public, 28 for speaking to superiors, and 13 for school. The directives range from the impossible ("approach near thy parents at no time without a bow"), to the practical dinner table instruction ("take no salt with a greasy knife"), to the amusing ("throw not anything under the table"), to the improbable ("be not hasty to run out" of Church "when worship is ended, as if weary of being there").[30] The *Christian Instructions for Youth* (1821) devoted 258 pages to the duties of young persons, ranging from how they should honor their parents, to how they should take correction, to the means of preserving their chastity, to choosing and maintaining friendships. Good manners also included a range of simple rules of etiquette: taking care to clean one's body, covering with clean and modest apparel, keeping elbows off the table at dinner, not drinking wine and ale excessively and preferably not at all, purity of speech in all encounters (not to swear, interrupt, or speak of vile things), not contending with another, humility, keeping to one's own affairs, and ignoring information one should not have overheard.[31]

According to many household manuals, humble and limited speech is

---

30. Moody, *School of Good Manners*, pp. 7-8, 11-12.

31. See, e.g., Desiderius Erasmus, *A Little Book of Good Manners* (London: Iohn Wallye, 1554); see also Desiderius Erasmus, *The Civility of Childhood* (London: John Tisdale, 1560); Robert Crowley, *The School of Virtue . . . Teaching Children and Youths Their Duties* (London: Printed by G. E., 1621); Robert Abbott, *A Christian Family Builded by God* (London: Printed by J. L., 1653).

a critical characteristic of a good and respectful Christian child. Evil speech and swearing are telltale signs of inner impurities and utter disrespect. But early manuals also warned children to limit their chatter (whether pure or not) and to speak to their parents and other adults only when absolutely necessary. Out of the duty of obedience and good manners, children were also required to listen attentively to parents and never to speak to them with derision or mocking tones. Luther remarked that honoring parents requires "that they be esteemed and prized above everything else as the most precious treasure we have on earth. That, in conversation with them, we measure our words, lest our language be discourteous, domineering, quarrelsome, yielding to them in silence, even if they do go too far."[32]

Some of the early household manuals called for a child to have complete control over his or her emotions in order to demonstrate this requisite respect. In his *Little Book of Good Manners* (1554), the great Dutch humanist Desiderius Erasmus (1469-1536) called children to be "merry and joyful" at the dinner table, and never "heavy-hearted." In his *The Civility of Childhood* (1560), Erasmus admonished children not to be "angry" when corrected or to "rejoice" when praised, for such habits were not becoming of a "courteous Christian child."[33] The child's duties to honor, love, obey, and respect parents, Erasmus insisted, require a child to exert and exercise full control over his emotional state, requiring tenderness in place of torment, happiness in place of heartache, and delight in place of despair.

Respect and Recompense

This calling of the child to respect parents continued into adulthood, even after the duty to obey parents in daily life had expired. American writer Timothy Shay Arthur (1809-1885) made this point in his *Advice to Young Men on Their Duties and Conduct in Life* (1848), a highly popular manual often reprinted on both sides of the Atlantic: "Although the attainment of mature age takes away the obligation of obedience to parents, as well as the right of dependence upon them, it should lessen in no way a young man's deference, respect, or affection."[34] William Blackstone wrote similarly in his *Commentaries on the Laws of*

---

32. Luther, *Large Catechism*, p. 66.
33. Erasmus, *The Civility of Childhood*.
34. T. S. Arthur, *Advice to Young Men on Their Duties and Conduct in Life* (Boston, 1848), p. 100.

England that as children we owe our parents "subjection and obedience during our minority, and honor and reverence ever after."[35]

One of the most important expressions of ongoing respect is the child's duty to "recompense his parents" for rearing him, especially if his parents fall ill or become poor. For younger children, the manuals insisted, the duty to recompense is bound up with the duty to obey. William Channing, for example, instructed children: "Do not expect that your parents are to give up every thing to your wishes; but study to give up every thing to theirs. Do not wait for them to threaten; but when a look tells you what they want, fly to perform it. This is the way in which you can best reward them for all their pains and labors."[36] Thomas Becon wrote that the child's duty of recompense also requires "concealing, hiding, covering and interpreting all their parents' faults and vices." Further, it requires "never objecting nor upbraiding them by any thing done amiss; but quietly and patiently to bear all things at their hands, considering that in thus doing [children] greatly please God, and offer unto him an acceptable sacrifice." "It becometh a good and godly child not to display, but to conceal the faults of his father, even as he wishes that God should cover his own offenses."[37]

For mature and emancipated children, the duty to recompense also requires them to give their parents aid, comfort, and relief in accordance with their own means and their parents' needs. The Catholic manualist Barthelemy Batt (1515-1559) put it thus in *The Christian Man's Closet* (1581): "To honor parents is to relieve and nourish their parents in case they fall into poverty and decay. And when they are old, to guide, lead, and bear them on their shoulders if need be." If the parents "shall fall into any grievous sickness, poverty or extreme old age, it shall be the children's duty willingly to relieve and comfort them by all possible means."[38] Luther taught similarly that honor is due to parents by our actions, "both in our bearing and the extension of aid, serving, helping, and caring for them when they are old or sick, frail or poor; and that we not only do it cheerfully, but with humility and reverence, as if unto God. For he who is rightly disposed to his parents will never let them suffer want and hunger, but will place them above and beside himself, and share with them all he has to the best of his ability."[39] Becon

35. Blackstone, *Commentaries*, I.16.
36. Channing, *Duties of Children*, p. 7.
37. Becon, *Catechism of Thomas Becon*, p. 358.
38. Barthelemy Batt, *The Christian Man's Closet* (London: Thomas Dawson, 1581), pp. 60-101, esp. 61, 71, 74.
39. Luther, *Large Catechism*, p. 66.

called for children "to requite their parents for . . . [the] great benefits as they
have received of God by them and their labors." And "if their parents be aged
and fallen by their own industry and labor, then ought the children, if they
will truly honor their parents, to labor for them, to see unto their necessity, to
provide necessaries for them, and by no means, so much as in them is, to suffer them . . . to lack for any good thing," because parents care and provide for
children when they are unable to provide for themselves.[40]

A child must discharge this duty of recompense even if the parent
does not deserve or appreciate it. Recompense is due to parents "in their
old age" even if they were "hard and cruel" earlier in life, or if they now be-
tray "unwieldy crookedness," wrote Heinrich Bullinger (1504-1575), the
sixteenth-century Swiss Protestant.[41] Luther counseled similarly that "even
though [parents] may be lowly, poor, frail, and peculiar, they are still father
and mother, given by God. Their way of living and their failings cannot rob
them of their honor."[42] Benjamin Wadsworth (1670-1737), American cler-
gyman and later Harvard president, insisted in his *The Well-Ordered Family*
(1712) that it was "a natural duty" for a child to take care of his parents
when they revert to the feeble and fragile state brought on by age and sickness, as a way of recompensing them for their earlier care of the child who
was once just as feeble and fragile. You are "bound in duty and conscience"
to "provide for them, nourish, support and comfort them."[43] "[T]he time is
coming when your parents will need as much attention from you as you
have received from them," Channing reminded children, "and you should
endeavor to form such industrious, obliging habits that you may render
their last years as happy as they have rendered the first years of your existence."[44]

The Duty (and the Right) to Be Loved

The child's duty to love, honor, obey, respect, and recompense his or her
parents and other guardians and loved ones was only one half of the domestic ethic envisioned by the household manuals. The manuals also

40. Becon, *Catechism of Thomas Becon,* p. 358.

41. Heinrich Bullinger, *The Christen State of Matrimony Moost Necessary and Profitable for All,* trans. Miles Coverdale (London: n.p., 1546), p. xxxiv.

42. Luther, *Large Catechism,* p. 66.

43. Wadsworth, *The Well-Ordered Family,* pp. 98-99.

44. Channing, *Duties of Children,* p. 9.

spoke of a child's "duty to be loved" by his or her parents and others. The child was regarded as both an agent of love and an object of love — one who discharged the duties of love and one who induced parents and others to discharge their reciprocal duties of love to that child. These twin duties of love *by* and *of* a child were interdependent. The child had to discharge his duties of love in part in order to make himself beloved and thus to become the object of the love of his parents. But these twin duties of love were not mutually conditional. The child had to discharge her duty of love to parents even if the parents did not or could not reciprocate. The parents, in turn, had to discharge their duty of love to the child, even if the child was incapacitated, recalcitrant, or unruly.

The later manuals sometimes put these duties of parental love for their children in sweeping emotional terms. T. S. Arthur's *Advice to Young Men on Their Duties and Conduct in Life* (1848), for example, described a mother's love thus: "She watched over you, loved you, protected and defended you; and all was from love — deep, pure, fervent love — the first love, and the most unselfish love that has or ever will bless you in this life, for it asked for and expected no return. *A mother's love!* — it is the most perfect reflection of the love of God ever thrown back from the mirror of the human heart."[45] Such talk of emotional love was largely absent from the earlier Catholic and Protestant household manuals. More typically, the duty of the child to be loved was expressed as the set of duties that Christian parents, guardians, and other members of the community had to rear and raise the child properly so that he could prepare properly for his Christian vocation.

The later manuals also sometimes translated the child's duty to be loved into the child's right to receive love, support, education, and nurture. As Charles Reid has shown, some medieval canonists and moralists spoke of the rights of the child in these terms.[46] None of the early household manuals that we have sampled, either Catholic or Protestant, spoke of "children's rights." In fact, this language was sometimes explicitly rejected. Anglican Bishop Jeremy Taylor, author of *Bishop Taylor's Judgment Concerning the Power of Parents over Their Children* (1696), for example, put it thus: "So long as the son is within the civil power of his father, so long as he lives in his house, is subject to his command, is nourished by his father's charge,

---

45. Arthur, *Advice to Young Men*, p. 101 (emphasis in original).

46. See Charles J. Reid Jr., *Power over the Body, Equality in the Family: Rights and Domestic Relations in Medieval Canon Law* (Grand Rapids: Eerdmans, 2004), pp. 213ff.

[he] hath no distinct rights of his own, he is in his father's possession, and to be reckoned by his measures."[47] This was doubly true for daughters, whom the manualists and common lawyers alike readily treated as the property of their fathers and families.

Explicit talk of a child's right to the love and support of his or her parents entered the manual tradition only at the turn of the eighteenth century, and it remained controversial. An early example was the three-hundred-page English manual, *The Infant's Lawyer* (1697), which gave a detailed guide to the status of children at common law and contended that "the law protects children in their persons, preserves their rights and estates, executes their laches and assists them in their pleadings."[48] This manual, which was largely a set of instructions to litigators, showed how children may not be convicted of felonies until "the age of discretion," and how even minor children can be protected in their "estates and rights."[49] Such language became more popular with the rise of Enlightenment thought, particularly through the influence of John Locke (1632-1704) and Jean Jacques Rousseau (1712-1778), though, as we shall see, children's rights language was sometimes staunchly resisted, especially by Protestant writers.

The manuals' dominant genre was a discourse of parental duty to children. On the one hand, the manuals encouraged active parental involvement and attentiveness to children, and chastised parents for neglecting their children's temporal and spiritual needs. On the other hand, the manuals increasingly sought to prohibit abusive parenting.

Parental Duties of Love

The manuals rooted the parents' duty to love and care for their child in the commandment that children must honor their fathers and mothers. The parents' duty to the child was the correlative and complement to the duty that the child owed parents — per this commandment and many later biblical instructions for children.[50] Luther put it thus: "Although the duty of

47. Jeremy Taylor, *Judgement Concerning the Power of Parents over Their Children* (London: n.p., 1696).

48. Anonymous, *The Infant's Lawyer* (London: n.p., 1697), p. A2.

49. *The Infant's Lawyer,* pp. 15-16.

50. See Marcia Bunge, *The Child in Christian Thought* (Grand Rapids: Eerdmans, 2000).

superiors is not explicitly stated in the Ten Commandments, it is frequently dwelt upon in many other passages of Scripture, and *God intends it to be included even in this commandment, where he mentions father and mother.*" "God does not purpose to bestow the parental office and government upon rogues and tyrants; therefore, he does not give them that honor, namely, the power and authority to govern, merely to receive homage. Parents should consider that they are under obligations to obey God and that, first of all, they are conscientiously and faithfully to discharge all the duties of their office; not only to feed and provide for the temporal wants of their children . . . but especially to train them to the honor and praise of God."[51] This was a typical sentiment of the household manuals, both Protestant and Catholic.

The manuals presented this parental duty to love one's child as a duty owed first and foremost to God. A child is made in the image of God, and as one of God's own is to be embraced and loved as such. But the child is also made in the image of the parent, and thus to love and embrace that child is, in a real sense, to love oneself. The duty to love one's child, therefore, is one of the most sublime gifts by which a parent can live out the primal command to love God, neighbor, and self at once.[52]

Right rearing of children involves constant attentiveness, the manualists insisted. Parents must not be lulled into a sense that "the parental office is a matter of your pleasure and whim, but remember that God has strictly commanded it and entrusted it to you, and that for the right discharge of its duties you must give an account." Parents are not blessed with children as merely "objects of mirth and pleasure" or "servants to use, like the ox or the horse." Nor are parents to raise children "according to [their] own whims — to ignore them, in unconcern about what they learn or how they live."[53] Children must not be neglected, but should be "objects of conscientious solicitude." They must be cared for, but not coddled. "If we wish to have worthy, capable persons for both temporal and spiritual leadership, we must indeed spare no diligence, time or cost in teaching and educating our children to serve God and mankind." Parents must know that, under the threat of "loss of divine grace," their "chief duty is to rear . . . children in the fear and knowledge of God; and, if they are gifted, to let them learn

---

51. Luther, *Large Catechism*, p. 77 (emphasis added).

52. Kolde, *Fruitful Mirror,* pp. 53ff.; see also Baxter, *Rules and Directions for Family Duties.*

53. Luther, *Large Catechism*, p. 77. See further such sentiments and other early Protestants in LP, pp. 262-77.

and study, that they may be of service wherever needed." "The children . . . we have are the children . . . we [must] rear." And, if we are negligent in this duty, not only will the child be harmed, but social discipline and peace will suffer.[54]

The manuals focused on four main duties of love and attentiveness that parents must discharge for their children. First, parents must instruct their children about God and God's commands — by baptizing the children, taking them to Church, teaching them about sacramental and virtuous living, and guiding them through catechism to confirmation.[55] This duty, the manualists emphasized, begins as soon as a child is able to speak. In *Of Weddid Men and Wifis and of Here Children Also,* Wycliffe opined that the greatest downfall of parents is in tending more to the temporal than to the spiritual welfare of their children.[56] Kolde's *Fruitful Mirror* emphasized that parents must discharge this first duty both by good instruction and by setting a good example of doing virtuous works. Parents must not curse, nag, or scold a child or do anything else to set a bad example for their children. Nor should they "constantly torment or beat or kick their children," thereby "inducing them to have evil thoughts." Kolde emphasized that "carelessness and neglect by parents who do not instruct their children well when they are young . . . is the main reason why people are so evil in the world and why so many evil afflictions and plagues come over the world. When children grow up doing and being as they please, they are without fear and anxiety and shame. And so they remain hard-headed, horrible, obstinate and disobedient." When these children are grown, "they ruin their parents and themselves as well," becoming poor and criminal, and they "often die in their sins and are damned. Thus they make themselves a whip and a rod to be beaten with."[57]

This points to the second main parental duty, namely, that of subjecting children to proper Christian discipline and correction. A few of the early manuals, both Catholic and Protestant, countenanced severe discipline and violence against children. John Bradford's (1510-1555) *A Letter Sent to Master A.B. from the Most Godly and Learned Preacher I.B.* (1548), for example, advocated violent beatings of children, and called parents to be

---

54. Luther, *Large Catechism,* p. 78.

55. Anonymous, *A Glass for Householders* (London: n.p., 1542).

56. John Wycliffe, *Of Weddid Men and Wifis and of Here Children Also* (1390), reprinted in *Selected English Works of John Wyclif,* ed. Thomas Arnold (Oxford: Clarendon, 1871), pp. 195-97.

57. Kolde, *Fruitful Mirror,* pp. 114-15.

"deaf" to their cries and moans of pain even while whipping and scourging "not only until the blood runs down, but even until we have left wounds in the flesh." Bradford believed that severe discipline is the only way to save a rebellious child from eternal damnation. He adduced the Bible in support of his views. Deuteronomy 21:18-21,[58] he argued, gives parents the right to take their rebellious children of any age before the town's people, who may stone them to death.[59] While stoning may no longer be expedient, Bradford argued, this passage underscores that parents have absolute control over their children, including the power to "scourge" them severely as needed.

But even the Reverend Bradford insisted that such harsh treatment be reserved for only the most rebellious child who was "more than twenty years old" and should by now know better. He further qualified his remarks by chastising the parents to whom he addressed his letter for failing to punish this particular son at a younger age, which would have spared all of them this later and greater severity of treatment: "If you had brought up your son with care and diligence, to rejoice in obedience toward his parents; and on the other side to be afraid to do evil and shun disobedience, and to fear the smart of correction, you would then have felt those comforts which happy parents receive from their good and honest children."[60] Because these lax parents had allowed their child to "run the course of his own will" in his early years, and had "foolishly foregone to spend the sharp rods of correction on the naked flesh of his loins," they were now required to save him from hell by making "his blood run[] down in streams, scourged loins, and forty days of pain." Any further indulgence or forbearance would put their son "in hazards of bitter confusion" and most assuredly put them in judgment before the Lord for "carelessly and negligently bringing up their children."

Most manualists, particularly by the sixteenth century, called for more "reasonable" forms of discipline and correction. A good early exam-

---

58. Deuteronomy 21:18-21 (NRSV) reads: "If someone has a stubborn and rebellious son who will not obey his father and mother, who does not heed them when they discipline him, then his father and his mother shall take hold of him and bring him out to the elders of his town at the gate of that place. They shall say to the elders of his town, 'This son of ours is stubborn and rebellious. He will not obey us. He is a glutton and a drunkard.' Then all the men of the town shall stone him to death. So you shall purge the evil from your midst; and all Israel will hear, and be afraid."

59. John Bradford, *A Letter Sent to Master A.B. from the Most Godly and Learned Preacher I.B.* (London: H. Jackson, 1548), A-Cii (modernized spelling).

60. Bradford, *Letter Sent to Master A.B.*, A-Cii.

ple was Alberti's (1404-1472) *Della Famiglia* (c. 1570). "Children must always be corrected in a reasonable manner, at times with severity, but always without anger or passion. We must never rage as some furious or impetuous fathers do, but must . . . not punish anyone without first putting anger aside." While "[i]t is a father's duty . . . to punish his children and make them wise and virtuous," punishment must be "reasonable and just."[61] Similarly, William Gouge's *Of Domestical Duties* (1622) taught that parental authority should evoke fear in children, but parental love should evoke affection in children. "Love, like sugar, sweetens fear, and fear like salt seasons love."[62]

The call for moderate and reasonable correction was even more pronounced in later manuals. In his *The Christian Home* (1860), for example, Samuel Phillips called parents to find a moderate middle way between "over-indulgence" and "the iron rod of tyranny." Parents must take steps to rule their households and execute their commands, or children will "end up ruling them." But no household should feature "parental despotism," "making slaves of children, acting the unfeeling and heartless tyrant over them . . . and making them obey from motives of trembling fear and dread." That is not only "un-Christian" but ineffective, said Phillips. Parental despotism engenders in children "the spirit of a slave," rooting out "all confidence and love" and making their obedience "involuntary and mechanical." A proper Christian home must find a middle way between these extremes: "It is mild, yet decisive," and it is "not lawless, yet not despotic." It "combines in proper order and harmony, the true elements of parental authority and filial subordination." In the Christian home, "[l]ove and fear harmonize; the child fears because he loves; and is prompted to obedience by both."

Phillips condemned those who favored severe corporal punishment in reliance on the Proverbial adage that "he that spareth the rod, spoileth the child." The term "rod," in this passage, he argued, does not necessarily mean "the iron rod of the unfeeling and unloving despot" but instead could be interpreted as the "rod of a compassionate father" who "does not always inflict corporal punishment," and, when he does, does so out of love. Phillips argued that corporal punishment does more harm than good, resulting

61. Leon Batista Alberti, *The Albertis of Florence: Leon Batista Alberti's Della Famiglia*, trans. Guido A. Guarino (Lewisburg, Pa.: Bucknell University Press, 1971), pp. 74-77.

62. William Gouge, *Of Domestical Duties* (London: John Haviland, 1622), pp. 498-99; see also pp. 427-96, on children's response to parental duties.

in "depravity" of character, resentment, and ultimately criminal acts against and by the children. "Christian correction is the interposition of love acting according to law in restraining the child." We should "correct but not punish" our children in a manner where "true severity and true sympathy . . . unite and temper each other."[63]

Third, beyond the parental duties of divine instruction and Christian discipline, the manuals emphasized that parents must teach a child a "trade" or "occupation" — or what the Protestant manualists frequently called "a divine calling" or "Christian vocation."[64] Heinrich Bullinger's instruction was quite typical. He emphasized that teaching a child a proper Christian vocation was a matter of "mutual discovery" for the parent and the child. Parents must observe and assess the child's talents and inclinations, and prepare and place the child in the occupation for which the child is best suited. This vocation should be one that is not only most conducive to the child's abilities and interests but also the "most profitable and necessary" for the Church and commonwealth. One of the chief parental responsibilities is to "place his children with expert and cunning workmen" who will "teach them some handicraft" and livelihood — or, as later manualists emphasized, to place them in a school to train them for their proper vocation. Placement in a job or a school should be determined by the "children's wit" and aptitude, and by mutual determination of where children would find the "most delight."[65]

Consideration of what vocation would bring the child the "most delight" became more explicit in later manuals — but principally for males. Most of the manuals restricted young women only to the vocation of being a wife and mother — or a nun or religious servant in a few of the late medieval Catholic manuals. Rather than seeking a vocation "most profitable and necessary for the commonwealth," the manuals encouraged that parents place daughters in a vocation "profitable for the family."

Fourth, the manuals emphasized the parents' duty to find a suitable mate for their children, the reciprocal of the child's duty to procuring parental consent before marriage. Bullinger insisted that while children "must" not marry without parental consent, "[s]o *should* not the parents without any pity compel their children to marry before their time, nor wickedly neglect

63. Phillips, *The Christian Home*, pp. 218-31.

64. Batt, *Christian Man's Closet*, p. 65; Bullinger, *Christen State of Matrimony*, pp. lxix-lxxii.

65. Bullinger, *Christian State of Matrimony*, pp. lxix-lxxi; Henry Bullinger, "The Fifth Precept of the Ten Commandments" [c. 1542], in *Decades of Henry Bullinger, Second Decade* (Cambridge: The University Press, 1849), pp. 267-98.

them, nor leave them unprovided for in due season."[66] This was a common sentiment in early modern Protestant and post-Tridentine Catholic circles that insisted on parental consent for valid marital formation.[67] While the children "must" obey parents in this matter, at least when they are minors, the parents "should" act reasonably. Children objecting to their parents' choice of a mate should do so "comely and with good manner," and recognize that the parental word is final in the matter.[68] Similarly, Nathaniel Cotton's (1705-1788) *Visions for the Entertainment and Instruction of Young Minds* warned young women "impatient of a parent's rule" not to rush into marriage without parental permission. Such foolish "rebels," Cotton warned, will only suffer a "joyless" life and, to add insult to injury, will become "barren."[69]

Evolving Ideals

Gender Roles

Not surprisingly, the manuals revealed the common double standards for men and women that prevailed in late medieval and early modern society. While much of the language in the household manuals was gender neutral and addressed to "children" or "youths," the manuals were directed principally at young men — as is clear from the prevalent warnings against "whoremongering" with women and proper habits of courting women. When the manuals did distinguish between gender roles, they generally called boys to learn to be bold and courageous and girls to be fearful and gentle. A 1542 manual made the father primarily responsible for rearing courageous and God-fearing young men and the mother responsible for raising gentle and virtuous females: "So in women . . . there is nothing more laudable than fearfulness and gentleness of manner. To the mother, your wife, give charge to do her duty in bringing up your women children virtuously and in the law and fear of God, as you do the men children."[70]

66. Bullinger, *Christen State of Matrimony,* pp. xv-xviii (emphasis added).

67. See examples in FSC; John Witte Jr. and Robert M. Kingdon, *Sex, Marriage, and Family in John Calvin's Geneva,* vol. 1: *Courtship, Engagement, and Marriage* (Grand Rapids: Eerdmans, 2005), pp. 165-201.

68. Bullinger, *Christen State of Matrimony,* pp. xv-xvii.

69. Nathaniel Cotton, *Visions for the Entertainment and Instruction of Young Minds* (Exeter, N.H.: Henry Ranlet, 1794), p. 76.

70. Anonymous, *A Glass for Householders* (modernized spelling).

The Christian Man's Closet (1581) set out a typical list of duties that were "especially applicable to daughters." These included (1) speaking and understanding (that is, learning) only about the fear of God; (2) not using filthy words; (3) modesty in appearance (meaning limited makeup and natural hair color); (4) avoiding wine and overindulgence in food; (5) learning to make woolen and linen cloth; (6) donning appropriate apparel without focus on silks; and (7) avoiding unvirtuous ("light") maidens.[71] Typically, in the early manuals, the duties of young women also included "shamefastness," meekness, chastity, modesty, "sadness," and sobriety. The most important thing for a daughter to learn and to be taught, the manuals emphasized, is "how to please her husband through gentle behavior, discreet conversation, prudence, wisdom, and virtue." As to education, "[d]aughters should be instructed in prayer and Christian knowledge, but should not be too busy in teaching and reasoning openly."[72]

A few of the manualists had other vocations in mind for young women beyond demure marriage and dutiful motherhood. Juan Luis Vives's (1492-1540) *Instruction of a Christian Woman* (1523), which appeared in some forty editions, was a good early example. Vives, a Spanish humanist and philosopher, recognized that many young women would pursue marriage, and their mothers had to teach them the proper ways and means of "keeping and ordering of a house." But other women "are born unto [learning], or at least not unfit for it." They were "not to be discouraged, and those that are apt should be heartened and encouraged." Vives acknowledged that "learned women are suspect to many." Thus "young women shall only study that which leads to good manners, informs her living and teaches the ways of a holy and good life." Eloquence and learnedness, while not necessary among women, are shameful only when they lead to indiscretion or deceit. Above all, women need goodness and wisdom. A woman is never to teach, however, because she is a "fragile thing" and, "like Eve," may be deceived by a weak argument.[73] These were only dim foreshadowings of the more ambitious vocations and aspirations for girls and young women projected by nineteenth- and twentieth-century feminist writers.

71. Batt, *Christian Man's Closet*, pp. 75-76.
72. Bullinger, *Christen State of Matrimony*, p. xxiv (modernized spelling).
73. Juan Luis Vives, *Instruction of a Christian Woman* (London: n.p., 1585), pp. 8, 18, 25-30, 322.

Enlightenment Influences

John Locke's *Some Thoughts Concerning Education* (1693) challenged many of the traditional notions of childhood, child rearing, and education. Locke advocated much more intimacy between parents and children. He rejected the idea that the child is marred by original sin, and instead saw the child as a free form ready to be shaped by experience and education. The parents' role was to guide and mediate those experiences for the benefit of the child. Education of children, Locke argued, is not simply for acquiring knowledge, but especially for building a virtuous and useful character. "Virtue is harder to be got than knowledge of the world; and, if lost in a young man, is seldom recovered." The aim of education is not simply knowledge, but to teach a child how to live life, and to live it well. Locke urged parents to teach their children self-discipline so that corporal punishment would be unnecessary. "I told you before that children love *liberty* and therefore they should be brought to do the things that are fit for them without feeling any restraint laid upon them. I now tell you they love something more: and that is *dominion*." He urged parents to restrain a child's cravings and desires by not giving in to the child's every whim.[74]

While Locke's treatise on education made a splash, Jean Jacques Rousseau's *Emile* (1762) changed the tide of childhood education. Rousseau wrote, "Everything is good coming from the Creator, everything degenerates at the hands of men." Thus a child ought to be free to experience life in every respect irrespective of potential harm, for a child's "joy of freedom compensates for many injuries." Rousseau criticized the heavily duty-bound ethic of earlier household manuals, catechisms, and educational texts; parents and others, he insisted, should "[n]ever tell the child what he cannot understand."[75] He minimized the importance of book learning and promoted instead the idea of educating a child's emotions and affections. Rousseau urged parents and teachers to focus on the passionate side of the child's human nature, something that earlier teachings had neglected, in his view. Like Locke, he specially recognized the virtue of a child's learning through experience — by trial and error, experiment and failure.

Rousseau's Enlightenment ideas of children and their education were highly controversial in their day, but they slowly found their way into the

---

74. John Locke, *Some Thoughts Concerning Education* (London: n.p., 1693), secs. 54-69.

75. Jean-Jacques Rousseau, *Emile* (Paris: n.p., 1769), pp. 292ff.

household manual tradition. Enos Weed's (1790-1813?) *The Educational Directory* (1803), for example, echoed Rousseau in arguing for a less rigid educational structure. Children should be exposed to a variety of experiences, and they must be allowed to question parents, teachers, and other authorities, especially as they grow older. Furthermore, while parents have a duty to correct children in all manner of wrongs, Weed warned against strict punishment. Good parenting requires taming an unruly will without breaking a child's spirit. A child's "trifling playish temper and disposition," which had been stifled by the strict traditional requirements, "should be encouraged, as being beneficial to them."

Weed, like Rousseau, criticized the heavily duty-bound ethic of the earlier manual tradition, calling for "very few" rules, lest the child's "natural development" be impaired and impeded. He had little sympathy for traditional instruction in decorum, etiquette, and manners, for this endless "heaping on them a large number of rules about their putting off their hats or making legs or courtesies" are mere "outward gestures to the neglect of their minds." Weed also railed against the earlier manualists' calls for emotional control of children, advising instead that children "should always . . . speak and act according to the true sentiments of their hearts." He despised compulsory use of courteous addresses made "for show and not from affection." Children should be free to express themselves to parents and other superiors according to the "true sentiments of their heart."[76]

Weed did not fully dispense with tradition. He thought that moderate corporal punishment to correct a child when necessary is best. He counseled that children should not be indulged in all their desires, and that they should be taught to dress modestly, eat moderately, and avoid wicked speech and actions. Parents should likewise provide a good example for their children, a common theme of the earlier manuals.

Tennessee Celeste Cook (1846-1923) went further in her chapter on children in *Constitutional Equality a Right of Woman* (1871). Cook was a feminist writer and reformer, most popular because her sister was the first woman to run for president of the United States. Cook wrote, "The teachings of Christianity are well; they have been taught persistently. But we have now arrived at that practical age of the world which demands adequate results as proofs of the validity of assumed positions." Among other things, practice has proved that while parental education and proper rear-

---

76. Enos Weed, *The Educational Directory Designed for the Use of Schools and Private Families* (New York: n.p., 1803), pp. 21-22.

ing of children are essential, "society is responsible for the character of the children which it rears." Till now, the household manuals had stressed the personal responsibility of the parent in rearing children, and the personal responsibility of the child to be well taught. Cook, following Rousseau and Locke, made this a paramount social duty as well, particularly through widespread schooling for young men and women.

Traditional schools, Cook argued, had failed to educate children in their duties as citizens of humanity: "We are arguing . . . [for] the rights of children . . . which shall make every child, male and female, honorable and useful members of society. . . . Scarcely any of the [traditional] practices of education . . . in regard to children are worthy of anything but the severest condemnation." Ignoring the child's "inherent rights," traditional schools cultivate virtues and "affections to the exclusion of all reason and common sense. They forget that the human is more than an affectional being; that he has other than family duties to fulfill, and that he belongs to humanity." Especially with respect to young women, Cook insisted, "[v]ery much of the fashionable external nonsense, which forms so great a part of young ladies' education might well be dispensed with, and they, instead, be instructed in their mission as the artists of humanity; artists not merely in form and feature, but in that diviner sense of intellectual soul." Cook viewed all children, male and female, as having both the ability and the responsibility to contribute to the common good. Indeed, she went so far as to urge the state to take children from parents not best suited to raise them in a vocation good for the commonwealth. "To make the best citizens of children, then, is the object of education, and in whatever way this can be best attained, that is the one which should be pursued, even if it be to the complete abrogation of the present supposed rights of parents to control them."[77]

While Weed and Cook were more radical than most, a number of more traditional manualists did absorb some of the Enlightenment concern for greater gender equality and greater respect for children's rights. A good example was the *Christian Home As It Is in the Sphere of Nature and the Church* (1860), authored by American minister Samuel Phillips. Phillips called the Christian home "a little commonwealth jointly governed by the parents," rather than principally governed by the paterfamilias. It is "the right of the parents to command; and the duty of the child to obey," he insisted. But "parental authority" must be limited, and parents must not "en-

---

77. Tennessee Celeste Cook, *Constitutional Equality a Right of Woman* (New York: Woodhull, Clafin, and Co., 1871), pp. 130-47.

act arbitrary laws." While they should not be "despotic" to their children, they must also not be "indifferent" or "permit children to do as they please, and to bring them up under the influence of domestic libertinism." While children must obey their parents, "obedience of the child is not that of the servile, trembling subject." This "is not unnatural" and results in *"no infringement upon the rights and liberties of the child"* because "[h]is subornation to the parent is the law of his liberty." Indeed, "he is not free without it."[78] According to Phillips, a home "destitute of reciprocated affection" between parent and child is lacking Christian family values.

Some Christian manualists were more critical of these new Enlightenment views. For example, John Wesley (1703-1791), the father of Methodism, derided Rousseau's *Emile* as "the most empty, silly, injudicious thing that ever a self-conceited infidel wrote." Upon reading Rousseau on matters of education, Wesley harshly commented that surely "a more consummate coxcomb never saw the sun!"[79] Joseph Benson's (1749-1821) *Hymns for Children,* collected from the works of John Wesley, included this hymn entitled "Obedience to Parents," to be sung in services and Sunday schools: "Children your parents' will obey, the Lord commands it to be done; and Those that from the precept stray, To misery and ruin run. . . . The disobedient children meet the vengeance of the Lord Most High; His curse pursues their wand'ring feet, And ere they reach their prime, — they die!"[80]

Summary and Conclusions

"We must not forget one very important admonition, which should be frequently inculcated to young students; that is, to pray often and fervently to God for his grace to know their vocation."[81] Amidst a litany of instructions, copious "how to's," and multitudes of good manner books, this simple counsel is the most timeless teaching of the household manuals.

The foundation of a child's Christian vocation is the love of God, most manuals insisted. The child truly loves God by living a life in profound, awe-filled reverence to God. This love for God involves a tenderness

78. Phillips, *The Christian Home,* pp. 213-17 (emphasis added).

79. John Wesley, "Entry of February 3, 1770," in John Wesley, *Journal and Diaries,* ed. W. Reginald Ward and Richard P. Heitzenrater, in *The Bicentennial Edition of the Works of John Wesley,* 34 vols. (Nashville: Abingdon, 1975), 5:214.

80. Joseph Benson, *Hymns for Children* (London: Geo. Story, 1806), p. 32.

81. *Christian Instructions for Youth,* p. 252.

of feeling and a deep personal attachment to God that flows from God's power and majesty as the giver and sustainer of life. Love of God, in accordance with the first commandment of the First Table of the Decalogue, leads a child to honor of parents, in accordance with the first commandment of the Second Table. Children are called to obey and respect their parents as a gift of God, to accept their correction and direction in life and learning, to cultivate the habits and manners of Christian living, to offer them recompense and support in their time of need, to accept their counsel in choosing a mate and in preparing for their own vocation in Church, state, family, and society.

The child's duty to honor and obey his or her parents also defines the parents' duty to nurture and educate their child. Parents are called to cherish their children as divine gifts who are images both of God and of themselves. They are to protect and support their children in their infancy, to teach them by word and example the norms and habits of the Christian life, to offer them correction and discipline, to prepare them for independence, and to direct them in their marriages and in their Christian vocations as adults.

Though sometimes quaint and idealistic, and occasionally offensive to modern ears, some of the lessons of these historical household manuals still ring true for young men and women struggling to find their direction and vocation in a world of conflicting loyalties and duties. On a practical level, the requirement that children be modestly dressed and primped says much to a culture numbed by the latest designer fashions for children. Cautions about moderation in food and drink provide an important message for a society with nearly half of its children suffering from obesity. The repeated instruction for children to work hard in school and to prepare for a vocation that serves the common good is good counsel for children who neglect or despise their education, and for parents who treat the school as a convenient child warehouse and day care center. For the older child, the duty to recompense, care, and honor parents in old age is a valuable lesson as aged parents struggle on social security or live their twilight years lonely and isolated in nursing homes. On a social level, the requirement of parental attentiveness and attention to children alerts parents of the dangers of placing other vocational duties before their principal vocation as a parent.

There is also a hard, but enduring, lesson in the traditional teaching that the duties of love by and for a child are mutually dependent, but not mutually conditional. The manuals make clear that the failure of the parent does not alter the duties of the child to that parent. Indeed, a parent's failure increases, rather than diminishes, the child's duties to irresponsible parents. Children reared by wicked, abusive, or drunkard parents, the manuals emphasize, must cover up the faults of their parents and "meekly" admonish them to return to their duties. A Christian child must fulfill her duties to God, including the duty to honor and love her father and mother, even if the parents are undeserving. This traditional teaching goes entirely against modern views that children are less culpable for their personal failures when they suffer from poor parenting. The household manuals call children to rise above poor parenting, to set aside excuses, and to fulfill their duties of love, even when they are hated and despised. Their duty of love to God demands no less. Overcoming child adversity and taking responsibility can be a source of great empowerment. When the child understands that she belongs to God, she also realizes that her vocation belongs to her. Outside forces do not absolve the child of her duty, but they also cannot deprive the child of her vocation.

The rich history in the household manual tradition reminds us of something else that we might be apt to forget in a modern Western world voracious in its appetites for the latest technological innovations. Reading these manuals allows our minds to drift to a historical place where father, mother, son, and daughter taught and learned the Christian traditions together by the soft glow of candlelight at the common dinner table. There is a great benefit to be derived from the familial bonds created by dinner conversations rather than by T.V. dinners, as several recent social science studies again underscore.[82] The unspoken, unwritten, and invaluable lesson of the household manual tradition lies in how those lessons were transmitted — a direct and loving line of communication between parents and children that requires the sacrifice and commitment of all parties.

82. See the summary of recent research on the importance of family table talk by Robyn Fivush, "The Family Narratives Project: Building Strength Through Stories" (March 23, 2005). (www.law.emory.edu/cslr/Fivushtext.pdf).

The Challenges of Christian Jurisprudence in Modern Times

Legal Positivism and the Rise of Interdisciplinary Legal Study

"The better the society, the less law there will be. In Heaven there will be no law, and the lion will lie down with the lamb. . . . In Hell there will be nothing but law, and due process will be meticulously observed."[1] So wrote Grant Gilmore to conclude his *Ages of American Law.* Gilmore crafted this catchy couplet to capture the pessimistic view of law, politics, and society made popular by the American jurist and Supreme Court Justice Oliver Wendell Holmes Jr. (1841-1935). Contrary to the conventional portrait of Holmes as the sage and sartorial "Yankee from Olympus,"[2] Gilmore portrayed Holmes as a "harsh and cruel" man, chastened and charred by the savagery of the American Civil War and by the gluttony of the Industrial Revolution. These experiences, Gilmore argued, had made Holmes "a bitter and lifelong pessimist who saw in the course of human life nothing but a continuing struggle in which the rich and powerful impose their will on the poor and the weak."[3] The cruel excesses of the Bolshevik Revolution, World War I, and the Great Depression in the first third of the twentieth century only confirmed Holmes in his pessimism that human life was "without values."[4]

1. Grant Gilmore, *The Ages of American Law* (New Haven: Yale University Press, 1977), pp. 110-11.

2. Catherine Drinker Bowen, *Yankee from Olympus: Justice Holmes and His Family* (Boston: Little, Brown, 1944).

3. Gilmore, *Ages of American Law,* pp. 48-56, 110, 147 n. 12.

4. Albert W. Alschuler, *Life without Values: The Life, Work and Legacy of Justice Holmes* (Chicago: University of Chicago Press, 2000).

This bleak view of human nature shaped Holmes's bleak view of law, politics, and society. Holmes regarded law principally as a barrier against human depravity — a means to check the proverbial "bad man" against his worst instincts and to make him pay dearly if he yielded to temptation.[5] Holmes also regarded law as a buffer against human suffering — a means to protect the vulnerable against the worst exploitation by corporations, Churches, and Congress. For Holmes, there was no higher law in heaven to guide the law below. There was no path of legal virtue up which a man should go. For Holmes, the "path of the law" cut a horizontal line between heaven and hell, between human sanctity and depravity. Law served to keep society and its members from sliding into the abyss of hell. But it could do nothing to guide its members in their ascent to heaven.

Holmes was the "high priest" of a new "age of faith" in American law, Gilmore wrote with intended irony, that replaced an earlier era dominated by the Church and the clergy.[6] The confession of this new age of faith was that America was a land "ruled by laws, not by men." Its catechism was the new case law method of the law school classroom. Its canon was the new concordance of legal codes, amply augmented by New Deal legislation. Its Church was the common law court where the rituals of judicial formalism and due process would yield legal truth. Its Church council was the Supreme Court, which now issued opinions with as much dogmatic confidence as the divines of Nicea, Augsburg, and Trent.

This new age of faith in American law was in part the product of a new faith in the positivist theory of knowledge that swept over America in the later nineteenth and twentieth centuries, eclipsing earlier theories of knowledge that gave religion and the Church a more prominent place. In law, the turn to positivism proceeded in two stages. The first stage was scientific. Inspired by the successes of the early modern scientific revolution — from Copernicus to Newton — eighteenth-century European and nineteenth-century American jurists set out to create a method of law that was every bit as scientific and rigorous as that of the new mathematics and the new physics. This scientific movement in law was not merely an exercise in professional rivalry. It was an earnest attempt to show that law had an autonomous place in the cadre of positive sciences, that it could not and should not be subsumed by theology, politics, philosophy, or economics. In

5. Oliver Wendell Holmes Jr., "The Path of the Law" (1897), in Oliver Wendell Holmes Jr., *Collected Legal Papers* (New York: Harcourt, Brace and Howe, 1920), p. 170.
6. Gilmore, *Ages of American Law,* pp. 41-67.

testimony to this claim, jurists in this period poured forth a staggering number of new legal codes, new constitutions, new legal encyclopedias, dictionaries, textbooks, and other legal syntheses that still grace, and bow, the shelves of our law libraries.[7]

The second stage of the positivist turn in law was philosophical. A new movement — known variously as legal positivism, legal formalism, and analytical jurisprudence — sought to reduce the subject matter of law to its most essential core. If physics could be reduced to "matter in motion" and biology to "survival of the fittest," then surely law and legal study could be reduced to a core subject as well. The formula was produced in the mid nineteenth century, most famously by John Austin (1790-1859) in England and Christopher Columbus Langdell (1826-1906) in America: law is simply the concrete rules and procedures posited by the sovereign and enforced by the courts. Many other institutions and practices might be normative and important for social coherence and political concordance. But they are not law. They are the subjects of theology, ethics, economics, politics, psychology, sociology, anthropology, and other humane disciplines. They stand beyond "the province of jurisprudence properly determined."[8]

This positivist theory of law, which swept over American universities from the 1890s onward, rendered legal study increasingly narrow and insular. Law was simply the sovereign's rules. Legal study was simply the analysis of the rules that were posited, and their application in particular cases. Why these rules were posited, whether their positing was for good or ill, how these rules affected society, politics, or morality were not relevant questions for legal study. By the early twentieth century, it was rather common to read in legal textbooks that law is an autonomous science, that its doctrines, language, and methods are self-sufficient, that its study is self-contained.[9] It was rather common to think that law has the engines of

---

7. I. Bernard Cohen, *Revolution in Science* (Cambridge, Mass.: Harvard University Press, 1985).

8. See esp. John Austin, *The Province of Jurisprudence Determined, Being the First of a Series of Lectures on Jurisprudence, or, The Philosophy of Positive Law* (London: J. Murray, 1861-1863); Christopher Columbus Langdell, *A Selection of Cases on the Law of Contracts* (Boston: Little, Brown, 1879), preface; Christopher Columbus Langdell, "Harvard Celebration Speeches," *Law Quarterly Review* 3 (1887): 123-25.

9. See, e.g., John Wigmore, "Nova Methodus Discendae Docendaeque Jurisprudentiae," *Harvard Law Review* 30 (1917): 812-29; Oliver Wendell Holmes Jr., "Learning and Science" and "Law in Science, Science in Law," in *Collected Legal Papers*, pp. 139, 231; Robert Stevens, *Law School: Legal Education in America from the 1850s to 1980s* (Chapel Hill, N.C.: University of North Carolina Press, 1983).

change within itself; that, through its own design and dynamic, law marches teleologically through time "from trespass to case to negligence, from contract to quasi-contract to implied warranty."[10]

Holmes was an early champion of this positivist theory of law and legal development. He rebuked more traditional views with a series of famous aphorisms that are still often quoted today. Against those who insisted that the legal tradition was more than simply a product of pragmatic evolution, he wrote, "The life of the law is not logic but experience."[11] Against those who appealed to a higher natural law to guide the positive law of the state, Holmes cracked, "There is no such brooding omnipresence in the sky."[12] Against those who argued for a more principled jurisprudence, Holmes retorted, "General principles do not decide concrete cases."[13] Against those who insisted that law needed basic moral premises to be cogent, Holmes mused, "I should be glad if we could get rid of the whole moral phraseology which I think has tended to distort the law. In fact even in the domain of morals I think that it would be a gain, at least for the educated, to get rid of the word and notion [of] Sin."[14]

Despite its new prominence in the early twentieth century, American legal positivism was not without its ample detractors. Already in the 1920s and 1930s, sociologists of law argued that the nature and purpose of law and politics cannot be understood without reference to the spirit of a people and their times — of a *Volksgeist und Zeitgeist,* as their German counterparts put it.[15] The legal realist movement of the 1930s and 1940s used the new insights of psychology and anthropology to cast doubt on the immutability and ineluctability of judicial reasoning.[16] The revived natural

---

10. Barbara Shapiro, "Law and Science in Seventeenth-Century England," *Stanford Law Review* 21 (1969): 728.

11. Oliver Wendell Holmes Jr., *The Common Law* (Boston: Little, Brown, 1881), p. 1.

12. *Southern Pacific Co. v. Jensen,* 244 U.S. 205, 222 (1917) (Holmes, J., dissenting); see also Michael H. Hoffheimer, *Justice Holmes and the Natural Law* (New York: Garland, 1992).

13. *Lochner v. New York,* 198 U.S. 45, 76 (1905).

14. Oliver Wendell Holmes Jr., "Letter to Sir Frederick Pollock (May 30, 1927)," in *Holmes-Pollock Letters: The Correspondence of Mr. Justice Holmes and Sir Frederick Pollock, 1874-1932,* ed. Mark DeWolfe Howe, 2 vols. (Cambridge, Mass.: Harvard University Press, 1941), 2:200.

15. See, e.g., Julius Stone, *The Province and Function of Law: Law as Logic, Justice, and Social Control* (London: Stevens, 1947); Gustav Radbruch, *Der Geist des englischen Recht* (Heidelberg: A. Rausch, 1946).

16. William W. Fisher, Morton Horwitz, and Thomas Reed, eds., *American Legal*

CONCLUSION

law movement of the 1940s and 1950s saw in the horrors of Hitler's Holocaust and Stalin's gulags, the perils of constructing a legal system without
transcendent checks and balances.[17] The international human rights
movement of the 1950s and 1960s pressed the law to address more directly the sources and sanctions of civil, political, social, cultural, and economic rights.[18] Marxist, feminist, and neo-Kantian movements in the
1960s and 1970s used linguistic and structural critiques to expose the fal-
lacies and false equalities of legal and political doctrines.[19] Watergate and
other political scandals in the 1970s and 1980s highlighted the need for a
more comprehensive understanding of legal ethics and political accountability.

By the early 1970s, the confluence of these and other movements had
exposed the limitations of a positivist definition of law standing alone.
Leading jurists of the day — Lon Fuller, Jerome Hall, Karl Llewellyn, Harold Berman, and others — were pressing for a broader understanding and
definition of law.[20] Of course, they said in concurrence with legal
positivists, law consists of rules — the black letter rules of contracts, torts,
property, corporations, and sundry other familiar subjects. Of course, law
draws to itself a distinctive legal science, an "artificial reason," as Sir Edward Coke (1552-1634) once put it.[21] But law is much more than the rules
of the state and how we apply and analyze them. Law is also the social activity by which certain norms are formulated by legitimate authorities and
actualized by persons subject to those authorities. The process of legal for-

Realism (New York: Oxford University Press, 1993); Wilfred E. Rumble, *American Legal
Realism: Skepticism, Reform, and the Judicial Process* (Ithaca, N.Y.: Cornell University
Press, 1968).

17. Charles Grove Haines, *The Revival of Natural Law Concepts* (New York: Russell and Russell, 1965); Roscoe Pound, *The Revival of Natural Law* (Notre Dame, Ind.:
University of Notre Dame Press, 1942).

18. RHR I and II.

19. Martha Albertson Fineman and Nancy Sweet Thomadsen, eds., *At the Boundaries of Law: Feminism and Legal Theory* (New York: Routledge, 1990).

20. Karl Llewellyn, *Jurisprudence* (Chicago: University of Chicago Press, 1962);
Lon L. Fuller, *The Morality of Law* (New Haven: Yale University Press, 1964); Jerome
Hall, *Studies in Jurisprudence and Criminal Theory* (New York: Oceana, 1958); Jerome
Hall, *Foundations of Jurisprudence* (Indianapolis: Bobbs-Merrill, 1973); Harold J. Berman,
The Interaction of Law and Religion (Nashville: Abingdon, 1974).

21. Anthony Lewis, "Sir Edward Coke (1552-1633): His Theory of 'Artificial
Reason' As a Context for Modern Basic Legal Theory," *Law Quarterly Review* 84 (1968):
330.

mulation involves legislating, adjudicating, administering, and other conduct by legitimate officials. The process of legal actualization involves obeying, negotiating, litigating, and other conduct by legal subjects. Law is rules, plus the social and political processes of formulating, enforcing, and responding to those rules.[22] Numerous other institutions, besides the state, are involved in this legal functionality. The rules, customs, and processes of Churches, colleges, corporations, clubs, charities, and other non-state associations are just as much a part of a society's legal system as those of the state. Numerous other norms, besides legal rules, are involved in the legal process. Rule and obedience, authority and liberty are exercised out of a complex blend of concerns, conditions, and character traits — class, gender, persuasion, piety, charisma, clemency, courage, moderation, temperance, force, faith, and more.

Legal positivism could not, by itself, come to terms with law understood in this broader sense. In the last third of the twentieth century, American jurists thus began to (re)turn with increasing alacrity to the methods and insights of other disciplines to enhance their formulations. This was the birthing process of the modern movement of interdisciplinary legal study. The movement was born to enhance the province and purview of legal study, to refigure the roots and routes of legal analysis, to render more holistic and realistic our appreciation of law in community, in context, in concert with politics, social science, and other disciplines.[23] In the 1970s, a number of interdisciplinary approaches began to enter the mainstream of American legal education — combining legal study with the study of philosophy, economics, medicine, politics, and sociology. In the 1980s and 1990s, new interdisciplinary legal approaches were born in rapid succession — the study of law coupled with the study of anthropology, literature, environmental science, urban studies, women's studies, gay-lesbian studies, and African-American studies. And, importantly for our purposes, in these last two decades, the study of law was also recombined with the study of religion, including Christianity.

In 1960, the catalogues of the thirty leading law schools listed a total of 56 interdisciplinary legal courses; by 2000, the number of such courses

22. Berman, LRI, pp. 4ff; Jerome Hall, *Comparative Law and Social Theory* (Baton Rouge: Louisiana State University Press, 1963), pp. 78ff.

23. See, e.g., Richard A. Posner, "The Present Situation in Legal Scholarship," *Yale Law Journal* 90 (1981): 1113-30; Robert C. Clark, "The Interdisciplinary Study of Legal Evolution," *Yale Law Journal* 90 (1981): 1238-74; Symposium, "American Legal Scholarship: Directions and Dilemmas," *Journal of Legal Education* 33 (1983): 403-11.

in these thirty schools had increased to 812.[24] In 1960, law libraries stocked 6 interdisciplinary legal journals; in 2000, the number of interdisciplinary legal journals had increased to 136, with many other traditional journals suffused with interdisciplinary articles.[25] The pendulum of the law has swung a long way from the predominantly positivist position of two generations ago.

The pendulum may well have swung too far. The interdisciplinary legal studies movement was born in an effort to integrate legal studies — both internally among its own subjects, and externally among the other disciplines. It is still doing that in some quarters. But in other quarters, ironically, integration is giving way to even further balkanization and isolation of the legal academy — in part because of this interdisciplinary legal studies movement. With so many rival methodologies emerging, different schools of interdisciplinary legal study have begun to clamor for legitimacy, even superiority. With so many new interdisciplinary legal terms and texts gaining legitimacy, whole quarters of legal study have become ever more intricate miniatures, increasingly opaque even to well-meaning fellow jurists.[26] All this has resulted in even further isolation of the legal academy than existed in the 1960s when a sustained interdisciplinary studies movement was born — isolation not only from other disciplines, but increasingly also from the bench and the bar.[27]

---

24. These numbers are based on a simple count of courses listed in the catalogues of the law schools at Harvard, Boston College, Boston University, Cornell, Yale, Pennsylvania, Columbia, New York University, Georgetown, George Washington, American, Virginia, William and Mary, Washington and Lee, Duke, Emory, Texas, Vanderbilt, North Carolina, Illinois, Notre Dame, Michigan, Chicago, Northwestern, Minnesota, Iowa, Stanford, Berkeley, UCLA, and USC. A more systematic curricular analysis was prepared for the American Bar Association by William B. Powers, *A Study of Contemporary Law School Curricula* (Chicago: American Bar Association, Office of the Consultant on Legal Education, 1987).

25. See listing in *Index to Legal Periodical Literature* (1958-1961), pp. 5-9, and Current Law Index (2000).

26. See, e.g., Reinhard Zimmermann, "Law Reviews: A Foray through a Strange World," *Emory Law Journal* 47 (1998): 659-95; Charles W. Collier, "The Use and Abuse of Humanistic Theory in Law: Reexamining the Assumptions of Interdisciplinary Legal Scholarship," *Duke Law Journal* 41 (1991): 191-273; Edward L. Rubin, "The Practice and Discourse of Legal Scholarship," *Michigan Law Review* 86 (1988): 1835-1905.

27. See, e.g., Harry T. Edwards, "The Growing Disjunction Between Legal Education and the Legal Profession," *Michigan Law Review* 91 (1992): 34-78; Harry T. Edwards, "The Growing Disjunction between Legal Education and the Legal Profession: A Postscript," *Michigan Law Review* 91 (1993): 2191-2219.

Legal study is more than the sum of its interdisciplinary parts — and should be more than a collection of the methods and manners of special interest groups. Law is an irreducible mode of human life and social living. Legal science offers unique forms of language, logic, and learning. Legal study should be enhanced, not eclipsed, by the methods and insights of other disciplines. The urgent task of our day is to create a new legal paradigm, or at least a new set of criteria to separate the legitimate from the illegitimate, the legally valuable from the legally spurious, methods of interdisciplinary study.

The Interdisciplinary Study of Law and Religion

Whatever the new paradigm of legal study might be, it will need to take full account of the religious sources and dimensions of law. For religion, in sundry forms, has proved its resilience — and inevitability. In the course of the twentieth century, religion has defied the wistful assumptions of the Western academy that the spread of Enlightenment reason and science would slowly eclipse the sense of the sacred and the sensibility of the superstitious. Religion has also defied the evil assumptions of Nazis, Fascists, and Communists alike that gulags and death camps, iconoclasm and book burnings, propaganda and mind controls would inevitably drive religion into extinction.[28] Yet another great awakening of religion is upon us — now global in its sweep and frightening in its power. Religion has proved to be an ineradicable condition of human lives and communities — however forcefully a society might seek to repress or deny its value or validity, however cogently the academy might logically bracket it from its legal and political calculus.

Indeed, today it has become increasingly clear — as it was in prior centuries — that religion and law are two universal solvents of human living, two interlocking sources and systems of values and beliefs that have existed in all axial civilizations. Law and religion, Justice Harry Blackmun once wrote, "are an inherent part of the calculus of how a man should live" and how a society should run.[29] In most eras and cultures law and religion

28. See introduction to Susanne Hoeber Rudolph and James Piscatori, eds., *Transnational Religion and Fading States* (Boulder, Colo.: Westview, 1997), pp. 6ff.

29. Harry A. Blackmun, foreword to John Witte Jr. and Frank S. Alexander, eds., *The Weightier Matters of the Law: Essays on Law and Religion* (Atlanta: Scholars, 1988), p. ix.

stand in a dialectical harmony, constantly crossing over and cross-fertilizing each other. Every major religious tradition strives to come to terms with law by striking a balance between the rational and the mystical, the prophetic and the priestly, the structural and the spiritual. Every legal tradition struggles to link its formal structures and processes with the beliefs and ideals of its people. Law and religion are distinct spheres and sciences of human life, but they exist in dialectical interaction.

It is these points of crossover and cross-fertilization that are the special province of the interdisciplinary field of law and religion, and the special opportunity for Christian reflection. How do legal and religious ideas and institutions, methods and mechanisms, beliefs and believers influence each other — for better and for worse, in the past, present, and future? These are the cardinal questions that the burgeoning field of law and religion has set out to answer. Over the past generation of scholarship, a number of tentative answers have begun to come forth, focused on the various modes of interaction between law and religion.[30]

For example, law and religion are institutionally related — principally in the relation between Church and state, but also in the relations among sundry other religious and political groups. Jurists and theologians have worked hand in hand, and sometimes combated hand to hand, to define the proper relation between these religious and political groups, to determine their respective responsibilities, to facilitate their cooperation, to delimit the forms of support and protection one can afford the other. Many of the great Western constitutional doctrines of Church and state — the two cities theory of Augustine, the two powers theory of Gelasius, the two swords theory of the High Middle Ages, the two kingdoms theory of the Protestant Reformation — are rooted in both civil law and canon law, in theological jurisprudence and political theology.[31] Much of our American constitutional law of Church and state is the product both of Enlightenment legal and political doctrine and of Christian theological and moral dogma.[32]

Law and religion are conceptually related. Both disciplines draw upon the same underlying concepts about the nature of being and order, of

---

30. See, e.g., F. C. DeCoste and Lillian MacPherson, eds., *Law, Religion, Theology: A Selective Annotated Bibliography* (West Cornwall, Conn.: Locust Hill, 1997) (a 326-page listing); *Journal of Law and Religion* 11 and 12 (2000-2001) (a comprehensive review of scholarship on law and religion published in the 1990s).

31. See Chapter 7 herein.

32. See Chapters 5-8 herein.

the person and community, of knowledge and truth. Both law and religion embrace closely analogous concepts of sin and crime, covenant and contract, redemption and rehabilitation, righteousness and justice that invariably combine in the mind of the legislator, judge, or juror.[33] The modern legal concept of crime, for example, has been shaped by an ancient Jewish and medieval Catholic theology of sin.[34] The modern legal concept of absolutely obligating contracts was forged in the crucible of Puritan covenant theology.[35] The modern legal concept of the purposes of punishment is rooted in Catholic doctrines of the causes of natural law and Protestant doctrines of the uses of moral law.[36] Both law and religion draw upon each other's concepts to devise their own doctrines. The legal doctrine that the punishment must fit the crime rests upon Jewish and Catholic doctrines of purgation and repentance.[37] The theological doctrine of humanity's fallen sinful nature is rooted in legal concepts of agency, complicity, and vicarious liability.

Law and religion are methodologically related. Both have developed analogous hermeneutical methods, modes of interpreting their authoritative texts. Both have developed logical methods, modes of deducing precepts from principles, of reasoning from analogy and precedent. Both have developed ethical methods, modes of molding their deepest values and beliefs into prescribed or preferred habits of conduct. Both have developed forensic and rhetorical methods, modes of arranging and presenting arguments and data. Both have developed methods of adducing evidence and adjudicating disputes. Both have developed methods of organizing, systematizing, and teaching their subject matters. These methods have constantly cross-fertilized each other; indeed, the same method is sometimes simply applied to both legal and religious subjects.[38] For example, the medieval

---

33. Mark C. Modak-Truran, "Corrective Justice and the Revival of Judicial Virtue," *Yale Journal of Law and the Humanities* 12 (2004): 249-98; Symposium, "Religion and the Judicial Process: Legal, Ethical, and Empirical Dimensions," *Marquette Law Review* 81 (1998): 177-567.

34. Jeffrie C. Murphy and Patrick M. Brennan, eds., "Special Issue on Religion and the Criminal Law: Legal and Philosophical Perspectives," *Punishment and Society: The International Journal of Penology* 5 (2003): 259-365.

35. See, e.g., Harold J. Berman, "The Religious Sources of General Contract Law: An Historical Perspective," *Journal of Law and Religion* 4 (1986): 103-24.

36. See Chapter 9 herein.

37. Patrick M. Brennan, "On What Sin (and Grace) Can Teach Crime," *Punishment and Society: The International Journal of Penology* 5 (2003): 347-65.

38. See, e.g., Jaroslav Pelikan, *Interpreting the Bible and the Constitution* (New Ha-

dialectical method of harmonizing contradictory legal and theological texts from the tradition emerged almost simultaneously in the twelfth century — with Gratian's 1140 *Concordance of Discordant Canons* and Peter Lombard's 1150 *Book of Sentences*.[39] The early modern "topical" methods of arranging theological and legal data under rhetorical and analytical loci or topoi emerged simultaneously among early Protestant theologians and jurists.[40]

These and other forms of interaction have helped to render the spheres and sciences of law and religion dependent on each other — indeed, as Harold Berman puts it, as "dimensions" of each other.[41] On the one hand, law gives religion its structure — the order and orthodoxy that it needs to survive and to flourish in society. Legal "habits of the heart" structure the inner spiritual life and discipline of religious believers, from the reclusive hermit to the aggressive zealot.[42] Legal ideas of justice, order, atonement, restitution, responsibility, obligation, and others pervade the theological doctrines of many religious traditions. Legal structures and processes — the Halacha in Judaism, the canon law in Christianity, the Shariʿa in Islam — define and govern religious communities and their distinctive beliefs and rituals, mores and morals.

On the other hand, religion gives law its spirit — the sanctity and authority it needs to command obedience and respect. Religion inspires the rituals of the court room, the decorum of the legislature, the pageantry of the executive office, all of which aim to celebrate and confirm the truth and justice of the law.[43] Religion gives law its structural fairness, its "inner morality," as Lon Fuller called it. Legal rules and sanctions, just like divine laws and promises, are publicly proclaimed, popularly known, uniform, stable, understandable, prospectively applied, equitably enforced.[44] Religion gives law its respect for tradition, for the continuity of institutions, language, and practice, for precedent and preservation. Just as religion has

---

ven: Yale University Press, 2004); Wolfgang Fikentscher, *Modes of Thought: A Study of the Anthropology of Law and Religion* (Tübingen: J. C. B. Mohr, 1995).

39. Berman, LR I, pp. 120-64.

40. LP, pp. 119-76; Theodor Viehweg, *Topics and Law,* trans. and ed. W. Cole Durham Jr. (Frankfurt am Main: Peter Lang, 1993).

41. See, e.g., Harold J. Berman, *Faith and Order: The Reconciliation of Law and Religion* (Atlanta: Scholars, 1993), pp. 1-29.

42. Robert N. Bellah et al., *Habits of the Heart: Individualism and Commitment in American Life* (New York: Perennial Library, 1986).

43. Berman, *Faith and Order,* pp. 1-29.

44. Fuller, *The Morality of Law,* pp. 33-94.

the Talmudic tradition, the Christian tradition, and the Islamic tradition, so law has the common law tradition, the civil law tradition, the constitutional tradition. As in religion, so in law, we abandon the time-tested practices of the past only with trepidation, only with explanation. Religion gives law its authority and legitimacy, by inducing in citizens and subjects a reverence for law and structures of authority. Like religion, law has written or spoken sources, texts or oracles, which are considered to be decisive in themselves. Religion has the Bible and the Torah and the pastors and rabbis who expound them. Law has the constitutions and the statutes and the judges and agencies who apply them.

Law and religion, therefore, are two great interlocking systems of ideas and institutions, values and beliefs. They have their own sources and structures of normativity and authority, their own methods and measures of enforcement and amendment, their own rituals and habits of conceptualization and celebration of values. These spheres and sciences of law and religion exist in dialectical harmony. They share many elements, many concepts, and many methods. They also balance each other by counterpoising justice and mercy, rule and equity, orthodoxy and liberty, discipline and love. Without law, religion decays into shallow spiritualism. Without religion, law decays into empty formalism.[45]

The Challenges of Christian Jurisprudence in the Twenty-First Century

Happily, in recent years, American legal education has become more open to studying the religious sources and dimensions of law. The Association of American Law Schools, the professional guild to which most American law professors belong, now has a substantial section of members on law and religion, and growing sections on Jewish law and Christian law. The *Index to Legal Periodical Literature* recently added "religion" as a legitimate subject under which to categorize articles. The libraries of our law schools and state bars now regularly carry stock periodicals like the *Journal of Law and Religion* and the *Journal of Church and State,* as well as a growing list of monographs, handbooks, and casebooks on law and religion. Virtually all law schools now have at least a basic course on religious liberty or Church-state relations. A growing number of law schools now also teach courses in

---

45. This is the thesis of Berman, *The Interaction of Law and Religion.*

Christian canon law, Jewish law, Islamic law, and natural law, and include serious consideration of religious materials in their treatment of legal ethics, legal history, jurisprudence, law and literature, legal anthropology, comparative law, environmental law, family law, human rights, and other basic courses. Several schools now have burgeoning interdisciplinary programs in law and religion and in law, religion, and ethics. Religion is no longer just the hobbyhorse of isolated and peculiar professors — principally in their twilight years. It is no longer just the preoccupation of religiously chartered law schools. Religion now stands alongside economics, philosophy, literature, politics, history, and other disciplines as a valid and valuable conversation partner with law.

Catholic and Protestant scholars have been among the leaders of this law and religion movement in American legal education — along with growing numbers of Jewish and Muslim scholars, and a growing number of specialists on Asian and Traditional religions. Legal scholars from these various religious traditions have already learned a great deal from each other and have cooperated in developing richer understandings of sundry legal and political subjects. This comparative and cooperative interreligious inquiry into fundamental issues of law, politics, and society needs to continue — especially in our day of increasing interreligious conflict and misunderstanding.

Christian scholars of law and religion, however, face some distinct challenges and opportunities in this new century that are worth spelling out. A first challenge is for us Western Catholics and Protestants to make room for our brothers and sisters in the Eastern Orthodox Christian tradition. Many leading Orthodox lights dealt with fundamental questions of law, politics, and society with novel insight, often giving a distinct reading and rendering of the biblical, apostolic, and patristic sources that Christians have in common. Moreover, the Orthodox Church has immense spiritual resources and experiences whose implications are only now beginning to be seen. These spiritual resources lie, in part, in Orthodox worship — the passion of the liturgy, the pathos of the icons, the power of spiritual silence. They lie, in part, in Orthodox Church life — the distinct balancing between hierarchy and congregationalism through autocephaly, between uniform worship and liturgical freedom through alternative vernacular rites, between community and individuality through a Trinitarian communalism, centered on the parish, on the extended family, on the wizened grandmother (the "babushka" in Russia). And these spiritual resources lie, in part, in the massive martyrdom of millions of Orthodox faithful in the last century — whether suffered by Russian Orthodox under the Communist Party, by Greek and Armenian Orthodox under Turkish and Iranian radicals, by Middle Eastern Copts at the hands of religious extremists, or by North African Orthodox under all manner of fascist autocrats and tribal strongmen.[46] These deep spiritual resources of the Orthodox Church have no exact parallels in modern Catholicism and Protestantism, and most of their implications for law, politics, and society have still to be drawn out.

A second challenge is to trace the roots of these modern Christian teachings into the earlier modern period of the seventeenth through nineteenth centuries. Scholars have written a great deal about patristic, scholastic, early Protestant, and post-Tridentine Catholic contributions to law, politics, and society. But many of the best accounts of the history of Christian legal, political, and social thought stop in 1625. That was the year that the father of international law, Hugo Grotius (1583-1645), uttered the impious hypothesis that law, politics, and society would continue even if "we should concede that which cannot be conceded without the utmost wickedness, that there is no God, or that the affairs of men are of no concern to him."[47] While many subsequent writers conceded Grotius' hypothesis, and embarked on the great secular projects of the Enlightenment, many great Christian writers did not. They have been forgotten to all but specialists. Their thinking on law, politics, and society needs to be retrieved, restudied, and reconstructed for our day.

A third challenge is to make these modern Christian teachings on law, politics, and society more concrete. In centuries past, the Catholic, Protestant, and Orthodox traditions alike produced massive codes of canon law and Church discipline that covered many areas of private and public life. They instituted sophisticated tribunals for the equitable enforcement of these laws. They produced massive works of political theology and theological jurisprudence, with ample handholds in catechisms, creeds, and confessional books to guide the faithful. Some of that sophisticated legal and political work still goes in parts of the Christian Church today. Modern

---

46. See further Chapter 4 herein; James H. Billington, "The Case for Orthodoxy," *The New Republic* (May 30, 1994), p. 24.

47. Hugo Grotius, *De Iure Belli ac Pacis* (1625), Prolegomena, no. 11. See discussion in Oliver O'Donovan and Joan Lockwood O'Donovan, *From Irenaeus to Grotius: Christian Political Thought, 100-1625* (Grand Rapids: Eerdmans, 1999); Brian Tierney, *The Idea of Natural Rights: Studies on Natural Rights, Natural Law, and Church Law, 1150-1625* (Atlanta: Scholars, 1997).

Christian ethicists still take up some of the old questions. Some Christian jurists have contributed ably and amply to current discussion of human rights, family law, and religious liberty. But the legal structure and sophistication of the modern Christian Church as a whole is a pale shadow of what went on before. It needs to be restored lest the Church lose its capacity for Christian self-rule, and its members lose their capacity to serve as responsible Christian "prophets, priests, and kings."

The intensity and complexity of the modern culture wars over family, education, charity, religious liberty, constitutional order, and other cardinal issues demand this kind of fundamental inquiry. Too often of late, Christians have marched to the culture wars without ammunition — substituting nostalgia for engagement, acerbity for prophecy, platitudes for principled argument. Too often of late, Christians have been content to focus on small battles like prayers in schools and Decalogues on courthouses, without engaging the great domestic and international soul wars that currently beset us. The Church needs to reengage responsibly the great legal, social, and political issues of our age, and to help individual Christians participate in the public square in a manner that is neither dogmatically shrill nor naively nostalgic but fully equipped with the revitalized resources of the Bible and the Christian tradition in all their complexity and diversity.

A fourth challenge is for modern Catholic, Protestant, and Orthodox Christians to develop a rigorous ecumenical understanding of law, politics, and society. This is a daunting task. It is only in the past three decades, with the collapse of Communism and the rise of globalization, that these three ancient warring sects of Christianity have begun to come together and have begun to understand each other. It will take many generations more to work out the great theological disputes over the nature of the Trinity or the doctrine of justification by faith. But there is more confluence than conflict in Catholic, Protestant, and Orthodox understandings of law, politics, and society, especially if they are viewed in long and responsible historical perspective. Scholars from these three great Christian traditions need to come together to work out a comprehensive new ecumenical "concordance of discordant canons" that draws out the best of these traditions, that is earnest about its ecumenism, and that is honest about the greatest points of tension. Few studies would do more both to spur the great project of Christian ecumenism and to drive modern Churches to get their legal houses in order.

A final challenge, and perhaps the greatest of all, will be to join the principally Western Christian story of law, politics, and society known in

North America and Western Europe with comparable stories that are told in the rest of the Christian world. Over the past two centuries, Christianity has become very much a world religion — claiming some two billion souls. Strong new capitals and captains of Christianity now stand in the south and the east — in Africa, Korea, China, India, the Philippines, Malaysia, and well beyond. In some of these new zones of Christianity, the Western Christian classics are still being read and studied. But rich new indigenous forms and norms of law, politics, and society are also emerging, premised on very different Christian understandings of theology and anthropology. It would take a special form of cultural arrogance for Western and non-Western Christians to refuse to learn from each other.

The Cathedral of the Law

A medieval diary included the following story: A traveler from Italy came to the French town of Chartres to see the great cathedral that was being built there. Arriving at the end of the day, the traveler went to the site of the cathedral just as the workmen were leaving for home. He asked one man, covered with dust, what he did there. The man replied that he was a stone mason. He spent his day carving rocks. Another man, when asked, said he was a glassblower, who spent his days making slabs of colored glass. Still another workman replied that he was a blacksmith who pounded iron for a living.

Wandering into the deepening gloom of this unfinished edifice, the traveler came upon an old widow, armed with a straw broom, sweeping up the stone chips, glass shards, and iron filings from the day's work. "And what are you doing?" he asked her. The woman paused, looked up, and said proudly, "Me? Why, I am building a cathedral to the glory of Almighty God."

The law is like a massive medieval cathedral, always under construction, always in need of new construction. It stands at the center of the city, at the center of matters spiritual and temporal, at the center of everyone's life. All live at times in the glory of this cathedral of the law. All live at times in its shadow. This cathedral of the law houses beautiful altars and hideous gargoyles, stained glass windows that capture the light of heaven and bleak marble monuments that signal the darkness of death. Though always under construction, this cathedral of the law is always open to those who knock. Its officials are always available to those who have need.

We members of the legal profession are at once the masters and the servants of this cathedral of the law. Some of us build on the edifice, some of us tend its doors. Some of us are the Michelangelos who paint frescoes with fine feathered brushes, others of us are the widows who sweep the floors with crude straw brooms. But we all have a craft; we all have a calling; we all have a place for our tools and our talents in this cathedral of the law.

The ethic of the widow in Chartres must be our ethic in the legal profession. We must not grow too proud in our own craft, too lost in painting our own frescoes, too confident that our little chapels of study are equivalent to the cathedral itself. We must not be too contemptuous of the past by removing or remodeling too easily what earlier workers have done. We must not be too contemptuous of the future, by believing that our formulations are beyond amendment and emendation. And most of all, we must not forget why we are here in this cathedral of the law — to give glory to Almighty God and to give loving service to our neighbor.

Permissions

I would like to thank the publishers and editors listed below for their permission to reprint excerpts and amplified versions of the materials cited below:

The Introduction is excerpted in part from "God's Joust, God's Justice: An Illustration from the History of Marriage Law," in *Christian Perspectives on Legal Thought,* ed. Michael W. McConnell, Robert F. Cochran Jr., and Angela C. Carmella (New Haven: Yale University Press, 2001), pp. 406-25, and from "Law and Legal Theory," in *The Encyclopedia of Christianity,* ed. Erwin Fahlbusch et al., vol. 3 (Grand Rapids: Eerdmans, 2003), pp. 219-26.

Chapter 1 is excerpted in part from "Rights," in *The Encyclopedia of Christianity,* ed. Erwin Fahlbusch et al., vol. 4 (Grand Rapids: Eerdmans, 2006), pp. 701-9.

Chapter 2 is excerpted in part from "Between Sanctity and Depravity: Human Dignity in Protestant Perspective," in *In Defense of Human Dignity: Essays for Our Times,* ed. Robert P. Kraynak and Glenn Tinder (Notre Dame, Ind.: University of Notre Dame Press, 2003), pp. 119-38.

Chapter 3 is excerpted in part from "A Dickensian Era of Religious Rights: An Update on *Religious Human Rights in Global Perspective,*" *William and Mary Law Review* 42 (2001): 707-70.

Chapter 4 is excerpted in part from introduction to *Proselytism and Orthodoxy in Russia: A New War for Souls,* ed. John Witte Jr. and Michael Bourdeaux (Maryknoll, N.Y.: Orbis, 1999), pp. 1-30, and in part from "Introduction — Soul Wars: The Problem and Promise of Proselytism in Russia," *Emory International Law Review* 12 (1998): 1-42.

Chapter 5 is excerpted in part from "The Biology and Biography of Liberty: Abraham Kuyper and the American Experiment," in *Religion, Pluralism, and Public Life: Abraham Kuyper's Legacy for the Twenty-First Century,* ed. Luis Lugo (Grand Rapids: Eerdmans, 2000), pp. 243-62.

Chapter 6 is excerpted in part from "Religious Rights in the Founding Era," in *Rights in the Founding Era,* ed. Barry Shain (forthcoming), and in part from "The Essential Rights and Liberties of Religion in the American Constitutional Experiment," *Notre Dame Law Review* 71 (1996): 371-445.

Chapter 7 is adapted in part from "That Serpentine Wall of Separation," *Michigan Law Review* 101 (2003): 1869-1905, and in part from "Facts and Fictions of Separation of Church and State in American Constitutional History," *Journal of Church and State* 48 (2006): 14-45.

Chapter 8 is excerpted in part from "'A Page of History Is Worth a Volume of Logic': Charting the Legal Pilgrimage of Public Religion in America," in *Religion, Politics, and the American Experience: Reflections on Religion and American Public Life,* ed. Edith Blumhofer (Tuscaloosa: University of Alabama Press, 2002), pp. 44-61, in part from "From Establishment to Freedom of Public Religion," *Capital University Law Review* 32 (2004): 499-518, and in part from "Publick Religion: Adams v. Jefferson," *First Things* 143 (March, 2004): 29-34.

Chapter 9 is adapted from "The Three Uses of the Law: A Protestant Source of the Purposes of Criminal Punishment?" in *Journal of Law and Religion* 10 (1994): 433-65 (with Thomas C. Arthur).

Chapter 10 is adapted from "An Apt and Cheerful Conversation on Marriage," in *A Nation under God? Essays on the Fate of Religion in American Public Life,* ed. R. Bruce Douglass and Josh Mitchell (Lanham, Md.: Rowman and Littlefield, 2000), pp. 91-110, and in part from "The Meanings of Marriage," *First Things* 126 (October, 2002): 30-41.

Chapter 11 is adapted from "The Goods and Goals of Marriage: The Health Paradigm in Historical Perspective," in *Marriage, Health and the Professions,* ed. John Wall, Don S. Browning, William J. Doherty, and Stephen G. Post (Grand Rapids: Eerdmans, 2002), pp. 49-89.

Chapter 12 is adapted from the introduction to *Covenant Marriage in Comparative Perspective,* ed. John Witte Jr. and Eliza Ellison (Grand Rapids: Eerdmans, 2005), pp. 1-25 (with Joel A. Nichols).

Chapter 13 was presented as the Richard Kessler Reformation Lecture at Candler School of Theology, October 22, 2002.

Chapter 14 is adapted from "Ishmael's Bane: The Sin and Crime of Illegitimacy Reconsidered," *Punishment and Society* 5 (2003): 327-46, re-printed in part as the afterword to *The Morality of Adoption,* ed. Timothy P. Jackson (Grand Rapids: Eerdmans, 2005), pp. 283-307.

Chapter 15 is a revised version of a chapter coauthored with my former student, Heather M. Good, J.D. and M.T.S. Emory (2005), which is forthcoming in a volume edited by Patrick M. Brennan and John E. Coons.

Chapter 16 is adapted in part from the introduction to *The Teachings of Modern Christianity on Law, Politics, and Human Nature,* ed. John Witte Jr. and Frank S. Alexander, 2 vols. (New York: Columbia University Press, 2006), 1:xxi-xxxvii (with Frank S. Alexander), and in part from "Law and Religion: The Challenges of Christian Jurisprudence," *University of St. Thomas Law Journal* 2 (2005): 439-52.

General Index

Abbott, Elizabeth L., 389n.2
Abbott, Robert, 431n.31
Abbott, Walter M., 46n.38, 83n.50, 342n.57, 381n.38
Abel, 59
Abington School District v. Schempp, 242n.124, 255n.32
abortion, 296, 299, 307, 309, 312, 341, 345, 366, 399, 412, 415, 421
Abraham, 144-45, 400-405, 416-17
Abrahamson, Mark, 414n.56
Abrams, Douglas E., 414nn.54-55
Adair, Douglass, 248n.14
Adair, Richard, 408n.34
Adam, 59, 145-46, 352-53
Adams, Abigail, 179n.38
Adams, Amos, 171n.6, 176n.27
Adams, Jaspar, 241n.121
Adams, John, 25; on church and state, 163, 226, 230, 234n.99, 246; on covenant, 143-44, 154-55; on religious equality, 180, 184; on religious liberty, 148-49, 172, 244, 246-53; on religious pluralism, 149-50, 178-79, 247
adoption, 309, 409, 412-13, 419, 421
adultery, 39-40, 62, 158, 277, 306-7, 332, 399; of Abraham, 405, 417; as grounds for divorce, 17, 57, 302, 313, 347; and illegitimacy, 307, 399, 407-8, 420
Adventists, 129, 250, 253

Advice to the Bride and Groom (Plutarch), 328-29
Advice to Young Men on Their Duties and Conduct in Life (Arthur), 432, 435
Africa, 64, 89-90, 252
Ages of American Law (Gilmore), 450
Agostini v. Felton, 210n.16, 256n.33, 256n.35
Aguilar v. Felton, 207n.2, 210n.16, 256n.33, 256n.35
Airhart, Phyllis D., 355n.96
Alabama, 364n.2
Alberti, Leon Batista, 440
Aleksii II, 96, 114, 119, 134n.64, 135
Alexander, Frank S., 5n.11, 91n.70, 95n.86, 224n.66, 457n.29
Alfred the Great, 11
Alleine, Richard, 146n.8
Almond, Gabriel A., 67n.15
Alschuler, Albert W., 450n.4
Alsted, Johann Heinrich, 145n.5
Althusius, Johannes, 37, 350-52
Amato, Paul R., 316n.36
Ambrose of Milan, 11
Amendments: First, 169, 183, 190-208, 225-26, 229, 237-40, 249, 254-56, 289, 396, 416; Fifth, 414; Tenth, 197; Thirteenth, 252; Fourteenth, 71, 206, 252, 254, 257, 399, 401, 414-15; Fifteenth, 252

Index to Biblical Sources